Exploring Global FinTech Advancement and Applications

Hamed Taherdoost
University Canada West, Canada

Nam Le
University Canada West, Canada

Mitra Madanchian
University Canada West, Canada

Yousef Farhaoui
Faculty of Sciences and Techniques, Moulay Ismail University of Meknes, Morocco

IGI Global
PUBLISHER of TIMELY KNOWLEDGE

A volume in the Advances in Finance, Accounting, and Economics (AFAE) Book Series

Published in the United States of America by
IGI Global
Business Science Reference (an imprint of IGI Global)
701 E. Chocolate Avenue
Hershey PA, USA 17033
Tel: 717-533-8845
Fax: 717-533-8661
E-mail: cust@igi-global.com
Web site: http://www.igi-global.com

Library of Congress Cataloging-in-Publication Data

Names: Taherdoost, Hamed, 1983- editor. | Le, Nam, 1987- editor. | Madanchian, Mitra, 1981- editor. | Farhaoui, Yousef, editor.
Title: Exploring global fintech advancement and applications / edited by Hamed Taherdoost, Nam Le, Mitra Madanchian, Yousef Farhaoui.
Description: Hershey, PA : Business Science Reference, [2024] | Includes bibliographical references and index. | Summary: "This valuable resource will have a significant impact on the research community, providing insights into regional FinTech growth, challenges, and opportunities for collaboration, as well as serving as a reference guide for academics, policymakers, investors, and industry professionals seeking to navigate the ever-changing landscape of financial technology globally"-- Provided by publisher.
Identifiers: LCCN 2023055016 (print) | LCCN 2023055017 (ebook) | ISBN 9798369315613 (hardcover) | ISBN 9798369315620 (ebook)
Subjects: LCSH: Finance--Technological innovations. | Digital currency.
Classification: LCC HG1710 .E97 2024 (print) | LCC HG1710 (ebook) | DDC 332.4--dc23/eng/20240105
LC record available at https://lccn.loc.gov/2023055016
LC ebook record available at https://lccn.loc.gov/2023055017

This book is published in the IGI Global book series Advances in Finance, Accounting, and Economics (AFAE) (ISSN: 2327-5677; eISSN: 2327-5685)

British Cataloguing in Publication Data
A Cataloguing in Publication record for this book is available from the British Library.

Advances in Finance, Accounting, and Economics (AFAE) Book Series

Ahmed Driouchi
Al Akhawayn University, Morocco

ISSN:2327-5677
EISSN:2327-5685

Mission

In our changing economic and business environment, it is important to consider the financial changes occurring internationally as well as within individual organizations and business environments. Understanding these changes as well as the factors that influence them is crucial in preparing for our financial future and ensuring economic sustainability and growth.

The **Advances in Finance, Accounting, and Economics (AFAE)** book series aims to publish comprehensive and informative titles in all areas of economics and economic theory, finance, and accounting to assist in advancing the available knowledge and providing for further research development in these dynamic fields.

Coverage

- Managerial Accounting
- Statistical Analysis
- Risk Analysis and Management
- Labor Economics
- Interest Rates and Annuities
- Health Economics
- Applied economics
- Auditing
- Economic Downturn
- Economic Policy

IGI Global is currently accepting manuscripts for publication within this series. To submit a proposal for a volume in this series, please contact our Acquisition Editors at Acquisitions@igi-global.com or visit: http://www.igi-global.com/publish/.

The Advances in Finance, Accounting, and Economics (AFAE) Book Series (ISSN 2327-5677) is published by IGI Global, 701 E. Chocolate Avenue, Hershey, PA 17033-1240, USA, www.igi-global.com. This series is composed of titles available for purchase individually; each title is edited to be contextually exclusive from any other title within the series. For pricing and ordering information please visit http://www.igi-global.com/book-series/advances-finance-accounting-economics/73685. Postmaster: Send all address changes to above address.

Titles in this Series

For a list of additional titles in this series, please visit:
http://www.igi-global.com/book-series/advances-finance-accounting-economics/73685

Democratization of Africa and Its Impact on the Global Economy
Ndwakhulu Tshishonga (University of KwaZulu-Natal, South Africa) and Icarbord Tshabangu (Leeds Trinity University, UK)
Information Science Reference • © 2024 • 487pp • H/C (ISBN: 9798369304778) • US $240.00

Digital Currency Assets and Challenges to Financial System Stability
Adekunle Alexander Balogun (University of Ibadan, Nigeria) and Yusuf Olatunji Oyedeko (Federal University Oye-Ekiti, Nigeria)
Business Science Reference • © 2024 • 227pp • H/C (ISBN: 9798369307700) • US $275.00

Algorithmic Approaches to Financial Technology Forecasting, Trading, and Optimization
Amandeep Singh (Chitkara Business School, Chitkara University, India) Sanjay Taneja (Graphic Era University (Deemed), India) and Pawan Kumar (Chandigarh University, India)
Business Science Reference • © 2024 • 266pp • H/C (ISBN: 9798369317464) • US $275.00

Econometric Analyses on Global Finance and Economic Development
Yekeen Oku Abdul-Maliq (University of Abuja, Nigeria)
Business Science Reference • © 2024 • 300pp • H/C (ISBN: 9798369316108) • US $265.00

Fintech Applications in Islamic Finance AI, Machine Learning, and Blockchain Techniques
Mohammad Irfan (Business School, NSB Academy, Bangalore, India) Seifedine Kadry (Noroff University College, Norway) Muhammad Sharif (Department of CS, COMSATS University Islamabad, Wah Cantt, Pakistan) and Habib Ullah Khan (Qatar University, Qatar)
Business Science Reference • © 2024 • 334pp • H/C (ISBN: 9798369310380) • US $265.00

Sustainable Investments in Green Finance
Sanjay Taneja (Graphic Era University (Deemed), India) Pawan Kumar (Chandigarh University, India) Simon Grima (Department of Insurance, Faculty of Economics Management and Accountancy, University of Malta, Msida, Malta & Faculty of Business, Management and Economics, University of Latvia, Riga, Latvia) Ercan Ozen (Usak University, Turkey) and Kiran Sood (Chitkara Business School, Chitkara University, India & Research Fellow at the Women Researchers Council (WRC) at Azerbaijan State University of Economics (UNEC), Azerbaijan)
Business Science Reference • © 2024 • 373pp • H/C (ISBN: 9798369313886) • US $275.00

IGI Global
PUBLISHER of TIMELY KNOWLEDGE

701 East Chocolate Avenue, Hershey, PA 17033, USA
Tel: 717-533-8845 x100 • Fax: 717-533-8661
E-Mail: cust@igi-global.com • www.igi-global.com

Table of Contents

Detailed Table of Contents

Financial technology (Fintech) has emerged as a disruptive force reshaping our conceptions of money, payments, investments, and banking. As the financial environment evolves, the importance of leadership in the Fintech industry grows. This chapter examines the dynamic intersection of leadership and Fintech, delving into leaders' unique challenges and opportunities in a landscape where innovation and regulatory complexities coexist. The reader will navigate the complexities of Fintech leadership, obtaining insight into the essential skills, strategies, and attitudes required to flourish in this swiftly evolving field. Various topics are covered, from fostering innovation and embracing risk to navigating regulatory obstacles and cultivating resilient teams.

This study explores the factors that contribute to the continual use of mobile banking apps by integrating design aesthetics, information quality, and perceived privacy with the expectation-confirmation information systems continuance model. A convenience sample of 300 respondents from two state-owned universities in Ghana provided survey data that was analyzed using the partial least squares-structural equation modeling technique. The results indicate that perceived usefulness is a significant factor in user satisfaction, while confirmation impacts both satisfaction and perceived usefulness. Additionally, design aesthetics and information quality have a significant influence on continual use. However, perceived security/privacy, satisfaction, and perceived usefulness have insignificant effects on continual use. By combining theoretical perspectives, this study offers a conceptual model for examining the factors that impact the use of mobile banking apps. These findings can be used by mobile app developers and marketers to develop effective marketing strategies.

Financial technology, aka Fintech, is poised to be the driving force of Southeast Asian economies in the future. While there are numerous studies of the development of Fintech in each ASEAN country, there has been a noticeable absence of a comprehensive report encompassing those nations as a whole. Hence, this report aims to scrutinize and analyze the development of Fintech in those ten nations in various aspects such as market size, Fintech adoption rate, types of Fintech, main players, new start-ups, technical infrastructure, government policy and regulation, the impact of Fintech on the local economy, security concern, and future trends meticulously. In order to achieve this objective, this study mainly uses a systematic review methodology with data from various trusted secondary sources such as governmental agencies, the World Bank, and academic studies. The results also reveal that Fintech in most ASEAN countries has grown significantly during the past years. Furthermore, specific recommendations for governments to foster their respective Fintech markets will be proposed.

The financial sector across the globe has been witnessing continuous disruptions every year. India is not an exception to the phenomenon. India figured in the list of economies where Fintech adoption was one of the highest in the year 2021. This kind of rare feat can be attributed to the conducive ecosystem that has been ensured by the state and subjects of the country over the years. During the past few years especially after 2016, there has been a paradigm shift in the Indian Fintech landscape. Numerous advancements have taken place in the sector and new players are emerging as serious threats to established financial institutions. Fintech has become synonymous with innovations and disruptions. This chapter aims to explain the current state of affairs and the innovations in the Indian Fintech landscape. The authors intend to show how new fintech players are coming up with out-of-the-box thoughts and disrupting the status quo of established financial institutions.

Healthcare organizations have unique challenges in preserving their financial stability. Due to the rising cost of healthcare, changing payment models, and the need to provide patients with high-quality treatment, hospitals are under continual pressure to optimize their financial operations. Conventional hospital accounting methods may not be enough in this rapidly evolving environment. The potential of artificial intelligence (AI) to transform hospital accounting and provide a means of enhancing financial stability is explored in this chapter. Automation, data analytics, and advanced machine learning algorithms are used in AI-driven hospital accounting to improve accuracy, speed up financial processes, and support well-informed decision-making.

This research delves into the adoption of financial technologies in Central America, also referred to as Fintechs, which hold great potential for financial inclusion and economic growth. By asking the question of how government support and regulatory framework affects the adoption of financial technologies, research is aimed towards the investigation of frameworks and its importance, the amount of government support, and the current market offering in the region. This research is significant per the authors given it highlights the opportunity to favor the adoption of financial technologies, not only for the chance to become an example but also a hub for innovation in the region. The investigation allowed to visualize the diverse landscape of Fintechs in the Central American market, such as adoption rate, level of priority, and the amount of support they receive per country. Some key findings include the high support from particular governments and the push of private organizations for the betterment of frameworks that will ease the development and operation of these companies.

The strategic emphasis of financial service providers on leveraging new technologies to enhance the accessibility and quality of financial services has given rise to the FinTech concept. The growing economies of Saudi Arabia, Qatar, and Turkey have actively embraced FinTech development in recent years. This chapter comprehensively examines the state of FinTech in these nations, offering insights into current dynamics and future trends. Evaluations underscore that banking and payment services are pivotal sectors in these countries' FinTech endeavors. However, concerns persist, particularly regarding legal frameworks and security risks associated with user financial transaction data. The financial and regulatory support extended by Saudi Arabia, Qatar, and Turkey to FinTech companies has spurred rapid growth in recent years. This upward trajectory is anticipated to persist, with these countries increasingly relying on technology to propel advancements in financial services.

FinTech investments in the Asia-Pacific region exceeded North America for the first time in 2017. These sources of FinTech come primarily from North-East Asia with fast-growing young markets such as China and mature economies like Japan and South Korea. As technologically fierce competition tackles

Preface

As Editors of *Exploring Global FinTech Advancement and Applications*, we are delighted to present this comprehensive reference book that delves into the transformative landscape of global financial technology. The dynamic collaboration of expertise from our esteemed authors, Hamed Taherdoost, Nam Le, Mitra Madanchian, and Yousef Farhaoui, brings forth a profound exploration of how FinTech is reshaping the world of finance.

The FinTech revolution has become a driving force, challenging conventional norms and ushering in an era of accessibility, efficiency, and security in financial transactions. In this book, we navigate through the intricate web of FinTech advancements, showcasing the impact on individuals, businesses, and entire economies. The innovative technologies of blockchain, AI-driven analytics, and mobile payment systems are not just trends but pivotal tools shaping the future of finance.

Our journey through this book spans across diverse global regions, providing in-depth country assessments that uncover the nuances of the FinTech landscape. From North America to Oceania, we explore market dynamics, adoption rates, services offered, key players, investments, government policies, and the broader economic implications. Each chapter serves as a valuable resource, offering insights into regional FinTech growth, challenges, and opportunities for collaboration.

This reference book is a crucial tool for various stakeholders:

Professionals in the Finance and Banking Industry: to stay informed about the latest FinTech trends shaping your industry.

Entrepreneurs and Startups in FinTech: to gain valuable insights into the competitive landscape and emerging opportunities.

Scholars, researchers, and students: to explore the intersection of finance, technology, economics, and business in the digital age.

Policymakers, regulators, and officials: to understand the evolving FinTech landscape to shape effective regulations and policies.

Tech Enthusiasts and Innovators: to stay abreast of cutting-edge technologies driving financial innovation.

Individuals engaged in cross-border trade and finance: to explore the global implications of FinTech on cross-border transactions.

The book is organized systematically, covering topics from the regulatory dynamics in North American FinTech to the growth of FinTech in Africa and the Asia-Pacific region. We delve into cryptocurrency adoption, financial inclusion challenges, and the future of global FinTech.

As Editors, we believe that this reference book will not only serve as a guide for academics but also as a source of inspiration for those driving change in the FinTech landscape. We extend our gratitude to the contributors for their invaluable insights, and we invite readers to embark on this journey of exploration into the vibrant world of global FinTech.

CHAPTER 1: LEADING THE FINTECH REVOLUTION NAVIGATING THE FUTURE OF FINANCE

Mitra Madanchian explores the dynamic intersection of leadership and FinTech, offering insights into the challenges and opportunities for leaders in this evolving landscape. The chapter covers essential skills, strategies, and attitudes required for success in the FinTech industry.

CHAPTER 2: DETERMINANTS OF CONTINUAL USE OF MOBILE BANKING APPLICATIONS – AN INTEGRATED THEORETICAL PERSPECTIVE

Ibrahim Issahaku, Eric Kuada, Peace Kumah, and Winfred Yaokumah explore factors influencing the continual use of mobile banking apps. The integrated theoretical perspective combines design aesthetics, information quality, and perceived privacy. The study offers insights into user satisfaction, confirmation, design aesthetics, information quality, and their impact on continual use, providing valuable input for mobile app developers and marketers.

CHAPTER 3: DETERMINANTS OF CONTINUAL USE OF MOBILE BANKING APPLICATIONS – AN INTEGRATED THEORETICAL PERSPECTIVE

Ibrahim Issahaku, Eric Kuada, Peace Kumah, and Winfred Yaokumah explore factors influencing the continual use of mobile banking apps. The integrated theoretical perspective combines design aesthetics, information quality, and perceived privacy. The study offers insights into user satisfaction, confirmation, design aesthetics, information quality, and their impact on continual use, providing valuable input for mobile app developers and marketers.

CHAPTER 4: DETERMINANTS OF CONTINUAL USE OF MOBILE BANKING APPLICATIONS – AN INTEGRATED THEORETICAL PERSPECTIVE

Ibrahim Issahaku, Eric Kuada, Peace Kumah, and Winfred Yaokumah explore factors influencing the continual use of mobile banking apps. The integrated theoretical perspective combines design aesthetics, information quality, and perceived privacy. The study offers insights into user satisfaction, confirmation, design aesthetics, information quality, and their impact on continual use, providing valuable input for mobile app developers and marketers.

CHAPTER 5: AI-POWERED HOSPITAL ACCOUNTING – TOWARDS SOUND FINANCIAL MANAGEMENT

Sabyasachi Pramanik explores the transformative potential of artificial intelligence (AI) in hospital accounting. The chapter delves into how AI, through automation and advanced machine learning algorithms, can optimize financial operations, enhance accuracy, and support well-informed decision-making in the unique challenges faced by healthcare organizations.

CHAPTER 6: CENTRAL AMERICA – PIONEERING INNOVATION AMIDST CHALLENGES

Rodrigo Romero, Luciana Gamarra Laguna, and Hamed Taherdoost investigate the adoption of Financial Technologies (FinTechs) in Central America. By assessing the impact of government support and regulatory frameworks on FinTech adoption, the research highlights opportunities for innovation and economic growth. Key findings include varying levels of government support and private sector initiatives promoting the development of FinTech companies.

CHAPTER 7: EXPLORING GLOBAL FINTECH ADVANCEMENT AND APPLICATION – CASE OF SAUDI ARABIA, TURKEY, AND QATAR

Behzad Najafi, Mohsen Amra, and Amir Najafi delve into the FinTech landscape of Saudi Arabia, Turkey, and Qatar. The chapter comprehensively examines the current state and future trends, emphasizing the strategic importance of banking and payment services. The authors address concerns related to legal frameworks and security risks, highlighting the financial and regulatory support propelling FinTech growth in these nations.

CHAPTER 8: FINANCIAL TECHNOLOGY – NORTH AND EAST ASIA

Marcela Alveno, Diego Gironda, Valeria Giraldo, Carlos Zamarron, and Paula Paez shed light on FinTech investments in the Asia-Pacific region, surpassing North America. Focusing on North and East Asia, the research explores the evolving financial landscape in countries like China, Japan, Taiwan, South Korea, and Mongolia. The study emphasizes the impact of data analytics, network externalities, and interwoven activities in the region.

CHAPTER 9: NORTH AMERICA DISRUPTING THE FINANCIAL GIANTS

Mitra Madanchian analyzes the dynamic forces causing significant changes in the financial industry of North America. The chapter provides an in-depth analysis of disruptive innovations challenging established financial institutions. It offers insights into the present condition, evolving rules and regulations, and potential future developments in the financial sector of North America.

CHAPTER 10: THE RISE OF AI IN MIDDLE EASTERN FINTECH WITH THE CASE STUDIES FROM THE UAE AND TURKEY

Hooman Razavi and Ali Habibnia delve into the FinTech landscape in the Middle East, focusing on the UAE and Turkey. The chapter explores the impact of Artificial Intelligence (AI) on FinTech, addressing challenges, opportunities, and future trends in these regional FinTech hubs. Tailored for finance professionals, policymakers, entrepreneurs, and academics, the chapter serves as a concise resource for navigating the evolving FinTech scene in the Middle East.

CHAPTER 11: SUSTAINABLE FINANCE STRATEGIES IN THE FORMULA 1 INDUSTRY – A FINTECH PERSPECTIVE

Jay Israni, Giovana Castanho, and Hamed Taherdoost explore sustainable finance mechanisms within the Formula 1 industry. The chapter investigates the integration of green bonds and impact investments to support the sport's goal of becoming carbon-neutral by 2030, offering a strategic approach for environmental change within a high-profile motorsport.

CHAPTER 12: FINTECH-ENABLED TELEMEDICINE- GLOBAL HEALTHCARE ADVANCEMENT

Shadi Askari, Alireza Ghofrani, and Hamed Taherdoost examine the collaboration between FinTech and telemedicine. The chapter explores the potential of this partnership to enhance global healthcare accessibility, affordability, and efficiency. Recommendations are provided for policymakers, healthcare professionals, and FinTech innovators to harness the full potential of this collaboration.

In closing, the culmination of our collective efforts as Editors and the invaluable contributions from our esteemed authors has given rise to "Exploring Global FinTech Advancement and Applications" – a compendium that delves into the transformative landscape of global financial technology. Through dynamic collaboration, Hamed Taherdoost, Nam Le, Mitra Madanchian, and Yousef Farhaoui have presented a profound exploration of how FinTech is reshaping the world of finance.

The FinTech revolution, which we've witnessed throughout the chapters, has emerged as a potent force challenging conventional norms and ushering in an era marked by accessibility, efficiency, and security in financial transactions. The innovative technologies of blockchain, AI-driven analytics, and mobile payment systems, highlighted across the book, are not mere trends but pivotal tools shaping the future of finance.

Our journey traverses diverse global regions, providing in-depth country assessments that uncover the nuances of the FinTech landscape. From Southeast Asia to North America and the Middle East, each chapter serves as a valuable resource offering insights into regional FinTech growth, challenges, and opportunities for collaboration.

This reference book is more than just a collection of chapters; it is a crucial tool for various stakeholders in the finance and technology realms. Professionals, entrepreneurs, scholars, policymakers, tech enthusiasts, and individuals engaged in cross-border trade and finance will find this book to be an indispensable guide to navigating the ever-changing landscape of global FinTech.

Organized systematically, the chapters cover a spectrum of topics – from regulatory dynamics and growth trends to the future of FinTech. The exploration of cryptocurrency adoption, financial inclusion challenges, and the rise of AI in Middle Eastern FinTech paints a comprehensive picture of the dynamic forces at play in the industry.

As Editors, we believe that this reference book will not only serve as a guide for academics but also as a source of inspiration for those driving change in the FinTech landscape. Our gratitude extends to the contributors for their invaluable insights, and we invite readers to embark on this journey of exploration into the vibrant world of global FinTech. Together, let us embrace the future of finance shaped by innovation, collaboration, and resilience.

Hamed Taherdoost
University Canada West, Canada

Nam Le
University Canada West, Canada

Mitra Madanchian
University Canada West, Canada

Yousef Farhaoui
Faculty of Sciences and Techniques, Moulay Ismail University of Meknes, Morocco

Chapter 1
Leading the Fintech Revolution: Navigating the Future of Finance

Mitra Madanchian
University Canada West, Canada

ABSTRACT

Financial technology (Fintech) has emerged as a disruptive force reshaping our conceptions of money, payments, investments, and banking. As the financial environment evolves, the importance of leadership in the Fintech industry grows. This chapter examines the dynamic intersection of leadership and Fintech, delving into leaders' unique challenges and opportunities in a landscape where innovation and regulatory complexities coexist. The reader will navigate the complexities of Fintech leadership, obtaining insight into the essential skills, strategies, and attitudes required to flourish in this swiftly evolving field. Various topics are covered, from fostering innovation and embracing risk to navigating regulatory obstacles and cultivating resilient teams.

INTRODUCTION

Fintech is the term for the application of technology to the provision of creative financial services. It includes a broad spectrum of technologies to digitalize and simplify traditional financial services, such as banking and payment procedures. With the introduction of online stock trading and electronic banking in the late 20th century, Fintech first emerged. Early in the new millennium, "Fintech" became widely used to characterize the growing convergence of technology and financial services, mostly due to the internet's and digital technologies' expansion. Fintech has developed over several historical periods, and major changes occur every. With origins in the late 19th century, when money could be transferred by telegrams and Morse code, it has shaped how people interact with their money for over a century (Giglio, 2021; Karkkainen, 2023).

Fintech has had a significant role in changing the financial services sector, upending established corporate structures, and opening new doors for individuals and companies in the consumer and enterprise markets. It has completely changed the financial landscape by erasing distinctions between established financial institutions and the financial sector, encouraging healthy competition and innovation, and pro-

DOI: 10.4018/979-8-3693-1561-3.ch001

pelling the creation of new financial goods and services. Fintech has also made examining and modifying supervision, supervisory, and regulatory frameworks necessary to ensure they continue serving their intended purposes and allow the authorities to promote a secure, effective, and inclusive financial system. Additionally, it has caused a change in the inclinations of consumer behavior and market structure, necessitating the proactive shaping of these changes to promote contestability and competitiveness in the financial sector. Fintech is positioned to change the future of finance and make it more accessible and equitable. Its influence is felt globally, helping new solutions to be adopted in underserved markets and digital banking to grow. Fintech is also critical in promoting financial inclusion, efficiency, and resilience.

The Fintech revolution is examined in this chapter, which traces its development from historical foundations to contemporary trends. Through case studies, it addresses important topics like blockchain, robo-advisors, and digital payments while emphasizing leadership qualities. Artificial intelligence (AI) and other technological advancements are considered regulatory challenges. With a forward-looking outlook on potential developments, the chapter offers readers a succinct yet thorough summary of Fintech's influence on the financial sector.

THE FINTECH LANDSCAPE

Overview of Current Fintech Trends

Digital Payments

Transferring money from one payment account to another using a digital device or channel is called a digital payment, sometimes called an electronic payment. This covers a range of payment options, including credit, debit, prepaid cards, bank transfers, mobile money, and QR codes. When given responsibly, digital payments—which can be partly, mostly, or digital—have the potential to advance decent employment and provide employees with more choice over their income and benefits. Transitioning from cash to digital payments is essential to laying the groundwork for upcoming investments in the world's poorest nations. Transparency, data and fund protection, accountability, fairness, and the capacity to operate across providers to guarantee competition and choice are characteristics of responsible digital payments.

The world of digital payments is changing quickly as more and more people accept peer-to-peer (P2P) payments, digital wallets, and "buy now, pay later" choices. Stronger fraud prevention and quicker access to funds are the main drivers of this trend. Financial institutions are adapting by implementing the newest payment technologies and forming partnerships with Fintech to fulfill the demands of evolving consumers better. Additionally, the epidemic has significantly increased user propensity to utilize digital payments, particularly in low- and middle-income economies, which has functioned as a driver for the development of cashless payments. The broad use of cell phones and related technology, infrastructural upgrades, and the release of international payment message standards have all made this easier.

Blockchain and Cryptocurrencies

The fundamental technology that makes cryptocurrencies like Bitcoin possible is called blockchain. Participants can confirm transactions without the need for a central clearing authority thanks to this P2P network's decentralized ledger of all transactions. Because of its capacity to offer safe, transparent, and decentralized transaction verification and recording, this technology has been hailed as a disruptive force in the finance industry, notably in payments and banking. Blockchain technology is a digital ledger that safely saves information about purchasing, selling, and exchanging cryptocurrencies by tracking and verifying cryptocurrency trades. Since no single authority is in charge of this data, it is possible to have a global currency with equal value everywhere. Blockchain technology has potential uses outside of cryptocurrency. It can track product paths, provide transparency, and spot problems in various industries, including the food supply chains. Like public internet protocols like HTML in the early days of the World Wide Web, blockchain is a quickly evolving technology that has the potential to alter many parts of our lives and work (Angrish, Craver, Hasan, & Starly, 2018; Mougayar, 2016).

Robo-Advisors and Wealth Management

With their ability to provide algorithm-driven investment management services with little human involvement, robo-advisors have become disruptive in wealth management. These platforms manage and distribute client assets, offer financial advice, and build ideal portfolios based on investor preferences, risk tolerance, and expected returns. The use of mathematical algorithms accomplishes all of these functions. Because they can provide typical investment management services at prices much lower than those of human financial advisors, robo-advisors are becoming increasingly popular among investors. Through web platforms and mobile applications, they also offer security, flexibility, and easy access to portfolio management tools. Robo-advisors are handling trillions of dollars worth of client assets, and the sector has grown exponentially. Although robo-advisors provide efficient and reasonably priced investment management services, they have come under fire for presuming that investors have specific goals and a thorough understanding of their financial situation and need more subjectivity to provide completely customized services. Despite these concerns, robo-advisors have grown in popularity and accessibility as a low-cost financial advising and investment management service provider for investors. Various robo-advisors are now offered to meet the needs and preferences of different investor types (Hakala, 2019; Sironi, 2016).

Insurtech

The creative application of technology in the insurance sector to improve efficiency and reduce costs within the existing insurance paradigm is known as insurtech, a subset of Fintech (Stoeckli, Dremel, & Uebernickel, 2018). It includes a broad spectrum of technologically enabled innovations that have surfaced to provide more straightforward products and optimize consumer experiences, drawing interest from traditional insurers and venture capital firms. With startups garnering large investments, the insurtech sector has grown significantly, changing the insurance industry's competitive environment and business models. The insurance value chain—including distribution, marketing, product design, underwriting, claims handling, and balance sheet management for all insurance lines, including life, health, and property and casualty—is covered by insurtech innovation. The influence of insurtech goes beyond increasing productivity; it also includes providing extremely tailored plans and using new data streams from Internet-enabled devices to price premiums depending on behavior seen dynamically. With the ultimate goal of offering an enhanced service of higher value to insurers and their clients, the sector is transforming insurance by giving clients and service providers a smooth, error-free, and secure means to do business (Pillay, 2018).

Lending and Crowdfunding

P2P lending, another name for lending-based crowdfunding, has become an important instrument for supporting innovation, particularly in the energy industry. Individuals can fund projects like building large-scale renewable energy plants through internet fundraising on specialized platforms. Citizens can benefit from this method by participating in the energy transition and receiving interest on their payments (Bottiglia, 2016).

P2P financing enables businesses to borrow directly from several people via online platforms, providing a substitute for traditional bank loans. To safeguard the interests of investors and businesses alike, borrowers can accept loan offers with the lowest interest rates after completing a thorough investigation for each loan request. P2P lending is a desirable choice for companies looking for alternative financing. It provides more flexibility regarding interest rates, the capacity to access funds even when a bank declines to approve a loan, and the ability to accommodate different loan amounts. Usually, the platform receives direct debits during the repayment process and distributes the money to the lenders. P2P financing is appropriate for companies that offer services and other types of businesses, giving them a practical source of finance (Milne & Parboteeah, 2016).

Key Players and Emerging Innovations

Established Fintech Companies

The term "embedded finance" describes how financial services, such as lending, payment processing, and insurance, can be integrated into the infrastructures of non-financial companies without sending customers to traditional financial institutions (Casper & Matthias, 2021; Omarini, 2023). Application programming interfaces (APIs) allow financial and non-financial businesses to integrate and provide services like payments, banking, lending, and insurance without establishing their financial infrastructure or becoming regulated as financial entities (Gochhwal, 2017). Businesses may improve customer experiences, generate new revenue streams, and upgrade the underlying payments infrastructure using embedded finance, eventually benefiting customers by giving them more ease and cost savings. Embedded finance is useful for companies looking to add financial tools and services to their products to make payments easier and quicker. This trend is driven by the growing consumer demand for faster and easier services and the desire for businesses to receive payments more quickly.

Startups Shaping the Industry

Fintech startups significantly influence how several industries, including banking, will develop. They bring about change, push the envelope, and upend established sectors with innovative ideas and state-of-the-art technology. Startups are pushing change in various industries, including healthcare and finance, and their impact is only expected to increase. Being an entrepreneur is exciting since the startup scene is always changing, and new ideas and technologies appear. Startups are bringing innovation to the forefront and upending well-established markets, helping the industry flourish. As technology progresses and novel prospects arise, startups are anticipated to sustain their pivotal position in molding the trajectory of sectors and propelling inventiveness ahead. With an emphasis on new opportunities and trends that are expected to influence the startup scene in the years to come, such as the development of AI, the emergence of the gig economy, and the influence of political and economic factors on investment trends, the future of startups is looking to be an exciting one.

Global Regulatory Landscape

Fintech is bringing about a paradigm change with several policy implications by quickly changing the financial sector landscape and erasing the distinctions between financial enterprises and the financial sector. These ramifications include expanding the scope of monitoring, reevaluating regulatory boundaries, encouraging beneficial innovation and competition, and keeping an eye on changing policy trade-offs as Fintech use increases. Regulatory, supervisory, and oversight frameworks are being examined to ensure they continue to serve their intended purpose and allow the authorities to promote a secure, effective, and inclusive financial system. Another important factor is anticipating and proactively shaping market structure tendencies to promote contestability and competitiveness in the financial sector. Aspects of the changing global regulatory landscape that are crucial to consider include modernizing and opening up financial infrastructures to promote contestability and competition, making sure public money is still appropriate for the digital age, and pursuing robust cross-border coordination and information sharing. The regulatory environment is changing to meet the opportunities and challenges of technology development, preserve financial stability, protect consumers, and foster innovation in the financial industry.

LEADERSHIP IN THE FINTECH SPACE

The financial markets and the availability of financial services have been significantly impacted by exceptional business ideas, matching services and products, new business models, and new technological applications. These have gained much attention due to their benefits, which include raising operational efficiency, cutting expenses, upending established industry structures, obfuscating boundaries between industries, enabling strategic disintermediation, opening up new avenues for entrepreneurship, and democratizing access to financial services. According to the study by Kuratko and Hornsby (Kuratko & Hornsby, 1999), economies are currently undergoing a surge in the entrepreneurial revolution as a result of nations and economies as a whole appreciating the work and value produced by small and medium-sized enterprises.

According to research by Zhou et al. (Zhou, Zhou, Zhang, Obschonka, & Silbereisen, 2019), many company executives and founders have distinctive entrepreneurial traits. These people have a reputation for taking risks, being confident in themselves, and having innate intuition. Companies of all sizes, especially start-ups, can gain a competitive edge and short- and long-term success by imitating their executives' entrepreneurial attitudes and behaviors (Latif, Afzal, Saqib, Sahibzada, & Alam, 2021). However, when the start-up develops into a full-fledged company, its leader or leaders take on new duties within the company; as a result, their focus shifts from innovation and creativity to more administration and organization of the entity, encompassing people management, organizational structures, culture, and philosophy, in addition to financial management (Latif et al., 2021).

Visionary innovation, flexible adaptability, and risk intelligence are traits of successful Fintech leaders who foresee trends and develop ground-breaking solutions while reacting quickly to shifts. Their customer-centric approach, collaborative leadership, and tech-savvy skills propelled personalized services, strategic alliances, and data-driven decision-making. These executives, who will continue to expand and innovate the financial industry, are resilient in the face of adversity and dedicated to lifelong learning. The key characteristics of effective Fintech executives are illustrated in Figure 1, which include creativity, flexibility, risk awareness, customer focus, collaborative leadership, and resilience.

Figure 1. Successful Fintech leaders

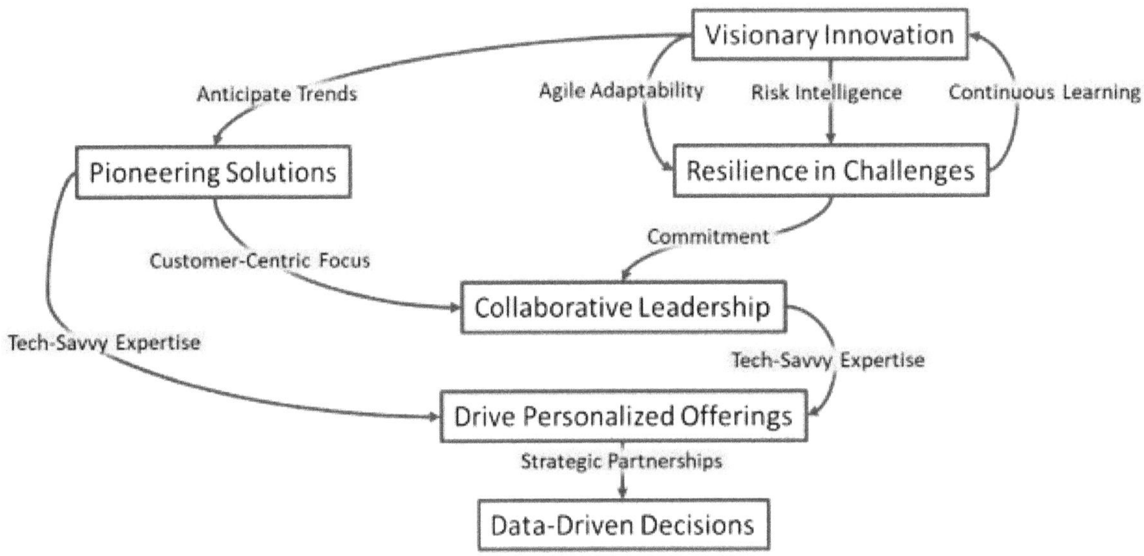

Innovation and Adaptability

Leaders in the Fintech industry who are adept at navigating this ever-changing landscape recognize how important it is to cultivate a continual innovation culture. This entails fostering proactive ideation and implementing iterative development procedures that enable the quick testing and improvement of innovative concepts. Leaders keep their companies at the forefront of industry evolution by fostering an environment that fosters creativity and rewards unconventional thinking.

Furthermore, these executives understand how important it is to be flexible to react to changes in the market and technological advances. Successful Fintech executives maintain a keen understanding of cutting-edge technology like blockchain, AI, and data analytics, making them known for their tech-savvy leadership. With this insight, they can strategically integrate new tools into their operations and make well-informed decisions. A crucial adaptation component is strategy flexibility; leaders are prepared to change course and modify business plans to take advantage of evolving markets and keep a competitive advantage.

Moreover, Fintech leadership innovation and flexibility go beyond technical considerations. Leaders adeptly handle regulatory changes by proactively incorporating compliance into developing new products and services. They achieve a careful balance between pursuing innovation and reducing possible hazards by working with regulatory agencies and utilizing risk-informed decision-making processes.

Risk Management and Compliance

Effective leaders understand that compliance and risk management are essential to long-term growth. Effective leadership is built on proactive engagement with regulatory agencies, which promotes openness and cooperation while keeping ahead of changing compliance requirements. To ensure compliance satisfies legal requirements and promotes innovation, leaders develop flexible compliance frameworks that adjust to regulation changes. This flexibility enables thorough risk evaluations to handle financial risks, weaknesses, and cybersecurity threats.

One of the most important aspects of effective Fintech executives' risk and compliance strategies is embracing technology. They incorporate state-of-the-art technologies like machine learning and AI to improve fraud detection, safeguard data, and automate compliance procedures. This technological ability puts the company at the forefront of innovation and increases compliance efficiency. Another important factor is ethics, where leaders cultivate a culture of moral behavior that extends beyond legal compliance to include fair company practices and appropriate consumer data use. Ongoing training for staff members guarantees that everyone in the team stays current on industry best practices and regulatory changes, demonstrating the dedication to negotiating the complexity of risk management and compliance with resilience and foresight.

Customer-Centric Approach

Fintech executives exhibit a dedication to comprehending their heterogeneous clientele via meticulous examination, utilizing instruments such as analytics and market research to generate all-encompassing consumer profiles. They use segmentation techniques because customized products for different consumer groups increase customer satisfaction.

A customer-centric strategy also entails personalization at scale, with leaders using cutting-edge data analytics to derive meaningful insights for customized financial advice and targeted marketing. To promote a culture of continuous improvement, proactive feedback systems are set up, enabling executives to develop products and services iteratively based on client input. Leaders need to prioritize trust and transparency by putting strong security measures in place to protect financial data and being transparent about how they use data and algorithmic processes. Adopting technology trends, forward-thinking leaders maintain their edge by incorporating cutting-edge technologies like blockchain and AI to improve user experiences.

NAVIGATING REGULATORY CHALLENGES

Overview of Fintech Regulations

A thorough grasp of the legal structures and compliance standards guiding the ever-changing field of Fintech can be gained by looking at Fintech legislation. Global regulatory organizations work to balance promoting innovation and guaranteeing consumer protection, financial stability, and compliance with legal requirements. At the same time, the Fintech sector is experiencing fast expansion and innovation. The following investigation explores important areas of Fintech legislation, illuminating the complex regulatory landscape (Figure 2).

First of all, different nations and areas have different regulatory strategies. Some governments have adopted a welcoming and pro-innovation posture, putting in place programs like sandboxes to promote experimentation. On the other hand, some adopt a more circumspect stance, prioritizing strict adherence and supervision to reduce hazards. Another important factor is licensing and registration requirements. According to laws in many countries, fintech companies need specialized licenses or registrations based on their activity, such as lending, payments, or cryptocurrency services. Understanding and meeting these regulatory requirements is critical for Fintech startups looking to operate legally.

A prominent issue in Fintech rules is consumer protection, which includes steps to guarantee equitable lending practices, open disclosure of terms and circumstances, protection of personal information, and establishment of dispute resolution procedures. Following these guidelines is not only required by law but also essential for preserving a good reputation and winning over new clients. Since Fintech businesses rely heavily on data, data security and privacy laws are more crucial than ever. Fintech businesses are usually required to put strong security measures in place to safeguard confidential client data, adhere to data protection regulations, and quickly notify any data breaches.

Fintech regulations also tackle the difficulties associated with Know Your Customer (KYC) and Anti-Money Laundering (AML) compliance. Because they handle financial transactions, Fintech companies are especially vulnerable to money laundering and other illegal activity. Strict customer verification procedures and reporting systems are required under rules about AML and KYC practices to stop financial crimes. Operating globally adds another layer of complexity, as Fintech businesses have to deal with cross-border regulatory issues such as managing cross-border transactions, traversing different frameworks, and adhering to different legal requirements. Sandboxes are regulated spaces created by some regulatory bodies where Fintech companies can test new goods and services while being closely monitored. Lastly, the constantly changing Fintech regulatory environment emphasizes the necessity of ongoing attention.

Strategies for Regulatory Compliance

Regulations about Fintech compliance are crucial for maintaining the integrity of financial services, safeguarding consumer safety, and preserving data privacy. These laws always change to prevent fraud and keep up with new technology developments. The financial services industry is experiencing a significant development in technology-enabled innovation, which has heightened the requirement for regulatory responses to precisely and quickly address new risks. Fintech is being utilized to increase compliance, create efficiency, and assist regulatory bodies in achieving their goals. The issues posed by Fintech have been met with various responses from regulatory bodies; therefore, regulation and supervision of Fintech should be adapted to the specifics of the innovation and its effects on the delivery of financial services.

Fintech companies should prioritize consumer protection, data privacy, and AML inspection to ensure regulatory compliance. They should also prepare ahead of time by making investments in regulatory technologies and fostering a compliance-oriented culture. Fintech companies may effectively traverse the intricate regulatory landscape and foster industry growth and innovation by keeping up with regulatory developments and engaging with regulatory organizations (Bains & Wu, 2023).

Figure 2. Fintech regulations: Global dynamics

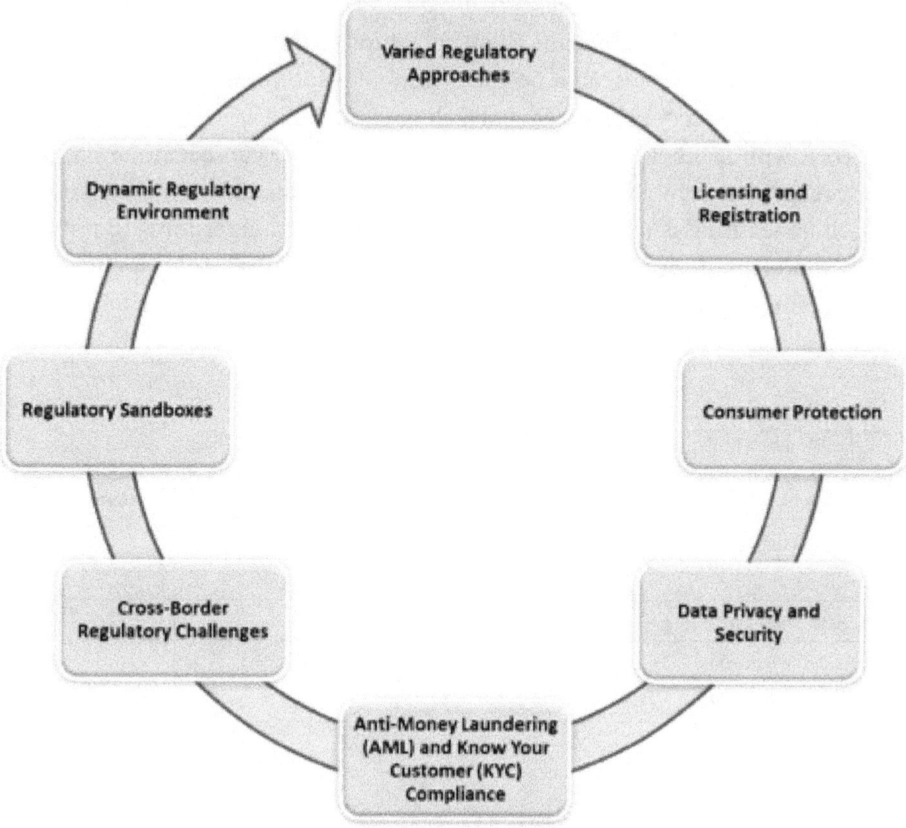

TECHNOLOGICAL INNOVATIONS SHAPING THE FUTURE

Technology advancements are crucial in determining how finance will develop in the future as the Fintech scene keeps changing. Using state-of-the-art technologies improves the effectiveness of financial services and creates new opportunities for both customers and enterprises.

Artificial Intelligence and Machine Learning in Fintech

AI and machine learning are fundamentally innovative technologies that are upending the financial services sector. It is changing the way that companies and people obtain and make use of financial services. AI can assist with activity recognition in various fields, including fraud detection and decision-making (Mahalakshmi et al., 2022). However, given this recent development, several studies have already been done on the effects of AI and Fintech on the financial sector. However, they need to address how large, established institutions worldwide use these technologies by employing specialized tools to help them carry out crucial tasks for the financial sector.

The progressive nature of AI sets it apart from other concepts highlighted in the 21st century as it continues to advance at a steady and fast pace. Stated differently, technological progress is unending.

Given that a new generation of consumers is growing more dependent on services that keep up with technological breakthroughs, the financial service sector has seen changes in response to these developments. New markets are being formed in the financial sector, and old ones are being redefined. Through simplifying processes, extensive research on the effects of AI and machine learning technologies has improved the industry's delivery quality (Mahalakshmi et al., 2022).

AI is concerned with technologies, systems, or processes that can accurately mimic how humans make decisions, respond to new information, communicate, listen, and comprehend language. On the other hand, machine learning is a subset of AI that uses data and algorithms to replicate how people learn, gradually improving its accuracy. Table 1 provides an overview of the application of AI and machine learning in Fintech, focusing on automation, real-time processing, data analysis, and flexibility in a range of critical roles.

Table 1. AI and machine learning aspects in Fintech

Aspect	Data Analysis	Real-Time Processing	Automation	Adaptability
Enhancing Customer Experience	✓	✓		✓
Fraud Detection and Security	✓	✓		✓
Credit Scoring and Risk Management	✓			✓
Algorithmic Trading and Investments	✓	✓		✓
Operational Efficiency and Automation	✓	✓	✓	✓

Enhancing Customer Experience

Machine learning (ML) and AI are key to improving consumer experience. This extends to individualized and user-centered financial services beyond simple transactional efficiency. Large-scale datasets, such as transaction histories, spending trends, and investment activity, are analyzed by AI-driven algorithms. Because of this analysis, Fintech platforms can provide consumers with highly customized financial advice. By delivering insights directly relevant to individual financial goals, AI improves the client journey through various applications, including budgeting assistance, investment opportunities, and spending habit optimization.

Virtual assistants and intelligent chatbots powered by machine learning algorithms transform consumer relationships. These virtual organizations can perform transactions, respond to standard questions, and offer real-time help, all of which increase the effectiveness and speed of customer care. These AI-driven interfaces adapt to better comprehend and meet user needs by continuously learning from consumer interactions.

By leveraging predictive analytics, fintech organizations may foresee client wants and challenges before they happen. AI can proactively address issues and lessen the need for reactive customer support by examining past customer interactions and common pain spots. This improves client happiness and loyalty while also streamlining the customer experience.

Fraud Detection and Security

Strong fraud detection and security protocols must be prioritized to preserve user confidence and guarantee the accuracy of financial transactions. Fintech businesses are increasingly using cutting-edge technologies to keep ahead of new dangers. This includes using multifactor authentication techniques to strengthen access controls beyond conventional username and password systems, such as biometric authentication (fingerprint, face, and voice recognition).

One crucial element of fintech security techniques is the monitoring of transactions in real time. Businesses use machine learning algorithms to instantly identify irregularities in transaction patterns and send out notifications or requests for authentication. Additionally, behavioral analytics are essential because they create a baseline of typical user behavior from which deviations that might indicate fraudulent activity can be quickly identified. By evaluating large datasets, such as transaction histories and external threat intelligence, AI proactively prevents fraud by spotting patterns suggestive of possible security risks.

Applications programming interface (API) security needs to be guaranteed since Fintech supports open banking and interconnected financial ecosystems. Fintech organizations employ robust encryption techniques to provide safe data transmission between platforms, shielding confidential data from unauthorized access and interception. Fintech companies actively engage with industry stakeholders, regulatory authorities, and law enforcement agencies to share information on new threats and best practices, further embracing a collaborative approach to security. By working together, we can better identify and stop fraud as a group, which creates a more stable and secure financial system.

Several academic papers shed light on how AI and machine learning are used in the financial sector for fraud detection and security. A computational model for quantitative methods-based financial reporting fraud detection has been proposed in one study by Glancy and Yadav (Glancy & Yadav, 2011). The use of data mining and machine learning techniques to detect financial scams is discussed in the paper by Sadgali et al. (Sadgali, Sael, & Benabbou, 2019). Furthermore, a report on methods by Aschi et al. (Aschi, Bonura, Masi, Messina, & Profeta, 2022) for detecting credit card fraud emphasizes using supervised and unsupervised learning to detect fraud in financial transactions. A further article by Boulieris et al. (Boulieris, Pavlopoulos, Xenos, & Vassalos, 2023) addresses automated fraud detection to protect user accounts. It highlights the difficulty presented by the rarity of confirmed fraudulent transactions and the significance of prompt identification in fostering and preserving client trust.

The Role of Big Data in Decision-Making

Big data is now a disruptive force in the finance industry, changing decisions and opening up previously unheard-of avenues for creativity. The enormous volumes of data produced by transactions, client interactions, and market dynamics provide a wealth of insights into the ever-changing field of Fintech. Fintech companies use big data analytics to find relevant patterns and correlations that help decision-makers get a detailed understanding of changing consumer habits and market trends. This data-driven strategy enhances strategic planning by refining existing products, generating specialized services, and keeping adaptable in response to changing customer preferences.

Furthermore, big data is essential to fintech risk management and fraud prevention. Risk mitigation methods can be implemented quickly thanks to proactive risk identification, made possible by analyzing historical and current data. By looking for odd trends in transaction data, machine learning algorithms improve fraud detection capabilities and protect consumers and the financial system's stability. Big data helps Fintech companies operate more efficiently, optimize costs, and reduce risk. To meet the demands of a financial landscape that is changing quickly, decision-makers can decrease costs, increase overall operational efficiency, and strategically deploy resources by automating repetitive work, optimizing internal procedures, and discovering inefficiencies.

Data Analytics for Personalization

Big data analytics within the Fintech sector extends beyond risk management, playing a pivotal role in delivering personalized and tailored financial services.

- *Customer-Centric Approach:* Fintech companies leverage advanced data analytics to gain deep insights into customer preferences and behaviors. These companies can create highly personalized financial products and services by analyzing transaction histories, spending patterns, and interaction data. This not only enhances the customer experience but also fosters stronger customer loyalty.
- *Targeted Marketing and Recommendations:* Big data enables Fintech firms to develop targeted marketing strategies by understanding the unique needs of individual customers. Through data-driven insights, companies can provide relevant and timely product recommendations, investment advice, and promotional offers, creating a more engaging and personalized customer interaction.
- *Customized Financial Solutions:* Big data analysis allows Fintech leaders to go beyond one-size-fits-all financial solutions. Personalized investment portfolios, insurance plans, and loan offerings can be tailored to match individual customers' financial goals and risk tolerance. This level of customization enhances the value proposition of Fintech services, attracting a diverse customer base.

Predictive Analytics for Risk Management

A key component of risk management is predictive analytics, which uses big data to produce predictive insights that improve risk assessment and assist in making decisions. The Fintech industry has transformed Risk management analysis by combining big data analytics, AI, and machine learning. This has increased its accuracy and compliance with legal requirements. Proactive and future-focused predictive analytics help identify possible dangers and possibilities, which helps financial organizations make wise investment decisions, spot fraud, and anticipate income accurately (Cornwell, Bilson, Gepp, Stern, & Vanstone, 2023). Furthermore, with the help of AI, predictive analytics provides crucial insights into consumer behavior, supply chains, and market trends, enabling companies to maximize performance and seize opportunities in a market that is changing quickly.

Predictive models use past data, credit ratings, and financial behavior to determine the probability of loan default or payback. This application of predictive analytics in Fintech extends to credit scoring and risk assessment. Predictive analytics can also identify the risks with the greatest potential for occurrence and financial impact, which helps identify appropriate risk management strategies.

FUTURE TRENDS AND PREDICTIONS

The Fintech business is evolving tremendously, and various significant trends and predictions influence its future. Both leaders in the Fintech industry and enthusiasts are keeping a close eye on these developments, predicting how they will affect financial services and the global economy.

The Rise of Decentralized Finance (DeFi)

The rise of Decentralized Finance (DeFi) represents a paradigm shift in the financial sector, upending established paradigms and promoting an environment that is more open and accessible. DeFi is a financial services reimagining platform based on smart contracts and blockchain technology. It does this by doing away with intermediaries and establishing P2P, decentralized networks for lending, borrowing, and trading. Smart contracts, the foundation of DeFi, automate the execution and enforcement of financial agreements, improving security and reducing procedures. Even with the advantages, the decentralized structure of DeFi presents difficulties, including security flaws and regulatory ambiguities, calling for industry-wide cooperation and the creation of regulatory frameworks.

With the introduction of cutting-edge financial tools like liquidity pools and decentralized lending, this paradigm shift offers consumers new opportunities for financial engagement and passive income. Furthermore, the community governance feature allows users to participate in decision-making processes actively. This is typically accomplished through Decentralized Autonomous Organizations (DAOs). However, issues with scalability—specifically, slow transaction speeds and network congestion—highlight the necessity of continuing to develop and apply scaling solutions. The decentralized structure of DeFi is causing governments and regulatory organizations to struggle; thus, maintaining a balance between innovation and regulatory compliance is essential to the ongoing development of this revolutionary financial environment.

Globalization of Fintech Services

Fintech is bringing in a new era of financial mobility, tearing down traditional boundaries, and bringing about a fundamental revolution in cross-border transactions. This development is driven by cryptocurrencies and digital payment methods, which provide a global financial transaction method. When these technologies become widely used, people and companies can conduct cross-border transactions quickly and efficiently. Governments and regulatory agencies worldwide are realizing how important it is to unify laws to support Fintech growth while maintaining consumer safety and financial stability. The emergence of collaborative efforts within regulatory frameworks creates a unified environment supporting Fintech services' worldwide expansion.

Fintech companies are forming multinational alliances in reaction to this profound change, utilizing one another's advantages to broaden their global presence. These partnerships, which include technology firms, startup enterprises, and well-established financial institutions, make it easier to share resources and experience and advance the creation of internationally compatible financial products. With digital financial services, the Fintech movement is reaching unbanked and underbanked communities worldwide and tackling financial inclusion issues on a never-before-seen scale. As governments aggressively promote their Fintech ecosystems to attract foreign talent and investment, Fintech diplomacy is rapidly becoming recognized as a strategic instrument in economic ties. Fintech services are becoming more globally distributed, offering many benefits but obstacles such as managing different legal environments and cultural quirks. Nevertheless, a crucial factor in determining the sector's success in leveraging the enormous potential of the global financial landscape will be its capacity to negotiate these complications skillfully.

Sustainability and Green Finance

By linking investors with projects centered on conservation, renewable energy, and other sustainable activities, Fintech platforms promote environmentally responsible investments. This change in thinking toward impact investment is part of a larger movement toward financial objectives matched with favorable social and environmental results. With a focus on blockchain technology, optimizing transactions for lower energy usage, and the creation of green data centers to minimize the carbon footprint associated with financial activities, Fintech companies are also actively addressing their operational impact.

Furthermore, governments and regulatory agencies are recognizing and influencing the integration of sustainability into Fintech through legislative measures, which are changing the landscape. Fintech's dedication to sustainable business practices is demonstrated by its role in creating and upholding green finance rules and by adopting standardized reporting standards for environmental, social, and governance (ESG) factors. Fintech companies are leading the way in developing cutting-edge green products that encourage consumers to make ecologically responsible financial decisions. Examples of these products include carbon-neutral payment options and eco-friendly banking solutions. In addition to promoting sustainability-related financial literacy, Fintech is using its power to increase public understanding of the environmental effects of financial decisions, helping to create a more environmentally conscious financial ecosystem. Key elements of Fintech's green activities are outlined in Table 2, which also covers impact investment, operational sustainability, regulatory compliance, cutting-edge products, and financial literacy initiatives.

Table 2. Fintech's green initiatives: Key focus areas

Aspect	Impact Investing	Operational Sustainability	Regulatory Compliance	Innovative Green Products	Financial Literacy and Awareness
Promotion of Eco-Friendly Investments	✓			✓	✓
Blockchain Technology for Reduced Energy Consumption		✓			
Green Data Centers for Reduced Carbon Footprint		✓			
Integration of Sustainability into Fintech Regulations			✓		
Standardized Reporting Frameworks for ESG Factors			✓		
Innovation in Green Financial Products	✓			✓	
Fostering Financial Literacy on Sustainability					✓

Evolution of Digital Identity Solutions

The financial industry is experiencing a significant shift in digital identity solutions due to the need for increased security, privacy, and consumer convenience. As a safe substitute for conventional passwords, biometric authentication techniques like fingerprint and facial recognition have become essential for digital identity verification. At the same time, the incorporation of blockchain technology is transforming identity management through decentralized and secure systems that give people more control over their data.

Digital identity is being shaped in large part by mobile technology, with cell phones acting as safe authentication mechanisms. Identity verification procedures easily incorporate mobile biometrics, such as fingerprint and facial recognition, and specialized ID apps function as digital wallets to help users safely access financial services. Using biometrics and extra security layers in multi-factor authentication techniques is becoming commonplace and improves transaction security overall. The progression also includes technologies that improve privacy, such as self-sovereign identity frameworks that give people more control over their identity information and zero-knowledge proofs that guarantee users can confirm their identity without compromising certain data.

As digital identification technologies advance, the financial sector is about to deliver a more secure, privacy-aware, and user-centric digital experience. These developments lead to a smooth and reliable global financial services-individual interaction while improving the security of financial transactions. The Fintech sector's dedication to offering creative and safe solutions for consumers' changing needs in the digital era is demonstrated by the continuous development of digital identity solutions. The development of Fintech's digital identification solutions is seen in Figure 3, which combines mobile, blockchain, biometrics, and privacy safeguards to provide a safe and user-friendly interface.

Figure 3. Digital identity

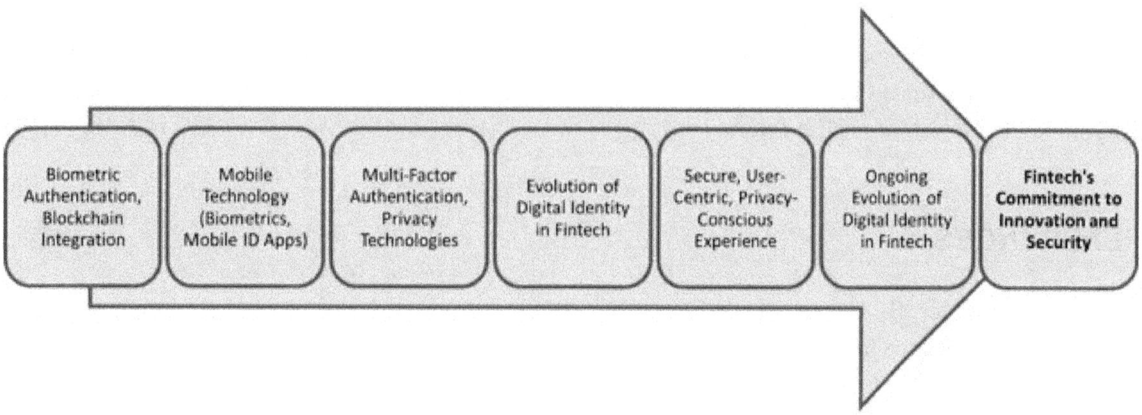

Adoption of Quantum Computing

The financial industry's adoption of quantum computing marks a revolutionary advance in processing capacity and analytical ability. Leveraging the concepts of quantum mechanics, quantum encryption has the potential to significantly increase the security of financial transactions by offering unmatched resilience to cryptographic attacks and eavesdropping. This improved security framework is needed as traditional encryption techniques become more vulnerable to hacking. Financial algorithms stand to benefit greatly from quantum computing's capacity for parallel processing. Fintech organizations are investigating quantum-resistant cryptography as a means of safeguarding confidential information. Additionally, the technology's capacity to expedite Monte Carlo simulations presents opportunities for more rapid and accurate risk assessments and portfolio improvements.

The implications of quantum computing go beyond security and into quantum machine learning. Quantum machine learning has the potential to transform fraud detection, credit scoring, and customer behavior analysis in Fintech applications by simultaneously recognizing complex patterns and trends. It also helps optimize portfolios more effectively by providing more educated risk management solutions and investing solutions. To fully realize the potential of quantum computing in the finance sector, however, obstacles like hardware development and smooth interaction with current systems need to be overcome.

CONCLUSION

In conclusion, strategic vision and creative leadership are essential for the Fintech revolution and the future of finance. This investigation has revealed the ever-changing Fintech sector, highlighting its revolutionary impact on conventional financial models. A customer-centric mentality, creativity, and agility are characteristics of successful leaders in this field, as demonstrated by case studies highlighting obstacles industry pioneers face. It became clear that navigating regulatory complexity was essential, and leaders were urged to use technology to ensure regulatory conformance and proactively integrate compliance measures. The effects of technology advancements on risk management, fraud detection, and customer experiences—including AI, machine learning, and big data—were closely examined. The emergence of decentralized finance (DeFi), the incorporation of cutting-edge technologies, and the internationalization of Fintech services indicate the direction of an intriguing and intricate future. The chapter acts as a call to action in this dynamic climate, imploring leaders to welcome innovation, cultivate resilience, and work together to create the changing financial landscape, where decisions taken today will determine the financial ecosystems of the future.

REFERENCES

Angrish, A., Craver, B., Hasan, M., & Starly, B. (2018). A case study for blockchain in manufacturing "FabRec": A prototype for peer-to-peer network of manufacturing nodes. *Procedia Manufacturing*, *26*, 1180–1192. doi:10.1016/j.promfg.2018.07.154

Aschi, M., Bonura, S., Masi, N., Messina, D., & Profeta, D. (2022). Cybersecurity and fraud detection in financial transactions. In *Big Data and Artificial Intelligence in Digital Finance: Increasing Personalization and Trust in Digital Finance using Big Data and AI* (pp. 269–278). Springer. doi:10.1007/978-3-030-94590-9_15

Bains, P., & Wu, C. (2023). *Institutional Arrangements for Fintech Regulation: Supervisory Monitoring*. Academic Press.

Bottiglia, R. (2016). Competitive frontiers in P2P lending crowdfunding. *Crowdfunding for SMEs: A European Perspective*, 61-92.

Boulieris, P., Pavlopoulos, J., Xenos, A., & Vassalos, V. (2023). Fraud detection with natural language processing. *Machine Learning*, 1–22.

Casper, S., & Matthias, Y. (2021). *Orientation in a New World of Technology and Finance Integration*. Exploring the Concept of Embedded Lending.

Cornwell, N., Bilson, C., Gepp, A., Stern, S., & Vanstone, B. J. (2023). The role of data analytics within operational risk management: A systematic review from the financial services and energy sectors. *The Journal of the Operational Research Society*, *74*(1), 374–402. doi:10.1080/01605682.2022.2041373

Giglio, F. (2021). Fintech: A literature review. *European Research Studies*, *24*(2B, 2B), 600–627. doi:10.35808/ersj/2254

Glancy, F. H., & Yadav, S. B. (2011). A computational model for financial reporting fraud detection. *Decision Support Systems*, *50*(3), 595–601. doi:10.1016/j.dss.2010.08.010

Gochhwal, R. (2017). Unified payment interface—An advancement in payment systems. *American Journal of Industrial and Business Management*, *7*(10), 1174–1191. doi:10.4236/ajibm.2017.710084

Hakala, K. (2019). *Robo-advisors as a form of artificial intelligence in private customers' investment advisory services*. Academic Press.

Karkkainen, T. (2023). *The FinTech Evolution: Technology Push, Market Pull Dynamics, and Inertia*. Tatja Karkkainen.

Kuratko, D. F., & Hornsby, J. S. (1999). Corporate entrepreneurial leadership for the 21st century. *The Journal of Leadership Studies*, *5*(2), 27–39. doi:10.1177/107179199900500204

Latif, K. F., Afzal, O., Saqib, A., Sahibzada, U. F., & Alam, W. (2021). Direct and configurational paths of knowledge-oriented leadership, entrepreneurial orientation, and knowledge management processes to project success. *Journal of Intellectual Capital*, *22*(1), 149–170. doi:10.1108/JIC-09-2019-0228

Mahalakshmi, V., Kulkarni, N., Kumar, K. P., Kumar, K. S., Sree, D. N., & Durga, S. (2022). The Role of implementing Artificial Intelligence and Machine Learning Technologies in the financial services Industry for creating Competitive Intelligence. *Materials Today: Proceedings*, *56*, 2252–2255. doi:10.1016/j.matpr.2021.11.577

Milne, A., & Parboteeah, P. (2016). *The business models and economics of peer-to-peer lending*. Academic Press.

Mougayar, W. (2016). *The business blockchain: promise, practice, and application of the next Internet technology*. John Wiley & Sons.

Omarini, A. (2023). From Digital Technologies to New Economics in Banking: How to Drive the Future of Digital Money and Data Information Knowledge. In Digital Transformation and the Economics of Banking (pp. 31-49). Routledge.

Pillay, T. (2018). *The influence of insurance on the existing insurance business model*. University of Pretoria.

Sironi, P. (2016). *FinTech innovation: from robo-advisors to goal-based investing and gamification*. John Wiley & Sons. doi:10.1002/9781119227205

Stoeckli, E., Dremel, C., & Uebernickel, F. (2018). Exploring characteristics and transformational capabilities of InsurTech innovations to understand insurance value creation in a digital world. *Electronic Markets*, *28*(3), 287–305. doi:10.1007/s12525-018-0304-7

Zhou, M., Zhou, Y., Zhang, J., Obschonka, M., & Silbereisen, R. K. (2019). Person–city personality fit and entrepreneurial success: An explorative study in China. *International Journal of Psychology*, *54*(2), 155–163. doi:10.1002/ijop.12451 PMID:28804917

Chapter 2
Determinants of Continual Use of Mobile Banking Applications: An Integrated Theoretical Perspective

Ibrahim Issahaku
Ghana Institute of Management and Public Administration, Ghana

Eric Kuada
Ghana Institute of Management and Public Administration, Ghana

Peace Kumah
Knutsford University, Ghana

Winfred Yaokumah
https://orcid.org/0000-0001-7756-1832
University of Ghana, Ghana

ABSTRACT

This study explores the factors that contribute to the continual use of mobile banking apps by integrating design aesthetics, information quality, and perceived privacy with the expectation-confirmation information systems continuance model. A convenience sample of 300 respondents from two state-owned universities in Ghana provided survey data that was analyzed using the partial least squares-structural equation modeling technique. The results indicate that perceived usefulness is a significant factor in user satisfaction, while confirmation impacts both satisfaction and perceived usefulness. Additionally, design aesthetics and information quality have a significant influence on continual use. However, perceived security/privacy, satisfaction, and perceived usefulness have insignificant effects on continual use. By combining theoretical perspectives, this study offers a conceptual model for examining the factors that impact the use of mobile banking apps. These findings can be used by mobile app developers and marketers to develop effective marketing strategies.

DOI: 10.4018/979-8-3693-1561-3.ch002

INTRODUCTION

Among the current trends in the financial sector is the development and adoption of mobile banking applications (apps). The uptake in the use of mobile banking apps can be associated with the increasing use of smartphones. However, despite the benefits of mobile banking apps, only a few people use this innovation in most countries in sub-Saharan Africa. In Ghana, for instance, there are 41.69 million mobile connections, representing 132.8% of the total population (Datareportal, 2021; Statista, 2021). Given this significant increase in mobile connectivity, statistics however show that only 7 percent of this mobile population performs some form of banking activity on their mobile devices (Statista, 2020). Promoting the use of mobile banking apps is therefore of particular importance to the banks as it reduces operational expenses and enhances customers' banking experience (Thusi & Maduku, 2020). One way to promote the acceptance of mobile banking apps is to increase their adoption among customers who can adapt quickly to innovation (Purani, Kumar, & Sahadev, 2019). Bajwa et al. (2022) predicted that financial technologies will likely be characterized by innovation and collaboration between traditional financial institutions and mobile banking platform developers.

Banks use various technologies to deliver mobile banking services, such as short messaging services (SMS banking) and unstructured supplementary service data (USSD) (Perlman, 2017). Mobile banking services cover a wide range of financial needs such as payments, savings, borrowing, risk management, and advisory (Wojcik, 2021). Mobile banking apps are a recent development in delivering mobile banking services. Users may have different perceptions of these technologies and so their acceptance of mobile banking services may differ according to which technology the bank uses. Despite these different approaches to mobile banking, research has largely focused on overall mobile banking technology rather than examining specific approaches (Thusi & Maduku, 2020). As a result, the user's perceptions of a particular delivery approach may be overlooked (Chen, Huang, & Davison, 2017). Given that banking apps are a recent phenomenon, particularly in developing countries, research on this delivery method is limited (Thusi & Maduku, 2020). A review of the literature identifies only a handful of studies on this subject most of which were conducted in developed nations. For example, Khurana (2023) indicates that the United States has made the most noteworthy contribution to the field of FinTech, producing the highest number of publications and citations in this area.

Recent studies investigate factors that determine the continual use of mobile banking applications in various contexts, including mobile wallets (Garrouch, 2021) and mobile payments (Pal et al., 2021). Specifically, Pan and Gao (2021) assess the perceived risks and the behavioral intention to use a mobile application. Pal et al. (2021) discuss the security risk and digital literacy issues of mobile payment systems. Solecki et al. (2020) explain the importance of usability and aesthetic features of mobile applications. Srivastava and Vishnani (2021) determine the effect of service quality on the continuance intention to use mobile banking. In general, these studies derived their constructs from a particular adoption model, without integrating factors from different theoretical perspectives. This current study proposes a conceptual model by integrating constructs from various theoretical perspectives to determine the factors that influence the continual use of mobile banking applications in a developing country. To achieve this objective, the study seeks to (a) determine the factors for the continual use of mobile banking applications, and (b) assess the factors that moderate the relationship between the determinants and the continual use of mobile banking applications.

BACKGROUND

Empirical Review

Advances in mobile technologies and the plethora of mobile applications (mobile apps) are bringing about behavioral changes in individuals and corporate users (Roy, 2017). Mobile technologies consist of physical mobile devices, the network connecting the devices, and the software that operates the devices (Yip et al., 2020). Mobile applications are application software that runs on mobile phones, tablet computers, and other mobile devices (Inukollu, Keshamoni, and Kang, 2014). Mobile applications span a wide scope of applicability, including marketing, m-health (Wang and Collins, 2021), advertising, news updates, manufacturing, education, and social networking. These make them extremely useful or powerful tools for everyday use (Cudjoe et al., 2015).

Qing and Haiying (2021) categorized mobile applications into branded and generic. Branded apps are software that displays brand identity, such as the app's name and business logo (Lim et al., 2021), while generic apps are not designed with any branding specifications. The branded apps are grouped into a) tool-centric (meant for identifying the motivations and requirements of consumers for using or buying products), b) entertainment and game-centric (designed with the aim of entertaining users), c) social-centric (for socializing with people online), d) m-commerce centric (for facilitating e-commerce transactions via mobile devices), and e) design-centric (for creating designs) (Filofteia, 2018). Other branded apps include a) standard web apps (which are mainly designed for desktop computer browsers), responsive web (web design with a different style), mobile web (websites dedicated to mobile devices), native apps (specific apps for mobile devices with particular features), and hybrid apps (mobile web applications packed into a native app). Mobile apps are deployed through app stores, including a) Amazon AppStore, b) Apple App Store, c) Windows Store, d) Google Play Store, and e) BlackBerry World (Filofteia, 2018).

Previous studies that investigated factors for the continual use of mobile banking apps found varying results. Zhou (2013) conducted a study to establish the determining factors of continuance intention to use mobile payment systems. Through structural equation modeling, the study found service quality as the key factor affecting trust, while system quality influenced user satisfaction. Also, service quality and information quality impacted positively on flow. Moreover, trust, flow, and satisfaction determined continuance intention to use mobile payment systems. Similarly, Kumar, Adlakaha, and Mukherjee (2018) investigated the influence of perceived ease of use, trust, perceived usefulness, perceived security, grievance redressal, and satisfaction on users' continual intention to use mobile wallets. Using the structural equation modeling, the study found that perceived ease of use and perceived usefulness strongly affect user satisfaction and intention to continue to use mobile wallets. The effect of perceived security on user satisfaction was found to be significant, whereas the grievance redressal mediated the effect of perceived security on the intention to continually use mobile wallets.

Likewise, Elmorshidy (2018) found that system quality, information quality, and service quality have a positive relationship with perceived usefulness and perceived ease of use of mobile applications. The system quality, information quality, and service quality positively influenced the actual use. Besides, Li, Sun, and Yang (2019) proposed a research model by applying a hierarchical regression technique to establish mobility as a moderator of the relationship between continuance usage of a mobile terminal and perceived ease of use. Also, Chaitanya and Gupta (2017) studied the factors that determine customer satisfaction with mobile apps. The study revealed that design aesthetics, information quality, and image-appealing nature have a significant impact on customer satisfaction. In a related study, Hanjaya, Kenny, and Gunawan (2019) found that usefulness and information quality significantly affect online purchase intention.

According to Das and Das (2020), the adoption of FinTech services is influenced by demographic characteristics such as gender, age, income, occupation, and educational qualification. The study found that the adoption of FinTech services is higher among males than females, and it is higher among millennials and Generation Z as compared with Generation X and baby boomers. Businessmen, professionals, and service holders are regular users of FinTech services as compared with agriculturists and housewives. The study also found that respondents with higher income and educational qualifications are more likely to adopt FinTech services. However, Khan et al. (2022) suggested that there are significant challenges that need to be addressed to facilitate the development of FinTech in the Gulf Cooperation Council (GCC) member countries. Cybersecurity threats, privacy laws, and concerns about terrorist funding can pose significant challenges for the emergence of FinTech-driven applications in the GCC region (Khan et al., 2022). The main perceived risk factors associated with fintech use in Pakistan are performance risk, financial risk, and overall risk. Performance risk refers to concerns about the reliability and effectiveness of the fintech service, while financial risk relates to concerns about the security of financial transactions and potential financial losses (Li et al., 2023).

Research Model and Hypotheses

The constructs used to develop the conceptual model are based mainly on the expectation-confirmation IS continuance (Bhattacherjee, 2001). The study draws from other theories, including the multi-motive information systems continuance model (Lowry, Gaskin, and Moody, 2015), the Information systems (IS) success model (DeLone and MacLean, 2003), and the unified theory of acceptance and use of technology (UTAUT) (Venkatesh et al., 2012). The constructs of the model include user satisfaction, confirmation, and perceived usefulness (Bhattacherjee, 2001) serve as the precursors to continuance intention to use information systems. Moreover, the current study believes that these constructs are inadequate to represent all the major determinants of continuance usage of mobile banking apps.

Accordingly, the design aesthetics were drawn from the Multi-motive information systems continuance model (Cyr et al., 2006; Lowry, Gaskin, and Moody, 2015), information quality from the IS success model (DeLone & MacLean, 2003), and the perceived security/privacy and the moderation variables (age and gender) from the unified theory of acceptance and use of technology (Puriwat & Tripopsakul, 2017; Venkatesh et. al., 2012). Thus, the current study extends the Expectation-Confirmation IS continuance model with new factors that can influence the continual use of mobile banking apps. Therefore, the conceptual model of this study posits that for mobile banking apps to be continually used, perceived usefulness, user satisfaction, confirmation, and information quality (Bhattacherjee, 2001), design aesthetics (Lowry, Gaskin, & Moody, 2015), and the perceived security/privacy (Puriwat and Tripopsakul, 2017) should be the determinants with age and gender as moderating factors (Venkatesh et al., 2011). Figure 1 shows the conceptual model and the hypothetical relationships among the constructs.

Based on the conceptual model developed (see Figure 1), this study proposes some hypotheses to ascertain the factors that determine the continual use of mobile banking applications.

Figure 1. Conceptual model of mobile banking apps continual use

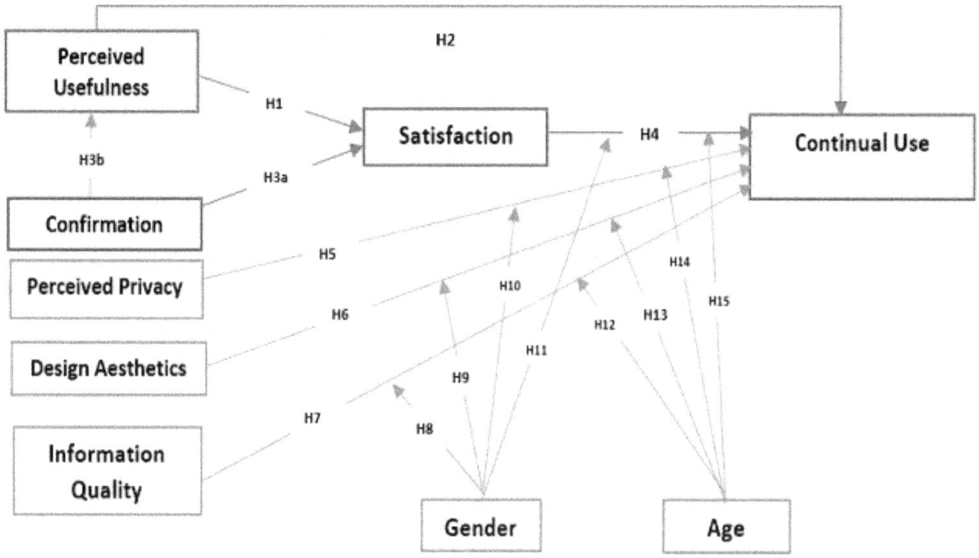

Perceived Usefulness. Perceived usefulness is the extent to which a user expects or anticipates an IS to serve his or her needs (Lwin, Ameen, & Nusarim, 2019). Perceived usefulness is one of the crucial determinants of continuance intention to use a system (Halawi, Mccarthy, and Farah, 2018; Liu & Tai, 2016). Perceived usefulness has been found to have a positive effect on the attitude to use a system. Masocha (2018) confirmed the relationship between the perceived usefulness of the information system to attitudes towards satisfaction with the system. Also, Alqahtani and Mohammad (2017) agreed that the high perceived usefulness of an IS leads to higher satisfaction. Hence, this study posits that:

H1: The perceived usefulness of mobile banking apps has a positive relationship with user satisfaction.

Using the Technology Acceptance Model, Masocha (2018) explored how perceived usefulness and perceived ease of use influence the user's behavioral intention to continually use a particular information system. The study established that the two constructs positively influence the continuance intention to use a system. Also, Liu and Tai (2016) indicated that perceived usefulness is one of the major indicators of an intention to use M-payment. Their conclusion was in agreement with that of Roy (2017), who found that perceived usefulness is a major predictor of continuance intention to use information systems. This implies that:

H2: Perceived usefulness of mobile banking apps has a positive effect on continuance intention to use the apps.

Confirmation. Bhattacherjee (2001) posited that confirmation has a positive relationship with satisfaction. With information via adverts, the user forms initial expectations about an app. Formation of expectation leads to the eventual use of the app. The eventual app usage (perceived performance) either confirms or disconfirms the initial expectations of the user. The user then forms satisfaction or dissatisfaction with the app. Therefore, the extent of the user's confirmation positively influences app satisfaction. Thus, this study proposes that:

H3a: Confirmation has a positive effect on user satisfaction with mobile banking apps.

Some researchers are of the view that people do not form opinions on a system and the intention to use the system from scratch but are rather influenced by prior ones. Bhattacherjee (2001) suggested that it is highly likely for perceived usefulness to be influenced, to a reasonable extent, by the experiences of confirmation. This is particularly true as the usefulness of a system initially perceived by a user may not be concrete since the user is uncertain as to what to expect from using the system. Therefore, the level of confirmation by a user consequently has a positive association with the perceived usefulness of the system. Hence, the study postulates that:

H3b: Confirmation has a positive relationship with the perceived usefulness of mobile banking apps.

Satisfaction. The issue of user satisfaction after using a system remains a constant construct in both the Expectation Confirmation Theory and the IS Continuance model (Lankton & Mcknight, 2012). Kumar, Adlakaha, and Mukherjee (2018) described user satisfaction as an emotion-based response to the target technology. The usage of the term in this study conforms to this definition as a technological phenomenon relating to the use of a mobile application. The definition also recognizes satisfaction as a post-purchase attribute. Using the expectation disconfirmation theory, Lankton and Mcknight (2012) found that a user's satisfaction with a system can strongly influence the decision to continually use that system. Therefore, the study proposes that:

H4: Satisfaction has a positive relationship with the continual use of mobile banking apps.

Perceived Privacy. Perceived privacy is used in this study to mean the confidentiality of the data transaction done with an app. Harris, Goodman, and Traynor (2013) explained that the increased ease of having access to personal information and the possibility of misusing this information has increased the level of privacy-related risks through mobile phone usage. Omolade (2017) argued that privacy can positively influence attitudes towards continuance intention to use a particular mobile application. People have become sensitive to the degree to which information about them is conveyed to other people (Omolade, 2017). Specifically, the rapid advancement of information exchanges has raised security concerns. For example, the main factors that affect the adoption of mobile payments in the Netherlands are safety and trust (Hasan, Islam, & Hossain, 2021). Similarly, Al Karim et al. (2023) mentioned that fraud, theft, customer security, and privacy threaten the Fintech business in Bangladesh. Therefore, this study posits that:

H5: Perceived privacy features of an app have a positive relationship with the continual use of mobile banking apps.

Design Aesthetics. Design aesthetics refers to how attractive the user interface can be to the user of the mobile app (Puriwat & Tripopsakul, 2017). Design aesthetics are particularly key in branded or commercial apps as it is believed to enhance the customer's interest in the app. The attractive user interface can make the user continue using the application. Chaitanya and Gupta (2017) pointed out that visual design appeals to the emotions and interest of the user, especially when various media such as animations, color, text, and music, font are carefully used. Such design features play a significant role in influencing the user's enjoyment and behavior towards usage of the app. Previous studies have established that a significant relationship exists between enjoyment, design aesthetics, and the usefulness of app usage (Puriwat & Tripopsakul, 2017). Hence, this study posits that:

H6: The design aesthetics of an app have a positive relationship with the continual use of mobile banking apps.

Information Quality. Information Quality is how current and accurate information on products or services provided by an app is to its users. In a generic sense, Elmorshidy (2018) defined it as the quality of the content of the information systems. The more a user finds the content of an app useful, the more it is considered to have quality information. If the information provided is quality it makes the app more valuable to the user, thus sustaining the user's attention and interest (Chen, Meservy, & Gillenson, 2012). If an app has excellent design but is poor in terms of information quality the customer may lose interest to further use it. However, if the information is quality, coupled with quality design, it increases the user's attention. This suggests that:

H7: Information quality has a positive relationship with the continual use of mobile banking apps.

Gender of the User as a Moderator to Continual Use. The interests and intentions concerning app usage vary among the two genders (Chaitanya & Gupta, 2017). Therefore, to understand the relationship between the continuance intention of the use of a mobile app, gender should be considered. Depending on the gender of the user, perception towards continuance usage of mobile apps might vary (Chaitanya & Gupta, 2017). This is consistent with the views of Williams, Rana, and Dwivedi (2015). Therefore, this study posited that the new constructs introduced have a moderation effect on gender. Hence, the following hypotheses:

H8: Gender moderates the relationship between information quality *and continual use of mobile banking apps.*

H9: Gender moderates the relationship between design aesthetics *and the continual use of mobile banking apps.*

H10: Gender moderates the relationship between perceived privacy *and continual use of mobile banking apps.*

H11: Gender moderates the relationship between user satisfaction *and continual use of mobile banking apps.*

Age of the User as a Moderator to Continual. The user's interests and intentions to continually use an app vary among the different age groups (Chaitanya & Gupta, 2017). This implies that in establishing the determinants of continuance intention of using mobile apps, one cannot overlook the moderating role of age. Depending on the age group, the user's perception towards continuance usage of mobile banking apps might differ. Therefore, this study posited that the new constructs introduced have a moderation effect with age. Hence, the following hypotheses:

H12: Age moderates the relationship between information quality and continual use of mobile banking apps.

H13: Age moderates the relationship between design aesthetics and continual use of mobile banking apps.

H14: Age moderates the relationship between perceived privacy and continual use of mobile banking apps.

H15: Age moderates the relationship between user satisfaction and continual use of mobile banking apps.

MATERIALS AND METHOD

Research Design

This study employed quantitative research and a survey approach. The target population for the study was made up of students in two major state-owned universities in Ghana. The population consisted of students who use smartphones or tablets. The sampling technique was based on the argument of Etikan, Musa, and Alkassim (2016) that the best way to sample the student population is to carry out a convenience sampling procedure. Four hundred questionnaires were distributed to respondents from which three hundred valid responses were received and used for the analysis. This represents a response rate of 75 percent. The items measuring the constructs were adapted from previous related studies. Measurement items for perceived usefulness, confirmation, user satisfaction, and continual use were adapted from Bhattacherjee (2001). The items used to measure perceived privacy were adapted from Puriwat and Tripopsakul (2017) and information quality was also adapted from DeLone and MacLean, (2003). The items for measuring design aesthetics were adapted from the multi-motive information systems continuance model (Lowry, Gaskin, and Moody, 2015). All items were measured on a five-point Likert scale with responses ranging from 1 (strongly disagree) to 5 (strongly agree).

Instrument Reliability

The reliability and validity of the questionnaire scale were significant for obtaining a meaningful result from the study (Yavuz, 2012). The reliability of the measures via Cronbach Alpha was within the acceptable range, between 0.65 and 0.85 (see Table 2). Pease and Rowe (2005) noted that the reliability of a scale for unwavering quality is the Cronbach Alpha where the coefficient ranges from 0 to 1 with an acceptable level of at least 0.6. Also, Puriwat and Tripopsakul (2017) mentioned three types of validity and described them as face validity or content validity, criterion validity, and construct validity. The study adopted construct validity because it involved the analysis of the data which supports the hypothesis testing (see Table 3).

Data Analysis Techniques

The tools used for the data analysis were the Statistical Package for Social Science (SPSS version 20.0) and Analysis of Moment of Structures (AMOS version 24). The data gathered was coded in SPSS and then transferred to AMOS for further analysis. Percentage summaries from itemized responses were evaluated and interpreted as per the study objective. The hypotheses were tested using SPSS and AMOS was used for the structural equation modeling.

RESULTS

Demography and Descriptive Statistics

Figures 2a, 2b, and 2c present the socio-demographic profile of all the respondents, and Table 1 depicts the means, standard deviations, skewness, kurtosis, validity, and reliability of the measures. The skewness and kurtosis values within ± 2.00 indicate the normal distribution of that dataset (George and Mallery, 2003). From the result, almost all the items have skewness and kurtosis values within the recommended values except one item that has a kurtosis value of 2.47. Also, the consistency level in the responses was examined using the Cronbach alpha (α). The alpha (α) takes values ranging from 0 to 1, values closer to 1 indicate a high internal consistency level. According to Griethuijsen et al. (2014), acceptable alpha values must be at least 0.70 to be considered. Observably, the constructs in this have reliability values ranging from 0.70 to 0.90, indicating that there is high internal consistency.

Structural Equation Modelling and Measurement Model

The analysis of data using structure equation modeling (SEM) has two main components, namely the measurement model and the structural model. The measurement model is used to establish the relationship between the constructs. The structural model examines the path strength and the direction of the

Figure 2. (a) Respondents' distribution by marital status, (b) respondents' distribution by age, (c) respondents' distribution by marital status

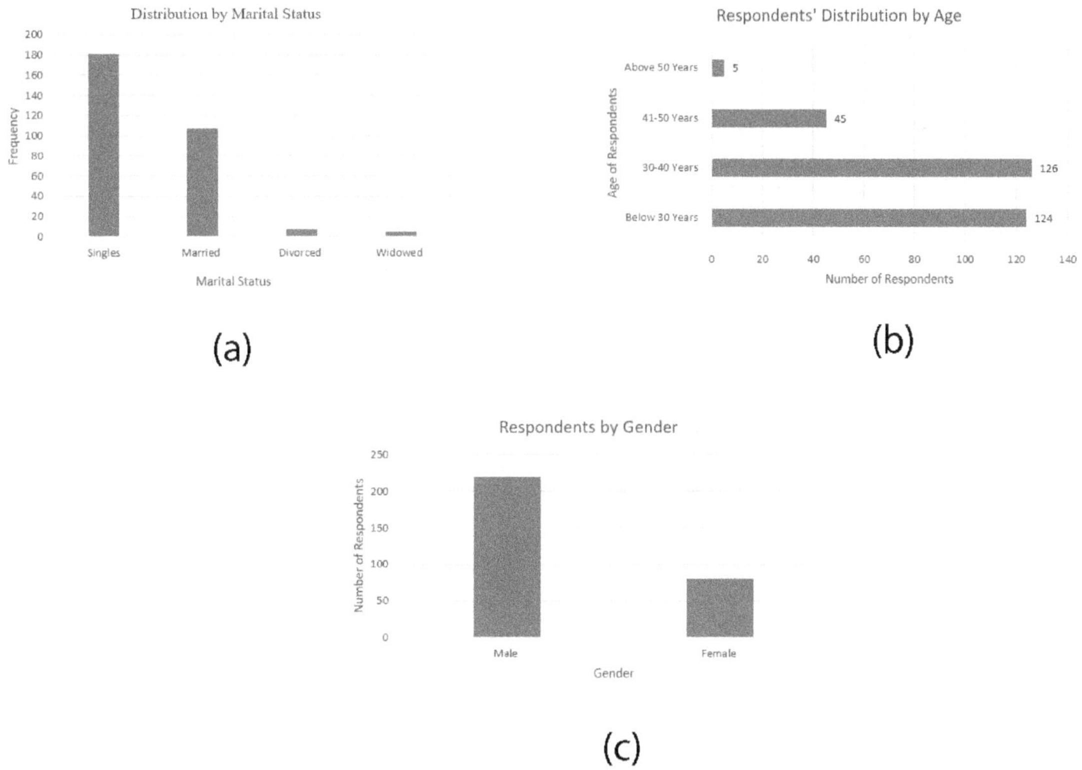

relationship that exists among the variables. The measurement of the model is tested to ensure that there is a satisfactory level of validity and reliability before testing for a significant relationship in the structural model (Ifinedo, 2006). Table 2 presents the psychometric properties of the measurement model in terms of reliability, convergent, and discriminant validity.

Reliability and Validity. The Composite Reliability (CR) was used to measure the reliability of the constructs in the measurement model. As evidenced in Table 3, almost all the constructs have composite reliability values of at least 0.70, indicating that there is a good and adequate reliability level (Hair et al., 2010; Hair et al., 2014). Also, the discriminant validity of the model was assessed by comparing the Average Variance Extracted (AVE) value with the squared correlation (Fornell & Larcker, 1981). The square root of the average variance extracted is indicated on the leading diagonal of Table 3. No correlations were equal to or greater than the square root of the AVE. As each AVE value was found to be more than the correlation square, discriminant validity is achieved thus indicating an absence of multicollinearity among the constructs (Byrne, 2016).

Model Fit. The confirmatory factor analysis using the Analysis of Moment of Structures (AMOS) was conducted to test the measurement model. The proposed model was checked with model chi-square goodness-of-fit and approximate fit indexes. For approximate fit indices, goodness-of-fit index (GFI) and insignificant model chi-square goodness-of-fit set at 0.05 signifies model fit (Bentler, 1990). Moreover, the normed fit index (NFI), relative fit index (RFI), incremental fit index (IFI), Adjusted Goodness of

Table 1. Descriptive statistics

Code	Constructs/Item	Mean	SD	Skew	Kurt	Loading	α
	Perceived Usefulness (Bhattacherjee, 2001)						
PU1	Using mobile banking apps improves my performance in managing personal finances.	3.95	0.84	-0.84	0.91	0.56	0.76
PU2	Using mobile banking apps increases my productivity in managing personal finances.	3.81	0.85	-0.61	0.10	0.53	
PU3	Using mobile banking apps enhances my effectiveness in managing personal finances.	3.60	0.79	-0.37	0.38	0.62	
PU4	Overall, mobile banking apps are useful in managing personal finances	3.67	0.87	-0.51	0.22	0.58	
	Confirmation (Bhattacherjee, 2001)						
CONF1	My experience with using mobile banking apps was better than what I expected.	3.20	0.97	-0.20	-0.54	0.73	0.85
CONF2	The services provided by mobile banking apps were better than what I expected.	3.56	0.81	-0.45	0.03	0.59	
CONF3	The benefits of using mobile banking apps were better than I expected.	3.38	0.88	-0.44	0.25	0.72	
CONF4	Overall, most of my expectations from using mobile banking apps were confirmed.	3.43	0.88	-0.50	0.10	0.71	
	Perceived Security/Privacy (Venkatesh et al., 2012)						
PPC1	Mobile banking apps would keep my sensitive data secure.	3.62	0.87	-0.78	0.73	0.73	0.78
PPC2	I trust the security of e-payment services so that no one can steal and successfully use my personal information.	3.69	0.93	-0.54	0.01	0.79	
	User Satisfaction (Bhattacherjee, 2001)						
USSAT1	I am satisfied with the support I receive from my current mobile banking app providers.	3.52	1.02	-0.77	0.17	0.70	0.78
USSAT2	I am content with the functions of the mobile banking apps I am currently using.	3.37	0.98	-0.62	-0.11	0.67	
USSAT3	Overall, I am satisfied with the experience of using my mobile banking apps.	3.50	0.94	-0.64	0.08	0.72	
	Information Quality (DeLone and MacLean, 2003)						
IQ1	The information generated by the mobile banking apps is correct.	4.21	0.73	-0.82	1.42	0.74	0.83
IQ2	The information generated by the mobile banking apps is useful for its purpose.	4.05	0.77	-0.67	0.63	0.81	
IQ3	I trust the information output of mobile banking apps.	4.08	0.73	-0.90	1.91	0.67	
	Design Aesthetics (Cyr et al., 2006)						
DA1	The mobile banking app design (i.e., text, animation, colors, boxes, menus, graphics, etc.) is attractive.	3.75	0.75	-0.08	-0.16	0.64	0.65
DA2	The mobile banking apps look professionally designed.	3.53	0.90	-0.58	0.41	0.61	
DA3	The overall look and feel of the mobile banking apps is visually appealing.	3.72	0.94	-0.77	0.68	0.60	

continued on following page

Table 1. Continued

Code	Constructs/Item	Mean	SD	Skew	Kurt	Loading	α
	Continual Use (Bhattacherjee, 2001)						
CU1	I intend to continue using mobile banking apps rather than discontinue their use.	3.84	0.86	-1.03	1.51	0.66	0.76
CU2	My intention is to continue using mobile banking apps rather than use any alternative means.	3.88	0.80	-0.92	1.19	0.74	
CU3	If I could, I would like to discontinue my use of mobile banking apps (reverse-coded)	3.83	0.78	-1.10	2.47	0.58	
CU4	I plan to continue using mobile banking apps.	3.87	0.78	-0.86	1.42	0.64	

Table 2. Reliability diagnostics and item loadings

Constructs	Composite Reliability	AVE	1	2	3	4	5
Information Quality (1)	0.71	0.59	*0.77*				
Design Aesthetics (2)	0.89	0.69	0.57	*0.83*			
Confirmation (3)	0.79	0.64	0.14	0.08	*0.80*		
Perceived Privacy (4)	0.69	0.59	0.04	0.02	0.59	*0.77*	
Perceived Usefulness (5)	0.77	0.54	0.11	0.06	0.64	0.68	*0.73*

Note: Values in italics are the square root of the Average Variance Extracted (AVE)

Fit Index (AGFI), Tucker-Lewis fit index (TFI) and comparative fit index (CFI) should all be above 0.9 to indicate a model fit (Bentler, 1990). Also, the root mean square error of approximation (RMSEA) value should be less than 0.08 (Tabachnick and Fidell, 2007).

Table 3 presents a summary of the model fit, the model adequacy test, and the goodness-of-fit indexes for the two models (*with* and *without* moderating effects). The $\chi^2/d_{f=}$ 2.51;2.06 for the two models is indicated in the model. Indices for the wit*hout moderating effect* are as follows; GFI=0.93; CFI=0.97; NFI=0.92; RMSEA=0.038; AIC=609.75. The model values are within the acceptable ranges; hence the model adequately fits the data. This allows for the testing of the hypotheses. In the case of the model wit*h moderating ef*fects, the fit indices are as follows: GFI=0.87; CFI= 0.94; NFI=0.85; RMSEA=0.04; AIC=2067.78. These values show an indication that the model fits the data, hence the hypotheses under it can be tested. Based on the Akaike information criterion (AIC) values, the model wit*hout moderating ef*fects performs better than the model wit*h moderating ef*fects. The model with the lowest AIC values is considered to be the best (Tabachnick and Fidell, 2007).

Testing of Hypotheses

The hypotheses of the study were tested as the model fit indices had met the recommended cut-off values. The testing of the hypotheses was conducted in two folds; *with* and *without* moderating effects.

Table 3. Summary of model fit

Index	Accepted Values	Model Without Moderating	Model With Moderating
		Model Values	Model Values
CMIN		489.75	1587.78
DF		193.00	772.00
P		0.00	0.00
CMIN/DF	<3.00	2.54	2.06
Goodness-of-fit index (GFI)	>0.90	0.93	0.87
Adjusted goodness-of-fit index (AGFI)	>0.90	0.89	0.81
Normed fit index (NFI)	>0.90	0.92	0.85
Incremental fit index (IFI)	>0.90	0.97	0.94
Tucker Lewis index (TLI)	>0.90	0.95	0.92
Comparative fit index (CFI)	>0.90	0.97	0.94
Root mean square error of approximation (RMSEA)	<0.08	0.038	0.04
AIC		609.75	2067.78
BCC		619.75	2177.69

Hypotheses Without Moderating Variables. Eight (8) main hypotheses were tested under this model at a 5% significance level and the results are summarized in Table 4 and Figure 3. It can be observed from the table that five of the hypotheses were supported and three were not supported.

Hypothesis H1 of the study states that the perceived usefulness of mobile applications has a positive relationship with satisfaction. The analysis of the data as indicated in Table 5 shows that perceived usefulness has a statistically significant and positive influence on satisfaction ($\beta=0.520$; $SE=0.146$; $Sig<0.05$), explaining about 52% of the variance. Hence, the hypothesis is significant and supported. Also, *Hypothesis H3a examines whether confirmation has a positive relationship with satisfaction.* The result obtained shows that confirmation has about ($\beta=0.339$; $SE=0.105$; $Sig<0.05$). This impact is statistically

Table 4. Summary of hypotheses testing results without moderating effect

				β	S.E.	C.R.	Sig	Remarks
H1	Satisfaction	<---	Perceived usefulness	0.520	0.146	4.718	0.000	Support
H3a	Satisfaction	<---	Confirmation	0.339	0.105	3.396	0.000	Support
H3b	Perceived usefulness	<---	Confirmation	0.767	0.066	9.313	0.000	Support
H6	Continual Use	<---	Design Aesthetics	0.841	0.085	12.169	0.000	Support
H7	Continual Use	<---	Information quality	0.098	0.047	2.375	0.018	Support
H2	Continual Use	<---	Perceived usefulness	0.122	0.087	1.426	0.154	Not support
H4	Continual Use	<---	Satisfaction	-0.023	0.065	-0.278	0.781	Not support
H5	Continual Use	<---	Perceived privacy	-0.092	0.037	-1.473	0.141	Not support

Note: β is the standardized regression weight

Figure 3. Path diagram of the model without moderating variables

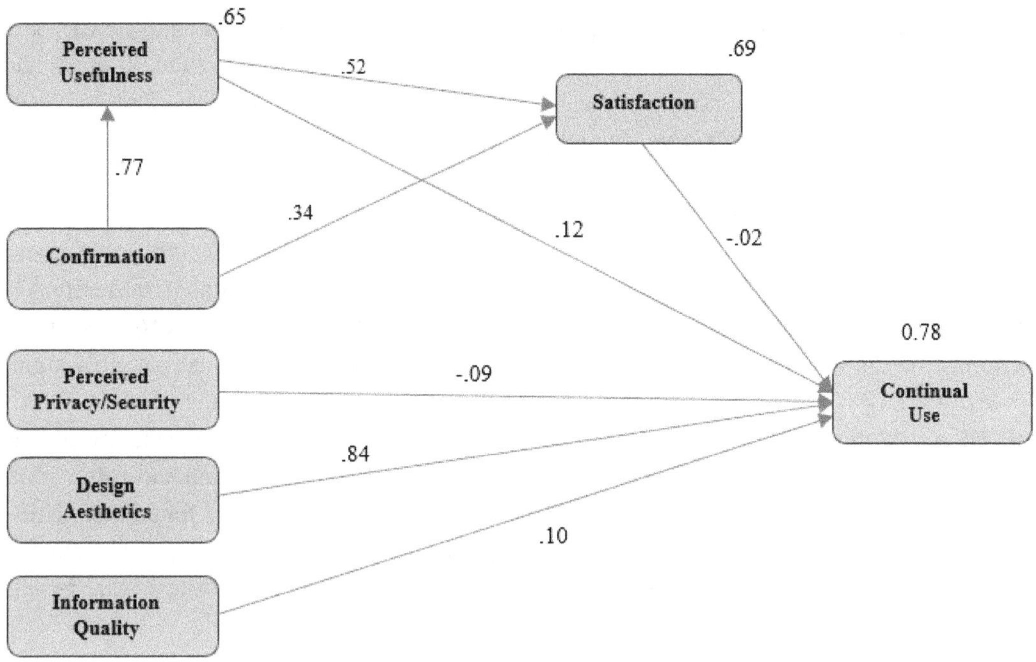

significant, contributing approximately about 34% to the satisfaction level. Hence, this hypothesis is positive and supported. Moreover, *Hypothesis H3b postulates that confirmation has a positive relationship with perceived usefulness.* The impact that confirmation has on perceived usefulness is estimated to be (*β=0.767; SE=0.066; Sig<0.05*). The result means that confirmation can influence the perceived usefulness of approximately 77%. This result is statistically and significantly positive. Therefore, the hypothesis is supported. Furthermore, *Hypothesis H6 of the study posits a positive relationship between design aesthetics and continual use.* The impact that design aesthetics has on continual use is statistically significant, estimated to be approximately 84% (*β=0.841; SE=0.085; Sig<0.05*). Thus, this hypothesis is significant and supported. Similarly, *Hypothesis H7 states that information quality has a positive relationship with continual use.* Based on the result obtained, there is statistically and significant evidence that information quality influences continual use. It has approximately 98% influence on continual use (*β=0.98; SE=0.047; Sig<0.05*). This means that the hypothesis is supported.

Moreover, *Hypothesis H2 seeks to examine whether the perceived usefulness of mobile applications has a positive effect on continuance intention to use mobile applications.* The result indicates that the perceived usefulness has no significant influence on continual use (*β=0.122; SE=0.087; Sig>0.05*). Therefore, the hypothesis is insignificant and not supported. Also, *Hypothesis H4 of the study examines whether satisfaction has a positive relationship with continual use.* The analysis of the data suggests that satisfaction has no significant influence on the continual usage of mobile applications (*β=-0.023; SE=0.065; Sig>0.05*). The impact that satisfaction has on continual use based on the result obtained suggests a negative relationship. Hence, the hypothesis is not supported. Moreover, *Hypothesis H5 postulates that perceived privacy features of the app have a positive relationship with continual use.*

The perceived privacy features have an insignificant influence on continual use (*β= -0.092; SE=0.037; Sig>0.05*). Thus, the hypothesis is not supported and indicates a negative relationship.

Hypotheses with Moderating Variables (Gender and Age). Multiple group analysis was carried out to estimate the moderating effects of gender (male and female) and age (less than 30 years and above 30 years). The following are the results of the formulated hypotheses with the moderating variables.

Gender is the moderation variable. Four hypotheses were tested using gender as the moderating variable. *Hypothesis H8 proposes that gender moderates the relationship between information quality and continual use.* As evident in Table 5, gender as a moderating variable between information quality and continual use is statistically significant. The impact of males is statistically significant, contributing about 35% (*β=-0.347; Sig<0.05*). However, females have an insignificant impact moderating between information quality and continual use (*β=0.057; Sig>0.05*). The overall impact of gender moderating between information quality and continual use is however statistically significant at a 5% significance level (*z-score =2.414*). Hence, the hypothesis is positively and statistically supported. In addition, *Hypothesis H9 postulates that gender moderates the relationship between design aesthetics and continual use.* The result obtained shows that gender has a statistical and significant impact on the relationship between design aesthetics and continual use (Z-Score=-3.681). Both males and females statistically and significantly influenced the relationship between design aesthetics and continual use. The males' impact on the relationship is estimated to be (β=0.741) and females (β=0.942). This shows that females were more influential in the relationship than males. The hypothesis is supported.

Table 5. Summary of hypotheses testing results with the moderating effect of gender and age

				Male		Remarks	Female		Remarks	Overall	Remarks
				β	*Sig*		*Estimate*	*Sig*		*z-Score*	
H8	Continual Use	<---	Information quality	-0.3147	0.004	Support	0.057	0.571	Not support	2.418**	Support
H9	Continual Use	<---	Design Aesthetics	0.741	0.000	Support	0.942	0.000	Support	-3.681***	Support
H10	Continual Use	<---	Perceived privacy	-0.126	0.075	Not support	-0.037	0.818	Not support	0.722	Not support
H11	Continual Use	<---	Satisfaction	0.064	0.514	Not support	-0.104	0.567	Not support	-0.850	Not support
	Age			***<=30 years***			***>30 years***				
H14	Continual Use	<---	Perceived privacy	-0.356	0.001	Support	0.032	0.657	Not support	2.811***	Support
H12	Continual Use	<---	Information quality	-0.235	0.080	Not support	-0.044	0.567	Not support	1.308	Not support
H13	Continual Use	<---	Design Aesthetics	0.621	0.000	Support	0.541	0.000	Support	-1.220	Not support
H15	Continual Use	<---	Satisfaction	0.142	0.377	Not support	-0.047	0.584	Not support	-1.032	Not support

Note: β is the standardized regression weight

Similarly, Hypothesis H10 seeks to examine whether gender moderates the relationship between perceived privacy and continual use. The result suggests that gender has no significant influence on the relationship between perceived privacy and continual use; Males (*β=-0.126; Sig>0.05;* females (*β=-*

0.037; Sig>0.05; Z-score=0.722). Therefore, the hypothesis is not supported. Moreover, *Hypothesis H11 of the study seeks to examine whether gender moderates the relationship between user satisfaction and continual use.* The result shows that gender does not moderate the relationship between satisfaction and continual use of the mobile application; *Males (β=0.064; Sig>0.05; females (β=-0.104; Sig>0.05; Z-Score=-0.850).* Hence, the hypothesis is not supported.

Age is the moderating variable. Four hypotheses were tested using *age* as the moderating variable. *Hypothesis H14 postulates that age moderates the relationship between perceived privacy and continual use.* The result reveals that age less than 30 years has a statistically significant influence on the relationship between perceived privacy and continual use (*β=-0.356; Sig<0.05*). The direction of the relationship that ages less than 30 years have between perceived privacy and continual use is however negative. The relationship is supported. Also, those above the age of 30 years show an insignificant relationship between perceived privacy and continual use (*β=0.032; Sig=0.657*). Although there is a positive relationship that age above 30 years has between perceived privacy and continual use, it is not a statistical and significant relationship. Overall age as a moderating variable has a statistical and significant influence on the relationship between perceived privacy and continual use (*Z-Score=2.811*). Hence, the hypothesis is supported. Also, *Hypothesis H12 states that age moderates the relationship between information quality and continual use.* Age as a moderating variable does not influence the relationship between information quality and continual use of the mobile application at each level and the overall level: age *<30 years (β=-0.235; Sig>0.05; age >30 years (β=-0.044; Sig>0.05; ZScore=1.308).* Therefore, the hypothesis is not supported.

Likewise, *Hypothesis H13 postulates that age moderates the relationship between design aesthetics and continual use.* The result suggests that at each level of age, there is a significant influence between design aesthetics and continual use: age *< 30 years (β=0.621; Sig<0.05; age > 30 years (β=0.541; Sig<0.05*). However, at the overall model level age has no significant influence on the relationship between design aesthetics and continual use (*Z-Score=-1.220*), hence the hypothesis is not supported. Finally, *Hypothesis H15 states that age moderates the relationship between user satisfaction and continual use.* Age as a moderating variable has no statistical and significant influence on the relationship that exists between satisfaction and continual use at the two age levels and on the overall level: age *<30 years (β=.0.142; Sig>0.377; age >30 years (β=-0.047; Sig>0.05; Zscore=-1.032*). Thus, the hypothesis is not supported.

DISCUSSION

The Expectation-Confirmation IS Continuance Model serves as the main theoretical guide for this study. As a whole, the findings of the proposed model align with some of the assumptions of the underlying model but disagree with some. The results are discussed in the following section.

Relationships Among the Constructs Without Moderating Variables

The hypothesis on the relationship between satisfaction and perceived usefulness is statistically significant. Perceived usefulness explains about 52% of users' satisfaction with mobile banking apps. Some studies validated a strong relationship between these two constructs. For example, Masocha (2018) found a significant relationship between the perceived usefulness of an information system and the user's satisfaction with the system. Likewise, Alqahtani and Mohammad (2017) agreed that high perceived usefulness leads to higher satisfaction. Moreover, confirmation has been found to have a positive relationship with satisfaction. The results show that confirmation accounts for about 34% of users' satisfaction with mobile banking apps. This finding is consistent with the Expectation-Confirmation IS Continuance model's assumption that confirmation has a positive relationship with satisfaction. Susanto, Chang, and Ha (2016) found that confirmation after the initial use of smartphone banking services has a significant impact on user satisfaction. In addition, this study found a positive relationship between confirmation and the perceived usefulness of mobile banking apps. The result shows that confirmation influences perceived usefulness by approximately 77%. This is in agreement with Bhattacherjee (2001), who found that the perceived usefulness of a system could be influenced by the users' confirmation of the system.

On the contrary, the perceived usefulness has no significant influence on continual use. However, some earlier studies established a significant relationship between perceived usefulness and continuance intention to use the system (Halawi et al., 2018). Liu and Tai (2016) found perceived usefulness as one of the determinants of the continuance intention to use the system. As stated earlier, in this study, the perceived usefulness was not found to directly affect the intention to continue using mobile banking apps. The perceived usefulness has a more mediated effect through satisfaction with continual use. Although it appears to be quite unusual, this result shares the findings of Chou and Lee (2013) and Hung et al. (2012), who established that users are not motivated by past benefits, but rather by future benefits. No matter how good the mobile app was in the past, its future use is based on the expectations of future benefits. Therefore, the inspiration to continue using mobile banking apps rests more on the anticipated future benefits rather than on the usefulness thereof.

Again, the relationships between design aesthetics and continual use and that of information quality and continual use were significant. The analysis reveals that design aesthetics has a positive influence on continual use. Design aesthetics of mobile banking apps influence continual use by approximately 84%. Also, information quality positively influences continual use. These findings confirm that of Chen, Meservy, and Gillenson (2012), who found that information quality influences continuance intention to use mobile banking apps. Besides, the result suggests that perceived privacy has an insignificant influence on continual use. This is inconsistent with the views of Omolade (2017), who argued that perceived security/privacy has a positive influence on attitudes towards continuance intention to use a particular mobile application. This finding may be a result of the fact that most of the respondents are not typical IT people and probably do not understand security/privacy issues. A related study conducted among organizations in a developing country did not find a significant impact of security on behavioral intention to use cloud computing (Yaokumah & Amponsah, 2017). Similarly, satisfaction has no significant influence on continual use. However, Lankton and Mcknight (2012) recognized that a user's satisfaction with a system can strongly influence the decision to continually use that system. This study also contradicts the Expectation-Confirmation IS Continuance model's (Bhattacherjee, 2001) assumption that satisfaction has a positive relationship with continual use.

Relationships Among the Constructs With Moderating Variables

Multiple group analysis was performed to estimate the moderating effects of gender (male and female) and age (less than 30 years and above 30 years). Interesting findings were observed from the results.

The Moderating Role of Gender. The result finds that the moderating role of gender on the relationship between information quality and continual use is statistically significant. Again, the result shows that gender has a statistical and significant impact on the relationship between design aesthetics and continual use. Both males and females were found to have a statistical and significant influence on the relationship between design aesthetics and continual use. But then females (β=0.942) influenced the relationship more than the males (β=0.741), hence the hypothesis is supported. However, gender has no significant influence on the relationship between perceived privacy and continual use. Again, gender does not moderate the relationship between satisfaction and continual use of mobile banking apps. Thus, according to Chaitanya and Gupta (2017), the interests and intentions concerning app usage vary among the two genders.

The Moderating Role of Age. The result reveals that participants with ages less than 30 years have a statistically significant influence on the relationship between perceived privacy and continual use. However, those above the age of 30 years show an insignificant relationship between perceived privacy and continual use. Again, age has an insignificant effect on the relationship between information quality and continual use of a mobile banking application. This finding is inconsistent with the views of Williams, Rana, and Dwivedi (2015). Moreover, the result suggests that age has no significant influence on the relationship between design aesthetics and continual use. This is inconsistent with the views that, depending on the age group, the customer's perception towards continuance usage of apps might differ. Again, this is inconsistent with an earlier study conducted by Williams, Rana, and Dwivedi (2015). Finally, age has no statistically significant influence on the relationship that exists between satisfaction and continual use at the two age levels and on the overall level.

RECOMMENDATIONS

The patterns and trends revealed by this study should be of primary concern to all who matter in the mobile apps industry including developers, marketers, users, and so on especially as the findings have to do with continual usage of these applications. The app developers must understand the decision to continually use an app is influenced by certain key factors. Factors such as aesthetics and information quality and so on as revealed by the study findings are crucial as they can help in planning their strategies to increase consumers' continuance intention to use their applications. The findings suggest that the user will be glued to any app that addresses concerns such as design aesthetics, information quality, and so on as well as factoring in features attractive to the different age groups and gender. The app producer or marketer who observes these as standards during the development phase will be able to attract a lot of users.

Additionally, it must be pointed out that because of the availability of other competing apps, it is easy for users to switch to other apps. Any dissatisfaction in that sense can force users to switch to other competing apps. App marketers must therefore be ready to enforce standards that take into consideration issues of perceived privacy, design aesthetics, and information quality seriously. This will help increase app downloads and continual use of these apps, retain their customer base, or even attract a section of "floating users".

The app industry still possesses the power to further revolutionize smartphones. For this reason, all who matter in the mobile banking applications industry must therefore take inspiration from this study in their next strategy development. Mobile App industry stakeholders that will take the perceived privacy, design aesthetics, and information quality seriously are the ones that will survive and possibly dominate the industry. This calls for collaboration between app industry stakeholders. The stakeholders must understand that there is going to be further evolution with similar new dynamics as smartphones and their users co-evolve by imposing new constraints that the industry must be willing to address. Therefore, any future regulatory strategy and policy must have a component that will satisfy perceived privacy, design aesthetics, and information quality serious

FUTURE RESEARCH DIRECTIONS

This study is of primary concern to the mobile apps industry including developers, marketers, financial institutions, and users of mobile banking apps especially as the findings have to do with the continual usage of these apps. The app's developers would understand users' decision to continually use the apps. For example, mobile banking app industry stakeholders that will take the design aesthetics, and information quality seriously are the ones that will survive and possibly dominate the industry. Therefore, any future regulatory strategy and policy must have a component that will satisfy design aesthetics and information quality.

This study has some limitations. The study was conducted in a developing country, which may have some unique dynamics, future studies must attempt to replicate and validate the study's outcomes for richer theory development in other contexts. Again, the study found that perceived privacy features have an insignificance influence on continual use. There was no statistically significant relationship between the two constructs. Further studies should look into this by using a more security-conscious or IT-inclined population. Moreover, though three (perceived privacy, design aesthetics, and information quality) new constructs were included in this study, other factors may exist that can be explored to enrich the theoretical foundation of the model.

CONCLUSION

The results revealed that the perceived usefulness of mobile banking apps has a significant influence on users' satisfaction with the apps. Confirmation has a significant impact on satisfaction. Perceived usefulness and design aesthetics have a significant influence on the continual use of mobile banking apps. Information quality has a significant influence on continual use. However, perceived usefulness has no significant effect on continual use, satisfaction has no significant influence on continual usage, and perceived security/privacy features have an insignificant influence on continual use. Moreover, gender moderates the relationships between information quality versus continual use and design aesthetics and continual use. However, gender does not moderate the relationships between perceived privacy and continual use as well as satisfaction and continual use. Besides, age moderates the relationship between perceived privacy and continual use. However, age does not moderate the relationships between information quality versus continual use, design aesthetics versus continual use, and satisfaction versus continual use.

REFERENCES

Al Karim, R., Rabiul, M. K., Taskia, A., & Jarumaneerat, T. (2023). Millennial customer engagement with Fintech services: The mediating role of trust. *Business Perspectives and Research*, 1–19. doi:10.1177/22785337231183275

Alqahtani, M., & Mohammad, H. (2017). Mobile Applications' Impact on Student Performance and Satisfaction. *The Turkish Online Journal of Educational Technology*, *14*(4), 102–112.

Antwi, S. K., & Hamza, K. (2015). Qualitative and Quantitative Research Paradigms in Business Research: A Philosophical Reflection. *European Journal of Business and Management*, *7*(3), 217–226.

Bajwa, I. A., Rehman, S. U., Iqbal, A., Anwer, Z., Ashiq, M., & Khan, M. A. (2022). Past, Present and Future of FinTech Research: A Bibliometric Analysis. *SAGE Open*, *12*(4), 1–22. doi:10.1177/21582440221131242

Bentler, P. M. (1990). Comparative fit indexes in structural models. *Psychological Bulletin*, *107*(2), 238–246. doi:10.1037/0033-2909.107.2.238 PMID:2320703

Bhattacherjee, A. (2001). Understanding Information Systems Continuance: An Expectation- Confirmation Model. *Management Information Systems Quarterly*, *25*(3), 351–370. doi:10.2307/3250921

Byrne, B. M. (2016). *Structural equation modeling with AMOS: Basic concepts, applications, and programming*. Routledge. doi:10.4324/9781315757421

Chaitanya, C., & Gupta, D. (2017). Factors Influencing Customer Satisfaction with Usage of Shopping Apps in India. *International Conference on Recent Trends in Electronics, Information and Communication Technology,* 1483–1486. 10.1109/RTEICT.2017.8256844

Chen, L., Meservy, T. O., & Gillenson, M. (2012). Understanding Information Systems Continuance for Information-Oriented Mobile Applications. *Communications of the Association for Information Systems*, *30*(9), 127–146. doi:10.17705/1CAIS.03009

Chen, X., Huang, Q., & Davison, R. M. (2017). Economic and social satisfaction of buyers on consumer-to-consumer platforms: The role of relational capital. *International Journal of Electronic Commerce*, *21*(2), 219–248. doi:10.1080/10864415.2016.1234285

Chou, C., & Lee, J. (2013). *Understanding Mobile Apps Continuance Usage Behavior and Habit: An Expectance-Confirmation Theory*. Academic Press.

Cudjoe, A. G., Anim, P. A., Gerald, J., & Tetteh, N. (2015). Determinants of Mobile Banking Adoption in the Ghanaian Banking Industry : A Case of Access Bank Ghana Limited. *Journal of Computer and Communications*, *3*(February), 1–19. doi:10.4236/jcc.2015.32001

Cyr, D., Head, M., & Ivanov, A. (2006). Design aesthetics leading to m-loyalty in mobile commerce. *Information & Management*, *43*(8), 950–963. doi:10.1016/j.im.2006.08.009

Das, A., & Das, S. (2020). Perception, adoption, and pattern of usage of FinTech services by bank customers: Evidence from Hojai district of Assam. *Emerging Economy Studies*, *6*(1), 7–22. doi:10.1177/2394901520907728

Datareportal. (2021). *Internet users in Ghana.* Retrieved July 10, 2021, from https://datareportal.com/reports/digital-2020-ghana

Elmorshidy, A. (2018). Factors Affecting Mobile Applications of Remote Security Cameras at Home and Office : An Empirical Investigation in Southern California. *The International Technology Management Review*, *7*(1), 93–111. doi:10.2991/itmr.7.1.9

Etikan, I., Musa, S. A., & Alkassim, R. S. (2016). Comparison of Convenience Sampling and Purposive Sampling. *American Journal of Theoretical and Applied Statistics*, *5*(1), 1–4. doi:10.11648/j.ajtas.20160501.11

Filofteia, T. M. (2018). Mobile Applications for Tourism. Study Regarding Their Use by Romanians. *Brâncuşi, Annals of the Constantin. Economic S*, (4), 78–84.

Garrouch, K. (2021). Does the reputation of the provider matter? A model explaining the continuance intention of mobile wallet applications. *Journal of Decision Systems*, *30*(2-3), 150–171. Advance online publication. doi:10.1080/12460125.2020.1870261

George, D., & Mallery, M. (2003). *Using SPSS for Windows step by step: a simple guide and Reference.* Academic Press.

Griethuijsen, R. A. L. F., Eijck, M. W., Haste, H., Brok, P. J., Skinner, N. C., & Mansour, N. (2014). Global patterns in students' views of science and interest in science. *Research in Science Education*, *45*(4), 581–603. doi:10.1007/s11165-014-9438-6

Hair, J. F., Black, W. C., Babin, B. J., Anderson, R. E., & Tatham, R. L. (2010). *Multivariate data analysis* (6th ed.). Pearson Prentice Hall.

Hair, J. F. Jr, Hult, G. T. M., Ringle, C. M., & Sarstedt, M. (2014). *A primer on Partial Least Squares Structural Equation Modeling (PLS-SEM).* SAGE Publications Ltd.

Halawi, L., Mccarthy, R. V., & Farah, J. (2018). Information Systems Continuance: Faculty Perceptions of Canvas. *Issues in Information Systems*, *19*(4), 171–175.

Hanjaya, M., Kenny, S. K., & Gunawan, F. (2019). Understanding Factors Influencing Consumer's Online Purchase Intention Via Mobile App: Perceived Ease Of Use, Perceived Usefulness, System Quality, Information Quality, And Service Quality. *MINIB*, *32*(2), 175–206. doi:10.2478/minib-2019-0035

Harris, A., Goodman, S., & Traynor, P. (2013). Privacy and Security Concerns Associated With Mobile Money Applications in Africa. *Washington Journal of Law, Technology and Arts*, *8*(3), 246–263.

Hasan, R., Islam, M. A., & Hossain, M. A. (2021). Evaluating drivers of fintech adoption in the Netherlands. *Global Business Review*, 1–14. doi:10.1177/09721509211027402

Inukollu, V. N., Keshamoni, D. D., & Kang, T. (2014). Factors Influencing Quality of Mobile Apps: Role of Mobile App Development Life Cycle. *International Journal of Software Engineering and Its Applications*, *5*(5), 15–34. doi:10.5121/ijsea.2014.5502

Khan, M. A., Alqahtani, F., Alqahtani, M., Alharthi, A., & Alghamdi, A. (2022). Utilizing the collective wisdom of FinTech in the GCC region: A systematic mapping approach. *Measurement and Control*, *56*(3-4), 717–725. doi:10.1177/00202940211042411

Khurana, K. (2023). A bibliometric study of publications on the adoption of FinTech using VOSviewer. *Journal of Educational Technology Systems*, *51*(4), 505–514. doi:10.1177/00472395231165715

Kumar, A., Adlakaha, A., & Mukherjee, K. (2018). The effect of perceived security and grievance redressal on continuance intention to use M-wallets in a developing country. *International Journal of Bank Marketing*, *4*(September), 1–22. doi:10.1108/IJBM-04-2017-0077

Lankton, N. K., & Mcknight, H. D. (2012). Examining Two Expectation Disconfirmation Theory Models : Assimilation and Asymmetry Effects Models : Assimilation and Asymmetry Effects. *Journal of the Association for Information Systems*, *13*(2), 88–115. doi:10.17705/1jais.00285

Li, A., Sun, Y., Yang, X., & Guo, J. (2019). Exploring the Relationship between Perceived Ease of Use and Continuance Usage of a Mobile Terminal: Mobility as a Moderator. *Sustainability (Basel)*, *11*(1128), 1–15. doi:10.3390/su11041128

Li, C., Khaliq, N., Chinove, L., Khaliq, U., & Oláh, J. (2023). Consumers' Perception of Risk Facets Associated With Fintech Use: Evidence From Pakistan. *SAGE Open*, *13*(4), 1–17. doi:10.1177/21582440231200199

Lim, X., Cheah, J.-H., Ng, S. I., Kamal Basha, N., & Liu, Y. (2021). Are men from mars, women from venus? examining gender differences towards continuous use intention of branded apps. *Journal of Retailing and Consumer Services*, *60*, 102422. Advance online publication. doi:10.1016/j.jretconser.2020.102422

Liu, G., & Tai, P. T. (2016). A Study of Factors Affecting the Intention to Use Mobile Payment Services in Vietnam. *Economics World*, *4*(6), 249–273. doi:10.17265/2328-7144/2016.06.001

Lowry, P. B., Gaskin, J. E., & Moody, G. D. (2015). Proposing the multimotive information systems continuance model (MISC) to better explain end-user system evaluations and continuance intentions. *Journal of the Association for Information Systems*, *16*(7), 515–579. doi:10.17705/1jais.00403

Lwin, N., Ameen, A., & Nusari, M. (2019). Mobile Banking Adoption among Customers within Private Commercial Banking Sector in Yangon, Myanmar. *International Journal of Management and Human Science*, *3*(2), 44–59.

Masocha, R. (2018). Adoption of Mobile Money Services and the Performance of Small and Medium. *Academy of Accounting and Financial Studies Journal*, *22*(3), 1–11.

Omolade, A. O. (2017). Predictors of Use of Mobile Applications by University Students in Oyo. *Journal of Information Science. Systems and Technology*, *1*(1), 34–47.

Pal, A., Herath, T., De', R., & Raghav Rao, H. (2021). Why do people use mobile payment technologies and why would they continue? An examination and implications from india. *Research Policy*, *50*(6), 104228. Advance online publication. doi:10.1016/j.respol.2021.104228

Pan, M., & Gao, W. (2021). Determinants of the behavioral intention to use a mobile nursing application by nurses in china. *BMC Health Services Research*, *21*(1), 228. Advance online publication. doi:10.1186/s12913-021-06244-3 PMID:33712012

Pease, W., & Rowe, M. (2005). An overview of information technology in the tourism industry. *Conference Proceedings-ICT Networks-Building Blocks for Economic Development*, 1–13. Retrieved from https://eprints.usq.edu.au/245

Perlman, L. (2017). *Technology inequality: Opportunities and challenges for mobile financial services.* Retrieved July 10, 2021, http://www.ruralfinanceandinvestment.org/sites/default/files/CFI_MFS_Tech_FINAL.pdf

Purani, K., Kumar, D. S., & Sahadev, S. (2019). E-loyalty among millennials: Personal characteristics and social influences. *Journal of Retailing and Consumer Services*, *48*, 215–223. doi:10.1016/j.jretconser.2019.02.006

Puriwat, W., & Tripopsakul, S. (2017). Mobile Banking Adoption in Thailand : An Integration of Technology Acceptance Model and Mobile Service Quality. *European Research Studies*, *20*(4), 200–210. doi:10.35808/ersj/885

Qing, T., & Haiying, D. (2021). How to achieve consumer continuance intention toward branded apps—From the consumer–brand engagement perspective. *Journal of Retailing and Consumer Services*, *60*, 102486. Advance online publication. doi:10.1016/j.jretconser.2021.102486

Roy, S. (2017). App Adoption and Switching Behavior: Applying the Extended Tam in Smartphone App Usage. *Journal of Information Systems and Technology Management*, *14*(2), 239–261. doi:10.4301/S1807-17752017000200006

Solecki, I., Porto, J., Alves, N. D. C., Gressevon, C., Hauck, J., & Borgatto, A. F. (2020). *Automated assessment of the visual design of Android apps developed with the app inventor.* Paper presented at the Annual Conference on Innovation and Technology in Computer Science Education. 10.1145/3328778.3366868

Srivastava, S., & Vishnani, S. (2021). Determinants of mobile bank usage among the bank users in north India. *Journal of Financial Services Marketing*, *26*(1), 34–51. doi:10.1057/s41264-020-00083-9

Statista. (2021a). *Online banking penetration forecast in Ghana 2010-2025*. Retrieved July 10, 2921, from https://www.statista.com/forecasts/1169529/online-banking-penetration-by-country

Statista. (2021b). *Penetration rate of Internet users in Ghana 2017-2021*. Retrieved July 10, 2021, from https://www.statista.com/statistics/1171435/internet-penetration-rate-ghana/

Susanto, A., Chang, Y., & Ha, Y. (2016). Determinants of Continuance Intention to Use the Smartphone Banking Services : An Extension to the Expectation-Confirmation Model information. *Industrial Management & Data Systems*, *116*(3), 508–525. doi:10.1108/IMDS-05-2015-0195

Tabachnick, B. G., & Fidell, L. S. (2007). *Using Multivariate Statistics* (5th ed.). Allyn and Bacon.

Thusi, P., & Maduku, D. K. (2020). South African millennials' acceptance and use of retail mobile banking apps: An integrated perspective. *Computers in Human Behavior*, *111*, 106405. Advance online publication. doi:10.1016/j.chb.2020.106405

Venkatesh, V., Thong, J. Y. L., Chan, F. K. Y., Hu, P. J., & Brown, S. A. (2011). *UTAUT predictors and the role of context*. doi:10.1111/j.1365-2575.2011.00373.x

Venkatesh, V., Thong, J. Y. L., & Xu, X. (2012). Consumer Acceptance and Use of Information Technology: Extending the Unified Theory of Acceptance and Use of Technology. *Management Information Systems Quarterly*, *36*(1), 157–178. doi:10.2307/41410412

Wang, Y., & Collins, W. B. (2021). Systematic evaluation of mobile fitness apps: Apps as the tutor, recorder, game companion, and cheerleader. *Telematics and Informatics*, *59*, 101552. Advance online publication. doi:10.1016/j.tele.2020.101552

Williams, M. D., Rana, N., & Dwivedi, Y. K. (2015). The unified theory of acceptance and use of technology (UTAUT): A literature review. *Journal of Enterprise Information Management*. doi:10.1108/JEIM-09-2014-0088

Wojcik, D. (2021). Financial Geography I: Exploring FinTech – Maps and Concepts. *Progress in Human Geography*, *45*(3), 566–576. doi:10.1177/0309132520952865

Yaokumah, W., & Amponsah, R. A. (2017). Examining the Contributing Factors for Cloud Computing Adoption in a Developing Country. *International Journal of Enterprise Information Systems*, *13*(1), 17–37. doi:10.4018/IJEIS.2017010102

Yavuz, A. (2012). Competing Paradigms : The Dilemmas and Insights of an ELT Teacher Educator. *International Education Studies*, *5*(1), 57–66. doi:10.5539/ies.v5n1p57

Zhou, T. (2013). An empirical examination of continuance intention of mobile payment services. *Decision Support Systems*, *54*(2), 1085–1091. doi:10.1016/j.dss.2012.10.034

Chapter 3
A Literature Review on the Development of Fintech in Southeast Asia

Ngoc Hai Truong
University Canada West, Canada

ABSTRACT

Financial technology, aka Fintech, is poised to be the driving force of Southeast Asian economies in the future. While there are numerous studies of the development of Fintech in each ASEAN country, there has been a noticeable absence of a comprehensive report encompassing those nations as a whole. Hence, this report aims to scrutinize and analyze the development of Fintech in those ten nations in various aspects such as market size, Fintech adoption rate, types of Fintech, main players, new start-ups, technical infrastructure, government policy and regulation, the impact of Fintech on the local economy, security concern, and future trends meticulously. In order to achieve this objective, this study mainly uses a systematic review methodology with data from various trusted secondary sources such as governmental agencies, the World Bank, and academic studies. The results also reveal that Fintech in most ASEAN countries has grown significantly during the past years. Furthermore, specific recommendations for governments to foster their respective Fintech markets will be proposed.

INTRODUCTION

Fintech's development has dramatically transformed the financial inclusion level in ten Southeast Asian countries, with the best catalyst of the last pandemic (United Overseas Bank Limited, 2022). Although ten ASEAN countries are at different developing paces of Fintech, all have witnessed an upward trend in Fintech, with more people embracing financial and technological products and services.

The main research objective of this report is to examine and analyze the development process of Fintech in ten Southeast Asian countries, including Brunei, Cambodia, Indonesia, Laos, Malaysia, Myanmar, Philippines, Singapore, Thailand, and Vietnam.

DOI: 10.4018/979-8-3693-1561-3.ch003

The purpose of the research is to understand the development of Fintech in ASEAN and the reason behind the differences in Fintech development in these nations. Thus, policymakers and investors can thoroughly consider this report's findings before investing or implementing new policies.

Regarding the research methodology, the report will employ a systematic approach to analyze and meticulously examine countless secondary data from various reliable sources such as the World Bank, governmental agencies, and trusted global audit companies. By extracting meaningful insights from these data, the report will summarize several critical findings before proposing specific initiatives for policymakers to make informed decisions.

Since the report is primarily built on secondary data, there could be chances that the data are incorrect or outdated. Moreover, this qualitative-based report does not apply any quantitative approach and thereby could not provide a comprehensive understanding of the significance of Fintech in the region.

Each country in the report will be analyzed in the following aspects: market size, Fintech adoption rate, types of Fintech, main players, new start-ups, technical infrastructure, government policy and regulation, the impact of Fintech on the local economy, security concern, literature reviews in the past five years and future trends.

BRUNEI

Market Size and Current Fintech Adoption Rate

Brunei is the least populous country in Southeast Asia, with only around 449,000 inhabitants (World Bank, 2023). However, the Fintech transaction value has increased significantly from $123.7 million in 2017 to approximately $244.7 million in 2022, expected to reach $353 million in 2026 (Statista, 2023). Moreover, the internet penetration rate has doubled from 56% in 2011 to around 95% in 2020 (Statista, 2023). The following chart illustrates the transaction value of Fintech in Brunei.

Figure 1. The transaction value of Fintech in Brunei from 2017 to 2026
Note. Adapted from Statista, 2023. Retrieved from https://www.statista.com/outlook/dmo/Fintech/brunei-darussalam

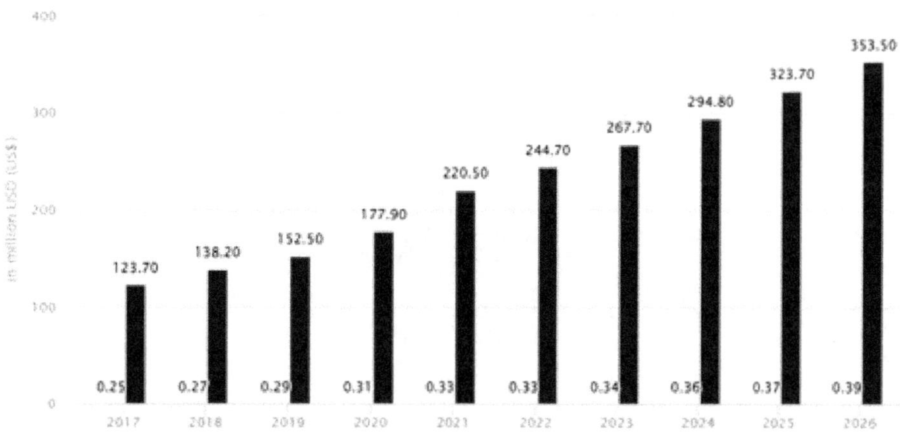

It is worth noticing that the Fintech adoption level in Brunei is comparatively high as internet users account for approximately 95% of the total population, and social media users account for 94% (Autoriti Monetari Brunei Darussalam, 2020). Undoubtedly, the country has various favourable conditions to thrive in the Fintech market.

Types of Fintech, Main Players, and Technical Infrastructure

With a humble population, Brunei has a few Fintech segments, such as digital payments, banking, crowdfunding, and remittance. There are a few giant companies in the digital payment sector, such as BIBD NEXGEN Wallet and Progresif. BIBD Nexgen wallet is backed by Bank Islam Brunei Darussalam with around 150,000 users and revenue of $126.9 million USD (The Asian Banker, 2022). The wallet offers various products and services to its customers, such as digital payments, online remittance, and investments. Another big mobile wallet app is Progresif Pay. The wallet is a joint investment effort between Bank Islam Brunei Darussalam and local telecommunication company Progresif. Progresif Pay wallet accounted for about 20% of the market share in 2023 (Payverse, 2023). Regarding the e-commerce sector, weelago is the largest e-commerce website platform in Brunei, with numerous products and sellers (Weelago, n.d). In addition, several incumbent banks have invested heavily in financial technologies to serve their customers better and fasten the processes, such as BIBD, Baiduri, and TAIB banks (Autoriti Monetari Brunei Darussalam, 2020).

Regarding the Fintech infrastructure and ecosystem in Brunei, the country has a clear organizational structure with different agencies handling different aspects. The Fintech ecosystem in Brunei is a joint effort from regulation, government, capital, talent, market, and infrastructure (Autoriti Monetari Brunei Darussalam, 2020). The following pie chart illustrates the Fintech ecosystem in Brunei.

Figure 2. Fintech ecosystem in Brunei

Note. Reprinted from Autoriti Monetari Brunei Darussalam, 2020. Retrieved from https://www.moneylaundering.com/wp-content/uploads/2021/01/Brunei.NA_.Fintech.2020.pdf

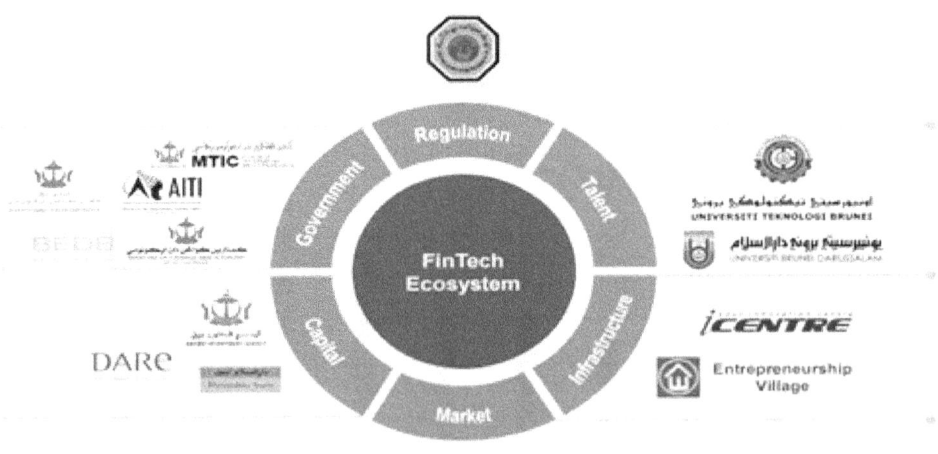

In addition, the telecommunication system has been upgraded, more people are using online payments, and the social media penetration rate was more than 90% in 2020 (Autoriti Monetari Brunei Darussalam, 2020). Overall, Brunei has various favourable conditions to develop further its Fintech industry.

New Investment and Startups

Currently, there are a couple of new startups in Brunei, and BruPay is one of them. The e-wallet provider app is being tested under the Fintech Regulatory Sandbox. BruPay was designed to help small businesses without POS terminals accept digital payments (Autoriti Monetari Brunei Darussalam, 2020). Another significant new Fintech startup is MoneyMatch. The online remittance platform enables customers to transfer their money to different destinations with low transaction fees, favourable exchange rates, and a digital identity verification process (MoneyMatch, n.d). The third new Fintech startup is Jana Kapital, a Syariah-based Peer-to-Peer (P2P) Crowdfunding platform. It allows small and medium enterprises to match and raise funds from other investors (Jana Kapital, n.d) with complete compliance with Sharia laws.

Government Policy, Regulation, and Impact of Fintech and Security Concerns

In Brunei, the Fintech sector is regulated by Autoriti Monetari Brunei Darussalam or Brunei Darussalam Central Bank. The central bank has implemented various regulatory frameworks to supervise the Financial Services sector, such as anti-money laundering and Counter-Terrorism Financing (Autoriti Monetari Brunei Darussalam, 2020). Moreover, the country has also created a Fintech Regulatory Sandbox to nourish potential Fintech startups with close supervision to minimize its negative impacts (Autoriti Monetari Brunei Darussalam, 2020). In addition, it is worth noticing that since Brunei is a Muslim country, all Islamic financial activities are regulated by the Islamic Banking Order, which was enacted in 2008 (Brunei Darussalam Central Bank, n.d)

Like other neighbouring countries, Fintech in Brunei has also brought various economic impacts. First, developing financial technologies has enhanced financial inclusion and improved customer experiences (Autoriti Monetari Brunei Darussalam, 2020). Second, Fintech has also posed challenges to the Islamic finance industry, as all financial activities must comply with Sharia requirements (Ali et al., 2019).

On the other hand, the growth of Fintech in Brunei has presented new security issues to the country, such as online fraud, scams, and cyber-attacks. In 2018, the country recorded more than 2900 cyber-attack incidents, a 39% increase compared to 2017 (Cyber Security Brunei, 2020). Overall, the government is supporting the development of Fintech despite certain negative impacts and security concerns.

Other Relevant Academic Research and Interesting Facts

During the past five years, a few studies have been conducted to understand better the Fintech landscape in Brunei. One of the common findings is that the Bruneian government has provided a supportive and favourable regulatory environment for the development of Fintech, such as Sandbox (Autoriti Monetari Brunei Darussalam, 2020; Ali et al., 2019). Another noticeable finding is that Fintech has brought significant impacts on the Islamic financial industry, where all financial activities must comply with Sharia laws (Ali et al., 2019; Hussain, 2018).

Furthermore, the government has launched several centers as a one-stop place for everything about startups and entrepreneurship. These centers were designed to bridge the startup world, the government, and other successful companies and investors (Autoriti Monetari Brunei Darussalam, 2020).

In addition, another wise initiative launched in Brunei was the digital payment hub. This hub was a joint effort between Darussalam Assets Sdn Bhd and local banks where funds would be transferred instantly, enhancing productivity and lowering transaction costs. In short, Brunei has favourable conditions to thrive in Fintech in the future (Othman, 2022)

CAMBODIA

Market Size and Current Fintech Adoption Rate

In 2022, the kingdom of Cambodia was home to more than 16 million inhabitants (World Bank, 2023). The country's Fintech market is promising, with a significant increase in total transaction value from $548 million in 2017 to almost $4 billion in 2022 and expected to reach around $8 billion in 2027 (Statista, 2023). The following chart illustrates the growth of Fintech in Cambodia.

Figure 3. Transaction value of Fintech in Cambodia
Note. Adapted from Statista, 2023. Retrieved from https://www.statista.com/outlook/dmo/Fintech/cambodia

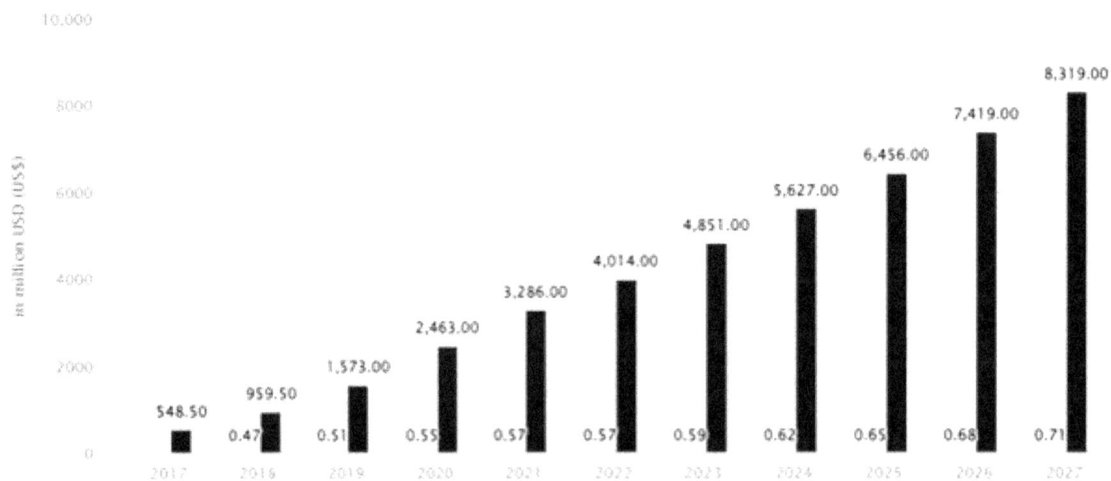

In 2019, the financial market had limited products, with approximately 3% of the population owning a credit card and 13% of Cambodian inhabitants using mobile payment (Kem et al., 2019). However, the Fintech adoption rate has grown dramatically, fueled by the high connectivity and mobile phone penetration level, around 124% of Cambodia's population, since one individual could have multiple mobile devices (Belaws Cambodia, 2022). Overall, Cambodia has vast potential to develop its Fintech market in the future.

Types of Fintech and Main Players

The types of Fintech market in Cambodia are relatively limited and consist of the following sectors: digital payment, insurtech, online lending services, accounting & banking, and crowdfunding (Aquarii, 2022). Regarding the digital payment segment, the leading players in Cambodia are PayWay, Pi Pay, and TrueMoney. PayWay is the leading online payment gateway, allowing all sizes of businesses to perform daily digital financial transactions (PayWay. n.d). In addition, PiPay is Cambodia's most famous payment platform because it offers a consumer-friendly app with merchant services. A local conglomerate backs the app and offers convenience and security for the customers (Pi Pay, n.d). Another key online wallet is TrueMoney, which is a Thai-based company. This Cambodia branch offered various financial products such as bill payments, money transfers, and phone top-ups. In 2021, the company recorded more than 1 million transactions (Firn, 2021). Regarding e-commerce, Cambodia is still in the nascent stage with a few famous platforms such as TinhTinh, Aliexpress, and Glad Market. Both TinhTinh and Glad Market are Cambodian companies, whereas AliExpress is from China (SCB, 2020).

New Investment and Startups

In 2020, the National Bank of Cambodia launched the first central bank digital currencies using cutting-edge blockchain technology (Belaws Cambodia, 2022). Moreover, there are a few new Fintech startups in the kingdom. Founded in 2018, Bongloy is one of them, providing an open API for digital payments and card issuance. The app also enables customers to receive payment from all over the world (Bongloy, n.d). Another interesting new startup in Cambodia is Boost Capital, where the app will allow customers to apply for loans, credit cards, and insurance online anytime (Boost Capitals, n.d).

Technical Infrastructure

In a report conducted in 2017, the coverage rate of 3G in Cambodia was around 80% of the population, and the 4G rate was approximately 50% (HBR, 2022). However, the mobile penetration rate has increased significantly, being in the world's top ten, with around 10.7 million phones connected to the internet in the country (Kem et al., 2019). According to Kem et al. (2019), more businesses aimed to transform digitally, fueled by more than 50,000 tech talents in Cambodia. The research above also estimated that the number of startups in Cambodia would double in the next few years.

Regarding the e-commerce sector, the market's total revenue is predicted to reach approximately $1 billion in 2023, with an annual growth rate of 12.24% (Statista, 2023).

Furthermore, Cambodians are highly interested in e-commerce due to the high internet access and the mobile phone penetration rate (Privacy Shield Framework, n.d). In terms of the digital banking system, in 2022, 69 financial institutions were offering mobile banking services in Cambodia (Mad, 2022). The pandemic also played an essential role in shifting the country's mindset towards digital transformation. While the kingdom had a slow start in adopting Fintech, the country is gaining pace with enormous potential to develop further.

Figure 4. The growth of eCommerce in Cambodia
Note. Reprinted from Statista, 2023. Retrieved from https://www.statista.com/outlook/dmo/ecommerce/cambodia

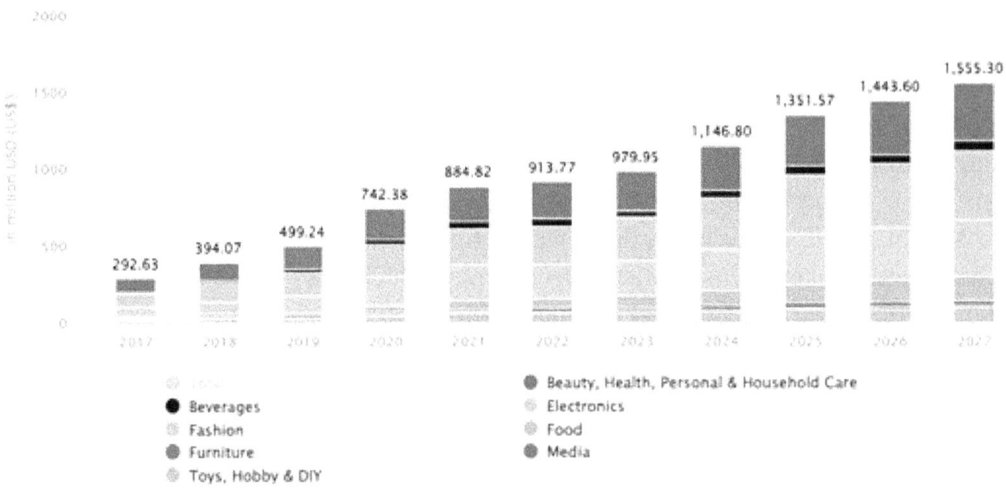

Government Policy, Regulation, and Impact of Fintech on the Economy

Understanding the importance of Fintech, the Cambodian government has enacted several encouraging initiatives and policies to support the tech startup ecosystem, including the Cambodia Startup Policy. This will be the first clear policy framework in the country regarding financial technology (Kem et al., 2019). Another key milestone in Cambodia's financial landscape was the launch of the Payment System Operator (PSO) by the National Bank of Cambodia (Acclime, 2023). The PSO will be used to regulate the payment service providers and ensure system security.

Moreover, the development of Fintech has presented various positive impacts. First, Fintech has boosted financial inclusion when more unbanked people can access and perform basic daily financial transactions (Kem et al., 2019). Second, the development of financial technologies has helped boost the growth of e-commerce in Cambodia, creating more employment opportunities (Banga & te Velde, 2020). The kingdom has been dominated by agriculture and textiles for a long time. Thus, the birth of Fintech is the catalyst to fuel the digital transformation process in Cambodia (Kem et al., 2019).

Along with the positive influences, the development of Fintech also poses certain threats to the cyber security of Cambodia. In 2022, the country deported 19 Japanese due to cyber scam suspects (Al Jazeera, 2023). Additionally, in the same year, the Cambodian police raided and arrested more than a hundred Chinese and Vietnamese immigrants linked to online frauds and scams (Dobberstein, 2022). Undoubtedly, the Cambodian government needs to work more to avoid future cyber-attack incidents.

Other Relevant Academic Research, Interesting Facts, and Trends

One of the most common academic findings for Fintech in Cambodia is that the development of financial technologies would improve the financial inclusion rate in the country (Kem et al., 2019; Makhija, 2019). In detail, Artificial Intelligence and Machine Learning technologies would help increase the accessibility to unbanked people in Cambodia. Another key finding is that the country should focus on developing its Fintech talents as the kingdom will need more high-skilled human resources to embrace the future digital transformation. (Kem et al., 2019; Makhija, 2019).

Furthermore, an interesting fact about the Fintech market in Cambodia is that the mobile data rates are among the cheapest phone plans in the world, around $1 for 10 gigabytes (Kem et al., 2019). This is a favourable condition for the unprivileged population to access the internet and enjoy the power of Fintech. In short, with the progression of financial technologies in Cambodia, the country will be a golden destination for Fintech companies to thrive.

INDONESIA

Market Size

Indonesia is the most populous country in Southeast Asia, with more than 275 million people in 2022 (World Bank, 2023). Moreover, Indonesia is known for having the largest population of Muslims in the world (Nurlatifah et al., 2022). Additionally, Indonesia ranks as the world's 10th-largest economy in terms of purchasing power parity (World Bank, 2022). In a survey conducted in 2019, the penetration of internet users in Indonesia was almost 171 million people, accounting for approximately 64% of its population (Abdillah, 2019). Lastly, the total value of Fintech transactions in this country has witnessed an impressive six-fold increase from around $13.9 billion in 2017 to almost $93 billion in 2022, with a forecast to reach $190 billion in 2027 (Statista, 2023). Obviously, Indonesia has been a fertile place for developing Fintech with a high level of internet users as well as its vast population.

Current Fintech Adoption Rate

Although Indonesia experienced significant growth in Fintech with strong support from the increasing numbers of internet users, its Fintech adoption rate was still comparatively low at almost 60% in 2020 (Haqqi & Suzianti, 2020). In a survey in 2022, just above 40% of correspondents replied that they had a banking app on their phones (Standard Insights, 2022). However, with the internet penetration rate growing to 8.9% in 2021, plus financial inclusion, Indonesia is expected to raise its Fintech adoption rate to a higher level (Kurniasari et al., 2022). Moreover, in 2020, there were around 63 million mobile wallet users, and the number is expected to hit almost 202 million users in 2025 (Fortumo, 2021).

Types of Fintech

Indonesia experienced rapid growth in the Fintech space, with many more Fintech start-ups being established. The number of Fintech start-ups went up from around 51 in 2011 to 334 in 2022, with the lending segment dominating the market share. The following figure illustrates how the change happened in the Indonesian Fintech landscape (Kumar et al., 2023).

Moreover, the Fintech landscape in Indonesia is relatively diverse, with various sectors such as P2P lending, digital payment, crowdfunding, wealth management, insurtech, and market provisioning (Batunanggar, 2019). The Indonesian Fintech market is clearly booming beyond P2P lending to include more complicated products and services. In addition, Indonesia has recently launched the world's first

Figure 5. The growth in the number of Fintech players by segment
Note. Reprinted from Indonesia's Fintech Industry Is Ready to Rise. Canada - EN. Retrieved from https://www.bcg.com/en-ca/publications/2023/Fintech-industry-indonesia-growth

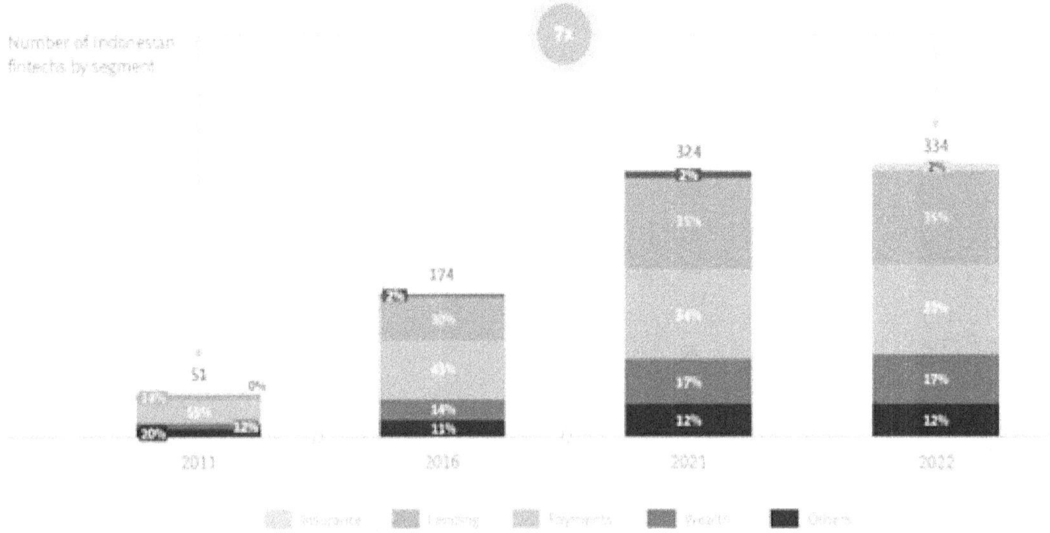

state-backed cryptocurrency bourse, where the government could regulate the new technology as well as encourage a fair and safe crypto trading platform (Medina, 2023).

Main Players

In 2022, there are five big Fintech companies dominating the digital online payment sector in Indonesia: Gopay, Dana, Ovo, Shopee Pay, and LinkAja. GoPay is a famous digital payment platform that allows its users to transact money directly from their mobile phones, whereas Dana was launched as a peer-to-peer payment platform and then expanded to process cashless transactions (GoPay, n.d; Dana, n.d). Shopee Pay is a part of the Shopee e-commerce platform that served as the default payment method for the platform, and LinkAja is a digital wallet that was formed by several state-owned enterprises (LinkAja, n.d). Gopay is the most popular e-wallet app used with more than 88% of total consumers in Indonesia in 2022, followed by Dana with around 83%, Ovo at almost 79%, Shopee Pay with 76%, and LinkAja at 30% (Kompas, 2022). The figure below depicts the share of respondents who used e-wallet apps to transact:

Regarding e-commerce platforms, there are numerous websites that Indonesians are using to shop online. However, only Tokopedia, Shopee, Lazada, and Bukalapak are leading the market. According to an analysis by iPrice Group (2022), Tokopedia and Shopee received the most visits from customers, with around 158 and 131 million web visits by monthly traffic, respectively. The following graph illustrates the leading e-commerce sites in Indonesia as of 2nd quarter of 2022:

In terms of digital banks, Indonesia has witnessed significant growth during the past decade (Kumar et al., 2023). Understanding the challenges of the country's geography and underbanked population, major banks have invested in financial technology and embedded it into their products and services to serve the customers better as well as generate more profits (Afif & Samsuri, 2022). For example, digital Seabank Indonesia, which was owned by Singaporean Sea Limited, experienced a double increase in

Figure 6. Most used e-wallet apps by consumers in Indonesia as of July 2022
Note. Adapted from the Most used e-wallet apps by consumers in Indonesia as of July 2022 Retrieved from https://www.statista.com/statistics/1327316/indonesia-most-used-e-wallet-apps/

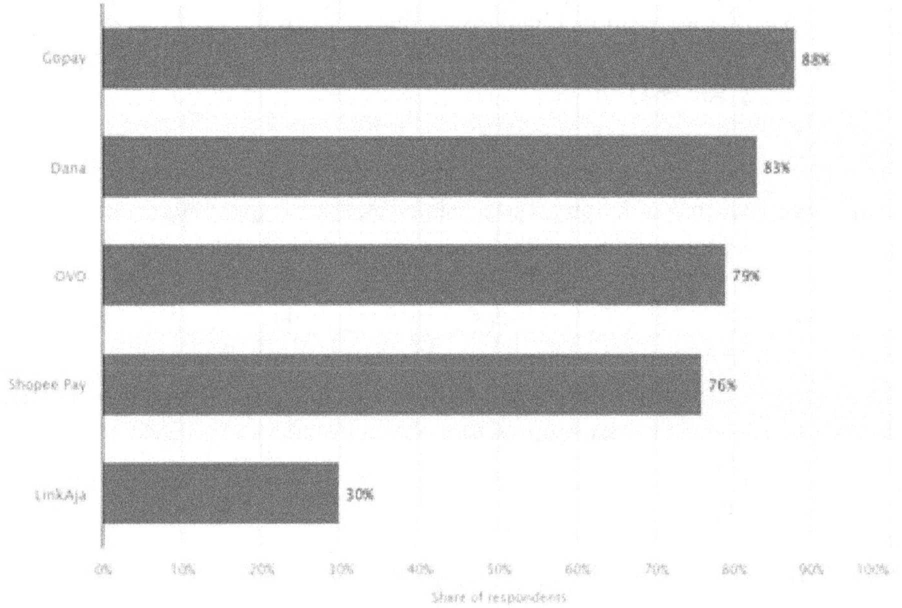

Figure 7. Leading e-commerce sites in Indonesia as of the 2nd quarter of 2022 by monthly traffic
Note. Adapted from Leading e-commerce sites in Indonesia as of the 2nd quarter of 2022 by monthly traffic (in million web visits). Retrieved from https://www.statista.com/statistics/869700/indonesia-top-10-e-commerce-sites/

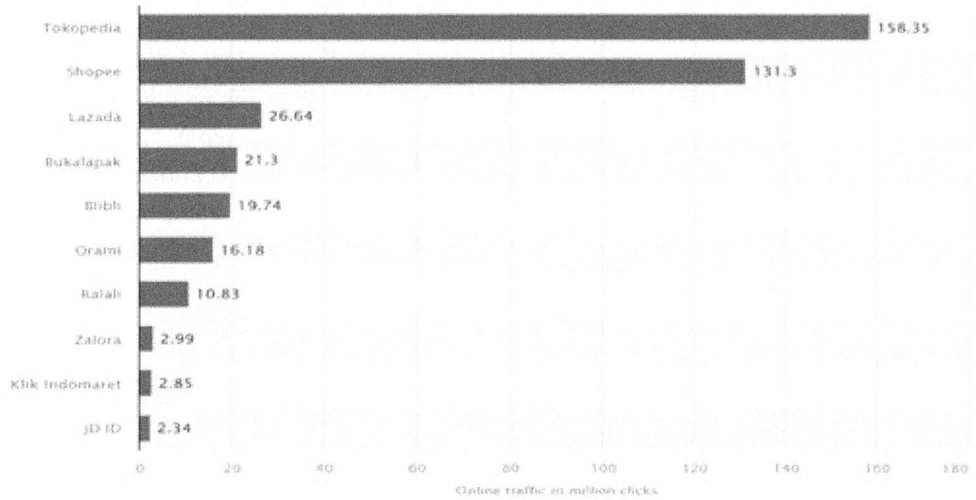

its total assets in 2022, around $1.4 billion (Kumar et al., 2023). The most known digital banks among Indonesians are Jenius, Bank Jago, Seabank, Neobank, Line Bank, and PermataME (Katadata, 2022). The growth of Indonesian digital banks can be attributed to various strategies, such as enhancing current revenue models and developing traditional banking businesses (Kumar et al., 2023).

New Investment and Start-Ups

With a huge population, Indonesia is home to various startups with huge funding. Pluang was founded in 2019 in Jakarta with the goal of helping Indonesians access micro-savings and micro-investments. The company has gone through several rounds of funding, with the total amount raised reaching more than $113 million (Pluang, n.d). The second new startup was UpBanx, founded in 2021 in Jakarta. Its business model is to provide a Fintech platform to accommodate the demands of creators, brands, free-lancers, and agencies (UpBanx, n.d). Another noticeable startup is Akseleran, which was established to offer a P2P lending platform to connect small and medium-sized firms with organizations or individuals willing to make those investments (Akselaran, n.d).

Technical Infrastructure

Indonesian Fintech ecosystem is unique and vibrant, where companies are investing heavily in financial technologies to gain their market shares. Numerous providers, such as e-commerce sites, e-hailing and food delivery firms, and Fintech solutions businesses, integrate their Fintech touchpoints through lending, online payments, and insurance (Kumar et al., 2023). However, the internet connection, especially 4G coverage, is still a big challenge for this archipelago nation. More than half of the Indonesian population in the eastern region has unstable access to the Internet due to geographical reasons (Saffa, 2023). The central government has accelerated the 4G coverage plan in rural areas to improve and ensure that its residents can access rapid internet connection. In terms of 5G technology implementation, the country is lagging behind its neighbouring countries with a slow penetration rate of 2.5% (Tomás, 2022).

However, regarding its e-commerce websites, the country experienced dramatical growth, becoming the ninth largest in the world, with an approximate value of $43 billion (International Trade Administration, 2022). Online purchases are gaining their paces, especially after the pandemic, with Tokopedia leading the market. On top of that, the growth of the Indonesian e-commerce sector is fueled by the development of digital wallets such as GoPay, DANA, and ShopeePay (International Trade Administration, 2022). On the other hand, digital banks have brought a huge positive impact on the Indonesian financial landscape when bridging the gaps for users in rural and remote islands (Kumar et al., 2023). It means that consumers from those areas can easily transfer money, shop online and enjoy more financial products and services. Overall, the Indonesian government is spending much effort to improve and enhance its Fintech infrastructure.

Government Policy and Regulation

In Indonesia, the Central Bank of Indonesia (BI) and the Financial Services Authority (OJK) are two independent financial authorities that were assigned to supervise and regulate the Fintech market (Aulia et al., 2020). The nation established its first framework for regulating electronic money and card payments in 2009. While BI aims to maintain a stable monetary system, OJK was formed to provide benefits to the economy (Aulia et al., 2020). Additionally, there is an association named Asosiasi Fintech Indonesia to gather Fintech firms. Furthermore, Indonesia has the most Islamic Fintech startups in the world, constituting one-third of the total Islamic Fintech startups worldwide (DIEDC, 2018).

Impact on the Economy

So far, Fintech has had several positive impacts on the Indonesian economy. First, the development of Fintech has helped the country connect the unbanked population from different regions in Indonesia and offered them a great variety of new financial products and services (Kumar et al., 2023). Second, Fintech helps the Indonesian economy close the funding gaps for various businesses, especially small and medium enterprises, increasing their revenue and leading to overall economic growth (Nugraha et al., 2022). On top of that, big digital wallets such as GoPay, Ovo, and Dana have allowed users to transact money more easily and securely. Another noticeable impact of Fintech is the development of Insurtech because companies in this area, such as PasarPolis and Qoala, used financial technology to simplify the entire insurance process from purchasing stage and claiming process to reimbursing (Wulandari et al., 2023).

Security Concern

The increasing volume of financial transactions, as well as customers' data, has come with the proliferation of cybersecurity threats and frauds, posing severe challenges for Fintech firms and authorities in Indonesia (Wulandari et al., 2023). For instance, recently, around 15 million account details from the Indonesian biggest bank, BSI, were published online, causing social chaos in the country (Reuters, 2023). Clearly, cybersecurity and consumer data are causing tough challenges for Fintech companies in Indonesia. Hence, companies should invest more to protect their data as well as their financial information to avoid any severe consequences (Wulandari et al., 2023).

Other Relevant Academic Research

Several studies about Indonesian Fintech have been conducted to point out the challenges and drawbacks of the current Fintech system. One of the common findings from recent studies is that the Indonesian Fintech market is encountering limited financial inclusion (Anifa et al., 2022; Kabulova & Stankevičienė, 2020). Despite having a large population, a significant portion of Indonesians, especially in remote areas, remain unbanked. Many individuals and businesses found difficulties when trying to enjoy basic financial services such as banking facilities, credit, and insurance. Another significant finding is the governmental regulatory environment. Although the government understands the importance of Fintech, there are bumpy roads for businesses to comply with time-consuming regulations and expensive licensing requirements (Wulandari, 2023; Batunanggar, 2019). New companies usually spend much time completing the registration and paperwork processes with the local authorities before officially operating. Since Fintech includes Regtech, the government could leverage and encourage further development of this technology sector to help reduce the red tape and embed digital transformation into traditional operations.

Furthermore, the third mutual finding is that the central government needs to devise a comprehensive plan with detailed strategies to establish a strong Fintech ecosystem with clear legal frameworks

(Batunanggar, 2019; Abdillah, 2019). Indonesia could consider and learn from Singaporean risk-based policies toward new Fintech startups as it would provide a more flexible way to regulate and establish an innovative environment for Fintech firms. In summary, the Indonesian government is advised to promote a broad financial inclusion approach, define a clear legal framework, and reduce the red-tape concerns.

Interesting Fact

Since the rapid development of Fintech in Indonesia, the country has several startups that could be classified in the Unicorn category, where each startup held a value of over $1 billion. These are Gojek, Traveloka, TokoPedia, BukaLapak and OVO. They are not only operating in Indonesia but also expanding to various Asian countries (Abdillah, 2019).

Furthermore, like Vietnam, the P2P lending sector is dominating the Fintech market. In 2019, more than 40% of Indonesian Fintech companies operated with P2P lending models, followed by payment and market provisioning. This is due to Indonesia's geographical distances, causing difficulties in accessing banking services (Batunanggar, 2019).

Trend and Future Aspects

Indonesia is experiencing growth in Superapps, which is an application consisting of various services. For instance, Shopee, Tokopedia, and Traveloka are offering their core products and introducing new services such as digital payments, buy-now-pay-later, or online micro-investments (United Overseas Bank Limited, 2021). In addition, the P2P lending trend will continue booming since a majority of the Indonesian population is still living in remote and rural areas on different islands (Kumar et al., 2023).

LAOS

Market Size and Current Fintech Adoption Rate

Laos, a landlocked country, is home to more than 7 million people (World Bank, 2023). Regarding Fintech adoption, the country's penetration rate of mobile phones in urban areas is comparatively higher than in rural areas, 47.3% compared to 23.9% (Morgan & Trinh, 2019). However, the Fintech transaction value in Laos has increased exponentially, from around $0.29 billion in 2017 to almost $1.15 billion in 2022, projected to reach approximately $2.76 billion in 2027 (Statis, 2023).

In addition, digital financial services in Laos are relatively limited, with only credit, insurance, and online payments through devices. According to Martina (2022), the Fintech market in Laos is still at a nascent stage. Overall, the market size of Fintech in Laos is considerably small, with a low adoption rate.

Types of Fintech, Main Players, and New Investment and Startups

The types of Fintech in Laos are relatively limited, with only a few basic segments, such as online savings, digital payments, and insurtech (Morgan & Trinh, 2019). The most famous Fintech app in Laos is the LaoPay Super App. The company was founded in 2019 with an aim to be the leading e-wallet and mobile payment app in the country. This go-to app soon became the first choice for Laotian users, where

Figure 8. Total transaction value of Fintech in Laos from 2017 to 2027
Note. Adapted from Fintech - Laos. Retrieved from https://www.statista.com/outlook/dmo/Fintech/laos#transaction-value

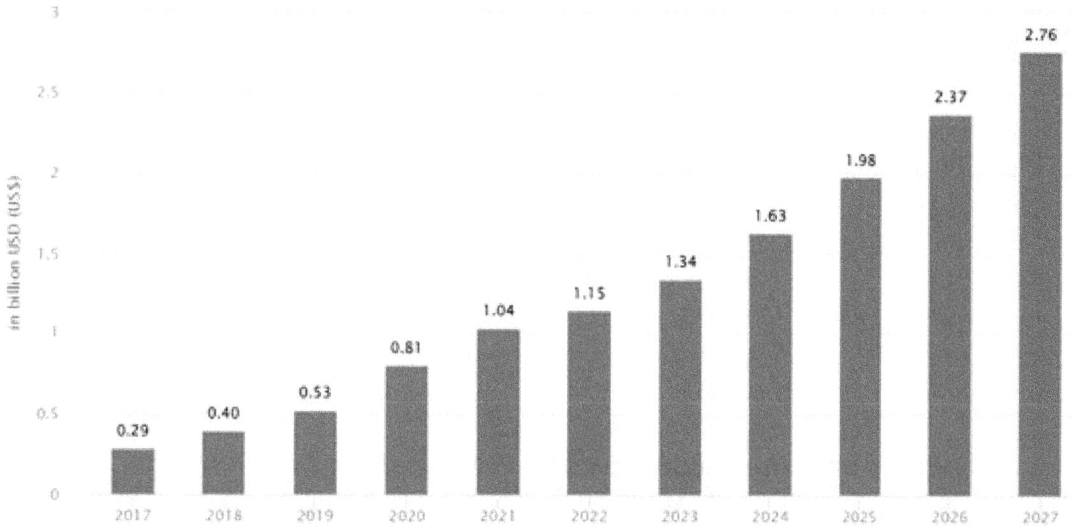

it offers various products and services such as paying bills, transferring money, online shopping, mobile top-up, travelling, and international remittance (LaoPay, n.d). Another main financial application in Laos is Loca. The company was established in 2018 as the first online ride-hailing platform but then soon adopted more new financial services such as Loca Pay (Loca, n.d). Moreover, it is worth noticing that there is no record of online P2P lending in Laos (Soriano et al., 2019). Overall, Laos's Fintech market is still nascent, with limited types and products for the customers.

Furthermore, there are a few new investments and startups in the country. Founded in 2019, LTS Ventures is offering a microfinance banking platform to remote populations, primarily rural areas. The app aims to educate and improve the financial literacy of the villagers (LTS Ventures, n.d). Another new startup is Cofarm, which was established in 2021. The app uses technology to match restaurant owners with high-quality products at reasonable prices from the farmers (CoFarm, n.d). Moreover, the National Bank of Laos has launched a pilot program for the digital Lao Kip, aiming to increase financial inclusion in the country (Medina, 2023).

Technical Infrastructure

In 2020, only around 63 out of 100 residents in Laos had a mobile subscription (The World Bank, 2020). Moreover, a report by the Lao Statistics Bureau indicated that in 2016, approximately 14% of the population owned a home telephone, 16% had computers, and 20% had access to the Internet (Martina, 2023). In short, the telecommunication system in Laos is outdated and not ready for adopting new financial technologies. Furthermore, e-commerce is not popular in Laos due to the lack of technologies, logistics, and formal banking and credit card usage (The International Trade Administration, 2022)

Government Policy, Regulation, and Impact of Fintech on the Economy and Security Concern

According to Morgan and Trinh (2019), in Laos, two governmental organizations regulate the Fintech market: the Ministry of Science and Technology and the Department of Small and Medium Enterprise Promotion. Moreover, the Laotian government does consider small businesses and startups to be the same. Thus, there are no clear legal framework or tax incentives for startups, especially Fintech ones. However, Martina (2023) believes that the development of Fintech in Laos would bring a significant impact on the local economy, enhancing online banking and payments and offering peer-to-peer lending. In addition, the introduction of Digital Lao Kip by the national bank would enhance financial inclusion for the unbanked population in Laos (Medina, 2023). Although Laos has yet to record any significant cyber-attacks, the country has started collaborating with foreign partners in Singapore and China to learn from their cyber security experiences as well as practices to protect data privacy (Data&StorageAsean, 2022).

Other Relevant Academic Research and Fintech Trend

The most common finding about Fintech in Laos is that the country has a low Fintech adoption rate and poor infrastructure preparation to embrace emerging financial technologies (Martina, 2022; Morgan & Trinh, 2019). The government should consider funding more Fintech projects as well as improving their technical infrastructure in order to embrace the development of Fintech in the future. In addition, the growth of Fintech in the country would be strongly supported by the public sector, with banks leading the trend (Fintechnews, 2023). Overall, the Laotian government needs to devise a master plan to regulate and nourish the development of Fintech.

MALAYSIA

Market Size

Located in the center of the Southeast Asian region, Malaysia is home to more than 33 million inhabitants (World Bank, 2022). The country experienced a dramatic growth in Fintech transaction value from $6 billion USD in 2017 to around $32 billion USD in 2022, with a forecast to reach $73 billion USD in 2027 (Statista, 2023). Malaysia is manifesting exponential growth with a 5-fold increase within five years. In addition, the number of Fintech companies in the country almost doubled, with 346 firms in 2017, obtaining 612 firms in 2022 (United Overseas Bank, 2022). These favourable factors would enable the country to thrive in Fintech further to compete with other ASEAN countries.

Current Fintech Adoption Rate

According to Chua et al. (2019), the adoption rate of Fintech in Malaysia was at the preliminary stage. However, the country witnessed a sharp increase in the adoption rate of Internet banking and mobile banks, with Internet banking transactions rising from around $500 million USD to more than

$2 billion USD in 2021 (Fintech News Malaysia, 2022). In addition, the Malaysian Fintech market is expected to thrive further in the future as more Fintech companies are gaining paces (Chua et al., 2019). In 2022, the Central Bank of Malaysia revealed in its annual report that around 79% of adults in Malaysia used digital payments for transactions (Central Bank of Malaysia, 2023). This is strong evidence of significant growth in the Fintech market in Malaysia, shifting from a preliminary stage to a high adoption rate.

Types of Fintech

Although Malaysia might not hold a primary position in Fintech in the ASEAN region, various sectors have embedded emerging technologies to improve their financial products and services. According to Zaghlol et al. (2021), the top Fintech business segments are payments, with a 20% market share, e-wallet with 15%, and lending with 14%. In addition, there are other Fintech business areas such as Insurtech, Wealthtech, Remittance, Blockchain/Crypto, and Regtech. Moreover, a unique Fintech sector in Malaysia is Islamic Fintech, accounting for 4% market share (Zaghlol et al., 2021). This is because more than 60% of the Malaysian population has faith in Islam (Statista, 2022). The figure below illustrates the percentage of Malaysian firms involved in Fintech in 2021.

Figure 9. Percentage of Malaysian companies involved in Fintech
Note. Reprinted from The Nexus between Fintech Adoption and Financial Development in Malaysia: An Overview, 2021. Retrieved from https://www.researchgate.net/profile/Nurasyiqin-Ramdhan2/publication/356194561_The_Nexus_between_Fintech_Adoption_and_Financial_Development_in_Malaysia_An_Overview/links/6191c63e61f09877209a322b/The-Nexus-between-Fintech-Adoption-and-Financial-Development-in-Malaysia-An-Overview.pdf

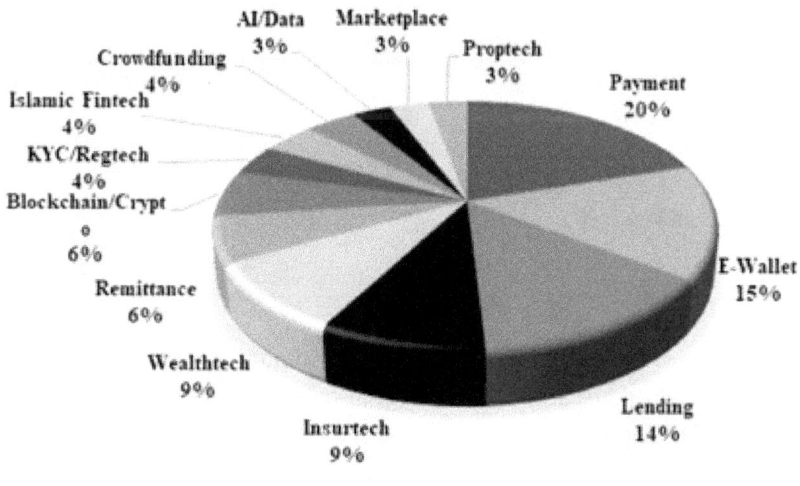

Like other ASEAN countries, payment, e-wallet, and lending sectors are leading the market, accounting for almost 50% of the market share. However, the adoption rate of blockchain technology is increasing significantly because it is heavily embedded in numerous industries, especially nine banks that have begun to accept Bitcoin as one of their payment methods (Ku-Mahamud et al., 2018).

Main Players

Regarding the e-wallet payment sector, a couple of giant tech companies are steering the Malaysian market. Grabpay is considered the most prominent e-wallet application, with more than 25 million users, followed by Touch'n Go, with more than 16 million users (Finextra, 2022). The total value of e-money transactions in Malaysia in 2022 already exceeded 65 million Malaysia ringgit (Bank Negara Malaysia, 2023). On top of that, other e-wallet companies also play crucial roles in the Malaysian market, such as Paypal, BigPay, Fave, and Ali Pay (Rakuten Insight, 2022).

In terms of the e-commerce market, it is gaining pace, especially after the pandemic. Shopee was the most visited platform in the second quarter of 2022, measured by monthly traffic, followed by PG Mall, Lazada, and Zalora, respectively. The following graph ranks the platforms by monthly traffic in 1,000 clicks.

Figure 10. Most visited e-commerce sites in Malaysia as of 2nd quarter 2022
Note. Adapted from Most visited e-commerce sites in Malaysia as of 2nd quarter 2022, by monthly traffic (in 1,000 clicks). Retrieved from https://www.statista.com/statistics/869640/malaysia-top-10-e-commerce-sites/

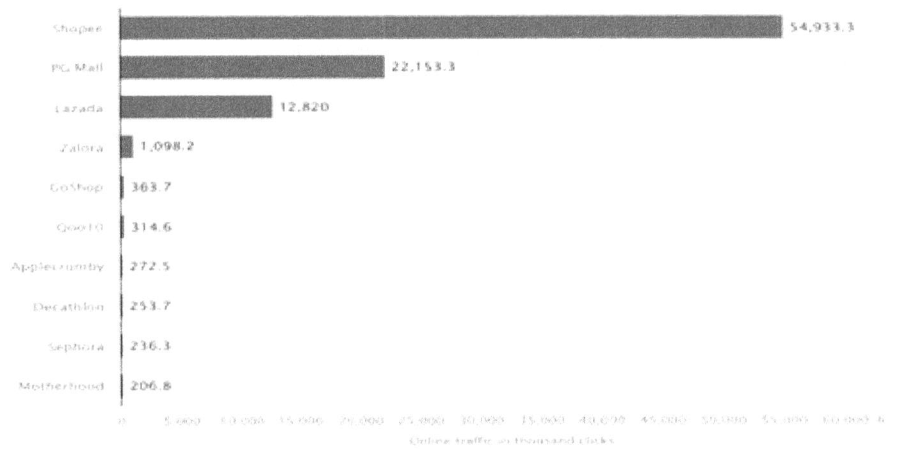

Malaysia has a couple of banks that are operating fully digital, to name a few: Boost Holdings, RHB Bank Berhad, and Kuok Brothers Sdn. All the digital banks needed to secure licenses from the Malaysian National Bank. Furthermore, Berhad cooperates with a joint venture between Singtel and Grab (RHB, n.d). Moreover, YTL Berhad of Malaysia partnered with Sea Limited, a growing tech company in Southeast Asia (YTL Corporation Berhad, n.d). Moreover, Islamic digital bank licenses were issued to Carsome and MoneyMatch, which KAF Investment Bank leads (Oi, 2023). Overall, the Fintech market in Malaysia is led by a few giant big tech companies, but their impact on the economy is enormous, especially with the development of Grab (Grab, 2019).

New Investments and Startups

New Fintech startups are proliferating in Malaysia and are used in diverse business sectors. PayWatch is a new Fintech startup, creating an online platform to enable employees to access the salary that they earned earlier in order to cover their financial needs (PayWatch, n.d). Another interesting new Fintech startup is Payd. The company established a common space to allow the entire nation to be involved in the financial ecosystem (Payd, n.d). Furthermore, Capsphere, a Sharia-compliant Fintech startup, was established in 2020 to provide financial solutions via a digital platform for the underserved and unserved population (Orpheus Capital, n.d). CapBay is another latest Fintech startup that created a peer-to-peer platform to finance supply chain operations, offering a simple process for businesses to access funds from financial institutions (CapBay, n.d).

Technical Infrastructure

Regarding internet coverage, Malaysia is believed to have a high mobile network coverage rate in the region. In 2021, more than 95% of the population was covered by a 4G LTE network (Malaysian Communications and Multimedia Commission, 2022). In 2023, 5G technology covered approximately 62.1% of populated areas in Malaysia (Nair, 2023). This is a powerful fundamental foundation for Fintech firms to thrive in the future.

In terms of the e-commerce market, Malaysia witnessed significant growth, and expected to increase by 20% yearly. In 2023, the e-commerce market in Malaysia is forecast to hit $10.19 billion USD, expecting to reach $16.98 billion USD in 2027. Shopee dominates the market with more than 55 million monthly visitors (Kashyap, 2023). The success of Malaysian e-commerce can be attributed to the seamless delivery process. This is because the country is separated into two main regions, which makes it easier to move things and reduce costs.

In addition, in 2021, more than 80 percent of the population could access the Internet, and the mobile phone penetration growth rate was high at 84.2 percent (International Trade Administration, 2022). Furthermore, the number of users of digital payments is picking up, increasing from 9.9 million users in 2018 to 15.72 million users in 2022 and is expected to hit 20.02 in 2027 (Statista, 2023). The following chart illustrates the dramatic growth in the number of digital payment users in Malaysia.

In short, with the above positive data, Malaysia has all the favourable conditions to thrive in Fintech further.

Government Policy and Regulation

Currently, there are two main acts to govern financial services and transactions, including Fintech. The first policy is the Financial Services Act which was bypassed in 2013 to promote a favourable environment for Fintech companies to develop with fair competition and create a common space for innovations (Central Bank of Malaysia, 2013). The act also aims to stabilize and regulate any new Fintech startups with a massive economic impact.

The second important act in Malaysia regarding Fintech firms is the Islamic Financial Services Act, which was also enacted in 2013. Since Malaysia has a significant Islamic population of more than 63.5%, they need to comply with the Sharia rules (Central Bank of Malaysia, 2013). The enactment of the Islamic Financial Services Act was initiated to better cater to the financial needs of this demographic. The

Figure 11. Number of users of digital payments in Malaysia 2018-2027
Note. Adapted from Number of users of digital payments in Malaysia 2018-2027 (in million users. Retrieved from https://www.statista.com/forecasts/1367668/malaysia-digital-payment-users

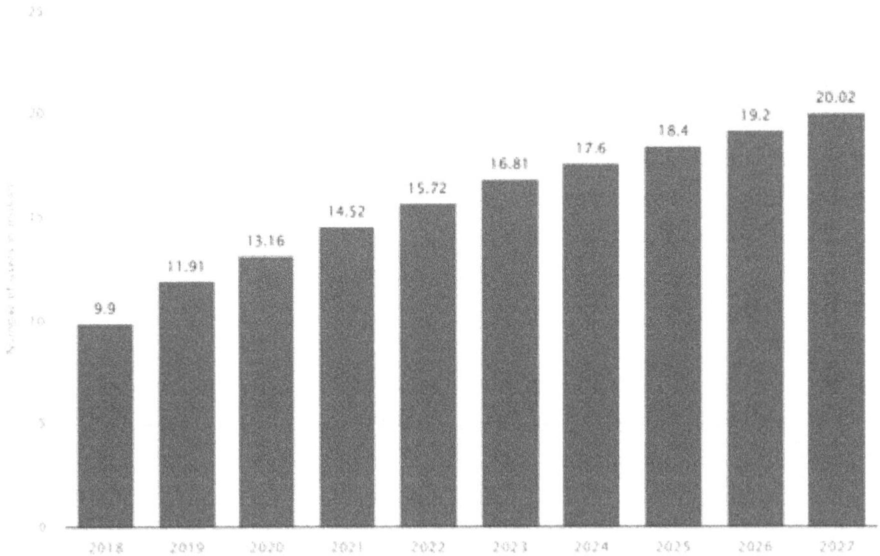

above fundamental financial acts serve as the main guideline to govern and regulate the Fintech market as well as establish a fair and robust Fintech ecosystem to thrive in the future.

Impact on the Economy

The development of Fintech has brought several significant impacts on the Malaysian economy. First, Fintech provided better financial inclusion, expanding financial services to a more unbanked population as well as offering more access to banking and insurance services (Yahaya & Ahmad, 2018). The second positive change from Fintech is that it enhances and facilitates several processes ranging from peer-to-peer lending and crowdfunding to alternative capital sources for small and medium-sized enterprises (Alam, Gupta, & Zameni, 2019). Additionally, the rapid development of Fintech could pose several regulatory challenges to the country, requiring the authorities to ensure financial stability and protection from money laundering and cyber securities, especially when dealing with Sharia rules (Ali, Abdullah, & Zaini, 2019).

Security Concern

As mentioned earlier regarding the security concern posed by the development of Fintech, the country experienced an upward trend of cybercrimes in recent years. The Royal Malaysia Police's office reported that over RM850 million was lost due to over 25,000 online fraud and scam incidents in 2022 (Chong, 2023). Obviously, the growth of Fintech has urged all financial institutions to devise an optimal mechanism to prevent online fraud, data violations, and cybercrimes. Otherwise, Fintech will be considered a new source for destabilizing the Malaysian economy.

Other Relevant Academic Research

Numerous studies have been conducted to analyze and understand better the development of Fintech in Malaysia. The most common finding is that emerging financial technologies must comply with Sharia rules, so they must be established with much caution and Islamic expertise (Ali et al., 2019; Ab Razak et al., 2020). Sharia rules require much more effort and prohibit various financial activities such as taking interest in loans, speculation, and gambling. Thus, separate Islamic banks were established to accommodate Islam fellows, including Alliance Bank Malaysia Berhad, Bank Islam Malaysia Berhad, and CIMB.

The second significant finding is that Fintech could pose certain risks to customers, especially financial frauds and cyberattacks. Therefore, the government should focus on creating a clear protection framework to address these concerns (Diniyya et al., 2020; Ali, Abdullah, & Zaini, 2019). The government should consider leveraging Regtech practices to prevent criminal activities as well as foster a transparent environment where Fintech firms comply with the country's rules. Overall, Malaysia has a vast potential to develop a strong Fintech ecosystem for Islam fellows as well as the non-Islam population.

Interesting Facts

Unlike other neighbouring countries, the Malaysian government needs to distinguish its policies to accommodate Islam and non-Islam citizens. The Financial Services Acts are prime examples of this practice. Regarding the Islamic Financial Services Act, the government aims to concentrate on Islamic Fintech solutions, with several Sharia-compliant investment and lending platforms (Ali et al., 2019). Another interesting fact about Fintech in Malaysia is that the country is leading the digital motor insurance market, with more than 63% of motor-insured transactions being purchased online (United Overseas Bank Limited, 2022). This is because bikers can easily purchase their motor insurance from their phones compared to conventional ways such as going to motor dealers or insurance offices. Furthermore, in a report conducted by PricewaterhouseCoopers in 2016, around 82% of Malaysian Financial Institutions considered Fintech a threat to their business models, and approximately 20% of Malaysian Financial Entities believed that they might lose their profits to Fintech firms (PwC, 2016).

Trend and Aspects

The funding trend for Malaysian Fintech is still in the digital payment sector. Several deals worth millions of USD have been closed for BigPay and TNG Digital (Fintech Malaysia, 2022). This is because the country aims to broaden its financial inclusion approach to help more unbanked population access the convenience of Fintech. Another promising trend is the rise of digital loans in Malaysia. Since it is easy to borrow money online, people tend to use these resources to fund their businesses, pay medical bills, and invest in other potential things (Tech Collective, 2023).

MYANMAR

Market Size and Current Fintech Adoption Rate

Myanmar is the only Southeast Asian country that has a land border with India and is home to more than 54 million people (World Bank, 2023). However, the total transaction value of Fintech is low, with only around $1.3 billion in 2017, and increased to approximately $3.6 billion in 2022 (Statista, 2023). Moreover, the pandemic was the latest catalyst to boost the adoption of Fintech in the country, with an example of a governmental distribution plan through local digital platforms such as Wave Money and OnePay (Oxford Business Group, 2020). In 2014, the mobile phone connection rate was less than 10% but increased significantly to around 95% in 2019 (International Trade Admission, 2021). According to Aye (2020), Myanmar's mobile phone penetration rate was almost 100 percent. Overall, the increase in mobile connectivity and penetration in Mynamar enables more people to access banking and financial services from their own phones.

Types Of Fintech and Main Players

In Myanmar, there are limited types of Fintech with two growing segments, which are digital payment and mobile wallets, with about ten Fintech companies offering these services (International Trade Admission, 2021). The Burmese mobile wallet market has increased exponentially from 1% in 2016 to approximately 80% in 2019 (Kyaw, 2022). In addition, the digital lending sector is also promising, where they could provide funds to the unbanked population, especially those in remote areas in Myanmar. Founded in 2016, the ZigWay app was designed to help the poor population in the country with a focus on women group by providing nano-loans with low interests (ZigWay, n.d)

In terms of the digital payment sector, there are a few main players, such as WavePay, KBZ Pay, and Aya Pay. Founded in 2015, WavePay is a non-bank digital wallet that recorded more than 1.1 million monthly active users in 2020 (Insider, 2020). The app was designed for Burmese citizens to transfer money more easily with their own phones as well as enhance the accessibility to formal banking services (Wave Money, n.d). Another significant digital payment app is KBZ Pay, which is backed by KBZ Bank. In 2020, the app had around 6 million users, with an expectation to reach 10 million users in the next ten years (DigFin, 2020). KBZ Pay offers various financial products and services ranging from transferring money to online lending (KBZ Pay, n.d). The third famous mobile platform in Myanmar is AYA Pay, which is also backed by Aya Bank. The app has an advanced ecosystem with several in-house services as well as fundamental financial products (Aya Pay, n.d).

Regarding the e-commerce sector, the platform shop.com.mm is the largest website in Myanmar, with more than 30,000 sellers and 5 million customers (SCB, 2020). The platform is backed by Alibaba, one of the largest e-commerce companies in China, with several latest technologies applied (Shop, n.d). Moreover, according to ecommerceDB (2023), food and personal care consisted of 35.9% of the Myanmar e-commerce revenue, followed by electronics & media with 28.8%, and furniture & and appliances with 15.0%. Fashion accounted for 14.3%, and Toys took 6.0% of the e-commerce revenue.

New Investment, Startups, and Technical Infrastructure

There are a few new Fintech established companies in Myanmar, and Waloan is one of them. Founded in 2019, the app was engineered to be a digital microfinance loan platform with an aim to provide loans to more people, especially the unbanked population, through various financial institutions (Waloan, n.d). Another new startup in Myanmar was AgriZay, which was established in 2020. The platform helps everyone grow and start an agricultural business remotely without physically owning the land (Fintech Energy, 2022). Another latest Fintech startup was NUGPay. The app was launched in 2022 to offer a new payment system for the Burmese (NUGPay, n.d)

Regarding the Burmese technical infrastructure, the country had around 124% mobile connection penetration rate, with 4G covering almost 90% of the area (Marek, 2020). Furthermore, there are approximately 24 million active mobile wallets in Myanmar (Greene, 2022). Another critical aspect of the Fintech ecosystem in Myanmar is its growing e-commerce market. The expected revenue of e-commerce in Myanmar is more than $3 billion USD in 2023, with a prediction of an annual growth rate of 13.2% (ecommerceDB, 2023). In addition, the number of e-commerce users is projected to reach more than 19 million people in 2027 (Statista, 2023). Overall, despite the economic downturn during the pandemic, the country has certain fertile grounds and room for thriving Fintech.

Government Policy, Regulation, and Impact on the Economy and Security Concern

Regarding the financial technology regulation in Myanmar, the Central bank governs the Fintech market. According to governmental regulation, a mobile financial services company must have at least 3 billion Myanmar kyat plus documentation and a business plan to apply for the permit (Central Bank of Myanmar, 2016).

Furthermore, the development of Fintech in Myanmar has significantly impacted the local economy. It has enhanced financial inclusion and transformed the Burmese economy digitally (Aye, 2020). Indeed, mobile wallets and digital payment apps have allowed more unbanked people in Myanmar to access fundamental financial services. However, the development of Fintech also posed certain threats to the national security. Recently, a joint effort between China and Myanmar has been implemented to arrest more than 200 Chinese for their suspected cyber scams (Ziwen, 2023). In short, Fintech could positively and negatively impact the Burmese economy.

Other Relevant Academic Research

During the past five years, the most common finding about the development of Fintech in Myanmar is that it has helped enhance financial accessibility and inclusion (Aye, 2020; Laik & Wei, 2019). Indeed, more unbanked Burmese have chances to access basic financial services as well as embrace new financial technologies.

It is worth noticing that the value of remittances from overseas Burmese has increased significantly from $1.64 billion in 2013 to around $2.67 billion in 2020, then a steep drop to $1.9 billion in 2022 due to the pandemic (World Bank, 2023). The following chart illustrates the growth of remittances received in Myanmar.

Figure 12. Value of remittances received in Myanmar from 2013 to 2022
Note. Adapted from Value of remittances received in Myanmar from 2013 to 2022 (in billion U.S. dollars). Retrieved from https://www.statista.com/statistics/880741/myanmar-value-of-remittances/

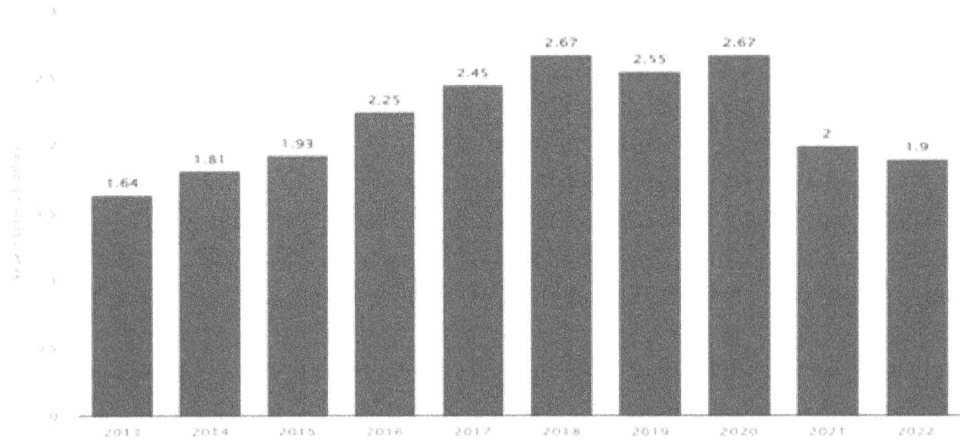

Overall, despite certain challenges in its Fintech infrastructure and applications, the country is attempting to build a cashless society and improve the national financial inclusion rate.

THE PHILIPPINES

Market Size

The Philippines has numerous favourable conditions for developing Fintech. Firstly, the country is the second most populous nation in the Southeast Asian region, with approximately 115 million people as of 2022 (World Bank, 2023). Moreover, internet penetration has grown significantly, reaching 73.93 percent and is expected to peak in 2028 (Statista, 2023). Additionally, the total transaction value of Fintech has increased dramatically from $10 billion USD in 2017 to $28 billion in 2022, with a forecast to reach around $56 billion in 2027. Lastly, the number of Fintech companies in the Philippines has risen from 177 in 2017 to around 289 firms in 2022 (United Overseas Bank, 2022). Undoubtedly, the Philippine Fintech market is promising and projected to thrive in the future.

Current Fintech Adoption Rate

In the past six years, the Fintech adoption rate was comparatively low, with more than 80 percent of adult Filipinos not having any bank account. In 2017, approximately 8 million Filipinos had a bank account to transact (Schellhase & Garcia, 2019). However, the Fintech adoption rate has increased dramatically recently. In 2022, more than 69.3 percent of the Philippine population embraced Fintech services in their daily lives, fueled by the boom of online shopping and e-commerce during the pandemic (The Fintech Times, 2023). Moreover, the Philippines has shown sustainable growth in mobile payment transactions, with around 24.6 million mobile wallet users in 2020. This figure is expected to reach 75.5 million users in 2025 (Fortumo, 2021).

Types of Fintech

Financial technologies have been applied in numerous business sectors in the Philippines, such as lending, payment, remittance, online wallets, blockchain, and insurtech. In 2020, Fintech in the lending sector accounted for 24% of the market share, whereas the payments segment consisted of 21% of the market. Interestingly, Fintech firms in the remittance area constituted 12%, the same as digital wallets with 12%. In addition, the blockchain and crowdfunding sectors made up 7% and 4%, respectively (Quimba et al., 2021). The following pie chart illustrates the market shares of Fintech firms in the Philippines in 2020.

Figure 13. Fintech firms in the Philippines in 2020
Note. Reprinted from Analysis of the Fintech Landscape in the Philippines (No. 2021-29). Retrieved from https://www.econstor.eu/bitstream/10419/256864/1/pidsdps2129.pdf

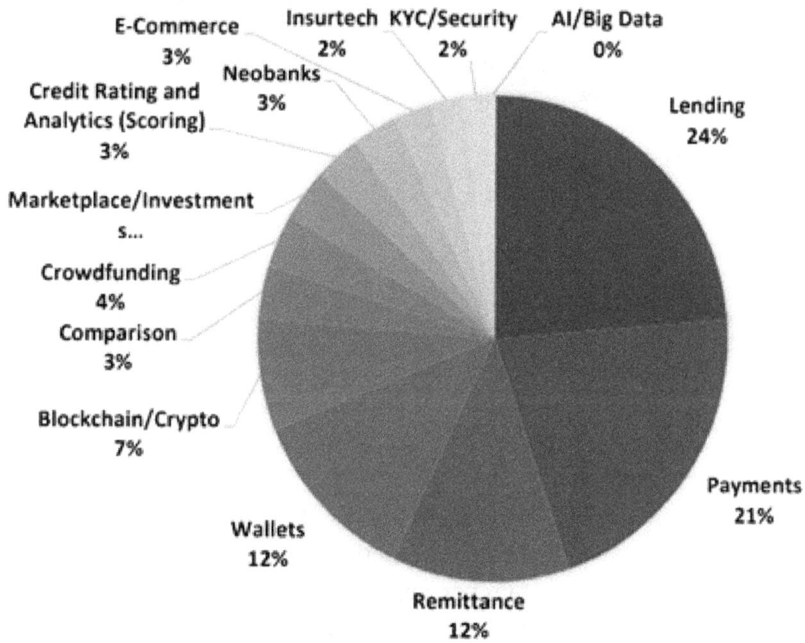

The Philippines also has a few new promising Fintech areas that are proliferating in the country, such as credit rating and analytics, regtech, and comparison. Overall, the Fintech landscape in the Philippines is diverse, with a primary focus on lending, payments, and remittance.

Main Players

Regarding the digital wallet segment, Gcash and Paymaya are the two applications leading the market, with the former accounting for 49.4% of the market share and the latter consisting of 41.9%. Grabpay is also a promising digital wallet, making up around 7.5% of the market (Fortumo, 2021). Both applications allow customers to transfer money and purchase goods with just a few touches.

In detail, Gcash is backed by Ant Group, an affiliate company of Alibaba Group from China, and Globe Group, the giant telecommunication company in the Philippines. Gcash offers various financial services and products such as fund transfers, online loans, crowdfunding, and online entertainment (Globe, 2023). On the other hand, Paymaya is an all-in-one money platform with an aim to address all the financial demands and needs of Filipinos. The app allows customers to perform numerous financial activities, such as shopping online, transferring money, buying flight tickets, and paying bills (Maya, n.d).

The following bar chart illustrates the market share of leading mobile wallet applications in the Philippines.

Figure 14. Market share of mobile wallet applications in the Philippines in 2020
Note. Adapted from Market share of leading mobile wallet applications in the Philippines in 2020. Retrieved from https://www.statista.com/statistics/1258098/philippines-mobile-wallet-apps-market-share/

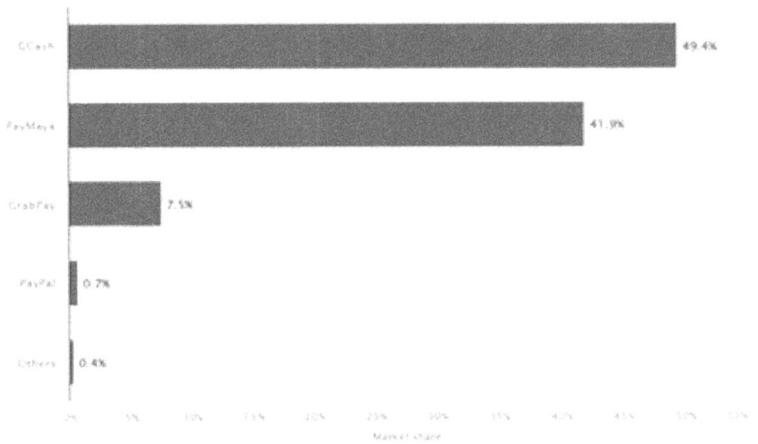

In terms of the e-commerce market, Lazada and Shopee dominate the market. In the second quarter of 2022, Shopee received the most visits from customers, with approximately 71.94 million web visits, while Lazada received around half of that number, approximately 36.55 million web visits (iPrice Group, 2022). Additionally, both e-commerce platforms offer a wide range of products and items from numerous merchants from both local and foreign markets.

Moreover, the Philippines is home to the most successful cryptocurrency exchange platform, named coins.ph. The company is the most famous crypto brand in the country, with more than 16 million users (Coins.ph, n.d). Regarding the digital banking sector, Maya Bank dominates the market, accounting for 61% (Philstar Global, 2023). In short, only a few companies are leading the Fintech market in the Philippines but are making significant impacts on the economy.

New Investment and Start-Ups

The Philippines has recently witnessed numerous new Fintech startups in various sectors. Fortune Pay, founded in 2019, is one of the latest Fintech digital payment platforms, enabling customers to transfer funds and perform basic e-wallet functions, as well as offering certain remittance benefits (Fortune Pay, n.d). Another promising new Fintech startup is Peddlr, established in 2021. The application is designed to be a free point-of-sale (POS) system for small and micro family businesses, helping them better organize and manage their transactions (Peddlr, n.d). A third noteworthy new Fintech startup is MarCoPay. Founded in 2019, this mobile app was created to provide an e-wallet platform mainly for seafarers and their families to improve their lives (MarCoPay, n.d). Lastly, PayMongo is a payment processing firm that offers APIs for use in mobile apps and websites (PayMongo, n.d). Undoubtedly, these new Filipino Fintech startups were created with the aim of offering better services and improving the quality of life for the population.

Technical Infrastructure

Speaking about the telecommunications network of the Philippines, as the country consists of more than 7,000 islands, it is challenging to provide nationwide coverage with the latest 4G and 5G technologies (International Finance, 2020). In a recent comparison report, 4G performance in the Philippines was lower than in other neighbouring countries such as Singapore, Vietnam, Thailand, and Malaysia. In detail, the median download speed in the Philippines was just around 5.14 Mbps, significantly behind Singapore, with a median of 44.11 Mbps, Vietnam, with 34.89 Mbps, and Thailand, with 24.86 Mbps (GSMA, 2022). Furthermore, 5G coverage is only available in limited major cities such as Metro Manila and Cebu (International Finance, 2020). Clearly, the Philippine government needs to accelerate efforts to expand 4G and even 5G coverage because the telecommunication network forms the backbone of the Fintech infrastructure.

Despite the challenges posed by the telecommunications network, the Philippines has a robust e-commerce market, which has grown from $3 billion in 2019 to $14 billion in 2022, with a forecast to reach $22 billion in 2025 (Bain & Company, Google, Temasek Holdings, 2022). Furthermore, the pandemic acted as a catalyst for the growth of e-commerce in the Philippines, with mobile penetration reaching 74.1% in 2021 (International Trade Administration, 2022). The following chart illustrates the dramatic growth of e-commerce in the country.

Figure 15. E-commerce market size in the Philippines

Note. Adapted from E-commerce market size in the Philippines in 2019 and 2021, with a forecast for 2022 and 2025 (in billion U.S. dollars). Retrieved from https://www.statista.com/statistics/1125455/e-commerce-market-size-philippines/

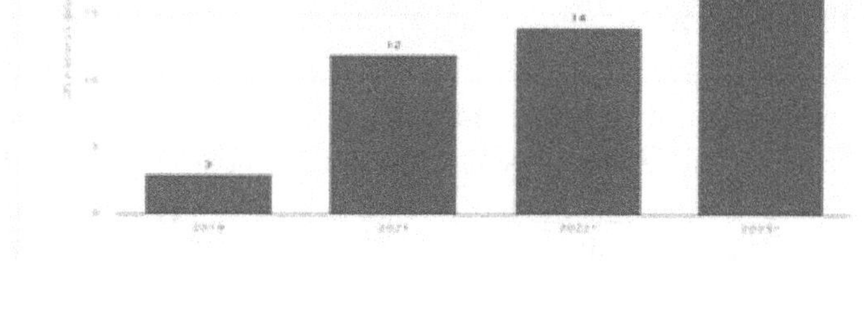

Furthermore, the number of active e-wallet users has grown exponentially, reaching almost 58 million in 2022, and is expected to reach 81 million users in 2025 (Asian Banking & Finance, 2022). Additionally, digital banks in the Philippines are gaining momentum with the emergence of various new institutions such as UnionBank, Tonik, and CIMB. Overall, despite the current limitations in its telecommunications network system, the Philippines offers enormous opportunities and potential for Fintech firms to thrive in the near future.

Government Policy and Regulation

The Philippine government, particularly the central bank (Bangko Sentral ng Pilipinas - BSP), has embraced the adoption of financial technologies. Instead of creating sandboxes like some neighbouring countries, the central bank established a "test and learn" regime, providing a space for new financial innovations and initiatives (Schellhase & Garcia, 2019). This open policy has led to the emergence of various payment systems, such as the National Retail Payment System, PESONet, and InstaPay. Moreover, the central bank has implemented supportive policies to regulate the Fintech market using appropriate approaches, with the goal of enhancing money service businesses and electronic payments (Ng Pilipinas, 2020). Furthermore, the BSP has also ventured into the application of artificial intelligence to support its mandate and supervise all financial institutions regarding their compliance (Dennis et al., 2022). In short, the Philippine government strongly supports the development of Fintech with numerous favourable policies.

Impact on the Economy

The development of financial technologies has brought significant changes to the economic landscape. Firstly, the introduction of digital banks in the Philippines has had a positive impact on the economy, enabling people in rural areas to transfer money more easily and securely (Jeník et al., 2020). Secondly, the Fintech boom has increased the level of financial inclusion in the country, providing greater financial accessibility to various demographic populations (Schellhase & Garcia, 2019). Indeed, more people, especially senior citizens in the Philippines, now have the opportunity to carry out basic daily financial transactions such as transfers via e-wallets and borrowing money online. Additionally, another significant impact on the economy is that Fintech has helped bridge the capital gaps and improve funds accessibility between SMEs and financial institutions (Schellhase & Garcia, 2019). With the current proliferation of Fintech, the Philippines can expect even more positive impacts from financial technology on its society.

Security Concern

Although there are merits to Fintech, it also entails several challenges, such as security and privacy. In a recent report, the Philippines ranked fourth among countries with the most cyberattacks, with over 3,000 cyber incidents recorded from 2020 to 2022 (GMA, 2023). Fintech risks in the country manifest in various forms, including cybersecurity issues, money laundering, fraud, and financial scams (Schellhase & Garcia, 2019). Moreover, given the relatively low level of financial literacy in the country, people are more susceptible to falling victim to new models of financial scams (Quimba et al., 2021). Therefore, the government should develop more policies to protect consumers and prevent future cyber incidents.

Other Relevant Academic Research

Over the past five years, various studies have aimed to better understand the Fintech landscape and situation in the Philippines. One of the most common findings is that the country faced challenges related to financial inclusion due to its geographical complexities (Karim et al., 2022; Schellhase & Garcia, 2019). Filipinos historically encountered difficulties in performing basic financial activities, such as sending money or making deposits, due to the lack of access to banking services in remote areas. Another consistent finding is that the government strongly supports and encourages the development of Fintech, particularly in the realm of cryptocurrencies (Quimba et al., 2021; Schellhase & Garcia, 2019). A recent report has revealed that more than 11 million Filipinos own digital assets (Mason, 2022). Recent studies also imply that the government should focus on strengthening the technical ecosystem to embrace future Fintech innovations and initiatives (Quimba et al., 2021; Schellhase & Garcia, 2019; Karim et al., 2022). The Philippine government's efforts to expand 5G technology coverage in various areas reflect its recognition of the technology's importance for Fintech development (Manila Bulletin, 2023).

Interesting Fact

Unlike other neighbouring countries, the remittance Fintech sector in the Philippines accounted for 12% in 2021 (Quimba et al., 2021). This is attributed to the fact that more than 1.8 million Filipinos were working abroad in 2021, leading to the launch of various financial products to cater to this large overseas workforce (PSA (Philippines), 2022). Most remittance Fintech solutions are digital payments, allowing overseas Filipinos to transfer their earnings home to support their families in the Philippines (JohnClements, 2023).

Another intriguing fact about Fintech in the Philippines is the increasing acceptance of Bitcoin payments by more businesses, with approximately 400 entrepreneurs reported in a recent study (Business World, 2023). This trend may be influenced by the government's friendly approach towards Fintech, particularly cryptocurrencies.

Trend, Future Aspect

In 2022, the central bank recorded a massive number of remittances, amounting to approximately $32.54 billion USD, placing the Philippines among the top four recipient countries for remittances (BSP, 2023). Experts predict that the trend of remittance Fintech will continue to flourish in the future (JohnClements, 2023). Additionally, blockchain and cryptocurrency Fintech will maintain their growth momentum with the introduction of more online financial products and platforms for the exchange and utilization of these digital assets (Schellhase & Garcia, 2019). In summary, various trends are expected to proliferate in the future in the Philippines.

SINGAPORE

Market Size

Singapore is one of the most developed countries not only in Southeast Asia but also in the world, with a GDP per capita of $82,807.6 USD in 2022 (World Bank, 2022). This tiny city-state has been a global financial and technological hub for a long time. Thanks to a transparent government with supportive policies towards tech startups and a highly skilled labour force market, Singapore has always been a leader in development in Asia, including the growth of Financial Technology (Tao & Azhgaliyeva, 2018). The Singaporean Fintech market, in terms of transaction value, has increased exponentially, from $5.55 billion USD in 2017 to $28.03 billion USD in 2022. The market is forecasted to reach $64.51 billion USD in 2027 (Statista, 2022). Although Singapore has a small population and limited natural resources, its Fintech market size is enormous, outperforming all other ASEAN neighbouring countries.

Current Fintech Adoption Rate

Ernst & Young Global Limited (2019), in a report, indicated that the Fintech adoption rate of Singapore was high at 67%, the same as Hong Kong and South Korea but comparably lower than China's 87% penetration rate. Moreover, in a survey conducted in 2021, the adoption rate of cashless payments in Singapore was much greater than in other Southeast Asian countries, 97% compared to an average of 93% (Visa Inc., 2022). Clearly, the adoption rate of Fintech in Singapore is relatively high, allowing it to embrace the processes of changes and innovations (Wyman, 2020).

Types of Fintech

Since Singapore is the leader of Fintech in the ASEAN region, there are numerous business areas in which Fintech is applied in the country (Huong et al., 2021). Currently, the dominating sectors of Singaporean Fintech companies are Blockchain/Cryptocurrency, Payments, Investment, Regtech, and Insurtech. The figure below illustrates a distribution of Fintech companies in Singapore in 2022.

On top of that, several Fintech segments are promising in the future, including personal finance, blockchain/cryptocurrency, and crowdfunding. Investors who can see the potential of these sectors and invest in them would probably earn huge profits.

Main Players

Regarding the digital online payments sector, there are a few giant companies dominating the Singaporean market. GrabPay is considered the market leader, consisting of 35.5% in 2020, whereas DBS PayLah and Singtel Dash accounted for 18.8% and 11.8%, respectively. EZ-Link shared 4.7% of the market, and the remaining 5.9% counted on others ("Popular payment methods in Singapore," 2022). Furthermore, GrabPay has secured a total of $16.5B in funding after 34 rounds, and this is a huge amount of money for a startup company (Crunchbase, 2023). On the other hand, DBS PayLah is backed by one of the biggest banks in Singapore, DBS, and Singtel is a Singaporean telecommunications conglomerate (Crunchbase, 2023). In general, the top Fintech payment companies in Singapore have strong financial backgrounds.

All major banks in Singapore have invested heavily in financial technology, and the city country was the first in Southeast Asia to formally implement a framework to license digital banking (Wyman, 2020). The banking industry in Singapore has recently welcomed several new full digital banks, such as Grab, GXS, MariBank, Trust Bank, and FairPrice Group (Fintech News Singapore, 2022).

Furthermore, Singapore has made a wise move when it comes to Blockchain and the cryptocurrency sector. There are currently numerous Fintech startups in this sector to name a few: Zipmex, Coinhako, and Crypto.com. In detail, Crypto.com is one the most popular online cryptocurrency trading platforms

Figure 16. Breakdown of Fintech companies in Singapore in 2022, by sector
Note. Adapted from Distribution of Fintech companies in Singapore in 2022, by sector. Retrieved from https://www.statista.com/statistics/1294130/singapore-Fintech-companies-share-by-sector/

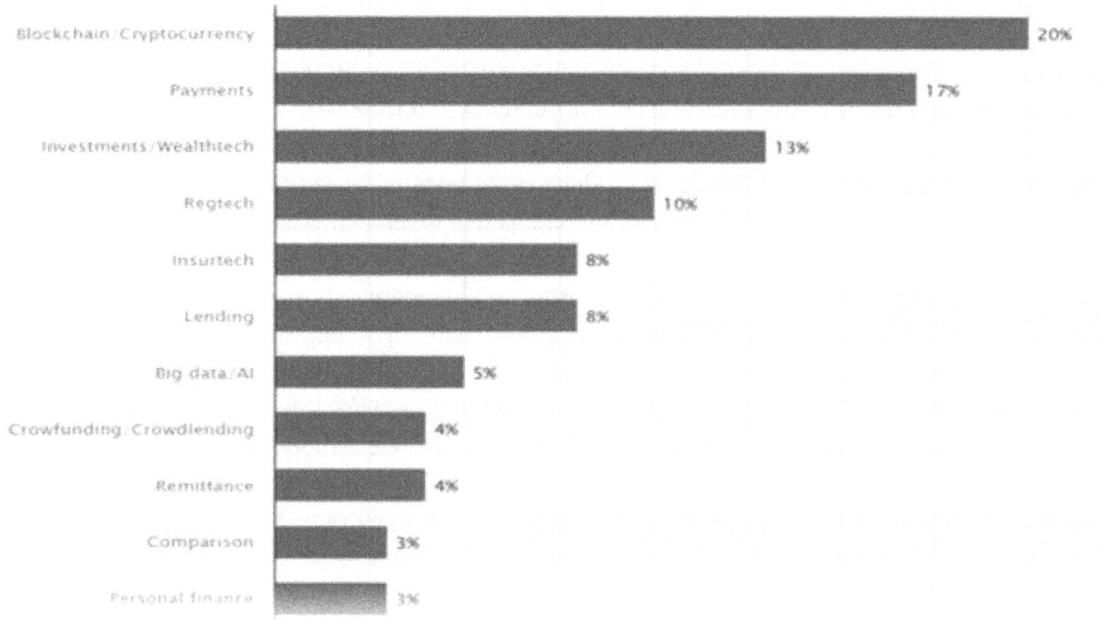

in the world, with more than 80 million active users and operating in more than 90 countries (Crypto.com, n.d). Moreover, Insurtech companies are proliferating in Singapore, expanding to many countries around the world. These global firms are PolicyPal, GrabInsure, FWD, and Igloo Insure, and they are heavily investing in financial technology to offer a wider range of products and services as well as allow customers to access and claim easily (Lin & Chen, 2020). On top of that, there are several Fintech startups in other trending sectors, such as Crowdfunding with Funding Societies, Fundnel, and Capital Match or Personal Finance with Moneko and Nugget. Fintech companies in the Wealthtech sector are gaining pace with 360F, Canopy, and Ayondo, whereas the Lending sector consists of Ablr, iLex, and Rely. In summary, Singapore has embraced financial technology across diverse business sectors, and numerous Fintech firms based in this city-state are operating on a global scale.

New Investment and Start-Ups

Singapore has always been the destination for creative ideas and innovations. There are numerous new Fintech startups catering to various customers' demands, and Volopay is one of them. This application digitalizes expense reports, making them faster and safer (Volopay, n.d). At the same time, the Gotrade startup allows anyone in the world to invest in US stocks fractionally without any commission (Gotrade, n.d). On the other hand, Cake Defi is a new Fintech allowing the owners of cryptocurrency to partake in certain decentralized financial services, such as staking or lending, in order to produce yields (Bake, n.d). The latest Fintech startup is Syfe, a digital wealth manager. The new application is a robo-adviser aiming to offer high-quality financial services to everyone. The company is reported to have more than

100,000 active users (Syfe, n.d). With diverse startups, Singapore has been a fertile ground for Fintech to develop further.

Technical Infrastructure

In the realm of the Fintech technical ecosystem, Singapore stands significantly ahead in comparison to its neighbouring countries, being the first country in the world to achieve full 5G coverage (Singtel, n.d). It means that all areas in this city country have full access to the 5G network, enabling the companies and individual users to connect faster and address more matters. In addition, 5G technology allows policymakers as well as companies to perform numerous deep-tech analyses such as video and image analytics, traffic analysis, safety and security, and facilities management (Huseien & Shah, 2022).

Another strong foundation for the technical ecosystem in Singapore is its e-commerce platform, which encourages people to shop online and use digital payment methods (Klenow, 2019). The Singaporean e-commerce market has grown dramatically, reaching $5.9 billion in 2021, and is expecting to increase to almost $10 billion in 2026 (International Trade Administration, 2022). The biggest e-commerce platforms in Singapore are Shopee, Lazada, Amazon, and Carousell, with Shopee being the market dominator (International Trade Administration, 2022). Furthermore, digital wallets have been widely used by 1.8 million users in 2020, and the number is forecast to reach more than 5 million in 2025 (Statista, 2022). GrabPay is considered the leading digital wallet in Singapore, with more than 4 million active users (Grab, n.d). The strong technical infrastructure has enabled the city-state to be poised for future growth, particularly for Fintech.

Government Policy and Regulation

Regarding government regulation and policy toward Fintech, the country has manifested strong support with a clear legal framework and numerous favourable policies (Pei, 2018). First, the government appointed the Monetary Authority of Singapore (MAS) to control, manage, and frame the policies for Fintech fully. MAS then established a dedicated group named Fintech & Innovation Group (FTIG) to be in charge of regulatory and developing strategies for the development of Fintech for better financial securities and risks as well as its efficiency.

Furthermore, the city-state opted for a modern and scientific approach based on risk management principles to cope with the rapid changes of Fintech and the uncertain future economy (Pei, 2018). This is a wise move from Singapore as it would allow the country to be flexible and easier to adopt new technologies and challenges instead of applying one universal Fintech policy for all entities. The risk-based approach to Fintech also allows more room for innovations and unregulated sectors (Pei, 2018). Because if the government had strict regulations at the early stage, it would suppress creative ideas and new Fintech innovations.

In addition, the country also proposed a free Sandbox space for trialling for new Fintech startups. They can freely create and innovate and get support from financial companies (Pei, 2018). Moreover, there are numerous Fintech events, with the Singapore Fintech Festival being the symbol. The Singapore Fintech Associate also offers financial support and provides certain available resources to new Fintech firms so they can overcome their initial technical and financial difficulties (Wyman, 2020). Overall, the country has a strong commitment to supporting and leveraging Fintech companies based on its profound technical infrastructure, clear legal framework, and enormous financial support.

Impact on the Economy

One of the noticeable Fintech impacts on the Singaporean economy is to reduce transaction costs, allowing consumers to increase their spending capacity and promote business growth (Agarwal et al., 2020). For instance, the introduction of financial technology in mobile payment showed significant growth for business-to-consumer industries by 8.9% per month compared to business-to-business (Agarwal et al., 2020). This is paramount for small and medium firms as they could overcome their payment challenges and generate more profits.

Another positive impact on the economy of Fintech is the attraction of talented foreign tech workers to come to work and settle in Singapore (Wyman, 2020). This high-skilled immigration influx also kept the economy growing and brought their expertise to the local companies. Obviously, the second positive impact helps Singapore strengthen its worldwide economic position as well as connect the country to the world and vice versa.

Security Concern

Since the beginning, the Singaporean authority has identified cybersecurity as the first priority to protect the financial sector. This is mainly because the financial services sector is always the first target of global cyber attackers (Didenko, 2020). The government has enacted several acts and policies to prevent these unexpected incidents, such as the Cybersecurity Act in 2018, several cyber crisis tests, and the annual Singapore International Cyber Week.

Despite strong preventive efforts from the government, the country has witnessed major cyber-attack incidents. For instance, the data breach of SingHealth records exposed more than 1.5 million customers' healthcare data in 2018 (Yu, 2019). In addition, Singapore experienced almost 2 million cyber attacks in the second quarter of 2022, with a 145% year-on-year increase compared to 2021 (International Trade Administration, 2023). It is worth noticing that the average cost of a cyber attack in Singapore is approximately $1.3 million, the highest rate in Asia-Pacific (International Trade Administration, 2023). Singapore witnessed significant growth in cybercrime from 2014 to 2021, illustrated in the figure below.

Other Relevant Academic Research

It has been observed that Fintech studies conducted in Singapore over the past years have revealed several significant findings. The government's smart, wise, and scientific approach to dealing with Fintech startups has received praise (Lin, 2019; Pei, 2018). Singapore's adoption of a risk-based approach and favorable policies to support Fintech companies has been a common highlight in the research (Wyman, 2020; Didenko, 2020). Moreover, financial technology has played a role in reducing transaction costs and increasing annual profits for banks and companies (Agarwal et al., 2020; Wyman, 2020; Didenko, 2020). Another key discovery is that Fintech's development in Singapore has attracted global talent and investment (Wyman, 2020; Didenko, 2020).

Interesting Facts

An interesting fact to note is the significant growth in funding for cryptocurrency companies in Singapore, surging from approximately $75 million in 2018 to nearly $375 million in 2021 (Statista, 2022).

Figure 17. Cybercrime as a share of total crimes in Singapore from 2014 to 2021
Note. Adapted from Cybercrime as a share of total crimes in Singapore from 2014 to 2021. Retrieved from https://www.statista.com/statistics/1267252/singapore-cybercrime-as-share-of-total-crime

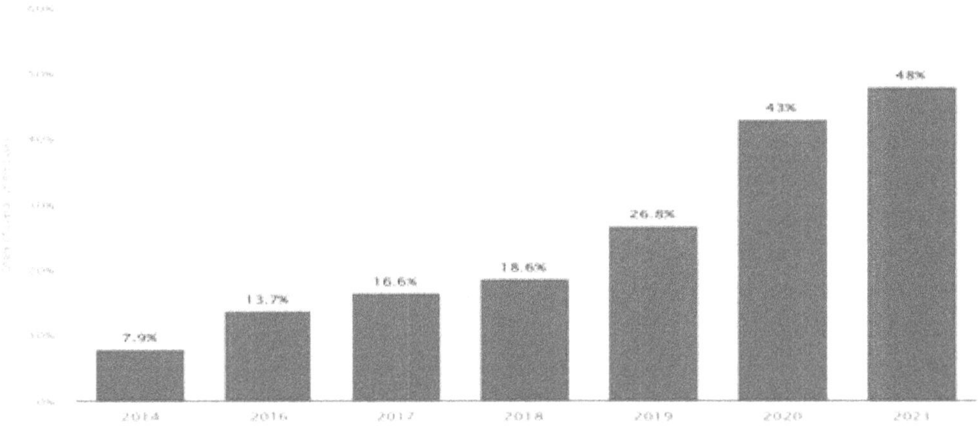

This serves as a strong testament to Singapore's pioneering spirit in embracing new technologies and its aim to strengthen and diversify the economy. Additionally, Singapore's Fintech ecosystem boasts a startup-focused environment, progressive regulatory support, a global mindset, and a large tech talent pool (Wyman, 2020), making it a prime example for other countries aspiring to lead in Fintech.

However, it is also essential to address the increasing rate of cybercrimes in Singapore, accounting for over 45% of the country's total crimes (CSA (Singapore), 2022). Therefore, a greater focus on preventing such crimes is imperative for the country's future.

Trend and Future Aspects

In terms of trends and future aspects, the Singaporean Fintech market has witnessed a decline in the average value per deal over the years, from around S$22.5 million in 2018 to S$17.3 million in 2020, suggesting increased investor caution and preference for pragmatic projects (PricewaterhouseCoopers, 2020). However, funding in Blockchain and AI startups has continued to grow, reaching more than $1 billion in 2019 (PricewaterhouseCoopers, 2020).

On a promising note, urban solutions and sustainability have emerged as potential growth areas. The urban transport sector, in particular, has proven to be a future aspect of the economy, addressing various city resident issues. Singaporean Fintech companies, exemplified by Grab and Ninjavan, are actively competing to lead in this domain (PricewaterhouseCoopers, 2020).

THAILAND

Market Size

Thailand ranks as the fourth most populous nation in Southeast Asia, home to approximately 72 million inhabitants (World Bank, 2023). The Fintech market in Thailand is still in its early stages, with a forecast for the digital economy to grow significantly by an average of 15% from 2022 to 2025. Moreover, the Thai digital economy would reach a total value of about $53 billion in 2025 and probably $100 billion in 2030 (Vigilia, 2023). However, in 2021, the total market value of Fintech in Thailand was reported to be around 37.6 billion Thai baths, which was equivalent to approximately 1 billion USD (Statista, 2022). Overall, Fintech in Thailand still has enormous room to thrive further, especially when more than 30% of the population is under 25 years old (Ernst & Young, 2019).

Fintech Adoption Rate

The Fintech adoption rate in Thailand is comparatively high compared to other developing ASEAN countries. This is because, in a survey conducted in 2021, more than 60% of the Thai population was aware of digital services and willing to use them (Asian Banking & Finance, 2021). However, the internet penetration rate in Thailand was around 69.66% in 2029 and increased slightly to 74.4% in 2022, with a forecast to hit 85.03% in 2028 (Statista, 2023). Furthermore, the cashless payments adoption rate in Thailand was at 94% in 2022 (Statista, 2022). These data have shown that although Thailand had a low Fintech adoption rate, it is gaining pace thanks to its current favourable conditions.

Types of Fintech

In Thailand, financial technology has been embedded into various business sectors, such as alternative lending, payments, cryptocurrencies, investment tech, financing and accounting, insurtech, banking, blockchain, and regtech. In 2021, Fintech firms in alternative lending accounted for 21% of the market share, whereas companies in payments and cryptocurrencies consisted of 20% each of the market share, followed by investment tech with 13%. On the other hand, banking tech and regtech firms only had 4% and 1% of the market share. The following chart illustrates the distribution of Fintech companies in Thailand in 2021.

Figure 18. Distribution of Fintech firms in Thailand in 2021 by type of firm

Note. Adapted from Distribution of financial technology (Fintech) firms in Thailand in 2021, by type of firm. Retrieved from https://www.statista.com/statistics/1293999/thailand-distribution-of-Fintech-firms-by-firm-type/

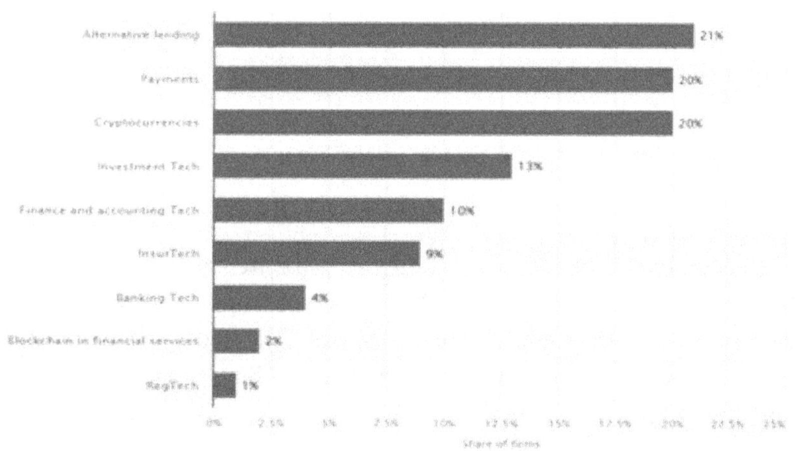

Cryptocurrency is a promising sector for Fintech companies in Thailand and has been on the rise recently (Statista, 2023). Additionally, blockchain and regtech firms also have opportunities to proliferate in the future, where the era of technology 4.0 is undeniable.

Main Players

Regarding the digital wallets segment, only a few giant Fintech companies are dominating the market. TrueMoney, an online wallet that processes daily digital transactions, is leading the Thai market. This is because the company is the child firm of the largest private company, C.P. Group, in Thailand (TrueMoney, n.d). In a report in 2020, TrueMoney accounted for around 52.6% of the market share, followed by Rabbit Line Pay at 24.7%, Airpay at 5.7%, mPay at 4.9%, and GrabPay at 6.9% (2c2p, 2022). Rabbit Line Pay is an extension branch of Line, which allows users to pay online bills, whereas Airpay was a Fintech initiative to help users pay their bills and purchase entertainment products such as movie tickets and games (Rabbit Line Pay, n.d; Airpay, n.d). The following pie chart illustrates the market shares of mobile wallet users in Thailand.

Figure 19. Market share of mobile wallet users in Thailand in 2020
Note. Reprinted from Popular Payment Methods in Thailand: What Consumers Want, 2022. Retrieved from https://2c2p.com/blog/thailand-payment-methods

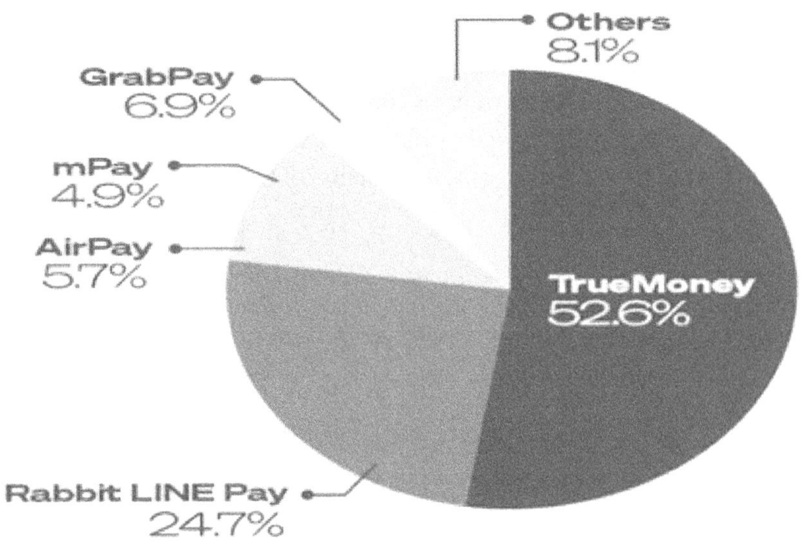

In terms of the e-commerce market, the leading players are Shopee, Lazada, Central Online, JD Central, and Homepro. In the first quarter of 2022, Shopee monopolized the market as the most clicked online e-commerce website, with around 57 million clicks, followed by Lazada with almost 37 million clicks. The other three aforementioned firms, Central Online, JD Central, and Homepro, only received around 2.5 million, 2.1 million, and 2 million clicks, respectively (iPrice Group, 2022). It is worth noticing that both Shopee and Lazada are not from Thailand but are leading the Thai e-commerce market. The following bar chart illustrates the list of the most visited e-commerce websites in Thailand.

Figure 20. Most visited e-commerce site in Thailand in the first quarter of 2022
Note. Adapted from Most visited e-commerce sites in Thailand as of 1st quarter 2022, by monthly traffic (in 1,000 clicks). Retrieved August 24, 2023, from https://www.statista.com/statistics/1117797/thailand-popular-e-commerce-sites/

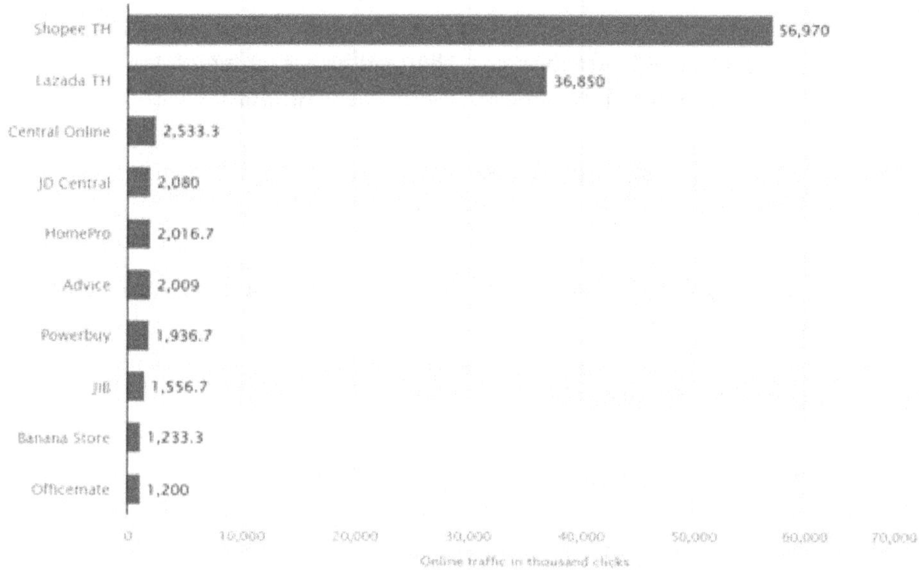

Unlike other neighboring countries, the Thai government and the Central Bank of Thailand have yet to establish any regulations or policies to supervise pure digital banks and their activities in the country. This means that no digital banks are operating currently, and the Central Bank of Thailand expects to have its first digital banks in late 2023 or in 2024 (Bank of Thailand, 2023).

New Investments and Startups

Thailand has been witnessing the proliferation of new Fintech companies recently. One promising new Fintech firm is Opn, established in 2020 and could raise funding worth more than $200 million (Opn, n.d). The company was an initiative to integrate contactless payments and e-wallet transactions, providing financial solutions to merchants and businesses. Another successful Fintech startup is Bitkub, Thailand's latest unicorn tech company (Thanthong-Knight, 2021). The company is Thailand's biggest cryptocurrency exchange platform, offering a place to trade various crypto coins (Bitkub, n.d). The third interesting new Fintech is 724market, an online insurance broker in Thailand. The company provides a friendly website interface where customers can easily choose from numerous insurance plans and purchase them online within a few clicks. (724market, n.d). The following new Fintech startup is Monix, founded in 2020. Monix uses a financial inclusion approach, providing legal funds to underbanked people in Thailand using cutting-edge digital technologies such as big data and machine learning (Monix, n.d).

Technical Infrastructure

The most important key driver for developing Fintech is the coverage rate of 5G technology. In 2022, Thai telecommunication operators covered more than 85% of the Thai population with 5G (Tomas, 2022). In addition, more than 56 million Thai people will be able to access the internet in Thailand in 2022, and this number is expected to hit 60 million in 2026 (Statista, 2023). These significant growth rates will benefit Fintech firms in the long run.

The E-commerce market is another strong foundation of technical infrastructure for Fintech in Thailand. In 2017, the e-commerce market value reached approximately 2.76 trillion Thai Bath and increased to $4.01 trillion in 2021 (ETDA, 2021). Moreover, Thailand has more than 50 million Facebook users, 45 million Line users, 42.8 million YouTube users, and another million TikTok, Instagram, and Twitter users (International Trade Administration, 2022). The driving factors have helped the country improve its logistics system, online payments, and customer experiences in digital technologies.

Although virtual banks have yet to be allowed to operate in the country, major banks such as Siam Commercial Bank (SCB) and Kasikornbank have heavily embedded financial technologies in a myriad of products and services (Kapron, 2023). Overall, Thailand has various favourable conditions and is building a robust fundamental technological infrastructure for the development of Fintech.

Government Policy and Regulation

The Thai government strongly supported the development of Fintech in the country as they valued the merits that financial technologies could bring to the economy (Ernst & Young, 2019). In 2019, the government established a sandbox for Fintech firms to test their business models, ideas, and products more quickly with less restriction from the authorities (Kijkasiwat, 2021). By creating a Fintech sandbox, new startups can freely design without fearing further legal action.

Furthermore, the Thai government is proactively utilizing financial technologies to improve operational efficiency. For instance, the Revenue Department incorporated a Promptpay payment solution to speed up the tax refund process and could refund in less than three business days. Another helpful feature of Promptpay is that whenever the users donate money to schools, the receipt will be sent directly to the Revenue Department for tax deduction purposes (Moenjak et al., 2020). In addition, in order to embrace the emerging technologies of blockchain and cryptocurrencies, the Thai Securities and Exchange Commission has enacted several acts and an Emergency Decree to supervise and regulate these digital assets (Chambers and Partners, 2023). Moreover, the Bank of Thailand has fully prepared to allow the operations of pure digital banks in Thailand (Bank of Thailand, 2023). Overall, the Thai government is trying step by step to embrace and regulate the Fintech market with proper practices.

Impact on the Economy

The emergence of Fintech in Thailand has resulted in diverse effects on the economy. First, the proliferation of financial technologies has rapidly changed Thai consumers' behaviours with online purchases and cashless transactions (Bank of Thailand, 2021). Consequently, Thai people can now quickly transfer their money to other people with dramatically lower transaction fees and time saved. Another significant positive impact of Fintech on the economy is that it promotes financial inclusion in Thailand, bringing convenience to elderly citizens (Bui & Luong, 2023). Because senior Thai people are the most vulnerable, and they are usually excluded from accessing banking services. However, with financial technology, they can now perform basic banking activities from their phones without visiting any physical branches. Despite the merits of Fintech, there is also a negative impact on corporate banks, which is the competition between Fintech companies and traditional banks (Kijkasiwat, 2021). People use digital payments to perform daily basic transactions because of its cost-effectiveness and time. However, this reduces the revenues that corporate banks used to generate.

Security Concern

While Fintech has brought various benefits to Thailand, it has presented certain security concerns. First, the number of cyber-attacks in Thailand is double the global average rate, with around 2388 times per week compared to around 1258 times globally (Leesa-nguansuk, 2023). Moreover, in 2022, approximately 367 threats of hacking websites and 48 times of data breaches were detected (National Cyber Security Agency, 2023). The following chart illustrates the number of cyber-attacks detected and settled in Thailand:

Figure 21. Number of cyber threats detected in Thailand in 2022
Note. Adapted from Number of cyber threats detected and settled by ThaiCERT in Thailand in 2022, by type of threat. Retrieved from https://www.statista.com/statistics/1154735/thailand-number-of-cyber-threats-by-type-of-threat/

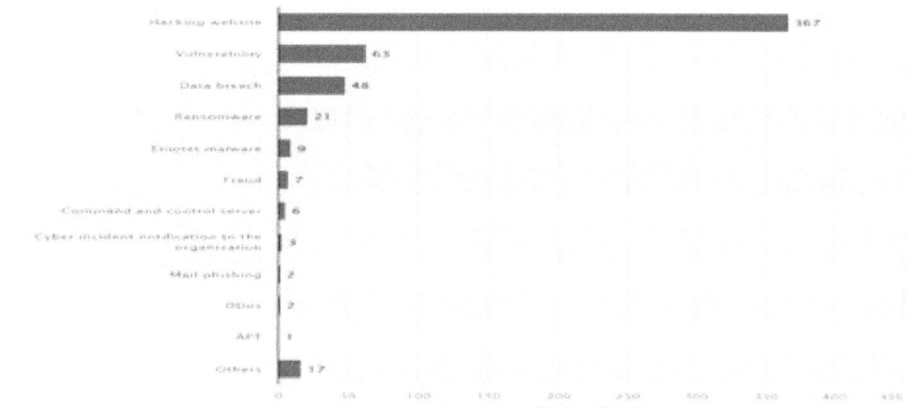

In order to help Thai residents adopt safely and effectively new financial technologies, the Bank of Thailand has launched several campaigns to educate, promote best practices, and raise public awareness (Moenjak et al., 2020).

Summary of Previous Research

Numerous studies have been conducted to examine, analyze, and propose recommendations for Fintech development in Thailand. The first significant finding from researchers is that the Thai government is strongly committed to supporting and leveraging new financial technologies for overall economic growth (Hasaka, 2019; Kijkasiwat, 2021; Postigo, 2023). Indeed, the Thai government has several initiatives to promote the development of Fintech, such as establishing a Sandbox space, hosting international Fintech fairs, and creating a sustainable Fintech ecosystem (Hasaka, 2019). The second important finding is the positive impact of Fintech on the Thai economy, enhancing financial inclusion (Loo, 2019; Bui & Luong, 2023). The emergence of digital and mobile payments has made it easier for senior Thai citizens to access banking services and perform daily basic activities. Another key finding about Fintech in Thailand is that the government approached and regulated the market with a clear legal framework (Kijkasiwat, 2021; Bromberg & Ramsay, 2017; Zheng et al., 2022). The central bank has precise guidelines for banks and Fintech firms as well as strong protection policies for the customers. In short, significant studies have indicated that the Thai government is well prepared for adopting Fintech.

Interesting Facts

In Thailand, the national bank has neither approved nor allowed pure digital bank operations. However, they are already in the final stage of drafting the policy and aiming to issue licenses to pure digital banks or virtual banks at the end of 2023 or 2024 (Bank of Thailand, 2023). Furthermore, although the government bans transactions using digital or cryptocurrency assets, Thailand has one famous Fintech unicorn startup named Bitkub. The company is the largest cryptocurrency exchange platform in Thailand (Reed, 2022). Moreover, the tourism authority in Thailand showed a strong interest in adopting cryptocurrencies as a new payment solution for travellers (United Overseas Bank Limited, 2021).

Trend and Aspects

With high expectations from the introduction of digital banks by the Bank of Thailand, virtual digital banks are expected to boom in the upcoming years (United Overseas Bank Limited, 2021). These neobanks would help the country promote deeper financial inclusion and better accommodate customers' expectations. Another significant trend in Thailand would be the emergence of blockchain and cryptocurrency firms, led by the Bitkub exchange platform (Chambers and Partners, 2023). With a friendly regulation approach from the government, Thailand is well-equipped to embrace the next development phase of Fintech.

VIETNAM

Market Size

Vietnam's economy has transformed dramatically from a post-war country to one of the promising economic tigers in Asia (Barker & Üngör, 2019). After the economic reforms (Doi Moi) in 1986, the country has successfully stepped into the middle-income nations group, reaching a GDP (Gross Domestic Product) per capita of approximately $4163.5 in 2022 (World Bank, 2022). One of the most important factors that fueled this rapid development is the abundance of the cheap labour force, especially the young, energetic generation (Cung, 2019)

Nowadays, this young talent group with fundamental knowledge of technology is propelling another key economic progress: the country's digital transformation. Especially with a wide coverage of the 4G network and a considerable unbanked population, Vietnam experienced rapid growth of Fintech during the past decades (Jung, 2019; Khue, 2021; World Bank, 2017). In terms of transaction value, the Vietnam Fintech market size experienced significant growth, reaching $9 billion USD in 2019 and is forecasted to increase to $41 billion USD in 2027 (Statista, 2022). Overall, the Vietnamese Fintech market still has a huge potential to grow further.

Current Fintech Adoption Rate

Regarding the Fintech Adoption rate, Vietnam is among one of the fastest-adopting countries in ASEAN. According to a sync report from Meta and Bain (2022), almost 60% of Vietnamese consumers have once used new financial technologies such as e-wallets, online money transfers, and banking solutions. The report also confirmed that the pandemic was the best catalyst to fuel this rapid move in Vietnam from a low-technology payment system to a cashless society. Furthermore, there are obvious distinctions in the Fintech adoption rate between age groups in Vietnam. Per a survey conducted by the Asian Development Bank in 2020, 37.95% of respondents who used Fintech services were under 30 years old, whereas 14.63% were between 30 and 60 years old. The rate for those over 60 years old was just above 5% (Statista, 2022). In summary, the Fintech adoption rate in Vietnam is relatively high and even is expected to increase further in the coming years.

Types of Fintech

Currently, there are countless applications of Fintech in Vietnam. However, these are the most dominating segments: digital payments, personal lending or P2P, wealth management, digital banking, buy now pay later, blockchain, and crypto (Khue, 2021). Moreover, there are certain applications that have just been initiated and have enormous room to grow exponentially in the future, such as Crowdfunding, Insurtech, Real Estate Fintech, and Regtech. The chart below lists the applications of Fintech in the Vietnam market in 2022.

Figure 22. Breakdown of Fintech startups in Vietnam in 2020
Note. Adapted from Breakdown of Fintech startups in Vietnam in 2020, by category. Retrieved from https://www.statista.com/statistics/1229955/vietnam-Fintech-startups-by-category/

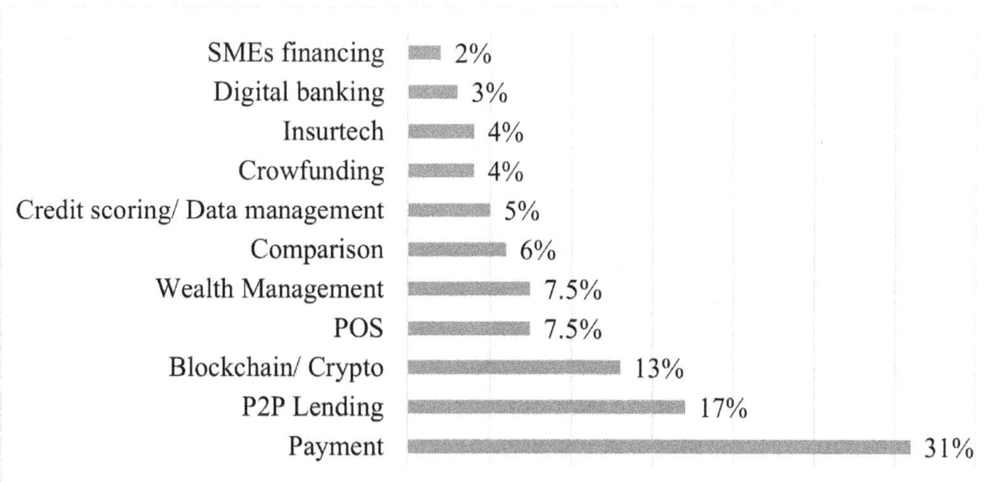

Main Players

Regarding online payment and e-wallets area, Momo, ZaloPay, Viettel Pay and VNPay are considered main players as described in the following chart.

Figure 23. Major e-payment services used among consumers in Vietnam as of October 2022
Note. Reprinted from Major e-payment services used among consumers in Vietnam as of October 2022. Retrieved from https://www.statista.com/statistics/1105406/vietnam-leading-e-payment-services/

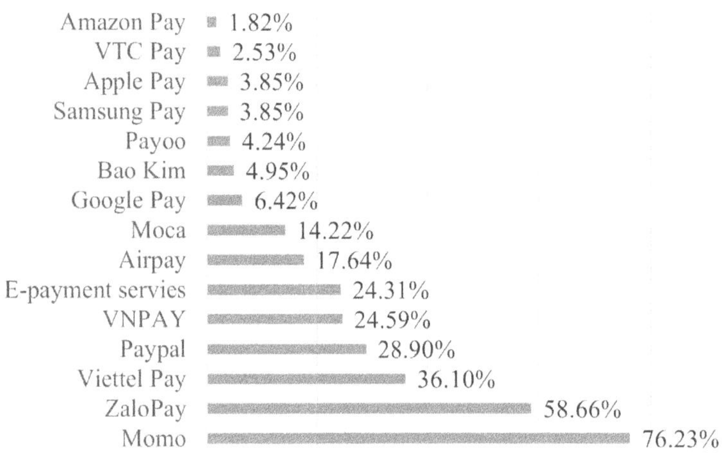

Momo Wallet was among the first "unicorn" start-ups in Vietnam. The company received several funding rounds from well-known global companies such as Warburg Pincus, Macquarie Capital, and Affirma Capital (Hoang, 2021). ZaloPay, on the other hand, is backed by Goldman Sachs (Hoang, 2021). According to Decision Lab (2022), both companies dominated the Vietnamese digital payment market, accounting for more than 80% of the users. On the other hand, Viettel Pay is backed by Viettel, a military government company, and VNPay also secured several funding sources from General Atlantic and Dragoneer Investment Group (General Atlantic, 2021). In general, the top Fintech payment companies in Vietnam share a common trait in that they are funded by various global investing companies or backed by the government.

Another developing Fintech segment in Vietnam is digital banking. There are a couple of new banks in Vietnam that operate completely digital, to name a few: Timo, TNEX, and Cake. However, the weakness of these financial institutions is that they are not giant and well-trusted banks in Vietnam. Moreover, several top traditional Vietnamese banks have heavily invested in and embedded financial technologies into their current systems, making it harder for these new digital banks to thrive. In addition, online e-commerce is a key battlefield for several Fintech companies. Vietnamese can enjoy and easily shop online from various platforms such as Shopee, Lazada, Tiki, or Taobao. Only Tiki is a Vietnamese company, whereas the other three came from China and Singapore. The competitive advantages of these companies are their strong capital and applications of various new financial technologies such as buy now pay later, digital wallets, and cross-border shopping experiences. In 2023, Tiki company only gained 5% of the market, where it is dominated by Shopee, accounting for around 73%, and Lazada almost 21% (Giang,

2023). Obviously, the only Vietnamese company Tiki, needs to do more to outperform those foreign companies in order to improve their market shares.

New Investment and Start-Ups

During the past few years, there have been numerous new start-ups established in Vietnam. One of the latest names is Metain which aims to make it easier to invest in real estate in Vietnam by embedding blockchain technology (Metain, n.d). Another startup in the blockchain segment is Realbox, which was founded in September 2021. Along with blockchain technology, the startup is incorporating other latest technologies such as encryption, NFT, and online consultation by AI in order to create and trade crypto assets (Realbox, n.d). Another healthcare solution is fueled by Heno. The startup aims to provide a smart payment gateway for healthcare and beauty services where patients and customers can use or buy now but pay later (Heno, n.d). This startup is a new blow in Vietnam, where the average household income is just above $3,500 USD annually. They do not have much dispensable income to spend on other non-essential healthcare and beauty products. Therefore, instead of spending much money on skin care products or high-end health care services at once, they can consider using the financial solutions provided by Heno by paying monthly. Furthermore, several new types of Fintech startups entered various segments, such as SME Lending and Accounting & Finance. To name a few, they are Dragon Lend, Validus for SMEs Lending, and TS24Corp, Vatnow. These new establishments will diversify the Fintech market as well as provide more solutions to current social and economic issues in Vietnam.

Technical Infrastructure

Vietnam has recently gradually improved and expanded its technical infrastructure to fuel the rapid development of Fintech. The core part of the Fintech infrastructure is the national telecommunication system. In 2020, the coverage of the 3G network reached more than 99.8 percent of the total inhabitants (Ministry of Information and Communications (Vietnam), 2021). Vietnam manifests a strong fundamental technical infrastructure to support the growth of Fintech.

Secondly, the digital transformation process started years ago in the Vietnamese banking system. There were two approaches to this long-term process. The first method involves the embedment of digitalization in current banks, whereas the second one is the establishment of pure digital-only banks (The Australian Trade and Investment Commission, 2020). All major banks opted for the former one by applying various of the latest financial technologies, such as using data in risk management, application of AI, QR code payment, or virtual chatbot assistants (The Australian Trade and Investment Commission, 2020). For the latter, a few digital-only banks were established, such as Timo, TNEX, and Cake. They aim to serve mainly the young generation who are familiar with technology and love shopping online. Moreover, the pandemic was the best catalyst to fuel the digital transformation in the banking industry in Vietnam. Nowadays, cashless transactions and online shopping have become norms.

Another strong pillar in the Vietnam Fintech infrastructure is the strong presence of digital wallets and online e-commerce platforms. Million customers in Vietnam have used E-wallets. They are using applications such as Momo, Zalopay, and Viettel to pay their bills, transfer money to their loved ones, buy associated insurance or simply order their favorite products online. People also use various platforms to trade and purchase items online, and to name a few: Shopee, Lazada, Tiki, or Taobao/Alibaba (Anh, 2021). On top of that, the E-commerce market value in Vietnam experienced significant growth from around \$2.97 billion USD in 2014 to approximately \$16.4 billion USD in 2022 (Ministry of Industry and Trade (Vietnam), 2022). The following bar graph illustrates a clear picture of this rapid change in the Vietnamese E-commerce market.

Figure 24. E-commerce market value in Vietnam from 2014 to 2022
Note. Adapted from E-commerce market value in Vietnam from 2014 to 2022 (in billion U.S. dollars). Retrieved October 14, 2023, from https://www.statista.com/statistics/986043/vietnam-ecommerce-market-value-revenue/

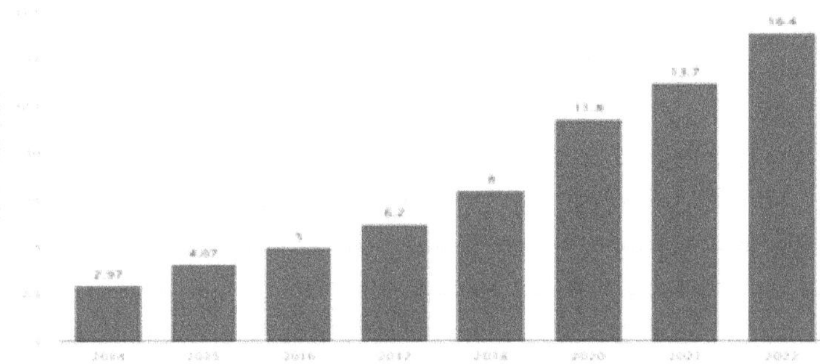

Overall, the Fintech infrastructure in Vietnam has been gradually improved to cope with the development pace of financial technologies. In addition, Vietnam has shown its readiness and competence to thrive further in the Fintech market.

Government Policy and Regulation

In all industries, the government has always played a crucial role in laying out the foundations with laws and acts to propel new things, including the Fintech environment. Understanding the benefits and importance of Fintech, the Vietnamese government has enacted several policies to support and motivate the Fintech market as well as new startups in this business area (Hao, 2020).

First and foremost, the government enacted a tax incentive policy to reduce the corporate tax income for Fintech companies, alleviating between 3% to 5% of their annual tax incomes (Hao, 2020). Secondly, the central government also founded a National Agency for Technology Entrepreneurship and Commercialization Development (NATEC) to support, mentor, and provide financial solutions to Fintech startups (Hao, 2020). Moreover, recently, the government has recommended schools instill tech startup spirit in young students by organizing regular competitions and collaborating with other successful Fintech startups to teach and train students (Giang, 2022). On top of that, the government also aims to seek more international cooperation, especially with global tech startups, to invest in Vietnam in order to learn from their expertise as well as improve the quality of domestic tech startups (Giang, 2022). Although there are certain favorable policies to support and encourage the development of Fintech in Vietnam, the central government still needs to work more on this new business area to leverage more initiatives and a clearer legal framework for tech startups. The government is expected to finalize the legal framework for Open Banking and Open API so banks and non-financial institutions like Fintech companies can share data and promote cooperation freely (Quang et al., 2022). In addition, the government must listen to the customers' voices and protect them from financial fraud, especially individual data privacy (Hao, 2020).

Fintech Impacts on The Economy

Financial technologies have made it easier to do banking in Vietnam and brought numerous positive impacts on the economy. Firstly, more Vietnamese people can now enjoy and perform any banking activities from their mobile phones with a few touches. It is truly convenient for the population, especially those living in remote areas. Secondly, by applying financial technologies, banks can improve their fee-based income, release more loans, and attract more deposits (Le et al., 2021). Fintech technology also helps banks reduce various transaction costs and improve efficiency. Thirdly, the proliferation of online payment services and digital wallets has solved the payment issues in Vietnam (Khue, 2021). No one can imagine that around ten years ago, it was still very hard to transfer money from a city to a small village in the mountain area. Nowadays, urban users can simply open their bank applications, and the money transfer transaction will be done within a few touches. On the other hand, Fintech also has a significant impact on the sphere of financial security. With the latest technologies, such as encryption, biometric identification, and artificial intelligence, banks can enhance their abilities to protect the customers' data and even extract meaningful insights from them (Khue, 2021). The central government and law enforcement can harness these powerful data findings to enact effective economic policies. In short, financial technology has changed and improved the quality of millions of lives in Vietnam.

Security Concern

Despite countless positive impacts brought by Fintech, there are certain challenges and concerns that it could induce. The most controversial part is the security matter. The development of Fintech is at the expense of cyber security risks. These risks come in different forms, such as money laundering, hacker attacks, or private data issues (Khue, 2021). In 2021, there were about 9,700 cyber-attacks occurred in Vietnam, a significant increase of 42.42 percent compared to 2020 (VSS, 2022). Moreover, recently, a data leak from a Vietnamese bank has sparked anger from social media, causing the government to further investigate and propose laws to protect more customers (Truong, 2023).

Other Relevant Academic Research

For the past few years, several studies have been conducted to understand more about the Vietnamese Fintech market. The first common finding is that the development of Fintech has helped banks reduce various related costs and significantly increase convenience for their customers (Khue, 2021; Hao, 2020). Another important implication from past studies was that the Vietnamese government had no clear legal framework for Fintech businesses, and they needed to work more to implement favorable policies for tech companies (Khue, 2021; Hao, 2020; Lien et al., 2020). The above authors also recommended the government create more innovative spaces for the young generation so they can freely create and invent new technologies. Training human resources and talent in the Fintech field is also a top priority.

In addition, various studies have also suggested that banks and non-financial institutions should promote cooperation, diversifying the banks' products and services as well as improving their system security (Lien et al., 2020; Quang et al., 2022). Moreover, the Vietnamese government is expected to simplify the investment process for foreign companies, especially tech firms, as well as create more Sandbox workspaces to nourish and develop more Fintech companies (Nathan et al., 2022; Quang et al., 2022).

Interesting Facts

Online lending platforms in various forms, like traditional financial institutions or P2P, are proliferating and ubiquitous in Vietnam nowadays. Major players for P2P applications are Vaymuon, Huydong, Mofin, and MoneyBank (Lainez, 2021). However, these new P2P lending applications also have posed certain threats to the customers, such as scams, financial traps, and money laundering (Minh, 2023). Financial technologies have helped the unbanked population connect and borrow money easily and simply get the money within a few minutes by using their phones. One reason is that around 60% of small and medium enterprises with insufficient credit or capital can secure their funds easily online via these lending platforms (Vietnam, 2021). However, this latest technology also poses several threats and risks to borrowers, such as scams, fraudulent loans, forged documents, and other unexpected consequences (Linh, 2022).

Another interesting fact about Vietnamese Fintech is that the adoption rate of cryptocurrency in Vietnam is among the highest in the world, figured by large transaction volumes (Julian et al., 2023). On top of that, the country also experiences a significant increase in blockchain and crypto startups, such as Sky Mavis, the developer of the famous mobile game Axie Infinity. They also became one of the first unicorn tech startups in Vietnam (Julian et al., 2023).

Trend and Future Aspects

Around the world, regulatory technology or Regtech, has been developed to manage regulatory compliance. The Vietnamese government should consider and encourage more Fintech companies and banks to embed and develop Regtech in order to follow the regulations as well as to prevent potential financial risks and threats. This also potentially mitigates the financial and cybersecurity risks.

Another promising Fintech trend in Vietnam would be the boom in healthcare and personal finance segments. Several tech startups have been launched in the healthcare sector to provide financial solutions as well as convenience for customers. On the other hand, since more Vietnamese move to the middle-class income, new financial solutions are expected to guide them in managing their wealth. Finally, Artificial Intelligence, Machine Learning, and Big Data technologies are poised to have a significant impact in the future.

COMPARISON AND ANALYSIS

By analyzing and examining various aspects of Fintech in ten Southeast Asian countries, we have gained a better understanding of the development of financial technologies in this region. In this section, we will further the report by comparing and analyzing these ten countries as a whole to assess their performance in the field of Fintech. This part also plays a vital role in summarizing all the key indicators, serving as a valuable resource for policymakers to make future informed decisions regarding Fintech.

In 2021, the population of ten ASEAN countries was approximately 666.19 million people (Statista, 2023), with tremendous opportunities to thrive in Fintech. However, according to Bain & Company, Google, and Temasek (2019), more than 70% of the adult inhabitants in this region remained unbanked.

The percentage of the unbanked population in each country was meticulously examined in the aforementioned country report.

Regarding the Fintech adoption rate in the region, there are different levels due to its diverse socioeconomic factors, regulations, and policies. The table below summarizes the Fintech adoption rate in each nation, extracted from the country report.

Table 1. Fintech adoption rate by country

Country	Fintech Adoption Rate
Myanmar	Low
Cambodia	Low
Laos	Low
Malaysia	Medium
Philippines	High
Indonesia	High
Singapore	High
Thailand	High
Vietnam	High
Brunei	High

Note. Data generated from the analysis of the earlier country report.

From the table, it is evident that six nations, including Singapore, Thailand, Vietnam, Brunei, the Philippines, and Indonesia, have high Fintech adoption rates, whereas Myanmar, Cambodia, and Laos adopted Fintech with low rates. Malaysia, in comparison, received a medium adoption rate. Hence, potential investors and policymakers in the region can consider the adoption rate factor in the region before making any investing decisions or implementing new Fintech policies.

Regarding the percentage of unbanked population by country in ASEAN in 2021, around 59% of the Vietnamese remained unbanked, whereas that figure in Indonesia was 48.3% and 44% in the Philippines. Thailand had the lowest share of the unbanked population, with only 4.5%, followed by Malaysia with 11.7% (Gantès et al., 2023). Although Vietnam, Indonesia, and the Philippines have high Fintech adoption rates, they still have almost half of their population unbanked. A few reasons behind this phenomenon could be summarized from the country report, such as inhabitants in these three countries embrace Fintech by using digital payment apps or mobile money without needing to open physical bank accounts.

Furthermore, the number of Fintech firms has increased significantly from 2,612 in 2018 to 4,030 in November 2023 in six ASEAN countries (United Overseas Bank Limited, 2022). The following bar chart illustrates the development of Fintech firms in ASEAN-6

In terms of Fintech funding, the region experienced an upward trend from around 2 percent in 2018 to approximately 7 percent in November 2022, being the region that received the lowest Fintech funding in the world (United Overseas Bank Limited, 2022).

However, during the report, people's behaviour changed when more people prefer cashless transactions, especially after the pandemic. According to United Overseas Bank Limited (2022), around 74% of the ASEAN-6 population used financial apps at least once a week, with Vietnam being on top with 85%.

Figure 25. Share of banked and unbanked by country in 2021
Note. Reprinted from On the verge of a digital banking revolution in the Philippines. McKinsey & Company. Retrieved from https://www.mckinsey.com/industries/financial-services/our-insights/on-the-verge-of-a-digital-banking-revolution-in-the-philippines

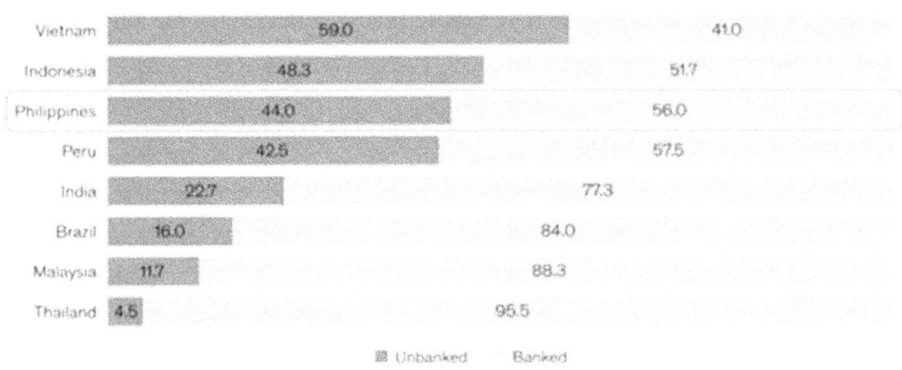

Figure 26. Growth in Fintech firms by country, 2018 - November 2022
Note. Reprinted from Fintech in ASEAN 2022: Finance, Reimagined. Retrieved from https://www.uobgroup.com/techecosystem/news-insights-Fintech-in-asean-2022.html

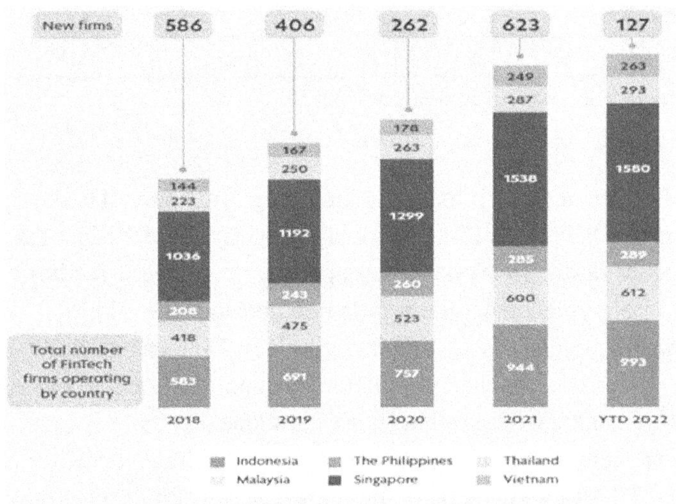

Moreover, ASEAN-6 witnessed a more diverse Fintech investment between 2021 and 2022, with the birth of Regtech accounting for 1% of the total funding. Till November 2022, the alternative lending sector experienced a decrease of 7%, followed by investment tech with a decline of 5%. Cryptocurrencies and blockchain sectors witnessed upward trends. More importantly, the payments segment still accounted for the largest market share of 45%. The pie charts below illustrate the funding breakdown by categories from 2021 to November 2022 (United Overseas Bank Limited, 2022).

Regarding the Fintech regulations, all ASEAN governments are supporting the development of financial technologies and trying different ways to nourish and boost this segment. Moreover, a couple of nations are implementing a Fintech-friendly approach with the introduction of Sandboxes: Singapore, Malaysia, Indonesia, Thailand, and the Philippines. With the launch of sandboxes in those countries,

Figure 27. Global Fintech funding split by region, 2018 – November 2022
Note. Reprinted from Fintech in ASEAN 2022: Finance, Reimagined. Retrieved from https://www.uobgroup.com/techecosystem/news-insights-Fintech-in-asean-2022.html

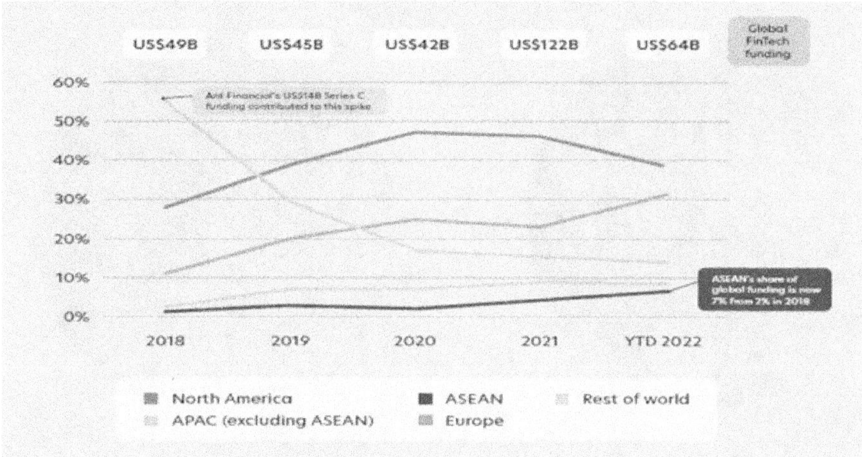

Figure 28. Frequency of usage of embedded finance apps across ASEAN-6
Note. Reprinted from Fintech in ASEAN 2022: Finance, Reimagined. Retrieved from https://www.uobgroup.com/techecosystem/news-insights-Fintech-in-asean-2022.html

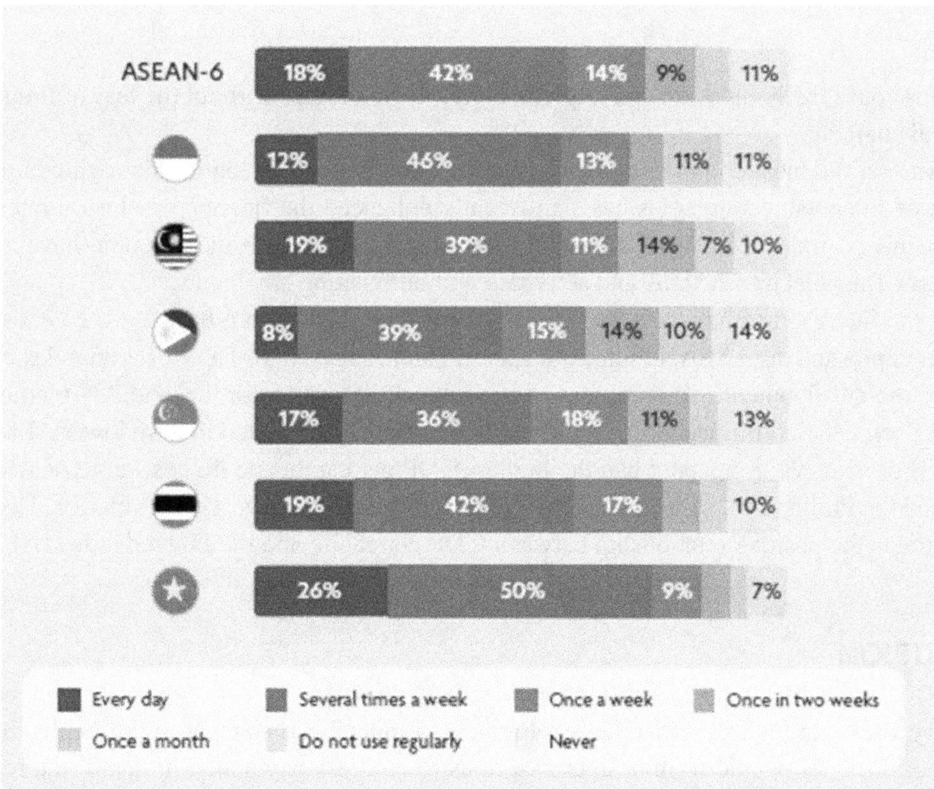

Figure 29. Breakdown of Fintech funding by categories from 2021 to November 2022
Note. Reprinted from Fintech in ASEAN 2022: Finance, Reimagined. Retrieved from https://www.uobgroup.com/techecosystem/news-insights-Fintech-in-asean-2022.html

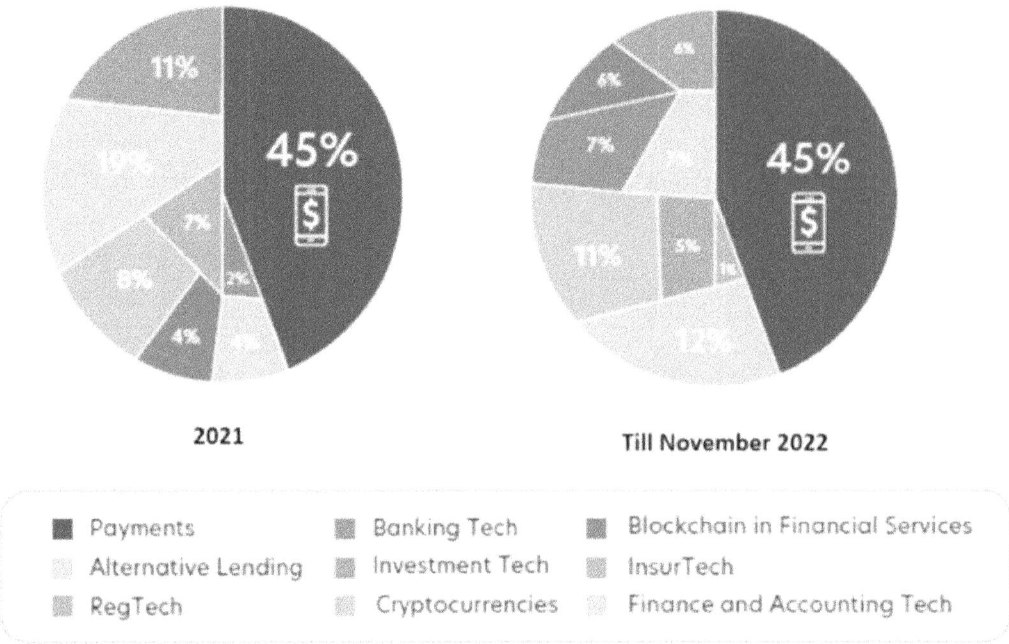

new startups could freely innovate and implement new technologies without the fear of future prosecution or legal challenges.

Furthermore, the most common academic research finding of Fintech in this region is that the development of financial technologies has significantly enhanced the financial inclusion rates in all the country members. Indeed, by using financial technologies, more unbanked people have a chance to perform daily financial transactions and activities without visiting any banks.

One of the interesting findings is that there is a positive relationship between the Gross Domestic Product per capita and the ASEAN Fintech Index (AFI) for ASEAN - 6. The AFI is an index constructed to measure the development and readiness of the Fintech ecosystem in the ASEAN-6 countries. According to Zheng et al. (2022), countries with low GDP per capita tended to have lower AFI scores and vice versa. For example, Singapore had the highest GDP per capita and highest score of AFI, whereas Vietnam and the Philippines, with low GDP per capita, received the lowest scores of AFI. The following chart illustrates the positive relationship between GDP per capita and the Fintech index (AFI).

CONCLUSION

In summary, the report indicates that the development of Fintech has changed significantly the financial behaviors of ASEAN people from cash transactions to cashless payments. In detail, the research has thoroughly scrutinized the development of Fintech in ten Southeast Asian countries by analyzing dif-

Figure 30. ASEAN-6 Fintech Index vs GDP per capita
Note. Reprinted from Examining the Fintech Ecosystem of ASEAN-6 Countries. Retrieved from https://www.dlsu.edu.ph/wp-content/uploads/pdf/research/journals/apssr/2022-June-vol22-2/2-zheng.pdf

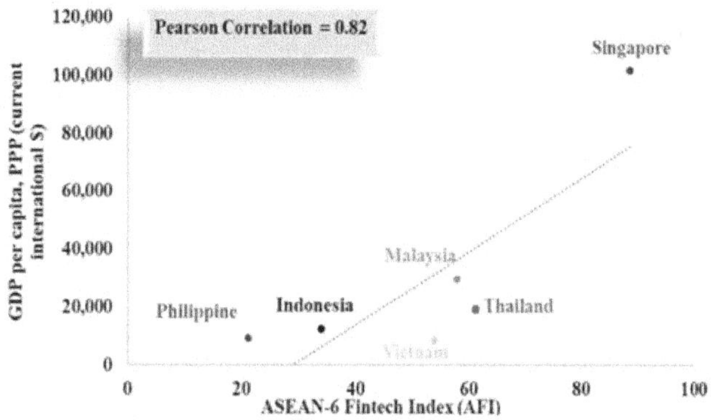

ferent aspects of each country member. The result reveals that Brunei, Vietnam, Thailand, Singapore, Indonesia, and the Philippines have high Fintech adoption rates, whereas Myanmar, Cambodia, and Laos received low adoption rates. While Malaysia has a medium adoption rate, the Fintech market in the country is projected to thrive in the near future.

Moreover, the report also suggests that the digital payment sector dominates the market share in most ASEAN nations. New emerging Fintech segments, such as remittance, blockchain, and cryptocurrency, were also mentioned with strong potential to develop further. Additionally, the technical infrastructures are being further developed with more 4G and even 5G coverages in various areas. Furthermore, several governments such as Singapore, Thailand, and the Philippines have implemented a friendly approach to Fintech by creating Sandboxes or testing schemes. These initiatives are strongly recommended to be applied to other nations. However, the development of Fintech has also posed certain security challenges, such as cyber-attacks, online frauds, and scams. Therefore, governments are advised to take courage to fuel the development of Fintech but with caution in security concerns. Overall, the report has gone through the development of Fintech in ASEAN countries with numerous key findings that policymakers and investors can consider before making informed decisions.

REFERENCES

2p. (2022). *Popular Payment Methods in Thailand: What Consumers Want*. Retrieved from https://2c2p.com/blog/thailand-payment-methods

Ab Razak, M. I., Dali, N. A. M., Dhillon, G., & Manaf, A. W. (2020). Fintech in Malaysia: Anappraisal to the need of shariah-compliant regulation. *Pertanika Journal of Social Science & Humanities*, *28*(4), 3223–3233. doi:10.47836/pjssh.28.4.40

Abdillah, L. A. (2019). An overview of Indonesian Fintech application. *Social Science Research Network*. https://papers.ssrn.com/sol3/papers.cfm?abstract_id=3512737

Acclime. (2023, August 31). *Fintech in Cambodia: An overview*. Retrieved from https://cambodia.acclime.com/insight/Fintech-overview/

Afif, M., & Samsuri, A. (2022). Integration of Fintech and Islamic Banking in Indonesia: Opportunities and Challenges. *Cakrawala: Jurnal Studi Islam*, *17*(1), 27–38. doi:10.31603/cakrawala.7051

AgarwalS.QianW.RenY.TsaiH. T.YeungB. Y. (2020). *The real impact of Fintech: Evidence from mobile payment technology*. doi:10.2139/ssrn.3556340

Airpay. (n.d.). *About us*. Retrieved from http://www.airpay.co.th/

Akselaran. (n.d.). *Blog*. Retrieved from: https://www.akseleran.co.id/blog/

Al Jazeera. (2023, April 11). *Cambodia deports 19 Japanese cybercrime scam suspects*. Retrieved from https://www.aljazeera.com/news/2023/4/11/cambodia-deports-19-japanese-cybercrime-scam-suspects

Ali, H., Abdullah, R., & Zaini, M. Z. (2019). Fintech and its potential impact on Islamic bankingand finance industry: A case study of Brunei Darussalam and Malaysia. *International Journal of Islamic Economics and Finance*, *2*(1), 73–108. doi:10.18196/ijief.2116

Ali, H., Abdullah, R., & Zaini, M. Z. (2019). Fintech regulation. *Fintech and Islamic Finance: Digitalization, Development and Disruption*, 137-158.

Anagnostopoulos, I. (2018, November). Fintech and Regtech: Impact on regulators and banks. *Journal of Economics and Business*, *100*, 7–25. doi:10.1016/j.jeconbus.2018.07.003

Anh, N. (2021, November 10). *Why do many Vietnamese people prefer to buy goods from Taobao and other Chinese e-commerce websites?* Vietnam Media Corporation Joint Stock Company - Vccorp. https://genk.vn/vi-sao-nhieu-nguoi-viet-thich-mua-do-tu-taobao-va-cac-trang-tmdt-trung-quoc-20210102101619171.chn

Aquarii. (2022, February 16). *Fintech And E-Commerce In Cambodia. Retrieved from*https://aquariibd.com/Fintech-and-e-commerce-in-cambodia/

Asian Banking & Finance. (2021). *Digital-savvy Thais push banks' Fintech adoption: S&P.*Retrieved from https://asianbankingandfinance.net/banking-technology/news/digital-savvy-thais-push-banks-Fintech-adoption-sp

Asian Banking & Finance. (2023, May). *Cards & Payments financial technology*. Retrieved From https://asianbankingandfinance.net/cards-payments/in-focus/filipinos-spent-over-4-million-hours-using-e-wallets-in-2022-study

Aulia, M., Yustiardhi, A. F., & Permatasari, R. O. (2020, January 1). An overview of Indonesian regulatory framework on Islamic financial technology (Fintech). *Jurnal Ekonomi & Keuangan Islam*, *6*(1), 64–75. doi:10.20885/jeki.vol6.iss1.art7

Australian Government. (n.d.). .https://www.austrade.gov.au/ArticleDocuments/4569/digital-banking-vietnam-report.pdf.aspx

Autoriti Monetari Brunei Darussalam. (2020). *The state of Fintech in Brunei Darussalam*. Retrieved from https://www.moneylaundering.com/wpcontent/uploads/2021/01/Brunei.NA_.Fintech.2020.pdf

Aya Pay. (n.d.). *Features*. Retrieved from https://www.ayapay.com/

Aye, T. (2020). *Adoption of Fintech and policy recommendations: The case for digital lending platform in Myanmar*. Retrieved from https://scholarbank.nus.edu.sg/handle/10635/192617

Bain & Company, & Google, & Temasek Holdings. (2022). *E-commerce market size in the Philippines in 2019 and 2021, with a forecast for 2022 and 2025 (in billion U.S. dollars)* [Graph]. Statista. Retrieved August 26, 2023, from https://www.statista.com/statistics/1125455/e-commerce-market-size-philippines/

Bake. (n.d.). *Control your financial destiny*. Retrieved from https://bake.io/about-us/

Banga, K., & te Velde, D. W. (2020). *Cambodia, COVID-19 and inclusive digitaltransformation: a seven-point plan*. Supporting Economic Transformation.

Bank of Thailand. (2021). *Fintech in Thailand*. Retrieved fromhttps://www.bot.or.th/en/financial-innovation/digital-finance/Fintech-in-thailand.html

Bank of Thailand. (2023). *Virtual Bank*. Retrieved from https://www.bot.or.th/en/financial-innovation/digital-finance/virtual-bank.html

Barker, T., & Üngör, M. (2019, January). Vietnam: The next Asian Tiger? *The North American Journal of Economics and Finance*, *47*, 96–118. doi:10.1016/j.najef.2018.11.010

Batunanggar, S. (2019). *Fintech Development and Regulatory Frameworks in Indonesia. ADBI Working Paper 1014*. Asian Development Bank Institute. Retrieved from https://www.adb.org/publications/Fintech-development-regulatory-frameworks-indonesia

Belaws Cambodia. (2022). *The rise of Fintech in Cambodia*. Retrieved fromhttps://www.belaws.com/cambodia/Fintech-in-cambodia/

Bitkub. (n.d.). *About us*. Retrieved from https://support.bitkub.com/en/support/solutions/articles/151000034649-who-is-bitkub-

Bodie, Z. H., & Merton, F. (2015). Design of financial systems: Towards a synthesis of functionand structure. *Journal of Investment Management*, *3*(1), 1–13.

Bongloy. (n.d.). *About us*. Retrieved from https://www.bongloy.asia/

Boost Capitals. (n.d.). *About us*. Retrieved from https://www.boostkh.com/

Borneo Bulletin. (2022, September 27). *Brunei sees acceleration of Fintech products, andservices*. Retrieved from https://borneobulletin.com.bn/brunei-sees-acceleration-of-Fintech-products-services/

Bromberg, L., Godwin, A., & Ramsay, I. (2017). Fintech sandboxes: Achieving a balancebetween regulation and innovation. *Journal of Banking and Finance Law and Practice*, *28*(4), 314–336.

Brunei Darussalam Central Bank. (n.d.). *Islamic Finance*. Retrieved fromhttps://www.bdcb.gov.bn/regulatory/islamic-finance

Bui, M. T., & Luong, T. N. O. (2023). *Financial inclusion for the elderly in Thailand and the role of information communication technology*. Borsa Istanbul Review. doi:10.1016/j.bir.2023.02.003

Business World. (2023, June 12). *More than 400 small businesses in the Philippines accept Bitcoin payments — Fintech firm*. Retrieved from https://www.bworldonline.com/sparkup/2023/06/12/527873/more-than-400-small-businesses-in-the-philippines-accept-bitcoin-payments-Fintech-firm/

Cafe, F. (2021). *Breakdown of Fintech startups in Vietnam in 2020, by category*[Graph]. In Statista. Retrieved July 23, 2023, from https://www.statista.com/statistics/1229955/vietnam-Fintech-startups-by-category/

CapBay. (n.d.). *The #1 Supply Chain Finance Company*. Retrieved fromhttps://capbay.com/about-us/

Central Bank of Malaysia. (2013a, March 22). *Financial Services Act 2013*. Retrieved fromhttps://www.bnm.gov.my/-/financial-services-act-2013

Central Bank of Malaysia. (2013b, March 22). *Islamic Financial Services Act 2013*. Retrievedfrom https://www.bnm.gov.my/documents/20124/8102422b-e6dd-d149-8db0-e3637e89ed5c

Central Bank of Malaysia. (2023c, March 29). Let's Go Digital Confidently. Annual Report 2022.Retrieved from https://www.bnm.gov.my/documents/20124/10150308/ar2022_en_box6.pdf

Central Bank of Myanmar. (2016). *Regulation on Mobile Financial Services*. Retrieved fromhttp://www.myanmar-embassy-tokyo.net/eco2017/Finance/Mobile-Financial-Services-regulation-2016.pdf

Chambers and Partners. (2023, March 23). *Thailand - Fintech Trends and Developments*. Retrieved from https://practiceguides.chambers.com/practice-guides/Fintech-2023/thailand/trends-and-developments

Chong, S. (2023, June 28). *Rising Cyber Crime, Financial Losses Will Test The Role Of Banks.Business Today*. Retrieved from https://www.businesstoday.com.my/2023/06/28/rising-cyber-crime-financial-losses-will-test-the-role-of-banks/

CoFarm. (n.d.). *About us*. Retrieved from https://cofarm.la/#about

Coins.ph. (n.d.). *About us*. Retrieved from https://coins.ph/about

Cortis, D., Debattista, J., Debono, J., & Farrell, M. (2019). InsurTech. *Disrupting finance:Fintech and strategy in the 21st century*, 71-84.

Crunchbase. (2023) *Grab Funding*. Retrieved from https://www.crunchbase.com/organization/grabtaxi/company_financials

Crypto.com. (n.d.). *Cryptocurrency in every wallet*. Retrieved from https://crypto.com/ca/about

CSA (Singapore). (2022, August 29). *Cybercrime as a share of total crimes in Singapore from2014 to 2021* [Graph]. Statista. Retrieved July 29, 2023, from https://www.statista.com/statistics/1267252/singapore-cybercrime-as-share-of-total-crime

Cung, N. H. (2019, November 30). Gross Domestic Product and Foreign Direct Investment: Empirical Evidence from Vietnam. *European Scientific Journal*, *15*(31). Advance online publication. doi:10.19044/esj.2019.v15n31p38

Cyber Security Brunei. (2020, February 6). *Brunei reports 39% rise in cyber attacks in 2018*.Retrieved from https://www.csb.gov.bn/brunei-reports-39-rise-cyber-attacks-2018#:~:text=BANDAR%20SERI%20BEGAWAN%20%E2%80%93%20Brunei%20has,its%20'Smart%20Nation'%20plans

DANA. (n.d.). *About DANA*. Retrieved from https://www.dana.id/en/about

Data&StorageAsean, (2022, August 9). *2022 Press Releases*. Retrieved fromhttps://datastorageasean.com/news-press-releases/digitalisation-being-bolstered-laos-countrys-government-which-concerned-about

Decision Lab. (2022). *The Connected Consumer*. https://www.decisionlab.co/connected-consumer#download

Dennis, Q., Divina, I., Neonette, P., & Kristina, N. (2022). *Law and Practice. Quisumbing Torres*. Retrieved from https://www.quisumbingtorres.com/-/media/minisites/quisumbing-torres/files/2022/quisumbing-torreschambers-and-partnersFintech-guid.pdf?sc_lang=en&hash=1ED0840A6D5998C2FC4F5C3330693962

Didenko, A. N. (2020). Cybersecurity Regulation in Singapore's Financial Sector: Protecting Fintech 'Ants' in a Jungle Full of 'Elephants'. *UNSW Law Research Paper*, 20-45.

DigFin. (2020, October 6). *Red app, blue app: KBZPay notches 6m Myanmar users*. Retrieved from https://www.digfingroup.com/kbz-pay/

Digital Financial Services. (n.d.). Bain & Company. Retrieved from https://www.bain.com/insights/fufilling-its-promise/

Dobberstein, L. (2022, September 22). *Cambodian authorities crack down on cyber slavery amid international pressure*. Retrieved from https://www.theregister.com/2022/09/22/cambodian_authorities_crack_down_on/

Dubai Islamic Economy Development Centre. (2018). *Islamic Fintech report 2018: current landscape & path forward*. Retrieved from https://www.dinarstandard.com/wp-content/uploads/2018/12/Islamic-Fintech-Report-2018.pdf

Dzhondzhorov, D. (2023, March 18). *Crypto Flourishes in Vietnam With 16.6 Million Holders (Report)*. CryptoPotato. https://cryptopotato.com/crypto-flourishes-in-vietnam-with-16-6-million-holders-report/

Dziawgo, T. (2021, September 1). Wealth Tech Impact on Wealth Management Sector. *European Research Studies, 24*(3B), 141–151. doi:10.35808/ersj/2463

E-commerce Driving Force for Growth. (n.d.). *Vietnam Business Forum of Vietnam Chamber of Commerce and Industry (VCCI)-Economy*. https://vccinews.com/news/48958/e-commerce-driving-force-for growth.html#:~:text=Shopee%20is%20the%20largest%20e,1%25%20of%20the%20market%20share.

eCommerceDB. (2023). *eCommerce market in Myanmar*. Retrieved fromhttps://ecommercedb.com/markets/mm/all

Eileen, Yu. (2019, March 6). *Hacker Group Behind SingHealth Data Breach Identified, Targeted Mainly Singapore Firms*. Retrieved from https://www.zdnet.com/article/hacker-group-behind-singhealth-data-breach-identified-targeted-mainly-singapore-firms/

Ernst & Young. (2019). *Thailand Fintech Landscape Report.* Retrieved fromhttps://www.researchgate.net/profile/Varun-Mittal-9/publication/337971279_Thailand_Fintech_Landscape_Report_Sanitized_by_Global_Markets_EY_Knowledge/links/5df8527aa6fdcc283726a7b3/Thailand-Fintech-Landscape-Report-Sanitized-by-Global-Markets-EY-Knowledge.pdf

Ernst & Young Global Limited. (2019). *Global Fintech adoption index 2019.* Retrieved fromhttps://www.ey.com/en_gl/ey-global-Fintech-adoption-index

ETDA. (October 13, 2021). *E-commerce market value in Thailand from 2017 to 2020, with a forecast for 2021 (in trillion Thai baht)* [Graph]. Statista. Retrieved August 19, 2023, from https://www.statista.com/statistics/1115125/thailand-e-commerce-market-value/

Fintech Energy. (2022). *Myanmar's 8 Fastest Growing Fintech Startups.* Retrieved from https://Fintech.energy/myanmars-8-fastest-growing-Fintech-startups/

Fintech Malaysia. (2022, July 18). *Fintech Report 2022: Malaysia Charts a New Path for Fintech Growth.* Retrieved from https://Fintechnews.my/31945/malaysia/Fintech-report-malaysia-2022/

Fintech Malaysia. (2022, May 11). *Top 5 Funded Fintechs in Malaysia.* Retrieved fromhttps://Fintech-news.my/31200/malaysia/top-5-funded-Fintechs-in-malaysia/

Fintech News. (2022, December 8). All 5 Singapore Digital Banks Are Now Members of the Credit Bureau. Lending Virtual Banking. Retrieved from https://Fintechnews.sg/67599/virtual-banking/all-5-singapore-digital-banks-are-now-members-of-the-credit-bureau/

Fintech News. (2022). *Distribution of Fintech companies in Singapore in 2022, bysector* [Graph]. Statista. Retrieved July 29, 2023, from https://www.statista.com/statistics/1294130/singapore-Fintech-companies-share-by-sector/

Fintechnews. (2023, January 10). *Laos' Fintech Revolution is Still Bank-Led, For Now.* Retrieved from https://Fintechnews.sg/68354/laos/laos-Fintech-revolution-is-still-bank-led-for-now/

Firn, M. (2021, July 15). *TrueMoney goal for 2 mn 2021 e-wallet transactions on target.* Retrieved from https://www.khmertimeskh.com/50894147/truemoney-goal-for-2-mn-2021-e-wallet-transactions-on-target/

Fortumo. (2021, July 27). *Market share of leading mobile wallet applications in the Philippinesin 2020* [Graph]. Statista. Retrieved August 26, 2023, from https://www.statista.com/statistics/1258098/philippines-mobile-wallet-apps-market-share/

Fortumo. (2021, September 28). *Number of mobile wallet users in Indonesia in 2020, with aforecast for 2025 (in millions)* [Graph]. Statista. Retrieved August 16, 2023, from https://www.statista.com/statistics/1327354/indonesia-mobile-wallet-users/

Fortune Pay. (n.d.). *About us.* Retrieved from https://fortunepay.com/about-us/

Gantès, G. D., Gerson, H., & Romano, K. (2023, May 3). *On the verge of a digital bankingrevolution in the Philippines.* McKinsey & Company. Retrieved from https://www.mckinsey.com/industries/financial-services/our-insights/on-the-verge-of-a-digital-banking-revolution-in-the-philippines

Giang, H. (2022, July 28). *Elevating the startup ecosystem through the innovative policies of the Government.* Government News. https://baochinhphu.vn/nang-tam-he-sinh-thai-khoi-nghiep-tu-nhung-chinh-sach-kien-tao-cua-chinh-phu-102220728140305108.htm

Giang, H. (2023, March 13). *E-commerce Driving Force for Growth.* Vietnam Business Forum.https://vccinews.com/news/48958/e-commerce-driving-force-for%20growth.html

Globe. (2023, August 9). *GCash: Everything You Need To Know To Make Life Easier.* Retrieved from www.globe.com.ph/go/technology/article/gcash-everything-you-need-to-know.html

GMA. (2023, April 12). *Philippines 4th in the world with most incidents of cyber attacks — DICT.* Retrieved from https://www.gmanetwork.com/news/scitech/technology/866755/philippines-4th-in-the-world-with-most-incidents-of-cyber-attacks-dict/story/

GoPay. (n.d.). *About us.* Retrieved from https://www.gopay.com/en/about-us/

Gotrade. (n.d.). *Making investing fun, fair and simple.* Retrieved from https://www.heygotrade.com/

Grab. (2019, December 20). *Grab Primed to Drive Digital Economy in Malaysia through e-Tunai Rakyat Programme.* Press Center. Retrieved from: https://www.grab.com/my/press/business/grab-e-tunai-rakyat-programme/

Grab. (n.d.). *Charging forward together.* Retrieved from https://www.grab.com/sg/about/

Greene, C. (2022, November 16). *Uproar in Mobile Financial Services.* Retrieved from

https://www.myanmarinsider.com/uproar-in-mobile-financial-services/

GSMA. (2022, July 4). *The Philippines is a Duopoly No More: Assessing DITO's Impact on 4G and 5G Performance.* Retrieved from https://www.gsma.com/membership/resources/the-philippines-is-a-duopoly-no-more-assessing-ditos-impact-on-4g-and-5g-performance/

Hao, V. (2020, January 1). Developing a Fintech Ecosystem in Vietnam: Opportunities and Challenges for Startups. *SHS Web of Conferences; EDP Sciences.* 10.1051/shsconf/20208904001

Haqqi, F. R., & Suzianti, A. (2020, June). Exploring risk and benefit factors affecting user adoption intention of Fintech in Indonesia. In *Proceedings of the 3rd Asia Pacific Conference on Research in Industrial and Systems Engineering* (pp. 13-18). 10.1145/3400934.3400939

Hasaka, K. (2019). *The Impact of Fintech innovations and financial standards on bank performance: Evidence from selected commercial banks in ASEAN.* Retrieved from https://ink.library.smu.edu.sg/cgi/viewcontent.cgi?article=1256&context=etd_coll

HBR. (2022). *Cambodia - Overview.* Retrieved from https://www.halberdbastion.com/intelligence/countries-nations/cambodia

Heno. (n.d.). *Introduction.* Heno. https://heno.vn/about/about-heno

Hoang, L. (2021, December 21). *Vietnam e-wallet MoMo gains unicorn status with $200m investment.* Nikkei Asia. Retrieved from https://asia.nikkei.com/Business/Technology/Vietnam-e-wallet-MoMo-gains-unicorn-status-with-200m-investment

Huong, A., Puah, C. H., & Chong, M. T. (2021). Embrace Fintech in ASEAN: A perception through Fintech adoption index. *Review of World Economics*, *12*(1), 1.

Huseien, G. F., & Shah, K. W. (2022, January). A review on 5G technology for smart energy management and smart buildings in Singapore. *Energy and AI*, *7*, 100116. doi:10.1016/j.egyai.2021.100116

Insider. (2020, October 30). Wave Money sets record breaking 1.1 Million Monthly ActiveUsers *of WavePay*. Market Insider. Retrieved from https://markets.businessinsider.com/news/stocks/wave-money-sets-record-breaking-1-1-million-monthly-active-users-of-wavepay-1029744558

International Finance. (2020, June 5). *5G is a logical solution to the Philippines*. Retrieved from https://internationalfinance.com/5g-is-a-logical-solution-to-the-philippines/

International Trade Administration. (2022, July 25). *eCommerce*. Retrieved from https://www.trade.gov/country-commercial-guides/philippines-ecommerce

International Trade Administration. (2022, April 20). *Singapore's e-commerce market*. Retrieved from https://www.trade.gov/market-intelligence/singapores-e-commerce-market

International Trade Administration. (2022, July 26). *eCommerce*. Retrieved from https://www.trade.gov/country-commercial-guides/thailand-ecommerce

International Trade Administration. (2022, November 23). Malaysia - eCommerce. Retrieved from https://www.trade.gov/country-commercial-guides/malaysia-ecommerce

International Trade Administration. (2023, February 7). Singapore cybersecurity market. Retrieved from https://www.trade.gov/market-intelligence/singapore-cybersecurity-marketInternational

iPrice Group. (2022, November 29). *Most visited e-commerce sites in Thailand as of 1st quarter 2022, by monthly traffic (in 1,000 clicks)* [Graph].In Statista. Retrieved August 24, 2023, from https://www.statista.com/statistics/1117797/thailand-popular-e-commerce-sites/

iPrice Group. (2022, November 7). *Leading e-commerce sites in Indonesia as of 2nd quarter 2022, by monthly traffic (in million web visits)* [Graph]. Statista. Retrieved August 05, 2023, from https://www.statista.com/statistics/869700/indonesia-top-10-e-commerce-sites/

iPrice Group. (2022, October 19). *Most visited e-commerce sites in Malaysia as of 2nd quarter 2022, by monthly traffic (in 1,000 clicks)* [Graph]. Statista. Retrieved August 12, 2023, from https://www.statista.com/statistics/869640/malaysia-top-10-e-commerce-sites/

Jana Kapital. (n.d.). *About us*. Retrieved from https://www.janakapital.com/about

Jeník, I., Flaming, M., & Salman, A. (2020). *Inclusive digital banking: Emerging markets case studies*. Consultative Group to Assist the Poor Working Paper. Washington, DC.

JohnClements. (2023). *Fintech Frontier: Trends And Innovations*. Retrieved from https://www.johnclements.com/the-looking-glass/featured/Fintech-frontier-trends-and-innovations/

Julian, H. L. C., Chung, T., & Wang, Y. (2023, January 6). Adoption of Metaverse in South East Asia. *Strategies and Opportunities for Technology in the Metaverse World*, 196–234. doi:10.4018/978-1-6684-5732-0.ch012

Kabulova, J., & Stankevičienė, J. (2020). Valuation of Fintech innovation based on patent applications. *Sustainability (Basel)*, *12*(23), 1–14. doi:10.3390/su122310158

Kapron, Z. (2023, April 12). *Incumbents Are Poised To Dominate Digital Banking In Thailand. Forbes*. Retrieved from https://www.forbes.com/sites/zennonkapron/2023/04/12/incumbents-are-poised-to-dominate-digital-banking-in-thailand/?sh=ef723811df9b

Kashyap, M. (2023, April 20). *Ecommerce in Malaysia: Growth, Trends & Opportunities. Capillary*. Retrieved from https://www.capillarytech.com/blog/ecommerce-in-malaysia-growth/

Katadata. (2022). *Most known digital banks among Indonesians in 2022*. Statista. Retrieved August 05, 2023, from https://www.statista.com/statistics/1326448/indonesia-leading-digital-banks/

Kem, B., Sou, J., Ng, Z., & Chan, P. (2019, January 1). *Cambodia's Vibrant Tech Startup Ecosystem*. Retrieved from https://static1.squarespace.com/static/56a87acd05f8e263f7b16c7f/t/5c9b07620852298 87ba9af72/1553663849501/Cambodian_Tech_Startup_Report_Final_250319.pdf

Khue, D. T. T. (2021, July 1). Recommendations contributing to the development of financial technology (Fintech) in Vietnam. *International Journal of Research in Finance and Management*, *4*(2), 74–80. doi:10.33545/26175754.2021.v4.i2a.110

Kijkasiwat, P. (2021). Opportunities and challenges for Fintech Startups: The case study of Thailand. *ABAC Journal*, *41*(2), 41–60.

Klenow, P. (2019). How valuable is e-commerce. *Stanford Institute for Economic Policy Research (SIEPR)*. Retrieved from https://siepr.stanford.edu/publications/policy-brief/how-valuable-e-commerce

Kompas. (2022, July 21). *Most used e-wallet apps by consumers in Indonesia as of July 2022* [Graph]. Statista. Retrieved August 05, 2023, from https://www.statista.com/statistics/1327316/indonesia-most-used-e-wallet-apps/

Ku-Mahamud, K. R., Abu Bakar, N. A. M., & Omar, M. (2018). Blockchain, cryptocurrency and Fintech market growth in Malaysia. *Journal of Advance Research in Dynamical & Control Systems, 10*(14 SI), 2074-2082.

Kumar, S., Li, A., Wong, H., Chauhan, H., Shubhankar, S., & Oetama, I. (2023, April 19). *Indonesia's Fintech Industry Is Ready to Rise. Canada - EN*. https://www.bcg.com/en-ca/publications/2023/Fintech-industry-indonesia-growth

Kurniasari, F., Tajul Urus, S., Utomo, P., Abd Hamid, N., Jimmy, S. Y., & Othman, I. W. (2022). Determinant factors of adoption of Fintech Payment Services in Indonesia using the UTAUT approach. *Asian-Pacific Management Accounting Journal*, *17*(1), 97–125. doi:10.24191/APMAJ.V17i1-04

Kyaw, E. N. (2022, June 3). *The revolution of Myanmar Fintech: Mobile payment applications*. Retrieved from https://www.myanmore.com/2022/06/the-future-of-myanmars-Fintech/

Laik, D. M. N., & Wei, C. M. H. (2019). *Creating a unique mobile financial services framework for Myanmar: A Review*. Retrieved from https://arxiv.org/ftp/arxiv/papers/1910/1910.03793.pdf

Lainez, N. (2021, January 6). *Navigating Vietnam's Lending App Maze. Fulcrum - Analysis on Southeast Asia.* https://fulcrum.sg/navigating-vietnams-lending-app-maze

LaoPay. (n.d.). *About us.* Retrieved from https://www.laopay.app/en/about-us

Le, T. T., Mai, H. N., & Phan, D. T. (2021, April 24). Fintech Innovations. *The Impact of.*

Leesa-nguansuk, S. (2023, August 1). *Thailand feels the force of cyber-attacks.* Bangkok Post. Retrieved from https://www.bangkokpost.com/business/general/2621385/thailand-feels-the-force-of-cyber-attacks

Lien, N. T. K., Doan, T. T. T., & Bui, T. N. (2020, September 30). Fintech and Banking: Evidence from Vietnam. *The Journal of Asian Finance. Economics and Business*, *7*(9), 419–426. doi:10.13106/jafeb.2020.vol7.no9.419

Lin, L., & Chen, C. (2020, March). The promise and perils of InsurTech. *Singapore Journal of Legal Studies*, 115-142.

Linh, D. H. (2022, April 18). P2P Lending's Credit Risk in Vietnam: Determinants and Discussions. *Journal of Economics. Finance and Management Studies*, *5*(4). Advance online publication. doi:10.47191/jefms/v5-i4-18

LinkAja. (n.d.). *About LinkAja.* Retrieved from https://www.linkaja.id/about-us

Loca. (n.d.) *Loca Pay.* Retrieved from https://loca.la/locapay/

Loo, M. K. L. (2019). Enhancing financial inclusion in ASEAN: Identifying the best growth markets for Fintech. *Journal of Risk and Financial Management*, *12*(4), 181. doi:10.3390/jrfm12040181

Mad. (2022). *The Landscape of Digital Banking in Cambodia.* Retrieved from https://www.mad.co/insights/the-landscape-of-digital-banking-in-cambodia

Makhija, A. K. (2019). *Accelerating Financial Inclusion in Cambodia Using Artificial Intelligence & Machine Learning.* Retrieved from https://ebook.cam-ed.com/public/images/sarana_file/1627893780.pdf

Malaysian Communications and Multimedia Commission. (2022, August 25). *Population coverage of 4G LTE mobile network in Malaysia from 2016 to 2021* [Graph]. Statista. Retrieved August 12, 2023, from https://www.statista.com/statistics/1051191/malaysia-4g-lte-population-coverage/

Manila Bulletin. (2023, July 12). *Fueling the country's digital shift with the 'real 5G'.* Retrieved from https://mb.com.ph/2023/7/12/fueling-the-country-s-digital-shift-with-the-real-5-g

MarCoPay. (n.d.). *About us.* Retrieved from https://www.marcopayinc.com/AboutUs

Marek, S. (2020, April). *Myanmar - Mobile Network Experience Report.* Retrieved from https://www.opensignal.com/reports/2020/04/myanmar/mobile-network-experience

Market Report. (2021, December 31). *Vietnam Fintech Report In 2021: Viet Nam.* Retrieved from https://marketreport.io/Fintech-vietnam-report

Marry, K., Nguonly, T., Makararavy, T., & Leakhena, C. (2020). *Financial Technology Landscape in the Kingdom of Cambodia.* Technical Report. Retrieved from https://digitaleconomy.gov.kh/public/images/mediahub/Fintech_Landscape_Report_in_Cambodia_Final_Submission.pdf

Martina, M. (2022). *Fintech and Financial Inclusion for MSMEs in Lao PDR* (Doctoral dissertation, School of Public Policy, The University of Tokyo). Retrieved from https://www.pp.u-tokyo.ac.jp/wp-content/uploads/2016/02/R8_Marsili-Martina.pdf

Mason, R. (2022, July 14). *Philippines' digital transformation could make it a new crypto hub. Cointelegraph.* Retrieved from https://cointelegraph.com/news/philippines-digital-transformation-could-make-it-a-new-crypto-hub

Maya. (n.d.). *About us.* Retrieved from https://www.maya.ph/about

Medina, A. (2023, July 25). *Indonesia Launches World's First State-Backed Cryptocurrency Bourse.* ASEAN Briefing. Retrieved from https://www.aseanbriefing.com/news/indonesia-launches-worlds-first-state-backed-cryptocurrency-bourse/

Medina, A. F. (2023, August 17). *Laos Launches Digital Currency Trial.* ASEAN Briefing. Retrieved from https://www.aseanbriefing.com/news/laos-launches-digital-currency-trial/

Meta Platforms, Inc, and Bain & Company, Inc. (2022, September). *Southeast Asia's digital consumers: A new stage of evolution.* Retrieved September 17, 2022, from https://www.edb.gov.sg/en/business-insights/market-and-industry-reports/southeast-asias-digital-consumers-a-new-stage-evolution.html

Metain. (n.d.). *What is Metain.* Metain Co-investment platform. https://metain.io/

Minh, P. (2023, June 17). *Lending money through the app is flourishing, but the risk of "falling into a trap" of black credit.* Vietnam Economic Association. Retrieved from:https://vneconomy.vn/cho-vay-tien-qua-app-no-ro-nguy-co-sap-bay-tin-dung-den.htm

Ministry of Industry and Trade (Vietnam). (2022, December 26). *E-commerce market value in Vietnam from 2014 to 2022 (in billion U.S. dollars)* [Graph]. Statista. Retrieved October 14, 2023, from https://www.statista.com/statistics/986043/vietnam-ecommerce-market-value-revenue/

Mobile Banking Apps on Bank Performance in Vietnam. (n.d.). *International Journal of Research and Review, 8*(4), 391–401. doi:10.52403/ijrr.20210446

Moenjak, T., Kongprajya, A., & Monchaitrakul, C. (2020). *Fintech, financial literacy, and consumer saving and borrowing: The case of Thailand (No. 1100).* ADBI Working Paper Series.

MoneyMatch. (n.d.). *About us.* Retrieved from https://moneymatch.com.bn/about-us

Monix. (n.d.). *About us.* Retrieved from https://www.monix.co.th/about-us

Moore, J. F. (1996). *The Death of Competition: Leadership and Strategy in the Age of Business Ecosystems.* HarperBusiness.

MorganP. L.TrinhL. Q. (2019). Fintech and Financial Literacy in the LAO PDR. *Social Science Research Network.* doi:10.2139/ssrn.3398235

Nair, K. (2023, June 7). *Fahmi: Malaysia's 5G coverage now at 62.1%.* The Star. Retrieved from https://www.thestar.com.my/business/business-news/2023/06/07/fahmi-malaysias-5g-coverage-now-at-621

Nathan, R. J., Setiawan, B., & Quynh, M. N. (2022, March 06). Vietnam during the COVID-19 Pandemic: In-Depth Descriptive Analysis. *Journal of Risk and Financial Management, 15*(3), 125. doi:10.3390/jrfm15030125

National Cyber Security Agency. (2023, April 20). *Number of cyber threats detected and settled by ThaiCERT in Thailand in 2022, by type of threat* [Graph]. Statista. Retrieved August 26, 2023, from https://www.statista.com/statistics/1154735/thailand-number-of-cyber-threats-by-type-of-threat/

Ng Pilipinas, B. S. (2020). *BSP digital payments transformation roadmap 2020-2023*. Retrieved from https://www.bsp.gov.ph/Media_And_Research/Primers%20Faqs/Digital%20Payments%20Transformation%20Roadmap%20Report.pdf

Ngoc, M. (2023, April 7). *MoMo and ZaloPay are leading the market for digital wallets*. Financial & Monetary Market Review. https://thitruongtaichinhtiente.vn/momo-va-zalopay-dan-dau-thi-truong-vi-dien-tu-trong-nuoc-45105.html

Nicoletti, B. (2017). *The Future of Fintech: Integrating Finance and Technology in Financial Services*. Palgrave Macmillan. doi:10.1007/978-3-319-51415-4

NUGPay. (n.d.). *About*. Retrieved from https://nugpay.app/

Nugraha, D. P., Setiawan, B., Nathan, R. J., & Fekete-Farkas, M. (2022). Fintech adoption drivers for innovation for SMEs in Indonesia. *Journal of Open Innovation, 8*(4), 208. doi:10.3390/joitmc8040208

Nurlatifah, H., Saefuddin, A., Nanere, M., & Ratten, V. (2022). Muslimpreneur: Entrepreneur potential characteristics in Indonesia as the country with the largest Muslim population in the world. *Entrepreneurial Innovation: Strategy and Competition Aspects*, 129-139.

Oi, R. (2023, February 21). *Digital Banks Could Be the Key to Promoting Financial Inclusion for Malaysia's B40*. Fintech Malaysia. Retrieved from https://Fintechnews.my/34216/financial-inclusion/digital-banks-could-be-the-key-to-promoting-financial-inclusion-for-malaysias-b40/

OpenGov Asia. (n.d.). https://opengovasia.com/expediting-4g-coverage-for-socio-economic-growth-in-indonesia/

Orpheus Capital. (n.d.). *About us*. Retrieved from https://orpheuscapital.com.my/en/about-us/

Oxford Business Group. (2020, September 23). *Covid-19 and Fintech: Myanmar's chance to expand financial inclusion?* Retrieved from https://oxfordbusinessgroup.com/articles-interviews/covid-19-and-Fintech-myanmars-chance-to-expand-financial-inclusion

PayK. B. Z. (n.d.). *About us*. Retrieved from https://www.kbzpay.com/en/about/

Payd. (n.d.). *Empowering Everyday People*. Retrieved from https://www.justpayd.com/about

Payverse. (2023). *A look at Brunei and Timor's major ewallets*. Retrieved from https://blogeromnet.com/brunei-and-timor-ewallets/?ckattempt=1

PayWatch. (n.d.). *About us*. Retrieved from https://www.paywatch.com.my/about-us

PayWay. (n.d.). *About us*. Retrieved from https://www.payway.com.kh/about-us

Peddlr. (n.d.). *About the product*. Retrieved from https://www.peddlr.io/en/faqs

Pei, S. F. (2018). Singapore approach to develop and regulate Fintech. In T. T. Kuo (Ed.), *R. H.*

Philstar Global. (2023, August 10). *Maya dominates digital banking*. Retrieved from https://www.philstar.com/business/2023/08/10/2287452/maya-dominates-digital-banking

Pi Pay. (n.d.). *Who we are*. Retrieved from https://www.pipay.com/#who-we-are

Pluang. (n.d.). *About us*. Retrieved from https://pluang.com/id/tentang-pluang

Postigo, A. (2023). *Governing the Digital Economy in Thailand: Domestic Regulations and International Agreements (No. 58/2023)*. Perspective.

PricewaterhouseCoopers. (n.d.). *Tech start-up funding trends and outlook: Singapore*. PwC. https://www.pwc.com/sg/en/financial-services/venture-hub/tech-startup-funding-trends-and-outlook.html

Privacy Shield Framework. (n.d.). *Cambodia - e-commerce*. Retrieved from https://www.privacyshield.gov/ps/article?id=Cambodia-eCommerce

PSA (Philippines). (2022, December 2). *Total number of overseas Filipino workers (OFWs) from 2017 to 2021 (in 1,000s)* [Graph]. Statista. Retrieved September 02, 2023, from https://www.statista.com/statistics/1287067/philippines-number-of-overseas-filipino-workers/PwC

Quang, D. P., Huu, T. K., & Manh, H. P. (2022). Fintech Development and Cooperation Strategies of Vietnamese Commercial Banks. *International Journal of Advanced Engineering and Management Research, 07*(01), 53–65. doi:10.51505/IJAEMR.2022.7104

Quimba, F. M. A., Barral, M. A. A., & Carlos, J. C. T. (2021). *Analysis of the Fintech Landscape in the Philippines (No. 2021-29)*. PIDS Discussion Paper Series.

Rabbit Line Pay. (n.d.). *About us*. Retrieved from https://pay.line.me/portal/th/main

Realbox. (n.d.). *The future of real estate investment*. Realbox. https://realbox.io/en

Reed, J. (2022, January 20). *Thailand's Bitkub plans crypto expansion in SE Asia*. Financial Times. Retrieved from https://www.ft.com/content/0aa3acff-e6c2-4482-8761-991f76cee7f7

Reuters. (2023, May 16). *Indonesia's biggest Islamic bank says customer data safe amid reports of breach*. Finance. Retrieved from: https://www.reuters.com/business/finance/indonesias-biggest-islamic-bank-says-customer-data-safe-amid-reports-breach-2023-05-16/

RHB. (n.d.). *Who we are*. Retrieved from: https://www.rhbgroup.com/others/about-us/who-we-are.html

Saffa, A. (2023, June 13). *Expediting 4G coverage for Socio-Economic growth in Indonesia*. Academic Press.

SCB. (2020). *Myanmar E-Commerce Market - Growing Trade Opportunities*. Retrieved from https://www.scb.co.th/en/personal-banking/stories/business-maker/myanmar-e-commerce.html

SCB. (2020). *Penetrate Cambodian Market through E-Commerce to Fight Against COVID-19*. Retrieved from https://www.scb.co.th/en/personal-banking/stories/business-maker/cambodia-e-commerce.html

Schellhase, J., & Garcia, A. (2019). *Fintech in the Philippines: Assessing the state of play*. Milken Institute.

Shop. (n.d.). *About us*. Retrieved from https://pages.shop.com.mm/wow/i/mm/about-us/about-us

Singapore, H. G. B. S. D. (2022, November 29). *Mobile wallet users Singapore 2020-2025*. https://www.statista.com/statistics/1325918/singapore-number-of-mobile-wallet-users

Singtel. (n.d.). *About 5G*. Retrieved from https://www.singtel.com/personal/products-services/mobile/5g

Soft Space. (n.d.). *About us*. Retrieved from https://www.softspace.com.my/about-us/

Soriano, M., Ziegler, T., Umer, Z., Chen, H., Jenweeranon, P., Zhang, B. Z., & Liu, K. (2019). *The ASEAN Fintech ecosystem benchmarking study*. Academic Press.

Standard Insights. (2022, September 13). *Share of Indonesians who owned a banking or insurance app on their phone in 2022* [Graph]. Statista. Retrieved August 16, 2023, from https://www.statista.com/statistics/1338322/indonesia-ownership-of-mobile-banking-or-insurance-app/

Statista. (2020). *Share of total population with 3G mobile network coverage in Vietnam from 2017 to 2020*. Retrieved from https://www.statista.com/statistics/1291551/vietnam-population-with-3g-mobile-network-coverage

Statista. (2022). *Fintech In Vietnam - Statista Digital Market Outlook – Market Report*. Author.

Statista. (2022). *Fintech industry market value Thailand 2018-2021*. Retrieved from https://www.statista.com/statistics/1284830/thailand-market-value-of-the-Fintech-sector/

Statista. (2022). *Fintech - Singapore*. Retrieved July 29, 2023, from https://www.statista.com/outlook/dmo/Fintech/singapore

Statista. (2022, June 27). *Cashless payments adoption rate SEA 2021, by country*. Retrieved from https://www.statista.com/statistics/1234061/sea-cashless-payments-adoption-rate-by-country/

Statista. (2022, November 29). *Mobile wallet users Singapore 2020-2025*. https://www.statista.com/statistics/1325918/singapore-number-of-mobile-wallet-users

Statista. (2022, November). *Funding value for cryptocurrency companies in Singapore*. Retrieved from https://www.statista.com/statistics/1294117/singapore-cryptocurrency-funding-by-deals-and-value/

Statista. (2023, April). *Cryptocurrencies in Thailand*. Retrieved from https://www.statista.com/outlook/dmo/Fintech/digital-assets/cryptocurrencies/thailand724market. (n.d). About us. Retrieved from https://insure.724.co.th/about

Statista. (2023, April). *Transaction Value. Fintech – Malaysia*. Retrieved from https://www.statista.com/outlook/dmo/Fintech/malaysia#transaction-value

Statista. (2023, August 14). *Internet penetration rate in Thailand 2019-2028*. Retrieved from https://www.statista.com/statistics/975067/internet-penetration-rate-in-thailand

Statista. (2023). *eCommerce - Cambodia*. Retrieved from https://www.statista.com/outlook/dmo/ecommerce/cambodia

Statista. (2023). *eCommerce - Myanmar*. Retrieved from https://www.statista.com/outlook/dmo/ecommerce/myanmar

Statista. (2023, February 13). *Internet penetration rate in Brunei from 2011 to 2020*. Retrieved from https://www.statista.com/statistics/767584/internet-penetration-rate-brunei/

Statista. (2023). *Fintech - Brunei*. Retrieved from https://www.statista.com/outlook/dmo/Fintech/brunei-darussalam

Statista. (2023). *Fintech - Cambodia*. Retrieved from https://www.statista.com/outlook/dmo/Fintech/cambodia

Statista. (2023). *Fintech – Indonesia*. Statista Market forecast. https://www.statista.com/outlook/dmo/Fintech/indonesia#transaction-value

Statista. (2023). *Fintech - Laos*. Retrieved from https://www.statista.com/outlook/dmo/Fintech/laos#transaction-value

Statista. (2023). *Fintech - Myanmar - Transaction Value*. Retrieved from https://www.statista.com/outlook/dmo/Fintech/myanmar

Statista. (2023). *Internet penetration rate in the Philippines*. Retrieved from https://www.statista.com/statistics/975072/internet-penetration-rate-in-the-philippines

Statista. (2023, June 26). *Number of users of digital payments in Malaysia 2018-2027 (in million users)* [Graph]. Statista. Retrieved August 12, 2023, from https://www.statista.com/forecasts/1367668/malaysia-digital-payment-users

Statista. (2023). *Number of internet users in Thailand from 2017 to 2020 with a forecast through 2026*. Retrieved from https://www.statista.com/statistics/553730/number-of-internet-users-thailand/

Statista. (2023). *Total population of the ASEAN countries from 2018 to 2028*. Retrieved from https://www.statista.com/statistics/796222/total-population-of-the-asean-countries/

Statista. (2023). *Transaction Value. Fintech in the Philippines*. Retrieved from https://www.statista.com/outlook/dmo/Fintech/philippines

Syfe. (n.d.). *The leading all-in-one digital investment platform for Asia-Pacific*. Retrieved from https://www.syfe.com/about-us

Tao, J., & Azhgaliyeva, D. (2018). *The role of green Fintech for Singapore: Risks and benefits*. https://scholarbank.nus.edu.sg/bitstream/10635/151199/1/4_Jacqueline_TAO_and_Dina_

Tech Collective. (2023, April 14). *Fintech trends: The rise of digital loans in Malaysia*. Retrieved from https://techcollectivesea.com/2023/04/14/Fintech-trends-digital-loans-malaysia/

Thanthong-Knight, R. (2021, November 30). *Thai Crypto Unicorn Plots Expansion in Bid to Be Asia's Coinbase*. Bloomberg. Retrieved from https://www.bloomberg.com/news/articles/2021-11-30/thai-crypto-unicorn-plots-expansion-in-bid-to-be-asia-s-coinbase?in_source=embedded-checkout-banner

The Asian Banker. (2022, May 26). *BIBD maintains leading market position in retail loans and deposits*. Retrieved from https://www.theasianbanker.com/updates-and-articles/best-retail-bank-in-brunei-bank-islam-brunei-darussalam-bibd-2022#:~:text=The%20bank's%20NEXGEN%20Wallet%20rec

The Australian Trade and Investment Commission. (2020). *Digital Banking in Vietnam*. Author.

The International Trade Administration. (2022, July 30). *Laos - eCommerce*. Retrieved from https://www.trade.gov/country-commercial-guides/laos-ecommerce

The World Bank. (2020). *Mobile cellular subscriptions (per 100 people) – Lao PDR, World*. Retrieved from https://data.worldbank.org/indicator/IT.CEL.SETS.P2?locations=LA-1W

Tomas, J. (2022, October 25). *Thailand to reach 5G coverage of 85% by end-2022*. Retrieved from https://www.rcrwireless.com/20221025/5g/thailand-reach-5g-coverage-85-end-2022-true

Tomás, J. P. (2022, October 26). *XL Axiata expects 5G momentum in Indonesia to start around 2025*. RCR Wireless News. https://www.rcrwireless.com/20221026/5g/xl-axiata-expects-5g-momentum-indonesia

TrueMoney. (n.d.). *About us*. Retrieved from https://www.truemoney.com/about/

Truong, N. (2023, June 20). *Employees of 13 banks questioned about selling customer data*. Academic Press.

United Overseas Bank. (2021, November 22). *Distribution of financial technology (Fintech) firms in Thailand in 2021, by type of firm* [Graph]. Statista. Retrieved August 19, 2023, from https://www.statista.com/statistics/1293999/thailand-distribution-of-Fintech-firms-by-firm-type/

United Overseas Bank. (2022, November 1). *Number of operating Fintech companies in the Philippines from 2017 to 2022* [Graph]. Statista. Retrieved August 26, 2023, from https://www.statista.com/statistics/1247613/number-of-Fintech-firms-philippines/

United Overseas Bank Limited. (2021, November). *Fintech in Thailand 3Q2021: Thailand 4.0 plots way forward*. Retrieved from https://www.uobgroup.com/techecosystem/news-insights-Fintech-in-thailand-3q-2021.html

United Overseas Bank Limited. (2022, April). *Shifting consumer habits drive Malaysia Fintech growth*. Fintech in ASEAN 2021 report. Retrieved from https://www.uobgroup.com/techecosystem/news-insights-consumer-research-malaysia.html

United Overseas Bank Limited. (2022, November). *Fintech in ASEAN 2022: Finance, Reimagined*. Retrieved from https://www.uobgroup.com/techecosystem/news-insights-Fintech-in-asean-2022.html

UOB. PwC, SAF. (2021). *Fintech in ASEAN 2021: Digital takes flight*. https://singaporeFintech.org/Fintech-in-asean-2021/

Vietnam, I. (2021, October 28). *5 Reasons Peer-to-Peer Lending is Really Hot in Vietnam*. InCorp Vietnam. https://www.cekindo.vn/blog/reasons-peer-to-peer-lending-hot-vietnam/

Vietnam as of October 2022 [Graph]. (n.d.). Statista. Retrieved July 23, 2023, from https://www.statista.com/statistics/1105406/vietnam-leading-e-payment-services/

Vietnam Social Security Portal. (2022, February 20). *Vietnam records nearly 1,400 cyber-attacks in January*. Retrieved from https://vss.gov.vn/english/news/Pages/external-information.aspx?ItemID=10306&CateID=184

Vietnam's service ecosystem. https://www.generalatlantic.com/media-article/vnlife-announces-series-b-funding-round-led-by-general-atlantic-and-dragoneer/

Vigilia, C. (2023, April 4). Thailand moves closer to the launch of digital-only banks. *The Asian Banker*. Retrieved from https://www.theasianbanker.com/updates-and-articles/thailand-moves-closer-to-creation-of-digital-banks

Visa Inc. (2022). *Cashless payments adoption rate in Southeast Asia in 2021, by country* [Graph]. Statista. Retrieved July 29, 2023, from https://www.statista.com/statistics/1234061/sea-cashless-payments-adoption-rate-by-country/

VNExpress. (n.d.). Retrieved from: https://e.vnexpress.net/news/news/employees-from-13-banks-investigated-for-allegedly-selling-customers-data-4619893.html

Volopay. (n.d.). *The financial control centre to manage*. Retrieved from https://www.volopay.com/sg/

Waloan. (n.d.). *About us*. Retrieved from https://www.waloan.app/en.html

Wave Money. (n.d.). *About us*. Retrieved from https://wavemoney.com.mm/about-us

Weelago. (n.d.). *Sellers center.* Retrieved from https://weelago.com/seller-center/#:~:text=Weelago.com%20is%20Brunei's%20No,and%20largest%20online%20shopping%20mall

World Bank. (2017). *The Global Findex Database*. Available online: https://globalfindex.worldbank.org/

World Bank. (2022). *GDP per capita (current US$) – Vietnam* [Data file]. Retrieved from https://data.worldbank.org/indicator/NY.GDP.PCAP.CD?locations=VN

World Bank. (2022). *World Development Indicators. GDP per capita (current US$) – Vietnam* [Data file]. Retrieved from https://data.worldbank.org/indicator/NY.GDP.PCAP.CD?locations=VN

World Bank. (2023). *Population, total - Brunei Darussalam*. Retrieved from https://data.worldbank.org/indicator/SP.POP.TOTL?locations=BN

World Bank. (2023). *Population, total - Cambodia*. Retrieved from https://data.worldbank.org/indicator/SP.POP.TOTL?locations=KH

World Bank. (2023). *Population, total - Lao PDR*. Retrieved from https://data.worldbank.org/indicator/SP.POP.TOTL?locations=LA

World Bank. (2023). *Population, total - Myanmar*. Retrieved from https://data.worldbank.org/indicator/SP.POP.TOTL?locations=MM

World Bank. (2023). *Population, total - Philippines*. Retrieved from https://data.worldbank.org/indicator/SP.POP.TOTL?locations=PH

World Bank. (2023). *Population - total Thailand*. Retrieved from https://data.worldbank.org/indicator/SP.POP.TOTL?locations=TH

World Bank. (2023, June 29). *Value of remittances received in Myanmar from 2013 to 2022 (in billion U.S. dollars)* [Graph]. Statista. Retrieved September 09, 2023, from https://www.statista.com/statistics/880741/myanmar-value-of-remittances/

Wyman, O. (2020). *Singapore Fintech Landscape 2020 and Beyond*. Singapore Fintech Association (SFA). Retrieved from: https://www.oliverwyman.com/content/dam/oliverwyman/v2/publications/2020/dec/singpore-Fintech-landscape-2020-andbeyond.pdf

Yahaya, M. H., & Ahmad, K. (2018). Financial inclusion through efficient zakat distribution for poverty alleviation in Malaysia: Using fintech & mobile banking. In *Proceeding of the 5th International Conference on Management and Muamalah* (pp. 15-31). Academic Press.

Zaghlol, A. K., Ramdhan, N. A., & Othman, N. (2021). The Nexus between Fintech Adoption and Financial Development in Malaysia: An Overview. *Global Business and Management Research*, *13*(4).

Zheng, A. H. Y., Ab-Rahim, R., & Jing, A. H. Y. (2022). Examining the Fintech Ecosystem of ASEAN-6 Countries. *Asia-Pacific Social Science Review, 22*(2). Retrieved from https://www.dlsu.edu.ph/wp-content/uploads/pdf/research/journals/apssr/2022-June-vol22-2/2-zheng.pdf

ZigWay. (n.d.). *Who we are*. Retrieved from https://www.zigway.co/

Ziwen, C. (2023, September 5). *Police in China and Myanmar detain 269 in cyber scam crackdown*. Retrieved from https://www.scmp.com/news/china/diplomacy/article/3233506/police-china-and-myanmar-detain-269-cyber-scam-crackdown

Chapter 4
Advancements in the Indian Fintech Landscape

Jigmet Stobdan
University of Ladakh, India

Sunil Kumar
University of Jammu, India

ABSTRACT

The financial sector across the globe has been witnessing continuous disruptions every year. India is not an exception to the phenomenon. India figured in the list of economies where Fintech adoption was one of the highest in the year 2021. This kind of rare feat can be attributed to the conducive ecosystem that has been ensured by the state and subjects of the country over the years. During the past few years especially after 2016, there has been a paradigm shift in the Indian Fintech landscape. Numerous advancements have taken place in the sector and new players are emerging as serious threats to established financial institutions. Fintech has become synonymous with innovations and disruptions. This chapter aims to explain the current state of affairs and the innovations in the Indian Fintech landscape. The authors intend to show how new fintech players are coming up with out-of-the-box thoughts and disrupting the status quo of established financial institutions.

INTRODUCTION

The terms financial inclusion and financial technologies have taken center stage in the business world in recent years. Fintech companies are known for disrupting the market and consequently reshaping it into a highly competitive one. The unfathomable progress in the digital technology arena in recent years has resulted in humans' over-dependence on technology (Wiyono & Kirana, 2021). The financial sector is not new to this new technological arena, with new-generation entrepreneurs and angel investors hoping to leverage game-changing innovation in financial services to bridge the lacuna that emerged in the aftermath of the crisis (Vives, 2019), and the turbulence has become a buzzword in the business sector. Technology in the financial sector has assumed the term "financial technology," popularly referred to as "FinTech"

DOI: 10.4018/979-8-3693-1561-3.ch004

(Campanella et al., 2023), and it has received due attention from academic and business practitioners recently, often features in public discourse and news (Lagna & Ravishankar, 2022). Essentially, it denotes harmonizing cutting-edge technology into financial services and processes. Identified as a key technical term, FinTech, short for financial technology, is mainly driven by innovative and emerging technologies (Li & Xu, 2021). It includes the application of computing and digital technologies in offering financial services, redefining how financial institutions operate, and significantly influencing our lives. This has given rise to the emergence of allied terms like PayTech, InsurTech, RegTech, and FinTech (Sangwan et al., 2019). According to Zavolokina et al. (2017), "FinTech" symbolizes the integration of finance and information technology. Gai et al. (2018) describe FinTech as an emerging term that represents the adoption of novel technologies by financial institutions. It includes various new business models, technological applications, and services that substantially affect the financial market and service delivery. Its rise to importance is linked to numerous benefits, such as enhancing operational efficiency, reducing costs, challenging traditional industry structures, blurring industry boundaries, fostering strategic disintermediation, creating new entrepreneurial opportunities, and making financial services more accessible (Agarwal & Zhang, 2020; Cao et al., 2020; Yang et al., 2020; Suryono et al., 2020). Key technologies in FinTech include internet technology like big data (Chen et al. 2017), distributed technologies (such as blockchain and cloud computing) (Belanche et al., 2019; Chen et al., 2019; Wamba et al., 2020), artificial intelligence (Belanche et al., 2019), Internet and the Internet of Things (Ruan et al., 2019), and security technologies (Wamba et al., 2020). These technologies have significantly altered the traditional development model of the financial sector (Li & Xu, 2021).

FINTECH IN INDIA

Fintech is among the fastest-growing sectors in the financial services arena worldwide and has emerged as the epicenter of customer-centric innovation, which disrupted financial sectors and brought a paradigm shift in how financial services are offered (BCG-FICCI, 2022). In sync with global trends, the Fintech sector in India has witnessed massive growth in recent years. The sector is primarily driven by innovative entrepreneurs (Firms) who have pooled their know-how and expertise to strengthen the Fintech ecosystem in India. They have converted the challenges thrown by the pandemic into opportunities by leveraging technologies to reach larger sections of society. Thanks to the substantial increase in smartphone penetration and easy access to high-speed internet, Fintech companies have been able to speedily spread their reach across the length and breadth of India. In a report by Netscribe on the Fintech market 2021, India had achieved the milestone of the highest financial technology adoption rate (87%) (Figure 1), greater than the average world rate of (64%). Moreover, the Indian fintech market size has been valued at US$ 584 Bn in the year 2022 and is estimated to touch US$ 2.1 Tn by the year 2030 at a CAGR of 18%, as per a report by Inc42. The Indian market is bestowed with a large proportion of the youth population, who are tech-savvy and love adopting new technologies in all spheres of their life, and finance is not an exception. There were 1145.45 million wireless subscribers in India as of 30th September 2022, comprising 518.31 million rural subscribers and the rest, i.e., 627.14 million from urban areas (TRAI, 2022). Fintech companies strive to fulfill consumers' unmet demands in financial sectors by leveraging cutting-edge financial technologies. In recent years, the Fintech adoption rate in India has witnessed a manifold rise, and a large number of Fintech start-ups have also entered the financial industry and achieved the Unicorns and Soonicorns status at a rapid pace but, at the same time, some are unable to keep up with the competition in the market.

The Fintech in India has evolved as one of the most dynamic sectors, rewriting the norms for financial service delivery. With an ever-increasing proportion of youth in the population and an increase in mobile subscribers, India offers a profitable opportunity for Fintech firms. Moreover, the government of India's historical initiatives, like JAM Trinity, has opened the financial market for fintech companies. India has a vibrant Fintech business ecosystem with platforms such as instant payments, investment advice, hassle-free and documentation-free, easy loan sanction, efficient insurance advisory and distribution, and a bouquet of other financial services previously done manually but now being digitalized. This chapter intends to explore the recent advancements in the Fintech sector of India.

DIGITAL PAYMENTS: A DRIVER OF GROWTH

Digital payments have been the most notable success story in the Indian Fintech landscape. The Unified Payments Interface (UPI), an instant real-time payment system developed by the National Payments Corporation of India (NPCI), has revolutionized the transactions system in India. The surge in mobile internet users has also facilitated the widespread adoption of digital wallets and online banking services. The digital payments sector has seen exponential growth in India. The introduction of the Unified Payments Interface (UPI) by the National Payments Corporation of India (NPCI) has simplified transactions, making digital payments accessible to a wider audience (Shah & Sinha, 2021).

After 2016, India has seen a substantial technological transformation in governance. Integrating state services with technology has gained growth momentum, enabling efficient last-mile delivery at the click of a mouse. As an aspect of the mission to digitalize the financial sector and the economy, the Government of India has been pushing hard to ensure a continuous rise in digital payment transactions. The prime goal of digital India is to attain a "Faceless, Paperless, Cashless" society and to ensure the attainment of this goal the Govt. has prioritised the large-scale promotion of digital payments. There has been a dramatic rise in digital payment transactions in India recently, especially after 2016 (Figure 2). Various easy-to-use digital payments methods like Bharat Interface for Money-Unified Payments Interface (BHIM-UPI), Immediate Payment Service (IMPS), prepaid payment instruments (PPIs), and the National Electronic Toll Collection (NETC) system have been downloaded by users in crores. These user-friendly apps have brought disruptions in the payment sectors, resulting in the substantial increase in Person-to-Person (P2P) and Person-to-Merchant (P2M) transactions. But, BHIM-UPI achieved the status of most popular method of payment among users. Moreover, the flagship initiative of the Government of India, Digital India program, intends to turn India into a digitally enabled community and knowledge-based economy. In this direction, the Ministry of Electronics & Information Technology (MeitY), Govt of India takes charge of popularising digital transactions, and the Ministry collaborates with other stakeholders like state governments, banks, and other financial service providers to ensure a high rate of adoption of digital payments in India. This kind of collaboration positively affects the adoption of digital payments in India. Moreover, contactless digital payment methods like BHIM-UPI were essential in ensuring social distancing with continuity in business operations, especially during the pandemic.

INNOVATION BY INDIA IN FINTECH: UNIFIED PAYMENTS INTERFACE (UPI)

Unified Payments Interface, popularly called UPI in India, is an innovative and watershed product from the National Payments Corporation of India (NPCI). UPI is seen as integrating a bouquet of several banking features to ensure smooth merchant payment and money transfer. It ensures prompt fund remittances, access to different bank accounts on the go, quick utility bill payments, Quick Response (QR) code payments, etc. After demonetization in 2016, most banks in India offer UPI-enabled services on their banking applications.

The peculiar features that make UPI popular are:

- One mobile application for accessing different bank accounts.
- Facility of round-the-clock fund remittance through mobile.
- Non-requirement of IFSC, card details, etc., for fund remittances. Only the virtual address of the customer is required, which provides a sense of security.
- Merchant Payment with a single application.

UPI was initially introduced as a pilot project on April 11, 2016, by then Reserve Bank of India Governor Dr. Raghuram Rajan in Mumbai. Since then, participating banks have developed their UPI-enabled apps on various mobile applications. Starting with a meager 1Mn transactions in 2016, UPI has achieved the level of 10Bn transactions in 2023 with highest ever volume record of 10.58 Bn transactions in August 2023, and experts estimate that the UPI platform will register daily transactions of 1 Bn by 2025.

LENDING: EASY ACCESS TO FINANCE

The recent report by Inc42 has estimated Indian lending tech to grow to the level of $270 Bn by 2030, and out of this, consumer lending is expected to be the most sought-after sector by investors owing to the size of the market and ever-increasing demand for consumer-led consumption in India. The digital lending sector has attained the status of a substantial facilitator of growth in India with rapid progress in past years. Commercial banks and various non-banking financial institutions are pushing hard on digital lending with new-age fintech companies. All the market participants strive hard to capitalize on this progressive path of transformation by introducing innovative approaches and offering a bouquet of new services with an eye on seizing market share. The customer orientation philosophy has become the main focus for lending tech companies in India. Lending tech companies are developing state-of-the-art technologies like, Artificial Intelligence (AI), Machine Learning (ML), APIs, etc. Moreover, the Central Bank of the Country (RBI) has offered its support to the digital lending sector by framing sound rules and regulations to ensure compliance and creating a congenial environment for entities to adapt their business models. In this direction, RBI has already notified guidelines on digital lending, co-lending, Co-Branded credit card, etc., and these measures are intended to give push to digital lending landscape by providing foundation for creating a conducive environment for speedy growth.

Lending tech firms have revolutionized the lending sphere in India by capitalizing on modern technology for evaluating the credit scores of potential clients and by offering mini-sized loans to meet the requirements of modern generations. The concept of Buy Now Pay Later (BNPL) is changing the landscape of short-term credit in India, allowing clients to pay for their purchases later, generally interest-free. The

BNPL's dramatic growth in India is incredible, and the report by Worldpay from FIS predicted that BNPL is emerging as the speediest growing e-commerce digital means in India and is forecasted to achieve the target of 9% of the total electronic commerce market share by 2024. In other words, lending tech firms have made credit easily accessible with lesser documentation and formalities, which consequently helps small businesses and individuals earlier excluded from conventional brick-and-mortar banking systems. Moreover, a new set of Peer-to-Peer (P2P) lending platforms developed by Fintech firms have gained the participants' attention as it offers an alternative to traditional banking services. These steps have made the Indian financial system genuinely inclusive. The explosion of embedded finance is expected to boost digital payments and credit penetration (BCG, 2022). Online market platforms like (Amazon, Flipkart), e-commerce enablers (Shopify, WooCommerce), traditional lenders (Bajaj Markets), and merchant discovery platforms (Zest, Simpl) now occupy various stages in the journey from product search, purchase, fulfillment, and financing via BNPL and India's BNPL systems are estimated to grow from ~INR 100,000 Cr.19 in FY21 to over INR 700,000 Cr.19 by FY26 (BCG, 2022).

BLOCKCHAIN: PROMOTING TRANSPARENCY AND A SENSE OF SECURITY

Blockchain is a digital, immutable, transparent, and distributed ledger system that chronologically records transactions in almost real-time (Coindesk, 2016). The introduction and record of transactions in a ledger are subject to the approval of all the participants (called nodes) of the Blockchain network (Chepurnoy et al., 2016). Furthermore, Blockchain records are immutable, transparently viewable, and accessible by all participants, which provides a persistent way of security and control of the data records by preventing their manipulation and errors (FinTech Futures, 2017)

Blockchain technology has been disrupting the fintech industry in many ways, for instance, minimising operational expenditure and time, quick identification process, non-requirement of third parties, etc. This technological intervention has helped the financial industry improve its transformation. Blockchain technology in India is being adopted to unleash its power to offer security and transparency in financial transactions and is gaining momentum in areas like Know Your Customer (KYC), fraud prevention, and payments.

India's serious inclination toward Blockchain-based FinTech applications can be witnessed from the proactive steps taken by the Reserve Bank of India (RBI), the country's central bank. Since 2017, RBI has carried out several studies on Blockchain and its Distributed Ledger Technology's (DLT) implementation for a decentralized and cashless financial system (Priyaranjan et al., 2020). In order to expedite the implementation of Blockchain technology, the country's Supreme Court permitted Indian commercial banks to get involved in the Blockchain Technology service and other allied businesses (Simms, 2020). Many provincial governments have already adopted this advanced technology to improve efficiency. For instance, one of the Indian states i.e, the Telangana government, has taken the decision to adopt Blockchain for digitising land records and other official data management (Sharma, 2018), and the Karnataka government hosts India's Centre of Excellence (CoE) for Blockchain Technology (Choudhury, 2020; THBL, 2018).

(PoC). These include trade finance, supply chain finance, E-KYC (Electronic – Know Your Customer) document management, cross border payments, and employee loyalty or rewards.

Figure 1 shows the Blockchain use cases in India developed into the proof of concept.

Figure 1. Fintech adoption rate in different countries
Source: https://www.ey.com

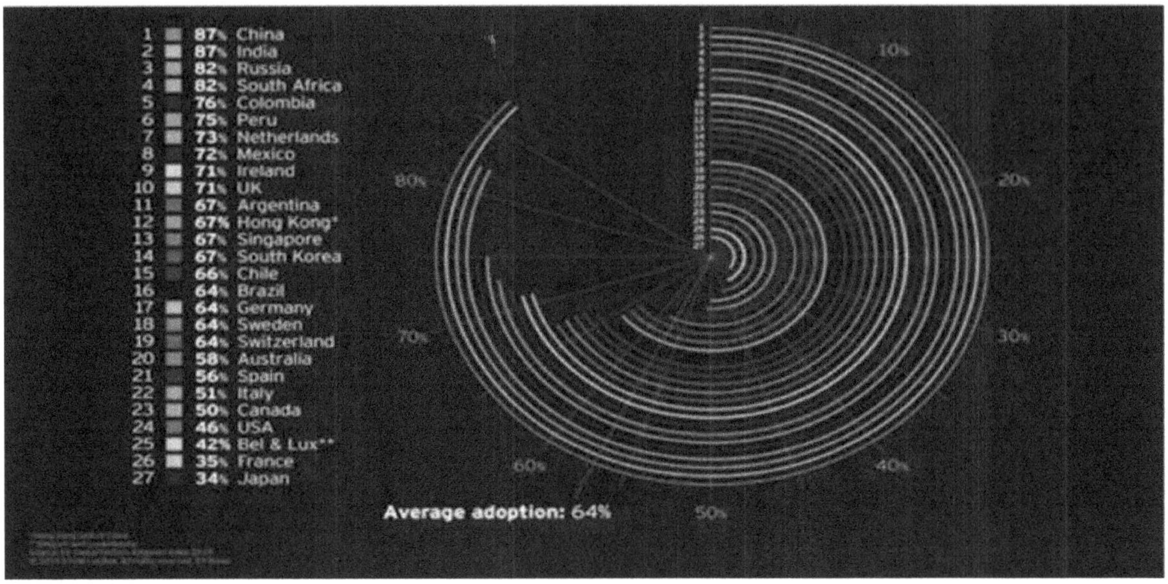

Figure 2. State of India's digital economy
Source: Statista, NPCI, Bain & Company, App Annie, Cable.co UK, Inc42.

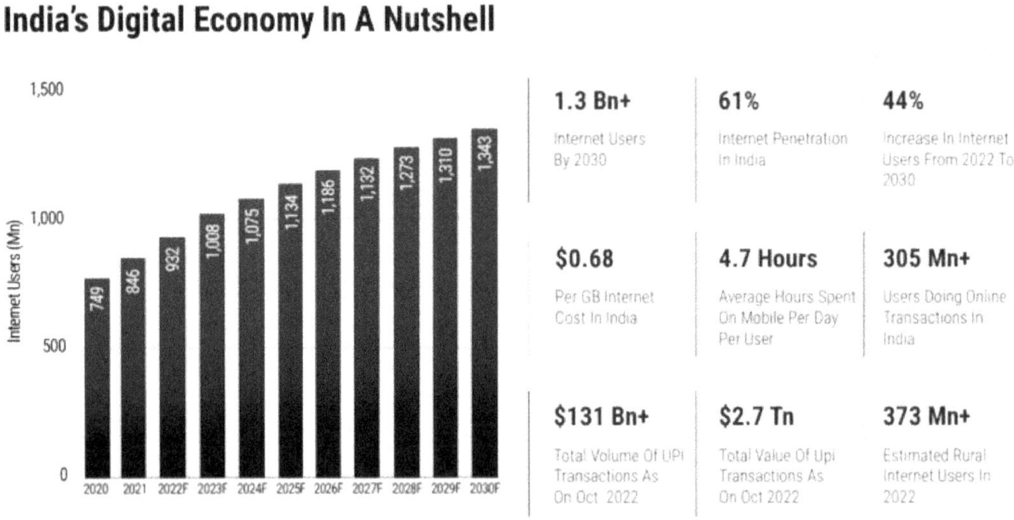

(PoC). These include trade finance, supply chain finance, E-KYC (Electronic – Know Your Customer) document management, cross border payments, and employee loyalty or rewards.

Figure 3. depicts the blockchain applications in India, which include areas like customer loyalty, trade finance, E-KYC electronics know-your-clients, foreign remittances, supply chain finance, etc. The main instances of blockchain applications by Indian entities are:

Figure 3. Blockchain applications by Indian financial entities
Source: Deloitte, 2017

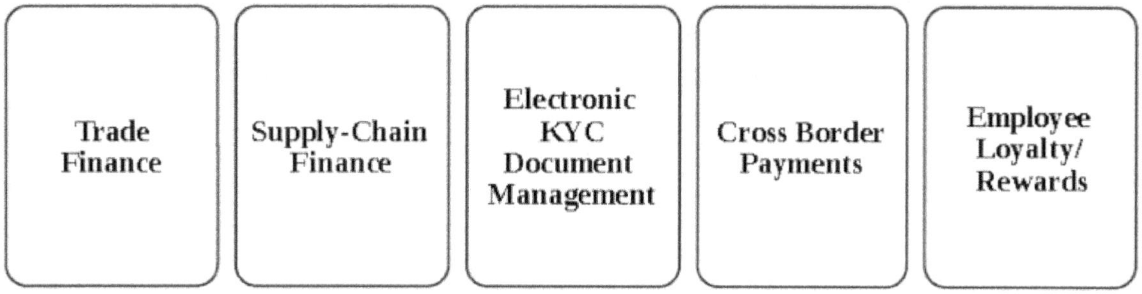

Customer loyalty and reward programs: Deloitte India introduced a Blockchain-based pilot project for maintaining transparency and seamless monetization of loyalty/rewards programs through e-wallets which minimize errors and easily cover the management of customer rewards and recognition programs (Deloitte, 2017).

Trade finance: ICICI Bank was India's first and one of the world's few banks to adopt blockchain technology for executing international trade finance and remittance in partnership with Dubai-based bank Emirate NBD.

E-KYC: Indian FinTech startup Elemential implemented E-KYC by collaborating with ICICI Bank, IDFC Bank, Kotak Mahindra Bank, IndusInd Bank, RBL Bank, and HDFC Securities (IFC, 2017).

Cross-border payments: Stellar India Consultants has partnered with four financial institutions to facilitate affordable international money transfers to the Philippines, as well as cross-border payments between India, Europe, Kenya, Ghana, and Nigeria. This initiative includes collaborations between Axis and Dubai-based RAKBank, as well as Yes, Kotak, and IndusInd, who are working in conjunction with RippleNet. These five private sector banks in India are presently engaged in trials of Blockchain technology, predominantly concentrating on cross-border remittances and trade settlements (VK, 2019).

Supply chain finance: Bajaj Electricals has adopted Blockchain-based 'smart contracts' for facilitating 'supplier finance' in partnership with Yes Bank, IBM and Cateina Technologies.

The implementation has enabled the organisation to reduce the time taken for payment processing to nearly instantaneous, a significant improvement from the earlier timeframe of 4-5 days (Manda & Polisetty, 2018).

REGULATORY FRAMEWORK: STRIKING THE BALANCE BETWEEN INNOVATION AND SECURITY

The regulatory environment for fintech in India is still in the evolving phase to keep pace with rapid advancements. Government and regulatory bodies in India have been providing perpetual support to nurturing innovation in the fintech industry while also ensuring the protection of consumer interests and the overall healthy development of the financial industry. This approach of government and regulatory authorities helps all stakeholders to prosper while working within the boundary of laid down guidelines.

In India, as of now, there is an absence of a uniform set of regulations that regulate all aspects of fintech services, and in a way regulatory framework for fintech is fragmented. This absence of a comprehensive set of regulations poses severe challenges in ensuring strict regulation of the industry and its growth. The central regulatory bodies that govern the fintech industry in India comprise the National Payments Corporation of India (NPCI), the Ministry of Corporate Affairs (MCA), the Ministry of Electronics and Information Technology (MEITY), the Reserve Bank of India (RBI), the Securities Exchange Board of India (SEBI), and the Insurance Regulatory and Development Authority of India (IRDAI). These regulatory bodies are doing their bit to promote the growth of the fintech industry in India. For example, in 2022, the RBI came up with its Payments Vision 2025, which strongly focuses on cross-border payments as a main thrust area in its recommendations. Similarly, to reach globally, the NPCI established NPCI International Payments Limited (NIPL), a wholly-owned subsidiary dedicated to promoting RuPay and UPI services in other countries. Through bilateral cooperation, agreements have been reached with countries like France, Singapore, the UAE, and the United Kingdom to promote UPI adoption. In the same vein, The RBI issued guidelines for Peer-to-Peer (P2P) Lending Platforms in 2017 and released the guidelines on digital lending, outlining eligibility criteria, prudential norms, and risk management practices to protect the interests of lenders and borrowers. Moreover, RBI's Payment Vision 2025 on the theme of 'E-Payments for Everyone, Everywhere, Everytime' shows clear intention on several goalposts focusing on themes like Innovation, Inclusion, Integrity, Institutionalization, and Internalization. It clearly shows a clear regulatory inclination towards growth and innovation with a simultaneous focus on enhanced scrutiny and audit. These kinds of initiatives will go a long way in pushing Fintech companies to build and strengthen organisational capabilities like sound risk management and stringent compliance. This payment vision by RBI is critical to achieving the intended outcomes.

Similarly, to safeguard policyholders' interests, promote innovation in the insurance industry, and ensure ease of transactions, IRDAI has also released its regulatory sandbox framework. The IRDAI has taken some proactive stances in encouraging fintech adoption in the insurance sector while ensuring that policyholders' and insurance product buyers' interests are protected.

Likewise, Securities Market regulator SEBI has issued relevant regulations that provide guidelines for establishing and operating Alternative Investment Funds (AIF), such as private equity funds, venture capital funds, and other similar investment vehicles. The regulations prescribe minimum disclosure obligations, guidelines for investor protection, registration criteria, investment restrictions, etc., for AIFs in India. These regulations are in the right direction for promoting transparency, investor confidence, and responsible practices among fintech-driven AIFs.

CHALLENGES AND FUTURE DIRECTIONS

Undoubtedly, the emergence of Fintech has disrupted the status quo of incumbent financial institutions. These new-age companies are rewriting the norms of the financial industry by challenging the conventional financial culture practiced by brick-and-mortar financial institutions, increasing user experiences, and ensuring financial inclusion. Fintech in India is still in its infancy and has brought a paradigm shift in the financial industry thanks to the India stack. As Fintech strives to reshape the country's financial landscape, more disruptive innovations are still in the store for the future. Moreover, addressing the challenges encountered by Fintech in India calls for a multi-faceted approach, which inter-alia includes technological intervention, strategic cooperation, regulatory intervention, etc.:

Improving Digital Infrastructure and Strengthening Cybersecurity: The government needs to invest in and improve digital infrastructure to ensure internet connectivity 24x7 across the length and breadth of the country. This can help in expanding the reach of FinTech services to underbanked populations. There is an urgent need to build sound cybersecurity protocols to safeguard against data thefts and cyber-attacks. Moreover, regular audits, adoption of advanced security tools, and regular employee training in cybersecurity best practices are indispensable.

Collaborations: For the healthy growth of the financial industry in India, both conventional financial institutions and new-age fintech firms need to collaborate with each other to capitalize on the synergistic effects of the collaboration. Collaboration between conventional financial institutions and new-age fintech companies will foster a conducive ecosystem of cooperation and innovation in the long run. Moreover, the synergy will help create a congenial environment for the generation of ideas, knowledge sharing, etc., which eventually will help promote a culture of innovation that helps in developing customer-centric solutions. Moreover, there is need to encourage a culture of innovation within the FinTech sector by supporting research and development and providing incentives for groundbreaking solutions.

Regulatory Support: Although government and regulatory bodies are striving hard to provide supportive policies for FinTech companies which includes streamlined processes for compliance, clear guidelines on new technologies like blockchain and cryptocurrencies, and support for innovation through sandboxes still, the sector needs handholding support from government and regulatory bodies to enact and enforce strong data privacy and protection laws to build trust among consumers. Clear guidelines on data usage, storage, and sharing are crucial. Regulatory bodies need to work for standardising protocols and systems to ensure seamless interoperability among different FinTech services for customer delight.

Leverage the latest technologies: Fintech companies need to leverage technologies like, AI, deep learning, and machine learning to minimise fraud and better risk management. Moreover, fintech firms to keep themselves updated about the latest trends in the global fintech sector.

By addressing these challenges, the FinTech sector in India can continue to grow and innovate, providing enhanced financial services and contributing to the country's overall economic development.

CONCLUSION

There is no denying the fact that the Indian Fintech sector is one of the quickest-growing sectors in the country. The Govt. of India has taken myriad initiatives to grow and strengthen the Fintech sector in the past several years, and as a result, today, India is at third position in terms of Fintech growth. The Indian Fintech landscape has witnessed phenomenal growth and resilience, mainly propelled by new-age innovation, industry-friendly policies, and the growing tech-savvy youth of India. As the sector continues to progress, it holds the enormous potential to transform the financial fabric of the country, making financial services inclusive, economical, and accessible to the remotest section of society. In spite of the huge progress, challenges such as financial literacy, cybersecurity risks, and the digital divide remain to be resolved in the near future. In the future, fintech companies in India need to take the full leverage of artificial intelligence and machine learning for more customized offerings with more stringent cyber security norms.

REFERENCES

Agarwal, S., & Zhang, J. (2020). FinTech, lending and payment innovation: A review. *Asia-Pacific Journal of Financial Studies*, *49*(3), 353–367. doi:10.1111/ajfs.12294

Belanche, D., Casaló, L. V., & Flavián, C. (2019). Artificial Intelligence in FinTech: Understanding robo-advisors adoption among customers. *Industrial Management & Data Systems*, *119*(7), 1411–1430. doi:10.1108/IMDS-08-2018-0368

Campanella, F., Serino, L., Battisti, E., Giakoumelou, A., & Karasamani, I. (2023). FinTech in the financial system: Towards a capital-intensive and high competence human capital reality? *Journal of Business Research*, *155*, 113376. doi:10.1016/j.jbusres.2022.113376

Cao, L., Yuan, G., Leung, T., & Zhang, W. (2020). Special issue on AI and FinTech: The challenge ahead. *IEEE Intelligent Systems*, *35*(2), 3–6. doi:10.1109/MIS.2020.2983494 PMID:35935446

Chen, M. A., Wu, Q., & Yang, B. (2019). How valuable is FinTech innovation? *Review of Financial Studies*, *32*(5), 2062–2106. doi:10.1093/rfs/hhy130

Chen, Z., Li, Y., Wu, Y., & Luo, J. (2017). The transition from traditional banking to mobile internet finance: An organizational innovation perspective-a comparative study of Citibank and ICBC. *Financial Innovation*, *3*(1), 1–16. doi:10.1186/s40854-017-0062-0

Chepurnoy, A., Larangeira, M., & Ojiganov, A. (2016). A prunable blockchain consensus protocol based on non-interactive proofs of past states retrievability. *arXiv preprint arXiv:1603.07926*.

Choudhury, M. D. (2020). *NIC sets-up CoE for Blockchain in Karnataka to enhance citizen services*. Express Computer. Available at https://www.expresscomputer.in/egov-watch/nic-sets-up-coe-for-block-chain-in-karnataka-to-enhance-citizen-services/45650/

Coindesk. (2016). *State of Blockchain q1 2016: Blockchain Funding Overtakes Bitcoin*. https://www.coindesk.com/state-of-blockchain-q1-2016/

Deloitte. (2017). *Blockchain technology in India Opportunities and challenges*. Deloitte and he Associated Chambers of Commerce of India. Available at https://www2.deloitte.com/content/dam/Deloitte/in/Documents/strategy/in-strategy-innovation-blockchain-technology-india-opportunities-challenges-noexp.pdf

Department of Banking Regulation Banking Policy Division. (n.d.). *Enabling Framework for Regulatory Sandbox*. the Reserve Bank of India. https://rbidocs.rbi.org.in/rdocs/PublicationReport/Pdfs/ENABLING79D8EBD31FED47A0BE21158C337123BF.PDF

Fosso Wamba, S., Kala Kamdjoug, J. R., Epie Bawack, R., & Keogh, J. G. (2020). Bitcoin, Blockchain and Fintech: A systematic review and case studies in the supply chain. *Production Planning and Control*, *31*(2-3), 115–142. doi:10.1080/09537287.2019.1631460

Gai, K., Qiu, M., & Sun, X. (2018). A survey on FinTech. *Journal of Network and Computer Applications*, *103*, 262–273. doi:10.1016/j.jnca.2017.10.011

IFC. (2017). *Blockchain in Financial Services in Emerging Markets.* EMCompass Note 43, International Finance Corporation. Available at: https://www.ifc.org/wps/wcm/connect/a3559b7c-19b7-4f8d-94be-30d1cf7e172b/EMCompass+Note+43+FINAL+8-21.pdf?MOD=AJPERES&CVID=lU51Cxz

Insurance Regulatory and Development Authority of India (Regulatory Sandbox) Regulations, 2019.

Lagna, A., & Ravishankar, M. N. (2022). Making the world a better place with fintech research. *Information Systems Journal, 32*(1), 61–102. doi:10.1111/isj.12333

Li, B., & Xu, Z. (2021). Insights into financial technology (FinTech): A bibliometric and visual study. *Financial Innovation, 7*(1), 1–28. doi:10.1186/s40854-021-00285-7 PMID:35024290

MandaV.PolisettyA. (2018). Status Check on Blockchain Implementations in India. doi:10.2139/ssrn.3265654

Priyaranjan, N., Roy, M., & Dhal, S. (2020). Distributed Ledger Technology, Blockchain and Central Banks. *RBI Bulletin.* Available at https://rbidocs.rbi.org.in/rdocs/Bulletin/PDFs/03AR_11022020510886F328EB418FB8013FBB684BB5BC.PDF

ReportB. C. G. (2022). Available at https://web-assets.bcg.com/e7/ab/51644cf944d686cd121d9c3f4bb4/future-of-fintech-july2022.pdf

Ruan, J., Wang, Y., Chan, F. T. S., Hu, X., Zhao, M., Zhu, F., Shi, B., Shi, Y., & Lin, F. (2019). A life cycle framework of green IoT-based agriculture and its finance, operation, and management issues. *IEEE Communications Magazine, 57*(3), 90–96. doi:10.1109/MCOM.2019.1800332

Sangwan, V., Prakash, P., & Singh, S. (2020). Financial technology: A review of extant literature. *Studies in Economics and Finance, 37*(1), 71–88. doi:10.1108/SEF-07-2019-0270

Sharma, T. K. (2018). *Blockchain technology in India – opportunities and challenges*. Available at <https://www.blockchain-council.org/blockchain/blockchain-technology-in-india-opportunities-and-challenges/

Simms, T. (2020). *India ban overturned, BTC owners warned they'll lose everything, holder's digest, Mar 2-8, Cointeregraph-the future of money*. Available at https://cointelegraph.com/news/india-ban-overturned-btc-owners-warned-theyll-lose-everything-hodlers-digest-mar-28

Suryono, R. R., Budi, I., & Purwandari, B. (2020). Challenges and trends of financial technology (Fintech): A systematic literature review. *Information (Basel), 11*(12), 590. doi:10.3390/info11120590

THBL. (2018). Karnataka to use blockchain technology for e-governance. *The Hindu Business Line*. Available at https://www.thehindubusinessline.com/news/karnataka-to-use-blockchain-technology-for-egovernance/article10035777.ece#

Vives, X. (2019). Digital disruption in banking. *Annual Review of Financial Economics, 11*(1), 243–272. doi:10.1146/annurev-financial-100719-120854

VK, A. (2019). 5 Indian banks That Are Rewriting The Payments Field With Blockchain. *Analytics India Magazine*. Available at: https://analyticsindiamag.com/5-indian-banks-rewriting-payments-field-blockchain/

Wang, Y., Xiuping, S., & Zhang, Q. (2021). Can fintech improve the efficiency of commercial banks?—An analysis based on big data. *Research in International Business and Finance*, *55*, 101338. doi:10.1016/j.ribaf.2020.101338

Wiyono, G., & Kirana Kusuma, C. (2021). Digital transformation of SMEs financial behaviour in the new normal era. *Jurnal Keuangan Dan Perbankan*, 191-211.

KEY TERMS AND DEFINITIONS

BNPL: It stands for buy now and pay later and is a payment method that allows clients to buy the products now and pay for them later, typically within a stipulated period.

IndiaStack: It is a set of Application Programming Interface (APIs) that enables startups, businesses, governments, and developers to use a unique digital Infrastructure to offer solutions for India's hard problems towards presence-less, paperless, consent layer, and cashless service delivery.

JAM Trinity: It refers to the government of India's initiative to link Jan Dhan accounts, Mobile, and Aadhaar for identification to implement direct subsidy transfer and prevent leakages of government's subsidy.

P2P Lending: It is an acronym for Peer-to-peer lending that offers an alternative funding source for those who face problems in getting loans through conventional channels. It functions as an online platform with ease of access, flexibility and choice of borrowing and lending for both borrowers and lenders.

UPI: Unified Payments Interface (UPI) is a real-time payment system in India. It enables users to send and receive money instantly and for free. It also enables users to synchronize many bank accounts into one application.

Chapter 5
AI-Powered Hospital Accounting:
Towards Sound Financial Management

Sabyasachi Pramanik
https://orcid.org/0000-0002-9431-8751
Haldia Institute of Technology, India

ABSTRACT

Healthcare organizations have unique challenges in preserving their financial stability. Due to the rising cost of healthcare, changing payment models, and the need to provide patients with high-quality treatment, hospitals are under continual pressure to optimize their financial operations. Conventional hospital accounting methods may not be enough in this rapidly evolving environment. The potential of artificial intelligence (AI) to transform hospital accounting and provide a means of enhancing financial stability is explored in this chapter. Automation, data analytics, and advanced machine learning algorithms are used in AI-driven hospital accounting to improve accuracy, speed up financial processes, and support well-informed decision-making.

INTRODUCTION

Artificial Intelligence, or AI for short, has emerged as one of the most innovative and interesting fields in computer science and technology. It encompasses a wide variety of methods, tactics, and technical developments that enable robots to emulate human intelligence and do tasks that were previously believed to be the exclusive domain of humans. This article examines the theoretical underpinnings of artificial intelligence (AI), shedding light on its many applications and subfields while also discussing its main concepts. The basic goal of artificial intelligence (AI) is to enable machines to learn, comprehend, and adapt in ways that are comparable to those of humans. This involves thinking, problem-solving, making decisions, and understanding spoken language. Systems using artificial intelligence (AI) are designed to handle massive amounts of data, spot trends, and use that information to make wise choices (Vesty, G. et al., 2023).

DOI: 10.4018/979-8-3693-1561-3.ch005

MACHINE LEARNING: THE AI MAINSTAY

Machine learning (ML) (Jayasingh, R. et al. 2022), a subset of AI, is its foundation. Machine learning approaches enable non-programmed systems to learn from data. Machines may recognize patterns and make predictions based on previously unknown data by being exposed to training data. A variety of techniques are included in multimedia learning (ML), such as supervised learning, which involves labeling data to train an algorithm, unsupervised learning, which involves identifying patterns in data, and reinforcement learning, which involves learning by interaction with the environment. Because deep learning, a kind of machine learning, is so adept at solving challenging issues, it has garnered a lot of attention. At the core of it all are artificial neural networks, which are inspired by the structure of the human brain. The neurons in these networks process data and are grouped into linked layers. Natural language processing, autonomous automobiles, picture and audio recognition, and other industries have profited tremendously from the implementation of deep learning. Natural language processing is a crucial component of artificial intelligence (NLP). The goal of natural language processing (NLP) (Andrushia, A. D. et al. 2023) is to enable computers to understand, interpret, and produce human language. Sentiment analysis, text generation, language translation, and chatbots all utilize it. With NLP technology, significant progress has been made in bridging the communication gap between people and robots.

APPLICATIONS OF AI

Numerous sectors, including robotics, healthcare, finance, and automotive, are affected by AI. In the healthcare sector, AI aids in drug development, patient care, and diagnostics. AI is utilized by financial organizations for risk assessment, investment strategies, and fraud detection. Artificial intelligence (AI) (Ashisha, G. R., et al. 2023) enables autonomous decision-making in industrial robots and self-driving autos, as well as voice recognition and natural language understanding in personal assistants like Siri and Alexa.

THE ASPECTS OF SOCIAL AND ETHICAL

Artificial intelligence (AI) raises ethical and societal questions despite its numerous advantages. The use of AI has raised many concerns, such as algorithmic bias, data privacy, job displacement, and the need for transparency in AI decision-making procedures. These problems need to be addressed in order to fully harness AI's potential. Artificial intelligence, with its roots in deep learning, machine learning, and natural language processing, is a prime example of technical advancement. From being only an idea, it has developed into the driving force behind several innovations and achievements in a variety of sectors. Understanding AI's underpinnings is necessary to appreciate the technology's potential and the continuous transformative implications it is having on our world. It will be our responsibility to navigate the ethical and social implications of AI as it advances while simultaneously appreciating its potential to benefit both local communities and the global community. Ultimately, enormous authority carries a great deal of responsibility.

THE ROLE AI IS CHANGING IN HEALTHCARE

Artificial intelligence (AI) in healthcare is a prime example of how technology may transform medical research, patient care, and operational effectiveness. AI is having a huge impact on healthcare (Pramanik, S. 2021) and will continue to do so in a variety of ways. This article looks at how artificial intelligence (AI) is developing in the healthcare sector and the many fields in which it is significantly influencing various fields, as seen in figure 1 below. *Illness identification and diagnosis:* One of the most significant applications of artificial intelligence in healthcare is in the field of diagnostics and illness detection. Machine learning algorithms may be used to analyze large amounts of medical data, such as test results, patient records, and medical imaging, in order to identify patterns and anomalies. Consequently, AI-driven diagnostic tools have been created for conditions including diabetes, cancer, and heart problems. Radiologists are now using AI to assist with the interpretation of MRIs (Praveenkumar, S. et al. 2023), CT images, and X-rays, leading to quicker and more precise diagnosis. *Customized Care Plans:* AI's ability to examine large datasets and extract insights enables the creation of individualized treatment plans for patients. By looking at genetic data, medical histories, and treatment outcomes, AI is able to offer tailored treatments and therapies. This improves patients' overall experience with healthcare by guaranteeing they get the finest treatment possible with the least amount of negative effects.

Figure 1. AI's impact on healthcare reform

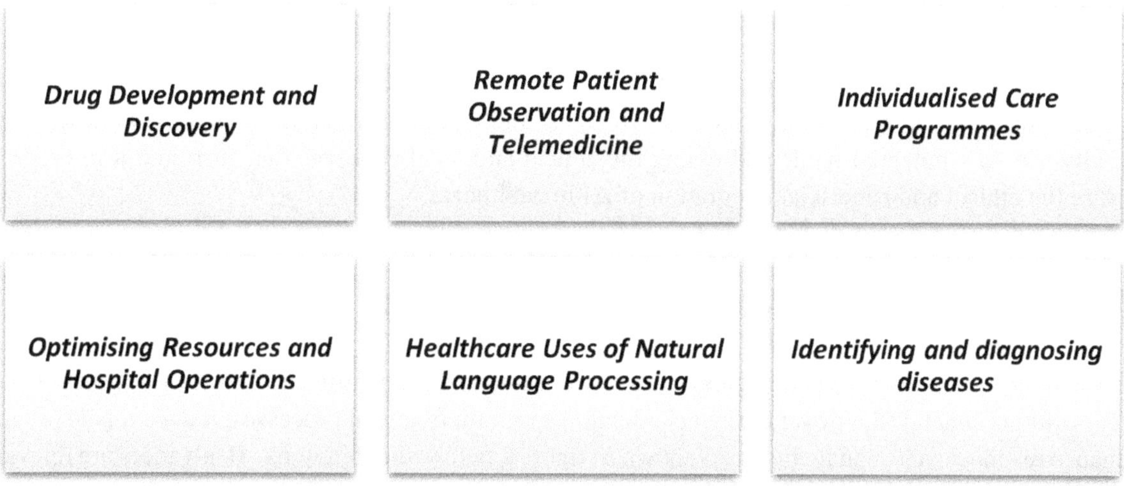

AI is critical to accelerating the discovery and development of novel medications in the drug development process. Pharmaceutical businesses utilize artificial intelligence (AI) to anticipate drug behavior, uncover potential treatment candidates, and simulate molecular interactions. This expedites the process of developing new medications while lowering associated costs. The hunt for treatments and vaccines against emerging diseases like COVID-19 has been greatly aided by AI. AI technology has proven important in propelling the uptake of tele-health and remote patient monitoring amidst the COVID-19 pandemic. This includes remote patient observation and telemedicine. AI systems are capable of analyzing patient data in real time that is gathered by Internet of Things sensors and wearable technology. Healthcare professionals may remotely check their patients' vital signs while they are at ease in their own homes, spot any anomalies, and take the necessary action. AI-powered telehealth services provide virtual consultations, which enable individuals in impoverished or rural areas to obtain treatment.

Allocating Resources and Improving Hospital Operations: AI is being used to improve hospital operations and resource allocation. Hospitals may alter staffing levels and resource allocation by utilizing predictive analytics to estimate patient admission rates. This assures the best possible use of the resources at hand, shortens wait times, and improves the overall experience of patients. Applications of Natural Language Processing in Healthcare: Natural language processing (NLP) is used to extract insights from unstructured medical data, such as electronic health records (EHRs) (VidyaChellam, V. et al. 2023), medical literature, and clinical notes. By automating coding, billing, and administrative activities, natural language processing (NLP) enhances the efficiency and precision of healthcare processes.

CHALLENGES AND ETHICAL CONCERNS

Artificial intelligence's expanding role in healthcare is not without challenges, despite its significant achievements. Algorithmic bias, data security, privacy, and the need for regulatory frameworks are still important considerations. Artificial intelligence-related ethical issues, such as the responsible use of patient data and transparency in AI decision-making, are often discussed in the context of healthcare. The evolving role of artificial intelligence (AI) in healthcare is marked by progress, innovation, and a commitment to improving patient outcomes and system efficacy. With the advancement of AI technology, healthcare may become more personalized and accessible, and we will be able to detect, treat, and prevent illnesses better. Technologists, policymakers, and healthcare practitioners must work together to fully use AI's potential while addressing the ethical and legal concerns that surround it in order to ensure the ethical and beneficial integration of AI in healthcare.

HOSPITAL ACCOUNTING-RELATED AI INNOVATIONS

Artificial intelligence (AI) technologies are essential to hospital accounting because they help healthcare organizations enhance their overall financial health, speed up financial processes, reduce mistakes, and enhance revenue cycle management. As shown in figure 2 below, the following AI advances are relevant to hospital accounting:

Robotic process automation (RPA): RPA uses software robots, sometimes referred to as bots, to automate repetitive, rule-based labor in accounting and financial operations. In hospital accounting, RPA is utilized for payroll processing, invoice processing, and accounts payable and receivable management. RPA may increase output, lower the rate of human error, and free up staff members to focus on more strategically significant financial tasks. *Predictive analytics uses artificial intelligence (AI)* systems to analyze historical financial data (Jain, V. et al. 2023) and project future trends. Hospital accounting may benefit from the use of predictive analytics to estimate revenue, detect potential issues, and improve financial planning. It may assist in the prediction of cash flow, patient numbers, and revenue cycle performance. *Anticipations for Claim Rejection:* Artificial Intelligence has the ability to predict which medical insurance claims are most likely to be turned down. By analyzing historical claim data and

Figure 2. Hospital accounting innovation using AI

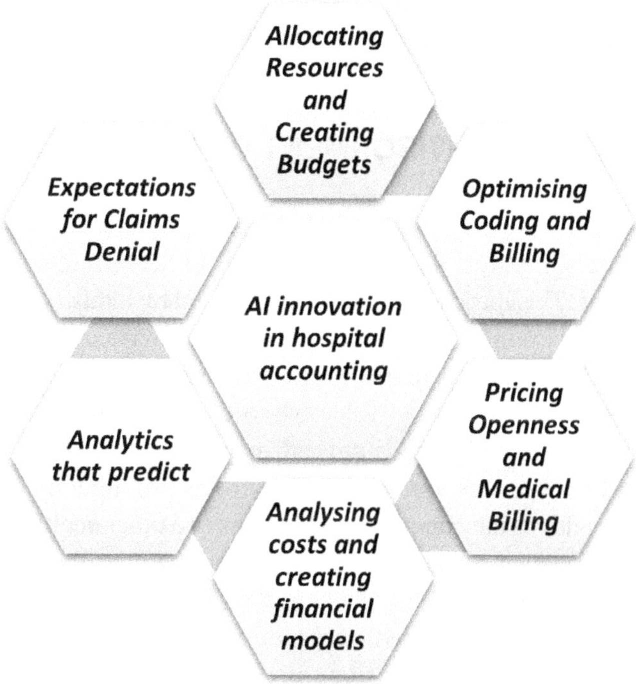

identifying recurrent rejection trends, AI technology may help hospitals reduce the number of claims denied. This may improve cash flow and reduce administrative costs.

Fraud Encounters: Artificial intelligence (AI)-based fraud detection systems may examine financial data to look for irregularities and potentially fraudulent activities. Avoiding financial losses due to dishonest accounting and invoicing practices is crucial. *Natural language processing, or NLP*, is a helpful technique for assessing unstructured data in contracts and other financial and accounting documents. It may help in gathering crucial information, identifying anomalies, and ensuring that accounting rules are followed. *Optimizing Coding and Billing:* Medical billing and coding may be made easier with the use of AI-powered solutions that suggest appropriate codes based on clinical documents. This ensures accurate invoicing, reduces mistakes, and expedites the reimbursement process. *Pricing Transparency and Medical Billing:* AI can assist by providing payers and patients with accurate cost estimates that account for available therapies and insurance coverage. It may also make it easier to create personalized billing statements and payment plans, which would improve the patient billing process. *Cost analysis and financial modeling:* Artificial intelligence (AI) tools can analyze financial data to provide insights into cost structures, identify areas for cost reduction, and provide financial modeling to assist hospitals in making data-driven financial decisions. *Allocating Resources and Creating Budgets:* Artificial intelligence (AI) may assist hospitals with resource allocation and budget planning by assessing historical financial data and optimizing budget allocation to different departments and projects. This ensures that financial resources are used effectively. *Support for Compliance and Audits:* AI may assist with the auditing of financial records and the observance of legal requirements. According to (Samanta, D. et al. 2021), it may help automate the tracking of financial transactions, which makes it easier to ensure compliance with financial rules. By utilizing these AI technologies, hospitals may increase income, reduce costs, enhance financial management, and improve their overall financial health. However, it is crucial that these technologies be used carefully to ensure patient and financial data security and privacy (Pramanik, S. 2023), as well as compliance with healthcare laws.

THE COMPLEX FINANCIAL ENVIRONMENT OF HEALTHCARE

The topic of healthcare finance is very dynamic and complicated, impacted by a wide range of factors, regulations, and stakeholders. It covers the financial aspects of healthcare delivery, administration, insurance, and reimbursement. This intricacy has to be understood by industry players, healthcare groups, and policymakers. Here, we'll examine some of the key components that make up the complex financial picture in the healthcare industry. There are many different complex types of healthcare payment plans. Among these are fee-for-service, capitation, value-based care, and bundled payments. These models sometimes need complex financial and administrative management and have an impact on how healthcare practitioners are paid for their services. *Health Insurance:* The proliferation of commercial and public health insurance providers adds to the complexity. Hospitals and other healthcare institutions must contend with various payer requirements, coding systems, and billing procedures. Health insurance claims, rejections, and reimbursements are strongly related to the financial operations of healthcare organizations. *Regulations and Compliance:* The healthcare industry is one of the most heavily regulated, with a myriad of federal and state regulations. Ensuring compliance with standards like the Health Insurance Portability and Accountability Act (HIPAA), the Affordable Care Act (ACA), and other Medicare and Medicaid requirements requires specialist expertise and dedicated financial resources. *Revenue Cycle Management:* The complex revenue cycle process in the healthcare sector includes patient registration, insurance verification, coding, billing, and collections. Any interruption to this cycle might lead to financial losses. Healthcare companies need advanced technology and specific skills to handle this cycle successfully.

Accounting and Reporting: Generally accepted accounting principles (GAAP) and specific healthcare accounting standards must be adhered to in financial reporting for the healthcare sector. Accounting for healthcare is a specialist profession. Accurate accounting and financial reporting are essential for regulatory compliance as well as financial transparency. *Costs and Pricing:* The costs of delivering healthcare are multifaceted, including capital project expenditures, administrative overhead, and regulatory compliance in addition to the direct costs of patient care. It may be difficult to estimate prices for services and procedures accurately, and agreements with payers and government efforts can have an influence.

Value-based Care: The shift to value-based care models aims to improve patient outcomes while cutting expenses. It will need significant investments in data analytics, infrastructure, and care coordination for this transformation to be financially viable and show benefit. *Investments in Technology:* Hospitals and other healthcare organizations must purchase state-of-the-art healthcare information systems in order to manage revenue cycle management, electronic health records (EHRs), and data analytics. These costs may mount up, and they need ongoing maintenance. *Financial Assistance and Charitable Care:* Healthcare institutions often provide financial assistance and charitable care to underinsured and uninsured patients. Due to this, financial management becomes much more challenging and calls for monitoring, reporting, and compliance with federal laws. *Economic Factors:* The status of the economy as a whole, which includes things like economic recessions, unemployment rates, and government fiscal policies, may have an influence on reimbursement rates, patient financial responsibility, and healthcare usage. *Acquisitions & Mergers:* Combining operations, systems, and financial reporting may provide financial issues during integration and consolidation in the healthcare industry. *Global Health Challenges:* The COVID-19 pandemic and other events have brought attention to the shortcomings in healthcare financing and have emphasized the need of emergency preparedness for healthcare facilities. To successfully navigate this complex financial environment, healthcare administration, finance, compliance, and technological experience are all prerequisites. Healthcare organizations need to make strategic choices and adapt to the shifting financial environment in order to sustain patient happiness, high-quality treatment, and financial sustainability. Policymakers and regulators also have a big influence on the financial scene via potential changes and improvements to healthcare financing systems.

THE DRAWBACKS OF TRADITIONAL HOSPITAL ACCOUNTING

Traditional hospital accounting methods have many shortcomings that may make it difficult for healthcare companies to handle their finances and make informed choices. A few of these limitations include: *Absence of detail:* Traditional accounting systems' financial reporting usually lacks enough information. They may not distinguish between different types of revenue and costs, which makes it difficult to identify specific examples of financial inefficiencies or possible areas for cost-cutting. *Inaccurate Cost Allocation:* When use conventional accounting techniques, costs could not be properly assigned to certain divisions, services, or activities. This might result in skewed cost data, which would make it difficult to determine the true profitability of different services or the cost of caring for a particular patient. *Complexity of Revenue Recognition:* The healthcare sector has a wide range of payment arrangements and revenue streams, including government grants, insurance reimbursements, and patient payments. As a result, the process of recognizing revenue is intricate. It's probable that traditional accounting methods aren't flexible enough to deal with this complexity in an effective manner. *Lack of openness:* The potential lack of financial reporting openness associated with conventional accounting systems may make it difficult for healthcare organizations to track and understand their financial performance. This might make it more difficult for them to identify areas that want improvement. *Limited Real-time Data:* Real-time financial data is scarce in conventional accounting systems since they usually depend on periodic financial statements. As a consequence, decisions may take longer to make and it might be harder to react quickly to financial opportunities or challenges. *Inefficient forecasting and budgeting:* Conventional accounting methods might be cumbersome for forecasting and budgeting in the quick-paced healthcare industry. It is challenging to model various situations and assess how changes in patient numbers, payment rates, and other factors may affect healthcare organizations using established approaches. *Inadequate for Value-Based Care:* As the healthcare industry transitions to value-based care, it may become more challenging for current accounting systems to fairly represent the quality and cost of patient treatment. Value-based care prioritizes patient satisfaction and results, which calls for more accurate cost assessment. *Difficulties with Regulatory Compliance:* Healthcare organizations may find it excessively challenging to adhere to intricate healthcare regulations like as HIPAA, the Affordable Care Act, and Medicare/Medicaid requirements while using conventional accounting methods. Noncompliance may result in monetary penalties.

Difficulty in Determining Cost Drivers: Traditional accounting may not have the tools and procedures required to accurately identify the sources of costs. Understanding the factors that affect costs is necessary to make informed decisions about the allocation of resources and price reductions. *Difficulties with Data Integration:* Accounting, revenue cycle management, electronic health records (EHRs), and other software programs are often used by healthcare organizations. It may be challenging to combine data from many disparate systems into a logical financial picture using standard accounting approaches. Many healthcare organizations are converting to more advanced financial management systems in order to circumvent these limitations. These systems are capable of handling the complex revenue and expense structures that are unique to the healthcare industry, provide real-time data, and offer robust financial analytics. These systems often contain elements of financial management and reporting that are unique to the healthcare business in order to better address the unique possibilities and challenges presented by the financial environment of the healthcare sector.

AI-POWERED REVENUE CYCLE MANAGEMENT

AI-powered predictive analytics may go through historical claims data to identify patterns and trends related to claim rejections. AI looks at a variety of data variables, including as patient data, billing information, and coding accuracy, to predict the likelihood that a claim would be denied. In order to avoid rejections, this enables healthcare companies to enhance documentation, code precisely, and adhere to billing rules. By resolving rejections before they occur, revenue is maximized and RCM becomes more efficient. *Increasing Coding Precision:* AI may significantly increase coding accuracy by giving medical coders access to coding help technologies. These systems use Natural Language Processing (NLP) and machine learning approaches to analyze clinical paperwork and offer suitable procedure and diagnostic codes. This reduces the possibility of coding mistakes and raises the possibility that the codes selected will be accepted by payers, leading to more accurate remuneration and increased revenue.

Optimizing the Patient Billing Process: AI technology may be used to enhance the patient billing process in a variety of ways. They may personalize billing statements, provide easy payment options, and provide a clear explanation of rates. AI is also capable of predicting a patient's financial status and modifying payment plans accordingly. This improves patient billing satisfaction and increases the likelihood of successful revenue collection. It also reduces the administrative burden related to patient billing by automating and streamlining several process processes. *Finding Inefficiencies and Revenue Leakage:* Artificial Intelligence (AI) can analyze financial and operational data to identify potential inefficiencies and revenue leaks. This involves determining whether services are underutilized, spotting issues with billing, and streamlining administrative processes. AI may also be used to identify opportunities for revenue growth and resource optimization. By fixing these issues, healthcare organizations can ensure that they collect all available funds and minimize inefficiencies that could lead to losses. In summary, integrating AI into revenue cycle management can improve operational efficiency, save costs, improve coding accuracy, and expedite patient billing processes. Furthermore, it enables proactive claim rejection management and detects potential revenue leakage and inefficiencies, all of which may improve financial outcomes and patient satisfaction. However, it's essential to use AI solutions with caution, ensuring that regulatory requirements are satisfied and patient data is kept private and safe.

AI-POWERED COST MANAGEMENT: MODIFYING PRECISION AND EFFECTIVENESS

Expense management is a critical part of financial control and optimization for businesses of all sizes. Effective cost tracking, evaluation, and management are essential for an organization to preserve its sustainability and financial soundness. In today's data-driven environment, artificial intelligence (AI) has emerged as a powerful instrument to revolutionize expenditure management. The benefits and drawbacks of artificial intelligence (AI)-driven expenditure management are discussed in this section, along with how this technology enhances the precision and effectiveness of financial processes.

THE ROLE OF AI IN COST MANAGEMENT

AI-driven expenditure management is the use of artificial intelligence technology to optimize, automate, and simplify the whole process of managing business spending. Numerous subjects are covered by this technique, including data analysis, processing of receipts, policy enforcement, and reporting of expenses. Let us look at the main ways that AI is transforming this industry. Automated Information Extraction and Receipt Scanning: Artificial intelligence (AI)-based expenditure management systems can automatically extract relevant information from invoices and receipts. Employees that do not have to manually input data will save a great deal of time and avoid mistakes. *Policy Enforcement and Compliance:* AI may police spending rules by detecting policy violations in receipts and expense reports. If an expense claim deviates from the company's rules, AI may flag it for further review or rejection. *Expense Categorization and Tagging:* AI can categorize and tag costs automatically, ensuring accurate and consistent accounting. This not only makes cost tracking simpler but also increases data accuracy for financial analysis. *Predictive analytics:* By examining historical data, AI-powered expenditure management systems may project future expenses. As a consequence, companies are in a better position to plan budgets, manage resources, and identify potential cost-saving opportunities early on. Artificial Intelligence (AI) can identify patterns of fraudulent cost submissions and irregularities in spending reports. By drawing attention to potential fraud scenarios for investigation, it may help businesses prevent financial losses. *Efficient Approval Workflows:* Artificial intelligence (AI) may enhance the efficiency of approval workflows by automatically allocating expenses to the appropriate staff. It may prioritize urgent or high-value charges for faster processing.

THE BENEFITS OF AI-POWERED EXPENSE MANAGEMENT

Organizations may benefit from incorporating artificial intelligence (AI) into expenditure management in the following ways:

Increased Efficiency: Manual cost management techniques are labor-intensive and prone to errors. AI has the ability to automate many of these tasks, freeing up employees to focus on more strategic work. *Cost savings:* By analyzing spending data and searching for inefficiencies or non-compliant expenditures, artificial intelligence (AI) may identify areas where money can be saved. *Enhanced Precision:* Data that is more precisely extracted by automation reduces the likelihood of accounting mistakes. *Enhanced Policy Compliance:* By guaranteeing that expense claims adhere to organizational rules, AI reduces the possibility of non-compliance. *Simplified Auditing:* AI can detect potential issues, which improves the precision and effectiveness of auditing. *Real-time Reporting and Insights:* Artificial intelligence (AI) provides firms with immediate access to expenditure data and insights, empowering them to take swift action on data-driven choices. AI-powered expense management is transformative for companies looking to improve their financial operations. It reduces the administrative burden and frees up staff workers to focus on other valuable initiatives since it offers efficiency, accuracy, and automation. AI has the potential to significantly impact an organization's bottom line by enhancing policy compliance, producing illuminating discoveries, and presenting cost-saving alternatives. As AI becomes more widely used in expenditure management, companies who adopt it will have a competitive edge in financial control and decision-making.

AI-POWERED EXPENSE MANAGEMENT: TRANSFORMING PRECISION AND EFFECTIVENESS

Expense management is a critical part of financial control and optimization (Pramanik, S. et al. 2022) for businesses of all sizes. Effective cost tracking, evaluation, and management are essential for an organization to preserve its sustainability and financial soundness. In today's data-driven environment, artificial intelligence (AI) has emerged as a powerful instrument to revolutionize expenditure management. The benefits and drawbacks of artificial intelligence (AI)-driven expenditure management are discussed in this section, along with how this technology enhances the precision and effectiveness of financial processes.

THE ROLE OF AI IN COST MANAGEMENT

AI-driven expenditure management is the use of artificial intelligence technology to optimize, automate, and simplify the whole process of managing business spending. Numerous subjects are covered by this technique, including data analysis (Veeraiah, V. et al. 2023), processing of receipts, policy enforcement, and reporting of expenses. Let us look at the main ways that AI is transforming this industry:

Automated Information Extraction and Receipt Scanning: Artificial intelligence (AI)-based expenditure management systems can automatically extract relevant information from invoices and receipts. Employees that do not have to manually input data will save a great deal of time and avoid mistakes. *Policy Enforcement and Compliance:* AI may police spending rules by detecting policy violations in receipts and expense reports. If an expense claim deviates from the company's rules, AI might flag it for further review or rejection. *Expense Categorization and Tagging:* AI can categorize and tag costs automatically, ensuring accurate and consistent accounting. This not only makes cost tracking simpler but also increases data accuracy for financial analysis. *Predictive analytics:* By examining historical data, AI-powered expenditure management systems may project future expenses. Consequently, companies may now more effectively allocate resources, create budgets, and identify opportunities for cost reduction up front. Artificial Intelligence (AI) can identify patterns of fraudulent cost submissions and irregularities in spending reports. By drawing attention to potential fraud scenarios for investigation, it may help businesses prevent financial losses. *Efficient Approval Workflows:* Artificial intelligence (AI) may enhance the efficiency of approval workflows by automatically allocating expenses to the appropriate staff. It may prioritize urgent or high-value charges for faster processing.

THE BENEFITS OF AI-POWERED EXPENSE MANAGEMENT

Organizations may benefit from incorporating artificial intelligence (AI) into expenditure management in the following ways:

Increased Efficiency: Manual cost management techniques are labor-intensive and prone to errors. AI has the ability to automate many of these tasks, freeing up employees to focus on more strategic work. *Cost savings:* By analyzing spending data and searching for inefficiencies or non-compliant expenditures, artificial intelligence (AI) may identify areas where money can be saved. *Enhanced Precision:* Data that is more precisely extracted via automation reduces the likelihood of accounting mistakes. *Enhanced Policy Compliance:* By guaranteeing that expense claims adhere to organizational rules, AI reduces the possibility of non-compliance. *Simplified Auditing:* AI can detect potential issues, which improves the precision and effectiveness of auditing. *Real-time Reporting and insights:* Artificial intelligence (AI) provides firms with immediate access to expenditure data and insights, allowing them to take prompt action on data-driven choices. AI-powered expense management is transformative for companies looking to improve their financial operations. It reduces the administrative burden and frees up staff workers to focus on other valuable initiatives since it offers efficiency, accuracy and automation (Khan, P. T. et al. 2023). AI has the potential to significantly impact an organization's bottom line by enhancing policy compliance, producing illuminating discoveries, and presenting cost-saving alternatives. As AI becomes more widely used in expenditure management, companies who adopt it will have a competitive edge in financial control and decision-making.

FINANCIAL FORECASTING DRIVEN BY AI

Financial forecasting is a crucial process that helps businesses and organizations plan ahead and make informed financial choices about their future. It comprises projecting future profits, expenses, and sales, among other financial outcomes. In recent years, artificial intelligence (AI) has shown to be a powerful tool to increase the accuracy and usefulness of financial forecasting. This section looks at the value of accurate financial predictions, the role AI models play in financial forecasting, and the importance of data-driven decision-making in this situation. Accurate financial projections are important for a number of reasons. Strategic planning relies heavily on financial estimates. They assist companies in determining their financial goals and formulating strategies to achieve them. *Resource Allocation:* Forecasts' advice has allowed budgets to be in line with projected financial demands. This prevents funds from being overspent or under spent in crucial areas. *Risk management:* By recognizing potential financial risks and uncertainties, organizations may develop backup plans and risk-reduction strategies. Forecasts that are accurate help to boost investor confidence. When determining whether to support or invest in a company, stakeholders, lenders, and investors need financial projections to make educated decisions. *Evaluation of Performance:* Forecasts are used as a point of reference to evaluate actual financial performance. By contrasting anticipated with actual outcomes, businesses may assess the effectiveness of their financial management.

FINANCIAL FORECASTING MODELS POWERED BY AI

AI algorithms have revolutionized financial forecasting by offering superior capabilities above outdated methods. A few AI-powered techniques for financial forecasting are as follows:

Machine Learning (ML): ML systems can analyze past financial data to identify patterns and correlations. Regression analysis, time series analysis, and deep learning techniques may all be used to predict future financial outcomes based on these patterns. To assess sentiment and extract information that might affect financial projections, natural language processing, or NLP, is used to analyze text data taken from social media, news articles, and financial reports. A branch of artificial intelligence called predictive analytics uses historical data to predict future financial performance. This is particularly useful for revenue forecasting, demand forecasting, and behavior analysis of customers. *AI-Enhanced Financial Models:* Artificial intelligence may enhance traditional financial models by providing more accurate inputs and real-time data updates. As a result, human data input mistakes are reduced and financial prediction accuracy is raised.

DATA-DRIVEN DECISION MAKING

Decision-making based on data is the cornerstone of AI-based financial forecasting. AI models are built on data, and the quality, quantity, and relevancy of the data employed influence the forecast accuracy. Furthermore, businesses that make decisions based on data are urged to:

Make Use of Real-Time Data: Businesses can react quickly to changing market conditions or financial challenges because to AI's capacity to manage enormous volumes of data in real time. *Adapt to Market Dynamics:* Financial forecasts must be flexible to take into consideration shifts in the market. AI models may provide ongoing insights and updates based on real-time data, ensuring that forecasts remain relevant and correct. *Determine opportunities and risks:* In addition to anticipating financial results, data-driven financial forecasting assists in identifying possible risks and opportunities for expansion. *Boost Resource Allocation:* By using data-driven forecasts, organizations may reduce waste and allocate resources more wisely. *Make Certain Financial Decisions Support the Overarching Mission:* Data-driven financial predictions help businesses make sure their financial goals align with broader strategic objectives. All things considered, the way firms create financial planning is being revolutionized by AI-powered financial forecasting. Since precise financial forecasts are the cornerstone of risk management, resource allocation, strategic planning, and investor confidence, their significance cannot be overstated. AI models that are driven by data-driven decision-making may be used by organizations to create more flexible and accurate financial predictions using state-of-the-art techniques and real-time data. This improves performance and financial decision-making.

HEALTHCARE FRAUD IS BECOMING A BIGGER PROBLEM, AND AI CAN HELP DETECT AND PREVENT IT

The integrity of international healthcare systems is threatened by the pervasive problem of healthcare fraud. Fraudulent activities cost billions of dollars annually and jeopardize the quality of treatment that patients get. Integrating AI algorithms is a crucial first step in ensuring compliance with legal standards, since traditional methods of preventing and detecting fraud are usually inadequate. This article looks at how artificial intelligence (AI) is being used to combat healthcare fraud, with a focus on how AI algorithms are being used to spot irregularities and ensure regulatory compliance.

The Growing Issue of Medical Fraud: Healthcare fraud encompasses a broad variety of unlawful activities, including identity theft, prescription fraud, kickbacks, and billing fraud. The increasing prevalence of healthcare fraud may be attributed to several factors, including the intricacy of healthcare billing systems, the expansion of telehealth services, and the growing reliance on electronic health records (EHRs). These challenges have made it harder to detect fraudulent activities using traditional methods. *AI Methods for Disparities:* Healthcare fraud is a serious problem that AI algorithms assist in resolving. These algorithms employ machine learning and data analytics to uncover abnormalities in massive datasets, which is important for spotting fraudulent activities. Here are a few crucial AI techniques for identifying fraud:

Machine Learning: Both supervised and unsupervised learning techniques are used in the analysis of healthcare data. Supervised learning models may be taught to recognize patterns connected to false claims, while unsupervised learning techniques can detect strange patterns or anomalies in the data. Textual data included in insurance claims and medical records is examined using natural language processing, or NLP. NLP analyses and interprets the text to find contradictions, inconsistencies, and strange language that may indicate fraud. *Prediction analytics:* AI-driven prediction algorithms may foresee future fraud incidents by analyzing historical data trends. This helps prevent deceit in advance and lessen financial damages. Huge datasets may include complex patterns and correlations that can be recognized by neural networks and other deep learning methods. This is particularly useful for spotting complex and dynamic fraud schemes. *Behavioral Analytics:* AI can provide a baseline of usual conduct for payers, patients, and healthcare providers. Flagging variations from these baselines as potential anomalies enables the early identification of fraud. Ensuring Specific Regulatory Standards Are Met:

AI algorithms are crucial for ensuring compliance with legal standards, in addition to helping identify fraud. To safeguard patient data and prevent fraud, regulatory bodies enact laws such as the Health Insurance Portability and Accountability Act (HIPAA) in the United States. AI is useful for the following tasks:

Real-time Monitoring: According to (Pramanik, S. et al. 2023), artificial intelligence (AI) may monitor healthcare transactions and data to identify any suspicious or non-compliant conduct and ensure that businesses are adhering to the law. Strong data encryption and access control systems may be implemented with the help of AI, safeguarding patient data and preventing unauthorized access. *Audit Trails:* By keeping a detailed record of all data accesses and transactions, AI-driven audit trails guarantee accountability and transparency, two aspects that are essential for compliance. *Reporting and Documentation:* Healthcare businesses may more easily demonstrate to auditors that they are following rules thanks to AI technologies' automated generation of compliance reports. In view of the rising issue of healthcare fraud, using cutting-edge technology, such as artificial intelligence (AI), is essential to effectively detecting and preventing fraudulent behaviors. A crucial component of this attempt is the use of AI algorithms (Bhattacharya, A. et al. 2021) to detect irregularities and processes to ensure compliance with regulatory standards. By using AI, healthcare organizations may secure patient data, save a substantial amount of money, and maintain the trust of patients and regulatory bodies. As the healthcare sector grows, artificial intelligence will play an ever larger role in reducing fraud and enhancing compliance.

AUTOMATION OF REPORTING AND COMPLIANCE IN HEALTHCARE: HANDLING THE REGULATORY LANDSCAPE

The regulatory framework in which the healthcare business operates is complicated because of the many rules and regulations that are in place to safeguard patient data, provide high-quality treatment, and maintain financial transparency. Automation technology may significantly increase the efficiency of financial reporting and compliance monitoring, two crucial aspects of hospital administration. This study looks at the healthcare industry's regulatory landscape, the role automation plays in managing compliance, and the benefits of simplifying financial reporting.

The Healthcare Regulatory Environment: The healthcare industry is subject to a plethora of municipal, federal, and international rules. Important regulatory regimes in the healthcare sector include:

The International Classification of Diseases (ICD) is a global standard for medical diagnosis coding. The Health Insurance Portability and Accountability Act (HIPAA) regulate the exchange of medical information and ensures the security and privacy of patient data. The Affordable Care Act (ACA) aims to improve access, affordability, and quality of healthcare in the US.

Food and Drug Administration (FDA) regulations: Control the development and approval of pharmaceuticals and medical equipment. The Clinical Laboratory Improvement Amendments (CLIA) establishes standards for the caliber of clinical labs. *Many accrediting agencies:* The Joint Commission and other institutions establish standards for the security and quality of medical service. *Medicare and Medicaid regulations:* Manage the funding and payment of healthcare services.

Automation in the Management of Compliance: Monitoring and ensuring that these regulations are followed requires automation. Automation may enhance healthcare compliance management in the following ways:

Continuous Monitoring: Automated technologies can keep an eye on data, processes, and transactions to identify any deviations from regulatory standards. This proactive approach facilitates prompt issue solutions. Automated solutions provide thorough audit trails that make it easier to manage and verify regulatory compliance. Automation may be used to enforce access controls and data encryption to ensure that patient data is kept secure and safe, as required by regulations like HIPAA. This is very helpful for doing audits. *Papers and Reports:* Automation can generate and maintain the records, papers, and reports required to demonstrate adherence to various regulatory requirements. *Risk assessment:* By using automated risk assessment systems, organizations may swiftly address non-compliance or vulnerabilities in healthcare operations. *Simplifying Accounting Reports:* Automation has the potential to significantly improve compliance management as well as financial reporting in the healthcare sector. Financial reporting in the healthcare industry is challenging due to many partners, large datasets, and stringent requirements. There are many ways that automation may improve the efficiency of this process:

Data Integration: Automated solutions may reduce the possibility of human error and laborious data input by combining financial data from several sources. *Real-time reporting:* Automation's capacity to provide real-time financial information allows healthcare organizations to act quickly and intelligently. *Standardized Reporting Templates:* When automation methods are used to produce standard financial reports that satisfy regulatory requirements, information may be communicated with relevant stakeholders more readily. *Predictive analytics:* By utilizing advanced analytics and forecasting models made possible by automation, healthcare companies can better understand their financial performance and be prepared for future issues. While navigating the regulatory environment in the healthcare industry can be challenging, financial reporting and compliance management are crucial to ensuring that healthcare organizations adhere to the law. Automation technology offers many advantages, such as streamlined processes, reduced chances of non-compliance, heightened efficiency, and enhanced quality of healthcare services overall. By adopting automation, healthcare companies may better meet their regulatory obligations while focusing more on patient care, research, and innovation. As the regulatory environment evolves, automation will become more important for healthcare reporting and compliance.

BETTER PATIENT EXPERIENCES AND TAILORED SERVICES: AI-POWERED PATIENT ANALYTICS IS REVOLUTIONIZING HEALTHCARE

Patient-centric healthcare has emerged as a critical paradigm change in the medical industry. Rather of using a one-size-fits-all approach, healthcare providers are beginning to realize how important it is to tailor their services to meet the individual requirements of each patient. Artificial intelligence (AI) is driving this change by facilitating the provision of personalized services that enhance patient experiences and provide valuable patient demographic data. This section covers the role of artificial intelligence (AI) in patient analytics, how it impacts patient-centric healthcare, and how it improves patient experiences.

Patient-First Medical Care: In patient-centric healthcare, the patient is at the centre of medical decision-making and treatment delivery. It prioritizes the needs, desires, and outcomes of the patient, with a focus on improving their overall health and well-being. One of the fundamental principles of patient-centric healthcare, along with collaboration, openness, and communication, is enabling people to make informed choices about their own health. *AI-Powered Patient Demographic Information:* Data Collection and Integration: AI systems are able to gather, analyze (Mandal, A. et al. 2021), and integrate vast amounts of patient data, including medical records and information on lifestyle, social determinants of health, and demographics. This thorough data collection allows medical personnel to get a more complete picture of every patient. *Predictive analytics:* AI systems can predict health risks and outcomes by analyzing patient data. By empowering medical providers to identify at-risk persons and take proactive efforts to address them, this improves patient outcomes and preventive therapy. *Segmentation and Personalization:* AI may classify patients based on demographics, health state, or preferences. This segmentation helps doctors better customize treatments, therapies, and communication to the unique needs of each group, resulting in more successful care. *Improved Patient Experiences with Tailored Services:* AI helps develop personalized treatment plans that include a patient's medical background, lifestyle decisions, and genetic predispositions. More effective and patient-specific treatments lead to better health outcomes. *Engagement and Communication:* Medical personnel may communicate with patients more promptly and personally thanks to AI-powered patient analytics. For example, AI-driven chatbots can instantly answer to patient questions, boosting satisfaction and engagement. *Medication Management:* Artificial intelligence (AI) may assist patients in better managing their medicines by monitoring adherence and sending out reminders. This customization helps to improve drug compliance and health management. *Telehealth & Remote Monitoring:* AI-driven remote monitoring solutions enable patients to get ongoing treatment while lounging in the comfort of their own homes. When required, prompt action is made possible by healthcare experts' real-time monitoring of vital signs and health data. *Data-Driven Insights:* Artificial intelligence (AI) leverages patient data to provide insights that are then utilized to inform choices about resource allocation, the construction of healthcare facilities, and general enhancements to the delivery of treatment, all of which have the potential to enhance the patient experience. AI-driven patient data is making patient-centric care the standard in the healthcare industry. It gives healthcare providers the information and tools they need to provide individualized care that improves patient outcomes, experiences, and happiness. As technology advances, artificial intelligence (AI) will play an ever larger role in healthcare, ultimately transforming the sector for the benefit of both patients and healthcare providers. The use of AI is one of the most crucial stages towards achieving the objective of truly patient-centric healthcare.

IMPLEMENTING AI-DRIVEN HOSPITAL ACCOUNTING: ENSURING ETHICAL OBLIGATION, DATA SECURITY, AND PERFORMANCE

AI-driven hospital accounting has the potential to revolutionize financial management in healthcare businesses. Artificial intelligence can automate accounting processes, improve accuracy, reduce costs, and optimize operations. However, the effective use of AI in this setting requires meticulous preparation, a focus on data security and privacy, and a commitment to addressing the ethical issues surrounding AI usage. This section discusses these three essential aspects of integrating AI into hospital accounting. *Requirements study:* Before incorporating AI into hospital accounting, it is essential to do a thorough requirements study. This involves understanding the infrastructure that is presently in place, identifying which specific accounting tasks may be automated, and connecting AI solutions with the hospital's financial goals. *Buy-in from Stakeholders:* Ensure that senior management, IT departments, and finance teams, among other pertinent stakeholders, are in favor of the execution plan. Training and good communication are necessary to win people over.

Selecting the Best AI Solutions: Select AI solutions that work with the hospital's accounting requirements. These solutions should be easily integrated with existing systems and adaptable to meet evolving needs. *Data Quality:* Having high-quality data is essential for AI-driven accounting to be successful. Hospitals should invest in data cleaning, normalization, and validation processes to ensure the accuracy and reliability of financial data. *Privacy and Security Considerations:* Regulation Compliance: Healthcare organizations must abide by data security rules, including the Health Insurance Portability and Accountability Act (HIPAA) and the General Data Protection Regulation (GDPR). These guidelines should be considered while developing AI systems. Protect sensitive medical and financial data from hackers and unauthorized access by encrypting it using strong data encryption algorithms (Bold et al., 2023). *Control Access:* Prevent unauthorized individuals from accessing financial information. Role-based access restrictions should be included into AI systems to safeguard user privacy. *Regular Audits and Monitoring:* Keep a careful check on AI systems and conduct frequent audits to spot any anomalies, security flaws, or inappropriate use of data.

CONSCIENTIOUS AI UTILIZATION AND ITS ETHICAL REPERCUSSIONS

Transparency: Artificial intelligence (AI) systems used in hospital accounting need to be able to explain their choices and be upfront about them. This openness helps to build trust among stakeholders.

Bias Mitigation: Hospitals should make a concerted effort to get rid of any biases that might exist in AI systems, especially in situations when making financial decisions is necessary. AI systems must be routinely audited for impartiality and bias. When using AI systems to manage financial transactions for patients, informed permission is a must. Patients must be informed about the potential financial consequences of the use of their data. *Responsibility:* Hospitals must establish separate avenues of responsibility for decisions made with AI. This means ensuring error-recovery protocols and assigning responsibility for the outcomes of AI-driven financial choices. Planning, data security, and ethical issues need to be taken into account even if integrating AI-driven hospital accounting has the potential to greatly enhance financial management. Healthcare institutions may employ AI while upholding patient privacy and public confidence by completing a thorough needs analysis, safeguarding data, and putting ethical AI practices into place. Successfully implementing AI-driven hospital accounting ultimately calls for a thorough plan that strikes a balance between responsibility and creativity.

REAL-WORLD EXAMPLES OF AI-POWERED HOSPITAL ACCOUNTING

Cleveland Clinic's AI-Enhanced Revenue Cycle Management: One of the top healthcare organizations, The Cleveland Clinic, has included AI into its revenue cycle management. AI-powered predictive analytics may be used to identify opportunities for improving financial performance, such raising revenue collection and lowering claim rejections. Their use of AI has greatly enhanced their financial processes.

Mayo Clinic's AI-Enabled Financial Forecasting: Known for its patient-centered care, the Mayo Clinic uses AI in its financial forecasting. They estimate patient flows, improve personnel levels, and efficiently allocate resources by using machine learning. This maintains a healthy balance between sound financial standing and first-rate medical care. *AI in Cost management at Intermountain Healthcare:* Intermountain Healthcare is a non-profit health system that uses AI in cost management. Algorithms powered by artificial intelligence (AI) go over the cost structure and help identify places where expenses might be reduced without compromising the quality of patient care. This approach has led to significant cost savings.

TOP TECHNIQUES AND INSIGHTS ACQUIRED

Quality of Data Is Crucial: Excellent data is the foundation for AI-driven hospital accounting that works. Hospitals should invest in data purification, validation, and normalization to ensure that AI systems are running on accurate and reliable data.

Clearly Stated Goals and KPIs: Prior to deployment, clearly state your goals and key performance indicators (KPIs). It is simpler to evaluate AI's influence when explicit objectives are set. *Interoperability and Integration:* Ensure that AI solutions are able to communicate with existing accounting and finance systems with ease. Interoperability has two advantages: it reduces friction and improves the flow of data and insights. *Engage Stakeholders:* During the planning and execution stages, it is essential to include finance teams, IT personnel, and upper management. Their collaboration, support, and contribution are essential to the outcome. *Regulation Compliance:* Healthcare facilities must ensure that AI-powered accounting systems comply with all applicable data security and healthcare legislation. There might be monetary and legal consequences if this isn't done. *Regular Updates and Training:* To make the most of AI systems, staff members need to continue learning about and being trained on them. When AI evolves, employees should be notified. To sustain ethical standards, hospitals should aggressively remove biases in AI systems and ensure transparency in their financial decision-making processes. When using AI ethically, consideration must be given to the impact on patients and the broader community.

Accountability and Recourse: Clearly identify the parties in charge of decisions made using AI, and provide protocols for addressing errors or unforeseen consequences. *Continuous Improvement:* Using AI in hospital accounting is an ongoing endeavor. Regularly assess and enhance AI systems to adapt to changing legal and financial contexts. *Patient Data Privacy:* When AI systems utilize patient data in financial transactions, informed permission and robust data privacy precautions are required. Patients should control their information and have knowledge about its utilization. These real-world examples and best practices demonstrate the potential benefits and challenges of AI-driven hospital accounting. AI may optimize financial operations, boost productivity, and enhance patient care if it is properly integrated into hospital financial management. However, this can only happen if the integration is done with careful planning, ethical responsibility, and compliance.

Future Hospital Accounting Solutions Powered by AI That Are Most Likely to Succeed:

Invest in AI Knowledge and Skill: Hospitals should make this investment if they want to hire and educate data scientists, financial analysts, and AI professionals who can manage the complexities of AI-driven accounting. Building an internal team with the necessary expertise is necessary for long-term success. *Adopt a holistic approach to AI:* Draught an AI strategy that addresses all financial functions, such as revenue cycle management, cost control, and forecasting. Verify that AI complies with the hospital's overall operational and budgetary goals. *Data Management and Governance:* Make data management and governance a top focus in order to protect high-quality data. Implement data governance policies, data cleaning techniques, and regular audits to ensure the accuracy of the data utilized to provide AI-driven insights.

Integration and Interoperability: Ensure that AI solutions are designed to be compatible with the current financial and accounting systems. Smooth data flow and integration between AI and older technologies may help improve financial processes and prevent data silos. *Monitor and Enhance AI Systems Regularly:* Keep an eye on AI systems and update your algorithms often to adapt to changing financial and legal environments. Artificial intelligence cannot be used only once; it requires ongoing maintenance and advancement. Hospitals must aggressively combat algorithmic biases and be transparent about their use of AI in financial decision-making. Ethical issues ought to have a major impact on AI adoption. *Patient Data Privacy and Informed permission:* When using patient data in financial transactions, get informed permission and ensure that robust data protection measures are in place. Patients should be in charge of their data and aware of how it is used. *Cooperation and Communication:* Promote collaboration and open communication across the financial, IT, and clinical departments. Effective cross-departmental cooperation may lead to improved patient care and more efficient financial operations. *Invest in Education and Training:* Employees should be provided with continual instruction on artificial intelligence (AI) and its potential applications in hospital accounting. A knowledgeable and educated workforce is better equipped to use AI technology to their full potential.

Regularly review and update compliance measures: Keep abreast on the most recent modifications to healthcare standards and data privacy. Regularly review and update compliance procedures to ensure AI-driven accounting is legal. *Establish Mechanisms for Accountability and Recourse:* Clearly define the lines of responsibility for decisions made using AI, and provide processes for remedy in the case of errors or unanticipated consequences. *Strategic Partnerships:* Consider establishing strategic partnerships with AI suppliers or consulting firms that focus in healthcare bookkeeping. The wealth of resources and smart insights from these partnerships may be advantageous for the hospital's AI efforts. *Evaluate and Share Success Stories:* Communicate success stories inside the organization and regularly monitor the results of AI-driven hospital accounting. Showcasing tangible benefits may help maintain buy-in and support from stakeholders. Future regulatory compliance, enhanced patient care, and improved financial operations are all possible with AI-driven hospital accounting. If hospitals embrace AI proactively, address privacy and ethical issues, and maintain data integrity, they will be well-positioned to thrive in this evolving environment.

Enhancing Financial Operations in Hospitals Using Artificial Intelligence

Enhance the Design of the Information Sharing Module

The primary objective of information sharing is to facilitate the effective interchange of financial data within hospitals. By utilizing this mode, the network information platform can integrate the financial data information from separate accounting units in each department. It can then transmit the required financial data to the financial management personnel. Subsequently, the content is defined and appropriate treatment plans are established for classified control. To ensure efficient data interaction and accurate information transmission within hospital departments, it is crucial to adhere to the principles of organized, rational, and comprehensive work. This approach minimizes the risk of redundant or erroneous information transmission. During the specialized preparation phase, the system database is used to determine the suitable report template based on the business development. Subsequently, the report data is extracted in accordance with the template specifications. The platform has the capability to examine, combine, and condense the data, as well as provide the analysis and explanation for the report.

Ultimately, facilitate the transfer of information across autonomous financial entities via an interactive platform. Simultaneously, the financial professionals have the ability to modify the structure of the financial report according to their own and the unit's requirements. They may conduct a thorough analysis and interpretation, with a particular emphasis on any atypical data, and then provide it to the management for evaluation.

Efficient Management of Hospital Expenses

An essential aspect of intelligent finance is the accounting treatment, specifically the accounting function. The intelligent design of the reimbursement module is to achieve the automation and intelligent execution of various tasks such as voucher recording, storage, and accounting inside the interactive system. With the use of AI technology, the system is capable of automatically recognizing the content of images and doing data analysis using large datasets. The rise in popularity of electronic invoicing has led to the development of intelligent financial systems that allow for deep interaction with invoice systems. These systems are able to record business credentials in the core accounting system. Through the use of artificial intelligence, key data from paper invoices such as billing information, tax price, and tax are identified and converted into digital language. This digital data is then stored in the cloud. Simultaneously, intelligent finance may integrate with the tax invoice inquiry system to verify the legitimacy of invoices and efficiently manage fraudulent enterprises.

The financial staff of the hospital must submit the examination and approval application electronically in the OA office system once it has been reviewed by the system according to the authorized settings. The application may then be signed and authorized inside the OA system. Following the OA review, the first voucher approval form and accompanying approval data will be sent to the financial accounting system. The financial professionals will examine the document information, which will then be encrypted by the intelligent financial system and shown as a QR code on the papers. This ensures the data's uniqueness and secrecy. Afterwards, the system automatically generates a hard copy of the accounting reimbursement papers, which are then placed by the financial professionals, together with the original vouchers, into the accounting file cabinet as per the regulations. The "smart finance" service mode incorporates memory feedback, enabling analysis of financial personnel's daily entry writing patterns and automated generation of accounting entries for specified economic business data. This feature saves time and facilitates subsequent review processes.

Simultaneously, the data before and after the review may coexist and it can be precisely and fully categorized and stored in accordance with accounting rules. The "smart finance" service is capable of managing the accounting vouchers in the financial budget processing, following the established processes. In order to examine the financial performance during the last 3-5 years, many budget models are integrated to conduct an initial estimation of the future cash flow of the economic enterprise. In the system, the major indicators of the current market environment and policy changes are entered based on many parameters. This allows for a realistic assessment of the unit's cash inflow and outflow, capital requirements, business outlook, and asset condition. The financial budget is developed based on this foundation. Following an assessment of the budget department, taking into account the viewpoints and recommendations of the budget stakeholders, the subsequent phase is now being implemented.

Efficient Management of Hospital Financial Records

Cost management accounting is an essential component of financial management. The "financial" system includes an intelligent cost accounting and management module, which promptly determines the current profit and loss accounting cost and cost responsibility centre in accordance with the cost accounting rules of the cost entity. If confirmation is not possible, predictions may be made based on historical practices and liquidation can be carried out at the conclusion of the accounting cycle. The cost management module primarily guarantees that the accounting items comprehensively include all aspects of the unit's economic activities. Cost control involves the division and quantification of expenses within separate economic departments. It further examines the real economic gains of independent financial units using cost analysis models, structural analysis, and trend forecast techniques. The cost control intelligence module may provide analysis reports for management to use when making adjustments to the organizational management structure and business model.

CONCLUSION

By integrating AI-driven technology into hospital accounting, a significant step has been achieved towards the financial stability and operational excellence of healthcare businesses. AI has the potential to revolutionize hospital financial administration by increasing accuracy, efficiency, and the ability to offer patient-centered care. Artificial intelligence (AI) has the potential to totally change financial management in the healthcare sector by enhancing revenue cycle management, cutting costs, and increasing forecasting accuracy. Artificial intelligence (AI) is shown to be more than just a theoretical concept but also a practical and tried-and-true solution for hospitals by the best practices and real-world examples given. If hospitals want to fully capitalize on AI's disruptive potential, they will need to make deliberate choices and substantial investments. This means resolving moral issues, ensuring data security and privacy, fostering a responsible and open culture, and encouraging high-quality data.AI-driven hospital accounting offers a practical path to operational improvement and financial stability as healthcare organizations continue to navigate the complex regulatory landscape and strive for patient-centered care. If hospitals deliberately embrace AI, include their stakeholders, and make knowledge and technology investments, they will be better positioned to thrive in this dynamic and evolving healthcare environment. They will be able to achieve financial stability and better care for patients and the community at large by doing this.

REFERENCES

Andrushia, A. D., Neebha, T. M., Patricia, A. T., Sagayam, K. M., & Pramanik, S. (2023). Capsule Network based Disease Classification for VitisVinifera Leaves. *Neural Computing & Applications*. Advance online publication. doi:10.1007/s00521-023-09058-y

Ashisha, G. R., Anitha Mary, X., George, T., & Martin Sagayam, K. (2023). Unai Fernandez-GamizHatıraGünerhan, M. N.Uddin and S. Pramanik, Analysis of Diabetes disease using Machine Learning Techniques: A Review. *Journal of Information Technology Management.*

Bhattacharya, A., Ghosal, A., Obaid, A. J., Krit, S., Shukla, V. K., Mandal, K., & Pramanik, S. (2021). Unsupervised Summarization Approach with Computational Statistics of Microblog Data. In D. Samanta, R. R. Althar, S. Pramanik, & S. Dutta (Eds.), *Methodologies and Applications of Computational Statistics for Machine Learning* (pp. 23–37). IGI Global. doi:10.4018/978-1-7998-7701-1.ch002

Jain, V., Rastogi, M., Ramesh, J. V. N., Chauhan, A., Agarwal, P., Pramanik, S., & Gupta, A. (2023). FinTech and Artificial Intelligence in Relationship Banking and Computer Technology. In K. Saini, A. Mummoorthy, R. Chandrika, N. S. Gowri Ganesh, & I. G. I. Global (Eds.), *AI, IoT, and Blockchain Breakthroughs in E-Governance*. doi:10.4018/978-1-6684-7697-0.ch011

Jayasingh, R. (2022). Speckle noise removal by SORAMA segmentation in Digital Image Processing to facilitate precise robotic surgery. *International Journal of Reliable and Quality E-Healthcare, 11*(1), 1–19. Advance online publication. doi:10.4018/IJRQEH.295083

Khanh, P. T., Ngọc, T. H., & Pramanik, S. (2023). Future of Smart Agriculture Techniques and Applications. In A. Khang & I. G. I. Global (Eds.), *Advanced Technologies and AI-Equipped IoT Applications in High Tech Agriculture*. doi:10.4018/978-1-6684-9231-4.ch021

Mandal, A., Dutta, S., & Pramanik, S. (2021). Machine Intelligence of Pi from Geometrical Figures with Variable Parameters using SCILab. In D. Samanta, R. R. Althar, S. Pramanik, & S. Dutta (Eds.), *Methodologies and Applications of Computational Statistics for Machine Learning* (pp. 38–63). IGI Global. doi:10.4018/978-1-7998-7701-1.ch003

Pramanik, S., & Bandyopadhyay, S. (2023). Identifying Disease and Diagnosis in Females using Machine Learning. In I. G. I. John Wang (Ed.), *Encyclopedia of Data Science and Machine Learning*. Global. doi:10.4018/978-1-7998-9220-5.ch187

Pramanik, S., Galety, M. G., Samanta, D., & Joseph, N. P. (2022). Data Mining Approaches for Decision Support Systems, *3rd International Conference on Emerging Technologies in Data Mining and Information Security*. 10.1007/s11042-023-16762-3,2023

Pramanik, S., Sagayam, K. M., & Jena, O. P. (2021). Machine Learning Frameworks in Cancer Detection. ICCSRE 2021, Morocco. doi:10.1051/e3sconf/202129701073

Praveenkumar, S., Veeraiah, V., Pramanik, S., Basha, S. M., Lira Neto, A. V., De Albuquerque, V. H. C., & Gupta, A. (2023). *Prediction of Patients' Incurable Diseases Utilizing Deep Learning Approaches, ICICC*. Springer., doi:10.1007/978-981-99-3315-0_4

Samanta, D., & Dutta, S. M. (2021). A Novel Approach for Web Mining Taxonomy for High-Performance Computing. *The 4th International Conference of Computer Science and Renewable Energies (ICCSRE'2021)*. 10.1051/e3sconf/202129701073

VidyaChellam. (2023). *A Machine Vision-based Approach for Tuberculosis Identification in Chest X-Rays Images of Patients, ICICC*. Springer. doi:10.1007/978-981-99-3315-0_3

Veeraiah, V., Thejaswini, K. O., Dilip, R., Jain, S. K., Sahu, A., Pramanik, S., & Gupta, A. (2023). *The Suggested Use of Big Data in Medical Analytics by Fortis Healthcare Hospital. In Adoption and Use of Technology Tools and Services by Economically Disadvantaged Communities: Implications for Growth and Sustainability*. IGI Global.

Vesty, G., Kokshagina, O., Jansson, M., Cheong, F., & Butler-Henderson, K. (2023). Accounting, valuing and investing in health care: Dealing with outdated accounting models. *Meditari Accountancy Research*, *31*(1), 52–77. doi:10.1108/MEDAR-06-2021-1334

Chapter 6
Central America:
Pioneering Innovation Amidst Challenges

Rodrigo Romero
University Canada West, Canada

Luciana Gamarra Laguna
University Canada West, Canada

Hamed Taherdoost
University Canada West, Canada

ABSTRACT

This research delves into the adoption of financial technologies in Central America, also referred to as Fintechs, which hold great potential for financial inclusion and economic growth. By asking the question of how government support and regulatory framework affects the adoption of financial technologies, research is aimed towards the investigation of frameworks and its importance, the amount of government support, and the current market offering in the region. This research is significant per the authors given it highlights the opportunity to favor the adoption of financial technologies, not only for the chance to become an example but also a hub for innovation in the region. The investigation allowed to visualize the diverse landscape of Fintechs in the Central American market, such as adoption rate, level of priority, and the amount of support they receive per country. Some key findings include the high support from particular governments and the push of private organizations for the betterment of frameworks that will ease the development and operation of these companies.

INTRODUCTION

The financial industry is presently undergoing a significant shift characterized by the extensive use of financial technology, commonly referred to as fintech, within conventional banking and financial services. Central America, a geographical area renowned for its rich cultural variety and distinctive topography, is not immune to this prevailing worldwide phenomenon. The Central American region has witnessed

DOI: 10.4018/979-8-3693-1561-3.ch006

a significant surge in the adoption of fintech solutions in recent years. This trend has brought about a transformation in the way citizens in these countries access and handle their financial matters. This study undertakes a thorough investigation of the captivating phenomena, the different aspects that affect the Fintech market of Central America.

The primary aim of this essay is to examine the significant influence exerted by regulatory frameworks and government backing in defining the fintech landscape of the region. The objective of our investigation is to examine the impact of regulatory frameworks on the rates of fintech adoption and assess their role in achieving broader goals of financial innovation and inclusiveness.

Moreover, this analysis transcends the boundaries of scholarly investigation, as it carries substantial policy ramifications for the governments of Central American nations. Policymakers within the region are consistently endeavoring to devise policies aimed at fostering economic growth while also safeguarding financial stability. Conducting a comprehensive examination of the consequences of policies connected to financial technology (fintech) can yield significant knowledge for the development of regulatory frameworks that facilitate financial innovation, protect consumer welfare, and encourage greater access to financial services.

Simply put, this essay argues that regulatory framework and government support of the fintech markets in their countries can have far-reaching effects in terms of economic growth, financial stability, and financial inclusion.

PROBLEM STATEMENT

The adoption of financial technology in Central American nations is a fascinating yet understudied topic, particularly in the area of government framework. This research aims to demonstrate the importance of the link between proper jurisdiction and how fintech might be able to shape the future of these nations.

Central American nations have long struggled with financial inclusion since they lack widespread access to formal financial services, leaving the fintech sector to advance slowly with a reduced.

The result that is hoped to achieve through this study is that it will have a big influence on public policy. Central American policymakers are constantly looking for new ways to promote economic growth while preserving a stable financial environment. through the reading of this paper, we hope that policymakers may create efficient regulatory frameworks that support greater financial inclusion and foster innovation specifically in financial technology sector by performing a thorough review of the long-term effects that fintech-related policies may have not only in each country but also in the entire region.

RESEARCH QUESTIONS AND OBJECTIVES

Given these factors, the main goal of this inquiry is to look into and assess the relationship between legal frameworks and the uptake of fintech in Central American nations. By looking at this connection, the research hopes to offer light on potential avenues for fostering financial innovation, accessibility, and inclusiveness in the area. By doing this, the study wants to advance the conversation on how fintech is fundamentally altering the economies and society of Central American nations. These facts lead to the formulation of the research question: How does government support and regulatory framework affect the adoption of financial technologies?

This study aims to provide insight into the current trend developments occurring in Central America related to Fintech, providing a glimpse into the transformative impact of financial inclusion and the innovation it brings to the region. It is hoped that this research will inspire others to further research the benefits fintech might bring to the Central American region, as well as to move legislators to review their current legal framework and create new laws to increase the rate of fintech adoption.

REVIEW OF LITERATURE

For the purpose of our literature analysis, we used four different areas as a foundation for our investigation: the different forms of fintech, the present offering, the present infrastructure, and the economic impact. In the course of our assessment of the relevant literature, we intend to collect this information from six countries in Central America: Guatemala, El Salvador, Honduras, Nicaragua, Costa Rica, and Panama, with a special mention to Belize. A general conclusion is drawn from the observations regarding wherever holes there are in the research. The review is sectioned by each of the previously mentioned aspects.

Influential Factors

A younger population that is more sensitive to technological innovations, higher smartphone penetration, and limited access to traditional financial services are just a few of the reasons why Central American nations are experiencing a spike in interest in fintech solutions. Other factors include the fact that these nations have limited access to traditional financial services. The rate at which countries adopt financial technology differs greatly from one another. For example, El Salvador, Costa Rica, Guatemala, Honduras, and Panama each have more than 20 financial technology companies registered in their respective countries. A growing number of individuals and businesses are providing online lending platforms, digital payment systems, and other financial services. Countries such as Costa Rica, Panama, and Guatemala were some of the first to adopt fintech. These nations had internet connectivity and digital infrastructure that was much superior to that of most others.

Classifications of Fintechs

A Fintech can be any type of technological financial service or tool, but we believe that Fonseca-Arguello (2021) classified them in the most effective way possible by dividing them into Tech for Financial Institutions, Payment Solutions, Alternative Financial Platforms, Enterprise Financial Management, and Alternative Scoring. In other words, Fintech is a broad concept that can refer to any type of technological financial service or tool. After doing some additional research, one can reach the conclusion that, due to the characteristics of the bulk of the businesses in Central America, they can be divided into two categories: payment solutions and alternative financial platforms.

Small Region, Big Players

Even though they only account for 6% of the total market, Central America is notorious for following growth trends in the predominant sectors, which are payments and lending (Fonseca-Arguello, 2021). The current offering of financial technology in Central America is relatively limited in comparison to the larger picture of financial technology in Latin America. As an illustration for the purpose of this discussion, we will be employing the type of financial technology that is most widely used in each nation.

Legislative Framework

Central American governments have been working hard to control the financial technology industry by passing legislation in recent years. Despite the fact that different countries go about it in different ways, all countries have the same overarching goal in mind, which is to foster financial innovation while also protecting consumers, ensuring anti-money laundering compliance, and maintaining overall financial stability. In order to establish regulations for the financial technology industry, Costa Rica is now engaging in discussions regarding the regulation of payment processors and electronic money. On the other hand, Panama achieved considerable progress by passing Law No. 122 in the year 2020. This law was enacted. In addition, the regulations that are outlined in this law apply to websites that facilitate peer-to-peer lending and crowdfunding, as well as digital wallets. Guatemala is looking into the regulations around online payments and crowdfunding as part of an effort to encourage innovation and expand access to financial services. In the meantime, a statute that establishes a robust legal framework for fintech services like digital wallets and electronic payments was just enacted in El Salvador, and Honduras is currently in the process of crafting legislation to govern electronic payment services. Both of these nations are in Central America.

RESEARCH METHODOLOGY

Our instrument of choice based on the requirements of our research and taking into consideration the kind of information that was required, we concluded that the best technique is to continue using the method of conducting a literature and article review.

The abundance of pertinent materials made it necessary for us to decide to depend only on already-published works, as well as news articles, websites, and publications from both public and private organizations. We did have a brief conversation with a government representative about the recently passed Fintech Law in El Salvador, but given the time constraints, it would have been impractical to do in-depth interviews, transcriptions, and analyses. Aside from conducting interviews with business owners and government officials, no other mode of data collection could adequately provide the information we needed.

As surveys would have added needless complexity and time requirements, we decided against employing them as well. We are more concerned with comprehending the regulatory dynamics and the causes driving Fintech expansion in Central America than we are with analyzing the general consensus. As many of the topics we are trying to answer can be answered by simple examination, surveys would not have contributed any insightful information to our research.

Our research instrument demonstrates strong support for our research objective, which is to acquire the data necessary for our study by supplying sufficient information. As a result, we do not need to rely on other research instruments such as surveys, interviews, or focus groups.

Given that it is more in line with our area of study, qualitative data will be prioritized in our analysis. We have access to both quantitative and qualitative data thanks to past studies and official records, but given the nature of our investigation, we continue to place a strong emphasis on qualitative data. Our data collecting strategy is further bolstered by the fact that it draws on peer-reviewed literature, expert opinions from the sector, and official government information, including legislation that has been passed.

The data utilized for this research was found through the use of Google Scholar and other similar online libraries, as well as official government websites to corroborate. Some of the keywords utilized in our research were "Fintech", "Central America", "Financial Inclusion", Fintech development", "Alternative banking", and "any country specific keywords such as regulatory body names, companies, and associations.

In addition, given the current state of affairs, we are unable to detect any ethical constraint to continuing our research. There is no requirement for permission to show opinions, there are no legal limits, and all of the data that was used is accessible to the public through official ways. As has been discussed throughout this document, the approach that we use to collect data does not require any additional complexity beyond the necessity to continue assessing past and current data in order to have a more thorough picture of the situation in Central America pertaining to fintech. Since this industry is undergoing rapid development at the time this paper was written, it will be helpful to make use of current and forthcoming information regarding the state of the fintech industry; accordingly, we will keep an eye out for any information that may become available.

The main interest from the research is to extract any information pertinent to each specific nation through readings of the literature found. First, the focus was to understand the current financial situation of each country, this allowed us to move to the second part of the research which was getting to know what Fintechs existed in each market and seek key players. The third and final part consisted of reviewing the government structure through the investigation and reading of current legislation. With the combined research it was possible to have a better understanding of the fintech landscape of Central America, further allowing us to draw individual and general conclusions about the state of legislation and financial inclusion.

INDIVIDUAL COUNTRY STUDY

Belize

For research purposes, it was decided to include Belize into this paper since even though there is minimal information related to Fintechs other than some superficial articles and a lack of regulatory framework, it serves a purpose for the general conclusion. Having a population of only around 400,000 Belize has a very saturated market and with many limitations to the banking system, an issue that can be addressed through the adoption of Fintechs.

Out of the seven countries of the region, Belize is the one with one of the largest amounts of Fintechs but least variety. Out of the 88 startups currently being developed in the country, the majority of these are related to Crypto and digital assets (Tracxn, 2023). The three fastest growing ones are Vconomics, PolkaFantasy, and Victorieum, the first two being Blockchain-based NFT marketplaces, with the third being a Crypto-based banking solution.

Guatemala

Current Fintech Landscape

The current state of Fintech in Guatemala seems promising, with the formation of the Guatemalan Fintech Association as a means to represent all these companies under one organization, Financial Technologies have gained more traction thanks to the continuous support of private equity.

"The Association's main objective is to bring together all companies in the country's fintech sector to offer its members and the general public an inclusive space for collaboration in which they are allowed to promote the evolution of the industry" (Fintech Guatemala, 2023). Additionally, they currently have 38 members in all the five areas previously mentioned, Paggo having the largest market share.

Key Player: Paggo

Paggo is currently the most widely adopted Fintech in Guatemala, it offers payment solutions for small and medium enterprises through links, QR codes, and POS terminals. Their intuitive approach to facilitating progressive business growth through the use of different levels of payment systems has led to them becoming the leaders in alternative payment solutions for the country.

Paggo has a user base of around 6,800 businesses and is available in the 22 departments of Guatemala. What's more, you can affiliate with any bank without the need for lengthy queues or opening new accounts. For businesses serving international customers, Paggo ensures that you can accept payments from visitors using international cards. With a competitive commission rate of 4.99% + VAT, Paggo stands as a cost-effective choice in the market for payment processing services.

Regulatory Framework and Government Support

Even though Guatemalan Fintechs are being supported greatly by private individuals and companies, there exists a lack of support from part of the government. As of writing, there exists no real law or framework related to Crypto and Digital Assets, but the regulations placed by the Superintendency of the country is being used for E-Money managed by banks, credit unions, and other users of digital currency; the SIB also has a branch dedicated to consultation of applicable laws and regulations related to Fintechs, but not much else is being done in terms of actually creating a framework.

El Salvador

Current Fintech Landscape

Out of the seven nations in the region, El Salvador has had the most publicly evident increase in support both by government and private enterprises. The rapid adoption of Fintech started in 2013 with the creation of YoVendoRecarga, which is a prepaid cell phone recharge app that removed the need for individuals to physically have to go and recharge their data, instead of simply doing it online. The current offering of Fintechs is ample, with payment solutions such as Teip, food and delivery services like Hugo and PedidosYa, and full-on traditional bank alternatives such as the government owned Chivo Wallet, which incorporates USD and the other official coin of El Salvador: Bitcoin.

Key Player: Chivo Wallet

Scale wise, the largest of all systems in Central America is Chivo Wallet, the privately owned-government managed wallet service provided free of charge to every citizen of the republic. Chivo Wallet falls into the category of alternative financial platform; it is an all-out traditional banking alternative that incorporates USD and the second official currency of El Salvador: Bitcoin. The app offers instant conversion between USD and BTC, QR codes for sending and receiving money, bill payment options, with a large Crypto ATM network that spans across the country that supports all transaction types related to Crypto.

Regulatory Framework and Government Support

The current administration of El Salvador has done extensive work in multiple areas of the country: Security, infrastructure, education, with Fintech support and financial inclusion being an area where special emphasis has been put in with the intention but improving the situation of the citizens while also attracting the interest of foreign investment towards the country.

The corpus Legis of El Salvador on Fintech activity is the following: Law for the Promotion of Innovation and Technological Manufacturing; Bitcoin Law; Guidelines for the authorization of the Operation of the Technological Platform of Services with Bitcoin and Dollars; Electronic Signature Law; Law to Facilitate Financial Inclusion; and the Technical Standards for the Constitution of Electronic Money Provider Companies;. There are also the Technical Standards to Facilitate the Participation of Financial Entities in the Bitcoin Ecosystem; Digital Asset Issuance Law and the Guide for Virtual Asset Service Providers that contains obligations.

The recent approval of the Law to Facilitate Financial Inclusion has brought new light to the subject of Fintechs, the object of it being to propitiate financial inclusion, foment competition in the financial system, reducing costs both for users and operators, as well as setting the minimum requirements for the creation, use, and transfer of Electronic Money. The law itself allows for all approved Fintechs to become part of the National Financial System as providers of E-money as well as all banks, cooperative banks, and credit unions also fall under the guidelines of this law, bringing commercial businesses and the traditional system to compete against one another.

Honduras

Current Fintech Landscape

In the aim of doing exhaustive research, we have decided to include Honduras in this study, despite the fact that there is very little information currently available on Fintech companies operating within the country, what is known is that the Covid-19 pandemic played a significant role into the development of the Financial Technology market, leading to a response from the government.

Key Player: TENGO

Despite there being few Fintechs in the Honduran market, TENGO' is by far the largest. TENGO is a flexible multi-bank solution made to make it easier for you to satisfy your financial commitments without spending any money. You can easily handle a range of transactions with the help of the TENGO app. You may easily manage utility bill payments, credit card settlements, loan repayments, cell phone top-ups, stadium ticket purchases, money transfers, and remittance collecting. TENGO provides personalized services for each customer, and what distinguishes it is its inclusivity — regardless of distances, the availability of bank accounts, or mobile service providers. TENGO meets your financial demands, assuring smooth transactions and increased convenience, whether you have a bank account or not. (TENGO, 2023)

Regulatory Framework and Government Support

In spite of the fact that the existing body of research provides only a surface-level grasp of the topic, there does exist a regulatory framework: the 2021"Decree No.83" established that legal entities that wish to provide payment and transfer services to natural and legal persons residing in Honduras must obtain authorization from the Central Bank of Honduras (BCH) or register in the registry that said Institution will maintain for this purpose, the above in accordance with the regulations issued by the BCH. Additionally in 2022, the "Regulation for Electronic Payment Service Providers" serves as an additional measure for all those entities that work with E-money for compliance with inclusion and financial stability and user protection policies. (Gov. Honduras, 2022)

Even though these measures serve a purpose, as of right now there still exist no law or regulation in relation to digital assets such as Crypto and NFTs, but it is still important to include Honduras in our analysis if we want to be able to draw full conclusions about the Fintech landscape in Central America.

Nicaragua

Current Fintech Landscape

Close to a dozen organizations have signed agreements with the Central Bank of Nicaragua (BCN) to supply fintech services in the country. These establishments include the country's biggest banks as well as newer, innovative fintech firms providing a wide range of services. Digital payment systems, currency exchange platforms, and services targeted toward virtual asset management are just a few of the important components of Nicaragua's remarkably varied financial technology ecosystem. The increased passion and capital infusion into the fintech sector across the nation are reflected by the broad selection of solutions already accessible to the public.

Regulatory Framework and Government Support

The Nicaraguan government's partnership with the BCN to establish and refine the regulatory framework is evidence of the government's support for fintech efforts. The Nicaraguan government's goal is to encourage both domestic and foreign fintech companies to set up shop in the country by cultivating an atmosphere that fosters innovation while also promoting safety and adhering to regulatory standards.

To protect its clients and guarantee the integrity of its financial system, Nicaragua has acknowledged the necessity to regulate fintech-related activity. The BCN's "Reglamento de los Proveedores de Tecnología Financiera de Servicios de Pago y Proveedores de Servicios de Activos Virtuales" (Regulation of Financial Technology Payment Service Providers and Virtual Asset Service Providers) was written with this end in mind. Providers of Financial Technology Payment Services and Virtual Asset Service Providers are both included in this all-encompassing rule.

Digital wallets, mobile POS systems, electronic money, online currency exchange, fund transfers, and payment gateways are only some of the electronic payment services provided by financial technology payment service providers. These services can be accessed from mobile devices. In order to legally conduct business in Nicaragua, they must first register with the BCN and the Financial Analysis Unit. Financial institutions that are currently licensed by the Superintendency of Banks and Other Financial Institutions or the National Microfinance Commission need not apply for a BCN license. However, they are still bound by the rules established here.

These companies help make possible the issuance, trading, and storage of virtual currencies, as well as the supply of related financial services. They, like their payment services industry contemporaries, are subject to BCN and Financial Analysis Unit registration requirements.

A new law backed by the BCN is now being drafted in Nicaragua; it is titled "Proyecto de Ley de Proveedores de Tecnología Financiera (Fintech)." Providers of Financial Technology Intermediation and Financing Services are the newest class to be established by this proposed law. The initiative gives rise to this class; nevertheless, it should be noted that it has not yet been brought to the National Assembly for consideration. This exemplifies Nicaragua's dedication to updating its regulatory framework to reflect the dynamic nature of the fintech sector.

Costa Rica

Costa Rica's Unique Financial Landscape

Nearly 79 percent of Costa Rica's population will have access to traditional banking services by the year 2020, earning the country the reputation as having an impressive banking rate. In addition, the country has a rate of phone service penetration that is greater than 169%, making it the highest in the world. Given this section of the population, sixty percent, has adopted fintech services (Fonseca-Arguello, 2021).

Because of its high phone service penetration and rising demand for internet-based financial services, Costa Rica stands out as one of the most banked countries in Latin America. At the same time, the country is undergoing a spike in development, highlighting the growing significance of technology-driven financial solutions (Ernesto, Gutiérrez, Schneider, 2019).

Regulatory Framework and Government Support

At the time of writing, Costa Rica does not have a formal law governing fintech. However, regulatory initiatives are already underway, and major institutions such as the Central Bank, the Superintendency, and CONASSIF (National Insurance and Financial Services Regulator) are working together to develop a complete regulatory framework. The goal of these efforts is to create an environment in which financial institutions can operate safely and securely. Existing legislation, such as SUGEF agreements 14-17, which cover the administration of information technologies, serve as a roadmap for the financial technology industry in Costa Rica, despite the fact that the absence of a specific law pertaining to fintech may appear to be a barrier.

The fact that Costa Rica is an active participant in the Fintech Association of Central America and the Caribbean is evidence of the country's dedication to promoting the expansion of the financial technology industry in the area. The number of financial technology firms in the country has exploded in recent years, growing from five in 2017 to an astonishing 25 in 2019.

Key Players

The landscape of the financial technology industry in Costa Rica is quite varied, spanning a variety of sectors such as Enterprise Financial Management, Payment Solutions, Alternative Financial Platforms, and Alternative Scoring, among others. WINK, Zunify, and Greenpay are three notable fintech businesses that have contributed in their own special ways to the expanding ecosystem of the financial technology industry.

Challenges and Opportunities

The requirement for regulatory frameworks that are both clear and robust is one of the most fundamental issues that the Costa Rican financial technology ecosystem must overcome. Uncertainty has arisen due to the lack of a formal law pertaining to Fintech, and players are working toward the establishment of a legislative framework that is open, well-balanced, and trustworthy in order to facilitate the expansion of the sector.

In addition, there is a demand for an all-encompassing public policy that includes both the public and commercial sectors, with an emphasis on the facilitation of business, the reduction of bureaucratic processes, and the active involvement of academia in research, training, and system evaluation.

Another essential component that must receive focus is the availability of financial backing for emerging fintech companies, particularly in the early phases of their development. During the early stages of a fintech enterprise, it is critical to locate potential funding sources and offer technical support in order to ensure the company's long-term viability and further growth.

WINK

Under the category of Alternative Financial Platforms, we have WINK, which is a mobile application that enables account opening in a matter of minutes. The application provides users with the ability to borrow money, manage their personal finances, make automatic payments to their bills, and obtain a debit card that can be used with any ATM network. Additionally, the application is connected to a national inter-institutional money transfer system known as SINPE.

Future Prospects

The environment of financial technology in Costa Rica is on the precipice of undergoing a substantial upheaval. In spite of the fact that it is one of the most banked countries in Latin America, the financial system is undergoing significant change as a direct result of the proliferation of fintech services. There is a deliberate effort being made to build a clear and supportive legal framework, despite the fact that regulatory challenges continue to exist.

There is a significant opportunity for innovation and economic growth in Costa Rica as the country works toward creating a more all-encompassing ecosystem for the financial technology industry. With ongoing cooperation between the public and commercial sectors, academic institutions, and international collaborations, Costa Rica has the ambition of establishing itself as a financial hub not just for Central America but also for the entirety of the Americas. As regulatory frameworks continue to develop and investments continue to stream in, the nation is well positioned for a fintech-driven future that offers greater financial inclusion and economic growth.

Panama

Current Fintech Offering

In a recent interview with La Estrella de Panama, Allen Cueli, regional leader of Visa Products for the Caribbean and Central America, discussed the critical importance of fintech technology in Panama. He argued that cutting out middlemen will allow financial transactions to be faster and more responsive.

There is already a large sum of fintech businesses in Panama that are making huge inroads. PayCaddy stands out as a notable competitor because of the innovative solutions it offers for digitizing banking and creating individualized financial technology solutions. Munily is another major player that has made its name by digitizing municipal services and payments.

Furthermore, the widespread availability of cutting-edge technology has significantly bolstered safety protocols. To make sure that only approved users may access their accounts, user authentication via mobile devices is becoming increasingly common. This level of safety is a giant step forward in protecting monetary transactions when compared to the operations of traditional banks.

Challenges and Future Prospects

Achieving financial inclusion is difficult in Panama because not all citizens have the digital credentials necessary to fully engage in the digital economy. It is crucial that we educate the public and enlist more participants from the general populace in this effort.

Allen Cueli agrees with the importance of increasing people's access to financial services and hopes that in the near future, more options will be made available to consumers. In order to bring this dream to fruition, he plans to increase the variety of payment methods available to the general public.

Raul Romero stresses the significance of user trust, especially among people who are unfamiliar with financial matters. The following steps must focus on establishing trust in the safety of digital transactions and guaranteeing flexibility in a wide range of economic contexts. (Panama Star, 2023)

Panama, despite these obstacles, has the potential to become a cashless society. Financial innovation flourishes there because of the country's cultural diversity and acceptance of online trade. If efforts are sustained, Panama might become the financial technology center of Central America. The government will then be in a better position to implement novel solutions and promote widespread access to financial services as a result.

Key Player: Nequi

Nequi is a Fintech company originally started in Colombia that gained traction in the Panamanian market. They are an app-based mobile payment platform that, in their own words: "Improves people's relationship with their money". They offer cellphone recharge, savings programs, online payments, and QR codes for money transfer. (Nequi, 2023)

In addition, both Nequi and Visa are helping to develop contactless payment systems, which are a safe and hassle-free method to do business. In fact, a staggering 73% of Visa transactions are currently conducted using this technology, demonstrating the widespread adoption of contactless payment methods in Panama. This change has been very helpful in maintaining good public opinion, especially through the difficult times brought on by the pandemic.

Fintech, as emphasized by Panama's Nequi head Raul Romero, is crucial for giving timely monetary answers. Although millennials make up the bulk of Nequi's user base, the platform is open to anybody interested in using its fast and secure financial services, regardless of age. Paying bills, adding money, transferring money, and doing other financial operations is much easier and faster on a platform like Nequi than it is with traditional banking.

The electronic banking channel for mobile payments or e-wallets governed by Agreement No. 006-2011 on Electronic Banking supports Nequi, a digital platform created by Banistmo S.A. It functions as a savings account that resides on your mobile device with the intention of improving your financial relationship and assisting you in reaching your objectives. Nequi gives you the tools to construct personalized compartments, set savings objectives, and provide a safety net for unforeseen costs.

A Nequi account is a personal savings account that has no monthly service charges. The account has limits that do not exceed $2,500 USD in monthly balance, and you have the option to keep a balance of zero if you so choose. This software offers a practical and user-friendly method of managing your money, encouraging better money management and command over your resources.

KEY TAKEAWAYS

Economic Impact

Fintech is contributing to financial inclusion, enhancing access to financial services, and fostering regional economic development. Particularly in rural and underdeveloped areas, the issue of limited access to traditional banking services was being addressed in part by fintech. Financial services were being made available to groups of people who had little or no access to them before thanks to mobile banking and digital payment systems. This practice promoted financial inclusion and increased economic participation for both individuals and small companies. Furthermore, a lot of Central American nations rely substantially on remittances from outside. Fintech solutions are offering more effective and affordable ways to send and receive remittances, decreasing the reliance on pricey traditional remittance channels and putting more money in the hands of recipients.

Additionally, fintech lending platforms opened up new pathways for regular folks and small businesses to get credit. These platforms used different types of information and creative ways to evaluate loan requests, which meant that fintech companies could lend money to people who might have been turned away by traditional banks. What's more, fresh and creative ideas were coming out of fintech startups, sparking new business possibilities. Entrepreneurs were coming up with solutions for local problems like funding for farmers, microinsurance, and supporting supply chains. This kind of innovation was not only driving economic growth but also generating more jobs. On top of that, fintech solutions often turned out to be more pocket-friendly than the usual banking methods. Take digital payments, for example—they cut down on the need for cash transactions, making things safer, and they also brought down transaction costs for both businesses and regular folks. Lastly, it's worth highlighting that the rules set by governments had a big say in how fintech impacted the economy. Places where regulations supported both new ideas and safeguarding consumers tended to become hotspots for fintech investment and progress.

Gaps in Research

The main identifiable gap in our study is simply the lack of research regarding the current and emerging trends in specific countries of the region, namely Belize, Guatemala, Honduras, and Panama; even though some nations have groups dedicated to furthering the presence of Fintechs, there are currently very few documents speaking in detail of these countries' specific situation.

In contrast, Costa Rica and El Salvador have many documented studies of their financial technology market, some going as far as making economic predictions and spot-on suggestions regarding the future of Fintech in each domestic market. There exist two issues here relating to studies: First, the lack of documentation from previous studies, and second; the lack of documentation of current events related to Fintech development, adoption, and government support.

It has been identified that an area of future research that could be developed is that of cross-border transactions. Currently each app works only within its country of origin, with few ones such as Nequi are present in multiple nations. By either spreading the coverage to be international or through a collaborative effort, the adoption of fintech could reach new heights in the region. The increased awareness and user base would also lead to higher rates of financial inclusion, leading to better management of finances and the betterment of individual and national economies.

It is not possible to retrospectively address the lack of documentation regarding Fintechs, but it is possible to produce records from here on out. It is of utmost importance to write the processes and innovations created by these pioneers so in the future it is possible to look back at the current Central American Fintech landscape and assess how it has changed through time, if any new key players have emerged, and if the government has given the support that they require to thrive. As well as this, it is important to document since it will guide future research efforts, allowing new developments to also look back and analyze situations to make educated guesses and decisions regarding future endeavors.

RECOMMENDATIONS

We recommend companies to keep proper documentation of processes is a key aspect of any development. Proper record taking of all advances made for the sake of future research and development is strongly advised since it will aid new and upcoming projects to make educated decisions based on previous research.

For the governments, it is suggested that proper Fintech laws and regulations are passed to manage them accordingly and ease their growth. Adequate framework will allow for greater development and public adoption of financial technologies, which in turn will positively affect the economy of each nation by increasing the threshold of financial inclusion.

CONCLUSION

In the past decade, fintech has shaken up the financial sector in Latin America providing innovations in lending, payments, insurance, and regulation and compliance (Bakker, 2023). The booming effect this market has had in the last 10 years has pushed the traditional banking system and the idea of financial inclusion to a new level.

Financial inclusion being one of the main drivers of the development of these new systems has resulted in an increase of in some cases up to 10-15% of users for both traditional and alternative systems, such as in the cases of El Salvador with the introduction of Chivo Wallet and Costa Rica with the use of BAC transfer and WINK.

Government support is another important aspect to this investigation, the conclusion that can be drawn related to this aspect is that all central American governments are interested in the implementation of financial technologies, but the level of support given depends on the priority this has to the country: Guatemala has a Private Fintech Association with almost 40 members pushing for the creation of a law that governs and facilitates their existence, but it simply isn't a priority of the administration. In contrast, Countries such as El Salvador which are interested in exploiting this market for the financial interest of the population and government, and the push from private organizations such as Asafintech have led to the creation of the Fintech Law in mid-2023 as a proper regulatory system for this developing market.

Finally, in countries such as Belize it can be determined that the priority is not financial inclusion, but to take advantage of the Crypto and Digital Asset bandwagon. Blockchain-based NFT markets and Crypto banking solutions are the main focus for these businesses, leaving a void for other Fintech solutions such as alternative scoring.

REFERENCES

Bakker, B. B. (2023). *The rise and impact of fintech in Latin America*. Imfsg. doi:10.5089/9798400235474.063.A001

Barsallo Rodríguez, R. (2018). *Propuesta De Regulación De Las Fintech En Panamá* (Doctoral dissertation). Universidad Santa María La Antigua.

Carare, A., Franco, L., Hadzi-Vaskov, M., Lesniak, J., Vasilyev, D., & Yakhshilikov, Y. (2022). *Digital Money and Remittances Costs in Central America, Panama, and the Dominican Republic*. Academic Press.

Consortiumadmn. (2023). *Estado de la Regulación Fintech en la Región Centroamericana*. Consortium Legal. https://consortiumlegal.com/2022/09/30/estado-de-la-regulacion-fintech-en-la-region-centroamericana/

Creación del marco regulatorio para Fintech en Costa Rica. (n.d.). https://revistas.uned.ac.cr/index.php/rna/article/view/4785/6664

Ernest, W., Gutiérrez, P., & Schneider, C. (2019). *FINTECH en Costa Rica: hacia una evolución de los servicios financieros* (Vol. 732). Inter-American Development Bank. doi:10.18235/0001754

Fonseca-Argüello, H. (2021, November 22). *Estado y tendencias del sector Fintech en Costa Rica*. http://201.196.25.14/index.php/actas/article/view/1328

Godoy-Troya, J. R., & de Velazco, T. (2022). Modelos de negocios basados en fintech y su impacto en el ecosistema financiero panameño. *Revista Científica Orbis Cógnita*, *6*(1), 111–127.

Guevara, H. R. L., & Domínguez, J. N. C. (2023). *Fintech: Modelo de negocio para plataforma digital de financiamiento colaborativo en Honduras*. Academic Press.

La Estrella De Panamá, G. -. (2023, December 1). *El futuro de las "fintech" en Panamá. La Estrella De Panamá.* https://www.laestrella.com.pa/cafe-estrella/tecnologia/230112/futuro-fintech-panama

Marqués, J. M., Ávila, F., Rodríguez-Martínez, A., Morales-Reséndiz, R., Marcos, A., Godoy, T., Villalobos, P., Ocontrillo, A., Lankester, V. A., Blanco, C., Reyes, K., Lopez, S. I., Fernández, A., Santos, R., Maza, L. Á., Sánchez, M., Domínguez, C., Haynes, N., Panton, N., ... Francis-Pantor, M. (2021). Policy report on FinTech data gaps. *Latin American Journal of Central Banking*, *2*(3), 100037. doi:10.1016/j.latcb.2021.100037

Nagaraji, S., & Gardeaszabal Monsalue, A. (2023). *Digital ecosystem in Guatemala*. Intl Food Policy Res Inst.

Paggo App I Crece tu negocio. (n.d.). https://www.paggoapp.com/

PerlmanL.GurungN.TrujilloV. (2021). Regulatory Technology ("RegTech") Readiness in Honduras. Available at SSRN 3887874.

Young El Salvador. (2019). *Retos de la industria: Banca tradicional vs. Fintech.* Realidad Empresarial, Recuperado el 25 de Octubre de 2020. doi:10.5377/reuca.v0i7.7831

Chapter 7
Exploring Global Fintech Advancement and Application:
Case of Saudi Arabia, Turkey, and Qatar

Behzad Najafi
Hamta Business Corporation, Canada

Mohsen Amra
https://orcid.org/0000-0002-5713-2800
Hamta Business Corporation, Canada

Amir Najafi
Hamta Business Corporation, Canada

ABSTRACT

The strategic emphasis of financial service providers on leveraging new technologies to enhance the accessibility and quality of financial services has given rise to the FinTech concept. The growing economies of Saudi Arabia, Qatar, and Turkey have actively embraced FinTech development in recent years. This chapter comprehensively examines the state of FinTech in these nations, offering insights into current dynamics and future trends. Evaluations underscore that banking and payment services are pivotal sectors in these countries' FinTech endeavors. However, concerns persist, particularly regarding legal frameworks and security risks associated with user financial transaction data. The financial and regulatory support extended by Saudi Arabia, Qatar, and Turkey to FinTech companies has spurred rapid growth in recent years. This upward trajectory is anticipated to persist, with these countries increasingly relying on technology to propel advancements in financial services.

INTRODUCTION

The emergence of Financial Technology (Fintech) in recent years has been driven by the desire to deliver financial services through innovative technologies that enhance quality, expedite service delivery, and improve customer experience (Nicoletti et al., 2017). Broadly defined, Fintech encompasses "innovative

DOI: 10.4018/979-8-3693-1561-3.ch007

technology-enabled financial services and the business models that accompany those services" (Mention, 2019), emphasizing the crucial element of "innovation."

Fintech startups have made significant contributions to the financial industry by offering several key advantages, such as establishing robust systems from inception, streamlining operational designs, and providing low-leverage solutions (Philippon, 2016). However, Fintech service providers must remain vigilant regarding cyber risks, data analysis constraints (including issues related to data access, hardware, algorithms, and expertise), facility implementation optimization, and the integration of data collected from diverse platforms (Gai et al., 2018). Therefore, a comprehensive and multi-dimensional examination is imperative to fully understand the state of Fintech, encompassing both the advantages and challenges associated with this dynamic landscape.

This article delves into diverse dimensions of Fintech, including market size, adoption rates, types, key players, new investments and startups, ecosystems, regulations, security, academic research, interesting facts, and future prospects. A primary goal is to make the article particularly relevant for researchers, and to achieve this, we narrow the scope to scrutinize the state of Fintech in specific countries.

Saudi Arabia, the world's largest oil exporter with 90% of its income dependent on oil, has recently shifted its focus toward developing a knowledge economy, recognizing the pivotal role of innovation and technology in achieving this goal (Nurunnabi, 2017). In Qatar, a burgeoning knowledge-based economy is receiving significant support from the government. As one of the developed countries and a growing economy in Asia, Qatar envisions a bright future for FinTech development (Ben Hassen, 2021). Turkey, with its emphasis on export-based strategies utilizing technology and low-cost labor, holds the potential for positive FinTech development (Erinç Yeldan and Ünüvar, 2016). As a case study, we concentrate on Saudi Arabia, Qatar, and Turkey in the Middle East, examining their unique contexts to gain insights into the state of FinTech.

FINTECH IN SAUDI ARABIA, TURKEY, AND QATAR

Market Size (Potential)

According to a report by the Saudi Arabian Fintech Association (SAFA), the size of the fintech market in Saudi Arabia is expected to reach $10 billion by 2025. The report also found that there are over 100 fintech companies operating in Saudi Arabia (SAFA, 2022). Reports from the FinTech Ecosystem in Turkey (2023) indicate that the FinTech market in Turkey, comprising over 200 companies, exceeds a size of 15 billion dollars (Deloitte, 2023).Qatar's fintech sector has substantial room for growth given the country's high digital finance adoption rate, tech-savvy demographics and supportive policy environment. Over 85% of Qatar's population already uses services like digital wallets and payment apps (Al Jaber, 2022).

Subsequently, we will delve into a more detailed discussion of the factors influencing this market size

A. Smartphone Penetration Rate

The smartphone penetration rate in Saudi Arabia has been steadily increasing in recent years, reaching 77.2% in 2023, according to Statista (2023). This growth is attributed to several factors, including rising disposable income, expanding internet connectivity, and a young, technology-savvy population (Al-Hashimi & Mehmood, 2022). According to Statista, the smartphone penetration rate in Saudi Arabia from 2018 to 2024 was 58.9%, 62.5%, 65.9%, 69.1%, 72%, 74.7%, and 77.2%, respectively. These figures indicate an increase in the use of smartphones in recent years. In 2023, there are over 30 million smartphone users in Saudi Arabia, and projections suggest that this number will increase to 36 million users by 2028. Samsung and Apple are the major companies operating in this sector in Saudi Arabia. Based on Graph 1, the penetration of Android-based smartphones in Saudi Arabia has increased significantly. In 2023, Android holds the top spot with a 72.3% share, while iOS holds the second spot with a 25.7% share.

Figure 1. Mobile operating system market share Saudi Arabia in Jan 2009 - Oct 2023

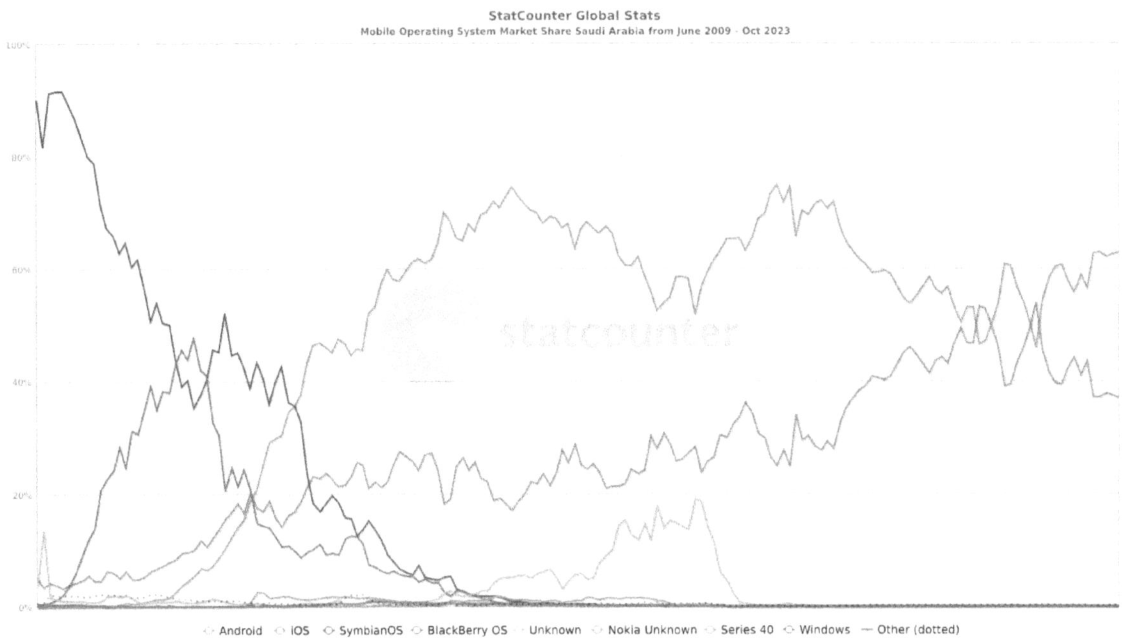

The smartphone penetration rate in Turkey has steadily increased from 61.22% in 2018 to 73.71% in 2024, according to Statista. This trend underscores the growing reliance on smartphones in recent years. As of 2023, Turkey boasts over 80 million smartphone users, with projections indicating a rise to 88 million users by 2028. Notably, Samsung and Apple emerge as the dominant players in this sector (Statista, 2023). Graph 2 depicts the Mobile Operating System Market Share in Turkey from Jan 2009 to Oct 2023. The graph reveals a significant rise in the penetration of Android-based smartphones (Statcounter,2023).

The smartphone penetration rate in Qatar has been steadily increasing in recent years, reaching 92% in 2023, according to GSMA Intelligence (2023). This growth is attributed to several factors, including rising disposable income, expanding internet connectivity, and a young, technology-savvy population (Al-Kaabi & Abushaiba, 2022).

According to GSMA Intelligence, the smartphone penetration rate in Qatar from 2018 to 2023 was 74%, 79%, 83%, 87%, 90% and 92%, respectively (GSMA Intelligence, 2023). These figures indicate a high level of smartphone adoption among the population. In 2023, there are over 2.6 million smartphone users in Qatar. Samsung, Apple and Huawei are among the top smartphone brands in Qatar (GSMA Intelligence, 2023).

B. The Young and Tech-Savvy Population of Saudi Arabia

Figure 2. Mobile operating system market share Turkey

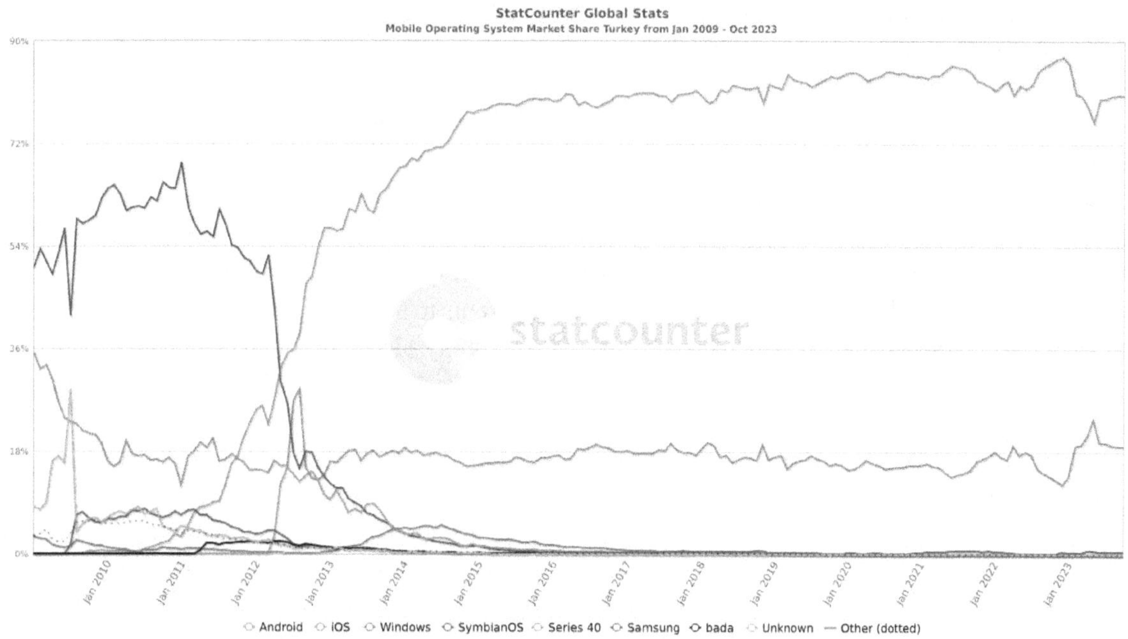

Figure 3. Mobile operating system market share Qatar 2009-2023

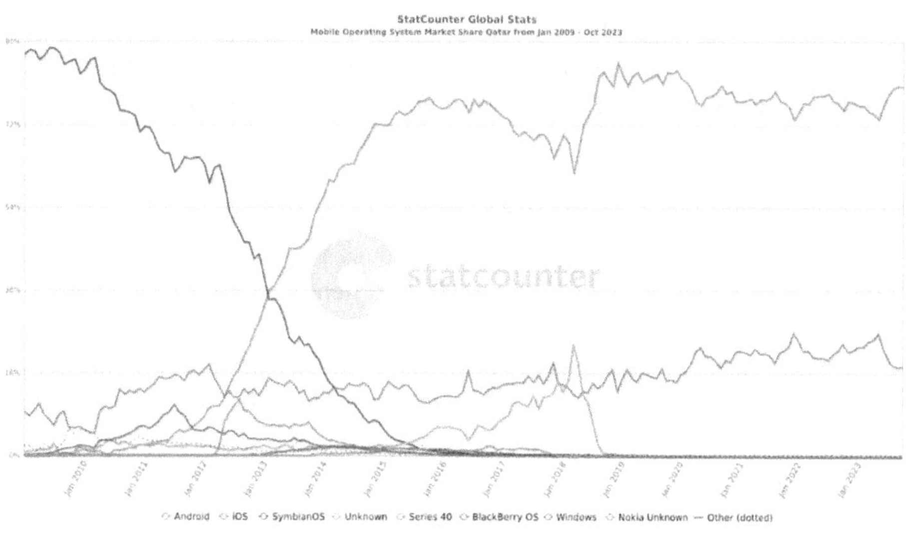

Statistics show that in 2023, 67.2% of the population of Saudi Arabia are between the ages of 15 and 64, with a median age of 32.5 (General Authority for Statistics, 2023). Specifically, 25.5% of the population of Saudi Arabia are between the ages of 18 and 34, indicating a young population (General Authority for Statistics, 2023). According to a report by WE ARE SOCIAL, the internet penetration rate in Saudi Arabia is 88.1% (WE ARE SOCIAL, 2023), with 42.1 million users of social media (WE

ARE SOCIAL, 2023). There are a total of 60.8 million mobile connections (90.9% of the total population) (General Authority for Statistics, 2023). Therefore, the presence of a young population and a high internet penetration rate and the availability of mobile phones indicate an acceptance of technology among young people in this country.

Also, Saudi Arabia has a young and tech-savvy population that is driving the country's digital transformation. According to the General Statistics Authority of Saudi Arabia, more than 70% of the population is under the age of 35, and 85% of the population has access to the internet (General Statistics Authority of Saudi Arabia, 2023). This young and connected population is driving demand for new technologies and services, and is creating opportunities for businesses of all sizes. A recent study by the Pew Research Center found that Saudi youth are more likely than their parents to use social media, watch online videos, and play online games (Gottfried & Shearer, 2022). The study also found that Saudi youth are more optimistic about the future than their parents, and are more likely to believe that technology will make their lives better (Gottfried & Shearer, 2022).

Statistics from 2022 reveal that 68.1% of Turkey's population falls within the age range of 15 to 64, with the country's average age being 33.5 (Turkish Statistical Institute, 2023). Notably, 26.3% of the Turkish population is specifically aged between 18 and 34, signifying a predominantly young demographic (WE ARE SOCIAL, 2023). According to a report by WE ARE SOCIAL, Turkey exhibits a high Internet penetration rate of 83.4%, with 62.55 million individuals using social networks and a total of 81.68 million mobile phone connections, encompassing 95.4% of the total population (WE ARE SOCIAL, 2023). Remarkably, 83.4% of the Turkish population actively engages with the Internet (WE ARE SOCIAL, 2023). This confluence of a youthful demographic, widespread Internet use, and mobile phone accessibility underscores the evident acceptance of technology, particularly among the youth in the country. Statistics show that in 2023, nearly 80% of Qatar's population is between the ages of 15 and 64, with a median age of 32.7 (MDPS, 2022). Specifically, over 30% of the population is between the ages of 25 and 44, indicating a high proportion of young working-age residents (MDPS, 2022).

The internet penetration rate in Qatar is over 99% (DataReportal, 2023), with 3.4 million social media users representing 115% social media penetration (DataReportal, 2023). There are over 4 million mobile connections in Qatar (ITU, 2023).

Therefore, Qatar boasts a predominantly expatriate young population that is tech-savvy and highly connected through mobile devices and the internet. This demography drives demand for consumer technology like smartphones.

The Qatari government has also emphasized technology and innovation as key pillars of the country's National Vision 2030 (General Secretariat for Development Planning, 2023). Significant investments are being made to nurture technology startups and build a vibrant ecosystem.

C. Government Support

The Saudi Arabian government supports the development of the fintech ecosystem through a variety of measures. The Saudi Arabian government has taken steps to create a regulatory environment that is favorable to fintech innovation. In 2022, the Saudi Arabian Monetary Authority (SAMA) established the Fintech Regulatory Sandbox, which allows fintech startups to test their products and services in a controlled environment. SAMA has also published a number of regulations that provide clarity and guidance for fintech companies (Al-Sartawi & Shamsudin, 2022; Al-Chalabi & Al-Qudah, 2022).

The Saudi Arabian government offers a number of financial incentives to encourage fintech innovation. These incentives include tax breaks, grants, and loans. For example, the Saudi Arabian General

Investment Authority (SAGIA) offers a 50% tax exemption for qualifying fintech companies (El-Haddad, 2023; Al-Chalabi & Al-Qudah, 2022).

The Saudi Arabian government supports collaboration and knowledge sharing among fintech companies. SAMA has established a number of initiatives to promote collaboration, such as the Fintech Saudi Hub and the Fintech Saudi Fellowship Program (Al-Sartawi & Shamsudin, 2022; Al-Chalabi & Al-Qudah, 2022). The Saudi Arabian government is investing in infrastructure that will support the growth of the fintech ecosystem. This includes investments in digital infrastructure, such as 5G and artificial intelligence (El-Haddad, 2023; Al-Chalabi & Al-Qudah, 2022).

The Turkish government actively supports the market development of fintech-based companies through various methods, including the establishment of a supportive regulatory environment (Turkish Ministry of Finance, 2023), providing financial incentives (S-GE, 2021), promoting collaboration and knowledge sharing (Ledger Insights, 2022), and supporting infrastructure development. Several noteworthy examples in this realm include the establishment of the Istanbul Finance Center (Turkish Ministry of Finance, 2023), the launch of the FinTech Istanbul initiative (S-GE, 2021), and the creation of the Regulatory Sandbox Turkey (Ledger Insights, 2022).

The government of Qatar supports the development of the fintech ecosystem through various programs and initiatives:The Qatar Central Bank (QCB) launched a regulatory sandbox in 2019 that allows fintech companies to test innovations in a controlled environment before full-scale deployment (Holla & Pasha, 2022).

QCB's Innovation Hub offers a collaborative platform for fintechs to engage with regulators and partners to develop solutions tailored for Qatar (Oxford Business Group, 2023).

Government funds like the Investment Promotion Agency's Launchpad and Qatar Development Bank's Al-Dhala Program offer financing to early-stage startups (Startup Qatar, 2023). Qatar's domestic fintech market will be worth over $550 million by 2022, according to estimates, with global expansion opportunities beyond (Holla & Pasha, 2022). There are over 46 fintech companies in Qatar spanning various segments like payments, regtech and blockchain (Fintech Galaxy, 2023).

Current FinTech Adoption Rate (Explaining, for Example, Why High or Low)

A. Identifying the level of acceptance based on reliable reports

According to the report "Saudi Arabia FinTech Landscape 2023" by KPMG (2023), the Digital Banking sector in Saudi Arabia is growing rapidly. In 2022, the market value of this sector reached $1.2 trillion and is expected to reach $2.5 trillion by 2027. This rapid growth is due to a number of factors, including the increasing use of smartphones, the development of digital infrastructure, and the increasing awareness of the benefits of digital banking.

According to the report "FinTech in Saudi Arabia: A Rising Force" by PwC (2023), the Digital Wealth Management sector is also growing rapidly in Saudi Arabia. In 2022, the market value of this sector reached $100 billion and is expected to reach $200 billion by 2027. This rapid growth is due to a number of factors, including the increasing wealth in Saudi Arabia, the increasing awareness of the benefits of digital wealth management, and the development of digital wealth management products and services.

According to the report "Fintech in the Middle East: The Next Frontier" by McKinsey & Company (2023), the acceptance rate of FinTech-based technologies in Saudi Arabia is increasing. In 2022, 60% of Saudi citizens used FinTech services. This figure is expected to reach 75% by 2027.

The 2023 report from Statista (Statista, 2023) on the role and adoption of FinTech in Turkey reveals that Digital Investment attracts the most capital, boasting an AUM of US$290.70 million. Projections indicate an average AUM per user in the Digital Investment market of US$121.00 for 2023. Furthermore, the report forecasts that by 2027, the number of active users in the field of digital payments will reach 67.99 million people, showcasing the widespread adoption of technology-based FinTech in Turkey.

According to "The State of FinTech Ecosystem in Türkiye" report, compiled by the Presidency of the Republic of Türkiye Finance Office in partnership with Startups. Watch, Türkiye registers 70.3 million active retail digital banking users (Presidency of the Republic of Türkiye Finance Office, 2023). In 2021, 1.7 million POS terminals, 52 thousand ATMs, 82.8 million credit cards, and 54.4 million prepaid cards were used, while contactless payment rate reached the level of 48 percent, and USD 48 million Fintech exits were recorded through 520 companies.

Qatar's fintech sector is nascent but growing rapidly, supported by high mobile and internet penetration rates. According to a 2023 report by QDB, 73% of Qatar's population uses fintech services, indicating a high level of acceptance (QDB, 2023).

Key drivers of fintech adoption in Qatar include:

- Increasing smartphone penetration (96% in 2023)
- High internet adoption (99% population coverage)
- Supportive regulatory environment
- Government promotion of digital economy
- Young, tech-savvy population

Fintech services seeing strong adoption in Qatar:

- Digital payments (90% aware, 65% use in 2023)
- Money transfers (75% aware, 55% use)
- Lending services (65% aware, 40% use) (KPMG, 2023)

This growth is expected to continue as connectivity and tech literacy improves further. Lack of awareness remains a barrier, indicating potential for further growth.

B. Identifying Factors Hindering the Development of Fintech Usage

Despite the high volume of investment in the Fintech sector in Saudi Arabia, there are some common concerns among customers regarding the adoption of Fintech, including security concerns, data privacy concerns, and limited government oversight (Arab Monetary Fund, 2022). These concerns are a general aspect of the reasons for non-adoption of Fintech by customers and are not limited to Saudi Arabia. In addition to security-related concerns, major challenges in Saudi Arabia that have also impacted the FinTech industry include the currency crisis (devaluation of the Saudi riyal), inflation, and strict regulations (Kaleido Intelligence, 2023). Overall, the adoption and development of Fintech in Saudi Arabia has been on the rise, and the FinTech market in Saudi Arabia is expected to grow by 14% annually (McKinsey & Company, 2021), indicating the high potential for Fintech development in Saudi Arabia, as confirmed by the Deloitte report (Deloitte, 2023).

To address the barriers to Fintech development in Saudi Arabia, the following actions can be taken, increase investment in ICT infrastructure, Strengthening the culture of innovation adoption, Streamlining

FinTech industry regulations: Raising awareness of Fintech, Promoting collaboration between traditional financial institutions and Fintech startups. By taking these actions, a conducive environment for the rapid and sustainable growth of the FinTech industry in Saudi Arabia can be created.

Despite the substantial investment volume in the Turkish FinTech sector, customers exhibit common concerns hindering widespread adoption. Predominant among these concerns are issues related to security, data confidentiality, and perceived limited government control (Mahmud et al., 2022). Notably, these concerns represent a universal aspect of the reasons for customer hesitation towards Fintech and are not exclusive to Turkey. In addition to security-related apprehensions, fundamental challenges impacting the Turkish FinTech industry include the currency crisis, marked by a decrease in the value of the Turkish lira, inflation, and stringent regulations (The Fintech Times, 2022).

While Qatar has high fintech potential, barriers slowing adoption include:

Lack of understanding: Low financial literacy limits understanding of fintech benefits (KPMG, 2023).

Security fears: Concerns around data privacy and fraud risk hinder adoption (KPMG, 2023).

Regulation uncertainty: Unclear regulations around some emerging fintech services causes uncertainty (Oxford Business Group, 2022).

Limited scale and collaboration: Qatar has a small population, limiting startup scale. More sector collaboration needed (Oxford Business Group, 2022).

As digital skills improve and regulations evolve to support fintech innovation while protecting consumers, these barriers can be addressed to realize Qatar's fintech potential.

Types of Fintech

In this section, we will discuss the most important Fintech technologies in Saudi Arabia, Turkey, and Qatar. In this regard, we will focus on the status of Payments, Investment, Lending, Banking, and Crypto technologies.

A. Payments

Payment technologies are becoming increasingly popular in Saudi Arabia. The use of digital wallets, digital payments, and contactless payments has grown significantly in recent years. This is due to a number of factors, including the rise of e-commerce, the increasing popularity of mobile devices, and the government's efforts to promote a cashless society.

The most popular payment methods in Saudi Arabia include credit cards, debit cards, and bank transfers (Saudi Payments, 2023). In 2023, the value of mobile banking transactions in Saudi Arabia reached SAR 1.3 trillion (Thunes, 2023). Digital wallets are another popular payment method in Saudi Arabia (Arab News, 2022). The most popular digital wallets in the country include Mada Pay, Fawry Pay, and Tap to Pay (Saudi Payments, 2022). the Saudi government is also playing a role in promoting the adoption of digital payments (Ministry of Finance Saudi Arabia, 2023). The Saudi Central Bank (SAMA) has launched a number of initiatives to encourage the use of digital payments, including the Saudi Instant Payment System (Sarie) (Saudi Payments, 2021).

According to the PYMNTS report (PYMNTS.com, 2022), the use of payment technologies during the coronavirus epidemic has surged, equivalent to a 15-year growth, showcasing widespread acceptance of FinTech payment services. In Turkey, popular digital payment methods include credit cards, debit cards, and bank transfers. Notably, in the final three months of 2022, mobile phone transactions alone accounted for TRY 1.3 trillion in bank transactions (Statista, 2023). Key players in the Turkish digital payment landscape include BKM Express, Paycell, and Gpay (Pay.com, 2023).

Digital payments are the largest fintech segment in Qatar in terms of adoption. In 2023, over 90% of the population is aware of digital payments and 65% actively use them, according to QDB (QDB, 2023).

Key payment fintechs in Qatar include:

MasterCard Payment Services: Provides digital payment processing infrastructure enabling digital wallet services like Apple Pay and Samsung Pay (Mastercard, 2022).

PayPal: Global payments platform launched localized Qatar services allowing users to make online payments (PayPal, 2023).

QNB Digital Wallets: QNB bank offers digital wallets on mobile apps enabling in-store, online and peer-to-peer payments domestically and abroad (QNB, 2023).

The Qatari government also supports payments innovation. The central bank launched a fast retail payment system to facilitate real-time transfers (Qatar Central Bank, 2022). These initiatives and services are advancing Qatar's transition to a cashless society.

B. Investment

FinTech is revolutionizing the investment landscape in Saudi Arabia, fostering financial inclusion, accessibility, and efficiency. Digital investment platforms, robo-advisors, P2P lending, and blockchain technology are just a few examples of FinTech innovations that are empowering individuals and institutions to make informed investment decisions and achieve their financial goals. As FinTech continues to evolve, it is poised to play an increasingly significant role in shaping the future of investment in Saudi Arabia and beyond.

Also, Asset and wealth management in Saudi Arabia is growing, and regulations, compliance, risk management, reporting, and taxation are subject to stricter and more complex rules (Capgemini, 2023). Promising forecasts are being published in the field of Robo-advisors in Saudi Arabia. It is estimated that the volume and number of users of the Robo-advisors market will reach 25.28 billion USD and 2.320 million users, respectively, between 2023 and 2027 (Boston Consulting Group, 2023). The number of online brokerage accounts in Saudi Arabia is 2.0 million. According to a brokerchooser report, some of the most important international online brokers in Saudi Arabia include Interactive Brokers, Saxo Bank, TradeStation Global, and Admirals (brokerchooser, 2023).

Additional information:

- The Saudi Arabian economy is growing, and the middle class is expanding. This is leading to an increase in demand for asset and wealth management services (World Bank, 2023).
- Robo-advisors are becoming increasingly popular in Saudi Arabia. They offer a convenient and affordable way to invest (Empaxis, 2023).
- The number of online brokerage accounts in Saudi Arabia is growing. This is due to the increasing popularity of online trading (Capgemini, 2023).
- Interactive Brokers, Saxo Bank, TradeStation Global, and Admirals are all leading international online brokers. They offer a wide range of services and products to Saudi Arabian investors (brokerchooser, 2023).

Investing in fintech in Turkey encounters several challenges. Insufficient information about fintech, concerns about the state of Turkey, and a lack of investors, including banks, contribute to a decrease in investment and attention in this sector (Yazici, 2019). One significant challenge in the investment domain is related to laws and government support, a hurdle that Turkey has addressed through the introduction of the special FDI law in 2003. This legislation supports foreign investors, as evidenced by Turkey attracting foreign capital amounting to 225 billion dollars (Republic of Turkey Ministry of Treasury and Finance, 2023).

The field of asset and wealth management in Turkey is experiencing growth, with regulations, compliance, risk management, reporting, and taxes becoming subject to stricter and more complex laws (PwC Türkiye, n.d.). Positive forecasts are emerging for Robo-advisors in Turkey, predicting that between 2023 and 2027, the market volume and the number of users will reach 21.67 billion dollars and 2.030 million users, respectively (Statista, 2023). The count of online brokerage accounts in Turkey stands at 1.9 million (Compare Brokers, n.d.). Notably, according to the brokerchooser report, prominent international online brokers in Turkey include Interactive Brokers, Saxo Bank, TradeStation Global, and Admirals (brokerchooser.com).

Qatar's investment fintech sector is small but innovative. A few promising startups are leveraging technology to make investing more accessible.

Sarwa, a UAE-based robo-advisory platform, expanded to Qatar in 2022. It automates portfolios using algorithms tailored to an investor's risk tolerance (Sarwa, 2022).

Qatar FinTech Hub launched an equity crowdfunding platform allowing startups and SMEs to raise capital from a wider pool of investors (Fintech Galaxy, 2022).

These startups are broadening investing opportunities. But adoption remains low (KPMG pegs investment fintech use at 20%). Strict regulations also limit platforms' offerings (Oxford Business Group, 2022). Targeted campaigns to educate investors on fintech benefits can boost adoption. As the ecosystem evolves, innovation can accelerate.

C. Lending

The average lending rate in Saudi Arabia between 1996 and 2023 was 5.50%, rising to 6.50% in October 2023, indicating an increase in borrowing costs in the country (Trading Economics, 2023). The Saudi Arabian Monetary Authority (SAMA) has recently taken new measures to control lending rates. These measures include:

- Raising the base interest rate from 2% to 2.5% (SAMA, 2023).
- Limiting the amount of loans that banks can issue (SAMA, 2023).
- Imposing new restrictions on the amount of loans that can be issued to individuals (SAMA, 2023).

These measures by the SAMA could have a variety of impacts on the fintech sector in Saudi Arabia. On the one hand, they could lead to increased financing costs for fintech companies. On the other hand, they could lead to increased competition in the sector. The Saudi Arabian government currently imposes various restrictions on the activities of fintech companies. Some of these restrictions include:

- Fintech companies must be licensed by the SAMA (Legal500, 2023).
- Fintech companies must have a minimum initial investment (Legal500, 2023).
- Fintech companies must comply with specific reporting requirements (Legal500, 2023).

These restrictions could pose challenges for the development of fintech in Saudi Arabia. Given the rising lending rates in Saudi Arabia, fintech companies in the country need to be prepared to face this challenge. They need to find ways to reduce financing costs and increase competition in the sector. They also need to adapt to existing government restrictions.

The average lending rate in Turkey between 1996 and 2023 was 32.10%, reaching 36.50% in October 2023 (thefintechtimes,2022). Recently, the Central Bank of Turkey has contemplated new measures to restrict credit card spending, potentially acting as a constraining factor for FinTech in the country (Bloomberg, 2023). Despite the absence of a specific law in Turkey to limit interest on loans (Legal500, 2023), the government has implemented measures to regulate this area, presenting both opportunities and threats to the FinTech sector. For instance, peer-to-peer lending is infrequently implemented in Turkey due to government laws and restrictions (thefintechtimes,2022).

Qatar's lending fintech landscape is nascent. P2P lending and digital banks are still uncommon compared to other fintech segments (Mordor Intelligence, 2022).

But increasing financial inclusion is a priority for Qatar. Supportive regulations can enable lending models that serve underbanked groups. The Qatar Development Bank already runs loan programs for SMEs and startups, paving the way for alternative digital lending (Qatar Development Bank, 2023).

As connectivity and data availability continues growing, lending fintechs can leverage technology to assess creditworthiness more inclusively. Banks too are building API infrastructures that enable interfacing with fintech lending apps to extend their services (Doha Bank, 2022). These trends point to a promising outlook for lending fintechs as the ecosystem evolves.

D. Banking

Despite the fact that fintech regulations in Saudi Arabia are mostly harmonized with those of the United States, fintech companies operating in the banking sector in Saudi Arabia face strict regulations that are leading to a decline in the sector's popularity in the country (Al-Hashimi, 2023). This does not mean that there are no active fintech companies in the banking sector in Saudi Arabia. For example, some of the most important fintech companies in Saudi Arabia that offer banking services include:

Baloot, a mobile banking app that allows users to open accounts, make payments, and transfer money. Tawadul, a digital investment platform that allows users to invest in stocks, bonds, and other financial products. Sadaaq, a crowdfunding platform that allows users to raise money for charitable causes.

These companies are providing innovative and competitive solutions in the banking sector, including mobile banking, digital investment, and crowdfunding. In the following, more information about the banking situation in Saudi Arabia is provided.

- As of 2023, there are over 100 fintech companies operating in Saudi Arabia (Fintech Saudi, 2023).
- The fintech sector in Saudi Arabia is expected to grow by 25% annually in the next five years (KPMG, 2023).
- The fintech sector in Saudi Arabia is still in its early stages of development, but it has the potential to revolutionize the way financial services are delivered in the country. The government of Saudi Arabia is supportive of the fintech sector and has taken steps to create a more favorable regulatory environment for fintech companies.
- In 2023, the Saudi Arabian Monetary Authority (SAMA) issued a new set of regulations for fintech companies (Saudi Arabian Monetary Authority, 2023). The new regulations are designed to promote innovation and competition in the fintech sector while protecting consumers.
- SAMA has also launched a number of initiatives to support the growth of the fintech sector, including a fintech accelerator program and a fintech fund (Saudi Arabian Monetary Authority, 2023).

Fintech companies operating in Turkey often require collaboration with banks, primarily through APIs (Degerli, 2019). This necessitates that fintech firms enter into a Bank Support Services Contract, which imposes specific duties and obligations upon them (Degerli, 2019). Notably, banks in Turkey have not demonstrated a particular inclination toward supporting financial institutions in the fintech sector (Yazici, 2019). Consequently, these fintech entities have shifted their focus towards offering innovative services to attract customers (Yazici, 2019).

Despite the alignment of most fintech regulations in Turkey with those of the European Union (EU), companies operating in the banking sector face stringent laws, leading to a decreased acceptance of the sector in Turkey (thefintechtimes.com, 2022). However, this does not signify the absence of fintech companies in the banking sector. Notable examples include Papara Turkish Online Bank, Payoneer, and Tosla e-Bank, which play a pivotal role in providing competitive, user-oriented solutions, cross-border payments, and mobile banking, respectively (imtilak.net, 2023).

Qatar's banking sector is evolving rapidly under the influence of technology and innovation. Both incumbent banks and specialized fintechs are deploying solutions to improve customer experience.

Doha Bank launched the country's first digital-only bank, Doha Bank Oasis, in 2022. This neobank targets tech-savvy youth and masses with lifestyle offerings beyond banking (Doha Bank, 2022). Qatar International Bank also unveiled an electronic onboarding app allowing digital account opening using national eIDs (The Peninsula, 2021). Banks like Commercial Bank are implementing integrated payment platforms enabling real-time account-to-account transfers domestically and globally in partnership with companies like TerraPay (TradeArabia, 2021).

Policy support for open banking is also accelerating - Qatar Central Bank recently instructed banks to give customer-permissioned access to third party providers to spur innovation (Gulf Times, 2022). These developments are positioning Qatar at the forefront of banking modernization in the region.

E. Crypto

Saudi Arabia is one of the fastest-growing crypto economies in the world, with transaction volume increasing by 12% from July 2022 to June 2023, reaching nearly $31 billion (Chainalysis, 2023). This growth is due in part to the increasing adoption of decentralized finance (DeFi), which offers a range of financial services without the need for traditional intermediaries like banks (Al-Monitor, 2023). While cryptocurrencies are legal in Saudi Arabia, there is currently no regulatory framework in place. The Saudi Arabian Monetary Authority (SAMA) has warned against the risks of investing in cryptocurrencies, but has also said that it is exploring the potential benefits of blockchain technology (SAMA, 2020).

Despite the lack of regulation, there is a growing interest in cryptocurrencies in Saudi Arabia. This is likely due to the country's young and tech-savvy population, as well as the increasing global adoption of cryptocurrencies (Chainalysis, 2023). The future of cryptocurrencies in Saudi Arabia is uncertain, but the country is clearly positioned to play a leading role in the development of this nascent industry.

According to Chainalysis' 2021 Geography of Cryptocurrency report, Turkey ranks as the second country in the Middle East for digital currency transactions, with an estimated volume of $130 billion (thefintechtimes.com, 2022). The Turkish government has demonstrated significant interest in digital currencies, as evidenced by its plans to implement a central bank digital currency (CBDC), a project initiated in September 2021 (cointelegraph.com, 2023). The CBDC project aims to establish a digital Turkish lira (nfcw.com, 2022). However, it is important to note that, currently, the use of digital currencies for payments is prohibited in Turkey, and organizations are not permitted to use crypto directly or indirectly for transactions (iclg.com, 2023).

Qatar has adopted a balanced approach toward cryptocurrency and blockchain technology - embracing potential benefits while closely managing risks.

In 2019, Qatar Central Bank banned trading of cryptocurrencies domestically while permitting investment in crypto assets internationally through regulated exchanges (Gulf Times, 2019).

More recently, the Qatar Financial Centre (QFC) introduced regulations allowing crypto trading by approved financial firms meeting strict standards aligned with global best practices (Arab News, 2022).

International players like BitOasis have received QFC crypto exchange licenses enabling access for Qatar-based investors to leading cryptocurrencies including Bitcoin, Ethereum and others (MENA Fintech Association, 2022).

As the market infrastructure improves with clear regulations around capital requirements, security protocols and transparency - Qatar aims to nurture financial innovation.

Key Players (Profile, Strengths, Weaknesses)

In this section, we present a comprehensive overview of key companies within the domains of Digital Wallets, Payment Gateways, Robo-Advisors, Neobanks, and Cryptocurrency Exchanges. Additionally, we explore the overarching concept of TechFin, with notable giants such as Alibaba, Amazon, and Apple leading the charge (Yazici, 2019). Subsequently, we will delve deeper into a more focused exploration of the prominent players within the fintech landscape.

A. Digital wallets and Payment gateways

The rapid advancement of digital technology has revolutionized the payment landscape in Saudi Arabia, fostering the adoption of digital wallets and payment gateways. These innovative solutions have simplified and streamlined financial transactions, offering a seamless and secure experience for both consumers and merchants. Digital wallets, such as STC Pay, Geidea Solutions, Hala, and UrPay, have emerged as popular tools for managing online and offline payments. These mobile applications enable users to store their financial information securely, make contactless payments, and transfer funds with ease. Their convenience and enhanced security have propelled their widespread adoption among Saudi Arabian consumers (Al-Shami, 2022).

Payment gateways, on the other hand, serve as intermediaries between merchants and payment processors, facilitating online transactions. Prominent payment gateways in Saudi Arabia include Moyasar, Payfort, Paytabs, and Hyperpay. These gateways provide merchants with a secure platform to accept payments from various card networks, including Visa, MasterCard, and Mada (Qureshi, 2023). The growth of digital wallets and payment gateways in Saudi Arabia is attributed to several factors, including the rise of e-commerce, the increasing penetration of smartphones, and the government's initiatives to promote a cashless society (Al-Zahrani, 2022). These developments have paved the way for a more digitalized economy, fostering financial inclusion and enhancing the overall payment experience for all stakeholders.

According to a report by Statista (2023), "credit cards issued by domestic banks like Yapi Kredi, QNB Finansbank, and Akbank made up nearly six out of 10 online transactions in Turkey in 2022" (Statista, 2023). However, despite the strong presence of these domestic banks, FinTech companies offering digital wallet services are actively making their mark. Key players in this domain include BKM Express (commencis.com, 2022), GPay (askwonder.com, 2023), Mobilexpress (askwonder.com, 2023), Papara (askwonder.com, 2023), and Pay Cell (askwonder.com, 2023).

Additionally, Iyzico, PayU, and Papara stand out as among the most important and popular payment gateways in Turkey (subscriptionflow.com, 2023). Their services encompass credit and debit card payment support, digital wallets, and bank transfers (subscriptionflow.com, 2023). The provision of digital wallet services necessitates access to mobile phone services along with the Internet, emphasizing the crucial role of telecommunication companies as major players in this field (Yazici, 2019).

As digital payments rise in Qatar, integrated fintech platforms are gaining ground by allowing users seamless payment experiences across channels.

Payment gateways:

- PayFort (Amazon partner): Payment gateway for online purchases supporting local acquiring capabilities in Qatar (Payfort, 2023).

Digital wallets

- QNB Digital Wallet: Full-service mobile wallet by QNB bank supporting money transfers, bill pay, mobile top-up/recharge, and payments at POS terminals (QNB, 2023).

Integrated payment platforms

- STC Pay: Digital wallet with payment processing, peer-to-peer transfers, and an ecosystem of value-added services like offers, loyalty programs etc. Has over 2 million users in Qatar (STC Pay, 2023).

These platforms leverage partnerships to enable payments across a wider network of merchants, both online and offline. High banking penetration also allows integration with bank accounts/cards for unified experiences. Developing holistic platforms tailored for local needs can drive higher adoption.

B. Robo-advisors

The Robo-advisors market in Saudi Arabia is a relatively new but rapidly growing sector (Statista, 2023). In 2023, the market is estimated to reach a value of €54.37bn, with a projected CAGR of 11.78% from 2023 to 2027 (Statista, 2023). Several factors are driving this growth, including:

- Increasing smartphone penetration (Statista, 2023)
- Growing awareness of financial literacy (Malaa, 2023)
- Rising interest in investment opportunities (Derayah Smart, 2023)
- Government support for fintech development (Saudi Arabian Monetary Authority, 2023)

Several Robo-advisors operate in Saudi Arabia, including Sarwa (Sarwa, 2023), Malaa (Malaa, 2023), and Derayah Smart (Derayah Smart, 2023). These Robo-advisors offer a variety of features, such as (Sarwa, 2023; Malaa, 2023; Derayah Smart, 2023) automated investment portfolios, low investment minimums, easy-to-use platforms, and customer support.

Robo-advisors offer several benefits to investors, including (Sarwa, 2023; Malaa, 2023; Derayah Smart, 2023) affordability, convenience, diversification, and professional advice. Robo-advisors are not without their risks, including (Sarwa, 2023; Malaa, 2023; Derayah Smart, 2023) potential for losses, lack of human interaction, limited investment options.

Overall, the Robo-advisors market in Saudi Arabia is promising. The market is expanding rapidly and is expected to continue to do so in the coming years. Robo-advisors offer several benefits to investors, including affordability, convenience, diversification, and professional advice. However, it is essential to understand the associated risks before investing in Robo-advisors.

The Robo-advisors market in Turkey is forecast to experience significant growth in the coming years, according to Statista (2023). Assets under management are projected to reach US$10.84 billion in 2023 and are expected to grow at an annual compound growth rate (CAGR) of 18.91% from 2023 to 2027, resulting in a projected total amount of US$21.67 billion by 2027. The number of users in the Robo-advisors market is expected to reach 2.03 million by 2027. The average assets under management per user in the Robo-advisors market is expected to amount to US$3.23 thousand in 2023.

In a global comparison, the United States has the highest assets under management in the Robo-advisors market, with US$1,172 billion in 2023 (Statista, 2023).

Qatar's robo-advisory ecosystem has a few new but promising startups leveraging algorithms to make investing more efficient.

Eqtor

Launched in 2021, Eqtor develops automated wealth management tools tailored to an investor's risk appetite and goals (Eqtor, 2023).

Strengths

- Algorithms quickly construct diversified portfolios matching investor goals
- Low fees due to automated advisory processes
- Accessible online platform requires low investment amounts

Weaknesses

- Limited track record and adoption (new player)
- Currently only stocks/ETFs - lacks other asset class offerings
- Understanding how algorithms guide choices may require investor education

Malaai

Qatar fintech app that automates halal stock portfolio construction and management aligned with Islamic investing principles (Malaai, 2023).

Strengths

- Caters to Islamic investors with dedicated Sharia screening
- Beginning advisory relationships includes assessing investor needs
- Low fees due to use of algorithms

Weaknesses

- Limited operating history
- Relies on Wahed Invest for execution, portfolio options - added layer between client and money manager

C. Neobanks

Neobanks, also known as challenger banks, are digital-only banks that operate without physical branches. They typically offer a wide range of financial services, including checking and savings accounts, debit cards, loans, and investment products. Neobanks are known for their innovative approach to banking, which often includes using technology to provide a more personalized and user-friendly experience for customers (Al-Hussaini & Alamro, 2023).

The neobanking industry in Saudi Arabia is still in its early stages of development, but it is growing rapidly. The Saudi Arabian Monetary Authority (SAMA) has been supportive of the development of neobanks, and has issued licenses to several new players in recent years (PwC, 2022). One of the most well-known neobanks in Saudi Arabia is STC Pay, which was launched in 2018. STC Pay is a subsidiary of Saudi Telecom Company (STC), one of the largest telecommunications companies in the Middle East. STC Pay offers a range of financial services, including money transfers, bill payments, and mobile top-ups. The company has over 8 million customers and is valued at over $1 billion (PYMNTS, 2023).

Another major player in the Saudi Arabian neobanking market is Saudi Digital Bank (SDB), which was launched in 2022. SDB is backed by Artar, a holding company with investments in real estate, construction, technology, and food. SDB is expected to offer a full range of banking services, including lending, savings, and investment products (HALA Ventures, 2023).

The neobanking industry in Saudi Arabia is expected to continue to grow in the coming years. This is due to a number of factors, including the increasing adoption of digital technologies, the growing demand for financial services among young Saudis, and the supportive regulatory environment (BCG, 2023). Neobanks are expected to play a significant role in the transformation of the Saudi Arabian banking sector. They are likely to put pressure on traditional banks to improve their digital offerings and provide more competitive rates and fees. Neobanks are also expected to expand the reach of financial services to underserved populations in Saudi Arabia.

In Turkey, commercial banks dominate the financial sector, holding over 90% of total assets (Bayram et al., 2022). Among Neobanks, key players with a significant market presence in Turkey have their headquarters in Hong Kong and the United Kingdom. Notable Neobanks include Neat, TransferGo, Wise (formerly Transferwise), and World Remit (Neobanks.app, 2023). According to Statista, the predicted value of transactions in Neobanks is expected to reach $36.24 billion in 2023, with a growth rate of 22.13% (Statista, 2023). This amount is projected to surge to $80.63 billion in 2027, translating to an average transaction of $15.28 thousand per user (Statista, 2023).

Qatar has a highly concentrated banking sector, with established players capturing most of the retail and SME market (Mordor Intelligence, 2022). But a growing fintech ecosystem is enabling neobank challengers to emerge and drive innovation.

Doha Bank Oasis

Doha Bank launched its Doha Bank Oasis digital-only subsidiary in 2022 as a standalone neobank (Doha Bank, 2022).

Strengths

- Leverages parent Doha Bank's resources and client base
- Features innovative lifestyle platform with rewards programs

Weaknesses

- Lacks brand recognition as a startup
- Faces competition from tech-savvy legacy banks

Collaboration between neobanks and incumbents can accelerate innovation. As legacy banks strengthen digital offerings, agile startups can differentiate with value-added services, capitalizing on banks' distribution infrastructure.

D. Cryptocurrency exchanges

Cryptocurrency exchanges are platforms that allow users to buy, sell, and trade cryptocurrencies (Chainalysis, 2023). They are an essential part of the cryptocurrency ecosystem, as they provide a way for people to convert their fiat currency into cryptocurrencies and vice versa.

Saudi Arabia is one of the most active cryptocurrency markets in the Middle East (Cointelegraph, n.d.). The country's young and tech-savvy population is driving adoption (Paxful, n.d.), and the government is taking a supportive stance towards the industry (Rain, n.d.). In 2020, the Saudi Arabian Capital Markets Authority (CMA) issued a regulatory framework for cryptocurrency exchanges (Chainalysis, 2023). There are a number of popular cryptocurrency exchanges operating in Saudi Arabia. Some of the most well-known include: BitOasis (Cointelegraph, n.d.), Rain (Rain, n.d.), Saudi-Emirati (Paxful, n.d.).

As a pioneer in digital currency transactions in the Middle East, Turkey is home to a thriving ecosystem of digital currency exchanges. The most prominent players in this domain are Paribu (50.5% market share), BtcTurk PRO (36.9% market share), Bitci (12% market share), and Bitlo (0.7% market share) (CoinGecko, 2023).

Qatar has adopted a cautious but open approach to cryptocurrency and related fintech innovation (Hassan, 2022). In 2022, the Qatar Financial Center (QFC) announced regulations allowing financial firms to trade crypto assets, provided they meet strict risk, security and disclosure requirements (Reuters, 2022).

BitOasis

Dubai-based BitOasis became one of the first fully QFC-regulated exchanges with approval to offer crypto trading to regional clients including Qatar (Arabian Business, 2022).

Strengths

- Strong brand recognition in MENA crypto sector
- QFC regulated since 2015 – longstanding regional experience
- Multi-coin offering – Bitcoin, Ethereum and others

Weaknesses

- Geographic focus leaves strategic gaps versus global exchanges
- Heavily reliant on UAE policy environment given operations center there

Regulations strike a balance between allowing well-managed innovation and addressing risks like money laundering. As the market infrastructure improves, Qatar can become a crypto hub. Government and industry collaboration to educate citizens on new asset classes will also boost adoption.

New Investment and Start-Up

Saudi Arabia is undergoing a significant transformation as it seeks to diversify its economy away from oil and embrace technology as a key driver of growth (Crunchbase News, 2023). The country has made substantial investments in its startup ecosystem, attracting both local and international investors (Techloy,

2023; Wamda, 2023). This has led to a surge in the number of startups operating in Saudi Arabia, with many innovative companies emerging across a wide range of sectors (Failory, 2023).

Several factors are driving the growth of investment and startups in Saudi Arabia:

- **Government initiatives:** The Saudi government has launched several initiatives to support startups, including the establishment of venture capital funds, accelerators, and incubators. These initiatives have provided startups with access to funding, mentorship, and resources, helping them to grow and succeed (The Banker, 2022).
- **Growing young population:** Saudi Arabia has a large and growing young population, which is a key driver of entrepreneurship. This young population is tech-savvy and eager to create new businesses, providing a strong foundation for the growth of the startup ecosystem.
- **Shift towards a knowledge-based economy:** The Saudi government is committed to developing a knowledge-based economy, and startups are seen as playing a crucial role in this transformation. Startups are creating new jobs and opportunities, and they are helping to diversify the economy and reduce reliance on oil.

Several Saudi startups have achieved significant success, attracting attention from investors and gaining recognition for their innovative products and services. Here are a few examples:

- **Careem:** A ride-hailing platform that has become the largest of its kind in the Middle East and North Africa (MENA) region.
- **STC Pay:** A mobile payment platform that is part of the Saudi Telecom Company (STC), one of the largest telecommunications companies in the Middle East.
- **Mrsool:** A food delivery platform that is one of the leading players in the MENA region.
- **Noon:** An e-commerce platform that is the largest in the Middle East.
- **Bayzat:** A cloud-based HR platform that is helping businesses to streamline their HR processes.

The FinTech landscape in Turkey is thriving, with over 520 FinTech companies operating in the country. Among these, payment companies hold the largest share, with 216 companies focusing on providing payment-related services (The Fintech Times, 2022). This highlights the growing importance of digital payments in Turkish society.

The Digital Assets market is poised to become the most significant FinTech segment in Turkey, with substantial capital expected to flow into this sector by 2027 (Statista, 2023). This growth is driven by the increasing adoption of cryptocurrencies and other digital assets.

Prominent Turkish FinTech companies, such as Birlesik Odeme, Papara, Iyzico, Figopara, Param, Moka, Ininal, and Paynet Odeme Hizmetleri, have successfully attracted significant capital (Formica AI, 2023). These companies are playing a crucial role in driving innovation and growth in the Turkish FinTech sector.

Emerging sectors in the FinTech field that are expected to garner attention in the coming years include Blockchain, robo-advisory, and alternative crowdfunding activities (Norton Rose Fulbright, 2023). These sectors are poised to disrupt traditional financial services and offer new opportunities for consumers and businesses.

Artificial intelligence (AI) technology is also expected to see significant investment in Turkey in the upcoming years (Politics Today, 2023). AI has the potential to revolutionize various aspects of the financial industry, from fraud detection to customer service.

Prepared by the Digital Transformation Office of the Presidency of the Republic of Turkey and the Ministry of Industry and Technology, the strategy, among others, laid out Turkey's aims to increase the share of artificial intelligence in its GDP to 5%, open 50,000 new jobs in the sector, and increase the number of AI postgraduate students to 10,000 by 2025. Within the same period, Turkey plans to become among the top 20 countries in the international AI indices.

Qatar is actively fostering its startup and fintech ecosystem through various government-backed initiatives that are attracting both local and foreign direct investment.

Factors Driving Investment and Startup Growth

Key factors spurring startup growth in Qatar include:

- Government support programs like the Qatar FinTech Hub and Digital Incubation Center which help startups with funding, infrastructure and regulatory advice (Qatar FinTech Hub, 2023).
- Strategic geographic location and business-friendly tax policies make Qatar an attractive startup hub (Cherif, 2022).
- Hosting of major sporting events like the FIFA World Cup 2022 provided a platform for showcasing Qatar's economic vision and startup ecosystem to global investors (Qatar Investment Authority, 2021).

Examples of Successful Fintech Startups

- **FinMkt:** Qatar based fintech startup focused on open banking and embedded financial solutions received $3 million in funding in 2022 (Salama, 2022).
- **Doha Bank Oasis:** Launched in 2022, this digital-only neobank aims to appeal to young, mobile-first users seeking a modern banking experience (Doha Bank, 2022).

Technical Infrastructure (Ecosystem), Discussion of Related Industry (E-Commerce)

Saudi Arabia has witnessed a remarkable transformation in its technical infrastructure and e-commerce landscape over the past decade. This transformation has been fueled by a combination of factors, including government initiatives, increasing internet penetration, and a growing tech-savvy population.

Saudi Arabia's internet penetration rate has reached 83% in 2022, significantly higher than the global average of 58% (Hoz 2022). This growth is attributed to the government's Vision 2030 initiative, which aims to increase internet accessibility and affordability.

Internet speed in Saudi Arabia has also improved significantly, with the average fixed broadband speed reaching 31 Mbps in 2022 (Statista 2023). Internet prices have also become more competitive, with the average monthly cost of 50 GB of data falling to around SAR 100 (USD 26) (Statista 2023).

The Saudi Arabian telecommunications market is dominated by three major players: Saudi Telecom Company (STC), Mobily, and Zain. These companies offer a wide range of communication services, including mobile, fixed broadband, and internet access. The penetration rate of smart and digital devices in Saudi Arabia is also increasing rapidly. In 2022, there were over 30 million mobile phone subscriptions in the country, with smartphone penetration reaching 75% (Hoz 2022). The number of internet-connected devices, including laptops, tablets, and smart home devices, is also growing rapidly.

The growth of Saudi Arabia's technical infrastructure has had a significant impact on the e-commerce industry. The increasing number of internet users, the availability of high-speed internet, and the widespread adoption of smart devices have all contributed to the growth of online shopping in the Kingdom. In 2022, the e-commerce market in Saudi Arabia was worth an estimated USD 18.5 billion (Statista 2023). This figure is expected to grow to USD 32.4 billion by 2025, driven by factors such as the increasing popularity of online shopping, the growing adoption of digital payments, and the expansion of e-commerce offerings by local and international retailers.

The FinTech ecosystem in Turkey is driven by several key components, including technology, telecommunication companies and infrastructure, startups, governments, financial institutions, customers, investors, and accelerators (Yazici, 2019). Startups in the Turkish FinTech sector are actively developing innovative solutions in areas such as card payment systems, wearable technologies, Internet of Things (IoT), Personal Assistants (e.g., Alexa, Siri, Bixby), chatbots, artificial intelligence, and Robotics Process Automation (RPA) software and applications (Yazici, 2019).

Turkey has made significant investments in information and communication technologies (ICT), with 82.5% of the population having internet access (Export.gov, 2018). This investment has resulted in the creation of 139,000 jobs and has fostered the development of technologies such as 5G, smart phones and tablets/IOT, cloud computing, M2M, data centers, disaster recovery, and IT services (Export.gov, 2018). Statista predicts that internet penetration in Turkey will reach 87.12% by 2028 (Statista, 2023), further demonstrating Turkey's commitment to ICT development.

Telecommunication companies play a crucial role in creating and developing a suitable platform for utilizing mobile phone-based technologies, particularly smartphones (Yazici, 2019). Major players in Turkey's telecommunications market include Turkcell (41.3% market share), Vodafone (36.6% market share), and Telekom (22.1% market share) (Export.gov, 2018).

Communication technology, information technology, and artificial intelligence are key enablers of FinTech in Turkey and are poised for substantial growth in the coming years (Yazici, 2019).

Qatar has invested substantially in modernizing its digital infrastructure and technical capabilities to establish a vibrant ecosystem for fintech and e-commerce innovation.

- National broadband provider Ooredoo provides high-speed 5G connectivity to 95% of Qatar's populated areas (Ooredoo, 2021).
- Microsoft partnership established the first cloud data centers in Qatar in 2021 to enable secure storage and processing for digital services (Qatar Tribune, 2021).
- New postal codes system implemented in 2022 helps enable efficient e-commerce deliveries (Q-Post, 2022).

These capabilities are driving rapid e-commerce growth. Qatar's e-commerce market is projected to reach US$2.1 billion by 2025 (IMF, 2022). Logistics players like Aramex and Talabat provide last-mile delivery solutions connecting retailers with Qatar's digitally savvy consumers (EdgePoint, 2021).

Government entities like the Qatar Free Zones Authority have introduced economic incentives and efficient clearance processes to attract e-commerce companies (QFZA, 2021). Qatar is also integrating virtual banking capabilities and payment systems into its digital ecosystem to facilitate online transactions (Cherif, 2022).

These initiatives are positioning Qatar as a competitive hub for emerging digital sectors – creating an economy centered on knowledge, technology and innovation in line with its National Vision 2030 (General Secretariat for Development Planning, 2022).

Government Policies, Regulations

Saudi Arabia's tax system is relatively straightforward compared to other countries in the region (SAGIA, 2023). The country has a corporate income tax rate of 20%, which is applied to all companies operating within the Kingdom. However, there are a number of tax exemptions and deductions available to businesses, which can significantly reduce their tax liability.

Foreign investors are eligible for a number of tax exemptions, including:

- A 10-year tax holiday for companies investing in specific sectors, such as manufacturing, technology, and renewable energy (SAGIA, 2023).
- A 50% reduction in corporate income tax for companies operating in strategic areas, such as infrastructure and tourism (PwC, 2023).
- A full exemption from customs duties and value-added tax (VAT) on imports of machinery and equipment used for industrial purposes (SAGIA, 2023).

SMEs are also eligible for a number of tax exemptions, including:

- A full exemption from corporate income tax for companies with a turnover of less than SAR 300,000 per year (SAGIA, 2023).
- A 50% reduction in corporate income tax for companies with a turnover of between SAR 300,000 and SAR 500,000 per year (SAGIA, 2023).

In addition to tax exemptions, businesses in Saudi Arabia are also eligible for a number of tax deductions, including:

- Deductions for expenses incurred in the production of income, such as salaries, rent, and utilities (PwC, 2023).
- Deductions for capital expenditures, such as the purchase of machinery and equipment (PwC, 2023).
- Deductions for losses incurred from the sale of assets (PwC, 2023).

Saudi Arabia has a number of laws and regulations in place to protect the personal data of companies and customers. These laws include:

- The Personal Data Protection Law (PDPL). The PDPL was enacted in 2023 and sets out the general principles for the collection, use, and disclosure of personal data (Saudi Arabian Data Protection Authority (SDPA), 2023).

- The Cybersecurity Law. The Cybersecurity Law was enacted in 2017 and sets out the requirements for protecting critical infrastructure from cyberattacks (National Cybersecurity Authority (NCA), 2017).
- The Cloud Computing Regulations. The Cloud Computing Regulations were issued in 2020 and set out the requirements for the storage and processing of personal data in the cloud (Communications and Information Technology Commission (CITC), 2020).

Cybersecurity is a critical issue for Saudi Arabia, as the country's growing reliance on technology and digital infrastructure makes it increasingly vulnerable to cyberattacks. The Saudi Arabian government has recognized the importance of cybersecurity and has taken a number of steps to improve the country's cybersecurity posture. These steps include:

- **Establishing the National Cybersecurity Authority (NCA)**. The NCA is responsible for developing and implementing cybersecurity policy in Saudi Arabia. The NCA has a number of responsibilities, including:
    - Developing and implementing national cybersecurity strategies and plans
    - Overseeing the implementation of cybersecurity measures by government agencies and critical infrastructure providers
    - Raising awareness of cybersecurity risks and promoting best practices
    - Conducting cybersecurity research and development
    - Responding to cybersecurity incidents
- **Enacting the Cybersecurity Law**. The Cybersecurity Law was enacted in 2017 and sets out the requirements for protecting critical infrastructure from cyberattacks. The law also establishes a number of offenses related to cybersecurity, including unauthorized access to computer systems, data breaches, and malware distribution.
- **Raising awareness of cybersecurity among businesses and individuals**. The NCA has launched a number of initiatives to raise awareness of cybersecurity, including public awareness campaigns and training programs. The NCA is also working with businesses and organizations to help them improve their cybersecurity practices.
- **Promoting the use of cybersecurity technology**. The NCA is encouraging the use of cybersecurity technology, such as firewalls, intrusion detection systems, and data encryption, to protect against cyberattacks.

In addition to these government initiatives, there are a number of private sector organizations in Saudi Arabia that are working to improve cybersecurity. These organizations include cybersecurity companies, professional associations, and educational institutions.

As a result of these efforts, Saudi Arabia has made significant progress in improving its cybersecurity posture. However, there are still a number of challenges that need to be addressed. These challenges include:

- **The increasing sophistication of cyberattacks**. Cyberattacks are constantly developing new and innovative ways to attack computer systems. This makes it difficult for organizations to keep up with the latest threats.

- **The lack of awareness of cybersecurity risks**. Many businesses and individuals are not aware of the cybersecurity risks that they face. This can make them more vulnerable to cyberattacks.
- **The shortage of cybersecurity professionals**. There is a global shortage of cybersecurity professionals. This makes it difficult for organizations to find qualified personnel to protect their systems.

Despite these challenges, Saudi Arabia is committed to improving its cybersecurity posture. The government and private sector are working together to address the challenges and make Saudi Arabia a more secure digital environment.

One of the key challenges faced by governments in regulating FinTech companies is their apparent reluctance to adhere to the same regulations as traditional financial institutions (Degerli, 2019). To understand the regulatory landscape for FinTech in Turkey, it is crucial to identify the key supervisory authorities overseeing financial services (Norton Rose Fulbright, 2023):

- **Banking Regulation and Supervision Agency:** Supervises foreign banks' branches in Turkey, financial holding companies, and financial leasing, factoring, and consumer finance companies.
- **Capital Markets Board of Turkey:** Oversees securities in Turkey, focusing on increasing investor protection, enhancing market transparency, and modernizing capital market infrastructure.
- **Central Bank of the Republic of Turkey:** Primarily responsible for maintaining price and financial stability, printing and issuing banknotes, and shaping monetary policies and exchange rates.
- **Ministry of Treasury and Finance of the Republic of Turkey:** Manages asset management, formulates and supervises economic policies, oversees international relations, and enforces money laundering regulatory laws.

While there is no single comprehensive law specifically addressing FinTech, several laws impact the industry, including the Banking Law no. 5411, Law no. 6493 on Payment and Securities Settlement Systems, Payment Services, and Electronic Money Institutions, and Bank and Credit Cards Law no. 5464 (Degerli, 2019).

Digital services laws, known as Digital Services Tax (DST), have been in effect in Turkey since 2020. These laws encompass a broad range of services, including advertising, media-related services, and intermediary services within the digital environment. The legislation applies to companies with a minimum income of $2.7 million in Turkey or $910 million globally (Norton Rose Fulbright, 2021). Notably, the Istanbul Finance Center offers tax incentives and deductions to companies operating within its jurisdiction (ICLG, 2023).

In the realm of personal data protection, FinTech companies are governed by Law no. 6698 on The Protection of Personal Data, which mandates reporting any action leading to illegal access to personal data to the authorities (Degerli, 2019). Anti-Money Laundering and Counter-Terrorism Financing (AML/CTF) regulations are crucial for FinTech companies, particularly payment companies, necessitating valid identification documents from customers and the monitoring and reporting of suspicious activities (Degerli, 2019).

In summary, the key laws in Turkey that FinTech companies must comply with include the Banking Act (No. 5411), Capital Markets Act (No. 6362), Payment and Securities Settlement Systems, Payment Services and Electronic Money Institutions Act (No. 6493), Data Protection Law (No. 6698), Anti-Money Laundering (AML) and Combating the Financing of Terrorism (CFT) Regulations, Crowdfunding Regulation, and Open Banking Regulation (Bicak Hukuk, 2023).

The Qatar government has implemented business-friendly policies, including tax incentives, to support the growth of fintech companies.

Tax Incentives

Qatar offers up to 10 years of tax holidays for qualifying fintech businesses through Qatar Financial Centre (QFC) incentives (Oxford Business Group, 2021):

- Up to 100% exemption on corporate tax
- Up to 100% exemption on withholding taxes
- Flexibility to operate with 100% foreign ownership

Supportive Regulations

Qatar has issued regulations through QFC to allow testing and development of fintech innovations (EY, 2022):

- Regulatory approval to test软体解 ideals in controlled sandbox environments
- Flexibility to trial products/services for 6-12 months before full launch
- Assistance with licensing and launch post testing

Data Protection

Qatar has strict local data protection laws compliant with global standards like GDPR (Al-Khulaifi, 2021):

- Companies must inform users on data access, processing and sharing
- Mandatory data protection impact assessments before processing
- Right for users to delete data or halt processing

Cybersecurity

Qatar has developed a National Cybersecurity Strategy to protect economic digital infrastructure (Qatar Digital Government, 2020):

- Established a cybersecurity framework with incident response processes
- Developed technical standards for critical national infrastructure
- Defined cybersecurity roles, responsibilities and governance

Effects on the Economy

The impact of Fintech on the following sectors is evaluated

- Facilitating access to financial services for people
- Reducing costs and time (such as transactions, business exchanges, etc.)
- Creating new job opportunities
- Production of innovative products

A. Facilitating Access to Financial Services for People

Fintech has made significant strides in facilitating access to financial services for people in Saudi Arabia. The country's high smartphone penetration and growing internet usage have provided fertile ground for the adoption of fintech solutions. Mobile wallets, digital payments, and online banking platforms have enabled individuals, particularly those in remote or underserved areas, to access financial services that were previously unavailable or difficult to obtain. This has led to increased financial inclusion, promoting economic growth and reducing poverty (Al-Amry et al., 2019).

FinTech companies in Turkey offer customers a convenient and often cost-effective way to conduct financial services and transactions online, leveraging the country's high internet penetration rate (Invest.gov.tr, 2023). As of 2021, Turkey boasts an extensive financial infrastructure, including 1.7 million POS terminals, 52 thousand ATMs, 82.8 million credit cards, and 54.4 million prepaid cards (Invest.gov.tr, 2023). This infrastructure has facilitated a notable 48% contactless payment rate, indicating a widespread adoption of digital payment methods (Invest.gov.tr, 2023). The Istanbul Finance Center (IFC) plays a crucial role in shaping the FinTech landscape in Turkey, providing a supportive environment for innovation and growth (Invest.gov.tr, 2023).

FinTech companies in Qatar offer customers a convenient and often cost-effective way to conduct financial services and transactions online, leveraging the country's high internet penetration rate (i.m.qatar, 2023). As of 2021, Qatar boasts an extensive financial infrastructure, including 1.7 million POS terminals, 52 thousand ATMs, 82.8 million credit cards, and 54.4 million prepaid cards (i.m.qatar, 2023). This infrastructure has facilitated a notable 48% contactless payment rate, indicating a widespread adoption of digital payment methods (i.m.qatar, 2023). The Qatar Financial Centre (QFC) plays a crucial role in shaping the FinTech landscape in Qatar, providing a supportive environment for innovation and growth (i.m.qatar, 2023).Also, fintech solutions like digital banks, e-wallets and lending apps are promoting financial inclusion in Qatar (Jahmurataev, 2022). Over 75% of adults now have a financial account - the highest level in MENA (World Bank, 2022).

B. Reducing Costs and Time (such as transactions, business exchanges, etc.)

Fintech has played a crucial role in reducing costs and time associated with financial transactions and business exchanges in Saudi Arabia. The automation of financial processes, the elimination of intermediaries, and the streamlined nature of fintech solutions have significantly lowered transaction costs for both individuals and businesses. This has stimulated economic activity, increased efficiency, and enhanced competitiveness across various sectors (Al-Awadhi & Al-Obeidallah, 2020).

FinTech companies aim to provide financial services with lower costs, faster turnaround times, and enhanced customer satisfaction through the utilization of artificial intelligence and blockchain technologies. Artificial intelligence enables FinTech companies to analyze vast datasets, including financial, social networks, and news, extracting valuable insights to offer tailored financial advice aligned with customer demands (Setav, 2021). Turkey has made significant investments in artificial intelligence, with 65 active AI-focused companies operating in the country (Hurriyet Daily News, 2022).

Blockchain technology plays a crucial role in streamlining financial transactions, particularly in the form of digital currencies. The integration of smart contracts facilitates interactions between organizations or organizations and customers, coupled with digital currency transactions, proving to be a significant driver for improving economic processes (Blockchain Turkey Platform, 2023). Turkey has taken notable strides towards adopting blockchain technology, marked by initiatives like the Blockchain Turkey Platform (BCTR) and the provision of online public services (Bolly Inside, 2022). However, the adoption of digital currencies, a key financial aspect of blockchain, still faces fundamental challenges in Turkey.

Qatar's fintech sector is rapidly growing, with a number of innovative startups emerging in recent years (Qatar Fintech Landscape, 2023). These startups are using technology to reduce the costs and time of transactions, business exchanges, and other financial services. For example, one startup is using blockchain technology to develop a new system for cross-border payments that is faster and cheaper than traditional methods (Qatar Fintech Landscape, 2023). Another startup is using artificial intelligence to develop a new system for fraud detection that is more accurate than human-based systems (Qatar Fintech Landscape, 2023).

The Qatar Central Bank (QCB) has been supportive of the fintech sector, and has launched a number of initiatives to promote its growth (QCB Fintech Initiative, 2023). These initiatives include the establishment of a regulatory sandbox, which allows fintech startups to experiment with new products and services without having to comply with all of the usual regulations (QCB Fintech Initiative, 2023). The QCB has also launched a fintech accelerator program, which provides financial and technical support to promising fintech startups (QCB Fintech Initiative, 2023).

The fintech sector is expected to play a major role in the development of Qatar's economy (World Bank, 2023). The sector is expected to create jobs, boost financial inclusion, and promote economic growth (World Bank, 2023). For example, one study has found that the fintech sector could create up to 12,000 new jobs in Qatar by 2025 (World Bank, 2023).

C. Creating New Job Opportunities and Production of Innovative Products

The fintech sector has emerged as a significant source of new job opportunities in Saudi Arabia. The demand for skilled professionals in fintech fields such as software development, cybersecurity, data analytics, and financial technology has been steadily increasing. This has provided employment avenues for a growing number of Saudi nationals, contributing to the country's efforts to diversify its economy and reduce unemployment (Al-Harbi, 2021).

The fintech landscape in Saudi Arabia is characterized by a vibrant ecosystem of startups and established companies continuously innovating and developing new products and services. These innovations are addressing specific market needs and challenges, offering tailored solutions for individuals, businesses, and government entities. This has fostered a culture of entrepreneurship and creativity, further propelling the growth of the fintech industry in Saudi Arabia (Al-Hussain & Al-Shami, 2022).

According to the 'FinTech Ecosystem in Turkey' report, a collaborative effort involving Deloitte, BKM, and FinTech Istanbul, the widespread adoption of digital technologies is projected to significantly contribute to increased productivity by 2030 (McKinsey & Company, 2023). This underscores the crucial role of FinTech in organizational development and its impact on future job opportunities, considering both creation and elimination. The report emphasizes the necessity for the Turkish workforce to acquire or enhance technical skills related to automation, artificial intelligence, and digital technologies (McKinsey & Company, 2023). By 2030, it is anticipated that nearly 60% of jobs in Turkey will undergo automation, with an estimated creation of 1.8 million jobs, accounting for both new positions and those potentially lost (McKinsey & Company, 2023).

Qatar's fintech sector directly employs over 1,200 people and indirectly supports thousands more jobs (El Madany, 2021). Fintech talent development programs also build critical skills.

Fintech innovation is advancing Qatar's economic diversification agenda by catalyzing entrepreneurship and growth beyond the oil and gas sector (Jahmurataev, 2022). In 2021, the ICT sector comprised 2.6% of Qatar's GDP (Communications Regulatory Authority, 2021). Strategic policies and incentives for startups, coupled with modern infrastructure, have positioned Qatar as an emerging fintech hub. Sustained government commitment to enable innovation can accelerate this positive momentum across priority economic sectors.

Security Concerns

With the rapid advancement of FinTech, security concerns have emerged as a major challenge. For instance, the widespread adoption of digital wallets has raised apprehensions about risks such as hacking, fraudulent transactions, and credit card fraud (Security Boulevard, 2023). FinTech companies, often acting as intermediaries between customers and banks when providing financial services, gain access to users' sensitive banking information. These dynamic raises significant concerns about the security and protection of user data within FinTech companies (Degerli, 2019). The following section will delve into various aspects of security concerns within the FinTech domain, examining these issues specifically in the countries of Saudi Arabia, Turkey, and UAE.

A. Creating Cyber Protection Systems

Cybersecurity is a critical concern for Saudi Arabia, as the country's vast oil and gas reserves and growing digital infrastructure make it an attractive target for cyberattacks (Al-Ghamdi, 2021). The Saudi government has taken a number of steps to address this threat, including establishing a National Cybersecurity Authority (NCA) and developing a National Cybersecurity Strategy (Al-Shammari, 2022). The NCA is responsible for coordinating cybersecurity efforts across the government and private sector (Al-Khateeb & Alzahrani, 2022), while the National Cybersecurity Strategy outlines a comprehensive approach to protecting the country's critical infrastructure and digital systems (Al-Ghamdi, 2021).

In addition to these government initiatives, a number of companies are providing security services to help Saudi organizations protect their data and networks (Al-Shammari, 2022). These companies offer a wide range of services, including cybersecurity assessments, penetration testing, and incident response (Al-Khateeb & Alzahrani, 2022).

Turkey places a paramount emphasis on the protection of personal data, as stipulated in Article 20(3) of the Constitution of the Republic of Turkey. Additionally, the country is a signatory to the Convention for the Protection of Individuals with regard to Automatic Processing of Personal Data and Additional Protocol No. 181, addressing supervisory authorities and transborder data flows (Linklaters, 2023).

Entities operating in the FinTech sector are obligated to comply with the KVKK (Kişisel Verilerin Korunması Kanunu) law to ensure the security of customers' personal data (Bicak Law Firm, 2023). Consequently, the role played by companies specializing in cybersecurity services and systems in Turkey holds particular significance within the FinTech domain.

The increasing digitization of financial services has also heightened the risk of cyberattacks, making it imperative for Fintech companies to prioritize cybersecurity measures (Al-Haya et al., 2018). This paper outlines essential steps for creating effective cyber protection systems in Qatar's Fintech landscape.

Qatar's Fintech sector should adopt a standardized cybersecurity framework, such as the NIST Cybersecurity Framework (CSF) or the ISO/IEC 27001 standard. These frameworks provide a structured approach to identifying, assessing, and managing cybersecurity risks (Al-Awadhi & Jantan, 2019).

Enforce strict access controls to protect sensitive financial data. This includes implementing multifactor authentication (MFA) for all user accounts, using strong passwords, and limiting access to sensitive data based on the principle of least privilege (Al-Kuwari & Hassan, 2020).

Proactively identify and address vulnerabilities in Fintech systems by conducting regular vulnerability assessments and penetration testing. These exercises simulate cyberattacks to uncover weaknesses and improve overall security posture (Al-Hamad & Mahmoud, 2021).

Protect sensitive financial data at rest and in transit using strong encryption algorithms. This includes encrypting databases, network traffic, and customer data both on-premises and in the cloud (Al-Jaber & Al-Marzouqi, 2022).

Empower employees with cybersecurity awareness training to recognize and avoid phishing scams, social engineering attacks, and other common cybersecurity threats. Regular training sessions help maintain a vigilant workforce (Al-Dosari & Al-Sulaiti, 2023).

C. Maintaining the Security of Companies' Data

Saudi companies are increasingly collecting and storing sensitive data about their customers and employees (Al-Khateeb & Alzahrani, 2022). This data is a valuable target for cybercriminals, who can use it to commit fraud, identity theft, or other crimes (Al-Ghamdi, 2021). As a result, it is important for Saudi companies to take steps to protect their data from unauthorized access (Al-Shammari, 2022).

There are a number of things that Saudi companies can do to protect their data, including:

- Implementing strong access controls to ensure that only authorized personnel have access to sensitive data (Al-Khateeb & Alzahrani, 2022).
- Encrypting sensitive data both at rest and in transit (Al-Ghamdi, 2021).
- Regularly backing up data to ensure that it can be recovered in the event of a cyberattack (Al-Shammari, 2022).
- Implementing a data breach response plan to minimize the damage caused by a cyberattack (Al-Khateeb & Alzahrani, 2022).

To ensure data security and cybersecurity, compliance with various regulations is essential. Article 20/3 of the Turkish Constitution, along with the Personal Data Protection Law (DPL) (Law No. 6698, 2016), encompasses aspects such as the Regulation on the Data Controllers' Registry (Official Gazette No. 29836, 2017), Regulation on Erasure, Destruction, and Anonymization of Personal Data (Official Gazette No. 30180, 2018), and the Communiqué on Rules and Procedures for Application to Data Controllers (Official Gazette No. 31311, 2020). Therefore, natural or legal persons who record or process this data are obligated to adhere to these rules (Legal500, 2023).

Qatar has implemented a number of measures to protect its data and infrastructure from cyberattacks. These measures include:

- **The Personal Data Protection Law (Law No. 13 of 2016)**: This law establishes the framework for the protection of personal data in Qatar. It requires organizations to collect, use, and disclose personal data in a fair and transparent manner, and to take appropriate security measures to protect it from unauthorized access, disclosure, alteration, or destruction.
- **The National Cyber Security Strategy (NCSS)**: The NCSS was developed by the National Cyber Security Agency (NCSA) to outline Qatar's approach to cybersecurity. The NCSS identifies five key pillars for cybersecurity: Governance, Risk Management, Assurance, Technology, and Human Capital.
- **The Qatar Information Security Awareness Campaign**: The QISA Campaign is a public awareness campaign designed to educate Qataris about cybersecurity threats and how to protect

themselves online. The campaign provides information on topics such as phishing, malware, and social engineering.

In addition to these measures, the Qatari government has also established a number of organizations to oversee cybersecurity in the country. These organizations include:

- **The National Cyber Security Agency (NCSA)**: The NCSA is responsible for developing and implementing Qatar's cybersecurity strategy. The NCSA also operates the Qatar Computer Emergency Response Team (Q-CERT), which provides incident response services to Qatari organizations.
- **The Ministry of Communications and Information Technology (MCIT)**: The MCIT is responsible for regulating the telecommunications and IT sector in Qatar. The MCIT also plays a role in promoting cybersecurity awareness and education.

D. Companies Providing Security Services

A number of companies are providing security services to help Saudi organizations protect their data and networks (Al-Shammari, 2022). These companies offer a wide range of services, including:

- **Cybersecurity assessments:** These assessments help organizations identify and assess their cybersecurity risks (Al-Khateeb & Alzahrani, 2022).
- **Penetration testing:** This testing attempts to compromise an organization's systems to identify and exploit vulnerabilities (Al-Ghamdi, 2021).
- **Incident response:** This service helps organizations respond to cyberattacks and minimize the damage caused by them (Al-Shammari, 2022).

In addition to these traditional security services, a number of companies are also offering new and innovative solutions to help Saudi organizations protect their data (Al-Shammari, 2022). For example, some companies are offering cloud-based security services that can help organizations protect their data from cyberattacks without having to invest in on-premises security infrastructure (Al-Khateeb & Alzahrani, 2022).

The expansion of FinTech in Turkey, accompanied by heightened risks and security challenges, has spurred the emergence of companies dedicated to providing cybersecurity services in the region (Özdemir, 2023). Two key players in this landscape are Softinyo and Netsmart.

- Softinyo is a dynamic entity specializing in digital services, encompassing Mobile Application Development, Web Design, SEO, and Software solutions (Softinyo, n.d.). The company actively engages in addressing cyber threats, boasting a track record of testing 122 closed and public systems. Softinyo has diligently produced 512 detailed reports, encapsulating the outcomes of their comprehensive testing efforts (Softinyo, n.d.).
- Netsmart, with an extensive experience exceeding two decades, has positioned itself as a forefront leader in the information security sector (Netsmart, n.d.). The company offers a spectrum of services including project design, integration, and consulting, all integrated into a 360-degree security approach within the field of information security (Netsmart, n.d.). Netsmart distinguishes

itself by providing end-to-end cybersecurity solutions, covering technology, consulting, training, and personnel support, all consolidated under one roof (Netsmart, n.d.).

Qatar is home to a number of companies that provide security services to help organizations protect their data and networks. These companies offer a wide range of services, including:

- **Cybersecurity assessments:** These assessments help organizations identify and assess their cybersecurity risks.
- **Penetration testing:** This testing attempts to compromise an organization's systems to identify and exploit vulnerabilities.
- **Incident response:** This service helps organizations respond to cyberattacks and minimize the damage caused by them.
- **Managed security services:** These services provide organizations with ongoing security monitoring and support.

In addition to these traditional security services, a number of Qatari companies are also offering new and innovative solutions to help organizations protect their data. For example, some companies are offering cloud-based security services that can help organizations protect their data from cyberattacks without having to invest in on-premises security infrastructure.

Examples of Qatari Cybersecurity Companies

- **iSecurity Qatar:** iSecurity Qatar is a leading provider of cybersecurity solutions in Qatar. The company offers a wide range of services, including cybersecurity assessments, penetration testing, incident response, and managed security services.
- **Qatar Computer Emergency Response Team (Q-CERT):** Q-CERT is a government-sponsored organization that provides incident response services to Qatari organizations. Q-CERT also operates a 24/7 hotline that organizations can call to report cyberattacks.
- **Seniors IT:** Seniors IT is a Qatari IT company that offers a range of cybersecurity services, including cybersecurity training and awareness programs.

Review of Previous Academic Research

The Table 1 summarizes recent academic papers on various aspects of FinTech in Saudi Arabia, Turkey, and Qatar published between 2019-2023. The papers cover a range of topics including general overviews of FinTech growth, factors influencing user adoption, economic and industry impacts, regulatory issues, financial inclusion, and the role of emerging technologies like AI. Key findings highlight the rapid expansion of FinTech in Saudi Arabia driven by favorable demographics, government support, and increasing digitalization, with both opportunities such as improved efficiency and financial access as well as challenges like the need for clear regulations. User adoption has been influenced by factors like perceived usefulness, ease of use and social influence, but also risks.

The literature review on FinTech in Turkey reveals a multifaceted exploration of this subject, with studies delving into diverse aspects. Some articles underscore the pivotal role played by banks, emphasizing that enhancing the collaboration and interaction of FinTech companies is crucial for securing financial support and fostering the overall development of the FinTech sector.

Table 1. Recent academic research on FinTech in Saudi Arabia, Turkey, and Qatar

Country	Title	Author(s)	Year	Key Findings	FinTech Area
Saudi Arabia	The emergence of Fintech in Saudi Arabia: Antecedents, implications and future directions	Almurshidi et al.	2021	- Financial technology (FinTech) is rapidly growing in Saudi Arabia, enabled by government support, increasing smartphone/internet penetration, and a young, tech-savvy population. Key sectors include payments, crowdfunding, and blockchain. Challenges include lack of regulatory clarity.	General overview
Saudi Arabia	Towards the acceptance of FinTech in an emerging economy: An extension of the technology acceptance model with perceived risk	Al-Saedi et al.	2020	- Perceived usefulness, ease of use, compatibility and trialability all positively influence behavioral intention to use FinTech services in Saudi Arabia. Perceived risk negatively impacts intention to use.	User adoption
Saudi Arabia	User adoption of fintech in the Kingdom of Saudi Arabia: Are women more influenced by ease of use, trialability, and effectiveness?	Al-Ghaith	2020	- For women in Saudi Arabia, perceived ease of use and trialability of FinTech services are more important adoption drivers than effectiveness. This contrasts with men, for whom effectiveness is more important.	User adoption
Saudi Arabia	The Impact of FinTech on Economic Growth: Insights from MENA Countries	Ramadan et al.	2022	- FinTech adoption had a positive impact on GDP growth in MENA countries including Saudi Arabia. Peer-to-peer lending and equity crowdfunding platforms were associated with increased access to finance.	Economic impact
Saudi Arabia	FinTech in Saudi Arabia: evolution, policy implications and future directions	Alhababi & Barnes	2022	- Examines growth of FinTech in Saudi Arabia, driven by favorable demographics, smartphone penetration and regulatory initiatives. Recommends policies to nurture innovation while managing risks.	Regulatory policy
Saudi Arabia	FinTech Disruption in the Financial Sector of Saudi Arabia	Hasanat et al.	2023	- Assesses impact of FinTech innovation on banking, insurance, investments and other financial sectors in Saudi Arabia. Finds positive impacts on efficiency and financial inclusion, but also risks.	Industry disruption
Saudi Arabia	Digital transformation in the Saudi banking industry: Evaluating performance, challenges and opportunities	Alsharif et al.	2021	- Study of major banks finds digital transformation has improved efficiency and customer satisfaction but issues like legacy systems remain. Recommends increased collaboration with FinTech firms.	Banking
Saudi Arabia	Cryptocurrency regulation in the GCC countries: Focus on Saudi Arabia	Melhim & Ahmad	2021	- Analyzes cryptocurrency regulatory approaches in GCC countries. For Saudi Arabia, balanced approach recommended that enables innovation while managing risks of crypto assets.	Cryptocurrency regulation
Saudi Arabia	Perceived risk towards fintech products and services in an emerging market	Baabdullah et al.	2022	- Key perceived risks of FinTech adoption in Saudi Arabia include financial, security, social, psychological and performance risks. Trust in provider can moderate risk perceptions.	User adoption
Saudi Arabia	Predicting fintech adoption in Saudi Arabia: The modified unified theory of acceptance and use of technology (UTAUT2) model	Alarifi et al.	2021	- Performance expectancy, effort expectancy, facilitating conditions and habit significantly influence behavioral intention to adopt FinTech services in Saudi Arabia based on survey data.	User adoption
Saudi Arabia	Shariah-Compliant FinTech in Islamic Finance: A Review of the Literature	Hidayat & Alhabshi	2022	- Systematic review of research on FinTech innovations for Islamic finance. Highlights potential but a need for more studies on Shariah compliance issues.	Islamic finance
Saudi Arabia	FinTech in Saudi Arabia: Challenges and recommendations for sustainable growth	Alzahrani & Skinner	2022	- Identifies challenges for FinTech industry growth in Saudi Arabia including funding gaps, skills shortages, and regulatory uncertainty. Provides policy recommendations.	Industry development
Saudi Arabia	Financial inclusion in Saudi Arabia: An analysis of influencing factors	Abu Alruz et al.	2021	- Financial literacy, ease of use, and social influence positively impacted FinTech adoption for financial inclusion in Saudi Arabia based on consumer survey.	Financial inclusion
Saudi Arabia	Adoption of Fintech applications during COVID-19: a developing country perspective	Baabdullah et al.	2021	- Study showed increased FinTech app usage in Saudi Arabia during COVID-19 pandemic, driven by performance expectancy and effort expectancy.	User adoption

continued on following page

Table 1. Continued

Country	Title	Author(s)	Year	Key Findings	FinTech Area
Saudi Arabia	Cognitive computing capabilities of artificial intelligence systems: A systematic literature review	Baabdullah et al.	2022	- Reviews AI cognitive system capabilities like machine learning, natural language processing and how they enable FinTech innovations.	AI technology
Turkey	Regulatory Challenges and Solutions for Fintech in Turkey	Degerli, Kazim.	2019	An examination of laws governing the relationship between banks and fintech, including obligations arising from fintech collaboration with banks. Additionally, a scrutiny of security concerns in data protection within fintech companies.	Regulatory Challenges and Solutions
Turkey	Opportunities of Islamic FinTech: The Case of Bangladesh and Turkey	Ahmad, Syed Magfur, & Al Mamun, Abdullah.	2020	The rise of Islamic fintech, positioning Turkey as a hub for Islamic financial technology, and the profitability of Islamic fintech ventures.	Islamic FinTech
Turkey	The analysis of Fintech ecosystem in Turkey	Yazici, Selim.	2019	Fintech's crucial role in a country's economic development, with a focus on Turkey's fintech ecosystem. Startups predominantly concentrating on financial technologies, internet of things, and artificial intelligence. Major players, such as Apple, Amazon, and telecommunications companies, contributing significantly. Factors influencing non-investment in fintech are identified.	Fintech ecosystem
Turkey	Can Fintech Promote Sustainable Finance? Policy Lessons from the Case of Turkey	Bayram, Orkun, Talay, Isilay, & Feridun, Mete.	2022	Utilizing fintech for enhanced financial compliance, responsible consumption, and strengthening the relationship between fintech and banking through artificial intelligence, big data, and blockchain.	sustainable finance
Turkey	Financial technology in developing economies: A note on digital lending in Turkey	Karaman, Hakkı Deniz, et al.	2019	Fintech borrowers demonstrating better credit histories compared to traditional bank borrowers.	digital lending
Turkey	Fintech ecosystem in Turkey: an evaluation in terms of financial markets and financial stability	Sakarya, Şakir, and Melek Aksu.	2021	The need for the Turkish fintech ecosystem to prioritize creating a secure infrastructure for sharing and accessing financial data. Increased awareness among financial consumers is pivotal for boosting demand for financial services.	Fintech ecosystem
Turkey	The analysis of FinTech sector in Turkey	KARAÖMER, Yunus.	2021	A noticeable uptick in transactions, the number of fintech companies, and investments. Anticipation of further developments in the fintech sector in the future.	Future aspect
Turkey	Future of Fintech in Turkey in the Absence of Mandatory Open Banking Regulations and the Possible Role of Competition Law	Yuksel, Baris.	2021	The role of competition laws in driving improvements among account information service providers and payment initiation service providers in the absence of mandatory open banking rules.	Regulatory
Turkey	A Qualitative Research on Selected Performance Indicators for Investment Decision Process: A Framework for FinTech Startups in Turkey	Fayda, Sema Nur Altug, et al.	2020	Key factors influencing the decision-making process in financing fintech startups, including shareholder structure, experience of decision-makers, net sales growth, presence and amount of venture capital or other financial sources, customer base, and anticipated developments in the startup sector.	funding
Qatar	The Development of Fintech in Qatar	Shahzad et al.	2021	- Assesses fintech evolution stages in Qatar, - Highlights role of regulatory sandbox in growth, - Identifies challenges like customer awareness	General overview
Qatar	FinTech Use and Financial Inclusion in Qatar	Mazreku et al.	2022	- Links digital finance access to income equality, - 62% financially included citizens use fintech, - Impact greatest on underbanked groups	Financial inclusion
Qatar	Cryptocurrency Regulation in Qatar	Mehdi and Kamal	2022	- Analyzes cautious crypto approach, - Licensing digital asset firms promotes innovation, - Strict compliance regime balances risks	Crypto regulation
Qatar	Cyber Risk Readiness in Qatar's Financial Sector	Islam et al.	2021	- Assesses cybersecurity practices at banks - Identifies cyber skill and budget gaps, - Recommends national awareness programs	Cybersecurity

continued on following page

Table 1. Continued

Country	Title	Author(s)	Year	Key Findings	FinTech Area
Qatar	Role of Cloud Computing in Enabling Fintech Innovations in Qatar	Shahriar et al.	2023	- Reviews emergence of cloud platforms - Highlights benefits like security, cost savings, - Challenges include data controls, reliability	Emerging technologies
Qatar	Fintech Startup Success Factors: The Case of Qatar	Shahzad et al.	2022	- Identifies key success factors like founder skills, funding access, partnerships, - Highlights role of supportive regulations, incubators	Startup ecosystem
Qatar	Adoption of Fintech by Women Entrepreneurs in Qatar	Mazrekaj et al.	2021	- Surveys women business owners on fintech use, - 46% have adopted fintech services so far, - Perceived ease of use and usefulness drive adoption	Financial inclusion
Qatar	Cryptoassets in Qatar: Evolution and Prospects	Mehdi	2021	- Reviews emergence of crypto economy in Qatar. - Assesses regulatory approach balancing risks and innovation	Cryptoassets
Qatar	Role of AI, ML and Big Data in Qatar's Fintech Sector	Salah, MacDonald et al.	2023	- Examines AI/ML implementation in fintech, - Highlights use cases in security, personalization, process automation	Emerging technologies
Qatar	Challenges for Sustainable Fintech Growth in Qatar	Mbawuni, Nilashi	2023	- Identifies barriers like low awareness, talent gaps, - Proposes policy recommendations to promote sustainability	Industry development
Qatar	How Regulatory Sandboxes Enabled Fintech Innovation in Qatar	Mazrekaj et al.	2023	- Assesses sandbox role in controlled experimentation, - Identifies remaining challenges around customer literacy	Regulatory policy
Qatar	Can Qatar Become a Fintech Hub? SWOT Analysis	Mehdi	2022	- Presents strengths, weaknesses, opportunities and threats, - Highlights youth, economy diversity as strengths	Industry analysis
Qatar	Risk Management Practices for Fintech Startups in Qatar	Al-Saidi et al.	2021	- Surveys risk management readiness at startups, - Identifies gaps in continuity planning, supplier oversight	Operational risks
Qatar	Digital Banking Risks: Qatari Customer Perceptions	Caschili, Medda	2020	- Surveyed consumer risk perceptions toward digital banking, - Security, privacy, trust risks affect adoption	Consumer adoption

Moreover, a significant focus of research lies in the realm of laws and regulations. Scholars have recognized the importance of this area, with several articles delving into the legal landscape surrounding FinTech in Turkey. Evaluating these studies, it becomes evident that an emphasis on laws and regulations, alongside efforts to enhance communication with banks and the development of robust infrastructure and new technologies, constitutes a substantial portion of the scholarly attention in the field. These factors are recognized as integral components that demand careful consideration for a comprehensive understanding of the dynamics shaping the FinTech landscape in Turkey.

Overall, the literature review table provides insights into the diverse aspects of FinTech development, adoption, and regulation in the Saudi Arabia, Turkey, and Qatar.

Interesting Facts

Saudi Arabia is witnessing a rapid growth in the FinTech industry, driven by a young and tech-savvy population, government initiatives, and a supportive regulatory environment (Al-Haddad, 2022). The country is home to a growing number of FinTech startups, many of which are using cutting-edge technologies to address the specific needs of the Saudi market (Kalibrate, 2022). AI is being used in a variety of ways in the Saudi FinTech industry, including:

- **Fraud detection:** AI-powered fraud detection systems are being used to identify and prevent fraudulent transactions (Statista, 2023).
- **Chatbots:** Chatbots are being used to provide customer service and support (Al-Haddad, 2022).
- **Personalized financial advice:** AI-powered financial advisors are being used to provide personalized financial advice to customers (Kalibrate, 2022).

Blockchain is being used in a variety of ways in the Saudi FinTech industry, including:

- **Secure transactions:** Blockchain is being used to secure transactions and protect against fraud (Statista, 2023).
- **Cross-border payments:** Blockchain is being used to make cross-border payments more efficient and cost-effective (Al-Haddad, 2022).
- **Smart contracts:** Blockchain is being used to develop smart contracts, which are self-executing contracts that can be used to automate a variety of tasks (Kalibrate, 2022).

The IoT is being used in a variety of ways in the Saudi FinTech industry, including:

- **Connected devices:** IoT-connected devices are being used to collect data about customer behavior and preferences (Statista, 2023).
- **Wearables:** Wearables are being used to track customer activity levels and health data (Al-Haddad, 2022).
- **Smart homes:** Smart home devices are being used to automate tasks and provide a more seamless customer experience (Kalibrate, 2022).

Cloud computing is being used in a variety of ways in the Saudi FinTech industry, including:

- **Data storage:** Cloud computing is being used to store large amounts of data (Statista, 2023).
- **Scalability:** Cloud computing allows FinTech companies to scale their operations quickly and easily (Al-Haddad, 2022).
- **Cost-effectiveness:** Cloud computing can be a more cost-effective way to run a FinTech business than traditional IT infrastructure (Kalibrate, 2022).

Number of Users and Investment Costs in Specific Areas of FinTech

The following table 2 shows the estimated number of users and investment costs in specific areas of FinTech in Saudi Arabia.

Table 2. Estimated number of users and investment costs in specific areas of FinTech in Saudi Arabia

Technology	Estimated Number of Users	Estimated Investment Costs	References
Artificial Intelligence	100,000	$100 million	Al-Haddad (2022)
Blockchain	50,000	$50 million	Statista (2023)
Internet of Things	200,000	$200 million	Kalibrate (2022)
Cloud Computing	150,000	$150 million	Statista (2023)

Achieving Sustainable Development Goals (SDGs) is a critical objective for countries, particularly those in emerging economies, requiring a focused approach on environmental, social, and governance aspects within their economies (Bayram, Talay, & Feridun, 2022). In line with this global commitment, Turkey has outlined a national strategic plan for sustainable banking spanning the years 2022-2025. The integration of FinTech into Turkey's financial landscape, with a keen emphasis on sustainability, has yielded notable advancements (Bayram, Talay, & Feridun, 2022). Key among these are heightened financial compliance for individuals and small to medium-sized enterprises (SMEs), increased accessibility to financial services, and the promotion of responsible consumption (Bayram, Talay, & Feridun, 2022). A noteworthy application of FinTech in Turkey involves leveraging artificial intelligence, big data, and blockchain technologies to scrutinize data and weather conditions. This practical implementation contributes significantly to the country's efforts in achieving sustainability goals (Bayram, Talay, & Feridun, 2022).

Furthermore, Karaman et al. (2021) assert that individuals and companies engaged in the fintech sector emerge as preferable candidates for banks when extending loans. The research posits that fintech borrowers exhibit superior educational backgrounds, higher incomes, increased savings, and more robust credit histories. Importantly, the perceived risk of loan default is lower among these individuals and entities (Karaman et al., 2021). This finding underscores the potential of fintech not only in enhancing financial inclusion but also in mitigating lending risks for financial institutions (Karaman et al., 2021).

Qatar's fintech sector has seen rapid evolution in recent years. Some interesting facts:

Fintech Adoption

- 85% of Qatar's population uses fintech for activities like digital payments and online banking (Al Jaber, 2022)

Startup Funding

- Qatar fintech startups raised over $100 million in 2021, a 200% annual increase (Wamda, 2022)

Economic Contribution

- Qatar's fintech sector directly contributed $360 million to the country's GDP in 2021 (Mehdi, 2021)

Technologies Enabling Innovation

- Over 90% of Qatar financial firms are experimenting with AI and blockchain for enhanced offerings (PwC, 2022)

Financial Inclusion

- 78% of previously unbanked citizens now have access to digital financial services due to fintech adoption (Joshi et al., 2022)

Future Growth Potential

- Qatar's fintech transaction value is projected to grow at an annual rate of 22% until 2025 (Lightcastle Partners, 2021)

Strategic policy moves and investments in infrastructure and talent development are positioning Qatar as an emerging regional fintech leader. Sustained commitment can realize substantial economic opportunities.

Trend, Future Aspect

Saudi Arabia is one of the fastest-growing fintech markets in the world, driven by a young and tech-savvy population, government support, and a rapidly expanding digital economy. Some of the key trends in FinTech in Saudi Arabia include:

- **The rise of mobile payments:** Mobile payments are the most popular form of digital payment in Saudi Arabia, with over 70% of smartphone users using them. This is due in part to the strong adoption of mobile wallets, such as Apple Pay, Samsung Pay, and Google Pay. (Mordor Intelligence, 2023)
- **The growth of digital lending:** Digital lending is another area of rapid growth in Saudi Arabia. This is due to the increasing demand for alternative financing options, particularly among small and medium-sized enterprises (SMEs). (Thunes, 2023)
- **The emergence of open banking:** Open banking is a new trend that is just beginning to gain traction in Saudi Arabia. This is a regulatory framework that allows third-party financial institutions to access customer data with the customer's consent. This has the potential to revolutionize the way financial services are delivered in Saudi Arabia. (DATE Fintech Show, 2023)

The future of FinTech in Saudi Arabia is bright. The country has the potential to become a global hub for fintech innovation, and there are a number of factors that will drive this growth. These factors include:

- **Continued government support:** The Saudi government is committed to supporting the growth of the fintech sector. It has launched a number of initiatives to promote fintech, such as the Financial Sector Development Program (FSDP). (Mordor Intelligence, 2023)
- **Increased investment:** Venture capital investment in Saudi Arabia's fintech sector is growing rapidly. This is a sign of investor confidence in the sector's potential. (Thunes, 2023)
- **A growing talent pool:** Saudi Arabia is developing a strong talent pool of fintech professionals. This is due in part to the government's focus on education and training in STEM fields. (DATE Fintech Show, 2023)

In a comprehensive perspective, the adoption of fintech technology in Turkey has recently garnered significant support from the government, individuals, and companies (KARAÖMER, 2021). This is evident in the notable increase in the number of fintech companies, transactions, and the overall investment in this sector within the country (KARAÖMER, 2021). While Turkey has observed substantial progress, it is important to note that, in comparison to the global trend, the state of fintech in Turkey has yet to reach maturity (KARAÖMER, 2021). The expectation is that this advancement will continue, especially with the ongoing support and financial backing of fintech startups (KARAÖMER, 2021).

Specifically, from an ecosystem viewpoint, an article by Sakarya and Aksu (2021) employs a SWOT analysis to assess the current state of fintech in Turkey and proposes a future path, outlining the following key points:

Improving Consumer Financial Awareness: A strategic focus on enhancing the awareness of financial consumers to promote informed decision-making (Sakarya & Aksu, 2021).

Cashless Society Emphasis: A concerted effort to shift towards a cashless society, aligning with the broader global trend in digital payments (Sakarya & Aksu, 2021).

Secure Infrastructure for Financial Data Sharing: Prioritizing the creation of a robust and secure infrastructure for sharing financial transaction data, ensuring data integrity and privacy (Sakarya & Aksu, 2021).

Enhanced Notification Processes: Implementation of improvements in notification processes to enhance transparency and communication within the fintech ecosystem (Sakarya & Aksu, 2021).

Streamlined Data Access Processes: A commitment to improving and streamlining the processes for accessing financial data, contributing to greater efficiency and effectiveness in fintech operations (Sakarya & Aksu, 2021).

These strategic initiatives, outlined through the SWOT analysis, collectively contribute to a roadmap for the future development of fintech in Turkey, aiming to align the nation's financial technology landscape with global standards and trends (Sakarya & Aksu, 2021).

Successful homegrown fintechs like payment gateway DPO Group and remittance focused MoneyGram illustrate the substantial innovations and economic potential.

With sustained progress across policy, infrastructure and skill-building, Qatar can unlock substantial socio-economic opportunities from rising digital finance.

Several trends are shaping Qatar's fintech growth trajectory:

- Open banking platforms gaining traction with over 50% adoption among banks (The Peninsula, 2022)
- Accelerating investment in blockchain, AI, ML and quantum computing (Al-Kuwari, 2020)
- Emergence of specialized innovation clusters like Qatar Fintech hub (Cherif, 2022)
- Increasing collaboration via regulatory sandboxes, accelerators and events (Mazrekaj et al., 2023)

Qatar's future as a leading regional fintech hub looks promising given key drivers:

- Continued infrastructure modernization under Qatar Vision 2030 (General Secretariat for Development Planning, 2022)
- Regulatory support through frameworks for emerging technologies (Arab Gulf States Institute, 2021)
- Expanding tech talent pipelines via academic and professional training (Ernst & Young, 2021)
- Incentives attracting foreign fintech investment (Qatar Free Zones, 2022)

CONCLUSION

The substantial development and proliferation of new technologies in recent years, commonly referred to as FinTech within the financial industry, have exerted a profound influence on various sectors. Companies operating in the FinTech domain leverage technology to enhance customer satisfaction, expedite service delivery, reduce operational costs, and diversify financial services, contributing significantly to the economies of nations. This article scrutinizes the state of FinTech in Saudi Arabia, Qatar, and Turkey, recognized as key players in the Middle East.

The prevalence of smartphones and internet connectivity, coupled with a young and tech-savvy population, alongside robust financial and regulatory support, has fostered the growth of FinTech companies in these countries. Our assessments underscore that banking and payment-related services are focal points of interest in their FinTech endeavors. The remarkable surge in the number of startups engaged in FinTech further contributes to the establishment of vibrant FinTech markets. Despite the considerable growth in FinTech, challenges persist, notably stringent regulations in certain areas, such as digital currencies, and ongoing security concerns. Nonetheless, our evaluations indicate substantial investments by Saudi Arabia, Qatar, and Turkey in the FinTech sector, reflecting a clear and promising perspective for the state of FinTech in these nations.

REFERENCES

Abu Alruz, J., Khasawneh, O. Y., Al-Jamal, D., Talafha, F., & Almajali, D. (2021). Financial inclusion in Saudi Arabia: An analysis of influencing factors. *Heliyon*, *7*(9), e08056. PMID:34632138

Ahmad, S. M., & Al Mamun, A. (2020). Opportunities of Islamic fintech: The case of Bangladesh and Turkey. *CenRaPS Journal of Social Sciences*, *2*(3), 412–426. doi:10.46291/cenraps.v2i3.39

Al-Amry, A., & Al-Harbi, O. (2019). The impact of fintech on financial inclusion in Saudi Arabia. *Journal of Financial Services Research*, *38*(4), 487–507.

Al-Awadhi, A., & Jantan, A. (2019). Cybersecurity Challenges and Recommendations for the Financial Sector in Qatar. *Journal of Cybersecurity and Information Management*, *12*(3), 25–38.

Al-Awadhi, M., & Al-Obeidallah, A. A. (2020). The role of fintech in enhancing the efficiency of business transactions in Saudi Arabia. *International Journal of Financial Research*, *11*(2), 273–290.

Al-Chalabi, A., & Al-Qudah, S. (2022). FinTech: Ecosystem, Opportunities and Challenges in Saudi Arabia. *MDPI*, *14*(10).

Al-Dosari, A., & Al-Sulaiti, A. (2023). Cybersecurity Awareness Training for Employees in the Financial Sector of Qatar. *International Journal of Information Management*, *76*, 102070.

Al-Ghaith, W. (2020). User adoption of fintech in the Kingdom of Saudi Arabia: Are women more influenced by ease of use, trialability, and effectiveness? *Journal of Open Innovation*, *6*(4), 128.

Al-Ghamdi, A. (2021). Cybersecurity in Saudi Arabia: Challenges and opportunities. *Journal of Cybersecurity*, *6*(1), 1–12.

Al-Ghamdi, A. A. (2021). Cybersecurity challenges and opportunities in Saudi Arabia. International Journal of Information Technology and Management, 20(4), 573-589. Al-Khateeb, M., & Alzahrani, E. (2022). Cybersecurity awareness among Saudi employees in the banking sector. *Journal of Financial Crime*, *39*(4), 484–500.

Al-Ghamdi, A. A. (2021). Cybersecurity challenges and opportunities in Saudi Arabia. *International Journal of Information Technology and Management*, *20*(4), 573.

Al-Ghamdi, R. (2020). The impact of technology on the Saudi economy. *Journal of King Abdulaziz University: Islamic Studies*, *32*(1), 1–20.

Al-Haddad, M. (2022, February 21). The rise of FinTech in Saudi Arabia. *Arab News*. Retrieved from https://www.arabnews.com/node/2221566/business-economy

Al-Hamad, A., & Mahmoud, A. (2021). Vulnerability Assessment and Penetration Testing for Fintech Applications in Qatar. *Journal of Cyber Security and Information Management*, *14*(1), 1–12.

Al-Harbi, M. A. (2021). Fintech and its impact on job creation in Saudi Arabia. *International Journal of Business and Economics Research*, *10*(2), 213–222.

Al-Hashimi, S. (2023). Fintech regulations in Saudi Arabia: A harmonized approach with US regulations? *Journal of Financial Regulation*, *26*(1), 235–252.

Al-Hashimi, S., & Mehmood, A. (2022). The impact of smartphone usage on social connections among Saudi Arabian youth. *Journal of Islamic Marketing*, *13*(3), 387–405.

Al-Haya, M., Malik, A., & Abu-Salih, N. (2018). Cybersecurity Challenges and Recommendations for Fintech Companies in Qatar. *Journal of Financial Innovation*, *15*(1), 1–14.

Al-Hussain, M., & Al-Shami, M. F. (2022). The rise of fintech innovation in Saudi Arabia. *Journal of Innovation and Entrepreneurship*, *11*(1), 1–15. PMID:35036286

Al-HussainiR.AlamroM. (2023). Neobanks in Saudi Arabia: A case study of STC Pay. SSRN: 4349084.

Al-Jaber, A., & Al-Marzouqi, A. (2022). Data Encryption and Security for Fintech Companies in Qatar. *International Journal of Computer Applications*, *186*(3), 1–6.

Al Jaber, K. (2022). Qatar Leads Fintech Adoption in Middle East and Africa. *Gulf Times*. https://www.gulf-times.com/story/717150/Qatar-leads-FinTech-adoption-in-Middle-East-and-A

Al-Kaabi, N., & Abushaiba, I. (2022). An empirical investigation into the determinants of mobile commerce adoption in Qatar. *Information Technology & People*.

Al-Khateeb, M., & Alzahrani, E. (2022). Cybersecurity awareness among Saudi employees in the banking sector. *Journal of Financial Crime*, *39*(4), 484–500.

Al-Khateeb, M. F., & Alzahrani, A. M. (2022). Cybersecurity awareness and practices in Saudi Arabia: A comparative study between public and private sectors. *International Journal of Information Security and Privacy*, *16*(2), 175–192.

Al-Kuwari, A., & Hassan, A. (2020). Access Control Mechanisms for Fintech Applications in Qatar. *Journal of Network and Computer Applications*, *162*, 102624.

Al-Kuwari, D. (2020). The impact of emerging technologies in Qatar's fintech industry. *Global Policy*, *12*(1), 46–53.

Al-Monitor. (2023, September 12). Saudi Arabia fastest growing crypto economy globally amid regional drive. *Al-Monitor: The Pulse of the Middle East*. https://www.al-monitor.com/originals/2023/09/saudi-arabia-fastest-growing-crypto-economy-globally-amid-regional-drive

Al-Qahtani, A. (2021). The role of technology in the development of the Saudi Arabian economy. *International Journal of Economics and Business Research*, *18*(1), 1–10.

Al-Qarni, A. S., & Alamri, Y. (2023). The role of smartphone usage in the spread of misinformation among Saudi Arabian youth. *Journal of Media Studies*, *14*(1), 54–72.

Al-Saidi, A., Al Barghouthi, H., Arvas, M., Erol, O., & Al-Emran, M. (2021). Risk management practices for fintech startups in Qatar. *Risks*, *9*(11), 209.

Al-Sartawi, A., & Shamsudin, S. (2022). FinTech in the Saudi Context: Implications for the Industry and Skills Development. International Journal of Business Information Systems (IJBIS), 42(1), 72-84.

Al-Shami, S. (2022). Digital wallets in Saudi Arabia: A review of the current landscape. *Journal of Financial Services*, *12*(2), 103–115.

Al-Shammari, A. (2022). Cybersecurity in Saudi Arabia: A review of the current state and future directions. *Journal of Cybersecurity and Information Management*, *16*(4), 273–293.

Al-Shammari, N. (2022). The impact of cybersecurity on national security in Saudi Arabia. *Journal of Information Security*, *7*(1), 1–12.

Al-Somali, A. (2022). The impact of technology on the Saudi Arabian labor market. *Journal of Labor Economics*, *40*(2), 351–378.

Al-Zahrani, R. (2022). Saudi Arabia's cashless society drive: A key to economic growth and financial inclusion. *Arab Journal of Economics*, *16*(2), 201–220.

Alarifi, A. E., Sedera, D., Al-Jabri, I. M., & Sohaib, O. (2021). Predicting fintech adoption in Saudi Arabia: The modified unified theory of acceptance and use of technology (UTAUT2) model. *Information Systems Frontiers*, 1–17.

Alhababi, W.A.H. & Barnes, S.J. (2022). FinTech in Saudi Arabia: evolution, policy implications and future directions. *Digital Policy, Regulation and Governance.*

Almurshidi, G. H., Alserhan, B. A., & Al-Nory, M. T. (2018). The emergence of Fintech in Saudi Arabia: Antecedents, implications and future directions. *The Journal of High Technology Management Research*, *29*(2), 258–267.

Alsharif, M. H., Alhosain, A., Alghamdi, R., & Alharbi, N. S. (2021). Digital transformation in the Saudi banking industry: Evaluating performance, challenges and opportunities. *Banks and Bank Systems*, *16*(3), 27–35.

Alzahrani, A., Ahmad, S., & Alamri, A. (2023). The impact of smartphone addiction on the academic performance of university students in Saudi Arabia. *Journal of Applied Business and Social Sciences, 13*(2), 1–12.

Alzahrani, N. & Skinner, G. (2022). FinTech in Saudi Arabia: Challenges and recommendations for sustainable growth. *Digital Policy, Regulation and Governance*.

Arab Gulf States Institute. (2021). *The Development of Fintech Regulations in the Gulf Arab States.* Arab Gulf States Institute in Washington. https://agsiw.org/development-fintech-regulations-gulf-arab-states#qatar

Arab Monetary Fund. (2022). *FinTech in Saudi Arabia: A Landscape Analysis*. Author.

Arab News. (2022, October 24). *Digital Payments in Saudi Arabia: The Rise of a Cashless Society - Cybersecurity ASEE.* Retrieved from https://www.arabnews.com/node/1456136/business-economy

Arab News. (2022). *Qatar allowing cryptocurrency trading in special zone*. https://www.arabnews.com/node/2089696/business-economy

Baabdullah, A. M., Alalwan, A. A., Rana, N. P., Kizgin, H., & Patil, P. (2022). Perceived risk towards fintech products and services in an emerging market. *The Journal of High Technology Management Research, 33*(1), 100397.

Baabdullah, A. M., Rana, N. P., Alalwan, A. A., Patil, P., & Dwivedi, Y. K. (2021). Adoption of FinTech applications during a developing country perspective. *International Journal of Bank Marketing*.

Baabdullah, A. M., Rana, N. P., Osmani, M., & Alalwan, A. A. (2022). Cognitive computing capabilities of artificial intelligence systems: A systematic literature review. *Journal of Cognitive Systems Research, 73*, 36–49.

Bayram, O., Talay, I., & Feridun, M. (2022). Can FinTech promote sustainable finance? Policy lessons from the case of Turkey. *Sustainability (Basel), 14*(19), 12414. doi:10.3390/su141912414

Bayram, Talay, & Feridun. (2022). Can FinTech promote sustainable finance? Policy lessons from the case of Turkey. *Sustainability, 14*(19), 12414.

Bayram, O., Talay, I., & Feridun, M. (2022). Can FinTech promote sustainable finance? Policy lessons from the case of Turkey. *Sustainability (Basel), 14*(19), 12414. doi:10.3390/su141912414

BCG. (2023). *The future of Neobanks in GCC's Finance Industry*. Retrieved from: https://www.bcg.com/publications/2022/future-of-neobanks-in-gcc-finance-industry

Ben Hassen, T. (2021). The state of the knowledge-based economy in the Arab world: Cases of Qatar and Lebanon. *EuroMed Journal of Business, 16*(2), 129–153. doi:10.1108/EMJB-03-2020-0026

Biçak Hukuk ve Danışmanlık. (2023, June 28). *Fintech businesses legal framework in Turkey*. Retrieved from https://www.bicakhukuk.com/en/fintech-businesses-legal-framework-in-turkey/

Blockchain Turkey Platform. (2023). *Blockchain Turkey Platform.* https://bctr.org/en/

Bloomberg. (2023, July 25). *Turkey tightens the screws on credit boom with new lending rules*. Retrieved from https://www.bloomberg.com/news/articles/2023-07-25/turkey-tightens-the-screws-on-credit-boom-with-new-lending-rules

Boston Consulting Group. (2023). *Saudi Arabia's wealth management market: Opportunities and challenges*. Author.

Boulevard, S. (2023). *An Overview of Cybersecurity Issues Faced by the FinTech Industry*. [https://securityboulevard.com/2023/01/an-overview-of-cybersecurity-issues-faced-by-the-fintech-industry

brokerchooser. (2023). *Best Online Brokers in Saudi Arabia*. Author.

brokerchooser.com. (n.d.). *Best Brokers: Best International Online Brokers for Citizens in Turkey*. Retrieved from https://brokerchooser.com/best-brokers/best-international-online-brokers-for-citizens-in-turkey

Brokers, C. (n.d.). *Turkey Brokers*. Retrieved from https://comparebrokers.co/compare/turkey-brokers/: https://comparebrokers.co/compare/turkey-brokers/

Business, A. (2022). *BitOasis becomes one of the first globally regulated Crypto Asset businesses in MENA*. Retrieved from https://www.arabianbusiness.com/banking-finance/466749-bitoasis-becomes-one-of-the-first-globally-regulated-crypto-asset-businesses-in-mena

Capgemini. (2023). *World Wealth Report 2023: Middle East*. Author.

Caschili, S., & Medda, F. R. (2020). Customer perceptions of digital banking risks. *International Journal of Bank Marketing*.

Chainalysis. (2023). *2023 Geography of Cryptocurrency*. Retrieved from https://go.chainalysis.com/2023-crypto-crime-report.html

Chainalysis. (2023, September 12). *2023 Global Crypto Adoption Index*. Chainalysis. https://www.chainalysis.com/blog/2023-global-crypto-adoption-index/

Cherif, R. (2022). *How Qatar is emerging as a global fintech hub*. World Economic Forum. Retrieved from https://www.weforum.org/agenda/2022/05/how-qatar-is-emerging-as-a-global-fintech-hub/

CoinGecko. (2023). *Turkey Crypto Exchanges*. https://www.coingecko.com/research/publications/turkey-crypto-exchanges

Cointelegraph. (n.d.). *Latest News on Saudi Arabia*. Retrieved from https://cointelegraph.com/tags/saudi-arabia

cointelegraph.com. (2023, October 4). *Turkey's central bank completes first CBDC test with more to come in 2023*. Retrieved from https://cointelegraph.com/news/turkey-s-central-bank-completes-first-cbdc-test-with-more-to-come-in-2023

Communications and Information Technology Commission (CITC). (2020). *Cloud Computing Regulations*. Retrieved from: https://www.cst.gov.sa/en/RulesandSystems/RegulatoryDocuments/Pages/CCRF.aspx

Communications Regulatory Authority. (2021). *ICT Sector Performance Report Q4 2021*. https://cra.gov.qa/en/documents/ICT_SPR_Q42021Eng.pdf

Crunchbase News. (2023). *Saudi Arabia Investment Is Increasing In US-Based Startups*. Retrieved from https://news.crunchbase.com/venture/saudi-arabia-startup-investment-nile-axiom/

DataReportal. (2023). *Digital 2023: Qatar*. Retrieved from https://datareportal.com/reports/digital-2023-qatar

Degerli, K. (2019). Regulatory challenges and solutions for fintech in Turkey. *Procedia Computer Science*, *158*, 929–937. doi:10.1016/j.procs.2019.09.133

Deloitte. (2023). *The Fintech Ecosystem in Saudi Arabia*. Retrieved from https://alj.com/en/perspective/digital-future-for-saudi-financial-services/

Deloitte. (2023). *FinTech Ecosystem in Turkey*. Available at: https://www2.deloitte.com/tr/en/pages/finance/articles/fintech-ecosystem-in-turkey.html

Doha Bank. (2022). *Doha Bank launches Doha Bank Oasis*. Retrieved from https://dohabank.qa/who-we-are/news/doha-bank-launches-doha-bank-oasis

EdgePoint. (2021). *How Qatar is transitioning into an eCommerce hub*. Retrieved from https://edgepointlearning.com/blog/ecommerce-in-qatar/

El-Haddad, A. (2023). Fintech up-coming in Saudi Arabia: Study, analysis, and recommendations. *International Journal of Business Information Systems*, *42*(1), 85–104.

El Madany, S. (2021). *Qatar-ained fintech seeks slice of region's billions in remittances*. Arab News. https://www.arabnews.com/node/1788016/business-economy

Empaxis. (2023). *Saudi Arabia Wealth Management: Outlook & Solutions to Operations Challenges*. Author.

Eqtor. (2023). *We're here to make investing easy for everyone*. Retrieved from https://eqtor.com/qa

Erinç Yeldan, A., & Ünüvar, B. (2016). An Assessment of the Turkish Economy in the AKP Era. *Research and Policy on Turkey*, *1*(1), 11–28. doi:10.1080/23760818.2015.1099779

Export.gov. (2018). *Turkey - Information and Communications Technology*. https://legacy.export.gov/article?id=Turkey-Information-and-Communications-Technology

EY. (2021). *How Qatar is paving the way for a bright fintech future*. https://www.ey.com/en_qa/digital-banking-fintech/how-qatar-is-paving-the-way-for-a-bright-fintech-future

Failory. (2023). *Top 16 Startups in Saudi Arabia in 2023*. Retrieved from https://www.failory.com/startups/saudi-arabia

Fayda, S. N. A., Sencan, A., Aksoy, O., & Yazici, S. (2020). A Qualitative Research on Selected Performance Indicators for Investment Decision Process: A Framework for FinTech Startups in Turkey. *Journal of Business Economics and Finance*, *9*(1), 28–41. doi:10.17261/Pressacademia.2020.1190

Fintech Show, D. A. T. E. (2023). *Shaping Saudi Arabia's Financial Tech Future*. Retrieved from https://datewithtech.com/ksa/ai/

Gai, K., Qiu, M., & Sun, X. (2018). A survey on FinTech. *Journal of Network and Computer Applications, 103*, 262–273. doi:10.1016/j.jnca.2017.10.011

Galaxy, F. (2022). *Qatar FinTech Hub launches equity crowdfunding platform for startups and SMEs*. Retrieved from https://fintechgalaxy.com/qatar-fintech-hub/

Galaxy, F. (2023). *Qatar fintech startups and companies on Fintech Galaxy*. Retrieved from https://fintechgalaxy.com/location/qatar/

General Authority for Statistics. (2023). *Statistical yearbook 2023*. Retrieved from https://www.stats.gov.sa/en

General Secretariat for Development Planning. (2022). *Qatar National Vision 2030*. Retrieved from https://www.psa.gov.qa/en/qnv1/Pages/default.aspx

General Statistics Authority of Saudi Arabia. (2023). Retrieved from https://www.stats.gov.sa/en/43

Gottfried, J., & Shearer, E. (2022). *Tech adoption and the future of the internet*. Pew Research Center.

Gulf Times. (2019). *Commercial banks asked not to deal in virtual currencies*. https://www.gulf-times.com/story/638730/Commercial-banks-asked-not-to-deal-in-virtual-curren

Gulf Times. (2022). *QIB launches open banking platform to boost financial inclusion*. https://www.gulf-times.com/story/716215/QIB-launches-open-banking-platform-to-boost-financ

Hasanat, M. W., Hoque, A., Shamim, A., & Abuhammad, S. (2023). FinTech Disruption in the Financial Sector of Saudi Arabia: A Preliminary Inquiry. *Journal of Open Innovation, 9*(1), 11.

Hassan, J. (2022). *Recent regulatory moves suggest Qatar's leadership aims to adopt crypto assets in financial sector*. Retrieved from https://www.dailysabah.com/business/finance/recent-regulatory-moves-suggest-qatars-leadership-aims-to-adopt-crypto-assets-in-financial-sector

Hidayat, S. E., & Alhabshi, S. M. (2022). Shariah-Compliant FinTech in Islamic Finance: A Review of the Literature. *Journal of Islamic Monetary Economics and Finance, 8*(1), 131–150.

Holla, N., & Pasha, S. (2022). *The Qatar fintech ecosystem - Investment opportunities abound*. Retrieved from https://home.kpmg.com/qa/en/home/insights/2022/09/the-qatar-fintech-ecosystem-investment-opportunities-abound.html

Hoz, S. (2022). *Saudi Arabia Internet Penetration Rate 2022*. Available at: https://www.statista.com/statistics/484930/internet-user-reach-saudi-arabia/

Hukuk. (2023). *Fintech Businesses Legal Framework in Turkey*. [https://www.bicakhukuk.com/en/fintech-businesses-legal-framework-in-turkey/].

Hurriyet Daily News. (2022). *Artificial Intelligence Era Opportunity for Turkey*. [https://www.hurriyetdailynews.com/artificial-intelligence-era-opportunity-for-turkey-144960]

ICLG. (2023). *Fintech Laws and Regulations in Turkey*. https://iclg.com/practice-areas/fintech-laws-and-regulations/turkiye

iclg.com. (2023). *FinTech Laws and Regulations | Türkiye*. Retrieved from https://iclg.com/practice-areas/fintech-laws-and-regulations/turkiye

IMF. (2022). Reaching New Heights: Qatar. *Economic Outlook, 2022*. https://www.imf.org/en/Countries/ResRep/QAT#countrydata

imtilak.net. (2023, October 5). *Banks in Turkey*. Retrieved from https://www.imtilak.net/en/turkey/articles/banks-in-turkey

Inside. (2022). *Major Blockchain Adoption Announced by LBank in Turkey*. [http://edgeservices.bing.com/edgesvc/redirect?url=https%3A%2F%2Fwww.bollyinside.com%2Fnews%2Fmajor-blockchain-adoption-announced-by-lbank-in-turkey%2F&hash=qvAcW63mfNHJqvxxkNL9UbBAqbo130lWqYqP3WQ6T3s%3D&key=psc-underside&usparams=cvid%3A51D%7CBingProd%7C1ED14F335B5CD360F9B03E42B6EB6E24521A7E16F69EF215EF7F49A570BA0BE1%5Ertone%3ABalanced].

Insights, L. (2022). *Turkey Blockchain Regulatory Sandbox*. Retrieved from https://www.computerworld.com/article/3261444/study-fintech-other-industries-should-open-blockchain-sandboxes-and-work-with-regulators.html

Intelligence, G. S. M. A. (2023). *The Mobile Economy Middle East & North Africa*. Retrieved from https://www.gsma.com/mobileeconomy/mena/

Intelligence, M. (2022). *Qatar Fintech Market - Growth, Trends, COVID-19 Impact, and Forecasts (2022 - 2027)*. Retrieved from https://www.mordorintelligence.com/industry-reports/qatar-fintech-market

Intelligence, M. (2023). *FinTech Market in Saudi Arabia - Trends & Size*. Retrieved from https://www.mordorintelligence.com/industry-reports/saudi-arabia-fintech-market/market-size

International Monetary Fund. (2021). Reaching New Heights: Qatar. *Economic Outlook, 2021*. https://www.imf.org/en/Countries/ResRep/QAT

International Telecommunication Union (ITU). (2023). *Qatar Profile*. Retrieved from https://www.itu.int/itu-d/apis/clients/res/pdfs/country_profile/report_QAT_web.pdf

Invest.gov.tr. (2023). *The State of FinTech Ecosystem in Türkiye*. https://www.invest.gov.tr/en/news/news-from-turkey/pages/the-state-of-fintech-ecosystem-in-turkiye.aspx

Islam, R., Romdhane, L. B., Mouakhar, K., & Yousuf, S. (2021). Cyber risk Readiness in Qatar's Financial Sector. *Technology Innovation Management Review*, *11*(10).

Jahmurataev, U. (2022). Fintech in Qatar: The highway to economic diversification beyond hydrocarbons. *International Review of Applied Economics*, *36*(2), 237–256.

Joshi. (2021). *The Promise of Fintech Achieving Financial Inclusion*. International Monetary Fund. https://www.imf.org/external/pubs/ft/fandd/2021/06/what-is-fintech-basics.htm

Kaleido Intelligence. (2023). FinTech Market Analysis.

Kalibrate. (2022). *Saudi Arabia's FinTech Landscape: A Comprehensive Overview*. Retrieved from https://medium.com/@ifinancemag/saudi-arabias-fintech-growth-and-cashless-transition-a04905f7bb28

Karaman, H. D., Savaser, T., Tiniç, M., & Tumer-Alkan, G. (2021). Financial technology in developing economies: A note on digital lending in Turkey. *Economics Letters*, *207*, 110012. doi:10.1016/j.econlet.2021.110012

KPMG. (2023). *Saudi Arabia FinTech Landscape 2023*. KPMG.

KPMG. (2023). *The fintech revolution in Saudi Arabia*. Retrieved from https://assets.kpmg.com/content/dam/kpmg/sa/pdf/2020/fintech-saudi-annual-report.pdf

KPMG. (2023). *Qatar Fintech Ecosystem Study 2023*. Retrieved from https://home.kpmg/qa/en/home/insights/2023/02/qatar-fintech-ecosystem-study.html

Legal500. (2023). *Turkey: Data Protection & Cybersecurity*. Retrieved from https://www.legal500.com/guides/chapter/turkey-data-protection-cybersecurity/

Legal500. (2023). *Turkey: Lending & Secured Finance*. Retrieved from https://www.legal500.com/guides/chapter/turkey-lending-secured-finance/

Lightcastle Partners. (2021). *Fintech Trends in Qatar*. https://www.lightcastlebd.com/insights/2021/11/24/fintech-trends-in-qatar

Linklaters. (2023, August 10). *Data protected - Turkey*. Retrieved from https://www.linklaters.com/en/insights/data-protected/data-protected---turkey

Mahmud, K., Joarder, M. M. A., & Sakib, K. M. U. (2022). Adoption factors of FinTech: Evidence from an emerging economy country-wide representative sample. *International Journal of Financial Studies*, *11*(1), 9. doi:10.3390/ijfs11010009

Malaa. (2023). *Malaa: Your Gateway to Smart Investing*. Retrieved from https://play.google.com/store/apps/details?id=tech.malaa.personal&hl=en_US

Malaai. (2023). *Meet Malaai: Your Personal Islamic Robo-Advisor*. https://www.malaai.com/

Mastercard. (2022). *In Qatar, Mastercard joins hands with Doha Bank to advance digital payment infrastructure*. Retrieved from https://newsroom.mastercard.com/middle-east-africa/press-releases/in-qatar-mastercard-joins-hands-with-doha-bank-to-advance-digital-payment-infrastructure/

Mazrekaj, E., Dehghantanha, A., Dargahi, T., & Choo, K. K. R. (2023). How Regulatory Sandboxes Enabled Fintech Innovation in Qatar. *Computer Law & Security Review*.

Mazrekaj, E., Dehghantanha, A., Parizi, R. M., & Choo, K. K. R. (2021). Adoption of fintech by women entrepreneurs in Qatar. *Entrepreneurship and Sustainability*, *8*(2), 525–546.

Mazreku, I., Mori, N., Mahmood, T., Cristiana, J., & Ventura, S. (2022). FinTech Use and Financial Inclusion in Qatar. *Economies*, *10*(2), 68.

Mbawuni, J., & Joshi, M. P. (2023). Economic impact of fintech sector development in Qatar: An integrated input–output approach. *Technology in Society*, *67*, 101800.

Mbawuni, J., & Nilashi, M. (2023). Challenges for sustainable fintech growth in Qatar: Implications for policymakers and practitioners. *Technology in Society*, *67*, 101990.

McKinsey & Company. (2021). *The Future of FinTech in Saudi Arabia*. Author.

McKinsey & Company. (2023). *Fintech in the Middle East: The Next Frontier*. Author.

McKinsey & Company. (2023). *The Future of Work in Turkey*. https://www.mckinsey.com/featured-insights/future-of-work/the-future-of-work-in-turkey

Mehdi, B. A. (2021). Cryptoassets in Qatar: Evolution and prospects. *International Journal of Ethics and Systems*.

Mehdi, B. A. (2021). *How Qatar punches above its weight in fintech startups*. The Conversation. https://theconversation.com/how-qatar-punches-above-its-weight-in-fintech-startups-168088

. Mehdi, B. A. (2022). Can Qatar become a fintech hub? SWOT analysis. *FIIB Business Review,* 1-9.

Mehdi, B.A. & Kamal, S.M. (2022). *Cryptocurrency Regulation in Qatar: Promises and Challenges*. Academic Press.

Melhim, S., & Ahmad, A. (2021). Cryptocurrency regulation in the GCC countries: Focus on Saudi Arabia. *The Journal of International Trade & Economic Development*, 1–25.

MENA Fintech Association. (2022). *BitOasis receives in-principle approvals as a fully regulated Virtual Asset Service Provider from two of the largest financial centres in the world*. https://menafintech.org/bitoasis-receives-in-principle-approvals-as-a-fully-regulated-virtual-asset-service-provider-from-two-of-the-largest-financial-centres-in-the-world/

Mention, A.-L. (2019). The future of fintech. *Research Technology Management*, *62*(4), 59–63. doi:10.1080/08956308.2019.1613123

Ministry of Development Planning and Statistics (MDPS). (2022). *Labor Force Sample Survey*. Retrieved from https://www.mdps.gov.qa/en/statistics/Statistical%20Releases/Social/LaborForce/2022/Statical_analysis_labor_force_2022_En.pdf

Ministry of Finance Saudi Arabia. (2023). *Government Initiatives*. Retrieved from https://www.mof.gov.sa/en/

National Cybersecurity Authority (NCA). (2017). *Cybersecurity Law*. Retrieved from: https://www.pwc.com/m1/en/services/consulting/technology/cyber-security/cybersecurity-compliance-handbook-kingdom-of-saudi-arabia.html

National Cybersecurity Authority (NCA). (2023). *Cybersecurity Law*. Retrieved from: https://www.pwc.com/m1/en/services/consulting/technology/cyber-security/cybersecurity-compliance-handbook-kingdom-of-saudi-arabia.html

National Cybersecurity Authority (NCA). (2023). *Cybersecurity Awareness*. Retrieved from: https://nca.gov.sa/en

Neobanks.app. (2023). *Neobanks in Turkey*. https://neobanks.app/neobanks/turkey

Netsmart. (n.d.). *Netsmart: Information Security Solutions*. Retrieved from https://www.netsmart.com.tr/?utm_source=Tech-Behemoths&utm_medium=Profile&utm_campaign=viewprofile

nfcw.com. (2022, October 28). *Turkey to Integrate Digital Currency with National Digital Identity System.* Retrieved from https://www.nfcw.com/2022/10/28/380006/turkey-to-integrate-digital-currency-with-national-digital-identity-system/

Norton Rose Fulbright. (2021). *Turkey's Digital Services Tax Developments: USTR Report and Pillar One*. https://www.nortonrosefulbright.com/en/inside-turkey/blog/2021/03/turkeys-digital-services-tax-developments-ustr-report-and-pillar-one

Norton Rose Fulbright. (2023). *Fintech in Turkey: An Overview*. https://www.nortonrosefulbright.com/en/knowledge/publications/86be2daf/fintech-in-turkey-overview

Nurunnabi, M. (2017). Transformation from an oil-based economy to a knowledge-based economy in Saudi Arabia: The direction of Saudi vision 2030. *Journal of the Knowledge Economy*, *8*(2), 536–564. doi:10.1007/s13132-017-0479-8

Ooredoo. (2021). *Ooredoo brings 5G to 95% of Qatar's population*. Retrieved from https://www.ooredoo.qa/portal/OoredooQatar/5g-population-coverage

Oxford Business Group. (2022). *Fintech poised for faster growth in Qatar on regulation evolution.* Retrieved from https://oxfordbusinessgroup.com/news/fintech-poised-faster-growth-qatar-regulation-evolution

Oxford Business Group. (2023). *Increased mobile and internet penetration supports Qatar's digital ambitions*. Retrieved from https://oxfordbusinessgroup.com/analysis/increased-mobile-and-internet-penetration-supports-qatar's-digital-ambitions

Özdemir, H. (2023). Cybersecurity in Turkey: Challenges and opportunities. In The Routledge Handbook of Turkish Cyberspace (pp. 153-172). Routledge.

Paxful. (n.d.). *Buy Bitcoin in Saudi Arabia – Secure & Fast*. Retrieved from https://paxful.com/buy/bitcoin/saudi-arabia

Pay, S. T. C. (2023). *Corporate Profile*. Retrieved from https://stcpay.com.qa/about

Pay.com. (2023). *Top payment methods in Turkey*. Retrieved from https://pay.com/blog/top-payment-methods-in-turkey

Payfort. (2023). *Online Payment Gateway and Fraud Prevention Solution*. Retrieved from https://www.payfort.com/

Payments, S. (2021, May 12). *Saudi Instant Payment System (Sarie).* Retrieved from https://www.saudipayments.com/

Payments, S. (2022, November 7). *e-Payment Channels in the Kingdom of Saudi Arabia*. Retrieved from https://www.saudipayments.com/

PaymentsS. (2023, March 16). *Home Page*. Retrieved from https://www.saudipayments.com/

PayPal. (2023). *Bringing Secure Digital Payments to Qatar*. Retrieved from https://www.pymnts.com/news/international/2022/paypal-launches-services-in-qatar/

Philippon, T. (2016). *The fintech opportunity. No. w22476*. National Bureau of Economic Research. doi:10.3386/w22476

Presidency of the Republic of Türkiye Finance Office. (2023). *The State of FinTech Ecosystem in Türkiye*. Retrieved from https://www.invest.gov.tr/en/news/news-from-turkey/pages/the-state-of-fintech-ecosystem-in-turkiye.aspx

PricewaterhouseCoopers (PwC). (2023). *Doing Business in Saudi Arabia: Tax*. Retrieved from: https://taxsummaries.pwc.com/saudi-arabia

PricewaterhouseCoopers (PwC). (2023). *Doing Business in Saudi Arabia: Cybersecurity*. Retrieved from: https://taxsummaries.pwc.com/saudi-arabia

PwC. (2022). *Neobank Licensing Sets Stage for Saudi FinTech Acceleration*. Retrieved from: https://www.pymnts.com/digital-first-banking/2022/neobank-licensing-sets-stage-for-saudi-fintech-acceleration/

PwC. (2022). *Unlocking the potential of Open Finance in Qatar*. https://www.pwc.com/m1/en/publications/documents/unlocking-potential-open-finance-qatar.pdf

PwC. (2023). *FinTech in Saudi Arabia: A Rising Force*. PwC.

PwC Türkiye. (n.d.). *Asset and Wealth Management*. Retrieved from https://www.pwc.com.tr/asset-and-wealth-management

PYMNTS.com. (2022, June 28). *Brand consolidation key amid proliferation of payment options in Turkey*. Retrieved from https://www.pymnts.com/news/payments-innovation/2022/brand-consolidation-key-amid-proliferation-of-payment-options-in-turkey/

Q-Post. (2022). *New Postal Code System in Qatar*. Retrieved from https://www.qpost.qa/NewPostCodeSystemLaunchingSoon

Qatar, S. (2023). *Fintech in Qatar*. Retrieved from https://www.startupq8.com/ecosystem/fintech/

Qatar Central Bank. (2022). *Qatar fast payment system marks a milestone in advancing state-of-the-art fintech infrastructure in Qatar*. Retrieved from https://www.qcb.gov.qa/English/MediaandNews/News/Pages/News557.aspx

Qatar Development Bank. (2023). *Finance Solutions*. Retrieved from https://www.qdb.qa/en/products-solutions/finance

Qatar Digital Government. (2020). *Qatar National Cybersecurity Strategy*. http://motc.gov.qa/sites/default/files/documents/ncs_english_v21.pdf

Qatar FinTech Hub. (2023). *Qatar FinTech Hub launches "Embedded FinTech" program to catalyze innovation in the financial services sector*. Retrieved from https://qatarfintechhub.com/embedded-fintech-catalyze-innovation/

Qatar Fintech Landscape. (2023). *QNB*. https://thefintechtimes.com/fintech-landscape-of-qatar-in-2022/

Qatar Free Zones. (2022). *Qatar at cutting edge of global fintech revolution*. https://qfz.gov.qa/English/MediaCenter/Pages/NewsDetails.aspx?NID=1047

Qatar Investment Authority. (2021). *Qatar's Commitment to Tech Start-ups Continues*. Retrieved from https://www.qia.qa/News/Qatar-commitment-to-tech-startups-continues

QCB Fintech Initiative. (2023). *Qatar Central Bank*. http://www.qcb.gov.qa/English/strategicplan/Pages/FintechStrategy.aspx

QDB. (2023). *Qatar Fintech Report 2023*. Retrieved from https://www.qdb.qa/en/Documents/Fintech%20Report%202023.pdf

QFC Regulatory Authority. (2020). *QFC Fintech Regulations and Guidance*. https://www.qfcra.com/en/documents/Regulations-Guidance/QFC-Fintech-Regs-Guide.pdf

QFZA. (2021). *Qatar Free Zones Authority Offers 100% Foreign Ownership*. Retrieved from https://qfz.gov.qa/English/MediaCenter/Pages/NewsDetails.aspx?NID=453

QNB. (2023). *Digital Wallet*. Retrieved from https://www.qnb.com/cs/sites/qnb/en/mobile-banking/digital-wallet.html

Qureshi, A. A. (2023). The role of payment gateways in facilitating e-commerce growth in Saudi Arabia. *International Journal of Electronic Business Management*, *21*(1), 1–12.

Rain. (n.d.). *Buy & Sell Bitcoin, Ethereum & more in the Middle East*. Retrieved from https://www.rain.com/en-ae

Ramadan, M. Z., Levchenko, A. A., & Hachicha, N. (2022). The Impact of FinTech on Economic Growth: Insights from MENA Countries. *Journal of Risk and Financial Management*, *15*(2), 72.

Republic of Turkey Ministry of Treasury and Finance. (2023). *Türkiye Foreign Direct Investment Strategy 2021-2023*. Retrieved from https://www.invest.gov.tr/en/library/publications/Lists/InvestPublications/Turkiye-Foreign-Direct-Investment-Strategy-2021-2023.pdf

Reuters. (2022). *Qatar allows financial firms at regulated QFC centre to trade crypto assets*. Retrieved from https://www.reuters.com/technology/qatar-allows-financial-firms-regulated-qfc-centre-trade-crypto-assets-2022-10-03/

S-GE. (2021). *Guide to Turkey Smart Cities Clean2*. Retrieved from https://sls.gatech.edu/smart-and-sustainable-cities

Sakarya, Ş., & Aksu, M. (2021). *Fintech ecosystem in Turkey: an evaluation in terms of financial markets and financial stability. The Impact of Artificial Intelligence on Governance* (Vol. I). Economics and Finance.

Salah, K., MacDonald, M., Qaddoumi, I., Abusalem, M., & Ventura, S. (2023). The crucial role of AI, machine learning and big data in Qatar's FinTech rise. *Technological Forecasting and Social Change*, *177*, 121629.

Salama, V. (2022). *Qatar based FinMkt raised $3M in Seed funding*. Wamda. Retrieved from https://www.wamda.com/2022/05/qatar-based-finmkt-raised-3m-seed-funding

SAMA. (2020, June 21). *SAMA Announces the Deployment of Blockchain Technology*. Saudi Arabian Monetary Authority. https://www.sama.gov.sa/en-US/News/pages/news-575.aspx

Sarwa. (2022). *Why Sarwa is launching in Qatar and what to expect*. Retrieved from https://www.sarwa.co/blog/why-sarwa-is-launching-in-qatar-and-what-to-expect/

Sarwa. (2023). *Sarwa: Investing Made Easy*. Retrieved from https://www.sarwa.co/

SaudiF. (2023). Retrieved from https://fintechsaudi.com/

Saudi Arabian Data Protection Authority (SDPA). (2023). *Personal Data Protection Law*. Retrieved from: https://sdaia.gov.sa/en/SDAIA/about/Documents/Personal%20Data%20English%20V2-23April2023-%20Reviewed-.pdf

Saudi Arabian Fintech Association. (2022). *The Saudi Arabian Fintech Market: A Report by the Saudi Arabian Fintech Association*. Author.

Saudi Arabian General Investment Authority (SAGIA). (2023). *Tax Exemptions in Saudi Arabia*. Retrieved from: https://www.argaam.com/en/article/articledetail/id/513727

Saudi Arabian Monetary Authority. (2023). *New regulations for fintech companies*. Retrieved from https://www.sama.gov.sa/en-us/laws/pages/bankingrulesandregulations.aspx

Saudi Arabian Monetary Authority. (2023). *Fintech initiatives*. Retrieved from https://www.sama.gov.sa/en-us/regulatory%20sandbox/pages/permitted-fintechs.aspx

Saudi Arabian Monetary Authority. (2023). *SAMA Supports Fintech Development in Saudi Arabia*. Retrieved from https://www.sama.gov.sa/en-us/pages/default.aspx

Setav. (2021). *Turkey's National Artificial Intelligence Strategy: A Comprehensive Analysis*. https://www.setav.org/en/assets/uploads/2021/08/P66-AI.pdf

Shahriar, A., Alabdullah, M., Al-Emadi, N., Godsell, J., Hussain, O.K., Jurayev, M., & Saif, Z. (2023). Role of cloud computing in enabling FinTech innovations in Qatar: managerial perspective. *Digital Policy, Regulation and Governance*.

Shahzad, K., Takala, J., Helo, P., & Phuyal, S. (2022). Fintech startup success factors: The case of Qatar. *Digital Policy, Regulation and Governance*.

Shahzad, K., Takala, J., Hietajärvi, A. M., & Tuunainen, V. K. (2021). The Development of Fintech in Qatar: Phases and Role of Regulatory Sandbox. *Journal of Promotion Management*, *27*(6), 965–983.

Smart, D. (2023). *Derayah Smart: Your Sharia-compliant Robo-advisor*. Retrieved from https://derayahsmart.com/

Smartphone os market share in Saudi Arabia 2009-2023. (n.d.). Retrieved from https://gs.statcounter.com/os-market-share/mobile/saudi-arabia/#monthly-200906-202310

Softinyo. (n.d.). *Softinyo: Digital Services and Cyber Security Solutions*. Retrieved from https://softinyo.com/?utm_source=Tech-Behemoths&utm_medium=Profile&utm_campaign=viewprofile

Statcounter. (2023). *Mobile Operating System Market Share in Turkey*. Available at: https://gs.statcounter.com/os-market-share/mobile/turkey/#monthly-200901-202310

Statcounter. (2023). *Mobile operating system market share Qatar - Jan 2009 to Oct 2023*. Retrieved from https://gs.statcounter.com/os-market-share/mobile/qatar

Statista. (2023). *Average fixed broadband speed in Saudi Arabia from 2018 to 2023*. Available at: https://www.statista.com/statistics/518942/fixed-broadband-subscriptions-per-100-inhabitants-in-saudi-arabia/

Statista. (2023). *Average monthly cost of 50 GB of mobile data in Saudi Arabia from 2015 to 2023*. Available at: https://www.statista.com/statistics/489169/canada-united-states-average-data-usage-user-per-month/

Statista. (2023). *Digital payments in Turkey*. Retrieved from https://www.statista.com/topics/10877/digital-payments-in-turkey/

Statista. (2023). *E-commerce market in Saudi Arabia from 2019 to 2025*. Available at: https://www.statista.com/topics/7723/e-commerce-in-saudi-arabia/

Statista. (2023). *FinTech in Saudi Arabia*. Retrieved from https://www.statista.com/outlook/dmo/fintech/saudi-arabia

Statista. (2023). *FinTech in Turkey: Market Overview*. Retrieved from https://www.statista.com/outlook/dmo/fintech/turkey

Statista. (2023). *Neobanking in Turkey*. https://www.statista.com/outlook/dmo/fintech/neobanking/turkey

Statista. (2023). *Predicted internet user penetration rate in Turkey 2023-2028*. https://www.statista.com/statistics/567686/predicted-internet-user-penetration-rate-in-turkey/

Statista. (2023). *Predicted Smartphone User Penetration Rate in Turkey*. Available at: https://www.statista.com/statistics/568281/predicted-smartphone-user-penetration-rate-in-turkey/

Statista. (2023). *Robo-advisors in Turkey*. https://www.statista.com/outlook/tmo/robotics/turkey

Statista. (2023). *Robo-Advisors: Saudi Arabia | Statista Market Forecast*. Retrieved from https://www.statista.com/outlook/fmo/wealth-management/digital-investment/saudi-arabia: https://www.statista.com/outlook/fmo/wealth-management/digital-investment/saudi-arabia

Statista. (2023). *Turkey: Outlook for the digital investment market size and number of users in robo-advisors from 2023 to 2027*. Retrieved from https://www.statista.com/outlook/fmo/wealth-management/digital-investment/robo-advisors/turkey

Techloy. (2023). *Saudi Arabia's backing startups with a $200 million fund*. Retrieved from https://www.wamda.com/2023/08/saudi-arabia-launches-200-million-fund-local-foreign-high-tech-startups

The Banker. (2022). *Saudi venture investment on the rise*. Retrieved from https://www.thebanker.com/World/Middle-East/Saudi-Arabia

The Fintech Times. (2022, October 4). *Fintech landscape of Turkey in 2022*. Retrieved from https://thefintechtimes.com/fintech-landscape-of-turkey-in-2022/

The Peninsula. (2021). *QIB unveils electronic account opening solution as part of digital transformation*. https://www.thepeninsulaqatar.com/article/05/12/2021/QIB-unveils-electronic-account-opening-solution-as-part-of-digital-transformation

The Peninsula. (2022). *Commercial Bank implements security solutions to adhere to compliance*. https://thepeninsulaqatar.com/article/13/09/2022/Commercial-Bank-implements-security-solutions-to-adhere-to-compliance

The Peninsula. (2022). *QIB launches open banking platform to boost financial inclusion*. https://thepeninsulaqatar.com/article/05/04/2022/QIB-launches-open-banking-platform-to-boost-financial-inclusion

thefintechtimes.com. (2022). *Fintech landscape of Turkey in 2022*. Retrieved from https://thefintechtimes.com/fintech-landscape-of-turkey-in-2022/

thefintechtimes.com. (2022). *Fintech landscape of Turkey in 2022*. Retrieved from https://thefintechtimes.com/fintech-landscape-of-turkey-in-2022/

Thunes. (2023, August 1). *Digital Payments In Saudi Arabia | Thunes*. Retrieved from https://www.thunes.com/

Thunes. (2023). *Is the Kingdom of Saudi Arabia the next fintech hotspot*. Retrieved from https://www.thunes.com/news/thunes-partners-with-saudi-arabias-new-digital-bank-d360-to-power-instant-cross-border-payments-across-mena-and-key-global-markets/

TradeArabia. (2021). *TerraPay ties up with Commercial Bank of Qatar for instant global payments*. https://www.tradearabia.com/news/BANK_396713.html

Tribune, Q. (2021). *Microsoft launches its first data centres in Qatar*. Retrieved from https://www.qatar-tribune.com/news-details/id/226004/microsoft-launches-its-first-data-centres-in-qatar

Turkish Ministry of Finance. (2023). *Istanbul Finance Center*. Retrieved from https://ifm.gov.tr/

Turkish Statistical Institute. (2023). *Results of Population Censuses, 1935-2000 and results of Address Based Population Registration System, 2007-2022*. Retrieved from https://www.tuik.gov.tr/en/

Ventures, H. A. L. A. (2023). *Neobanks and Saudi Arabia Banking Industry*. Retrieved from: https://www.hala.vc/neobanks-and-saudi-arabia-banking-industry/

Wamda. (2022). *Fintech in Qatar*. https://www.wamda.com/research/whitepaper/the-state-of-fintech-in-qatar

Wamda. (2023). *Saudi Arabia launches $200 million fund to back local, foreign high-tech startups*. Retrieved from https://www.wamda.com/2023/08/saudi-arabia-launches-200-million-fund-local-foreign-high-tech-startups

WE ARE SOCIAL. (2023). *Digital 2023: Saudi Arabia*. Retrieved from https://datareportal.com/reports

WE ARE SOCIAL. (2023). *Digital 2023: Turkey*. Retrieved from https://datareportal.com/reports/digital-2022-turkey

World Bank. (2022). *Global Findex Database 2021*. https://globalfindex.worldbank.org/

World Bank. (2023). *Saudi Arabia Overview*. Author.

World Bank. (2023). *Mena FinTech: Embracing financial inclusion and innovation for the digital era.* https://www.worldbank.org/en/news/press-release/2022/07/21/world-bank-support-to-the-middle-east-and-north-africa-exceeds-us-5-billion-helping-to-mitigate-impacts-of-covid-19-and-

Yazici, S. (2019). The analysis of Fintech ecosystem in Turkey. *Journal of Business Economics and Finance*, *8*(4), 188–197. doi:10.17261/Pressacademia.2019.1162

YukselB. (2020). *Future of Fintech in Turkey in the Absence of Mandatory Open Banking Regulations and the Possible Role of Competition Law*. doi:10.2139/ssrn.3622317

Yunus, K. (2021). The analysis of FinTech sector in Turkey. *Journal of Politics Economy and Management*, *4*(2), 128–139.

Chapter 8
Financial Technology:
North and East Asia

Marcela Alveno
University Canada West, Canada

Diego Sebastian Gironda
University Canada West, Canada

Valeria Giraldo
University Canada West, Canada

Carlos Zamarron
University Canada West, Canada

Paula Paez
University Canada West, Canada

ABSTRACT

FinTech investments in the Asia-Pacific region exceeded North America for the first time in 2017. These sources of FinTech come primarily from North-East Asia with fast-growing young markets such as China and mature economies like Japan and South Korea. As technologically fierce competition tackles the industry, data analytics, network externalities, and interwoven activities in the North and East Asia region made them stand out. By shedding light on the journey of FinTech adoption across the region, this research seeks to provide a comprehensive understanding of China, Japan, Taiwan, South Korea, and Mongolia`s evolving financial landscape in the FinTech setting.

INTRODUCTION

FinTech is increasingly a global phenomenon. Over 64% of consumers globally have used a FinTech product (Lazarow, A. 2020). FinTech refers to the term *financial technology* and is characterized by providing solutions to customers, innovation, technological alternatives, and financial and economic development. In North and East Asia, countries like China, Japan, Taiwan, and South Korea are leading

DOI: 10.4018/979-8-3693-1561-3.ch008

the way to FinTech growth while Mongolia is still behind. FinTech advancement in these countries is due to the consumers' tendency to switch and search for digital alternatives.

As stated in the article written by M. Joshi, President of Infosys, "Asian countries, especially China – home to 4 of the biggest FintTech Unicorns: Ant Financial, Lufax, JD Finance and Qufenqi – along with Japan and Korea are leading the world in FinTech innovation" (Joshi, 2023). North and East Asia has four of the strongest companies in FinTech currently, just behind the U.S. which is the first in the world of financial technology development (Joshi, 2023).

Financial technology or "FinTech" has been defined in various ways. Bettinger defined the concept in 1972, as "…an acronym which stands for financial technology, combining bank expertise with modern management science techniques and the computer" (p. 2). Nearly five decades later, the definition has relevance and importance. The widespread adoption of technology such as mobile connectivity and the internet, has paved the way for FinTech to transform the provision of financial services. Through the application of information technology (IT), the financial landscape has thrived in new business models, products, applications, and processes (Feyen et al., 2023).

The correlation between technology and finance has in fact been intertwined since the 19th century. The first wave of FinTech was prompted in 1866 by the first transatlantic telegraph cable where "finance gradually shifted from analogue to digital" (Hernàndez, 2019, p.2). This was followed by a second wave in the 1950s and 1960s with the introduction of the automated teller machine (ATM). Now, we are experiencing a third wave with the emergence of new players and financial channels such as mobile money accounts and electronic transactions (Hernàndez, 2019).

Since banking engages with high-value activities there has always been an enticement to use the latest technology. The constant innovation has promoted transparency, high speed, interconnectivity, security, and most importantly, the availability of more tailored financial services (Feyen, et al., 2023). As technologically fierce competition tackles the industry, data analytics, network externalities, and interwoven activities in the East-Asia region made them stand out.

According to United Nations Escap (2018) the FinTech investments in the Asia-Pacific region have exceeded North America for the first time at $11.2 billion in 2017 -more than doubled from 2016. These sources of FinTech come primarily from North-East Asia with fast-growing young markets such as China and mature economies like Japan, dominating the global market. By shedding light on the journey of FinTech adoption across the region, this research seeks to provide a comprehensive understanding of China, Japan, Taiwan, South Korea and Mongolia`s evolving financial landscape in the FinTech setting.

CHINA

Market size

China has recently been a global leader in the development of the FinTech business because "its economic development and transformation have enabled it to invest heavily in research and development, foster entrepreneurship and attract foreign direct investment" (Santosdiaz, 2023). The FinTech environment in China offers a wide range of opportunities and challenges in a variety of industry sectors, influenced by the financial ecosystem of the country. The year 2013 is widely recognized as the onset of the boom. Since then, major segments of the FinTech market – namely online peer-to-peer lending, online wealth management, digital insurance, and third-party payment – have on average doubled or even tripled every year" (Cheng.Sheng.Yi., 2017). According to Zhou (2022), the Chinese FinTech market size was projected in 2019 to reach USD $ 85.7 billion by the beginning of 2023. Accurately, the market in fact generated a revenue of USD $85 billion in 2022 and is poised to "achieve a compound annual georth rate, CAGR, of 18.05% for the forecast period" (China FinTech Mordor Intelligence, n.d.). The organic growth allowed China to continue to be the world`s leading FinTech investor since 2018 (Zhou, 2022).

Current Adoption Rate

China`s adoption rate in FinTech rate is extremely high. According to the Global FinTech Adoption Index (2019) the nation represents the highest penetration rate of FinTech services in major economies at 87%. Companies aim to develop technological resolutions to increase fficiency and adaptability to achieve new outcomes such as the proper management of economic resources. The high adoption rate is a result of the widespread use of financial platforms and ecosystems (EY, 2019).

Businesses significantly increased their use of technology to replace face-to-face contacts during the COVID-19 epidemic. China took advantage of this trend at the time by embracing e-commerce. In fact, according to G.E.'s 2022 study, FinTech companies are expected to expand their operations outside of the mainland two years after the epidemic by joining virtual banks and launching new products that employ more linked API access. According to G.E.'s 2022 report, businesses in less developed regions, including small and medium-sized enterprises (SMEs), are using fintech solutions for things like auditing, tax compliance, business liability insurance, and payment services to make up for the absence of traditional incumbents.

Types of FinTech

The Chinese FinTech market is segmented (in order of usage) as digital payments, personal finance, alternative peer-to-peer lending. According to Statista (2023), in 2021, more than 987 million people used digital payments in China. Chinese founders, first and foremost, have brought to the table a distinct perspective and understanding of where the gaps exist within their respective focus industries — for payments Alipay, WeChat Pay, QQ Pay, and Baidu Wallet, for wealth-tech Lufax, Yu'eBao, and LiCaiTong, for insurtech ZhongAn Insurance, and for lending HuaBei and MyBank.

Main Players

Within China, the main players in the market these are Alipay, WeChat, Tencent and Lufax. Their lasting legacy and integration with e-commerce and social media platforms have been well unified into the life of the Chinese consumer. The platforms Alibaba and WeChat are collectively known as the predominant services contributing to the nation's overall revenue of USD $85 billion in 2022 and "is poised to achieve a CAGR of 18.05% for the forecast period" (Mordor Intelligence, n.d.)

Alipay, owned by Ant Financial in partnership with Alibaba, is an e-payment provider that allows users to save their debit and credit card details and use them to make online and in-store payments. (Erinflolami, 2021) One of their strengths that has aided their development is the Chinese national credit evaluation system. Similar cocenpt to Venmo, Alipay in the US, overtook as the world`s largest digital e-wallet payment platform in 2013.By the end of 2015, China's third-party payments transaction volume was over RMB 10 trillion (US$1.56 trillion), which surpassed Western counterparts such as Paypal" (Briefing, 2018b).

By 2019, Alipay smashed new e-commerce records by having 674 million active monthly users - representing 60% of the entire Chinese e-commerce market. (O`connell, 2020) Despite the owner, Jack Ma, not being the CEO for several years, Alibaba continues to thrive dominating the market along with WeChat. WeChat, owned by Tencent Holdings, is the most popular social messaging app in China. Just like WhatsApp, it supports video, text chat, and voice to stay connected with other individuals. According to Connell (2023), Tencent possesses 55% of all mobile time in China. To combat the possible monopoly, regulations have recently been handed out to fight the two main giants: Tencent and Alibaba. However, it's important to understand that the government has a loose regulatory environment.

Internationally recognised leaders in the FinTech sector include Ant Group, Tencent, and Lufax. Ant Group stands out among them as a trendsetter. According to figures from the business and its cooperating partners, Ant Financial served 870 million clients globally by March 2018. Several well-known companies fall under the Ant Financial umbrella, including Alipay, Ant Fortune, Yu'e Bao, Zhima Credit, MYbank, and Ant Financial Cloud. Tencent, in comparison.Therefore, "As of 2021, it owns 30.86% through Prosus, which also owns a stake in Tencent's sister companies, such as OLX, VK, Trip.com Group, Delivery Hero, Bykea, Meesho, Stack Overflow, Udemy, Codecademy, Brainly and PayU, having a growing net income of CN¥227.81 billion"(Wikipedia, 2023).

New Investment and Start-Ups

Most of the Chinese FinTech startups offer financial services between mobile payment, digital banking, crowdfunding and cryptocurrencies. From the 2,160 upcoming startups the majority targets middle class in the sectors of wealth management and 18 are already considered unicorns (Vyshnavi, 2021). In fact, China has the largest sector of unicorn with 79. The term unicorn allocates when a startup company its already valuated at $1 billion. (Vyshnavi, 2021)

Tencent, comes at first place, with a funding of USD$12.6 billion and dominant investors such as Lippo Group, PCCw and IDG Capital (Vyshnavi, 2021).Through the app of WeChat Pay they increased its valuation to USD$21 billion in 2018. Other companies include Chinese Edtech startup established in 2014. With already valuated at USD$10 billion, the company is gaining recognition and is known as a top tech Unicron company (Vyshnavi, 2021).

Technical Infrastructure

The development of the Telecommunication network in China has represent growth within its infrastructure, "China has built 6 times the number of 5G towers in 3 months than the US has installed in 2 years. China built 600,000 5G base stations from April to June, 2023. This means China has already reached its goal of having 2.9 million stations built by the end of 2023" (South China Morning Post, 2023).

As mentioned, the importance of the Telecommunication system signifies a vital part of the country "Telecommunications growth has also been linked to other stimulants like increased education, improved access to information, development of research centers and other positive changes on an economy and a culture. The telecommunications sector in China has been one of the fastest growing sectors in China" (WebenertiaAdmin, 2016).

On the other hand, e-commerce is a vibrant and quickly developing industry in China that has profoundly altered how people purchase and conduct business. Its success demonstrates the nation's capacity for innovation and adaptation in the digital era, making it a focal point for companies and businesspeople throughout the world eager to enter this lucrative sector. According to Statista, "The emergence of China's e-commerce market inaugurated a new era in the country's economy. In 2021, the added value of the digital economy accounted for nearly 40 percent of the country's GDP. More than a quarter of China's physical goods retail sales were sold online, far above the global average of 18.8 percent" (Ma,2023).

Government Policies and Regulations

Through the years, the development of FinTech in China has revealed different barriers for the country to grow in this sector with various challenges and opportunities in regard., However, the situation has improved significantly due to supportive policies from the government.

The Chinese government's supportive policies and its loose regulatory environment have been conducive to innovations and developments in the industry. The industry has also helped to serve the demands of groups that were previously excluded from traditional banking, such as small and medium-sized enterprises (SMEs) and low-income earners. Further to this, Chinese consumers are more open to sharing data, especially the generations of the 1980s and 1990s who are the main users of FinTech. (Briefing, 2018)

Furthermore, in the actuality the People Bank Of China, relentless efforts to promote a secure environment for FinTech innovation through sandbox initiatives and the investigation of cross-border regulatory sandboxes demonstrate its commitment to building an adaptable and dynamic financial ecosystem. As these measures progress, they have the potential to transform the landscape of financial regulation and innovation, propelling China's FinTech sector to new heights while retaining a sound regulatory basis. According to Thomson Reuters practical law article, "The long-awaited Chinese FinTech regulatory framework was fully completed in 2019 with the release of the PBOC's FinTech Development Plan (2019-2021). A set of thorough, scientific, and quantitative evaluation standards for the development and optimisation of financial technology in China is what the FinTech Development Plan seeks to achieve. (2000) Huang and Chiang. In addtion according to an article released on 2023 "China broadened its clampdown on the industry in 2021, and declared all cryptocurrency-related transactions illegal. The motive, it said, was to maintain national security and social stability" (Kowsmann & Ostroff, 2023).

The Chinese government regulations for mobile payments had represent a significant step for the development of these companies, therefore, with over a billion users, leading mobile payment services Alipay and WeChat Pay are paving the way. Alipay is a mobile payment software and digital wallet that also lets users order taxis, apply for credit cards, and purchase insurance. According to Hersey (2017), "the government will mandate that all mobile payments be cleared through the PBOC, putting all mobile payment transactions into the Chinese Communist Party's (CCP) hands." The PBOC's stated justification for enforcing this law is to prevent fraud and money laundering. Zheng (Zheng, 2023).

Impacts on the Economy and Previous Academic Research

Numerous academic sources have examined the complicated and diverse subject of how FinTech is affecting Chinese economy. The authors give a thorough assessment of the literature in this area in "FinTech and the Economy: A Review and Synthesis of the Literature." The authors draw attention to the major transformations brought about by FinTech technologies across a range of economic sectors.

Greater financial inclusion is one of the main effects of FinTech on the economy. Access to financial services has increased because of FinTech solutions, especially for underprivileged groups and areas. This may lessen wealth disparity and promote economic expansion.

The study's conclusions have substantial practical consequences for Chinese policymakers. The findings indicate that FinTech, as well as its sub measures of third-party payment, credit, and insurance, are key determinants of China's economic growth. As a result, this study suggests that policymakers should encourage the growth of FinTech in China. (Song & Appiah-Otoo, 2022)

Nevertheless, "Digital investing platforms are also gaining popularity, as people look for low-cost and user-friendly investment solutions. Additionally, because it offers a quick means to acquire money, digital capital raising has grown in popularity as an alternative for startups and SMEs. For investors and traders, the advent of digital assets like cryptocurrencies and NFTs has opened up new possibilities. Finally, by offering creative, customer-focused solutions that meet the demands of today's tech-savvy consumers, neobanks have challenged the traditional banking business (Statista, n.d.).

In conclusion, FinTech has had a big influence on the economy by fostering financial inclusion, raising competitiveness, and enhancing financial sector effectiveness. To maintain its development and advantages, it also presents security issues that must be solved. This compilation of academic studies sheds important light on both the promise and the hazards involved with the complicated interaction between FinTech and the economy.

Security Concerns

Due to the rising reliance on digital platforms for financial transactions, effective cybersecurity measures are increasingly necessary to guard against attacks and data breaches. For FinTech to remain trustworthy and to continue growing, these security issues must be addressed. Strong cybersecurity measures are becoming increasingly important as the dependence on digital platforms for financial transactions increases in order to guard against possible attacks and data breaches. For FinTech to remain trustworthy and to continue growing, these security issues must be addressed "China is increasingly emphasising government sovereignty on cyberspace and data, rapidly evolving its cybersecurity and data regime, enacting numerous rules and policies, and formulating national standards for cybersecurity and data protection" (PricewaterhouseCoopers, n.d.).

Interesting Facts

- Chinese consumers are the world's largest users of mobile payments. Millions of transactions take place every second thanks to services like WeChat Pay and Alipay, which have become indispensable to daily life. Even tiny businesses and street sellers accept payments using QR codes.
- The nation is progressing towards being a cashless society. People frequently conduct their everyday affairs without having access to cash. Even in remote locations, mobile payment methods are commonly accepted.

- Neobanks, often known as digital banks, have grown in popularity in China. Players like WeBank and MYbank provide totally digital banking services, upending the established banking industry with cutting-edge, client-focused strategies.

Trends and Future Aspects

China's FinTech Development Plan for 2022-2025 outlines the government's commitment to growing FinTech innovation, ensuring financial inclusion, strengthening regulatory oversight, and promoting sustainable finance. "By 2025, China wants to achieve leapfrog improvement in the FinTech sector, in which data is fully realised as a factor of production, high-quality digital transformation of the financial sector is advanced, FinTech governance is improved, key technology application is deepened, and digital infrastructure development becomes more advanced" (Zhoau,2022). Furthermore, it underlines the importance of ethical behaviour in the FinTech business, as well as the critical function of digital money. This plan demonstrates China's ambition to efficiently handle risk elements while maintaining its leading position in global FinTech growth.

TAIWAN

Market Size

With a population over 23 million people, Taiwan is one of the most advanced countries in terms of technology. The technological infrastructure, high internet penetration, and financially educated population allow them to have quite a robust market, despite its geographical condition. With a GDP of over $790.7 billion and a growing middle class, the country offers a proper environment for the FinTech industry to perform and cater to diverse financial needs (Tseng et al. n.d).

Current Adoption Rate

Taiwan's current FinTech adoption rate stands at a moderate level. While digital payments and mobile banking services are widely used, the adoption of more advanced FinTech services, such as investment platforms and cryptocurrencies, is relatively slower due to various factors, such as cautious consumer behavior and complex regulatory processes. Traditional banking dominance and security concerns also influence this rate. However, the tech-savvy nature of the population, increasing digital literacy, and growing awareness of FinTech's benefits are gradually fostering higher adoption rates. As these trends continue and regulatory frameworks evolve, the adoption rate is expected to rise, driving further integration of FinTech into the daily financial lives of Taiwanese consumers (KPMG. 2023).

The Taiwainesse government stated that the use of mobile payment in the country increased significantly last year, driving up usage fields, age, frequency, and consumption amount; new services, such as web banking, smart customer service, and Robo-advisors have pretty much become essential to financial institutions (KPMG, 2023). Large-scale financial holding companies were even more aggressive in establishing specialized units, such as customer experience and data analysis, in recent years, which brought efficiency and good performance. Overall, FinTech in Taiwan is gradually advancing, but compared with the development and scale in other countries, there is still room for improvement (KPMG, 2023).

Types of Fintech

- Peer-to-Peer Lending: Online lending platforms connect borrowers with investors, catering to both individuals and small businesses seeking funding. For example Lend&Borrow (Pitchbook. 2023).
- Crowdfunding: Platforms facilitate fundraising for creative projects, startups, and social causes, enabling broad community participation. FlyingV is a typical comprehensive fundraising platform and the most influential crowdfunding platform in Taiwan (Airfunding. 2019).
- Digital Banking: Innovative digital banks and neo-banks provide streamlined services like account opening, transfers, and financial management. Rakuten is one of the major players on the online banking landscape (Rakuten. 2023).
- Cryptocurrencies and Blockchain: Taiwan hosts cryptocurrency exchanges, and blockchain-based solutions are explored across various industries, from supply chain to digital identity. The leader on this area is Bito.Ex (Bito.Ex. 2023)
- Cross-Border Payments: Services facilitate swift and cost-effective international money transfers and currency exchange. Wise is one of the most used services in the country for cross-border transactions (Wise. 2023).

Main Players

The main players on Taiwan Fintech market are E.Sun Bank, Rakuten Card, and BitoEx. SUN Bank, also known as E.SUN Commercial Bank, is a financial institution based in Taiwan. It is one of the leading banks in Taiwan and operates both domestically and internationally (E.SUN, 2023). The bank's strength lies in its established presence as a traditional bank, allowing it to leverage customer trust and infrastructure. It offers a wide range of digital banking services, embracing innovation to cater to evolving customer preferences. However, they lack rapid technological changes, and competition from specialized FinTech startups can be challenging. As a traditional player, regulatory compliance might also slow down agility in innovation (Rakuten, 2023).

Rakuten Card excels in digital payment solutions, leveraging its brand recognition and extensive customer base (Rakuten, 2023). Its established platform and customer trust provide an advantage for expansion into new FinTech areas. One of its weaknesses is heavy reliance on its core business (credit card services) might limit diversification. Staying ahead in the rapidly evolving FinTech landscape requires continuous innovation and adaptation (Rakuten, 2023).

And finally, we have BitoEX, a prominent player in the cryptocurrency space, offering users a way to buy, sell, and manage cryptocurrencies. Its focus on blockchain technology and cryptocurrency services positions it as a pioneer in this niche (Tseng et al., n.d.). Yet, cryptocurrency markets are inherently volatile, exposing BitoEX to significant market risks.

Regulatory uncertainties in the crypto space can impact its operations and growth potential (Tseng et al., n.d.).

New Investment and Start-Ups

Taiwan's FinTech situation is experiencing a large increase of new investments and startups. Emerging players like BSL and MobiX focus on blockchain solutions and digital identity verification, respectively, while NextBank aims to revolutionize mobile banking (Tracxn. 2023). These startups attract investor interest due to their cutting-edge technologies and potential to reshape financial services. Government support through grants and incubators further nurtures the growth of these ventures, creating a dynamic ecosystem that positions Taiwan as a hub for FinTech innovation in the Asia-Pacific region. So far, 98 FinTech startups have been registered on Taipei, Taiwan (Tracxn, 2023).

If the government offers a friendly environment for startups based on their (startups) opinions and boldly makes reforms, perhaps it can train more startups that will draw worldwide attention in the international market and drive up FinTech development and business opportunities in Taiwan to make a breakthrough.

Technical Infrastructure

The country has a gigantic technical infrastructure that supports its FinTech ecosystem and eCommerce environment. With high-speed internet connectivity, widespread smartphone usage, and a digitally literate population, the foundation is strong" Statista. 2023). Taiwan`s eCommerce market projecs revenues reaching a significant US$12.21 billion in 2023. As the digital shopping landscape continues to evolve, user penetration is anticipated to increase steadily, with a projected 80.7% in 2023 and a promising rise to 90.6% by 2027 (Statista, 2023). This surge in user engagement is set to translate into an average revenue per user (ARPU) of approximately US$633.10, underlining the immense potential for businesses and investors in the eCommerce sector. The market's anticipated annual growth rate (CAGR) of 8.67% from 2023 to 2027 reflects the continuous innovation and adaptability of the eCommerce industry in Taiwan (Statista, 2023).

About its infraestructure, Taiwan is a country that relies heavily on its highly advanced ICT's. Allowing the industry to grow rapidly compared to most of the countries worldwide. By offering a great business environment, a large number of companies offer advanced ICT products and services. Taiwan is also one of the world leaders regarding 5G technology, which have helped the indutry to reach new technological strengths and provide competitive advantage against other industries (ITA, 2022). As a result of this highly developed technological advances, TSMC has developed advanced chips that require complex software with the most updated technology, making Taiwan the larger supplier of this technology in the world, providing almost all the advanced processors (Miller, 2022).

This ecosystem enables seamless online transactions, fosters innovation in payment gateways, and drives data-driven business strategies. The synergy between FinTech and eCommerce creates a dynamic environment where technological advancements enhance user experiences and drive economic growth.

Government Policies and Regulations

The country has a gigantic technical infrastructure that supports its FinTech ecosystem and eCommerce environment. With high-speed internet connectivity, widespread smartphone usage, and a digitally literate population, the foundation is strong. (Statista, 2023). This ecosystem enables seamless online transactions, fosters innovation in payment gateways, and drives data-driven business strategies. The synergy between FinTech and eCommerce creates a dynamic environment where technological advancements enhance user experiences and drive economic growth.

Impacts on the Economy

In 2017, Taiwan Executive Yuan established the Anti-Money Laundering Office, aimed at strengthening money laundering prevention before the third evaluation round of the Asia Pacific Group on Money Laundering (APG). In August 2019, Taiwan was promoted to APG's "regular follow-up" category, which is the most favorable category (Falgright, 2023). Successful money laundering prevention depends upon industry-wide cooperation with regulatory reporting systems and use of proper RegTech solutions, including risk analysis tools, abnormal activity monitoring, and due diligence tasks through various data sources, like social media, and trade surveillance. Providers of such technologies will continue to enjoy a strong market in Taiwan as the FinTech industry expands (Lee & Li, 2023).

Taiwan's FinTech sector follows significant trends emerging across key market segments. Digital Investment stands as a dominant force with an anticipated AUM of US$1,375 million in 2023, reflecting the growing interest in tech-driven financial management (KPMG, 2023). This market's vitality is underscored by an average AUM per user projected to reach US$651.1 in the same year. Meanwhile, the Digital Assets domain charts an impressive growth trajectory, with a projected 42.9% revenue increase anticipated for 2024. Simultaneously, the Digital Payments market anticipates a burgeoning user base, estimated to reach 14.1 million users by 2027. This multifaceted FinTech arena defies a singular numerical representation due to its diverse KPIs, highlighting the nuanced and dynamic nature of this sector (KPMG, 2023).

Security Concerns

The rapid growth of FinTech in Taiwan has led the evolution of the financial services but has also raised significant security concerns. After several cyber-attacks over the last few years, data security remains as one of the major concerns as the digitization of financial services continues, necessitating rigid measures to safeguard sensitive customer information and protect against data breaches and cyberattacks (Eldon, 2016). The evolving threat landscape of cybersecurity poses an ongoing challenge, demanding continuous investment in security measures to avoid potential hacking, ransomware, and other cyber threats. These security challenges underscore the critical need for collaboration between financial institutions, FinTech companies, regulatory authorities, and law enforcement agencies to foster a secure and trustworthy FinTech ecosystem in Taiwan (Eldon, 2016).

Synthesize Previous Academic Research

Taiwan's FinTech landscape, presents a promising environment for financial technology innovation. Although the current FinTech adoption rate in Taiwan is moderate, with digital payments and mobile banking being widely used, the adoption of more advanced FinTech services like investment platforms and cryptocurrencies has been slower due to cautious consumer behavior and regulatory complexities (KPMG, 2023). Nevertheless, the tech-savvy nature of the population, increasing digital literacy, and growing awareness of FinTech benefits are gradually driving higher adoption rates. Large-scale financial holding companies in Taiwan have been proactive in establishing specialized units to improve efficiency and performance, indicating a growing commitment to FinTech integration. Additionally, the emergence of new FinTech startups and investments in blockchain and digital identity verification technologies further solidify Taiwan's position as a hub for FinTech innovation in the Asia-Pacific region (Tracxn, 2023).

Taiwan's advanced technical infrastructure, including high-speed internet connectivity and widespread smartphone usage, provides a strong foundation for its FinTech ecosystem and eCommerce industry (Statista, 2023). The eCommerce market in Taiwan is projected to reach significant revenues of $12.21 billion in 2023, with a growing user base and promising future growth. The country's emphasis on advanced information and communication technologies, including 5G technology, has positioned it as a global leader, particularly in semiconductor manufacturing (ITA, 2022). This technological ecosystem enables seamless online transactions, fosters innovation in payment gateways, and supports data-driven business strategies. As Taiwan continues to invest in FinTech and eCommerce, it is expected to have a positive impact on its economy, with the potential to drive growth, create jobs, and enhance financial services for its population (Statista, 2023).

Interesting Facts

When consumers handle financial services, the identity verification mechanism of each business operator is time-consuming and not universal. Can the government promote the mechanism of data integration and verification in a unified manner? For example, fully implementing digital ID cards so that consumers do not have to manage too many passwords?

Each financial institution has its own KYC (Know Your Customer) policy. In addition to the requirements from the regulatory authority, the other required information is also similar. If consumers are dealing with businesses from different financial institutions, they must go through tedious re-registeration procedures such as uploading information (KPMG, 2023). Perhaps this can be led by a government unit to stipulate an unified KYC data format and verification mechanism. For example implementing the use of digital ID cards for authentication, which avoids the time-consuming application process and improves overall convenience (KPMG, 2023).

Trends and Future Aspects

The foreseeable future of the FinTech landscape in Taiwan shows significant potential for growth and innovation. In particular, the digital investment sector is set to dominate the market, with projected assets under management (AUM) reaching the US$1,375.00 million in 2023 (Statista, 2023). This sector's growth is highlighted by an average AUM per user of US$651.10, reflecting the increasing interest in digital investment platforms. Meanwhile, the digital assets market is set for substantial revenue growth of 42.9% in 2024, indicative of the rising importance of cryptocurrencies and blockchain technologies. The digital payments market is expected to experience an increase on users, reaching 14.1 million users by 2027 (Statista, 2023).

JAPAN

Market Size

Japan has a large consumer economy and a strong consumer market, with an income per capita of about $43,000 (International Trade Administration, 2022). In terms of population distribution, Japan has mostly an aging population, whereby 2022, the population growth was -0.44% compared with 2021; also, in terms of the fertility rate, by 2021, it was 1.3 children per woman, whereas by 2016 was 1.44, showing an evident diminution in the fertility rate; finally, the age distribution of Japan is increasing for the group of 65+ and decreasing in the group of 0-14 years with the time pass, whereby 2021 only 11.77% of the population is people between 0-14 years old, and 29.79% is 65+ (Statista, 2022). All the above evidence shows the presence of an aging population in Japanese society.

In 2015, Japan accrued investments worth USD$360.2 million but regarding the market size in the financial technology sector, early predictions showed that the nation's FinTech sector would increase by 51% yearly to $11 billion by 2022 (Japan Brandvoice, 2021).

Current Adoption Rate

The current landscape for Japanese society in terms of FinTech is approximately 113 million users distributed between Digital Payments, with the most users, 102.5 million, followed by Digital Investment, 7.5 million, Neobanking, 3.92 million and Digital Capital raising, 0.01 million (Statista & Statista Digital Market Insights, 2022). The determining factor for adaptation to FinTech in terms of electronic payments is financial literacy, where more educated people tend to adapt easier and use the new payment methods more than people with low education in the finance sector (Long, 2023). At the same time, another determining factor of adopting and using electronic payments is people's risk tolerance, where risk-averse people are less likely to accept and use electronic payments than people with herd behaviour (Long, 2023).

Japan leads other nations with a 20% increase in the use of digital wallets, whereby in the third quarter of 2022, Japan took the lead in digital wallet adoption compared to other eleven countries, including Singapore, Germany, and Italy (Pymnts, 2023).

Types of FinTech

Breaking down the digital payments type, in 2022, the most amount of digital payments were made by credit cards at 30.4% of the total cashless payments, followed by debit card payments at 1%, electronic money payments at 2%, and QR code payments with 2.6% (Statista & Statista Digital Market Insights, 2022).

Regarding digital investment, cryptocurrencies are the most popular method used in Japan. The most used cryptocurrency by 2021 is Bitcoin, with a trading value of over 15,000 billion in Japanese Yen, followed by Ethereum at 5,000 billion in Japanese Yen (Statista & Statista Digital Market Insights, 2022). It is also important to mention that crypto-asset exchange is regulated under Japan's Financial Services Agency (FSA), with specific guidelines for supervising crypto-asset exchange service providers (Financial Service Agency, 2023). For digital capital raising, by 2023, there were a total of 41 million online brokerage accounts at securities companies (Statista & Statista Digital Market Insights, 2022).

Main Players

The three main start-ups in Japan are Kyash, Money Design and Tranako, all founded in Tokyo (Monteiro, 2023). Kyash is looking forward to the next generation of infrastructure for money exchange by offering mobile payments and banking to customers and a financial platform for enterprises (Monteiro, 2023). Money Design offers online consulting services and automated investment management on currencies and stocks, through an AI and algorithms-powered robot advisor called Theo (Monteiro, 2023). Finally, Tranako allows users to invest extra change they have accumulated from daily purchases and automatically make global investments (Monteiro, 2023).

New Investment and Start-Ups

Considering the Asian-Pacific region, Japan has the seventh major FinTech company, Rakuten, based on the total funding amount, with a funding of $2.26 billion (Statista & Statista Digital Market Insights, 2022).

Digital payments and digital investment hold the most attention in Japan since it's the sector with the most users. For digital payments, several startups are located in Japan, such as Paidy, PayPay, and others, which mainly provide a customer solution for online payments. In this case, Paidy is software already acquired by PayPal that allows the consumer to make online payments without registering a credit card (Crunchbase, 2023). Some of the most popular companies for digital investment are bitFlyer, Liquid Global, and Coincheck, which mainly provide access to a secure digital wallet to use, buy and sell cryptocurrencies. In the case of bitFlyer, it has total funding of $37.5 million and provides the consumer with a Bitcoin exchange and marketplace (Crunchbase, 2023).

The other start-ups are Opn and Netstarts. Opn is an e-wallet that provides contactless payment solutions for businesses and consumers, which also lets companies collect payments online and offline using credit/debit cards, bank transfers, and other methods (Tracxn, 2023). On the other hand, Netstars is a hardware-based terminal for payment acceptance, making it easier to receive credit and debit card payments, as well as making payments using QR codes (Tracxn, 2023).

Technical Infrastructure and Ecosystem

One of the greatest e-commerce marketplaces in the world is Japan, which is distinguished by the predominance of business-to-business transactions, with an increasing emphasis on business-to-consumer sales, and an emerging consumer-to-consumer market (Diep, 2023). The shifting of most businesses towards the online world is mainly developed thanks to the availability of internet connection almost nationwide, and the strong postal service of the country. Moreover, major companies such as Amazon dominate online retail (Diep, 2023).

Additional, supporting government regulations have played an important role when it comes to the shifting of business to business towards the online world (Diep, 2023). At the same time, another factor that contributed to the shift to e-commerce is the recent Covid-19 pandemic (Diep, 2023).

Government Policies and Regulations

When it comes to the leading sectors for startups in Japan in 2021, FinTech occupied the ninth position by capital raised with $1.82 million (Statista & Statista Digital Market Insights, 2022). One main characteristic that is helping Japan to move towards FinTech is the regulatory transformation, where the regulatory authority for financial services in Japan, the Financial Services Agency (FSA), has created a supportive environment for FinTech and innovation. A clear example of the abovementioned is the FinTech conference that has been held since 2016 till the present year. In the last conference, Fintech, the era of "Neoteric Individual" 2023, a 1-million-yen prize was offered to participating startups that offered a social-solving problem with their innovative FinTech (FIN/SUM, 2023).

Besides, since 2017 Japan has been conducting international joint research on blockchain with the collaboration of different institutions, such as MIT Media Lab in the

US, Canada's Central Bank, Singapore's MAS, and other foreign organizations (Japan External Trade Organization, 2017). Japan strongly supports the development of FinTech; one example of it is FINOLAB, a FinTech incubator that offers support to startups by connecting them with corporate members to raise funds, providing physical spaces to develop their business, and providing professional advice in different areas (O'Hanlon, 2020).

The main concern for the regulatory agencies is to promote innovation through FinTech but, at the same time, make sure that the customers and their data are secured. The Financial Services Agency, established in 2000, is the one in charge of overseeing financial services, including FinTech (Kagan, 2022). However, the regulatory agencies are not meant to stop innovation. Japan's action plan to ensure that it does not happen developed a regulatory sandbox, allowing innovative startups to test initial products before complying with the official regulatory requirements (Cabinet Secretariat, n.d.).

Impacts on the Economy

It is clear that FinTech is restructuring the economy in every way; one example is globalizing transactions, which will be time-consuming and take many steps to get done. However, FinTech has provided inclusion by offering many traditional banking services to online services. It has also increased competition among financial institutions, creating room for improvement in customer service (Nakaso, 2016). Another point to highlight is the accessibility to different investment platforms, where the population can easily make transactions with non-traditional currencies, for example, with Bitcoin as legal tender (Nakaso, 2016).

Security Concerns

Regarding data protection, the Personal Information Protection Commission Japan is an independent organ in charge of protecting the rights of FinTech users and, at the same time, considering the effective use of personal information (Personal Information Protection Commission Japan, n.d.).

Synthesize Previous Academic Research

Project Stella's goal is to investigate how distributed ledger technology (DLT) may be used to Financial Market Infrastructure FMIs, also called financial market infrastructures. The project is divided into two phases, each of which deals with a unique facet of DLT deployment in FMIs. Real-time gross settlement systems, a crucial aspect of central bank operations, are performance-required, and phase one of the project demonstrated that DLT applications could achieve these criteria, whereas phase two demonstrated that cross-ledger delivery-versus-payment (DVP) functionality could be provided across many ledgers without requiring physical links between them. This research is part of a larger trend where central banks and securities exchanges are investigating the possibilities of DLT in the financial infrastructure of different countries, and shows both opportunities and challenges in further investigation (Kishi, 2019).

Interesting Facts

By 2019, there were more than 500 start-ups registered and functioning in Japan, most of them focused on online payments and digital wallets, and a few more regarding cryptocurrencies (Tracxn, 2023). Japan was one of the first countries in the world to recognize cryptocurrencies legally, and ever since it has been facilitating its usage among the population, opening a new investment option for society (Deloitte, 2017). The fact that digital currencies have been far more successful in Japan than in other nations is another noteworthy feature of the nation, showing that Japan is unique in its attempts to spread e-money (Deloitte, 2017).

Trends, Future Aspect

The future job market in Japan regarding FinTech is mostly seeking software engineers, data engineers and security engineers who have experience in the payment industry (Computer Futures, 2022).

As mentioned earlier, Japan is doing better than other countries in including and recognizing cryptocurrencies legally. One of the future aspects to look forward to is InvestTech and digital asset management (Kajihara, 2023)

SOUTH KOREA

Market Size

South Korea plays an important role in the North and East Asia region since their country`s FinTech is booming. In the space of 50 years, Korea has transitioned from an agricultural economy to one driven by technology in sectors such as automotive, shipbuilding, and manufacturing (Intralink, 2020). They have climbed out of poverty to a powerhouse fueled by technology, creativity, and innovation. Introducing several ICT infrastructures in smartphone penetration, broadband speed, and information communications.

With a population of 51.7 million, the country is the world`s 11th largest economy with a GDP of one trillion (Intralink, 2020). According to the World Bank (2023) South Korea has maintained strong annual growth -close to 2.6%. When it comes to the experience of digital finance, South Korea takes the lead in the Asia-Pacific region. Over half, 67%, of digitally active citizens have adopted the use of digital financial services in their routines (Nam & Lee, 2022). This high rate is rdue to government support and accessible policies and regulations.

Current Adoption Rate

South Korea `s FinTech adoption rate has grown significantly in the last few years. The massive mobile and technology adoption has made the country one of the biggest e-commerce markets globally and has paved the way for its high consumption. The market increased since 2017 from 32% to 67% in 2019 regarding the digitally active adult population (Statista, 2023). A rate that continued to grow for the years to come despite the COVID-19 pandemic.

Similar to China and other countries, the COVID-19 pandemic forced Koreans to embrace contactless financial services to minimize face-to-face interactions. According to the Bank of Korea (2022), the volume of banking transactions increased by 19.6% from USD $50 billion between 2020 and 2021 and mobile banking by 36.3% respectively. The rate, volume and number of transactions were increasing; however, the pandemic motivated further adoption (Nam & Lee, 2022).

Types of FinTech

The Korean business models of FinTech continue to evolve with contemporary financial innovations such as mobile payments, digital banking, robo-advisors, peer-to-peer (P2P) lending, and cryptocurrencies. Nevertheless, the strongest growth is in digital payments. Followed by P2P loans, investments and blockchain technology. These digital payments continued to grow with online service giants: Kakao Pay and Naver Pay. Followed by global companies: Samsung Pay, Lotte Group`s L Pay; and startups such as Toss and Viva Republics (Intralink, 2020).

Main Players

The leading FinTech companies in South Korea in 2021 are (in order by registered users) Kakao Pay, Naver Pay, Toss, Kakao Bank and Payco. Kakao Pay takes the lead in the market with 37 million users (Statista, 2023). Launched in 2014 by DaumKakao and LG CNS, is a digital financial platform where payments and transfers are the main source to purchase things online. According to Expat Guide Korea (2020) "three in every four people over the age of 15 are now using it. Kakao Pay has attracted more than 30 million users in the past few years" (para. 3) Now, the company is seeking to expand to international waters and dominate new economies. CEO of Kako Pay, Alex Ryu, stated in 2019 that "cross-border payments will become more important in the near future, which creates new partnership opportunities between Korean and overseas FinTech firms, such as those from the UK" (Intralink, 2020).

Similarly, Naver Pay promotes a shopping experience through the mobile experience. It was launched in 2015 by Naver Corp, and by 2021 they attracted 35 million users (Statista, 2023). One of their strengths is that the platform is encouraged by the largest and first South Korean search engine: Naver. By the end of 2021, Google, the long-standing worldwide search engine leader, lost its influence in the nation`s market due to the dominance of Naver. According to a survey by Statista (2023) 94% of the surveyed individuals stated that "they used Naver when they were looking for information during the last month" (Josbt, 2023).

Both of these are well supported by the government, and that is one of the main reasons the adoption rate keeps getting higher. And they could still take the amount even higher if they supported other submarkets such as peer-to-peer lending, the second most popular. The P2P loan market is growing rapidly from 16 platforms in 2016 to 150 in 2020. Despite the expansion, not enough regulations let P2P companies experience difficulties like fraud, embezzlement, and bankruptcy (Intralink, 2020). To handle the circumstances, the government began working with market leaders to pass new tailored regulations designed to improve the market. This way they support and nurture the growth of the FinTech industry.

The most known P2P app in Korea is Toss (Viva Republica) launched in 2015 with more than 25 financial services. Credit scores, customized loans, stocks, and insurance are a few that are featured in that the apps. Once they started working with Kleiner Perkins and PayPal they raised their value to 18.72 billion in 2020 (Intralink, 2020). The third area for Korean FinTech growth is blockchain and its cryptocurrency adoption. The size of cryptocurrencies is being endorsed by large market players. Shinsegae Duty-Free, partnered with Bithumb, to encourage online purchases through the use of cryptocurrencies (Intralink, 2020). It might seem low compared to other submarkets but it's growing and gaining traction in the nation helping with the FinTech growth.

New Investments and Start-Ups

New investment and investements are growing due to the South Korean government pledging a US$781 million fund until 2028 (Lee, 2022), which stimulated the creation of new companies. As of July 2023, they are 687 FinTech startups in South Korea (Tracxn, 2023). The multiple enterprises vary from different contexts from artificial intelligence to cryptocurrency.

Qraft Technologies is gaining traction since they are incorporating AI into the practice management solutions for asset managers. They are seeking to leverage AI by crafting quantitive solutions for their clients, which is an innovative idea. Since its creation in 2016, they have gathered a funding of around US$163 million and fostered good relations with their critical investors such as SoftBank Group, IBK Capital and Hana Financial Group (Tracxn, 2023). One of their long-term goals is to "increase the accessibility of financial products for people everywhere" (Qraft, 2023).

Other startups worth mentioning include Carrot, internet`s first online platform for non-life insurance and Dunamu an online exchange platform for cryptocurrency (Tracxn, 2023). Both exciting projects in the industry that are gaining recognition and new investors such as Affairma Capital and Altos Ventures Managment (Tracxn, 2023). But it seems that Toss, an app for banking and investment, holds the first spot in the list of most exciting FinTech startups in South Korea (Tracxn, 2023).

Toss, also known as Viva Republica, is the most disruptive startup in the country ranking 35 on KPMG`s top 100 FinTech Companies in 2017 (James, 2018) Valued at US$7 billion in December 2022, Tosss has made the Korean market more competitive and demanding by including international participation from Paypal. (FinTech News Hong Kong, 2018)

Technical Infrastructure

The South Korean technical infrastructure is quite dominant since the society consumes an estimation of 93% of internet usage rate (Statista, 2023). With the great number of people using the internet daily, it is no surprise how e-commerce holds a strong status among the public. The e-commerce sector saw an increase of sales for online shopping for a variety of products such as food, beverages and home appliances (Statista, 2023). The pandemic of Covid-19 encouraged people to rely on online and mobile purchases to avoid face-to-face interactions. The platform *coupang.com* continues to be the most popular online shopping property since their approach of next-day delivery service continues to appeal to the masses

(Statista, 2023). Its popularity overtook the famous marketplace G-market marketplace and introduced a solution for fast delivery of food and groceries.

Government Policies and Regulations

While regulations continue to be conservative, the Korean government`s support has encouraged entrepreneurs to innovate through a favourable policy environment. Fintech used to be held back, "but deregulation is on the horizon" (Intralink, 2020, p. 18). The most important policy came into effect in April 1, 2019 known as the Regulatory Sandbox Program. It basically secures companies to develop products and services while ensuring security to users through a live audience in a controlled environment (Malyshev, 2021). Firms can pre-launch under certain conditions, controlled scale, and location and if the FSC determines are deemed "innovative" they can be exempted from regulations for up to two years (James, 2019).

Back to the government being a factor in slowing peer-to-peer loans, they tried to change that in 2019 by establishing a good legal framework. The Financial Services Commission (FSC) intends to amend the Credit Information Act to facilitate the use of big data in the P2P2 sector. Furthermore, Korean policymakers have been highly receptive of tech-driven new entrants with barely any restriction on them (Mahapatra, 2023). These elements can work cohesively and improve the country`s economy.

Impacts on the Economy

Korea possesses an extraordinary opportunity for economic growth through the FinTech industry. Choi and Shin (2019) acknowledge that it`s feasible for the FinTech industry to be a platform for sustainable economic growth and prompter of the fourth industrial revolution since the FinTech businesses depend on innovation. It is not only a good intermediate between the national demand and the final good but also the thing that might stimulate the fourth industrial revolution: artificial intelligence.

It has the power to transform all business models and nationwide economic structures into innovative and advanced ones, such as Toss. Modern technologies and players like blockchain and insurance are now executed with higher security and creating new smart infrastructure and ecosystems (Choi & Shin, 2019). Indirectly contributing to other industries such as investment or banking. The connection ultimately impacts the country`s economy by increasing financial/monetary-related activities (Choi & Shin, 2019).

Security Concerns

South Korea has implemented several security practices regarding the financial technology sector. The FSC developed policies that ensure the security and reliability of electronic transactions by "clarifying their legal relations and promoting financial conveniences for people and developing the national economy…" (Financial Sector Assessment Program, 2020, p.13). This means that they are seeking the safety of payment services and providers as well as ensuring safety of customer funds and data. It`s a balance between security and consumer protection through multiple periodic reviews and testing.

Synthesize Previous Academic Research

The concept of FinTech has developed throughout the years by reshaping products, payments, business models, market players and money itself. But it has also come with challenges. A study by Nam and Lee

(2023) recognized the socioeconomic inequalities when it comes to using digital financial services. After the COVID-19 pandemic, many ATMs and major banks closed branches which implies there are fewer options for individuals who do not have access to the internet. Certain groups, old people or low-income families, are left without the necessary resources to continue their monetary-related activities. In fact, Oh and Kim (2019), came up with a similar premise suggesting that online channels are stable among older adults but the challenging thing is the lack of knowledge when it comes to using it, especially in financial services.

Choi and Shin (2019) argued that FinTech is not an expansion of the ordinary or a traditional paradigm in financial industry but its an inclusive factor in "transforming all industries toward value creation networking" (p. 18). Which ultimately, encourages innovation through automatic synchronized economic activities. However, one of the limitations was that the Korean government`s policies were deregulating the industry. But in the same year, 2019, the Regulatory Sandbox Program came into effect; securing startups and established companies with innovation and a supported environment. Perhaps new studies, Korean-focused, should base their studies on how the upcoming regulations` affect businesses models.

Interesting Facts

The emergence of South Korea in FinTech is gaining recognition after being overshadowed by Japan, China and India for many years. Now, its vibrant and dominant tech ecosystem is flourishing and growing exponentially. Like other dominant markets, Covid-19 accelerated the shift to digital platforms, especially in payment and banking (Mahapatra, 2023). In 2020, Kakao Pay, the main player, recorded over 140 billion South Korean won in revenue. This was the first time a FinTech company gained more than 100 billion South Korean won in revenue. (Statista, 2022)

Trends and Future Aspects

South Korea`s future seems promising in the financial technology sector since the rate of adoption reached 67% among the adult population in 2019 and had the highest internet penetration in the Asia Pacific at 90% (James, 2018). It is evident that consumers are trying to relate to domestic FinTech products and also embrace new solutions. These brand-new domestic financial technologies are still solidifying their position in the market such as Toss. On the other hand, well-established enterprises such as Kakao Pay or Naver Pay are seeking overseas markets to overcome the limitations of the local market size (Park, 2023).

During the Korea Fintech Week 2023, FSC Vice Chairman Kim So, elaborated that the collaboration between FinTech giants and start-ups in B2B areas is "expected to lead to new growth in both the FinTech sector and major financial groups" (Park, 2023). With the help of the Financial Services Commission (FSC)`s new regulations they`ll allow various to forms of collaboration with international financial organizations. In fact, during the global expo of Korea Fintech Week 2023, World Bank, EBRD and Unido participated while exploring possible and promising startups in Korean FinTech firms (Park, 2023). In addition, the government proposed a new business agreement aimed at helping the local FinTech industry through new fund of US$781 million until 2028 (Lee,,2022).

MONGOLIA

Market Size

According to the World Bank, (2023), Mongolia's economic development is looking forward to increasing by 5.2% by the end of 2023, focusing on the mining sector and the recuperation of tourism. By the end of 2022, the Gross Domestic Product marked $16,810,883,361, while GDP per capita in the same year, with a population of 3,398,366 marked $4,242. From 2021 to 2022, Mongolia's GDP presented a growth rate of 4.85% (Worldometer, n.d.).

According to Statista, (2023), the FinTech Mongolia growth of market size projection for 2023 is 0%, although the digital payment market is projected to grow by 17.19% in the next 4 years and digital development is expected to grow by 94% by 2024. This doesn't mean that Mongolia has no opportunity to grow the FinTech size market, there's no exact number for the potential, but only 15% of Mongolia's population has "formal access to banking" (ISPs, 2023), which gives space to companies and digital banking startups to begin spreading FinTech in Mongolia.

Current Adoption Rate

The global adoption rate of Fintech users happens to be 64%, and, as stated by the Mongolian Fintech Association (2023) "93% of FinTech users agree that technology saves them time". Additionally, according to the Mongolian FinTech Association (2023), the adoption rate of Financial Technology has shown a large growth in the last few years all over the world, with payment apps being used by about 70% of Financial Technology adopters. The current FinTech adoption rate in Mongolia is relatively high, as stated before, the use of digital wallets has grown, helping individuals who do not have access to formal banking. Also, in Mongolia, 10% of families receive international remittances, with the help of FinTech (ISP, 2023).

Furthermore, ISP (2023) mentions that, "financial technology, has become a major player in the Mongolian financial sector, and telecommunications has played a significant role in its growth." As mentioned in the article about Mongolian FinTech by ISP, (2023), "many people live in remote areas, with limited access to banking", which is why, the ease of having their banking app on their phones gives them the opportunity to be part of this growth.

Types of FinTech

The main actors in FinTech according to Statista (2023) in Mongolia are ranked by relevance.

- Digital payments: The most used platforms for e-payments include PayPal, BitPay, Paysera, UnionPay and Skrill. This type of payment has led to the growth of digital commerce by younger generations (Statista, 2023).
- Digital remittances: One of the currently popular actors for FinTech gives people the opportunity to connect monetarily with their family and friends. According to Statista, (2023), "The Digital Remittances market in Mongolia is projected to grow by 8.37% (2023-2027) resulting in a market volume of US$9.38m in 2027".

- Digital capital raising: Gives Mongolians the opportunity to invest digitally in personal businesses connecting them with banking digital solutions. "Total transaction value in the Digital Investment market is projected to reach US$194.90m in 2023" (Statista, 2023).

Main Players

As stated, the main media players include, the Mongolian FinTech Association. This is a non-profit association interested in the development of FinTech with growing technologies. They are in charge of promoting collaboration, startups, and the growth of the FinTech environment. Collecting updated information about financial technologies in Mongolia. Despite being widely recognized they are still a new association founded in late 2019 (Mongolian FinTech Association, 2023).

On the other hand, GrapeCity Mongolia was founded in the year 2000 and concentrated on the development of "banking and payment solution software" (Monteiro, 2022), due to its positioning, it became the market leader in the sector. "Of the 12 commercial banks in Mongolia, 11 use its software products, and 9 are operating on its Core Banking system" (Monteiro, 2022).

Furthermore, Most Money is associated with XXBank and Capriton Bank, letting their customers move their money digitally. According to Monteiro, (2022), "The company encrypts and sends information to meet end-to-end security requirements, and uses OTP to securely protect its users' privacy from third parties". As stated in the last sentence, one of the main concerns of the company is its users' privacy, which is something that might attract new consumers.

Another main player in Mongolia's FinTech is SendMN, founded in 2016, which had the objective of providing great and low-priced international transfer solutions. "SendMN NBFC allows its customers to transfer money to more than 170 countries and more than 400,000 agents in just 10 minutes using their mobile phones" (Monteiro, 2022).

Another key player is MineSec. Best known for coming directly from Singapore, Minesec provides Point Of Sale (POS) mobile solutions for Mongolian businesses and customers. "MineSec's white-label SoftPOS solution meets international standards set by payment schemes like Visa, Mastercard, Discover, AMEX, UnionPay and JCB, enabling customers to scale confidently and competitively amid the international market's unique evolving needs" (PR Newswire, 2023). It has paved a fresh journey for Mongol iD in their POS mobile solution development. As stated by PR Newswire (2023) "Mongol iD will utilize the SoftPOS solution from MineSec for the newly released MinuChat." In addition, F6s.com, (n.d.), states that one of its founders, Angus Chiu is the main, and appears to be the only, investor in the company, which means that the main weakness of the company is the lack of investors.

Golomt Bank integrates FinTech solutions, one of the key banks of Mongolia, "Investing on a brighter future" (Golomt Bank, n.d.). They are one of the main systematic banks in Mongolia. Founded in 1995, was a pioneer in Western Union transfers, international payment card systems, smart-phone banking apps, as well as "SocialPay digital wallet, a Fintech product based on advanced technology, easy-to-use, and the simplest solution for saving time" (Golomt Bank, n.d.). They don't only give big market share but provide outstanding service quality. One of their weaknesses is the barrier of government regulations, tax, and inflation (Apollo.io, n.d.).

Finally, we have Mongol ID. A company focused on developing technologies in Mongolia. Founded in 2016 it has a little more experience than the others since the previous were "relatively new" in the industry. Yet, their recognition and growth have not been good; they have only grown 16.7% in the last couple of years (Apollo.io, 2020).

New Investment and Start-Ups

Statista (2023) states that digital investment is going to be the biggest market in the FinTech area in Mongolia with an AUM of US$2,794k by the end of the present year. Here are some of the companies investing in Mongolia's FinTech development.

- SBI Holdings: a Japanese company that invested in the Singapore FinTech startup called AND Global which provides micro-loans to Mongolia (SBI Holdings, n.d.).
- AND Global Pte.: Launched LendMD in 2016, and helps start-ups to involve AI in their services and FinTech products (AND Global, n.d.).
- ORDA Wealth Tech: Manages investors' profiles with all of the requirements to match them with an investment after detailed analysis (Themefisher, n.d.).

It also, includes some of the main players in the FinTech sector of Mongolia as;

- Grapecity Monol LLC: This specializes in digital banking growth and "payment solution software" (Monteiro, 2022).
- MOST Money: Moneiro (2022) states that, is a "public electronic payment service" that gives fast and easy payment solutions from your phone.
- SendMN: This is a "non-bank financial institution", as mentioned by Monteiro (2022) which has the objective of providing cheap and easy abroad money transfers.

Technical Infrastructure

The e-commerce market in Mongolia is not the biggest compared to other countries in East and North Asia. As mentioned in the statistics by E-commerce Market Mongolia, (n.d.), by the end of 2023, the e-commerce market revenue is expected to be US $381.3 M, and is expected to grow 12.4% by 2027. The most common e-commerce sector is Fashion, with 29.4% of the revenue. Then they have Electronics and Media, with 27.7%, followed by Food and Personal Care with 26.9%. Furniture and Appliances get 10.4% of the revenue, and other departments, (Toys, Hobbies, among others), get 5.5% (E-commerce Market Mongolia, n.d.).

The FinTech sector in Mongolia is closely linked to the ecosystem of technical infrastructure and a number of adjacent sectors, including e-commerce through the online experience. For the expansion and advancement of the FinTech sector, a solid technical infrastructure is essential. It includes data centers, telecommunications networks, internet connections, and electronic payment systems. A robust technical foundation fosters digital innovation, enables quick adoption of FinTech solutions, and makes financial transactions safe and efficient.

Government Policies and Regulations

"The rapid growth has raised novel and complex regulatory challenges, with implications for financial stability, consumer borrowing and credit protection practices, cybersecurity, money laundering risks, data protection, and data privacy" (Asian Development Bank, 2022). As mentioned in the last paragraph, among Mongolia's government policies, we can find the data protection law, which is focused on ensuring the user's privacy. Mongolia is also allowed to collaborate internationally in order to expand the country's FinTech. Also, the regulatory environment is in charge of maintaining the regulatory bodies of the Fintech associations and environment, as well as helping in the promotion of the legal and regulatory frameworks, which includes the implementation of infrastructure and creating a regulatory system for FinTech companies (Asian Development Bank, 2022).

Impacts on the Economy

As mentioned in the report *Developing Financial Technology Legal and Regulatory Frameworks for Mongolia*, by the Asian Development Bank, (2022), FinTech has helped in the expansion of the financial sector in Mongolia, by providing new and different solutions and also expanding the financial and economic market. Also, with external investment, Mongolia is prone to see economic growth from foreign market collaborations. As mentioned by the Asian Development Bank (2022) "MSMEs are one of Mongolia's most dynamic sectors in Mongolia from a development perspective, contributing 17.8% of gross domestic product and employing 72% of the total workforce." MSMEs are important because they build a great piece of the FinTech sector, and, the growth and development of financial technologies help the recuperation of Mongolia's economy post-COVID-19 (Asian Development Bank, 2022).

SESE (2019) mentions that "the government is fully behind the blossoming IT industry. In 2018, it launched the Hub Innovation Center, the nation's first facility that directly supports startups" which is an essential fragment of the economy's growth in the technological and that being so, the financial sector, leading to the external interest of investors in the countries' FinTech expansion, "This makes fertile ground for new types of financial services" (SESE, 2019).

Security Concerns

As mentioned by the Asian Development Bank (2022) "The sector is innovating rapidly, which requires an agile, risk-aware and functional regulatory approach". And, as specified in the Government, Policies and Regulations, FinTech has shown a higher growth rate in the last 3 years, which can compromise users' cybersecurity if not regulated. The lack of regulatory frameworks around Fintech in Mongolia, has provided a route to originate new laws that help with cybersecurity and privacy issues, "The TA will develop a comprehensive roadmap for FinTech legal and regulatory frameworks that identify the avenues of intervention" (Asian Development Bank, 2022).

Synthesize Previous Academic Research

In the Comparative Analysis of Financial Advancements in Mongolia, the financial background of the country is discussed in relation to the economy, "Right now, Mongolia is at 127th position in the world ranking in terms of economic strength with a freedom score of 55.9 on the economy" (Heritage, 2020). On the other hand, Chuluunbat, (2021) mentions that by 2021, mining constituted around 90% of Mongolia's "exports" and talks about the lack of regulatory frameworks in the financial (and other) sectors in the country. Also, the advancement that can be done when focusing on financial areas and its expansion is soon to be noticed in hand with the financial recovery (Chuluunbat, 2021). "These technologies have revolutionized the buyer-seller interactions, the overall business model, and the current and future financial sector" (Bakkar, n.d.).

Bakkar, (n.d.), states the importance of switching to online/digital solutions, which is one of the reasons why international e-commerce is increasingly expanding all over the world. He also supports the fact that FinTech gives great solutions to individuals with limited access to in-person banking, "Access to under-banked and un-banked consumers is allowing FinTech companies to reach and capitalize on markets that have been underserved to date, particularly in Asia and the Southern Hemisphere" (Bakkar, n.d.).

Interesting Facts

- Artificial Intelligence: Woffenden (2022), states, "Artificial intelligence is being used to credit scoring and provide short-term consumer loans". This helpful tool has been part of Mongolia's FinTech growth and user adoption, which is also a feature of the E-Mongolia platform.
- E-Mongolia platform: Imparts government services digitally, including passport assistance, and license services, among others. "Over 75 percent of the adult population is now using E-Mongolia on daily basis" (Woffenden, 2022).

Trends and Future Aspects

Woffenden (2022) talks about a possible financial relationship with the United Kingdom, as, Mongolia has a "tax-friendly environment" which is attractive to other countries in terms of investment and start-ups, and it is a great opportunity for FinTech market expansion due to East Asia high rate adoption. "The Ministry of Digital Development and Communications is paying great attention to nurturing and developing IT startups, in addition to the national digital transformation" (Woffenden, 2022). Previous paragraphs already mention the support of the government on FinTech development, which if continuous, will lead the way for Mongolia to be one of the strongest countries in the sector.

As for privacy concerns, banks and digital payment apps are going to seek privacy protection of their consumers, as well as a high percentage of digitalization, which will have an impact on the users, "is to be expected that customer loyalty in the future will be even more strongly determined by the efficiency, flexibility, reliability and customer friendliness of the online access offered by the individual banks" (Gayabazar, 2021). The switch from in-person banking to online banking is already happening, "For the bank of the future, this means a restructuring through digitization, because only in this way can banks remain attractive and profitable" (Gayabazar, 2021). In conclusion, whether digitalized or not, most of the market has shown some interest in online banking solutions, given their efficacy and accessibility, we can expect the rates of digitalization to go higher in the next 4 years.

COMPARISON AND ANALYSIS

The comprehensive understanding of China, Japan, Taiwan, South Korea, and Mongolia`s evolving financial landscape in the FinTech setting displayed a good comprehensive reflection between each one. It provided evidence on how technological adoption, companies, regulations, and market maturity vary from country to country. It became evident that these regions are eager to harness the potential of FinTech to keep increasing economic progress and innovation in the industry.

Predominantly, the usage of mobile payments became *the* critical factor in each territory analyzed. China stands out with Tencent and Alipay, Japan with PayPay and Paidy,

Taiwan with Regutan Card, South Korea with Kakao Pay and Naver Pay, and Mongolia with Mobile POS Payments. However, when it comes to their plans for the next few years, they vary.

China, along with South Korea and Japan, is seeking to go beyond its domestic market. Perhaps their well-established position across their microeconomy promotes seeking macro integration with international markets and partnerships across borders. On the other hand, Taiwan and Mongolia (a smaller player on a global stage) are embracing the FinTech landscape through regional counterparts and seeking the government's aid and cooperation. Compared to mature markets, they need to expand and be deeply consistent within the country before going to other economies. It might take years but there is promise for both nations in the increase of financial technology advancements- better with the government's support.

In addition, the inclusion and audience vary surprisingly for each country. Japan is focusing more on the quality of financial services rather than seeking young individuals since they want the old population to manage their wealth efficiently. Mongolia, still geographically rural, is seeking the integration of easy access in those limited geographical and technological territories where digital financial tools are not easily accessed.

CONCLUSION

After having analyzed the Fintech Landscape in East Asia, reviewed over 40 different articles and documents, and compared, and contrasted each country's situation by very specific parameters, we have come to the following resolution.

The study of China, Japan, Taiwan, South Korea, and Mongolia's evolving FinTech landscapes emphasizes the intricate interplay of technological innovation, regulatory frameworks, market dynamics, and strategic aspirations. Mobile payments have emerged as a key force driving FinTech growth across all the examined regions. Remarkably, each has developed its own distinct leader in the mobile payment arena, signifying the prevalence of digital transactions as a fundamental aspect of modern financial ecosystems.

China, Japan, and South Korea, having solidified their domestic FinTech bases, are aiming to broaden their influence on the global stage. This pursuit of macro integration highlights their intent to establish international partnerships and collaborate across borders, capitalizing on their well-established microeconomic positions. However, Taiwan and Mongolia, are presenting distinct market conditions, where they focus on fostering FinTech growth through more localized and regional approaches.

Each country's trajectory is a testament to its unique circumstances, and while the path ahead may differ, the common idea remains the commitment to attaching FinTech's potential for economic growth and enhanced financial services, ensuring a future shaped by both domestic prowess and international collaboration.

REFERENCES

About Us. (n.d.). Golomt Bank. https://www.golomtbank.com/en/about-bank

About Us: MineSec white-label softpos. MineSec. (n.d.). https://www.theminesec.com/about-us

Airfunding. (2019). *5 kinds of Taiwan Crowdfunding Platforms*. Airfunding Blog. https://blog.airfunding.net/crowdfunding/5-kinds-crowdfunding-platform/#:~:text=flyingV%20is%20a%20typical%20comprehensive,and%20divided%20into%2012%20categories

Alda, T. (2022b, October 24). FinTech in China. *Statista*. https://www.statista.com/topics/6893/FinTech-in-china/#editorsPicks

Apollo.io. (2022). https://www.apollo.io/companies/Mongol-iD/556cf15c73696412081d5a00?chart=count

Asian Development Bank. (2022). Mongolia: Developing Financial Technology Legal and Regulatory Frameworks for Mongolia. Asian Development Bank.

Bakkar, A. (n.d.). *FinTech and the Future of Finance. The Global Advisory and Account in Network*. https://www.hlb.global/FinTech-and-the-future-of-finance

Banking. (n.d.). https://www.boj.or.jp/en/about/press/koen_2016/data/ko161118a.pdf

Banking and Fintech. (n.d.). Invest in Mongolia | Ministry of Economy and Development. https://invest-mongolia.gov.mn/banking-and-FinTech/

Beijing's intentions. (n.d.). China Briefing News. https://www.china-briefing.com/news/a-close-reading-china-FinTech-development-plan-for-2022-2025/

Bito.Ex. (2023). *About Us*. Bito.Ex. https://www.bitoex.com/?locale=en

Briefing, C. (2018b, January 22). China's FinTech Industry. *China Briefing News*. https://www.china-briefing.com/news/chinas-FinTech-industry/

Briefing, C. (2022, July 21). *China's Fintech Development Plan for 2022-2025: Understanding Beijing's intentions*. China Briefing News. https://www.china-briefing.com/news/a-close-reading-china-FinTech-development-plan-for-2022-2025/

CAG. (2021). DERIN, The FinTech revolution in China: opportunities and threats. *FinTech Magazine*. https://FinTechmagazine.com/financial-services-finserv/FinTech-revolution-china-opportunities-and-threats

CFMI - China Fintech market insights. (n.d.). https://www.mordorintelligence.com/industry-reports/china-FinTech-market#:~:textChina%20Fintech%20Market%20has%20generated,the%20FinTech%20space%20in20China

Choi, Y., & Shin, Y. (2019, September 23). Feasibility of the Fintech Industry as an Innovation Platform for Sustainable Economic Growth in Korea. *MDPI*, *11*, 5351. doi:10.3390/su1119535

Connell, A. (2022). 33 Latest WeChat Statistics And Trends For 2022. *Blogging Wizard*. https://bloggingwizard.com/wechat-statistics/

Crunchbase. (2023). *BitFlyer*. Crunchbase Website. https://www.crunchbase.com/organization/bitflyer

Crunchbase. (2023). *Paidy*. Crunchbase Website. https://www.crunchbase.com/organization/paidly

Deloitte. (2017, October 23). *How does FinTech in Japan compare to the rest of the world*. Deloitte. https://www2.deloitte.com/jp/en/pages/financial-services/articles/bk/jp-fi-FinTech-in-japan.html

Diep, C. (2023, August 31). *E-commerce in Japan - statistic & facts*. Statista. Retrieved September 3, 2023, from https://www.statista.com/topics/5262/e-commerce-in-japan/#topicOverview

Digital Investment - Mongolia. (n.d.-a). *Statista market forecast*. Statista. https://www.statista.com/outlook/dmo/FinTech/digital-investment/mongolia

Digital remittances - Mongolia: Statista market forecast. (n.d.). Statista. https://www.statista.com/outlook/dmo/FinTech/digital-payments/digital-remittances/mongolia

Ecommerce Market Mongolia - Data & Trends | ecommercedb.com. (n.d.). https://ecommercedb.com/markets/mn/all

Eldon, Y. (2016). *Information Security Challenges in the New Era of Fintech*. AIS Electronic.

E.SUN. (2023). *Brand Story*. E.SUN FHC. https://www.esunfhc.com/en/about-esun/intro/commitment

Expat Guide Korea. (2020, July 23). How to Set Up Kakao Pay: the best mobile payment service in Korea. *Expat Guide Korea*. https://www.expatguidekorea.com/article/how-to-set-up-kakao-pay-the-best-mobile-payment-service-in-korea.html

Falgright. (2023). The Future of Reg Tech in Taiwan. *Fintech Global*. https://FinTech.global/2023/05/22/the-future-of-regtech-in-taiwan

Feyen. (2023). Fintech and the Future of Finance. *World Bank Group*. https://documents1.worldbank.org/curated/en/099450005162250110/pdf/P17300600228b70070914b0b5edf26e2f9f.pdf

Financial Service Agency. (2023). *Laws & Regulations: FSA*. FSA. https://www.fsa.go.jp/en/laws_regulations/index.html

FIN/SUM. (2023). *Fintech, the era of "Neoteric Individual"*. FIN/SUM 2023. https://www.finsum.jp/en_index.html

Fintech - Mongolia: Statista market forecast. (n.d.). Statista. https://www.statista.com/outlook/dmo/FinTech/mongolia

Fintech News Hong Kong. (2020, February 10). *Fintech In South Korea: Regulators Step In To Boost Innovation*. Fintech Hong Kong. https://FinTechnews.hk/4823/FinTechkorea/FinTech-south-korea-regulators-step-boost-innovation/F6s.com

FinTech sector? (n.d.). *McKinsey & Company*. https://www.mckinsey.com/~/media/mckinsey/industries/financial%20services/our%20insights/whats%20next%20for%20chinas%20booming%20FinTech%20sector/whats-next-for-chinas-booming-FinTech-sector.ashx

Futures, C. (2022, October 2). *The Future of Fintech in Japan: Top Fintech Trends to watch in 2023*. Computer Futures. https://www.computerfutures.com/en-jp/knowledge-hub/financial-technology/the-future-of-FinTech-in-japan-top-FinTech-trends-to-watch-in-2023/#jobs

Gayabazar, U. (2021). Future tendencies in the financial markets in Mongolia and worldwide. *Int. J. Foresight and Innovation Policy, 15*(1-3), 187–203.

Global, E. (2022). What is next for Asia in FinTech adoption. *EY - Global*. https://www.ey.com/en_gl/banking-capital-markets/what-is-next-for-asia-in-FinTech-adoption

Golomt bank - banking - overview, competitors, and employees. (n.d.). Apollo.io. https://www.apollo.io/companies/Golomt-Bank/5f3db67ee06ba3000173b9e1?chart=count

Heritage (2020). *2020 Index of Economic Freedom: Mongolia*. Author.

Hernàndez, P. (2019, Nov 19) Financial technology: the 150-year revolution. *Basel Committee on Banking Supervision and Governor of the Bank of Spain*. https://www.bis.org/speeches/sp191119.htm

Huang, Chiang FinTech in China: overview. (2021). *Practical Law*. https://uk.practicallaw.thomsonreuters.com/w-019-4896?transitionType=Default&contextData=(sc.Default)&firstPage=true#:~:text=The%20People's%20Bank%20of%20China%20(PBOC)&text=Control%20and%20supervision%20of%20the,finance%2Drelated%20laws%20and%20regulations

International Monetary Fund. (2020, September) *Republic of Korea: Financial Sector Assessment Program*. IMF Country Report No. 20/280.

International Trade Administration. (2022, November 4). *Japan - Market Overview*. International Trade Administration. https://www.trade.gov/country-commercial-guides/japan-market-overview

International Trade Organization. (2020). *Taiwan Fintech Market*. Market Intelligence. https://www.trade.gov/market-intelligence/taiwan-FinTech-market

Internship golomt bank. (n.d.). https://app.emaze.com/1927358/internship-golomt-bank#/12

Intralink. (2020). *Fintech South Korea: Market Intelligence Report. Innovation is Great*. www.intralink-group.com/Syndication/media/Syndication/Reports/Korean-Fintech-report-Oct-2020.pdf

ISP. (2023, June 27). *The growth of Fintech in mongolia: How telecommunications is shaping the financial sector*. https://isp.page/news/the-growth-of-FinTech-in-mongolia-how-telecommunications-is-shaping-the-financial-sector/

ITA. (2023). *Taiwan - Country Commercial Guide*. https://www.trade.gov/country-commercial-guides/taiwan-information-and-telecommunications-technology

James. (2019, August 19). The future of FinTech in South Korea - QARA - Medium. *Medium*. https://medium.com/qara/the-future-of-FinTech-in-south-korea-37a0a1315742#:~:text=Compared%20to%20the%20U.S.%20or%20China%2C%20South%20Korea%E2%80%99s,2018%20and%2045%20million%20users%20expected%20by%202022

Japan External Trade Organization. (2017). Japan's Fintech Ecosystem Transformation Today and toward 2020. *JETRO*. https://www.jetro.go.jp/ext_images/canada/pdf/FinTechseminaroct1817maeda.pdf

Kagan, J. (2022, October 30). *Financial Services Agency (FSA)*. Investopedia. https://www.investopedia.com/terms/f/financial-services-agency-fsa.asp

Kajihara, A. (2023, February 20). FinTech in Japan. Trends for 2023. Wahl+Case. https://www.wahlandcase.com/blog/FinTech-predictions-2023

Kishi, M. (2019). *Project Stella and the impacts of FinTech on financial infrastructures in Japan*. ADBI Working Paper Series.

Kowsmann, P., & Ostroff, C. (2023, August 2). Crypto is illegal in China. Binance does $90 billion of business there anyway. *WSJ*. https://www.wsj.com/articles/crypto-is-illegal-in-china-binance-does-90-billion-of-business-there-anyway-2a0af975

KPMG. (2023). 100 Questions: FinTech Development In Taiwan. *KPMG International Cooperative*. https://assets.kpmg.com/content/dam/kpmg/tw/pdf/2020/07/tw-100-Questions-FinTech-Development-in-Taiwan.pdf

Lee & Li. (2023). First-step analysis: FinTech regulation in Taiwan. *Lexology*. https://www.trade.gov/market-intelligence/taiwan-FinTech-market

Library (AISeL). (n.d.). https://aisel.aisnet.org/cgi/viewcontent.cgi?article=1038&context=iceb2016

Long, T. Q. (2023, June 11). *Financial literacy, behavioral traits, and ePayment adoption and usage in Japan*. Financial Innovation. https://jfin-swufe.springeropen.com/articles/10.1186/s40854-023-00504-3

Mahapatra, J. (n.d.). *South Korea - The Fintech Growth Story*. https://www.linkedin.com/pulse/south-korea-FinTech-growth-story-jagdish-mahapatra/

Malyshev. (2021 Oct 25) Regulatory quality and competition policy in Korea. *OECD*. https://www.oecd.org/country/korea/thematic-focus/regulatory-quality-and-competition-policy-in-korea-e5b4137d/

Miller, C. (2022). The Chips That Make Taiwan the Center of the World. *TIME*. https://time.com/6219318/tsmc-taiwan-the-center-of-the-world/

Mongolia GDP. (n.d.). Worldometer. https://www.worldometers.info/gdp/mongolia-gdp/#:~:text=GDP%20Growth%20Rate%20in%202022,3.3%25%20in%20GDP%20per%20capita

Mongolian FinTech Association. (2023, May 11). *Fintech statistics*. www.mongoliaFinTech.org. https://www.mongoliaFinTech.org/52/bitem

Monteiro, L. (2023, February 15). *3 FinTech companies in Japan to watch out for in 2023*. IBS Intelligence. https://ibsintelligence.com/ibsi-news/3-FinTech-companies-in-japan-to-watch-out-for-in-2023/

Mordor Intelligence. (n.d.). China Fintech Market Size. *Mordor Intelligence Industry Reports*. https://www.mordorintelligence.com/industry-reports/china-FinTech-market/market-sieç

NamY.LeeS. T. (2022). Behind the growth of FinTech in South Korea: Digital divide in the use of digital financial services. *Social Science Research Network*. doi:10.2139/ssrn.4295694

Newswire, P. R. (2023, March 16). *MINESEC empowers Mongol ID as Mongolia's pioneering FinTech with softpos launch*. https://www.prnewswire.com/apac/news-releases/minesec-empowers-mongol-id-as-mongolias-pioneering-FinTech-with-softpos-launch-301771327.html

O'Hanlon, J. (2020, May 18). *FINOLAB: driving innovative startups in FinTech.* FinTech Magazine. https://FinTechmagazine.com/company-reports/finolab-driving-innovative-startups-FinTech

Park, A. J. (2023, August 31). Korea Fintech Week 2023 brings financial giants and startups together. *Koreatimes.* https://www.koreatimes.co.kr/www/biz/2023/08/126_358142.html

Personal Information Protection Commission Japan. (n.d.). *Roles and Responsibilities.* Roles and Responsibilities |PPC Personal Information Protection Commission, Japan. https://www.ppc.go.jp/en/aboutus/roles/

Pitchbook. (2023). *Lend & Borrow (Taiwan) overview.* Pitchbook. https://pitchbook.com/profiles/company/266998-15#overview

PricewaterhouseCoopers. (n.d.). *A comparison of cybersecurity regulations: China.* PwC. https://www.pwc.com/id/en/pwc-publications/services-publications/legal-publications/a-comparison-of-cybersecurity-regulations/china.html#:~:text=China%20is%20increasingly%20emphasising%20government,for%20cybersecurity%20and%20data%20protection.pymnts

Rakuten. (2023). *About Us.* Rakuten. https://global.rakuten.com/corp/about/company/FinTech.html

Santosdiaz, R., & Santosdiaz, R. (2023). How China became a leader in digital payments and wider digitalisation. *The Fintech Times.* https://theFinTechtimes.com/how-china-became-a-leader-in-digital-payments-and-wider-digitalisation/#:~:text=However%2C%20with%20its%20population%20of,for%20innovation%2C%20technology%20and%20adoption

SBI Holdings. (n.d.). Japanese Site. https://www.sbigroup.co.jp/english/

Secretariat, C. (n.d.). *Regulatory Sandbox|Cabinet Secretariat Website.* 内閣官房. https://www.cas.go.jp/jp/seisaku/s-portal/regulatorysandbox_e.html

SESE. (2019, November 11). *Mongolia's emerging it sector leads economy in New Direction.* Nikkei Asia. https://asia.nikkei.com/Business/Technology/Mongolia-s-emerging-IT-sector-leads-economy-in-new-direction

Song, N., & Appiah-Otoo, I. (2022). The Impact of Fintech on Economic Growth: Evidence from China. *Sustainability (Basel), 14*(10), 6211. doi:10.3390/su14106211

South China Morning Post. (2023, July 20). *China far outpaces the US in 5G base-station construction.* https://www.scmp.com/video/technology/3228390/china-has-built-6-times-number-5g-towers-3-months-us-has-installed-2-years

Statista & Statista Digital Market Insights. (2022). *Digital & Trends: FinTech in Japan.* Statista. https://www-statista-com.ezproxy.myucwest.ca/study/111372/FinTech-in-japan/

Statista. (2022). *Countries & Regions: Japan.* Statista. https://www-statista-com.ezproxy.myucwest.ca/study/10007/japan-statista-dossier/

Statista. (2023, August 8). *Fintech adoption rate South Korea 2017-2019.* https://www.statista.com/statistics/1125349/south-korea-FinTech-adoption-rate/

Statista. (2023). *eCommerce - Taiwan.* Statista. https://www.statista.com/outlook/dmo/ecommerce/taiwan

Statista. (2023). *FinTech - China | Statista market forecast.* https://www.statista.com/outlook/dmo/FinTech/china#analyst-opinio

Statista. (2023). FinTech – Taiwan. *Statista.* https://www.statista.com/outlook/dmo/FinTech/taiwan#key-market-indicators

Statista. (2023a, March 13). *Main information channel when looking for information South Korea 2022.* https://www.statista.com/statistics/1115944/south-korea-main-service-used-to-search-for-information/#:~:text=According%20to%20a%20survey%20in%202022%2C%20close%20to,Korean%20website%20to%20feature%20its%20own%20search%20engine

The World Bank in Mongolia. (2023, June 19). World Bank. https://www.worldbank.org/en/country/mongolia/overview

Themefisher. (n.d.). *About Orda.* ORDA. https://orda.mn/about/

Toplist Joint Stock Company. (n.d.). *Top 10 biggest FinTech companies in China - Toplist.info.* toplist.info. https://toplist.info/top-list/biggest-FinTech-companies-in-china-by-market-cap-10577.htm

Tracxn. (2023). *Fintech Start Ups in Taipei.* Tracxn. https://tracxn.com/explore/FinTech-Startups-in-Taipei

Tracxn. (2023, July 9). *FinTech Startups in Japan.* Tracxn. https://tracxn.com/explore/FinTech-Startups-in-Japan

Tracxn. (2023, September 2). South Korea. *Geographies | Tracxn.* https://tracxn.com/d/geographies/south-korea/__us6kb0pJxXgamA9AipJbdHh7DP6AZ-jAWckbXbAmAhQ/companies

Tseng. (n.d.). Taiwan Fintech. *The Legal 500.* https://www.legal500.com/guides/chapter/taiwan-FinTech/

United Nations Escap. (2018, April) Potential of financial technology in East and North-East Asia. *MPFD policy briefs. No.73.* https://www.unescap.org/sites/default/d8files/knowledge-products/MPFD%20Policy%20Brief%2073_FinTech%20in%20ENEA.pdf

Vyshnavi - StartupTalky. (2023, June 20). StartupTalky. https://startuptalky.com/author/pv/

Webenertia_Admin. (2016, April 6). *White Paper: How China Telecom's transformation enables growth.* China Telecom Americas. https://www.ctamericas.com/blog/china-telecoms-transformation-enables-growth/#:~:text=Telecommunications%20growth%20has%20also%20been,fastest%20growing%20sectors%20in%20China

Woffenden, C. (2022, October 20). *Digital Transformation in mongolia: Insight from the Ministry of Digital Development.* The Fintech Times. https://theFinTechtimes.com/digital-transformation-in-mongolia-insight-from-bolor-erdene-battsengel/

Writer, S. (2021, July 6). *SBI invests in AI-powered microlender serving Mongolia.* Nikkei Asia.https://asia.nikkei.com/Business/Finance/SBI-invests-in-AI-powered-microlender-serving-Mongolia

Zheng, H. (2023). China's experience with mobile payments highlights the pros and cons of a cashless society. *The Conversation.* https://theconversation.com/chinas-experience-with-mobile-payments-highlights-the-pros-and-cons-of-a-cashless-society-201177#:~:text=Leading%20mobile%20payment%20platforms%20Alipay,credit%20card%20and%20buy%20i

Chapter 9
North America:
Disrupting the Financial Giants

Mitra Madanchian
University Canada West, Canada

ABSTRACT

North America is an influential region that garners the interest of prominent financial institutions and industry frontrunners worldwide. This vast and heterogeneous continent, comprising the economic superpowers of Canada and the United States, has been at the forefront of financial innovation, fundamentally transforming our understanding of investments, money, and the financial sector itself. This chapter provides an in-depth analysis of the dynamic forces that are causing significant changes in the financial industry of the continent. This inquiry scrutinizes the present condition of affairs and illuminates the disruptive innovations that have started to pose a challenge to well-established financial behemoths. This chapter provides an overview of the continuous changes affecting the financial sector, from the integration of cutting-edge technologies to the constantly evolving rules and regulations. Furthermore, it analyzes forthcoming developments, uncovering potential scenarios and trends that will persistently impact the financial terrain of North America.

INTRODUCTION

North America is widely recognized as a dominant financial region, exerting substantial sway over the worldwide economic sphere. Fundamental to this concept are the economic powerhouses of the United States and Canada, whose institutions and financial markets have a significant impact on the course of global finance. The continent is home to a multifaceted and resilient economy, distinguished by advancements in technology, innovation, and an intricate web of financial institutions (Pramanik, Kirtania, & Pani, 2019).

The financial and economic environment of North America is changing dramatically; the continent is only now beginning to integrate economically, and at this point, it is only integrating in specific areas like commerce and investment (Reyes, 1999). The United States and Canada have become increasingly dependent on each other economically as a result of the North American Free Trade Agreement (NAFTA)

DOI: 10.4018/979-8-3693-1561-3.ch009

of 1994, and Mexico has also started to integrate its economy with the United States more deeply. As a result, a robust economic bloc that is almost as integrated as the European Union has emerged, and NAFTA's economic integration is expanding more quickly (Rugman, 2004). North America's smaller countries stand to benefit most from these opportunities, but there are necessary conditions to boost investment, increase production, and make it easier for workers to find gainful employment (Horton, 1979).

The financial industry is experiencing a rapid acceleration of technological development, with huge technology corporations and innovative start-ups posing a threat to established players in the market (Rugman, 2004). The integration process in North America has sparked debate about whether it can accomplish more than just trade and investment, taking into account structural elements such as national identities, cultural distinctions, nation-building experiences, internal strife, and homogenization (Reyes, 1999).

Collectively, these countries propel financial services innovation, consistently challenging the limits of conventional banking. The financial ecosystem in North America is distinguished by a dynamic interaction among well-established financial behemoths, adaptable Fintech firms, and a regulatory structure that endeavors to strike a balance between stability and innovation. In addition to financial markets, North America serves as a fertile ground for innovation, fostering the development of groundbreaking financial solutions and technological advancements. Fintech centers in cities such as San Francisco and Toronto, along with Silicon Valley, contribute significantly to the advancement of financial technology on the continent. This, in turn, impacts global trends. The importance of North America is reflected in the actions and strategies of its preeminent financial institutions and corporations, which have an impact on international finance.

This chapter provides an exhaustive examination of the transformative forces that are influencing the financial sector in North America. It commences with a comprehensive outline of the present condition before exploring technological disruptions, regulatory intricacies, and evolving consumer patterns. Using case studies, this article illustrates how established financial behemoths are being challenged by disruptive innovators. With an eye toward the future, the chapter examines potential scenarios and trends, offering valuable perspectives on the dynamic financial sector of North America. The objective is to provide readers with a succinct yet perceptive comprehension of the obstacles and prospects associated with the continuous metamorphosis of prominent financial institutions in the area.

Current State of North America's Financial Industry

Overview of the United States and Canada as Economic Powerhouses

The economies of Canada and the United States are, respectively, two of the largest and most prosperous in the world. Canada is one of the wealthiest nations globally, surpassing the majority of countries in the Americas in terms of relative prosperity. In contrast, the United States possesses the most expansive economy worldwide. The two countries have a rich historical background of economic cooperation, which culminated in the North American Free Trade Agreement (NAFTA), an exemplary trade agreement of an international scale. The agreement was superseded by the United States-Mexico-Canada Agreement (USMCA), which offers insight into the structure of a forthcoming epoch in global economic governance (Puig, 2019).

According to a study conducted by Harvard University, significant economic growth has occurred in both the United States and Canada throughout the information age (Jorgenson, 2004). Adoption and advancement of information technology have been identified as factors that have contributed to increased economic growth and productivity in both countries, according to the study.

An alternative inquiry illustrates that the historical progression of Canada's economic growth can be deduced through an analysis of three notable inequalities in quality of life within the nation: the division between the First Nations and the rest of Canada, the distinction between French and English Canadians, and the division between Atlantic Canada and the rest of Canada. An analysis of these three discrepancies can provide valuable understanding regarding the critical significance of institutions in establishing the relative poverty and wealth levels between Canada and the United States (Geloso, 2022).

An opinion expressed in a recent article suggests that the unification of the United States and Canada would constitute a North American superpower. The merged nation would be an economic and energy superpower, boasting a magnitudeier economy than, among others, the European Union, Japan, China, and Germany (Francis, 2014).

Regulatory Landscape Shaping the Financial Sector

The regulatory framework is of utmost importance in shaping the trajectory of the financial sector in North America, particularly in the economic powerhouses that are the United States and Canada. Significant transformations have occurred in the regulatory domain in recent years due to the repercussions of the 2008 financial crisis and the ongoing proliferation of technological innovations. These modifications are analyzed in depth in this section, with an emphasis on the ramifications for financial institutions. An extensive analysis is conducted on the regulatory landscape, encompassing a vast array of topics such as the complex transformations brought about by the Dodd-Frank Act and the recent adjustments implemented to accommodate the progress of financial technology (fintech). The narrative emphasizes the intricate relationship between promoting innovation and preserving stability, in addition to the impact that current legislation is having on the functioning of major financial establishments.

Conventional financial institutions encounter a distinct array of obstacles in the regulatory landscape. To effectively navigate the complexities presented by stringent compliance regulations, including those concerning data protection, cybersecurity, and anti-money laundering protocols, one needs to possess navigational expertise. This segment of the chapter examines the compliance obstacles encountered by prominent financial institutions, such as investment firms and banks, and illustrates how challenging it is for these establishments to synchronize their activities with the perpetually evolving mandates of regulatory agencies. Moreover, the debate revolves around the paradoxical function of regulations, which may serve as impediments to progress or as drivers of innovation. This chapter uses case studies and real-world examples to illustrate instances in which regulations have either effectively promoted responsible innovation or unintentionally impeded developments. To attain a nuanced equilibrium between fostering innovation and safeguarding consumer interests, the chapter underscores the criticality of ongoing dialogues between regulatory bodies and industry stakeholders.

Forces of Transformation

The financial environment in North America is currently undergoing a significant shift, which can be accelerated by three critical factors: technological advancements, regulatory development, and shifting consumer patterns. This continent, which is host to economic powerhouses including the United States and Canada, maneuvers through the ever-changing currents of the international financial arena. A new era is ushered in by the synergy of these forces.

Technological Innovations

Technological advancements have emerged as the principal drivers behind the disruption of the largest financial institutions in North America. The rapid and continuous progress of information technology has ushered in a transformative period in the finance industry, which has disrupted conventional business models and altered the conceptualization and provision of financial services. How fintech disrupts conventional banking using heightened competition, digital payment systems, blockchain integration, and adaptable modifications to meet customer demands and regulatory obstacles is illustrated in Figure 1.

Figure 1. The evolution of banking: Fintech's impact

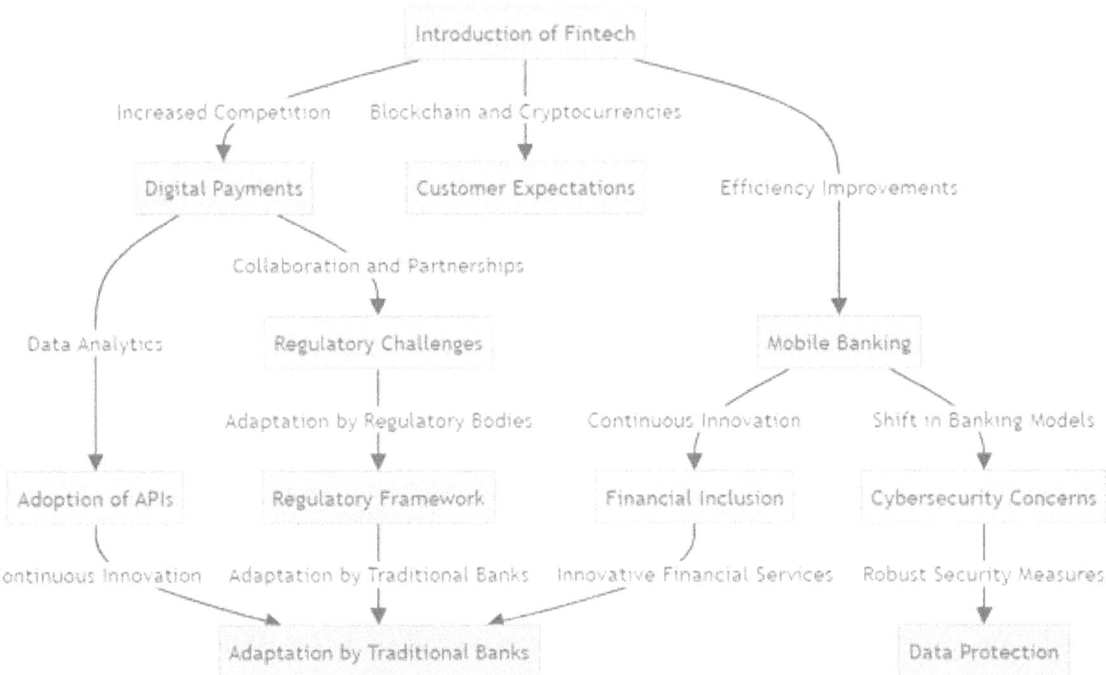

Impact of Fintech on Traditional Banking

Geographically speaking, the peer-to-peer lending market is segmented into the following regions: Asia-Pacific, Europe, North America, South America, the Middle East, and Africa. North America, which is home to renowned platforms such as LendingClub, Prosper, Upstart, CircleBack, and PeerForm, dominates this landscape. In this region, the United States is distinguished by having the highest number of FinTech adopters and the largest FinTech industry, per Ernst and Young (Ernst, 2014).

The World Payment Report for 2019 identifies the United States and the Eurozone as the leading two markets in terms of non-cash transactions when compared across regions. Nevertheless, mature markets, including North America and Europe, exhibit a comparatively sluggish growth rate of 7%. This can be attributed to the greater prevalence of digitization in those regions (Agarwal & Zhang, 2020).

Buchak et al. (Buchak, Matvos, Piskorski, & Seru, 2018) and Fuster et al. (Fuster, Plosser, Schnabl, & Vickery, 2019) examine the impact of FinTech lending on the mortgage market in the United States. The 20% reduction in mortgage processing time attributed to FinTech lenders such as LendingClub, Prosper, Upstart, CircleBack, and PeerForm is emphasized by Fuster et al. In contrast to the efficiency exhibited by conventional lenders, default rates for loans originated by FinTech are 25% lower. This finding poses a challenge to the "lax screening" hypothesis. Moreover, according to Jagtiani et al. (2019), FinTech lending is correlated with an increased likelihood of refinancing, the transmission of market interest rates to households, and the broadening of consumer credit accessibility.

The intelligent utilization of big data to evaluate credit risks is a significant benefit introduced by FinTech, as it contributes to the establishment of a more stable and diverse credit sector (Fuster, Goldsmith-Pinkham, Ramadorai, & Walther, 2022). The application of novel predictive algorithms is assessed, and the distributional ramifications of implementing machine learning methods in the mortgage market of the United States are investigated. The primary observation is that although a more advanced statistical technology aligns more closely with the predicted outcome variable, it is capable of producing more scattered predictions in comparison to the technology that came before it.

Crowe et al. (Crowe, Rysman, & Stavins, 2010) redirect attention toward the obstacles and potential of mobile payments within the market in the United States. The authors draw attention to supply-side obstacles, such as the absence of consolidation in the financial services and telecommunications sectors, which hinder the ability of a single company to spearhead and negotiate fruitful joint agreements. One obstacle to demand is the substantial expense associated with adopting new technologies, which is problematic considering the firmly established electronic payment system for credit and debit cards in the United States.

The substantial investments in Canada, where on the order of one hundred fintech start-ups, demonstrate that fintech's influence extends beyond lending, are further indications of this. In the previous year alone, nearly $20 billion was invested in fintech on a global scale. In Canada and other regions, a multitude of services are currently being implemented, encompassing robo advisors for investment advice, Apple Pay, Google Wallet, and peer-to-peer lending platforms such as the Lending Club. The fintech industry is an ever-changing landscape, with the prospect of further service developments (Wilkins, 2016).

Blockchain and Cryptocurrency

Regarding the introduction of blockchain technology, North America, particularly the United States, is the foremost region (Cywinska & Zawadzki, 2018). The advent of blockchain technology and cryptocurrencies in North America has brought about a contrast between obstacles and prospects, thereby transforming the conventional financial environment. One aspect that hinders the widespread adoption of cryptocurrencies is regulatory uncertainty, which arises from inconsistent regulations in different jurisdictions, resulting in a complex regulatory environment.

The absence of clarity hinders the integration and adoption of established financial systems by the general public. Furthermore, significant security concerns are present, having been exacerbated by prominent cryptocurrency breaches and frauds that have undermined confidence in the resilience of blockchain networks. These obstacles are exacerbated by the inherent volatility of cryptocurrency markets, which poses dangers for both businesses and investors. Further impediments to the technology's capacity to effectively manage the increasing volume of transactions are scalability concerns.

Notwithstanding these obstacles, nevertheless, there exists a terrain brimming with prospects for ingenuity and metamorphosis. Blockchain's decentralized architecture offers a distinctive prospect to democratize financial services by expanding accessibility to populations that are presently unbanked or have limited access to them. By providing access to traditional banking infrastructure for those without it, cryptocurrencies have the potential to revolutionize financial inclusion. Furthermore, the effectiveness improvements enabled by the immutability and transparency of blockchain technology can optimize financial procedures, diminishing dependence on intermediaries and decreasing operational expenditures.

Blockchain and cryptocurrencies are not only facilitating efficiency improvements but also stimulating a surge of innovation in the financial industry. The tokenization of assets and the emergence of decentralized finance (DeFi) are examples of how these technologies are generating new investment opportunities and financial instruments. In addition, cryptocurrencies provide a remedy for the inefficiencies inherent in cross-border transactions by facilitating remittances and international transactions that are both expedited and economical.

In light of the numerous challenges and opportunities that blockchain and cryptocurrency present, the financial sector in North America is poised to embark on a voyage that will fundamentally alter the course of finance in the area. Cryptocurrencies have been actively regulated in the United States and Canada, which have also supported Blockchain-based innovations and research. Canada is the global leader in blockchain technology (Li et al., 2021).

In March 2016, TMX Group, Payments Canada, and the Bank of Canada launched Project Jasper, a collaborative research initiative to investigate the prospective effects of distributed ledger technology (DLT) on Canadian payments. Beyond its toleration policy in the financial sector, the Canadian government actively engages in the investigation and implementation of Blockchain technology. This innovation serves to enhance administrative transparency by granting the public access to records about government expenditures. The website provides access to government expenditure records for the general public.

Furthermore, several governmental entities and organizations in Canada, such as the Bank of Canada, the Ontario Provincial Government, and the City of Toronto, are actively engaged in Blockchain research initiatives spearheaded by the Blockchain Research Institution (BRI). BRI was constructed in 2017 in Toronto. It is a preeminent research institution for commercial applications and Blockchain technology on a global scale. In approximately seventy initiatives, it has worked in tandem with nearly forty global authorities on a variety of subjects, such as Tencent, IBM, Microsoft, and others (Li et al., 2021).

Artificial Intelligence in Financial Decision-Making

Anticipated market dominance is in the North American region, where technologies such as artificial intelligence, machine learning, and digital learning were earlier adopted. The aforementioned supremacy can be ascribed to North America's preeminence in technological innovations and advancements, which are propelled by substantial investments in AI research and development. North America is anticipated to maintain its lead in artificial intelligence technologies for education (Osetskyi, Vitrenko, Tatomyr, Bilan, & Hirnyk, 2020).

The ubiquitous impact of artificial intelligence is apparent in its utilization for system operation and evaluation, disease diagnosis, suspect identification, industrial process optimization, document translation, text analysis, outcome prediction, and decision-making influence across diverse sectors. A Directive has been formulated by the federal government in North America to guide the implementation and utilization of automated decision systems. This action demonstrates the considerable attention that the government has paid to automated decision-making (Martin-Bariteau & Scassa, 2021).

Canada has established a notable standing in the field of AI development and deployment, boasting the third-highest number of AI experts worldwide. International corporations, investments, and the establishment of AI research centers are drawn to the nation. Prominent Canadian financial institutions have incorporated artificial intelligence (AI) advancements, thereby augmenting client offerings and provisions, specifically in the domains of wealth management and financial planning. Additionally, Canadian startups' AI applications in financial and business processes attract investor interest (Clements, 2019).

AI applications have a positive impact on the Canadian financial services sector by facilitating cost reductions in back-office operations, enhancing customer service, and automating processes. Through regtech innovations, AI improves advisory services, facilitates inter-application user enhancements, oversees portfolio allocation and client risk profiles, assists in credit assessment and underwriting, sustains research and valuation, and decreases the expense of regulatory compliance. In Canada, insurance companies and financial institutions employ AI to manage internal risks, a critical function in light of the global financial crisis of 2008. Automated contract analysis and other AI developments have the potential to significantly alter the Canadian legal services industry (Clements, 2019).

A multitude of disciplines, such as business, computer science, engineering, and medicine, have made extensive use of machine learning algorithms to forecast forthcoming occurrences. The surge in fraudulent activities within Canada's financial markets has engendered deliberation regarding the critical function that machine learning can play in forecasting and identifying indicators of fraudulent activity. Significantly, an area of research that requires attention is the application of machine learning to the prediction of fraudulent activities in financial markets (J. Perols, 2011; J. L. Perols, Bowen, Zimmermann, & Samba, 2017).

Prominent financial institutions in Canada are actively engaged in the digitalization competition, as evidenced by the double-digit annual growth of technological budgets at the largest banks. Financial services providers are placing increasing emphasis on artificial intelligence and big data, capitalizing on Canada's prowess in these domains. Customer relationship management, robo-advisory, and pilot systems for investment decision-making all make extensive use of these technologies. Nevertheless, the Canadian financial sector faces obstacles in its extensive implementation of novel technologies. These obstacles include the effectiveness of platforms, the quality of customer service, the education and training of human resources personnel, and the mitigation of adverse labor market effects. All of this needs to be done in the context of escalating technological expenditures and intensifying competition (Khoroshilov, 2018).

Regulatory Evolution

Not solely technological advancements but also dynamic regulatory modifications are causing a profound shift in the North American financial sector. Regulatory bodies and governments are currently reassessing their supervision frameworks to adapt to the swift rate of change and strike a balance between promoting innovation and preserving stability.

Government Policies Shaping the Financial Landscape

The financial landscape of North America is substantially shaped by government policies, which need to strike a delicate equilibrium between encouraging innovation and ensuring stability. To foster an environment conducive to innovation, numerous governmental bodies proactively assist in fintech ventures via regulatory sandboxes, grants, and partnerships with influential industry participants. The objective of this proactive strategy is to facilitate technological progress in the financial industry, thereby enhancing the region's competitiveness on an international level.

Concurrently, endeavors toward digital transformation emphasize the acknowledgment of the imperative to adjust to changes in technology. To reduce dependence on conventional currency transactions, governments promote the extensive implementation of digital payment systems and allocate resources towards infrastructure development that fosters the growth of a resilient digital financial ecosystem. Governments are promoting the development of inclusive financial products that are tailored to diverse demographics and implementing programs to bring banking services to marginalized areas as part of a broader strategy to increase financial inclusion.

With the continuous evolution of the financial landscape, there is an increasing emphasis on sustainability, cybersecurity, and consumer protection. Governments enforce rigorous data protection legislation, tackle concerns such as fraudulent activities, and promote openness in the disclosure of environmental, social, and governance (ESG) metrics. Concurrently, regulatory frameworks are implemented to strengthen cybersecurity protocols and guarantee the ability of financial institutions to withstand the increasing menace of cyber assaults. The comprehensive strategy outlined above demonstrates a deliberate attempt to seize the advantages brought about by technological advancements while also minimizing potential drawbacks and protecting the welfare of customers in a financial environment that is progressively becoming more digital. Within this ever-changing context, the interdependence of the public and private sectors assumes utmost significance, necessitating the implementation of cooperative approaches that harmonize inventive thinking with efficient risk mitigation.

Compliance Challenges and Opportunities

Established financial institutions, rooted in traditional methods, face the challenging endeavor of adapting to digital changes, which requires significant modifications to current compliance systems. The incorporation of disruptive technologies has both advantages and challenges for traditional banks. While legacy banks encounter obstacles throughout this transition, those with a proactive mindset capitalize on the chance to enhance compliance processes by implementing automation, artificial intelligence, and machine learning. These tools provide opportunities to improve efficiency in risk assessment, fraud detection, and regulatory reporting.

In terms of regulations, the increasing control of Know Your Customer (KYC) and Anti-Money Laundering (AML) standards presents difficulties for institutions in the whole financial industry. Fintech businesses face limitations in resources as they work towards meeting these changing criteria. However, this challenge presents a chance for innovation. Entrepreneurs in the field of financial technology are investigating innovative methods, utilizing technologies such as blockchain to ensure secure and transparent verification of identities. By doing this, they not only tackle compliance difficulties but also can completely transform the way financial institutions interact with regulatory regimes.

Within the domain of cryptocurrencies, there is a significant presence of regulatory ambiguity, which makes it challenging to ensure compliance. The decentralized and transnational characteristics of these digital assets pose a difficulty for governments in defining precise categorizations and formulating taxation rules. Nevertheless, this lack of clarity provides opportunities for actively engaging with regulators. By actively engaging in the process of developing Bitcoin rules, companies may establish themselves as industry leaders in compliance, thereby cultivating confidence among users and investors. Furthermore, the inclusion of digital financial services brings an additional level of intricacy due to the associated issues regarding privacy. Organizations that place high importance on implementing strong data protection measures, according to requirements like the General Data Protection Regulation (GDPR), not only guarantee compliance but also establish confidence with customers, thereby fostering a resilient and responsible financial environment.

Changing Consumer Behavior

The financial terrain of North America is seeing a significant transformation in reaction to evolving consumer behaviors. This section examines the evolving changes in how individuals engage with and perceive financial services.

Shifts in Consumer Interaction with Financial Services

The way consumers engage with financial services is seeing significant changes due to the combination of technical improvements, societal expectations, and growing preferences. The primary change is the widespread use of digital channels, with consumers increasingly preferring online platforms and mobile applications for a range of financial activities. The digital transformation not only improves convenience but also establishes new benchmarks for the velocity and effectiveness of financial services.

Concurrently, the emergence of fintech platforms has upset the conventional banking model by providing inventive and customer-focused solutions. Consumers currently interact with a wide range of fintech services, including digital wallets, robo-advisors, and peer-to-peer lending platforms. The agility and customer-centric attitude of fintech are fundamentally transforming the way individuals access and utilize financial products. The disruption also affects the personalization and customization of financial experiences, where advanced analytics and artificial intelligence are used to customize services based on individual preferences, risk tolerance, and financial objectives. The shift away from standardized banking practices is raising client standards and creating a need for customized financial solutions.

Furthermore, the growing importance lies in the smooth incorporation of several financial services into a cohesive user experience. Consumers anticipate a comprehensive approach that integrates banking, investment, insurance, and budgeting into a unified platform. This phenomenon is promoting cooperation between conventional financial institutions and fintech companies to provide all-encompassing services. Moreover, with the advancement of technology enabling broader access to financial services, there is a growing focus on ensuring security and fostering trust. The industry is making significant investments in strong cybersecurity safeguards and transparent processes to build consumer confidence in the protection of their financial data.

Rise of Digital Banking and Online Financial Management

The rise of digital banks, which operate solely online, is overshadowing traditional brick-and-mortar banking models. These digital banks provide users with unparalleled convenience and accessibility. These establishments provide convenient access to financial services using online platforms and mobile apps, removing the necessity for physical branches. Digital banks improve cost efficiency by reducing overhead costs related to traditional infrastructure. This results in cheaper fees, more competitive loan conditions, and greater interest rates on savings, which makes them increasingly attractive to consumers who are mindful of costs.

Concurrently, the increase in digital banking is accompanied by the upsurge in online financial management tools that enable individuals to assume authority over their accounts. Personal finance applications, which include functions for monitoring expenses, creating budgets, and setting financial objectives, have become essential tools for contemporary consumers. Moreover, robo-advisors, which are automated investing platforms guided by algorithms, provide customers with convenient entry to diversified investment portfolios at reduced costs in comparison to conventional investment management services. In this era of online financial management, there is also a connection with the growing interest in cryptocurrencies. This integration enables users to monitor and manage both traditional and digital assets through a single interface.

Nevertheless, the rise of digital banking and online financial management is not devoid of obstacles. Financial institutions and service providers need to carefully evaluate security risks, regulatory difficulties, and the need to find a balance between innovation and risk management. As customers progressively adopt new digital solutions, the financial industry needs to effectively address these difficulties to guarantee the ongoing prosperity and safety of these developing financial ecosystems.

Generation-Specific Trends Influencing Financial Preferences

Distinct financial preferences and behaviors are observed among different generations in North America, influenced by their individual life experiences and the changing technology world. Individuals belonging to the baby boomer generation, born from 1946 to 1964, typically exhibit a strong inclination towards conventional banking systems, favoring physical bank branches and making conservative investing decisions. The current generation places great importance on retirement planning, highlighting the necessity for financial goods and services that are specifically designed to cater to their focus on stability.

Generation X, born from 1965 to 1980, seeks a harmonious equilibrium between conventional practices and progressive approaches when it comes to their financial preferences. Although they are at ease with traditional banking methods, they are open to embracing new financial instruments and advancements. The investment methods of Gen X are influenced by their prioritization of goals such as housing and wealth creation. Their varied lifestyle requirements, which encompass a strong emphasis on maintaining a healthy equilibrium between work and personal life, contribute to a sophisticated approach to financial management.

Millennials, individuals born between 1981 and 1996, are early adopters of fintech and digital banking. The current generation demonstrates a pronounced inclination toward utilizing mobile banking applications, digital wallets, and other modes of payment. Millennials exhibit a strong inclination towards socially responsible investing and express a desire for sustainable financial choices. Additionally, they encounter distinctive obstacles such as burdensome student loan debt and postponed acquisition of homes. Generation Z, born after 1996, is identified as digital natives who are actively influencing the future of finance. They have a strong preference for cutting-edge financial technologies and prioritize efficiency and swiftness in transactions. This indicates a tendency towards entrepreneurial pursuits and a keen curiosity in exploring various investment opportunities at an early stage.

These generational groupings share shared characteristics such as a growing inclination towards socially responsible investing, a desire for clear and open communication from financial institutions, and the emergence of robo-advisors and AI-powered financial planning tools. Furthermore, there is a growing prevalence of collaborative financial arrangements, such as shared financial objectives within families. This emphasizes the need for financial institutions and fintech companies to modify their services to cater to the varied and changing requirements of consumers across various age demographics.

Disruptive Innovations

Identifying Up-and-Coming Innovations Poised to Reshape the Industry

North America's financial industry is seeing a wave of transformational innovations that are challenging old standards and creating new approaches to offering financial services. These nascent trends can profoundly transform the industry. The initial wave of advancements centers around decentralization, as shown by the emergence of Decentralized Finance (DeFi). This encompasses an investigation into the fundamental ideas of DeFi and its influence on conventional banking, along with an analysis of decentralized systems for lending, borrowing, and trading. Furthermore, the focus is on Open Banking Initiatives, clarifying the ideas, presenting successful implementations through case studies, and examining the advantages and difficulties for both consumers and institutions.

The subsequent wave of advancements explores state-of-the-art technologies. RegTech advancements provide insights into the uses and role of Regulatory Technology (RegTech) in compliance operations, as well as the integration problems and possibilities encountered by financial institutions. Quantum Computing in Finance examines the implementation of quantum computing and its significance, as well as possible uses in risk management, portfolio optimization, and cryptography. The study of Biometric Security and Authentication focuses on the application of fingerprint and facial recognition technology in the field of finance, to improve security measures in digital transactions. It also takes into consideration the complex relationship between security and privacy issues.Finally, the concept of Embedded Finance is examined, encompassing its precise definition, illustrating instances of embedded finance models, and examining the partnership between conventional financial institutions and non-financial organizations, as well as its consequences for customer experience and market expansion. The last innovation emphasized is Sustainable and Impact Investing, which explores the increasing interest in investments that are ecologically and socially responsible. This includes the incorporation of ESG considerations in financial decision-making and its impact on investment strategies and market dynamics. Table 1 provides a concise overview of significant advancements in finance throughout North America. It specifically

Table 1. Up-and-coming innovations in North American finance

Innovation	Description	Impact
DeFi	Decentralized finance, disrupts traditional banking	Increased inclusion, regulatory challenges
Open Banking	Shares data, improves experience, raises concerns	Enhanced competition, privacy issues
RegTech	Streamlines compliance faces integration challenges	Better compliance, adoption hurdles
Quantum Computing	Accelerates finance tasks, challenges in implementation	Faster calculations, high implementation costs
Biometric Security	Enhances digital security, balances privacy concerns	Improved authentication, privacy considerations
Embedded Finance	Integrates into non-financial platforms, regulatory challenges	Seamless services, regulatory hurdles
Sustainable Investing	Focus on ESG, influences investment strategies	Ethical investments, standardization challenges

focuses on the characteristics and effects of these innovations, ranging from the transformative impact of decentralized finance to the ethical considerations associated with sustainable investing.

Potential Challenges and Opportunities for Early Adopters

Identifying Up-and-Coming Innovations Poised to Reshape the Industry

Individuals who readily adopt disruptive ideas need to confront both problems and opportunities that can significantly influence their market positions. A significant obstacle arises from the lack of clear regulations in response to the rapid advancement of innovative technologies such as blockchain and cryptocurrencies. Those who embrace new technologies at an early stage may encounter a challenging environment, dealing with regulatory requirements that may result in legal complications and operational difficulties. Furthermore, the incorporation of novel technologies into well-established financial institutions that utilize outdated systems poses an additional challenge, characterized by intricacies in data management, apprehensions regarding security, and difficulties in achieving interoperability.

Notwithstanding these difficulties, individuals who embrace new ideas and technologies have the potential to achieve significant advantages. Market leadership is a significant benefit that enables pioneers to establish themselves as frontrunners in the market and acquire a competitive advantage over slower competitors. This can enhance the reputation of the business and appeal to a consumer base that is actively seeking cutting-edge financial solutions. The adoption of emerging technologies can bring about enhanced operational efficiency, decreased transaction costs, and novel service delivery, therefore paving the way for cost efficiency and innovation. Establishing strategic alliances with fintech startups and technology suppliers presents additional prospects, granting entry to innovative solutions, broadening the range of services, and facilitating a more adaptable reaction to changing market requirements. Figure 2 provides a graphic representation of the obstacles, opportunities, and strategic factors in North America's financial business. It emphasizes the crucial importance of embracing disruptive ideas early on to achieve success.

Figure 2. Financial industry: Challenges and opportunities

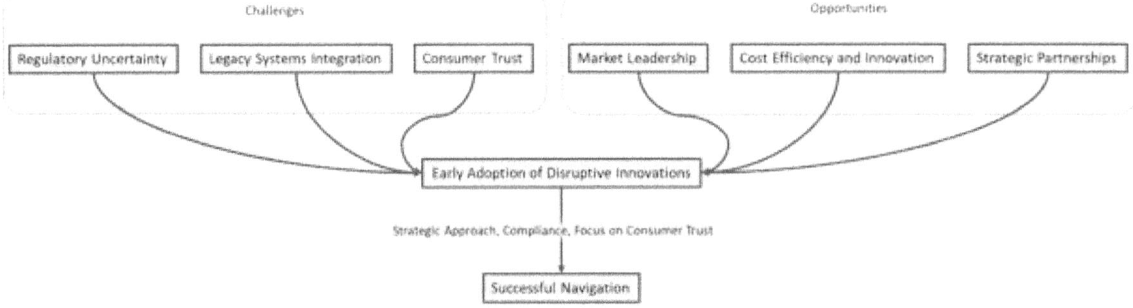

Future Scenarios and Trends

Scenario Analysis

A strategic framework for imagining possible futures in the financial sector of North America is offered by scenario analysis. It is possible to obtain insights into the variety of possibilities that could influence the environment in the years to come by exploring a variety of scenarios. In the first scenario, dubbed the Status Quo Continuation, steady economic conditions, slow technical improvements, and little regulatory changes characterize a future in which existing trends continue without major disruption. In this context, established financial behemoths continue to rule the market by gradually adapting to changing customer demands. In the second scenario, Regulatory Overhaul, regulatory agencies adopt significant changes in the future to handle new opportunities and difficulties, especially in fintech, cryptocurrency, and consumer protection. While clear regulations encourage innovation, institutions first encounter difficulties while adjusting to new compliance standards.

The final scenario, titled "Technological Revolution," imagines a day in the future when cutting-edge innovations in blockchain, artificial intelligence, and quantum computing completely alter a sector. The financial industry's power dynamics are altered as a result of this disruption, which gives rise to new, tech-driven competitors. The fourth scenario, Global Economic Shifts, imagines a future in which trade disputes, geopolitical upheavals, or economic crises have a major impact on global economic changes and North American banking. In this scenario, financial institutions navigate obstacles and take advantage of new opportunities as they adjust to a shifting global marketplace. The final scenario, "Consumer-Led Transformation," imagines a time when changing customer preferences will force financial services to change. Traditional institutions are under pressure to change as consumer-focused fintech disruptors rise in prominence. These forces include a growing demand for individualized, tech-savvy services as well as a desire for sustainable and ethical investments. The sixth scenario, "Cybersecurity Crisis," examines a future in which the financial industry is severely disrupted by a major cybersecurity compromise. Widespread assaults on financial institutions can hurt consumer confidence by eroding trust, raising regulatory scrutiny, and focusing more attention on cybersecurity measures. Stakeholders in the North American financial sector should strategically position themselves to prosper in a changing and dynamic environment by examining these situations. Table 2 presents six possibilities for the financial sector in North America, outlining the relevant elements and consequences, including regulatory modifications, technological advancements, and effects on the world economy.

Predictive Trends

Several significant factors that will shape the financial landscape of North America in the future highlight the necessity for financial institutions to continue being adaptable and progressive. A big change is occurring with the emergence of Decentralized Finance (DeFi), as decentralized platforms pose a threat to established intermediaries. Blockchain and smart contracts have the potential to have a significant impact on lending, borrowing, and investment practices. As this impact grows, there will also be a greater focus on dangers and regulatory issues in the developing DeFi field.

Table 2. North American financial industry scenario analysis

Scenario	Key Factors	Implications
Status Quo Continuation	Stable economy, gradual tech advances, minimal regulations	Traditional giants maintain dominance and incremental changes.
Regulatory Overhaul	Focus on fintech, cryptocurrency, consumer protection	Regulatory clarity drives innovation and initial adaptation challenges.
Technological Revolution	Advances in AI, blockchain, quantum computing	Disruption of traditional models, the rise of tech-driven entrants.
Global Economic Shifts	Trade tensions, geopolitical shifts, economic crises	Financial institutions adapt, navigate challenges, and seize opportunities.
Consumer-Led Transformation	Demand for personalized, tech-savvy, sustainable services	Pressure on traditional institutions, the rise of consumer-centric fintech.
Cybersecurity Crisis	Large-scale cyberattacks, trust loss, increased regulation	Focus on cybersecurity, shifts in consumer confidence.

Concurrently, the financial industry is changing due to the increased incorporation of Artificial Intelligence (AI). As big data analytics and AI combine to provide more accurate risk assessments and individualized financial advice and decision-making, ethical questions about responsibility and transparency are brought to light. Furthermore, an increasing desire for investments that are in line with environmental, social, and governance (ESG) principles is reflected in the growth of sustainable and socially responsible investing. This strategy entails pushing financial institutions to contribute to sustainability, influencing market dynamics, and incorporating ESG metrics into conventional investing methods.

Furthermore, the investigation of digital currencies and central bank digital currencies (CBDCs) is changing the financial landscape. This covers the function of stablecoins and cryptocurrencies in day-to-day transactions, the efforts made by central banks to put CBDCs into effect, and the consequences for monetary policy, financial stability, and international trade. Additionally, Open Banking is speeding up, encouraging cooperation between fintechs and traditional banks, giving users more control over their financial data, and opening up access to a wider range of financial services. However, in a networked financial ecosystem, this evolution creates security and privacy concerns. The financial sector needs to be strengthened against cyber risks, and industry stakeholders and regulators need to work together to implement strong measures to counter evolving cyber threats, such as integrating cutting-edge technologies like blockchain. Cybersecurity stands out as a top priority at the same time. Finally, the financial sector expects regulatory adaptations to continue, emphasizing the need for international collaboration in developing uniform regulatory frameworks while striking a balance between innovation consumer protection, and financial stability. Financial institutions hoping to prosper in the changing financial landscape of North America will need to recognize these trends and take proactive measures to adjust to them.

CONCLUSION

In summary, the North American financial system is poised for an unparalleled metamorphosis. This chapter has carefully looked at the current situation in the continent's financial sector, highlighting the powerful presence of long-standing giants and the complex regulatory framework that has historically controlled their activities. But this is only the beginning of the story; there are more disruptive forces at work that are changing the core structures of finance.

Innovative technology, changing consumer habits, and developing regulatory frameworks have come together to create a tsunami of innovation that is upending the status quo. Blockchain and artificial intelligence-driven fintech companies are upending established banking practices and bringing in a new era where financial services are experiences rather than just transactions. As a result of the shift in consumer behavior brought about by digital natives, online banking and financial management are now the standard rather than the exception.

The chapter has examined case studies of prosperous disruptors to show how agile and creative businesses are making their way in a sector that has historically been dominated by giants. Patterns show through from these case studies, suggesting new directions that will continue to shape North America's financial scene for years to come.

Going ahead, industry players can use the future scenarios and predictive patterns presented in this chapter as a reference. To succeed in a constantly changing environment, both new and established institutions will need to be able to innovate and adapt. External influences will add layers of complexity, requiring an agile and proactive approach to navigate the unpredictable terrain. Examples of these factors include global events and economic developments.

REFERENCES

Agarwal, S., & Zhang, J. (2020). FinTech, lending and payment innovation: A review. *Asia-Pacific Journal of Financial Studies*, *49*(3), 353–367. doi:10.1111/ajfs.12294

Buchak, G., Matvos, G., Piskorski, T., & Seru, A. (2018). Fintech, regulatory arbitrage, and the rise of shadow banks. *Journal of Financial Economics*, *130*(3), 453–483. doi:10.1016/j.jfineco.2018.03.011

Clements, R. (2019). Fintech in Canada. In Research Handbook on the Law of Fintech. Digital Innovation and Technology Law Lab, Digital Law Network, University of Padova.

Crowe, M. D., Rysman, M., & Stavins, J. (2010). *Mobile payments in the United States at retail point of sale: current market and future prospects*. FRB of Boston Public Policy Discussion Paper (10-2).

Cywinska, M., & Zawadzki, K. (2018). Performance appraisal system for administrative staff: A pilot implementation study at the University of Warsaw. *Economic and Social Development: Book of Proceedings,* 332-340.

Ernst, Y. (2014). *Landscaping UK Fintech*. Ernst and Young LLP.

Francis, D. (2014). Should the US & Canada merge? Journalist Diane Francis argues that it would create an unstoppable North American superpower! *New York Times Upfront, 147*(6), 8-13.

Fuster, A., Goldsmith-Pinkham, P., Ramadorai, T., & Walther, A. (2022). Predictably unequal? The effects of machine learning on credit markets. *The Journal of Finance*, *77*(1), 5–47. doi:10.1111/jofi.13090

Fuster, A., Plosser, M., Schnabl, P., & Vickery, J. (2019). The role of technology in mortgage lending. *Review of Financial Studies*, *32*(5), 1854–1899. doi:10.1093/rfs/hhz018

Geloso, V. (2022). The Historical Evolution of Canadian Living Standards. In Oxford Research Encyclopedia of Economics and Finance. doi:10.1093/acrefore/9780190625979.013.791

Horton, J. (1979). *Financing North American economic cooperation*. Paper presented at the Forum for Social Economics.

Jorgenson, D. (2004). *Economic Growth in Canada and the United States in the Information Age*. Academic Press.

Khoroshilov, E. (2018). New Technologies in Canadian Financial Sector: Artificial Intelligence and Big Data. *Ekonomika, Politika, Kultura*, (10), 50-65.

Li, Z., Zhong, R. Y., Tian, Z.-G., Dai, H.-N., Barenji, A. V., & Huang, G. Q. (2021). Industrial Blockchain: A state-of-the-art Survey. *Robotics and Computer-integrated Manufacturing*, *70*, 102124. doi:10.1016/j.rcim.2021.102124

Martin-Bariteau, F., & Scassa, T. (2021). *Artificial intelligence and the law in Canada. Artificial Intelligence and the Law in Canada*. LexisNexis Canada.

Osetskyi, V., Vitrenko, A., Tatomyr, I., Bilan, S., & Hirnyk, Y. (2020). Artificial intelligence application in education: Financial implications and prospects. *Financial and Credit Activity Problems of Theory and Practice, 2*(33), 574-584.

Perols, J. (2011). Financial statement fraud detection: An analysis of statistical and machine learning algorithms. *Auditing*, *30*(2), 19–50. doi:10.2308/ajpt-50009

Perols, J. L., Bowen, R. M., Zimmermann, C., & Samba, B. (2017). Finding needles in a haystack: Using data analytics to improve fraud prediction. *The Accounting Review*, *92*(2), 221–245. doi:10.2308/accr-51562

Pramanik, H. S., Kirtania, M., & Pani, A. K. (2019). Essence of digital transformation—Manifestations at large financial institutions from North America. *Future Generation Computer Systems*, *95*, 323–343. doi:10.1016/j.future.2018.12.003

Puig, S. (2019). *The United States-Mexico-Canada Agreement: a glimpse into the geoeconomic world order*. Academic Press.

Reyes, E. D. (1999). Regionalism: The Case of North America. In Economic Integration in NAFTA and the EU: Deficient Institutionality (pp. 161-177). Springer.

Rugman, A. M. (2004). *North American Economic and Financial Integration*. Emerald Group Publishing Limited. doi:10.1016/S1064-4857(2004)10

Wilkins, C. (2016). *Fintech and the Financial Ecosystem: Evolution or Revolution?* Remarks to Payments Canada.

Chapter 10
The Rise of AI in Middle Eastern Fintech With the Case Studies From the UAE and Turkey

Hooman Razavi
https://orcid.org/0009-0005-7944-672X
Tecnologico de Monterrey, Mexico

Ali Habibnia
Virginia Tech, USA

ABSTRACT

This chapter explores the dynamic FinTech landscape in the Middle East with a focus on the UAE and Turkey by considering the impact of cutting-edge technologies, particularly artificial intelligence (AI). Amidst rapid economic changes and a burgeoning youth population, FinTech has emerged as a pivotal force driving innovation. The UAE and Turkey, positioned as regional FinTech hubs, attract significant investments, fostering vibrant startup ecosystems. Analyzing statistical insights and technological trends, this chapter unravels the unique factors propelling FinTech adoption. It delves into the integration of emerging technologies and addresses challenges, opportunities, and future trends. Tailored for finance professionals, policymakers, entrepreneurs, and academics, this chapter aims to provide a concise resource for navigating and contributing to the evolving FinTech scene in the Middle East.

INTRODUCTION

The strategic global location of the Middle East emerges as a foundation for the thriving FinTech landscape within the region. Functioning as a financial gateway that seamlessly connects Asia, Europe, and Africa, the Middle East becomes an enticing hub for international trade and investment (Akmal, S., 2023). This positioning not only appeals to financial institutions but also draws FinTech companies seeking access to a well-connected market (Abdeldayem, M., 2023). The region's proximity to major trade routes and shipping lanes further elevates its significance as a hub for financial activities, making it an

DOI: 10.4018/979-8-3693-1561-3.ch010

attractive destination for businesses engaged in cross-border transactions and trade finance (Lukonga, I., 2021). The Middle East's strategic location, fostering global connectivity, is particularly advantageous in the FinTech sector, where digital financial services transcend national borders. This connectivity not only attracts investments but also positions the region as an ideal environment for the development and deployment of innovative FinTech solutions (Saba, I., 2019). Overall, the Middle East's strategic global location serves as a catalyst for the robust growth of FinTech, offering unparalleled opportunities for international collaboration, trade, and technological innovation.

Beside this, The Middle East boasts immense potential across various sectors, presenting a fertile ground for growth and innovation. In terms of human resources, the region is endowed with a young, dynamic population that is increasingly tech-savvy and well-educated. This demographic dividend positions the Middle East as a pool of talent ready to drive innovation and entrepreneurship (Cusolito, 2022). The startup ecosystem is growing, with cities like Dubai, Istanbul and Riyadh emerging as dynamic hubs for innovation and technology (Baird, 2023; Gur, N., 2023). Government initiatives supporting entrepreneurship and the establishment of startup accelerators have further fueled the ecosystem's growth. Additionally, the Middle East's sizable and interconnected population creates a substantial market for FinTech. As the region increasingly embraces digital transformation, the FinTech market is poised for significant expansion, with opportunities to address financial inclusion challenges and cater to the diverse financial needs of the population. The convergence of a youthful workforce, a thriving startup ecosystem, and a rapidly evolving FinTech market positions the Middle East as a dynamic player on the global stage, poised for substantial contributions to the future of human capital, entrepreneurship, and financial technology (Evron, 2024). Human resource excellence serves as the heartbeat of organizational growth, while young talent injects innovation and vitality, propelling the company towards a dynamic and prosperous future (Mason, 2022). In Figure 1, a global map is depicted, showcasing the years when

Figure 1. Year in which deaths started to outnumber births by country
(Buchholz, 2022).

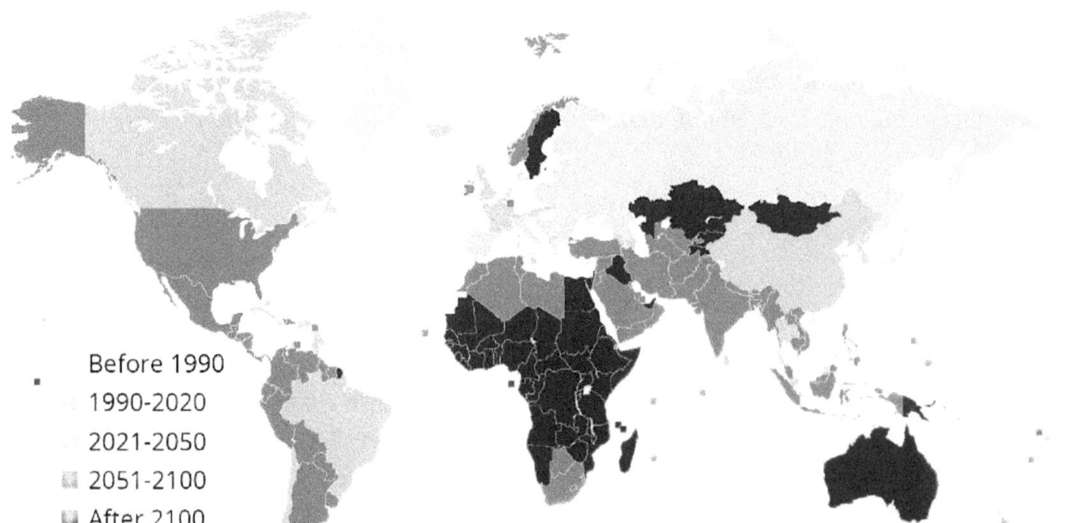

deaths surpassed births by country. Notably, the Middle East and Africa emerge as regions characterized by a steadily increasing young population. This demographic potential in terms of human resources stands as a significant catalyst for development. The burgeoning youth population in the Middle East and Africa represents a valuable asset, offering the prospect to leverage this demographic advantage for sustained and impactful development. As these regions progress through the demographic transition (figure 2), strategic investments in education, healthcare, and employment opportunities have the potential to unlock the full economic and innovative potential of this youthful demographic, shaping the course of global development.

Situated at the crossroads of Asia and Europe, Dubai stands as a vibrant hub for commerce within the Gulf region. Its strategic location, coupled with visionary infrastructure development, has transformed the city into a global epicenter for trade and business activities (Sharafi, 2022). Dubai's meteoric rise as a commercial hub is not merely confined to its geographical advantage but is underscored by a commitment to innovation, creating an environment conducive to international investment and trade. The city's bustling ports, cutting-edge free zones, and a dynamic business ecosystem make it an indispensable player in shaping the economic landscape of the Gulf and beyond (Yasin, 2022). Similarly, Istanbul, straddling two continents, acts as a bridge between Asia and Europe, further enhancing the global economic significance of the region (Cengiz, 2019). The city's unique position along the Bosphorus Strait has historically made it a pivotal center for trade and cultural exchange. Today, Istanbul continues to play a crucial role in connecting East and West, fostering economic cooperation and facilitating the seamless flow of goods and ideas. With its rich history, diverse cultural influences, and strategic location, Istanbul serves as a conduit for businesses looking to capitalize on the synergies between two continents, contributing to the broader narrative of global economic integration (Dogan, 2017). This chapter focuses on dissecting and comparing the FinTech scenes in the UAE and Turkey, providing insights into their emerging trends and key players.

Figure 2. Total population across the Middle East and North Africa from 1990 to 2050 (UN DESA, 2019)

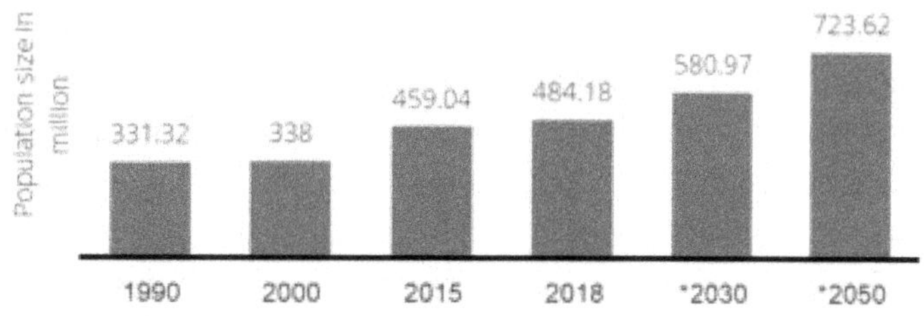

The FinTech revolution unleashes a transformative wave, fundamentally reshaping how we perceive, access, and interact with financial services in an era of unprecedented technological advancements (Barroso, 2022). At the heart of this transformative wave in FinTech lies AI, a technological juggernaut that is redefining how financial services are conceived, delivered, and experienced (Acemoglu, D., & Restrepo, P., 2020). AI, with its capacity for advanced data analysis, pattern recognition, and machine learning, is revolutionizing the financial landscape (King, 2018). It empowers institutions to enhance customer experiences through personalized services, streamline operations for greater efficiency, and mitigate risks with predictive analytics (Comin, D., & Mestieri, M., 2022). From algorithmic trading to credit scoring, AI algorithms are optimizing decision-making processes, fostering a more agile and responsive financial ecosystem. This infusion of intelligence into financial technologies not only augments traditional services but also opens doors to innovative solutions, shaping the future of finance in ways that were once deemed futuristic. As AI continues to evolve, its role in FinTech is set to deepen, ushering in an era where smart technologies drive financial inclusivity, resilience, and unparalleled user experiences (Ruslan, 2022). According to a September 2022 survey by Insider Intelligence involving 600 senior technology professionals in financial firms (Figure 3), the anticipated growth in the adoption of artificial intelligence (AI) within the finance sector is evident. In 2022, nearly half of executives foresaw widespread AI adoption in their companies, with expectations that, by 2025, this ratio would be surpassed, particularly in critical AI implementation. The results of the survey indicate a notable upward trajectory in the adoption of artificial intelligence (AI) within the finance sector.

Figure 3. AI adoption rate in financial businesses worldwide in 2022 and 2025
(Insider Intelligence, 2022)

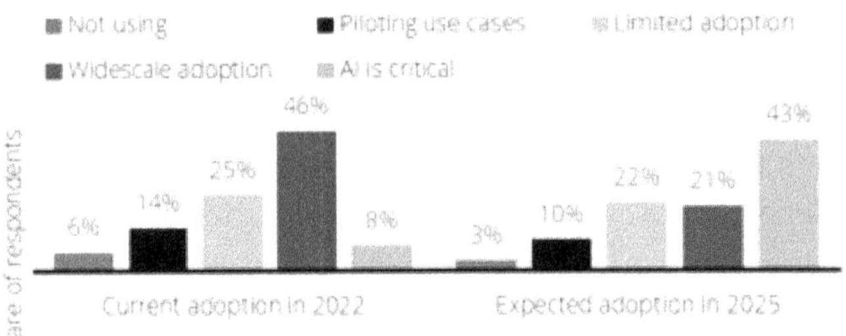

FinTech plays a pivotal role in the economic growth and developmental infrastructure of business activities, emerging as a critical component for global progress. In the Middle East, a region poised for significance in the future world, the importance of FinTech is expected to amplify. As Middle East positions itself as a hub for innovation and economic advancement, the role of FinTech becomes increasingly vital in shaping the future of the region. Notably, the trajectory of FinTech startups in the Middle East is driven by key factors such as AI and digital technologies, acting as the primary catalysts propelling development in this dynamic sector. The integration of these technologies not only fosters innovation but also positions this region as a frontrunner in the global FinTech landscape, contributing to the overall progress of the region. The primary objectives in conducting these investigations are to offer valuable insights that can guide strategic decision-making and advance the ongoing discourse surrounding the evolution of FinTech in the Middle East. The focal motivations of this chapter include:

- **Analyzing the Capacity of the Middle East for FinTech:**
    - Understand the readiness of the Middle East for FinTech integration.
    - Assess the digital infrastructure and technological landscape.
    - Evaluate regulatory frameworks and financial literacy in the region.

- **Characteristics of FinTech in the Middle East:**
    - Identify unique features defining the FinTech sector in the Middle East.
    - Explore prevailing technologies and market dynamics.
    - Understand specific challenges and opportunities in the regional context.
- **Addressing Challenges, Opportunities, and Future Trends:**
    - Recognize and discuss obstacles faced by the Middle East's FinTech industry.
    - Explore potential growth areas and developmental opportunities.
    - Anticipate and analyze future trends shaping the FinTech landscape.
- **Notable FinTech Startups in the Middle East:**
    - Highlight innovative FinTech startups in the region.
    - Understand the business models and contributions of these startups.
    - Recognize the impact of startups on the broader FinTech ecosystem.
- **Analysis of Statistical Insights of Middle East Growth:**
    - Examine quantitative indicators to gauge the growth of FinTech.
    - Analyze investment levels, user adoption rates, and transaction volumes.
    - Gain insights into the trajectory and evolution of the FinTech industry.
- **Islamic Banking and Regulation:**
    - Explore the role of Islamic banking in the Middle East.
    - Understand regulatory frameworks governing FinTech in compliance with Islamic principles.
    - Examine how FinTech aligns with Islamic finance and the measures ensuring adherence.

In the subsequent sections of this chapter, we embark on a comprehensive exploration, beginning with a detailed "background" analysis that draws on recent research to establish a robust foundation for understanding the contemporary FinTech landscape in the Middle East. Progressing from there, the "FinTech Landscape in the Middle East" segment provides a panoramic overview of the region's financial technology ecosystem, laying the groundwork for a nuanced comprehension. The narrative then delves into the "Country-Specific Focus: UAE and Turkey," where two compelling cases are thoroughly examined, offering insights into the unique dynamics of FinTech within these pivotal regional hubs. The investigation extends its reach into "Investments and Startups," a crucial section dedicated to scrutinizing investment trends and profiling noteworthy startups shaping the FinTech landscape. The spotlight then shifts to "Technological Integration in FinTech," where a focused discussion unfolds on the cutting-edge technologies driving the evolution of FinTech in the Middle East, with a specific emphasis on Artificial Intelligence (AI). Navigating through the intricate terrain of challenges and opportunities, "Challenges and Opportunities" provides a comprehensive understanding of the obstacles faced and potential avenues for growth within the FinTech sector in the Middle East. The exploration continues with "Future Trends and Forecasts," projecting anticipated trends in the region's FinTech landscape. Gazing towards the future, "Future Research Directions" outlines envisioned paths and capacities for ongoing research, creating a roadmap for sustained scholarly inquiry. Finally, the "conclusion" section synthesizes the wealth of findings and insights accumulated throughout the chapter, providing a conclusive perspective on the dynamic and evolving FinTech scene in the Middle East.

BACKGROUND

The burgeoning interest in Financial Technology within the Middle East is evident through a myriad of studies that provide insights into the evolving dynamics of the region. In recent years, numerous researchers have dedicated their efforts to exploring the emergence of FinTech in Middle Eastern countries and charting the substantial growth witnessed in this sector. The spotlight on technological advancements and innovative financial solutions in the region reflects a profound interest in leveraging cutting-edge technologies to transform the traditional financial landscape (Razavi, H., 2023a). These studies not only shed light on the evolving nature of FinTech but also contribute valuable insights into the transformative journey of the financial industry across the Middle East.

Several researchers have undertaken an exploration of the FinTech landscape in Turkey, delving into the unique perspective and dynamics shaping the financial technology sector in the country. In the study conducted by (Fayda, 2020), the emphasis lies on aiding investors in their decision-making process when funding FinTech startups. Through structured interviews with angel investors and venture capitalists, Fayda establishes a framework of key performance indicators (KPIs). These indicators, such as shareholder structure, decision-makers' experience, net sales increase, funding sources, client base, and sector developments, provide valuable insights for effective financial resource allocation. Selim Yazıcı et al. (2019) takes a different approach by adopting a self-reflection methodology in his work. As the co-founder of FinTech Istanbul Platform, Yazıcı leverages his experience to analyze the dynamics of creating a healthy FinTech ecosystem. The study identifies eight essential components for a thriving ecosystem, including new technologies, telecom and technology infrastructure, innovative startups, regulatory bodies, financial institutions, end-users, and entities supporting innovation financially and spatially. Kazim Degerli (2019) into the regulatory aspects of FinTech in Turkey. Highlighting regulators' common approaches of ignoring, likening, or regulating, Degerli sheds light on the challenges faced by FinTech companies in navigating the diverse regulatory landscape. Through examples of both successful and unsuccessful projects, the study offers remediations for better integration within the Turkish financial sector. The intersection of FinTech solutions and sustainable finance in Turkey is the focal point of research conducted by Orkun Bayram et al. (2022). Progress in financial inclusivity, responsible consumption, and the assessment of climate-related financial risks in the country is examined, showcasing the potential of FinTech in promoting sustainability. The pivotal role in this endeavor is played by collaborative efforts between the banking and FinTech sectors, supported by regulatory institutions.

In concert, these studies provide a holistic understanding of the FinTech landscape in Turkey. From investment dynamics to ecosystem development, regulatory challenges, and the role of FinTech in sustainable finance, these insights collectively form a robust foundation for further exploration and analysis within the field. Current research on FinTech in Turkey has highlighted key areas such as technology, investment indicators, ecosystem dynamics, regulatory challenges, and sustainable finance. However, numerous unexplored opportunities exist within these realms for future research. Examining evolving technologies, emerging investment indicators, understanding ecosystem dynamics, addressing regulatory challenges, and exploring innovative approaches to sustainable finance promotion present promising avenues for further investigation. Future research in these areas can enhance our understanding of the dynamic FinTech landscape in Turkey.

The UAE, emerging as a significant startup hub, holds strategic importance in the realm of FinTech. Fueled by stable financial and economic conditions, the region has become a focal point for researchers investigating the dynamics of FinTech in recent years. The exploration of FinTech in the UAE unfolds through a diverse array of research endeavors, shedding light on various facets of this rapidly evolving landscape. Banerjee (2020)'s investigation illuminates the radical transformation occurring in FinTech across the Gulf and MENA region, with a particular focus on the UAE, Bahrain, and Saudi Arabia. Government-led initiatives and large private sector investments underscore the UAE's central role in leading the FinTech revolution, though challenges and bottlenecks persist. Pradeep Dwivedi et al. (2021) delves into the impact of FinTech on the competitiveness and performance of the UAE banking industry, employing empirical testing with 76 banking professionals from Dubai. Findings highlight the significant influence of FinTech adoption on competitiveness and its subsequent impact on banking industry performance, crucial insights given the UAE banking industry's diverse customer base.

The vital role of venture capital in ensuring the success and survival of FinTech ventures in the UAE. In a comprehensive study by Hajer Zarrouk et al. (2021), which contributes valuable insights into the emergence of the UAE as a regional FinTech hub, emphasizing the need for empirical evidence regarding the determinants of FinTech success and survival. Through a meticulous analysis of factors such as the business model, access to finance, and the regulatory environment, the study provides essential guidance for policymakers and underscores the critical role of resources, particularly venture capital, in the success and survival of UAE-based FinTech ventures. The investigation into Dubai's proactive approach to the digital transformation of the financial sector and the growth of FinTech is undertaken in (Schilirò, D., 2021). The paper underscores Dubai's dynamic financial ecosystem, marked by innovative startups, collaboration with the private sector, an adaptive regulatory regime, and supportive government policies. The portrayal of the emirate's FinTech ecosystem as a challenging paradigm for the business world is attributed to the contribution of all these elements. Another research that provides valuable insights that can inform industry professionals, policymakers, and academics, offering a comprehensive view of FinTech's impact and potential within the UAE and beyond, is (Alblooshi, 2022). In this study, Fatima Saif Ahmed Kameel Alblooshi explores diverse dimensions of FinTech, including its evolution, impact on the financial services industry, and its relationship with Islamic Finance. The chapter underscores the UAE's pivotal role as a global and regional FinTech hub, contributing significantly to FinTech empowerment during challenging times such as the Covid-19 pandemic. A well-structured conceptual framework for FinTech laws and regulations in the Middle East is vital for legal clarity, encouraging innovation, and fostering investor confidence. This framework ensures consumer protection, facilitates international integration, and promotes adaptability to technological changes. By establishing consistency across jurisdictions, it enhances regulatory effectiveness, manages emerging risks, and creates a conducive environment for the growth and sustainability of the rapidly evolving FinTech sector in the region. Mohammad Essa Yousuf Majid Al Suwaidi et al. (2022) focuses on the development of a conceptual framework for FinTech laws and regulations, with a particular emphasis on their impact on risk management in UAE financial institutions. This research not only addresses the strategic aspects of FinTech but also underscores its potential to align with regulatory requirements. Another comprehensive study conducted by Mohamed Bouteraa et al. (2023) explores the consumer-side dynamics of FinTech adoption in the UAE, utilizing the Unified Theory of Acceptance and Use of Technology (UTAUT). This comprehensive model identifies barriers hindering consumer acceptance and usage, offering a pioneering exploration that encompasses organizational, technological, individual, and environmental aspects.

Despite the valuable insights provided by existing research on FinTech in the UAE, several potential gaps and avenues for further exploration are apparent. These include a deeper investigation into specific regulatory challenges faced by FinTech ventures and potential solutions, a more nuanced exploration of how FinTech aligns with Islamic Finance principles, a prolonged assessment of the long-term sustainability of FinTech ventures, a more extensive examination of consumer attitudes and barriers to adoption, a detailed analysis of cross-border collaborations, and a broader exploration of the impacts of digital transformation on the financial sector. Addressing these gaps would contribute to a more comprehensive understanding of the dynamic FinTech landscape in the UAE.

Several noteworthy studies examining FinTech in the MENA[1] regions have been presented in recent years. Noha Emara takes a broader perspective, analyzing the impact of FinTech on Sustainable Development Goals (SDGs) and highlighting positive correlations between FinTech measures and poverty alleviation in the MENA region (Emara, N., 2021). A conceptual piece outlining the pillars of FinTech growth in MENA is contributed by (Chinnasamy, 2021), with an emphasis on sustainability, infrastructure, human resources, and government support. Tahanout Kheira in (Kheira, T., 2021) focuses on enhancing financial services for the unbanked and SMEs in MENA through FinTech. In another valuable research by M. Kabir Hassan and his coauthors (Hassan, 2022) visualizes the FinTech ecosystem in MENA, emphasizing the region's efforts to establish a conducive environment for FinTech startups. Jaber and Issa delves into disruptive innovation in emerging markets, emphasizing the role of capital resources in driving competitive advantage for Middle Eastern FinTechs (Jaber, J., 2022). Covid-19 impacted the growth of FinTech and online banking services across all industries, bringing forth various challenges in the process. So, Farah Naz et al. explore FinTech's growth during COVID-19 in MENA, presenting challenges like privacy issues and cybercrimes alongside potential benefits such as cost-effectiveness and financial outreach (Naz, F., 2022). A recent study by Mohammad Abdel Mohsen Al-Afeef investigates the mediating effect of perceived ease of use on FinTech adoption in the Middle East, providing insights into factors influencing users' intention to use financial technology (Al-Afeef, 2023).

Several studies in the literature specifically delve into the realm of FinTech within individual Middle Eastern countries. Anjum Razzaque's study in Bahrain assesses users' willingness to continue using FinTech services, focusing on the impact of perceived benefits and risks (Razzaque, 2020). The embrace and implementation of FinTech in Oman are explored by (Kukreja, 2021), with an examination of its influence on the country's banking and finance industry. Mansour Saleh Albarrak describes the features of the Saudi Arabian FinTech landscape, highlighting changes within the ecosystem, including a cautious approach by Saudi banks and the government's emphasis on regulations (Albarrak, M., 2021). Ayman Mansour Khalaf Alkhazaleh provides a comprehensive review of FinTech in the Arab world, emphasizing global strides and addressing challenges in the region in (Alkhazaleh, 2021). A shift in focus to the Gulf and MENA region, acknowledging radical changes in FinTech and exploring challenges and opportunities, is undertaken by (Banerjee, A., 2020). Maryam Mirzaei presented a comprehensive study on the Iranian FinTech market underscores its rapid growth, with a focus on electronic payments and emerging trends like bank-independent financial management and crowdfunding. Despite great potential and infrastructure, there's a need for increased integration compared to regional hubs like Abu Dhabi and Dubai. (Mirzaei, 2022). Hossam Hussein's research presents an in-depth analysis of Egypt's financial inclusion challenges, emphasizing the role of government, collaborative efforts, and FinTech innovation, supported by empirical data from the World Bank's Global Findex database (Hussein, 2020). Examination of consumers' awareness, readiness, and perceptions toward FinTech products and services in Kuwait is conducted by (Rabaa'i, A. A., 2021). Haya Yusuf Mohamed provides a comprehensive review of the FinTech discipline, exploring its history, evolution, and categories in Bahrain, specifically emphasizing the role of women in the FinTech sector and initiatives aimed at empowering them within the industry. (Mohamed, 2021). The capacity of FinTech for the Islamic economy is crucial, given that Islamic Shari'a rules have both direct and indirect effects on banking and business in most Middle Eastern countries. Mustafa Raza Rabbani delves into challenges and opportunities awaiting Islamic financial institutions with the rise of FinTech (Rabbani, 2022).

The literature on FinTech in the Middle East region places a substantial emphasis on several key areas that have garnered significant attention from researchers. In both Turkey and the UAE, a notable focus is on investment dynamics, with studies exploring the decision-making processes of investors when funding FinTech startups. This includes the examination of KPIs such as shareholder structure, experience of decision-makers, net sales increase, funding sources, client base, and sector developments. Additionally, the literature extensively delves into the regulatory landscape, addressing common approaches taken by regulators and the associated challenges faced by FinTech companies in navigating diverse regulatory environments. The emphasis on ecosystem development is another recurrent theme, particularly evident in studies exploring the essential components for a thriving FinTech ecosystem, encompassing new technologies, infrastructure, startups, regulatory bodies, financial institutions, end-users, and entities supporting innovation. Sustainable finance and the intersection of FinTech solutions with environmental and social considerations also receive noteworthy attention, reflecting a growing interest in promoting financial inclusivity, responsible consumption, and assessing climate-related financial risks. Furthermore, the literature underscores the vital role of venture capital in ensuring the success and survival of FinTech ventures, with a focus on empirical evidence regarding determinants of FinTech success and survival. In the UAE, there is an additional emphasis on government-led initiatives, large private sector investments, and the overall transformative impact of FinTech on the competitiveness and performance of the banking industry. The literature collectively reflects a holistic exploration of the multifaceted landscape of FinTech, ranging from investment and regulatory aspects to ecosystem dynamics, sustainability, and the role of various stakeholders in fostering innovation and growth.

Despite the extensive research on FinTech in the Middle East, there is a noticeable gap in the literature concerning the exploration of Artificial Intelligence (AI) potential within the FinTech landscapes of the UAE and Turkey. While existing studies offer valuable insights into investment dynamics, regulatory challenges, and sustainable finance, a comprehensive examination of the specific role and impact of AI in shaping the financial technology ecosystems of these two countries is conspicuously absent. The transformative influence of AI technologies, encompassing machine learning, natural language processing, and predictive analytics, on FinTech globally necessitates a focused investigation into their adoption and adaptation within the financial sectors of the UAE and Turkey. This research gap highlights the need for a deeper understanding of how AI is employed in these regions, addressing its applications, challenges, and opportunities. Such exploration would not only bridge a significant gap in the existing literature but also provide essential knowledge for policymakers, industry practitioners, and academics aiming to navigate the evolving landscape of financial technology in the UAE and Turkey.

This identified research gap highlights the urgency of investigating the detailed dimensions of AI in FinTech within these regional contexts. Understanding the specific applications, challenges, and opportunities presented by AI in the financial landscapes of the UAE and Turkey is not only essential for scholarly exploration but also holds practical implications for policymakers, industry professionals, and academics. Bridging this gap in the literature would not only contribute to a more comprehensive understanding of the evolving FinTech landscape but also provide actionable insights for those navigating the intricate intersection of Artificial Intelligence and financial technology in these dynamic regions.

FINTECH LANDSCAPE IN THE MIDDLE EAST

The Middle Eastern banking and payment sector is currently experiencing a profound evolution driven by the integration of advanced technologies such as artificial intelligence (AI), blockchain, big data, and cloud computing (Taherdoost, H., 2023a). This shift is prompted by the escalating demand for more secure, convenient, and rapid payment methods, compelling established financial institutions to make substantial investments in bolstering their digital capabilities. In a departure from traditional models centered around physical branches and operations, financial institutions are now collaborating with FinTech firms to devise innovative solutions (Razavi, H., 2023b). This signifies a shift towards a model that places a premium on back-office transformation and adopts a more customer-centric approach.

The contemporary financial landscape encompasses telecommunications firms, retailers, and FinTech entities, all competing for market dominance in an era characterized by streamlined payments. However, financial service providers are required to match the innovation and technological adeptness of their clients, offering products that prioritize a digital-first, mobile-first, and user experience (UX)-first approach. In the Middle East and North Africa (MENA) region, where 55% of the population is under 30 (Adeleye, B. N., 2022), catering to the preferences of the 'Instagram and TikTok generation' is not just a preference but a necessity. Yet, The World Bank reports (Demirgüç-Kunt, A., 2022) a staggering 1.4 billion adults worldwide remain unbanked, highlighting a significant gap despite the 2.8 billion people residing in the MENA region.

In the dynamic landscape of the Middle Eastern FinTech sector, the intersection of diverse customer needs and a significant expatriate presence in the Gulf Cooperation Council (GCC) creates a fertile ground for innovation. FinTech firms, recognizing the substantial opportunity at hand, are strategically positioning themselves to cater to the varied requirements of this population. Simultaneously, traditional banks are proactively adapting to this changing environment by investing in digital capabilities and engaging in partnerships with FinTech companies. This collaborative approach aims to develop cutting-edge solutions, ensuring the continued relevance and competitiveness of traditional banking institutions.

As the banking industry undergoes this rapid transformation, a multifaceted competitive landscape emerges. Telecommunications companies, retailers, and agile FinTech startups are actively entering the market, intensifying the competition for a share of the financial services sector. Notably, the rise of neobanks, representing a digital-only banking model, disrupts traditional banking paradigms and prompts non-banking entities to explore untapped opportunities in this dynamic and evolving space.

This transformative environment is further bolstered by the Middle East's favorable macroeconomic conditions, which serve as a cornerstone for the sustained growth of its flourishing FinTech sector. The various elements contributing to this positive outlook collectively delineate a narrative of prosperity within the Middle Eastern FinTech market. In essence, the region's economic vibrancy and the agile response of financial institutions to evolving consumer demands converge, setting the stage for an exciting and innovative future in the realm of financial technology.

1. **Unbanked Population:** The Middle East's positive macroeconomic situation is driven, in part, by a significant proportion of unbanked individuals. Millions in the region lack access to basic banking services, creating ample opportunities for growth in FinTech, particularly in open banking, cryptocurrency, and stock trading.
2. **Internet and Smartphone Penetration:** The region's FinTech growth is further fueled by the increasing affordability and penetration of the internet and smartphones. Notably, the United Arab

Emirates leads with 99% internet access, while markets like Egypt present untapped potential with 71% internet penetration. This index in Turkey is 82%.

3. **Young Demographic:** The Middle East's advantageous demographic factor is its youthful population, with an average age of around 30-31 years. This demographic, born around the turn of the millennium, proves to be highly adaptive to technological innovations, contributing to the flourishing FinTech sector.
4. **Government and Regulatory Support**: The FinTech boom in the Middle East is supported by proactive government and regulatory initiatives. Authorities in the region have responded to digital advancements by introducing new standards and rules. Recent updates in regulatory frameworks, including open banking, cryptocurrency, digital banking, and payments, create a conducive environment for FinTech companies to develop disruptive applications and services. Open banking, in particular, stands out as a crucial component of this regulatory landscape.
5. **FinTech Hubs and Free Zones in the Middle East:** Numerous Middle Eastern countries, including Saudi Arabia, the UAE, Bahrain, and Egypt, have embraced the concept of FinTech sandboxes as of today. Concurrently, there is a concerted effort in constructing FinTech hubs. These hubs, as outlined in Appendix 1, play a crucial role in supporting startups by offering a conducive environment for skill enhancement. They serve as platforms for startups to not only refine their capabilities but also to explore opportunities for collaboration, connect with potential partners, and even contemplate expansion into different countries. In the Middle East, the presence of diverse FinTech hubs underscores the commitment to fostering a robust ecosystem that propels innovation and facilitates strategic partnerships within the burgeoning field of financial technology.

FinTech Hubs in The Middle East

Within the Middle East region, the diversity is striking, comprising a spectrum of social, economic, and cultural backgrounds that span some of the wealthiest and most impoverished nations globally. Consequently, when evaluating these hubs, it becomes imperative to consider a broad range of economic development indicators, particularly those related to technology, digital infrastructure, and fintech. To categorize fintech hubs across the ME region, one can delineate them into three tiers (Figure 4) based on their economic development and fintech prominence:

1. Tier-one – Premier Global Fintech Hubs:
    - **Robust Economies:** Both nations boast well-developed economies, characterized by a high standard of living, attracting diverse talent from around the globe.
    - **Key Commercial and Tech Hubs:** Israel and the UAE are home to major commercial, financial, and technological centers. Tel Aviv in Israel stands out as a significant innovation hub, while the UAE hosts Dubai and Abu Dhabi, which play pivotal roles in fintech development.
    - **Entrepreneurial and Business-Friendly Environments:** Evidenced by the proliferation of fintech and tech companies, both nations are recognized as entrepreneurial hubs. The UAE, in particular, hosts over half of the fintechs in the Middle East and Africa (excluding Israel and Turkey). Israel surpasses the rest of the MENA region, producing numerous fintech unicorns.

- ◦ **Innovation-Supportive Policies:** The governments of Israel and the UAE actively prioritize innovation. Israel is a major investor in Research and Development (R&D), while the UAE envisions a future dominated by blockchain technology and the metaverse.

2. Tier-two – Emerging Fintech Hubs:

Saudi Arabia and Turkey fall into the Tier-Two category, specifically in the higher range. Bahrain, Qatar, Kuwait, Egypt, Oman, Jordan is classified in the Tier-Two middle range, while Lebanon is placed in the Tier-Two lower range. Common characteristics within the Tier-Two category, whether in the higher, middle, or lower range, include:

- **Diverse Populations:** Many countries in this tier, such as Turkey and Saudi Arabia, boast large populations, while others with smaller populations maintain an outward-looking perspective.
- **Government Focused on Fintech:** Governments in this tier express aspirations for fintech and implement pro-business policies. Fintech has played a significant role in their economic development, contributing to enhanced GDPs and overall quality of life. This focus on fintech aligns with broader initiatives to promote business, attract foreign direct investment (FDI), and stimulate entrepreneurship. Some countries in this tier, historically or presently, serve as financial or commercial hubs, including Bahrain, Kuwait, and Lebanon.

3. Tier-three – Early-Stage Fintech Hubs:

The remaining countries in the Middle East that haven't been mentioned fall into the tier-three fintech hubs category with some similar characteristics:

- **Fintech in Infancy:** Countries in this category lack well-established fintech-specific derivatives or financial services infrastructure. While some may have aspirations and governmental support for the growth of these sectors, they remain in their infancy compared to both global standards and their higher-ranked Middle Eastern peers. Many in this category still lack a specific strategic government vision and its effective implementation to propel these sectors forward.
- **Economic Development Impact:** These nations typically have middle or lower-middle-income, or low-income economies. The level of economic development directly influences their infrastructure and current technological accessibility. Limited technology and accessibility hinder innovations in fintech or make them entirely inaccessible. This shared characteristic is a common challenge among these tier-three fintech hubs.
- **Aspirations for Future Economy:** Despite facing various challenges, countries in this tier express aspirations for long-term development. The goal is to elevate their income status, utilizing technology and digital advancements to alleviate poverty and foster economic growth.

Legal Considerations and Regulation in ME FinTech

In this segment, we delve into several prevalent legal considerations that individuals contemplating investments in the Middle East's FinTech sector should take into account. These concerns may find alleviation or resolution through recent advancements in the market or the existence of applicable frameworks.

Figure 4. Three tiers of fintech hubs in the Middle East region
(Santosdiaz, 2023)

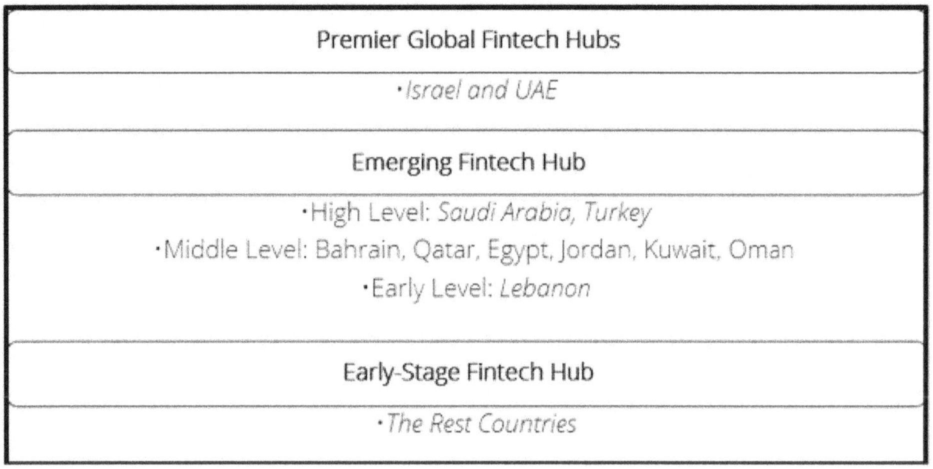

Moreover, the evolving landscape and available structures may offer avenues for addressing these legal considerations effectively.

The development and expansion of fintech startups are significantly influenced by four key areas that collectively shape the fintech ecosystem. These domains comprise policies and regulations, human capital, support and investment, and markets and demand (Igor Tomych, 2023). Together, they play a crucial role in determining the number of startups launched and the success rate of those experiencing rapid growth. Entrepreneurs in this field encounter various challenges, with only around 10% of startups managing to achieve significant growth by effectively navigating these obstacles. Due to the confidential nature of customer data and financial metrics, directly tracking this phenomenon proves difficult (Xu, Y., & Bao, H., 2023). In the region, only a handful of countries offer a conducive environment for business startups, and the strict regulations around fintech often impede growth potential. Licensing laws, initially designed for traditional banks, create uncertainty for startups entering the financial services space. Many startups operate in a gray area, seeking partnerships with established banks for compliance. However, fostering innovation and industry growth requires a more adaptive regulatory framework that recognizes the unique characteristics of fintech (CCAF, 2021).

1. Uncertainty

The Middle East has traditionally been slow to adopt international standards or enact modernizing changes in its legal systems, leading to uncertainties in enforcing rights and obligations. Factors such as linguistic or cultural approaches and the prioritization of core structural reforms for economic and social stability contribute to this uncertainty. Additionally, varying degrees of application of Shari'a laws across the region, with examples such as Shari'a being a source of law in the UAE and Egypt but the actual law in Saudi Arabia, introduce complexities. Shari'a laws can impose restrictive penal provisions, particularly concerning online content deemed offensive to public morals, potentially hindering or adding uncertainty to technological advancements.

Potential Resolutions: Specific licensing regimes in the Middle East address issues of uncertainty, such as the financial regulatory regimes in UAE financial free zones. These zones operate under an English common law approach in their court systems, providing greater certainty in commercial transactions. Addressing Shari'a developments, Islamic finance is evolving alongside modern finance and could potentially extend to FinTech. Leading practices in Islamic Finance, like Clifford Chance, have been instrumental in creating innovative structures to offer compliant finance and insurance products. Shari'a scholars recognize the necessity of modern financial services solutions. The parallels between innovation in Islamic finance and FinTech are evident, as seen in the issuance of a Shari'a standard on trading in gold by AAOIFI in November 2016, followed by the issuance of several gold-linked ICO[2]s in the UAE.

2. Regulations:

The regulatory environment for fintech in the Middle East region is intricate and varies from country to country, with each nation having its own distinct set of rules and regulations. Some countries, such as the United Arab Emirates with its Dubai Financial Services Authority (DFSA) and BRSA[3] in Turkey, have established specific frameworks and regulatory policy principles to facilitate sustainable development and equitable growth within the tech industry.

Conversely, other countries in the region are still in the process of developing such frameworks, with varying requirements ranging from mandatory licenses or registrations to restrictions on the types of financial services offered. Adhering to these regulatory requirements is crucial, as non-compliance may lead to fines, reputational damage, and legal consequences. Therefore, understanding the common factors influencing collaboration with Middle East countries is paramount. Key factors include:

a. *Licensing and Authorization:* Many regulatory authorities mandate that fintech companies obtain a license before operating in the Middle East region. This ensures compliance with legal frameworks and regulatory standards.
b. *Data Privacy and Protection:* Fintech companies in the Middle East are obligated to safeguard customer data, adhering to data protection laws that restrict its misuse or unauthorized access.
c. *AML[4] and KYC[5]:* Fintech firms must comply with AML and KYC regulations to prevent money laundering and terrorist financing. This involves verifying customer identities and monitoring transactions for potential suspicious activities.

While the ME region is a hub for fintech innovation, navigating the diverse licensing requirements can pose challenges for companies seeking to establish a presence. To successfully navigate these complexities, it is advisable to seek expert guidance and consult professionals well-versed in the local regulatory landscapes of each Middle Eastern country.

Potential Resolutions: To successfully address the intricate regulatory challenges in the Middle East region's fintech landscape, a comprehensive approach is recommended. Initiating a thorough regulatory due diligence process is crucial, involving in-depth research into the specific licensing, data protection, and AML/KYC requirements of each targeted country. Collaborating with local legal experts or law firms specializing in fintech regulations within the region provides valuable insights and guidance on compliance procedures. Building relationships with regulatory authorities fosters open communication and facilitates a smoother approval process. Tailoring fintech solutions to align with individual country regulations ensures local compliance and acceptance (Daza Jaller, L. S., & Molinuevo, M., 2020).

Prioritizing robust data protection measures and implementing ongoing staff training on AML and KYC regulations contributes to a culture of compliance within the organization. Active participation in industry associations and engaging in government relations and advocacy efforts further solidify the company's position within the evolving regulatory landscape. Continuous monitoring and adaptability are key, allowing fintech companies to stay abreast of regulatory changes and swiftly adjust to maintain compliance. This holistic strategy enables companies to navigate the diverse regulatory requirements, fostering a strong and compliant presence across the ME region (Susanto, H., 2022).

3. Challenges in Engagement:

Historically, language barriers and limited resources have posed significant challenges for many firms seeking to connect with the right audience and facilitate their entry into Middle Eastern markets.

Potential Resolutions: Governments and supporting departments, particularly in the UAE, have displayed a commendable level of responsiveness and adaptability in supporting FinTech initiatives. This responsiveness is indicative of FinTech aligning with central principles in government agendas focused on the future advancement of technology and innovation, as well as the recognition of the necessity to diversify from reliance on natural resources. The youthful demographic in the Middle East contributes to a widespread acceptance of new technologies in the region. Recent experiences highlight that governmental authorities have dedicated resources to establish networks and collaborations in the FinTech space, demonstrating a willingness to collaborate with both prospective and established participants.

4. Challenge for International Entry:

In certain jurisdictions like the UAE and Qatar, non-nationals (or non-GCC) are restricted to holding a maximum of 49% ownership in a company. This limitation can lead investors to hesitate in committing capital to establish a presence, especially without a reliable local partner or network.

Potential Resolutions: In various jurisdictions, foreign investment is on the rise, and restrictions have been eased in certain sectors, most recently in engineering. Despite these changes, many investors continue to opt for collaboration with local partners due to practical business considerations. Another viable solution is the incorporation of companies in UAE free zones, applicable in numerous scenarios. However, challenges may arise when conducting operations outside the free zone, particularly in visiting and contracting with customers. A thorough cross-border analysis is necessary in each case to address these challenges effectively.

5. Perceived Risks and Sensitivities:

Cyber risks have become focal points for organizations worldwide, given their prominence in global news and the consequential disruptions and reputational harm they cause. In the Middle East, there's an amplified sense of concern due to geographical proximity to regional instability, with media reports underscoring the susceptibility of businesses across the region. Privacy laws, often designed to safeguard national security, may be constrained in certain jurisdictions. Additionally, the region's specific concern about terrorist financing poses a potential threat, and the laws aimed at countering this may inadvertently impede the growth of the FinTech sector.

Potential Resolutions: Many regions in the Middle East possess robust tools to effectively safeguard against cyber threats, akin to any other jurisdiction. Notably, local firms frequently leverage international data hosting services within the EU, such as Amazon Web Services, viewing this issue as a global threat addressable through tools available worldwide, rather than being region-specific. The absence of comprehensive data protection regimes can contribute to managing compliance costs during initial setup, provided there are adequate disclosures to customers and counterparties regarding data usage. It is advisable for firms to maintain access to international solutions to ensure enhanced protections, aligning with international standards for the secure storage and integrity of data.

6. Underdeveloped Intellectual Property (IP) Landscape:

While IP protection laws are in place across the Middle East, and brand rights are duly acknowledged, the region's IP regime is still evolving. Although it is now possible to secure patents covering the entire GCC, the examination and enforcement framework for copyright, industrial design, and patents lags behind some other jurisdictions. This developmental gap may instill hesitation among FinTech entrepreneurs contemplating capital investments in the Middle East. Intellectual property poses a unique concern for FinTech engineers due to the prevalence of open-source code, engagement with third-party developers, and the collaborative nature of the industry.

Potential Resolutions: Entrepreneurs might explore obtaining patents not only within the GCC but also in more mature jurisdictions such as the US, Europe, and Japan. This strategy enhances protection against international infringement. Additionally, innovators can deploy alternative methods to safeguard their intellectual property, including the protection of trade secrets and the use of digital rights management technologies. For practical management, it is advisable for firms to regularly secure confirmations of IP assignments from contractors and employees upon termination, a measure that should be feasible for many organizations.

7. Compliance Expenses:

Operating locally may entail substantial expenses related to Know Your Customer (KYC) and Customer Due Diligence (CDD) checks, along with efforts to mitigate compliance risks.

Regtech Innovations: Numerous local FinTech initiatives are emerging in the regulatory technology (regtech) domain. Local authorities are strategically embracing technology, exemplified by initiatives like the Dubai Blockchain Strategy. These endeavors aim to enhance transparency and prioritize the prevention of money laundering and other financial crimes.

Notable Startups in The Middle East

FinTech startups are generating significant excitement in the region, having secured over $100 million in funding over the past five years. This investment trend is justified, especially considering the limited success of traditional banks in a region where 70% of the population lacks a bank account (Forbes Middle East, 2023).

Addressing challenges related to financial inclusion, these startups are tackling issues such as limited financial knowledge, restricted access to finance, and expensive, inadequate financial options for small businesses. Notable examples include yallacompare and Souqalmal.com, which enable users to compare and choose the most suitable financial products from a plethora of options. Crowdfunding platforms like Beehive and Eureeca play a crucial role in bridging the gap between investors and businesses, offering affordable finance to fledgling companies while providing investors with attractive returns.

The 20 FinTech startups on Forbes' list have collectively raised over $99 million in venture funding, with many planning additional fundraising this year. Topping the list is Paytabs, a payment platform backed by Saudi Aramco, having raised $20 million for expansion into 17 countries. The United Arab Emirates (UAE) emerges as the FinTech hub, hosting half of the listed startups, while Jordan closely follows with four entries. Forbes compiled the rankings by engaging with various FinTech startups, gathering details about their businesses, funds raised, and business models. To qualify for the list, startups had to be founded in 2011 or later and have received external funding. Forbes assessed companies based on the funds raised, giving it the highest weight, and also considered the quality of investors and the business models of the startups. Table 1 provides a summary of the top 10 startups in this influential list.

Table 1. Top 10 FinTech startups in the Middle East (Forbes Middle East, 2023)

Rank	Startup	Description	Founders	Funding	Investor	Country
1	PayTabs	Online payment processing solutions	Abdulaziz Fahad Aljouf	$20 M	Saudi Aramco's Wa'ed, Angel investment	Saudi Arabia
2	Souqalmal	Financial products comparison site	Ambareen Musa	$15.2 M	HummingBird Ventures, NNS Capital, 500 Startups, Riyad Taqnia Fund, Angel investors	UAE
3	Bayzat	Online health insurance and HR solutions provider	Talal Bayaa, Brian Habibi	$12.6 M	BECO Capital, Precinct Partners, RAED Ventures, Delta Partners Group, WOMENA, Silicon Badia, Vision Ventures, undisclosed investor	UAE
4	Beehive	SME focused peer2peer lending platform	Craig Moore	$11.5 M	Riyad TAQNIA And Mohammed Bin Rashid Funds, Angel investors	UAE
5	Yallacompare	Financial products comparison site	Jon Richards, Samer Chehab	$10.1 M	STC Ventures, Wamda Capital, Dubai Silicon Oasis, Saned, Mulverhill Associates, others	UAE
6	Eureeca	Crowdfunding platform	Christoper Thomas, Sam Quawasmi	$7.1 M	Singularity Investments, Bahraini Investment bank, Saudi Financial Institution, crowd and other angel investors	UAE
7	MadfooatCom	Electronic bill presentment and payment service	Nasser Saleh	$7 M	Oasis500 (Accelerator), 2P Company, AlSulmi and Sons company, Capital bank, Cairo Amman bank, AlEtihad bank and other angel investors	Jordan
8	liwwa	Peer-to-peer lending platform	Ahmed Moor, Samer Atiani	$5.6 M	MENA Venture Investments, DASH Ventures, Bank al Etihad, Badia Impact Fund, Samih Toukan	Jordan
9	Remitr	Money transfer app	Kanchan Kumar, Sandeep Jhingran, Altaf Ahmed, Sandeep Todi	$2 M	Professional angel investors, family & friends	UAE
10	Ajar Online	Rent payment and property management	Shaheen AlKhudhari	--	Beco Capital, Sharq Ventures	Kuwait

COUNTRY-SPECIFIC FOCUS: UAE AND TURKEY

Turkey and the United Arab Emirates (UAE) stand out as robust representatives for the broader Middle East when examining the evolution of FinTech within the region. Firstly, both nations boast diverse economic models that mirror the varied economic landscapes found across the Middle East. Turkey, positioned as a transcontinental country, serves as a microcosm of the region, blending European and Asian influences. Its economic dynamism and substantial market size make it a compelling case study, showcasing adaptability to different economic structures and challenges. On the other hand, the UAE, particularly Dubai and Abu Dhabi, serves as a key financial hub in the Gulf Cooperation Council (GCC), epitomizing the unique economic dynamics of oil-rich nations diversifying their wealth. Secondly, the regional influence of Turkey and the UAE cannot be overstated. Turkey's historical and cultural ties with many Middle Eastern countries, coupled with its geopolitical significance, position it as a bellwether for regional FinTech trends. Similarly, the UAE's leadership role in the GCC and its global business engagement make it a pivotal player with insights applicable to neighboring countries. Thirdly, the government initiatives and regulatory approaches in both countries serve as benchmarks for Middle Eastern nations navigating the delicate balance between fostering FinTech innovation and ensuring regulatory oversight. Turkey's regulatory reforms and incentive programs provide a blueprint for nurturing a conducive environment for FinTech startups, while the UAE's proactive measures, such as regulatory sandboxes, offer valuable lessons in regulating a rapidly evolving sector. Additionally, the cultural and demographic diversity in Turkey and the UAE reflect the broader Middle East, enabling a nuanced understanding of how various population segments respond to FinTech innovations. Lastly, the global connectivity of both nations, driven by their strategic geographical locations, showcases how FinTech can play a pivotal role in facilitating international transactions and collaborations, providing crucial insights for other Middle Eastern countries aspiring to enhance their global financial presence. In essence, Turkey and the UAE emerge as rich case studies that encapsulate the economic, cultural, regulatory, and global dimensions of FinTech in the Middle East, offering valuable lessons for the entire region.

FinTech in United Arab Emirate

In recent years, the FinTech landscape in the UAE has witnessed a remarkable evolution, marked by robust growth in digital payments even prior to the onset of the Covid-19 pandemic. Notably, the annual rate of consumer digital payments transactions in the UAE surged by more than 9 percent between 2014 and 2019, outpacing Europe's average growth rates. The pandemic further accelerated this momentum, with 80 percent of payments practitioners in the region estimating that noncash payments increased by more than 10 percent, and 43 percent believing it exceeded 20 percent due to pandemic-induced shifts. Remarkably, respondents expect this digital transformation to be enduring, with 90 percent predicting that at least half of new users will sustain their adoption of digital payments. Looking ahead, more than half of survey participants anticipate robust growth in noncash payments over the next five years, projecting a cumulative increase of over 50 percent above 2020 levels. These trends underscore a dynamic FinTech landscape in the UAE, poised for sustained digital innovation and a reshaped financial ecosystem.

The United Arab Emirates is emerging as a prominent FinTech hub in the Middle East for several compelling reasons. Firstly, the UAE government and business community are actively collaborating to bolster the country's standing as a global hub, fostering an environment conducive to both new and established FinTech companies. Through strategic initiatives, the UAE aims to leverage a combination of substantial market opportunities, supportive government policies, and a burgeoning FinTech ecosystem.

One key factor contributing to the UAE's FinTech growth is the vast commercial opportunities available in the Middle East region. Unlike more mature markets, a significant portion of the population in the region is either underbanked or unbanked. The UAE and the wider ME region offer FinTechs access to a large pool of potential customers, particularly given that 136 million adults in the Middle East fall into these categories. This demographic provides a fertile ground for FinTechs to expand their customer base and concurrently promote financial inclusion. Moreover, the demographic profile of the ME region, characterized by a sizable population below the age of 30 and a strong inclination towards technology, presents substantial opportunities for FinTech innovation. The region's tech-savvy population, coupled with a desire for products offering speed, reliability, and convenience, creates an ideal market for FinTech services.

Government support plays a pivotal role in the UAE's FinTech ascendancy. The UAE government has implemented various initiatives to nurture entrepreneurship, including the establishment of special economic zones with business-friendly regulations, zero tax on business income and profits, and no restrictions on foreign exchange or capital repatriation. Golden visa schemes, allowing foreigners to live, work, and own businesses with 100% ownership on the UAE's mainland, further attract international players.

Access to funding is another critical aspect contributing to the UAE's FinTech growth. The government's concerted efforts, such as the establishment of free zones and initiatives like the Dubai Future District Fund and Abu Dhabi Catalyst Partner's $1 billion fund, have created a supportive funding environment. In 2021, Forbes Middle East reported that 22 of the 50 best-funded start-ups in the ME region were based in the UAE, with 13 of them being FinTech. This significant investment reflects a robust investor appetite in the tech sector.

As a result of these factors, the UAE is positioned as a hub of FinTech innovation in the ME region, with a mature digital economy, favorable regulations, and ongoing efforts to attract top entrepreneurial talent. The region's commitment to digital payments, expected to account for 73% of transaction volume by 2023, underscores the UAE's trajectory as a major player in the global FinTech landscape.

To comprehend the UAE's pivotal role in evolving into a fintech hub within the region, it is essential to delve into the investments made in fintech startups. The UAE proved to be a magnet for venture capital, pulling in an impressive sum exceeding $1.47 billion in 2021. This positive trend continued with a significant surge in 2022, where companies within the UAE secured a notable $699 million in the first half of the year. This places the Emirates in a prominent position as the primary country for venture capital financing in the Middle East region, a testament to its growing influence and appeal to investors, as illustrated in Figure 5.

Figure 5. Top Arab Countries for VC funding in the first half of 2022
(Magnitt, 2022)

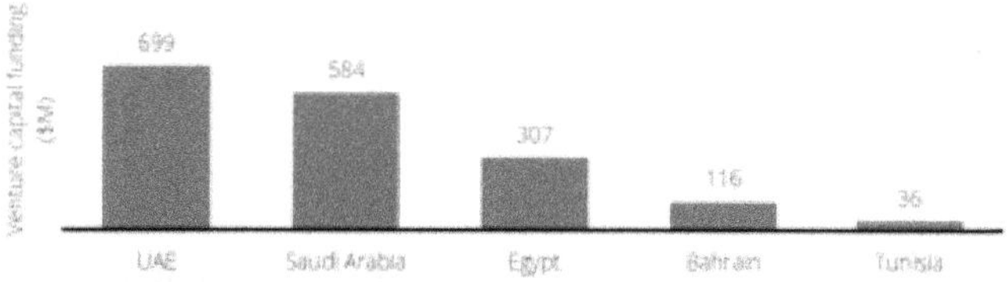

The critical insight conveyed in Figure 6 is that one-third of the overall venture capital funding across various sectors is directed towards FinTech startups. This significant allocation underscores the UAE's emergence as a focal point for fintech within the region and potentially on a broader scale.

Figure 6. Top sectors in the UAE for VC funding in the first half of 2022
(Magnitt, 2022)

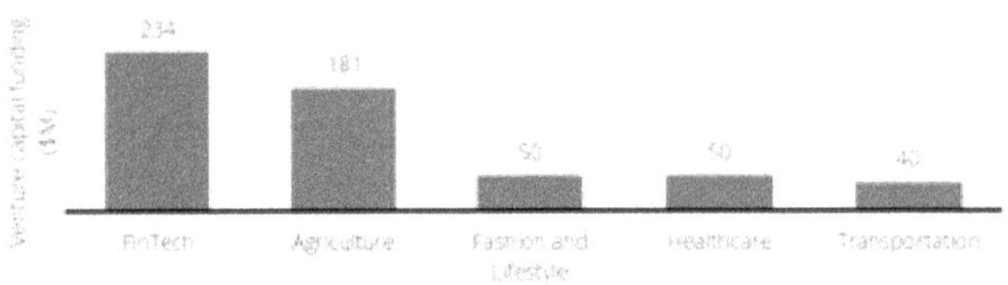

Examples of FinTech Firms in UAE

Souqalmal: Souqalmal, a trailblazer in digital financial product comparison across the Middle East, commenced its journey in 2012. Having empowered over 600,000 customers, the company serves as a thought leader in personal finance and financial education in the region. As a member of the United Arab Emirates National Debt Panel, Souqalmal plays a crucial role in assisting those in need of financial guidance, enabling individuals to make informed decisions about their personal finance options.

Bayzat: Bayzat, a prominent FinTech company, offers a comprehensive HR and employee benefits platform. Through automation of HR, payroll, and insurance processes, companies can optimize resources for more critical tasks. Bayzat's payroll services facilitate multi-currency payments, generate payslips, and automate gratuity payments effortlessly. In the realm of insurance, the platform simplifies medical policies, providing real-time employee additions and deletions, health benefits, and analytics, thereby streamlining HR and benefits management for businesses.

Beehive: Beehive pioneers Peer-to-Peer (P2P) lending, a form of crowdfunding that connects investors directly with businesses, eliminating traditional intermediaries. Utilizing the internet as a platform, Beehive facilitates businesses in securing finance from a diverse crowd of potential investors. This innovative approach to lending redefines the landscape of business financing, offering a decentralized and efficient funding alternative.

yallacompare: Formerly known as Compareit4me, yallacompare is a leading comparison platform based in Dubai, United Arab Emirates. Specializing in financial products, the platform allows users to compare and apply for bank accounts, insurance policies, loans, and car deals. Targeting individuals and businesses seeking diverse financial and insurance products, yallacompare has been a key player in simplifying and streamlining the decision-making process for its users since its founding in 2011.

Eureeca: Eureeca stands out as an equity crowdfunding platform with a global presence, spanning Europe, the Middle East, and South East Asia. Offering a unique opportunity for early-stage businesses and SMEs, Eureeca enables them to raise capital from a diverse group of investors, ranging from individual and angel investors to institutional firms. In exchange for equity, businesses can access funding through this innovative crowdfunding platform.

Remiter: Remiter, a UAE-based money transfer app, has carved a niche in the MENA business landscape by offering agile, convenient, and accessible financial services. The platform champions the successes of small businesses, providing a reliable and efficient means for money transfers within the region.

Tabby: Tabby, a FinTech based in the UAE, introduces a flexible payment option for consumers to pay for both online and offline purchases. Offering the choice between a single payment at a later date or multiple interest-free instalments, Tabby streamlines the payment process. With a quick and hassle-free experience, customers can split their purchases into four payments, all without additional fees or interest, making it a convenient solution for modern consumers.

Cashew Payments: Cashew, a financing company focused on payment solutions in the MENA region, addresses consumer challenges in accessing finance at the point of sale. Committed to providing a faster and fairer way to pay, Cashew aims to simplify important purchases for individuals. Embracing diversity and actively listening to customer needs, Cashew aspires to become a more inclusive organization that reflects the broader community it serves.

NymCard: NymCard, a unique BaaS (Banking as a Service) provider in the Middle East, offers a modern payment issuing and processing platform. Catering to startups, FinTechs, large enterprises, and banks in the MENA region, NymCard enables instant creation, control, and distribution of virtual or physical cards through its public API platform. Simplifying financial services integration, NymCard empowers payment innovators to enhance customer journeys.

BitOasis: BitOasis, headquartered in the UAE, stands as the largest cryptocurrency platform in the MENA region since its establishment in 2015. A pioneer in the region's cryptocurrency ecosystem, BitOasis caters to both novice and expert traders. With a commitment to offering a secure and regulated infrastructure, BitOasis aims to be the premier platform for buying, selling, and trading cryptocurrencies. The platform prioritizes user-friendliness, security, and compliance, establishing itself as the go-to destination for cryptocurrency enthusiasts across the region.

FinTech in Turkey

Turkey has firmly established itself as a significant player in the fields of banking, technology adoption, and digitalization, backed by compelling statistics that highlight its global financial prominence. Seizing the 7th spot globally with 93.8 million credit card holders and ranking 6th in credit card transactions, Turkey showcases a robust financial infrastructure. The country boasts 1.8 million POS devices, 52,200 ATMs, and an impressive 86.7 million active retail digital banking customers, solidifying its leadership position in the banking sector.

The driving force behind Turkey's FinTech prowess lies in its regulatory environment, which actively fosters innovation. The FinTech ecosystem has experienced continuous growth, with 629 active FinTechs, 74 licensed payment and electronic money institutions, and 8 crowdfunding platforms. FinTech startups in Turkey have garnered favor not only from banks but also from venture capital funds. Recognizing the potential of FinTech, banks invest in these startups through established funds and contribute to ecosystem expansion through acceleration programs.

The regulatory landscape in Turkey has been instrumental in propelling FinTech advancements, particularly from 2019 to 2021. During this period, regulatory innovations were introduced, laying the groundwork for subsequent successes. The issuance of a communiqué on equity-based crowdfunding in 2019 marked a pivotal moment. Fast-forwarding to 2022, 46 campaigns were successfully completed through equity-based crowdfunding platforms, emerging as a noteworthy alternative financing source for entrepreneurs seeking seed investment. The year 2021 saw the introduction of regulations governing digital banking, leading to the licensing of four institutions to establish digital banks in 2022. Turkey's FinTech journey is not only defined by impressive statistics but also by a regulatory environment that actively nurtures innovation, setting the stage for sustained growth and success in the years ahead (Sakarya, Ş., 2021).

The Turkish banking sector has consistently been a pioneer of innovation, spearheading transformative changes in financial transactions within Turkey and across Europe. Key milestones include the introduction of Turkey's first credit card in 1968 and the deployment of the country's inaugural electronic Point of Sale (POS) terminal in 1991. The establishment of Kredi Kayıt Bürosu in 1995, a collaborative effort involving nine banks, led to groundbreaking services such as the Information Verification System (2002), Individual Credit Rating (2004), and the Internet Fraud Alert System (IFAS-2007). In 2006, Turkey made history by becoming the first European country to adopt contactless credit cards and the third in Europe, following France and the UK, to implement the chip & pin application (Mikhaylov, 2023).

Turkey's forward-thinking approach is further evident in its early adoption of loyalty cards and debit cards with installment options for store purchases. In the 1980s, stores allowed installment-based payments using store cards for a nominal fee. By 1998, these cards evolved into the first installment credit cards in both Turkey and Europe. As of August 2022, Turkey ranks 7th globally and 1st in Europe for credit card ownership, boasting an impressive 93.8 million credit cards. In terms of credit card transactions, Turkey holds the 6th position globally and again secures the 1st position in Europe. The country's financial infrastructure is robust, featuring 1.8 million POS devices and 52,200 ATMs (BKM, 2022). According to the June 2021 Digital, Internet, and Mobile Banking Statistics released by the Banks Association of Turkey, the number of active retail digital banking customers surged to an impressive 86.7 million, underscoring Turkey's pivotal role in shaping the digital banking landscape.

The data on fintech startup activities in Turkey in 2021, depicted in Figure 7, reveals intriguing insights into the dynamic landscape of financial technology in the country. The substantial number of 589 fintech startups indicates a robust entrepreneurial ecosystem, signifying a growing interest and investment in innovative financial solutions. The dominance of payment services, with over 200 new startups, underscores the significance of this sector in meeting evolving consumer needs. The subsequent ranking of activities, ranging from banking and crypto money to insurance and corporate finance, reflects a well-diversified fintech landscape, with entrepreneurs exploring various facets of the financial industry. This diversity suggests a comprehensive approach to addressing different aspects of financial services, showcasing the adaptability and responsiveness of the Turkish fintech sector to a wide array of financial needs. The emphasis on information security and the inclusion of emerging technologies like blockchain also highlight a commitment to ensuring the security and technological advancement of financial services in the country. Overall, the data paints a picture of a thriving fintech ecosystem in

Figure 7. Number of fintech startups in Turkey by activity
(Turkish Competition Authority, 2021)

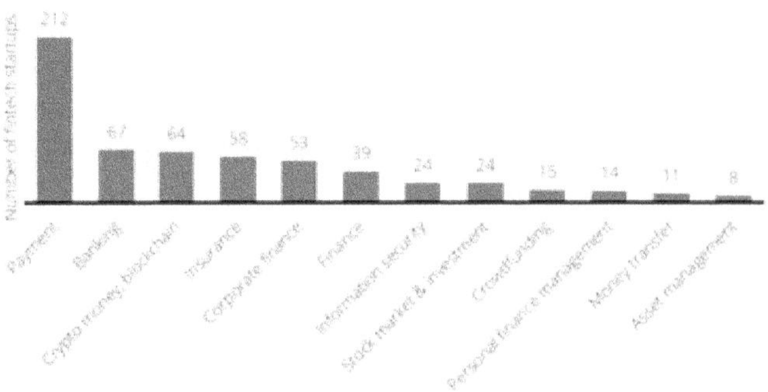

Turkey, with a strong foundation in payment services and a multifaceted approach to addressing diverse financial challenges.

Examples of FinTech Firms Turkey

Tekkredi: Tekkredi facilitates debt consolidation for individuals by connecting with various financial institutions. Providing a lending option to pay off multiple previous loans, Tekkredi empowers consumers to choose a bank for opening a new loan account, simplifying the debt management process.

Ininal: In 2012, a group of developers launched Ininal, a new generation payment processing technology serving individuals and small businesses. Acquiring an electronic money operating license from the Banking Regulation and Supervision Agency (BRSA) in 2017, Ininal provides prepaid cards and a wallet app across numerous locations in Turkey. Offering business clients an API platform, co-branded cards, and streamlined bulk payment solutions, Ininal continues to benefit hundreds of thousands of users with its affordable and user-friendly financial services.

Paraşüt: Paraşüt, a cloud-based pre-accounting tool launched in 2013, focuses on empowering small and medium-sized firms (SMEs) in the Turkish economy. Offering essential financial operations features such as invoice and current account management, income tracking, and reporting, Paraşüt serves as a financial management panel designed for business owners. The user-friendly platform ensures accessibility for individuals unfamiliar with invoicing, contributing to the continuous improvement efforts by the Mikrogrup family in support of SMEs.

iPara: Founded in 2012, iPara Bilgi Teknolojileri A.Ş. swiftly rose to prominence as Turkey's premier online payment service provider. Pioneering online purchasing convenience, iPara is committed to delivering value-added services to member businesses and partners. Emphasizing innovation and continuous improvement, iPara strives to expand its product and service offerings while maintaining a leadership position in the industry.

KolayBi: KolayBi, through partnerships with top banks, e-commerce platforms, e-invoice integrators, and payment systems, is dedicated to meeting clients' e-transformation needs efficiently. Leveraging cutting-edge technological infrastructure and a talented team, KolayBi ensures seamless digital solutions for clients, contributing to the ongoing transformation of digital processes.

PayCore: Founded in 2001, PayCore is a comprehensive payment technology solutions provider serving clients in banking, telecommunications, payment service provision, public service, and retail industries. With over 250 institutional partners across 30+ countries, PayCore is a recipient of 30+ local and international awards. Recognized for PCI DSS, BKM, MasterCard, and Visa certifications, PayCore's Processing Center serves over 65 customers, offering cutting-edge solutions in card management, digital payment, EMV solutions, processing services, and secure hardware devices.

Moka: Moka, a subsidiary of Turkey İş Bankası, is a financial technology firm providing clients with advanced payment options. Launched in 2014, Moka aims to deliver fast, convenient, and practical payment solutions. With an e-money license acquired in 2022, Moka serves as a bridge between traditional and digital payment industries, offering rapid and competitive services. Focused on cutting-edge financial technology solutions, Moka prioritizes overall customer experience through novel business models and anticipating customer needs.

Papara: Established in 2016 by Ahmed Faruk Karsli and Ilker Diker, Papara is an electronic money and payment services provider challenging traditional financial executions with innovative and user-friendly solutions. Offering a novel and convenient way to make payments, purchase items, and transfer money,

Papara enhances financial control for users. Notable clients, including Uber, BiTaksi, and Yemeksepeti, attest to the company's success, further boosted by a $2 million investment in 2016.

Colendi: Colendi, established with a mission to provide simple, accessible financial products, focuses on democratizing banking services. Offering embedded FinTech services, Colendi's cutting-edge scoring technology assesses creditworthiness based on real data and machine-learning algorithms. The company empowers individuals and organizations to start fresh, unburdened by their financial past.

Arf: Arf enables financial institutions to make instant, compliant international payments using regulated stable coinage. Offering a range of services, including custody, redemption, tokenization, settlement, and foreign exchange (FX), Arf serves licensed money service businesses and financial institutions. With native on-ramp and off-ramp capabilities, Arf provides digital asset-based working capital and settlement services, contributing to efficient financial operations.

AI INTEGRATION IN FINTECH

The integration of artificial intelligence (AI) into the realm of FinTech has sparked a revolution in the financial sector, introducing enhancements in efficiency, precision, and the overall customer experience (Brynjolfsson, E., 2018). AI, driven by sophisticated machine learning algorithms, equips financial institutions with the capability to analyze extensive datasets, enabling the pinpointing of fraudulent activities, meticulous evaluation of credit risks, and the crafting of personalized investment strategies (Taherdoost, H., 2023b). Projections from Accenture underscore the substantial impact of AI, estimating a cumulative value addition of $1.2 trillion to the financial industry by 2035. Additionally, insights from a PwC study reveal a significant trend, with 77% of financial service providers anticipated to embed AI as a fundamental component of their business operations within the upcoming three years. This strategic incorporation not only optimizes operational processes but also empowers companies to deliver bespoke financial solutions, thereby reshaping the landscape of FinTech.

The infusion of Artificial Intelligence (AI) and machine learning into the financial services sector is delivering substantial value by automating and refining diverse processes (Agrawal, A., 2018). Within the realms of banking and finance, AI empowers organizations to swiftly and accurately distill insights from massive datasets, thereby enhancing decision-making processes (Rock, D., & Sorkin, I., 2021). Its applications in finance span a wide spectrum, encompassing functions from fraud detection, credit assessment, and customer service to risk management, investment strategies, and trading. AI's role extends to aiding institutions in portfolio management through the analysis of market trends, offering real-time insights into dynamic market conditions. Moreover, it proves instrumental in minimizing risks and optimizing returns, ultimately boosting profitability. Implementing AI in the financial sector brings about a notable efficiency boost by automating mundane tasks like data entry, allowing employees to redirect their efforts towards intricate and strategic initiatives. This shift not only heightens operational efficiency but also leads to cost reductions. In the realm of customer service, the integration of AI-driven chatbots and virtual assistants plays a pivotal role, addressing inquiries promptly and enhancing response times, ultimately resulting in elevated customer satisfaction. The application of Artificial Intelligence in banking and finance proves instrumental in effective risk management (Razavi, H., 2019). By analyzing market trends and providing real-time insights, AI empowers organizations to make well-informed decisions, thus contributing to more robust risk management practices. Moreover, in the crucial area of fraud detection and prevention, the deployment of AI-powered tools proves invaluable. Swift and accurate identification and prevention of fraudulent activities not only enhance security but also translate into substantial monetary savings for organizations.

The global private investments in artificial intelligence (AI) for 2022 are visually represented in Figure 8. Notably, the combined investments in FinTech and insurtech have soared to a remarkable 7.24 billion dollars, establishing it as the leading investment category among various industries. This financial commitment suggests a recognition of AI's potential to drive innovation, enhance efficiency, and transform traditional financial services. The significant capital influx indicates a collective belief in the future trajectory of AI in FinTech, anticipating a continued trend of integration and development. As AI applications become more sophisticated and tailored to the financial landscape, these investments signal a broader industry consensus that AI will play a pivotal role in shaping the future of FinTech, ushering in advancements, improved customer experiences, and new possibilities.

Figure 8. AI private investment worldwide in 2022, by industry
(Stanford University, 2023)

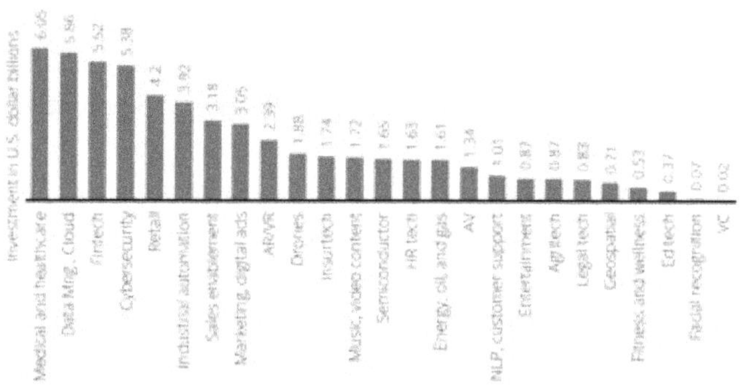

Figure 9 provides a compelling insight into the anticipated impact of Artificial Intelligence (AI) on the UAE within the Middle East and North Africa region. The forecast for 2030 indicates that the UAE is poised to experience the most significant influence of AI, constituting a noteworthy 14 percent of the country's Gross Domestic Product (GDP). This translates to an estimated value of approximately 96 billion U.S. dollars, underscoring the substantial economic contribution expected from advancements in AI technology. A remarkable aspect is the UAE's exceptional growth in AI contribution, boasting an

Figure 9. Average annual growth and share of GDP of AI in the ME from 2018 to 2030, by region
(PwC., 2018)

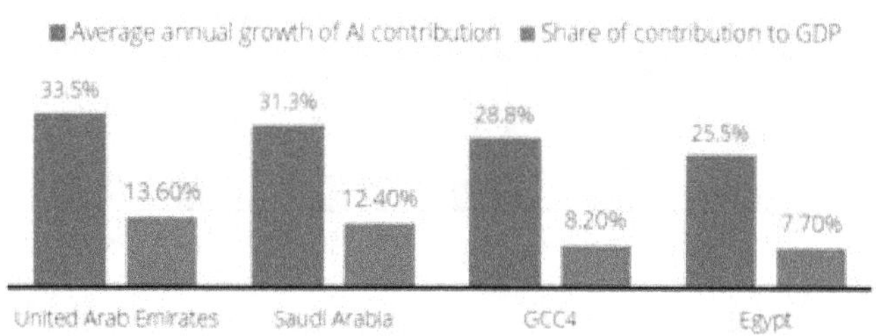

average annual growth rate of around 33.5 percent from 2018 to 2030. This accelerated growth is a clear reflection of the UAE's strategic investments in AI technology. The figure also offers a comparative perspective, including other key countries in the region such as Saudi Arabia and Egypt, alongside the collective impact of the Gulf Cooperation Council (GCC4), comprising Bahrain, Kuwait, Oman, and Qatar. This forecast emphasizes the UAE's pivotal role in spearheading the AI landscape in the Middle East, signaling a transformative journey with significant economic implications. The analysis of Figure 9 suggests a promising future trend for the UAE in the field of Artificial Intelligence (AI). The projected substantial contribution of AI to the UAE's GDP, reaching 14 percent by 2030 with an estimated value of around 96 billion U.S. dollars, indicates a robust and transformative economic trajectory. This trend underscores the UAE's commitment to harnessing AI technologies for sustainable growth and innovation.

The noteworthy annual growth rate of approximately 33.5 percent between 2018 and 2030 further accentuates the proactive measures taken by the UAE in embracing and investing in AI. This rapid acceleration in AI contribution signals a trajectory of continuous advancement, positioning the UAE as a global leader in AI adoption and development. While the statistics does not delve into the specifics of other countries in the region, the comparative analysis implies that the UAE is emerging as a standout player in the regional AI landscape. This comparative advantage is likely to fuel the UAE's influence in shaping the future of AI adoption in the Middle East. Additionally, the inclusion of GCC4 countries in the analysis provides a broader regional perspective, indicating the potential for collaborative efforts and shared advancements in AI technology.

Understanding the array of AI applications employed by banks is crucial for gaining insights into the evolving landscape of financial technology. As of 2020, a comprehensive survey of investment banks worldwide highlighted the prevalent utilization of machine learning as the foremost AI application in the industry (figure 10). A majority of respondents, constituting 63%, acknowledged the widespread adoption of machine learning, attesting to its significance in enhancing operational efficiency and decision-making processes. Following closely, predictive analytics secured the second position with 60% of respondents leveraging its capabilities for data-driven insights and forecasting. Virtual assistant technologies emerged as another notable AI application, embraced by 58% of respondents, underscoring the sector's inclination towards leveraging intelligent automation for improved customer interactions. Additional AI applications included image analysis and natural language processing, both standing at 52%, reflecting a diverse integration of technologies to address varied banking challenges. Robotic process automation, at 45%, rounded out the array of AI applications. However, it is noteworthy that the development of these technologies is hindered by a common challenge faced by fintech activities in this region—the

Figure 10. Share of investment banks worldwide using (AI) as of 2020, by types of application (Forbes, 2020).

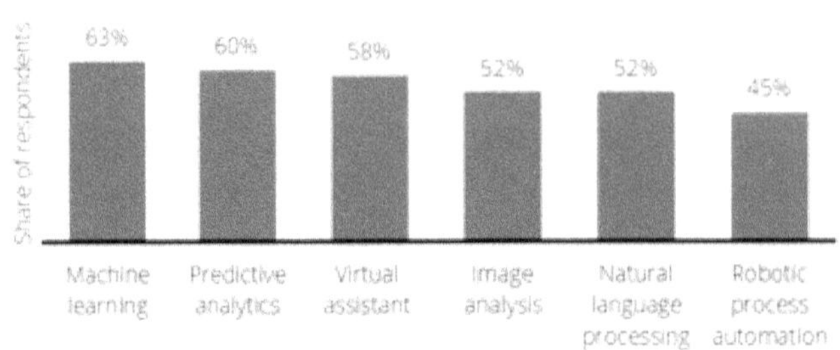

acquisition of talented hu,man capital. Struggling with the recruitment of skilled professionals poses a hurdle in fully harnessing the potential of these advanced technologies within the fintech landscape.

CHALLENGES AND OPPORTUNITIES

In the Middle East region, FinTechs address challenges like financial inclusion, with 136 million adults being underbanked or unbanked. Despite obstacles such as market asymmetries and inconsistent regulations, FinTechs introduce innovative solutions, including alternative payments and blockchain technologies. (Milken Institute, 2019) notes a rise in FinTech adoption from 13% in 2017 to 18% in 2020 in the ME region. The region's SMEs face a $260 billion credit gap, offering a substantial opportunity for FinTechs. Saudi Arabia, aiming to contribute $1.2 billion to its GDP by 2025, aligns FinTech goals with its Vision 2030 plan. Increased digital financial transactions could boost GDP per capita by 1.1 percentage points. However, with FinTech advancements come new challenges, including cyber threats. Regulatory barriers concern 67% of ME FinTech firms, with 46% citing cybersecurity issues. The lack of comprehensive frameworks and constraints on balance sheets pose hurdles. Governments and regulators must collaborate with industry stakeholders to foster a conducive environment for FinTech innovation.

In conclusion, FinTech holds the potential to reshape the ME region's financial landscape, fostering economic growth and financial inclusion. Addressing challenges and seizing opportunities will enable FinTechs to make a lasting impact in the digital age.

Main Challenges for FinTech in ME:

1. Infrastructure Challenges: Many countries in the Middle East face a shortage of high-speed internet connections, constraining the expansion of digital offerings and restricting their availability to the public.
2. Digital Literacy Concerns: Despite technological proficiency among the younger demographic, a significant segment of the population lacks digital literacy, resulting in a digital disparity that needs to be addressed through educational efforts and skill development programs.
3. Cybersecurity Risks: The rapid growth of digital technologies exposes the Middle East to potential cyber threats, emphasizing the crucial need to ensure the safety and security of digital systems to maintain public trust and encourage further adoption.
4. Legal and Regulatory Framework Issues: The Middle East lacks comprehensive legal and regulatory frameworks for addressing crucial issues such as data protection, privacy, and intellectual property rights, leading to uncertainty that hinders the growth of digital industries.
5. Regulatory and Market Harmonization Challenges: Regulatory changes across the region are uneven, creating differences in legal frameworks for setting up digital businesses and obtaining licenses. Greater collaboration and alignment across markets are needed to facilitate scaling.
6. Talent Acquisition and Development: Attracting experienced talent, particularly in areas such as engineering and product management, poses a challenge due to high demand and increased costs. Government-mandated localized hiring targets further emphasize the need to upgrade skills and train local talent.
7. Diversity in Leadership: The representation of women in leadership positions in the Middle East's startups is limited (only 9 percent). Increasing gender diversity is crucial for a broader range of perspectives and enhanced organizational performance.

8. Partnerships for Value Creation: Collaboration between incumbents and startups in the Middle East is below 50 percent, highlighting the need for more aggressive approaches to partnering. Creating compelling propositions and discussions with regulators are essential for upgrading the value proposition and preventing market share loss.

Main Opportunities for FinTech in ME:

1. Youthful Demographic and Digital Adoption: The Middle East boasts a young, educated population with some of the world's highest rates of mobile, internet, and smartphone penetration. This demographic, constituting a third of the population under 30, signals an opportunity for FinTech to address the financial needs of tech-savvy individuals entering adulthood.
2. Digital Payment Growth: The acceleration of noncash payments during the COVID-19 pandemic, exemplified by the rise from 39% to 73% in cardless payments in the United Arab Emirates, underscores a growing demand for digital financial products. FinTech can capitalize on this trend by offering innovative digital payment solutions.
3. Financial Inclusion: With only 17% of consumers in the Middle East currently using digital banking, there is substantial room for FinTech to enhance financial inclusion. By providing accessible and user-friendly financial services, FinTech can reach a broader segment of the population.
4. Economic Diversification and Job Creation: Regional governments' commitment to economic transformation, private sector engagement, and reducing the public sector's role aligns with FinTech's potential to diversify the economy and create jobs.
5. Venture Funding Opportunities: Despite current challenges and a slowdown in venture funding, FinTech in the Middle East has attracted significant investment, with funding expected to increase from \$1.5 billion in 2022 to \$3.5–\$4.5 billion by 2025. This presents opportunities for FinTech startups to secure funding and scale their operations.
6. Regulatory Reforms: The region's regulatory environment, while protective, is recognized as having the greatest potential for reform among emerging market economies. Regulatory harmonization and policies that level the playing field for incumbents and newcomers can create a conducive environment for FinTech growth.
7. Ecosystem Development: Countries such as Abu Dhabi, Bahrain, Dubai, and Riyadh are actively vying to become FinTech hubs. FinTech startups and companies can benefit from the development of these ecosystems, fostering collaboration, innovation, and the exchange of ideas.
8. Market Scalability: Despite challenges in regulatory fragmentation and high scalability costs, there is an opportunity for FinTech companies to adopt a regional, multimarket approach. This can help them achieve growth targets and develop sustainable, profitable business models.
9. AI and Technological Advancements: The emergence of artificial intelligence (AI) presents opportunities for FinTech to disrupt traditional financial services. AI can enable sophisticated analysis of complex data sets, leveling the playing field for FinTech startups and facilitating innovation in the sector.
10. Policy Support for Innovation: Policymakers in the region are recognizing the importance of FinTech for financial inclusion and economic growth. Recent policy actions, such as Saudi Arabia's open banking framework and Egypt's digital payment regulation, indicate a commitment to creating a favorable regulatory environment for FinTech.

FUTURE TRENDS OF FINTECH IN MIDDLE EAST

The financial landscape in the Middle East is undergoing rapid transformation, propelled by technological advancements and shifting consumer preferences. The region is emerging as a dynamic frontier for the fintech industry, experiencing growth fueled by a combination of favorable demographics, economic prospects, digital enthusiasm, and widespread mobile penetration. By the year 2030, the FinTech sector was anticipated to play a substantial role, contributing approximately 13.6% to the GDP of the Middle East region, with artificial intelligence being a significant driving force. Projections suggested that the UAE would take the lead in the region's development and adoption of AI technologies (figure 11).

Figure 11. Forecasted contribution of AI to GDP in the Middle East in 2030, by industry
(Oxford Business Group, 2021)

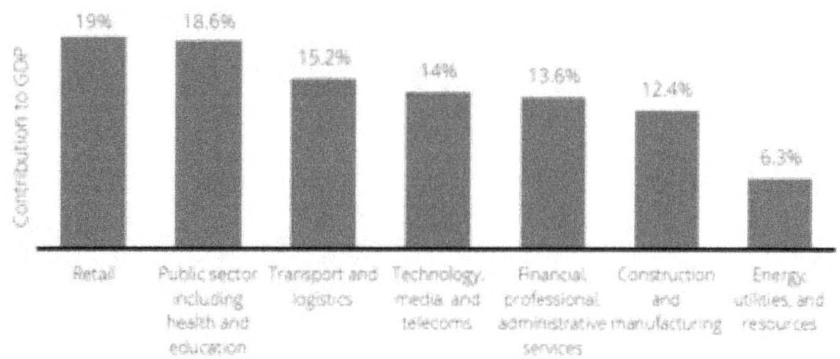

The foundation of developing AI stands on robust data infrastructure, and the Middle East is in the nascent stages of establishing comprehensive data sharing practices (Razavi, H., 2017). For instance, according to the Global Data Barometer, the UAE, Jordan, and Oman received overall data scores of 26.7, 34.5, and 14.1, respectively. In comparison, countries like the UK and Estonia received scores of 64.5 and 67.4, emphasizing the region's early progress in this domain. Examining specific instances like open banking and data sharing underscores the critical role of data. Access to financial data in the Middle East is still evolving, prompting the introduction of open banking to emphasize the importance of liberating financial data. Traditionally held by banks, this initiative shifts ownership to customers, who now have the authority to grant consent on sharing their data and specify the type of data they wish to share.

To address the early stages of data access in the Middle East, fintech companies are taking proactive measures to bridge the data gap. Collaboration with various stakeholders, including governments, financial institutions, and technology partners, becomes pivotal in this process. Several countries in the Middle East have already embarked on the journey towards open banking. Bahrain, for instance, launched its Open Banking Framework in October 2023. In March 2023, Qatar's Central Bank outlined a Fintech Sector Strategy Summary, with a significant focus on open banking architecture. Jordan released its Open Finance Framework in November 2022, and the UAE introduced its Financial Infrastructure Transformation Program, slated for full implementation by 2026. These initiatives collectively signify the region's commitment to advancing data sharing practices and fostering a conducive environment for the growth of AI and fintech.

Figure 12 illustrates the future potential of five ME countries, highlighting a notable trend of high and continually increasing digital penetration. The infrastructure in these nations is generally more advanced, with Bahrain trailing somewhat behind. Despite varying degrees of economic challenges, all countries in the group are confronted with less-than-ideal economic outlooks. Projections indicate that Bahrain is anticipated to experience the slowest growth within the group, while the UAE is expected to demonstrate the fastest, although still moderate, growth.

Figure 12. Assessment of FinTech growth potential across ME countries
(Velmie, 2023)

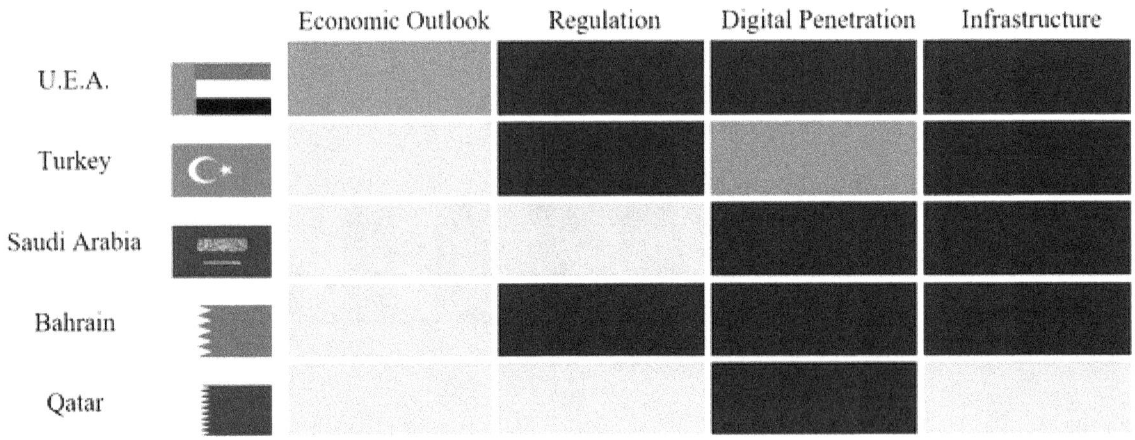

Current Landscape:

- The Gulf nations are heavily investing in becoming global AI hubs, with a particular emphasis on the banking, healthcare, and transportation sectors.
- Turkey and the UAE are at the forefront of developing AI strategies, regulations, and applications, including chatbots, fraud prevention, and personalized marketing.
- There is a growing interest in blockchain due to its crypto appeal, supported by proactive regulations from countries like the UAE and Bahrain.
- Cloud connectivity is of utmost importance for fintechs and neobanks aiming for rapid scalability in the Middle East.
- However, the growth of cloud technology faces challenges, notably talent shortages and stringent cross-border data regulations.
- Open banking has commenced data sharing, underscoring the importance of platforms to bridge data gaps.
- Balancing privacy and security risks is crucial, with fintechs prioritizing the protection of consumer data.

Future Outlook:

- AI is reshaping the retail payments ecosystem, with machine learning tools enabling neobanks to offer customized services at a pace traditional banks struggle to match.

- AI could transform various sectors if challenges related to implementation and regulation are effectively addressed.
- Blockchain startups and innovations are expected to thrive with continued government support.
- Progress in cloud technology requires updated regulations and skills development.
- Managing risks related to data sharing will be critical as open banking continues to expand.
- The Middle East is well-positioned to emerge as a global fintech leader snd hub with the right policies and investments.

Key Technologies Impacting the Sector:

1. Artificial Intelligence:

In the Middle East, AI is poised to revolutionize the FinTech landscape by introducing unprecedented levels of efficiency and personalization. AI-powered algorithms can analyze vast datasets, facilitating more accurate credit assessments, personalized financial advice, and precise fraud detection. Chatbots and virtual assistants, driven by AI, enhance customer interactions, providing instant support and improving overall user experience. With a projected 20% improvement in operational efficiency, AI is set to be a game-changer, streamlining processes and elevating the quality of financial services across the region.

2. Cloud Technology:

Cloud computing is set to reshape the infrastructure of FinTech in the Middle East, offering scalable and cost-effective solutions. Cloud-based platforms enable financial institutions to store and process vast amounts of data securely, fostering innovation in product development and service delivery. The flexibility of cloud technology facilitates seamless collaboration, accelerates time-to-market for new financial products, and ensures the scalability needed to meet the region's growing demand for digital services. As a result, cloud adoption is poised to be a key driver in transforming the agility and responsiveness of the FinTech sector in the Middle East.

3. Open Banking:

Open Banking is ushering in a new era of collaboration and customer-centricity in the Middle East's financial ecosystem. By allowing secure data sharing between financial institutions and third-party providers, Open Banking fosters the development of innovative financial products and services. Customers gain greater control over their financial data, leading to personalized and tailored offerings. With the increased competition and innovation spurred by Open Banking, consumers in the Middle East can expect a diverse array of financial products, improved transparency, and enhanced financial inclusivity.

4. Blockchain:

Blockchain technology holds immense potential to transform the Middle East's financial landscape by providing transparency, security, and efficiency. In a region known for its global economic connectivity, blockchain can streamline cross-border transactions and reduce the complexities associated with international payments. Smart contracts on blockchain facilitate secure and automated transactions, reducing the risk of fraud and errors. Additionally, blockchain's decentralized nature enhances the security and integrity of financial data. As governments and financial institutions embrace blockchain, it is poised to be a game-changer in reducing costs, mitigating risks, and enhancing the overall efficiency of financial processes in the Middle East.

CONCLUSION

This chapter aims to unravel the intricate dynamics of the FinTech landscape in the Middle East, with a keen focus on the UAE and Turkey. Our primary objectives are twofold: to meticulously examine the ongoing transformations within the region's FinTech ecosystem and to assess the profound impact of Artificial Intelligence (AI). Tailored for finance professionals, policymakers, entrepreneurs, and academics, this chapter serves as a comprehensive resource, providing nuanced insights into the forces that shape the FinTech narrative.

Our journey through the multifaceted Middle Eastern FinTech sector commences by delving into the technological integration of AI, blockchain, big data, and cloud computing. We illuminate their transformative effects on the banking and payment sector, elucidating the paradigm shift towards customer-centric, digital-first approaches. Emphasizing collaborative initiatives between established financial institutions and nimble FinTech startups underscores the industry's responsiveness to evolving consumer needs.

The exploration extends to the intersection of diverse customer needs and the considerable expatriate presence in the GCC, serving as catalysts for innovation. By dissecting the competitive landscape featuring telecommunications firms, retailers, and neo-banks, we gain insights into the intensified competition within the financial services sector. Addressing challenges and opportunities, especially in catering to the financial preferences of the youthful population and acknowledging global issues of unbanked adults, paints a comprehensive picture of the sector's intricacies.

Looking forward, the future of FinTech in the Middle East holds promise, driven by favorable macroeconomic conditions. The anticipated continued collaboration between traditional banks and FinTech entities is poised to yield cutting-edge solutions, ensuring sustained growth and competitiveness. The economic vibrancy of the Middle East, coupled with the agility of financial institutions, establishes a foundation for an era marked by continued innovation in financial technology. As we navigate this ever-evolving landscape, future research extends its focus across several dimensions. The evolving regulatory environment's impact on FinTech development requires in-depth exploration, providing critical insights for stakeholders. Further research into specific applications and successes of AI, blockchain, big data, and cloud computing within the region is essential for a comprehensive understanding of their transformative potential. Efforts are concentrated on developing strategies to address financial inclusion challenges, particularly for the unbanked population, with a keen eye on collaborative models between traditional banks and FinTech firms. Comparative studies with global FinTech trends could offer valuable perspectives, positioning the Middle East within the broader context of the global FinTech ecosystem.

In summary, this chapter stands as a stepping stone for those interested in the Middle Eastern FinTech scene. The objectives of dissecting the FinTech landscape, evaluating technological impacts, and providing a resource for stakeholders are achieved. As the FinTech journey unfolds, the roadmap ahead holds exciting prospects for innovation, collaboration, and continued growth in the financial technology domain of the Middle East.

REFERENCES

Abdeldayem, M., & Aldulaimi, S. (2023). Entrepreneurial finance and crowdfunding in the Middle East. *The International Journal of Organizational Analysis, 31*(4), 927–944. doi:10.1108/IJOA-03-2021-2684

Acemoglu, D., & Restrepo, P. (2020). Robots and jobs: Evidence from US labor markets. *Journal of Political Economy, 128*(6), 2188–2244. doi:10.1086/705716

Adeleye, B. N., Bengana, I., Boukhelkhal, A., Shafiq, M. M., & Abdulkareem, H. K. (2022). Does human capital tilt the population-economic growth dynamics? Evidence from Middle East and north African countries. *Social Indicators Research, 162*(2), 863–883. doi:10.1007/s11205-021-02867-5

Adrian, T., & Mancini-Grifoli, T. (2019b, September 19). *Digital Currencies: The Rise of Stablecoins.* Retrieved from https://blogs.imf.org

Agrawal, A., McHale, J., & Oettl, A. (2018). *The Impact of Artificial Intelligence on Innovation.* National Bureau of Economic Research, Working Paper 24284. February 2018.

Akmal, S., Talha, M., Faisal, S. M., Ahmad, M., & Khan, A. K. (2023). Perceptions about FinTech: New evidences from the Middle East. *Cogent Economics & Finance, 11*(1), 2217583. doi:10.1080/23322039.2023.2217583

Al-Afeef, M., Fraihat, B., Alhawamdeh, H., Hijazi, H., AL-Afeef, M. A., Nawasr, M., & Rabi, A. M. (2023). Factors affecting middle eastern countries' intention to use financial technology. *International Journal of Data and Network Science, 7*(3), 1179–1192. doi:10.5267/j.ijdns.2023.5.006

Al Suwaidi, M. E. Y. M., Sidek, S. B., & Al-Shami, S. A. (2022). *A Conceptual Framework of FinTech Laws and Regulations on the Risk Management of Financial Institutions in UAE.* Mathematical Statistician and Engineering Applications, 71(3), 01-07.

Albarrak, M. S., & Alokley, S. A. (2021). FinTech: Ecosystem, opportunities and challenges in Saudi Arabia. *Journal of Risk and Financial Management, 14*(10), 460. doi:10.3390/jrfm14100460

Alblooshi, F. S. A. K. (2022). FinTech in the United Arab Emirates: a general introduction to the main aspects of financial technology. In Entrepreneurial Rise in the Middle East and North Africa: The Influence of Quadruple Helix on Technological Innovation (pp. 163-178). Emerald Publishing Limited. doi:10.1108/978-1-80071-517-220221010

Alkhazaleh, A. M. K. (2021). Challenges and Opportunities for FinTech Startups: Situation in The Arab World. *Academy of Accounting and Financial Studies Journal, 25*(3), 1–14.

Baird, N., Blevins, J., Scheerschmidt, T., Vecchi, N., & Weiße, L. (2023). Dubai: A City of Contradictions. In *The Strategic Management of Place at Work: Why, What, How and Where* (pp. 377–393). Springer Nature Switzerland. doi:10.1007/978-3-031-29463-1_20

Banerjee, A. (2020). FinTech revolution in the gulf countries and mena region. *Entrepreneurial Finance in Emerging Markets: Exploring Tools, Techniques, and Innovative Technologies*, 335-344.

Barroso, M., & Laborda, J. (2022). Digital transformation and the emergence of the FinTech sector: Systematic literature review. *Digital Business, 2*(2), 100028. doi:10.1016/j.digbus.2022.100028

Bayram, O., Talay, I., & Feridun, M. (2022). Can FinTech promote sustainable finance? Policy lessons from the case of Turkey. *Sustainability (Basel), 14*(19), 12414. doi:10.3390/su141912414

BKM. (2022*). Report on the Number of POS, ATM, ÖKC Software.* bkm.com.tr

Bouteraa, M., Chekima, B., Lajuni, N., & Anwar, A. (2023). Understanding Consumers' Barriers to Using FinTech Services in the United Arab Emirates: Mixed-Methods Research Approach. *Sustainability (Basel), 15*(4), 2931. doi:10.3390/su15042931

Brynjolfsson, E., Rock, D., & Syverson, C. (2018). Artificial Intelligence and the Modern Productivity Paradox: A Clash of Expectations and Statistics. *The American Economic Review, 108*(6), 1259–1266.

Buchholz, K. (January 19, 2022). *The End of Natural Population Growth?* [Digital image]. Retrieved November 12, 2023, from https://0-www-statista-com.biblioteca-ils.tec.mx/chart/26634/start-year-of-negative-net-births-by-country

CCAF. (2021). *Fintech Regulation in Sub-Saharan Africa*. CCAF. www.jbs.cam.ac.uk/faculty-research/centres/alternative-finance/publications/fintech-regulation-in-sub-saharan-africa

Cengiz, S., Atmiş, E., & Görmüş, S. (2019). The impact of economic growth oriented development policies on landscape changes in Istanbul Province in Turkey. *Land Use Policy, 87*, 104086. doi:10.1016/j.landusepol.2019.104086

Chinnasamy, G., Madbouly, A., & Reyad, S. (2021). FinTech: A pathway for MENA region. *The fourth industrial revolution: implementation of artificial intelligence for growing business success*, 135-151.

Comin, D., & Mestieri, M. (2022). Artificial Intelligence and Economic Growth: A Review of the Literature and Directions for Future Research. *Annual Review of Economics, 14*, 743–767.

Cusolito, A. P., Gévaudan, C., Lederman, D., & Wood, C. (2022). *The upside of digital for the Middle East and North Africa: how digital technology adoption can accelerate growth and create jobs*. World Bank Publications.

Daza Jaller, L. S., & Molinuevo, M. (2020). *Digital Trade in MENA: Regulatory Readiness Assessment*. World Bank Policy Research Working Paper, (9199).

Degerli, K. (2019). Regulatory challenges and solutions for FinTech in Turkey. *Procedia Computer Science, 158*, 929–937. doi:10.1016/j.procs.2019.09.133

Demirgüç-Kunt, A., Klapper, L., Singer, D., & Ansar, S. (2022). *The Global Findex Database 2021: Financial inclusion, digital payments, and resilience in the age of COVID-19*. World Bank Publications. doi:10.1596/978-1-4648-1897-4

Dogan, E., & Stupar, A. (2017). The limits of growth: A case study of three mega-projects in Istanbul. *Cities (London, England), 60*, 281–288. doi:10.1016/j.cities.2016.09.013

Dwivedi, P., Alabdooli, J. I., & Dwivedi, R. (2021). Role of FinTech adoption for competitiveness and performance of the bank: A study of banking industry in UAE. *International Journal of Global Business and Competitiveness, 16*(2), 130–138. doi:10.1007/s42943-021-00033-9

Emara, N., & Mohieldin, M. (2021). Beyond the Digital Dividends: FinTech and Extreme Poverty in the Middle East and Africa. *Topics in Middle Eastern & North African Economies: Proceedings of the Middle East Economic Association,* 23.

Evron, Y., Kowner, R., & Kumaraswamy, P. R. (2024). East and West Asia in the Twenty-First Century: From Bilateral to Interregional Relationships. In East-West Asia Relations in the 21st Century (pp. 3-14). Routledge.

Fayda, S. N. A., Sencan, A., Aksoy, O., & Yazici, S. (2020). A Qualitative Research on Selected Performance Indicators for Investment Decision Process: A Framework for FinTech Startups in Turkey. *Journal of Business Economics and Finance*, *9*(1), 28–41. doi:10.17261/Pressacademia.2020.1190

Forbes Middle East. (2023). *Top 20 Fintech Startups in the Middle East*. Retrieved November 13, 2023, from https://www.forbesmiddleeast.com/list/top-20-FinTech-startups-in-the-middle-east

Forbes. (2020). *Share of investment banks worldwide using artificial intelligence (AI) as of 2020, by types of application* [Graph]. Statista. Retrieved November 18, 2023, from https://0-www-statista-com.biblioteca-ils.tec.mx/statistics/1246874/ai-used-in-investment-banking-worldwide-2020

Gur, N., Babacan, M., Aysan, A. F., & Suleyman, S. (2023). Firm Size and Financing Behavior during COVID-19. In *Pandemic: Evidence from SMEs in Istanbul*. Borsa Istanbul Review.

Hassan, M. K., Rahiman, H. U., Rabbani, M. R., & Alhomaidi, A. (2022). The future of finance and FinTech: Visualizing the opportunities for FinTech in the MENA region. In *FinTech in Islamic Financial Institutions: Scope, Challenges, and Implications in Islamic Finance* (pp. 89–111). Springer International Publishing. doi:10.1007/978-3-031-14941-2_5

Hussein, H. (2020). The impact of financial technology on financial inclusion: The case of Egypt. *IOSR Journal of Economics and Finance*, *11*(6), 35–51.

Igor Tomych. (2023). *Fintech Compliance In MENA: Navigating Regulations and Security Requirements*. Retrieved from https://dashdevs.com

Insider Intelligence. (2022). *Artificial intelligence (AI) adoption rate in financial businesses worldwide in 2022 and 2025* [Graph]. Statista. Retrieved November 13, 2023, from https://0-www-statista-com.biblioteca-ils.tec.mx/statistics/1346736/ai-function-adoption-rates-business-finance

Jaber, J., & Issa, H. (2022). Disruptive innovation in the middle eastern FinTech sector: Resource-based view. *International Journal of Technology and Human Interaction*, *18*(1), 1–21. doi:10.4018/IJTHI.299069

Kheira, T. (2021). Financial technology prospects in the Middle East and Africa. *Journal of Economic Growth*, *4*(3), 14–25.

King, B. (2018). *Bank 4.0: Banking everywhere, never at a bank*. John Wiley & Sons. doi:10.1002/9781119506515

Kukreja, G., Gupta, R., & Gupta, A. (2021). FinTech in Oman: Present and future scenario. *Applications of Artificial Intelligence in Business, Education and Healthcare*, 173-183.

Lukonga, I. (2021). Fintech and the real economy: Lessons from the Middle East, North Africa, Afghanistan, and Pakistan (MENAP) region. The Palgrave handbook of fintech and blockchain, 187-214.

Magnitt. (2022). *UAE H1 2022 Venture Investment Report*. magnitt.com.

Mason, A., Lee, R., & Network, N. T. A. (2022). Six ways population change will affect the global economy. *Population and Development Review*, *48*(1), 51–73. doi:10.1111/padr.12469

Mikhaylov, A., Dinçer, H., & Yüksel, S. (2023). Analysis of financial development and open innovation oriented FinTech potential for emerging economies using an integrated decision-making approach of MF-X-DMA and golden cut bipolar q-ROFSs. *Financial Innovation*, *9*(1), 1–34. doi:10.1186/s40854-022-00399-6

Milken Institute. (2019). *The Rise of FinTech in the Middle East*. Retrieved from https://milkeninstitute.org

Mohamed, H. Y., Hamdan, A., Karolak, M., Razzaque, A., & Alareeni, B. (2021). FinTech in Bahrain: The role of FinTech in empowering women. In The Importance of New Technologies and Entrepreneurship in Business Development: In The Context of Economic Diversity in Developing Countries: The Impact of New Technologies and Entrepreneurship on Business Development (pp. 757-766). Springer International Publishing. doi:10.1007/978-3-030-69221-6_57

Naz, F., Karim, S., Houcine, A., & Naeem, M. A. (2022). FinTech growth during COVID-19 in MENA region: Current challenges and future prospects. *Electronic Commerce Research*, 1–22. doi:10.1007/s10660-022-09583-3

Oxford Business Group. (2021). *Forecasted contribution of artificial intelligence to gross domestic product in the Middle East and North Africa region in 2030, by industry* [Graph]. Statista. Retrieved November 18, 2023, from https://0-www-statista-com.biblioteca-ils.tec.mx/statistics/1272197/mena-ai-contribution-to-gdp-by-industry

PwC. (2018). *Forecasted contribution share of Artificial Intelligence to GDP in the Middle East and North Africa in 2030, by region* [Graph]. Statista. Retrieved November 18, 2023, from https://0-www-statista-com.biblioteca-ils.tec.mx/statistics/1181489/mena-forecasted-gdp-contribution-of-ai

PwC. (2021). *US$320 billion by 2030? The potential impact of AI in the Middle East*. Retrieved from https://www.pwc.com/m1/en/publications/potential-impact-artificial-intelligence-middle-east.html

Rabaa'i, A. A. (2021). FinTech in Kuwait: A survey study. *International Journal of Business Information Systems*, *1*(1), 10042271. doi:10.1504/IJBIS.2021.10042271

Rabbani, M. R., Hassan, M. K., & Rashid, M. (2022). Introduction to Islamic FinTech: a challenge or an opportunity? In *FinTech in Islamic Financial Institutions: Scope, Challenges, and Implications in Islamic Finance* (pp. 1–27). Springer International Publishing. doi:10.1007/978-3-031-14941-2_1

Razavi, H., & Ghasemi, A. (2017). Multi-Objective Optimization of a QoS-Aware Channel Allocation in Cognitive Radio Networks using NSGA-II Algorithm. *Journal of Control*, *11*(1), 1–9.

Razavi, H., Jamali, M. R., Emsaki, M., Ahmadi, A., & Hajiaghei-Keshteli, M. (2023, September). Quantifying the Financial Impact of Cyber Security Attacks on Banks: A Big Data Analytics Approach. In *2023 IEEE Canadian Conference on Electrical and Computer Engineering (CCECE)* (pp. 533-538). IEEE. 10.1109/CCECE58730.2023.10288963

Razavi, H., Jamali, M. R., Emsaki, M., Gholian-Jouybari, F., Bonakdari, H., & Hajiaghaei-Keshteli, M. (2023, September). Statistical and Data Analytics Approaches to Parameter Tuning for Enhancing QoS of E-Banking Transactions: A Case Study of Sample Bank. In *2023 IEEE Canadian Conference on Electrical and Computer Engineering (CCECE)*. 10.1109/CCECE58730.2023.10288713

Razavi, H., Sarabadani, H., Karimisefat, A., & Lebraty, J. F. (2019, February). Profitability prediction for ATM transactions using artificial neural networks: A data-driven analysis. In *2019 5th Conference on Knowledge Based Engineering and Innovation (KBEI)* (pp. 661-665). IEEE.

Razzaque, A., Cummings, R. T., Karolak, M., & Hamdan, A. (2020). The propensity to use FinTech: Input from bankers in the Kingdom of Bahrain. *Journal of Information & Knowledge Management, 19*(01), 2040025. doi:10.1142/S0219649220400250

Rock, D., & Sorkin, I. (2021). *Artificial Intelligence and the Future of Work: The Role of Corporate Social Responsibility.* National Bureau of Economic Research, Working Paper 29992.

Ruslan, R. A. H. M., Ibrahim, M. A., & Abd Hamid, N. H. (2022). Application of artificial intelligence in FinTech: the decision of youth investors to use robo-advisor platform as micro-investing alternative. *Journal of Entrepreneurship, Business and Economics, 10*(2S2), 38-54.

Saba, I., Kouser, R., & Chaudhry, I. S. (2019). FinTech and Islamic finance-challenges and opportunities. *Review of Economics and Development Studies*, *5*(4), 581–890. doi:10.26710/reads.v5i4.887

Sakarya, Ş., & Aksu, M. (2021). FinTech ecosystem in Turkey: An evaluation in terms of financial markets and financial stability. *The Impact of Artificial Intelligence on Governance, Economics and Finance*, *I*, 11–31.

Santosdiaz, R. (2023). *Fintech Hubs In The Middle East and Africa.* Retrieved April 24, 2023, from http://thefintechtimes.com

Schilirò, D. (2021). FinTech in Dubai: Development and Ecosystem. *International Business Research, 14*(11), 61–70. doi:10.5539/ibr.v14n11p61

Sharafi, A. (2022). A survey of the innovation ecosystem in the United Arab Emirates. *Journal of Economic and Social Thought*, *9*(3), 163–177.

Stanford University. (2023). *Artificial intelligence (AI) private investment worldwide in 2022, by industry* [Graph]. Statista. Retrieved November 15, 2023, from https://0-www-statista-com.biblioteca-ils.tec.mx/statistics/1381487/ai-private-investment-focus-worldwide

Susanto, H., Ibrahim, F., Rosiyadi, D., Setiana, D., Susanto, A. K. S., Kusuma, N., & Setiawan, I. (2022). Securing Financial Inclusiveness Adoption of Blockchain FinTech Compliance. In FinTech Development for Financial Inclusiveness (pp. 168-196). IGI Global. doi:10.4018/978-1-7998-8447-7.ch010

Taherdoost, H. (2023a). Fintech: Emerging trends and the future of finance. *Financial Technologies and DeFi: A Revisit to the Digital Finance Revolution*, 29-39.

Taherdoost, H. (2023b). Drivers of Financial Technologies. In *Mainstreaming Cryptocurrency and the Future of Digital Finance* (pp. 1–30). IGI Global. doi:10.4018/978-1-6684-8368-8.ch001

Turkish Competition Authority. (2021). *Number of fintech startups in Turkey in 2021, by activity* [Graph]. Statista. Retrieved November 17, 2023, from https://0-www-statista-com.biblioteca-ils.tec.mx/statistics/1295524/turkey-fintech-startup-number-by-activity

UN DESA. (2019). *Total population across the Middle East and North Africa from 1990 to 2050 (in million)* [Graph]. Statista. Retrieved November 12, 2023, from https://0-www-statista-com.biblioteca-ils.tec.mx/statistics/978535/mena-total-population

Velmie. (2023). *Middle East Digital banking Outlook.* www.velmie.com

Xu, Y., & Bao, H. (2023). FinTech regulation: Evolutionary game model, numerical simulation, and recommendations. *Expert Systems with Applications*, *211*, 118327. doi:10.1016/j.eswa.2022.118327

Yasin, N., & Khansari, Z. (2022). Exploring the Enterprise Landscape for Business Incubators in the UAE. In *Entrepreneurship and Change: Understanding Entrepreneurialism as a Driver of Transformation* (pp. 191–208). Springer International Publishing. doi:10.1007/978-3-031-07139-3_8

Yazici, S. (2019). The analysis of FinTech ecosystem in Turkey. *Journal of Business Economics and Finance*, *8*(4), 188–197. doi:10.17261/Pressacademia.2019.1162

KEY TERMS AND DEFINITIONS

AI Integration: AI integration involves incorporating various artificial intelligence tools into existing business processes to enhance efficiency, functionality, and communication.

Angel Investor: An angel investor is a wealthy individual who invests capital in startups in exchange for equity or convertible debt, often providing mentorship and industry connections.

Emerging Technologies: Refers to innovative and advanced technologies that are in the early stages of adoption and have the potential to significantly impact various industries, including finance.

FinTech: A portmanteau of "financial technology," FinTech encompasses the use of cutting-edge technology to enhance and streamline financial services, covering areas such as digital payments, online banking, and financial management.

Gulf Cooperation Council (GCC): Refers to a regional alliance formed in 1981, comprising six Middle Eastern countries: Bahrain, Kuwait, Oman, Qatar, Saudi Arabia, and the United Arab Emirates. Designed to enhance economic cooperation and regional stability, the GCC focuses on fostering collaboration among member states in areas such as economic development, security, and cultural exchange.

Islamic Shari'a: Islamic Shari'a is the legal and ethical framework based on Islamic principles, governing aspects of life including finance, family, and societal conduct, derived from the Quran and Hadith. In finance, it emphasizes ethical transactions and prohibits interest.

Middle East: A region that includes Western Asia and parts of North Africa, known for its geopolitical and cultural significance. In the context of the chapter, it specifically pertains to the dynamic FinTech landscape in countries such as the UAE and Turkey.

Regional Hub: A central location or area recognized for its concentration of specific activities or industries. In the context of FinTech, a regional hub is a geographic location that serves as a focal point for FinTech-related activities, investments, and innovations.

RegTech: Regtech, short for regulatory technology, refers to the use of advanced technologies, such as artificial intelligence, blockchain, and data analytics, to streamline and enhance regulatory compliance processes in various industries.

Startup: A startup is a newly formed business known for its innovation, scalability, and focus on addressing specific market needs.

Startup Ecosystems: The interconnected network of startups, investors, mentors, and support organizations within a specific geographic area. In the context of FinTech, startup ecosystems contribute to the growth and development of financial technology initiatives.

ENDNOTES

1 Middle East North Africa

2 Initial Coin Offering

3 Banking Regulation and Supervision Agency

4 Anti-Money Laundering

5 Know Your Customer

Chapter 11
Sustainable Finance Strategies in the Formula 1 Industry: A Fintech Perspective

Jay Ramesh Israni
University Canada West, Canada

Giovana Castanho
University Canada West, Canada

Hamed Taherdoost
https://orcid.org/0000-0002-6503-6739
University Canada West, Canada

ABSTRACT

This chapter explores the integration of sustainable finance mechanisms, such as green bonds and impact investments, within the Formula 1 as a strategic approach to facilitate the realization of its goal to become a carbon-neutral sport by 2030. In the context of a rapidly evolving global landscape characterized by heightened environmental consciousness and sustainable finance paradigms, this study investigates how Formula 1, a high-profile motorsport, can leverage innovative financial tools to drive meaningful environmental change while ensuring its long-term growth and relevance. This research delineates a pathway for harnessing sustainable financial mechanisms to support and advance the sport's sustainability agenda.

INTRODUCTION

With 34 participating nations, 20 drivers, 10 teams, and billion-plus fans, Formula 1 is a well-known sport that has a significant environmental impact. It produces more than 250,000 tonnes of CO_2 emissions annually, demonstrating the urgent need for sustainability measures (Redahan, 2022). The race among the fastest drivers in the world is also the competition among the best engineers in the world. Formula

DOI: 10.4018/979-8-3693-1561-3.ch011

1 Racing is one of the biggest sports in the world and it is a pioneer in technology and innovation in automotives. This money sport holds the steering wheel in a global level of tourism and influence for 23 cities in an almost year-long season. Situations similar to those of 2012 and 2015, where the economic impact in Austin, Texas resulted in about 25,000 jobs surrounding the event, adding about $2.8 billion to the economic flow of the city (Storm et. al., 2020) make us analyze the immensity of influence and the number of countries involved in the planning, maneuvering, and realizing of the sport. The chapter believes such dimensions result in an immense natural resource consumption and in the consumption of materials with a difficult recyclable life.

Sustainability has been an ongoing conversation over the last decade. Comments about how we can reduce waste, how much reduction is needed to provide number of extra years before the world collapses, and how we can stop pollution are ongoing in most Environmental, Social, and Governance goals, also known as ESG goals, on most company websites. Sustainability today has shifted from the necessity of reduction of negative impact into ways of providing positive impact that will rather benefit society and the environment, from its core (Juntunen et. al., 2019, p. 332). Although there has been a societal change in perspective towards becoming sustainable, companies struggle from moving away from the reduction mindset, trying to reduce consumption and waste, due to the complexities that follow this new methodology which entails not creating such waste in the first place. Juntunen et al. describe it as a need for an institution remodeling involving new models for business conduction, through changes in product, service and systems (2019, p.334).

Fintech has a role in the application of this new methodology of sustainability and the authors argue it is the ultimate solution for effective implementation of sustainable practices in businesses. Formula 1 CEO, Chase Carey states they are now focusing on becoming the first net-zero sport in the world. The goal to achieve this by 2030 is that they believe they can "create positive environmental outcomes through their progressive innovations" (Lowrey, 2020). The authors believe that through the application of green bonds and impact investments in the teams in Formula 1 Racing, the sport will be able to achieve said "progressive innovations" towards their new zero goal by 2030 and influence other sports to follow the same financial investment structure. The primary source of funding for Formula One is sponsorships. If these sponsors can be persuaded to uphold an ESG pledge, which denotes a commitment to environmental, social, and governance norms, it will essentially bind the sport's financial ecosystem to work together to advance it. Such a commitment would start a chain reaction that would get the sport closer to its sustainability goals.

The authors hypothesise that, to achieve its goal as a sustainable sport, Formula 1 has to integrate into its sponsorship plans, the use of Green Financial resources such as Green Bonds and Impact investments. According to our hypothesis, a key component of Formula 1 team sponsors' financial sponsorship plans is the use of financial resources, such as bonds and investments. As Cobbs et al, has described in their 2017 paper that earlier studies have mostly focused on sponsors' survival rates and how they affect team performance, our study aims to set a new standard for the field. In particular, the authors want to investigate the viability and effects of changing the Formula 1 sponsorship structure to include sustainable financial options. The dynamics of sponsorship relationships within Formula 1 are being changed by our investigation into the adoption of sustainable finance practices among sponsors. The authors hope to learn that with the change in these financial tools will contribute towards the sustainability of teams as well as contribute to the sport's larger sustainability goals.

BACKGROUND

This chapter will analyse the integration of sustainable finance structures such as green bonds and impact investments within the Formula 1 Racing sport in their objective of becoming a Net Zero sport. Research objectives include an examination of the extent to which Formula 1 has pursued its net zero objective in context of it structure and assess its standing in sustainability efforts which will be measured by the extent of goal achieved by the sport of its promised timeline and to examine the extent of the Net Zero objective to its partners. The study also seeks to set a new standard by investigating the viability and effects of altering the Formula 1 sponsorship structure to incorporate sustainable financial options. While the scope for the analysis will be based on the sponsorship of all Formula 1 teams in analysis to how they perform towards the sport's sustainable goals.

The Authors will use Qualitative and Inductive Approach in analysis of multiple Sustainability, F1 and Fintech reviews. These were carefully chosen reviewed articles to assess Formula 1's progress towards achieving its net zero goal. These articles were used to establish the individuality of each of the three themes and will also be used to synthesize each other. As it is the case with articles by Schneider and ClausB, Intonti, Cobbs, Jensen, & Tyler, and many others, this chapter will discuss whether green bonds and impact investments are an active solution for F1 in achieving sustainable finance and positive change for the sports future in sustainability. Previous studies have focused primarily on sponsors' survival rates and their impact on team performance. This points towards a gap in literature in context to the financial implication on the sustainability goal of the sport. These articles were used to reshape the dynamics of sponsorship relationships in Formula 1 through the adoption of sustainable finance practices among sponsors.

This research framework has been based on an overall analysis of different abstracts related to each theme and collection of several reviews. Once main articles were established, a pathway was established to start collecting valuable information from each in the construction of Literature Reviews for each which gave access to synthesize the correlation between each before all of them were read. Following this step, came researching these articles and collecting common information to then synthesize and transform what has developed into this essay.

This chapter follows qualitative and inductive research approach. This approach gives space to theorize and hypothesize based on observations of data. Feeding into exploratory nature, investigating, and reaching insights that have not yet been approached (Taherdoost, 2022). Sustainable finance in the Formula 1 industry involves numerous interconnected factors, including financial practices, environmental impacts, technological innovations, and stakeholder perspectives. The inductive research approach allows for a holistic examination of these factors, enabling a comprehensive understanding of the industry's efforts to achieve its sustainability goals while still having flexibility in adapting to emerging trends and new developments within the Formula 1 industry. The understanding to the structure of chapter can be depicted in Figure 1. As the diagram showcases the layer of topics explored to the construction of chapter can provide the understanding to the background and foreground of the topic. Layer one, showcases individual topics of Formula 1, Fintech and Sustainability, which is explored into the relationship among each of the given with other to establish the topic in the chapter.

Figure 1. Structure of chapter

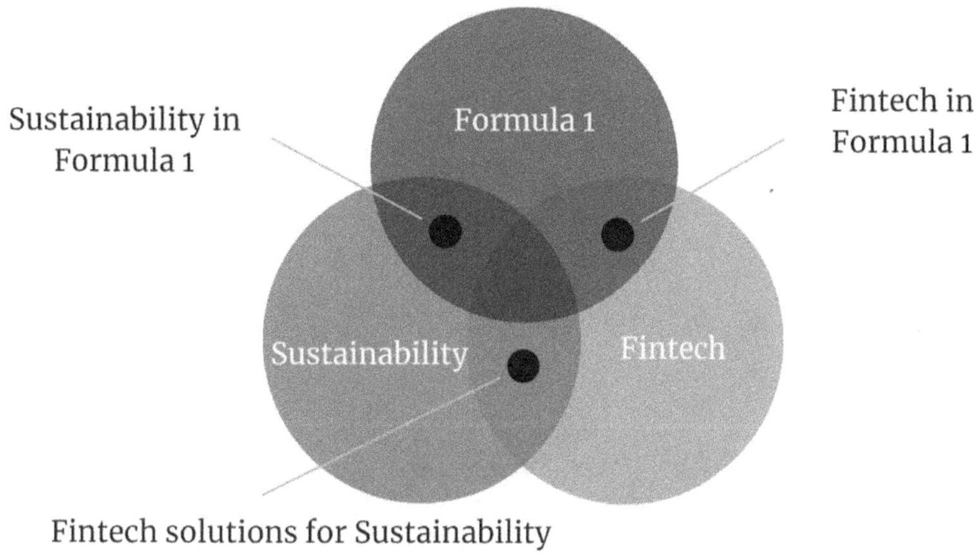

Literature Review

This research has been constructed based on a diverse list of references from well recognized authors. The following were some of the most relevant when it came to the analysis of F1's application of sustainable finance structures in green bonds and impact investments.

In "Prioritizing Sponsorship Resources in Formula One Racing: A Longitudinal Analysis" by Cobbs, J., Tyler, B. D., Jensen, J. A., & Kwong Chan in 2017, the authors delved into the crucial matter of resource acquisition and exploitation focusing on Formula One Racing. Corporate sponsorships' pivotal role in securing resources is underscored, with recognition of the heterogeneous benefits they offer and their varying contributions to team survival. Resource-based, the study emphasizes that sponsorship effectiveness depends on factors such as resource type and the sport's institutional context. This is beneficial to this research to help us analyze the current financial standings and roles of sponsorship for F1 teams.

The following, written in 2021 with some of the same authors, Jensen, J. A., Cobbs, J. B., Albano, B., & Tyler, B. D, is named "Analyzing Price Premiums In International Sponsorship Exchange: What Drives Marketing Costs In Formula One Racing?". This research draws attention to a crucial aspect of sponsorship investment. The analysis reveals fascinating conclusions after examining Formula One sponsorship rates over multiple years. While sponsorship and industry level were taken into account, characteristics including congruence, clutter, sponsor size, and sponsored company performance had a small effect on sponsorship prices. The data and results from the current sponsorship programs are compared with the application of green bonds and impact investments for this chapter.

Smoking Gentlemen—How Formula One Has Controlled CO2 Emissions. Sustainability, written by Paulo Reis Mourao in 2018 focuses on analyzing the steps taken by Formula 1 to minimize its level of CO2 emissions. The article highlights the two capacities in CO2 emissions, one being followed by tourism and the attraction of the amount of people to each city for each race regarding their CO2 emissions in traveling, while the second discusses the emissions per test round, qualifying races and the Sunday races. The data from this scholar article is beneficial in reporting the environmental damage caused by the Formula 1.

Figure 2. The pictorial depiction of the flow of money in the sport through sponsorship

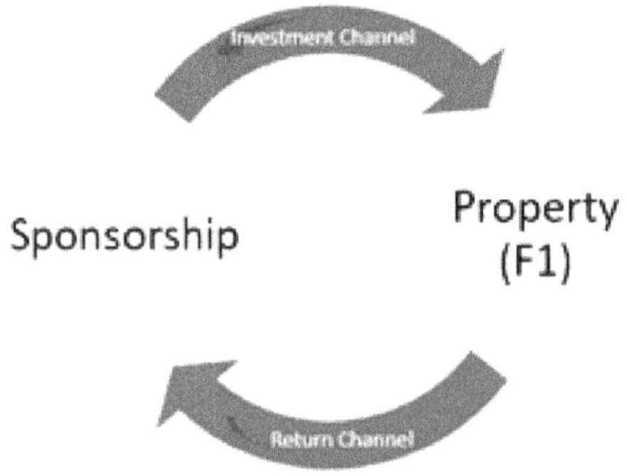

The final highlighted review holds an investigation of stakeholder integration tactics within new product development processes and offers insightful information about sustainable innovation. The study emphasizes the challenges of effectively incorporating stakeholders while acknowledging the complex interplay between sustainability and innovation. The strategies provided in this resource to develop the sustainable projections discussed towards the Formula 1 Sponsorship Program. This article was written by previously mentioned Juntunen, J. K., and also Halme, M., Korsunova, A., and Rajala, R. in 2019.

Noted that these were influential resources for the development of this chapter, although not limited. These articles provided guidance and knowledge for its development to supply rich supporting evidence.

MAIN FOCUS OF THE CHAPTER

Formula 1 (F1) is a billion-dollar industry, and in recent years has been gaining popularity among its viewers. According to Ernst and Young (2011), the 2011 Australian Grand Prix has 120,000 unique spectators and 20 million record followers on television across European countries. According to *Forbes* Formula 1 has seen $2.573 billion in the year of 2022. (Brown, 2023) Therefore before exposing sustainable fintech elements to the industry, it is crucial to understand the financial workings of the industry.

When planning, executing, and managing events, event planners typically devote enormous amounts of resources, and these expenditures frequently cause them to worry about their return on investment (ROI) because of costs. (Gao, 2018). As any major sport, the financial structure of Formula 1 starts with Sponsorship. According to Cobbs, Jensen and Tayler (2022) a typical cycle of F1 starts with sponsorship money rolling in from team sponsors which is presented to the property (F1) via investment channels, these resources can include In-kind, Monitory or Intangible resources, property then uses the resources in the sport and upon result returns investments resources of promotional or technical through return channel. Upon receiving this money, the property divides money based on allocation which is used by teams to create their cars and compete in the race and with viewership, and tickets F1 generates revenue. This revenue is allocated in results and presented back to the team sponsors as return on investments

(Petroczy and Csato, 2021). *Figure 1* provides a clear visual picture of the flow of money inside Formula 1, streamlining the complex process of money transfer between sponsors and the governing corporation (F1) through the Investment and Return Channels. It demonstrates how sponsors contribute money to Formula 1 through investment channels and how Formula 1 returns money to sponsors through return channels.

Sponsorship In F1

As the chapter dives into Formula One's Financial Structure, the influence of sponsorships stands out, as in most sports. Sponsorship in the F1 funds up to 70% of the team's budgets, which brings light to how specific sponsors might be crucial to the team's performance during the season (Cobbs et. al, 2017). Money invested in the teams in exchange for public display of the brand and demonstration of the product within the sporting context is what this chapter will be referring to as sponsorships. The money allocated by different companies is visualized by them by marketing expenses and investments (Jensen et al., 2021). The allocation of money made by these sponsorships is responsible for paying salaries, suits, meals, trips and stays in each of the countries throughout all the races.

An example given by Cobbs et al. (2017) is the sponsorship deal made by the F1 through a bidding system that gave the tire manufacturer, Pirelli, the authority of being the only supplier for every team in the F1 races in the Formula 1. This example of regulation can be both exceptionally significant for the sport and the company while it can also be limiting and such monopoly might cause delay in technology.

The Formula One sponsorship usually works within an oligopoly system, where a set of small number of enterprises will partner with specific teams to collectively compete amongst the competition to sell more of its product and stand out. (Budzinski & Müller-Kock, 2017). When applying such monopolistic incentives like the one made in 2011, Formula 1 is limiting competition and therefore, innovative technology in the tires for the races; this behavior can be applied to the sustainable efforts and become a deal breaker in sponsorships for the Formula 1.

Significance of Financial Sponsorship

Due to its crucial role in determining the financial landscape of Formula 1, the authors lay a lot of attention on financial sponsorship in this article. Financial sponsorship stands out as a type of investment that not only provides the sport with necessary funding, but also operates with a clear focus on how sponsors will use their money over the long term. Due to this distinctive quality, financial resources are effectively converted into a type of collateral, underscoring their crucial relevance to our subject. The significance of financial sponsorship resides in its capacity to give an organization financial flexibility.

Financial resources can frequently be easily transformed into other resources that are now viewed as being crucial to the success of the team because they are frequently extremely liquid. Racing teams and other entrepreneurial businesses may quickly react to shifting demands and possibilities because of this liquidity. Researchers in the fields of entrepreneurship and organizational development have noted that other types of resources directly related to performance and operations may take precedence over financial resources, particularly in the early phases of an organization's growth (Cobbs et. al.,2017).

Fintech in Sports and Its Relevance to Formula 1

Formula 1, despite its global popularity and financial success, appears to lack socially responsible investments, as evidenced by the Norwegian Government Pension Fund-Global's involvement with Delta Topco, the holding company of Formula 1. The Norwegian Oil Fund, managed by Norges Bank Investment Management, is mandated to uphold socially responsible investment principles through its Council of Ethics. Considering reports on the intertwined nature of political economy and sporting events, it becomes evident that Formula 1, as an entity, may not fully embrace socially responsible investments (Naess, 2019).

Integrating Fintech Solutions Into Formula 1

Sports club management now uses fintech, which includes a variety of cutting-edge financial technologies and applications, as a beneficial tool. These technologies give sports teams cutting-edge options for managing their finances, interacting with fans, and growing their businesses. Fintech enables sports clubs to increase their income streams and financial efficiency through everything from optimizing ticket sales and merchandising transactions to improving payment processing for memberships and sponsorships. Additionally, clubs are given the ability to make informed judgments about player acquisition, team performance analysis, and fan engagement tactics thanks to fintech-driven analytics and data management technologies. The incorporation of fintech into sports clubs' management not only updates their financial procedures but also aids in their general expansion and sustainability in a sector of the sports industry that is becoming more and more cutthroat (Wang, 2022).

Fintech Solutions in Formula 1

Fintech solutions have streamlined financial processes, making them safer and more effective. This includes everything from ticketing and product sales to managing athlete contracts and sponsorship agreements. Furthermore, the industry's capacity to make educated judgments about performance, team tactics, and fan engagement has improved as a result of fintech's integration with sports analytics and data management systems. In addition to streamlining financial operations inside sports organizations, this technology advancement has increased data interchange transparency and accessibility, guaranteeing a safer and more dependable environment for all parties concerned (Ata et al 2023). As a comparative to other sports, fintech solutions can also be applied to Formula 1.

Connecting Fintech to Formula 1

This investigation got underway by determining the importance of fintech in the sports industry. As the authors investigated its use in other sports, it became clear that fintech techniques might change and improve Formula 1. Formula 1 may be able to streamline financial operations, improve data analytics for team performance and fan engagement, and ultimately strengthen its financial viability through the gradual implementation of fintech tools and tactics.

This cutting-edge strategy fits in perfectly with current trends in the sports business. Formula 1 can respond to the rising demand for socially responsible investments by enhancing financial management through fintech. It gives the sport the capacity to make more educated and data-driven decisions, opening up options to maximize revenue sources and keep a competitive edge in the increasingly cutthroat sports market.

A strong theory may be built on top of this foundation of improved financial management and fintech integration. It makes us wonder if sponsors may use fintech components, like green bonds and impact investments, as substitutes for current financial techniques. These fintech-driven financial instruments could help Formula 1 get closer to its sustainability objectives by adapting and changing it association with investments that also support the environmental cause, which would be a big step in the sport's quest of ethical and socially conscious practices. This constitutes that F1 will be promoting sustainability as a "mobilizer" and by requiring its stakeholders and investors to adapt. Providing them the space to invest in such operations through their new policies.

Table 1. Sustainable Fintech investments definition

Green Bonds	A financial instrument known as a "green bond" is one that is issued particularly to raise money for programs and projects that benefit the environment. Projects including renewable energy, environmentally friendly transportation, climate change mitigation, and other green initiatives are frequently funded with the help of these bonds.
Impact Investment	Impact investing is the practice of making investments with the goal of producing both financial returns and beneficial social or environmental impact. It seeks to achieve commercial results while addressing societal and environmental concerns.

Sustainable Investments (FinTech)

Now that the chapter has defined financial sponsorship as our main area of interest and talked about how to incorporate fintech into sports, it's time to look at the essential components of our suggested structure. *Table 2* explains these factors in more detail and gives definitions for the two essential elements of sustainable fintech solutions. The first is a financial asset that is relatively new and inventive called a "green bond," which has become increasingly popular in diverse investment portfolios due to its special combination of financial resources and environmental protection features. Green bonds are comparable to traditional fixed-income corporate bonds in certain ways, but what sets them apart is their

Table 2. Comparison between traditional bonds and green bonds, analysis by author based on Intonti et al. (2023)

Environmental and Social Focus	Green Bonds are designed with a specific environmental and social purpose, which can include funding projects related to renewable energy, clean technology, or social welfare. Traditional Bonds, on the other hand, do not have these specific sustainability objectives. (Intonti et al, 2023)
Investor Behavior	The greenium measurement suggests that investors might be willing to accept different yields or prices for Green Bonds compared to Traditional Bonds. This could be driven by investors' preference for socially responsible or environmentally friendly investments. (Intonti et al, 2023)
Liquidity Influence	Liquidity appears to play a role in the pricing of Green Bonds. This means that factors related to the ease of trading and market liquidity could affect the greenium for Green Bonds. (Intonti et al, 2023)
Determinants of Pricing	Specific characteristics of Green Bonds, such as currency, issuance quantity, credit rating, and issuer type, can impact the greenium, indicating that these factors are considered by investors when valuing Green Bonds. (Intonti et al, 2023)
Impact of COVID-19	The analysis suggests that the COVID-19 pandemic had an influence on the greenium, with government Green Bonds being more affected than corporate ones. This implies that external events and economic conditions can impact the relative pricing of Green Bonds and Traditional Bonds. (Intonti et al, 2023)

special function: they only make money from green initiatives. In other words, the money raised through green bonds is used to support programs that benefit the environment. Investors and issuers alike have expressed a great deal of interest in this environmental focus (Le et. Al., 2020).

The fact that green bonds are a type of financial instrument particularly adapted for advancing the shift to a low-carbon economy is one of the main factors contributing to their rising popularity. Green bonds have become an effective tool for financing environmentally friendly innovations and long-term sustainable investments as nations and organizations throughout the world step up their efforts to address environmental concerns. Green bonds are a desirable alternative for investors wishing to align their portfolios with sustainability goals due to their twin benefits of improving financial performance and environmental results. (Le et. Al., 2020). The paper have provided the following *Table 3* to compare traditional and green bonds in-depth, outlining their key similarities and differences.

The second is Impact investing, often known as socially responsible investing or triple impact investing, is notable for its simultaneous commitment to generating both financial returns and favourable social and environmental results. Impact investing is focused on triggering significant societal and ecological changes, as opposed to standard investments that are only motivated by financial rewards. Impact investment, in particular within the context of social enterprises, emerges as a key contributor, offering crucial financial assistance required for their long-term growth and viability (Bacuilima et. al., 2023).

Fintech's Catalyst Role and the Potential of Green Bonds and Impact Investments in Formula 1 Sustainability

As Wang et. al. (2022) have already established in their paper clear empirical evidence that fintech plays a positive role in advancing corporate sustainability efforts, particularly in emerging markets. It not only underscores the impact of fintech but also sheds light on how it can be harnessed as a catalyst for positive ESG outcomes in the corporate sector, emphasizing the growing importance of technology-driven financial solutions in promoting sustainability.

Integration to

The question remaining is towards how Green Bonds and Impact Investments will be applied in the Formula 1 sport. As aforementioned, establishing policies is the best way to develop substantial change within the Formula 1 industry, as it happened in 2011 with Pirelli. A way to collectively influence all of the sports sponsors is to create a green policy which states that enterprises who wish to sponsor require minimum ESG behavior and influence in the stock market. Establishing a green financial policy will also strengthen the willingness of the people around it to also collaborate in it such as the cities who will be influenced and other brands trying to get into the market. This domino effect will cause "high-pollution" companies to follow the green transition (Liu & Nie, 2022). Sponsor companies will have to choose between accepting the transition or not being a recognized sponsor of Formula 1. Believing that they will not want to be left out of the marketing opportunity, Formula One teams will continue to receive their money, people will see the green influence of the sport through the sponsorships and they will continue to invest in these brands, generating more profit for the sponsoring companies.

DISCUSSION

Recognizing the urgency of sustainability, there has been a growing impetus, fueled by peer pressure, mandates, and consumer expectations, compelling industries to play a more active role in addressing these societal and environmental concerns. This shift has led to an evolving landscape where firms are increasingly compelled to integrate contributions to ecological and social needs into their core business activities, moving beyond profit maximization as their sole focus. Consequently, a sustainable business model that combines economic, ecological, and social value contributions has become imperative. This paradigm shift also reflects similarly on sponsors of the Formula 1 team with a broader movement wherein industry and sponsors alike are embracing the concept of social businesses, not only as economically viable entities but also as positive contributors to the environment and society at large. Such a shift towards sustainable business models is critical in fostering a harmonious and responsible coexistence between businesses and the broader global community while actively working towards addressing our most pressing challenges (Schneider and ClausB, 2019).

Formula 1 is focusing on becoming the first net-zero sport in the world by 2030 and is responsible for this matter in the world of motorsports (Lowrey, 2020). Being one of the priciest sports, the use of these bonds will work on the objective of Responsible Sourcing and provide expedition in 100% renewable powered sport (Mourao, 2018). According to independent news sites, Formula 1 is on-track in becoming net zero sport, but has been lacking in its responsible sourcing objective. Abdul-Rahim et al (2022) demonstrates as well that perceived benefits have a major impact on FinTech adoption, in contrast to perceived risk, which in case of formula 1 would be beneficial as all the stakeholders are willing to work towards change.

In Intonti (2023), the main goal was to answer whether Green Bonds fintech's are more like traditional bonds or investments. This study focused on utilizing the fintech's instead of the traditional bonds, showing the potential for sustainable interaction and the cross-pollination of complementary business models. The main contribution of this chapter was that the application approaches of fintech's follow those of existing structure, having a revenue model much more scalable than that of a typical government. Fintech's may provide a solution for sustainable finance with Impact Investments, among others.

The FinTech phenomenon from an ecosystem point of view is analyzed in Wang et. al. (2022). According to this analysis the integration of any fintech model into the formula 1 sport is both practical and transitional due to the updating nature of the sport. In effect, this study explored the FinTech ecosystem application in Formula 1 in order to understand sustainable business model innovation based on underlying ecosystem dynamics whilst focusing on the specific role of cross-sector actors. Adopting a comparative case study method by considering the broad fintech spectrum and Formula 1 financial model, the study's findings indicated that sustainable business model developments based on existing financial tools and scale-based resources by cross-sector Fintech render a functional perspective on the fast- developing Formula 1 industry practical. The successful integration of this fintech investment model would support the sport in the zero carbon emission goal by changing its association with similar brands and investing in green solutions. This also brings into considerations the potential risks and challenges that will come with the applications of change into a fintech model investment. Potential hurdles could be the barriers over smooth transition between investment channels, variable market factors and including brand resistance due to potential higher costs for implementation. But as we understand changes cause resistance in any aspect of discussion. Therefore, as per our analysis, teams and stakeholders of sport would have a period of resistance towards this new implementation before they support the application.

Thus, this manuscript contributed to the scant literature on FinTech ecosystems and comparative to their sustainable development of Formula 1.

FUTURE PROSPECTS AND LIMITATIONS

Based on the presented results we can dive into future prospects for Formula 1 Racing and what would some limitations for the sports be. With proper implementation of green bonds, impact investments and other sustainable finance mechanisms, the sport could undergo positive growth in social and environmental popularity and consequently increase its investor base with the new environmental investors in the game. Future prospects would include an increase in monetary base, higher sustainable influence and becoming a reference sport in the sustainability aspect. Limitations, however, are inevitable as we are dealing with a sport who has the resources to implement such mechanisms and are yet failing to do so. It is perceived that the leaders in the industry fail to value the vital importance of this matter and for this same reason have lacked in providing vital change to the matter. The continuum of this worldview towards the sustainable embrace is the sport's biggest limitation to reach its net zero goal by 2030.

CONCLUSION

The existing state of Formula 1 has, as argued in this article, allowed its net zero charge to proceed but has lagged in its efforts toward responsible sourcing. In the current climate, several fintech tools can be crucial in modernizing the sport. The adoption of sustainable financial instruments like green bonds and impact investments can support the sport's long-term growth. With high hopes for expansion, Formula 1 is growing in popularity. The Fintech sector also promotes sustainable economic growth and has several positive consequences on social, environmental, and ecological benefits. The use of sustainable fintech can encourage the usage of finances for financial sponsorships in F1 in order to advance environmental and ecological growth.

With the use of technologies like impact investments and green bonds, among other things like crowdfunding, big data analytics, blockchain technology, and artificial intelligence, fintech demonstrates consistency and continuity with ESG criteria. As mentioned above, there are numerous similarities between sustainable finance and fintech, and fintech's promotion of green financing can make Formula 1 more environmentally friendly as a whole. The financial framework of Formula 1 is created, the strategic viewpoint of Fintech is discussed, and via a thorough assessment of the literature, it is possible to investigate the connection between Fintech and sustainability. The case of Formula 1 has also been used to apply the theoretical framework and demonstrate how to establish sustainable behaviours and encourage green investment.

Based on all the key elements discussed along this research, the authors encourage the stakeholders of the Formula 1 to act out towards change in the sport. To introduce this ideal this chapter recommend the discontinuation of partnership and investment with brands that have presented negative impacts on environment, instead commit with companies that have made their operations sustainable to the environment. By supporting green companies rather than the ones who ignore their ecological impact, the sport will be able to contribute and further commit towards change.

REFERENCES

Abdul-Rahim, R., Bohari, S. A., Aman, A., & Awang, Z. (2022). Benefit–Risk Perceptions of FinTech Adoption for Sustainability from Bank Consumers' Perspective: The Moderating Role of Fear of COVID-19. *Sustainability (2071-1050), 14*(14). doi:10.3390/su14148357

Ashta, A. (2023). How Can Fintech Companies Get Involved in the Environment? *Sustainability (2071-1050), 15*(13), 10675. doi:10.3390/su151310675

Ata, S. N., Hassan, A. K., Selim, H. S., Hammad, B. E., Abdelhalim, H. M., & Abdelhalim, A. M. (2023). The Use of Blockchain Technology and Its Reflection in the Financial Performance of Investment Projects Developed by the Ministry of Sports. *Economies, 11*(5), 140. doi:10.3390/economies11050140

Bachman, J. R. (2020). Motorsport Event Attendees: Who are They, What is Their Environmental Worldview, And How Does It Relate to Trip Spending? *Event Management, 24*(5), 629–644. doi:10.3727/152599519X15506259856264

Bacuilima, E., Morocho, J., Aguirre, J., Coronel-Pangol, K., & Mora, P. (2023). Financing Ecuadorian Social Enterprises: What Is the Role of Impact Investment? *Sustainability (2071-1050), 15*(14), 11210. doi:10.3390/su151411210

Bag, S., Gupta, S., Kumar, S., & Sivarajah, U. (2021). Role of technological dimensions of green supply chain management practices on firm performance. *Journal of Enterprise Information Management, 34*(1), 1–27. doi:10.1108/JEIM-10-2019-0324

Bayram, O., Talay, I., & Feridun, M. (2022). Can Fintech Promote Sustainable Finance? Policy Lessons from the Case of Turkey. *Sustainability (2071-1050), 14*(19), 12414. doi:10.3390/su141912414

Bittini, J. S., Rambaud, S. C., Pascual, J. L., & Moro-Visconti, R. (2022). Business Models and Sustainability Plans in the FinTech, InsurTech, and PropTech Industry: Evidence from Spain. *Sustainability (2071-1050), 14*(19), 12088. https://doi-org.ezproxy.myucwest.ca/10.3390/su141912088

Brochado, A., Dionísio, P., Leal, C., Bouchet, A., & Conceição, H. (2021). Organizing sports events: the promoters' perspective. *Journal of Business & Industrial Marketing*. doi:10.1108/JBIM-10-2020-0451

Brown, M. (2023, March 30). Inside the numbers that show formula 1's popularity and financial growth. *Forbes*. https://www.forbes.com/sites/maurybrown/2023/03/29/inside-the-numbers-that-show-formula-1s-popularity-and-financial-growth/?sh=3288d45d4df6

Budzinski, O., & Muller-Kock, A. (2018). Is the Revenue Allocation Scheme of Formula One Motor Racing a Case for European Competition Policy? *Contemporary Economic Policy, 36*(1), 215–233. doi:10.1111/coep.12247

Choi, G., & Cho, S. H. (2022). Effect of market versus nonmarket environmental policy stringency on knowledge sourcing behavior for green technology: Evidence from OECD countries. *Review of International Business & Strategy, 32*(1), 72–93. doi:10.1108/RIBS-09-2020-0113

Chueca Vergara, C., & Ferruz Agudo, L. (2021). Fintech and Sustainability: Do They Affect Each Other? *Sustainability (2071-1050), 13*(13), 7012. doi:10.3390/su13137012

Cobbs, J., Tyler, B. D., Jensen, J. A., & Chan, K. (2017). Prioritizing Sponsorship Resources in Formula One Racing: A Longitudinal Analysis. *Journal of Sport Management*, *31*(1), 96–110. doi:10.1123/jsm.2016-0115

Cobbs, J. B., Jensen, J. A., & Tyler, B. D. (2022). The sponsorship performance cycle: Longitudinal evidence of sponsors' contribution to Formula One team achievement. *Journal of Business and Industrial Marketing*, *37*(1), 103–114. doi:10.1108/JBIM-06-2020-0299

Cooper, A. (2023, June 14). *F1 reports progress towards 2030 net zero target. Motorsport.com: F1 News, MotoGP, NASCAR, Rallying and more*. https://www.motorsport.com/f1/news/f1-reports-progress-towards-2030-net-zero-target/10482379/#:~:text=Formula%201%20says%20that%20the,with%20much%20more%20to%20come.&text=F1%20reduced%20its%20carbon%20footprint,figures%20yet%20to%20be%20finalised

Cruz Rambaud, S., & López Pascual, J. (2023). Insurtech, Proptech, and Fintech Environment: Sustainability, Global Trends and Opportunities. *Sustainability (2071-1050), 15*(12), 9574. https://doi-org.ezproxy.myucwest.ca/10.3390/su15129574

de Araujo Silva, C., & Walter Wildauer, E. (2023). Modelo De Expansão Sustentável Para Um Ecossistema De Fintech. *Revista Gestão & Tecnologia*, *23*(1), 298–315.

Ernst & Young. (2011). *The economic impact of the 2011 Formula 1TM Australian Grand Prix*. Retrieved from https://www.tourism.vic.gov.au/images/stories/Documents/FactsandFigures/2011_gp_eco_impact_final_21_07_11.pdf

Fallahpour, A., Yazdani, M., Mohammed, A., & Wong, K. Y. (2021). Green sourcing in the era of industry 4.0: Towards green and digitized competitive advantages. *Industrial Management & Data Systems*, *121*(9), 1997–2025. doi:10.1108/IMDS-06-2020-0343

Gao, F. (2018). Leveraging a mega sport event: Lessons for the 2019 FIBA world cup. *Sport & Entertainment Review*, *4*, 59–63.

Gupta, V., & Zhang, Y. (2020). Investigating Environmental Performance Management. *Revista Brasileira de Gestão de Negócios*, *22*(1), 5–48. doi:10.7819/rbgn.v22i1.4034

Halme, M., Rintamäki, J., Knudsen, J. S., Lankoski, L., & Kuisma, M. (2020). When Is There a Sustainability Case for CSR? Pathways to Environmental and Social Performance Improvements. *Business & Society*, *59*(6), 1181–1227. doi:10.1177/0007650318755648

Intonti, M., Serlenga, L., Ferri, G., De Leonardis, M., & Starace, G. (2023). The "Greenium" in Green Bonds: How Did It Change with COVID-19? *Sustainability (2071-1050), 15*(7), 5631. https://doi-org.ezproxy.myucwest.ca/10.3390/su15075631

Jain, R., Kumar, S., Sood, K., Grima, S., & Rupeika-Apoga, R. (2023). A Systematic Literature Review of the Risk Landscape in Fintech. *Risks*, *11*(2), 36. doi:10.3390/risks11020036

Jensen, J. A., Cobbs, J. B., Albano, B., & Tyler, B. D. (2021). Analyzing Price Premiums In International Sponsorship Exchange: What Drives Marketing Costs In Formula One Racing? *Journal of Advertising Research*, *61*(1), 44–57. doi:10.2501/JAR-2020-018

Jones, C. W., Byon, K. K., & Huang, H. (2019). Service Quality, Perceived Value, and Fan Engagement: Case of Shanghai Formula One Racing. *Sport Marketing Quarterly*, *28*(2), 63–76. doi:10.32731/SMQ.282.062019.01

Liu, X., & Nie, W. (2022). Study on the coupling coordination mechanism of green technology innovation, environmental regulation, and green finance. *Environmental Science and Pollution Research International*, *29*(47), 71796–71809. doi:10.1007/s11356-022-20905-8 PMID:35599286

Lowrey, T. (2020). *Sustainability*. Formula One World Championship Limited. https://corp.formula1.com/corporate-responsibility/sustainability/

Miller, T. (2016). Greenwashed sports and environmental activism: Formula 1 and FIFA. *Environmental Communication*, *10*(6), 719–733. doi:10.1080/17524032.2015.1127850

Mourao, P. R. (2018). Smoking Gentlemen—How Formula One Has Controlled CO2 Emissions. *Sustainability (Basel)*, *10*(6), 1841. doi:10.3390/su10061841

Næss, H. E. (2019). Investment Ethics and the Global Economy of Sports: The Norwegian Oil Fund, Formula 1 and the 2014 Russian Grand Prix. *Journal of Business Ethics*, *158*(2), 535–546. doi:10.1007/s10551-017-3751-8

Ojekemi, O. S., Rjoub, H., Awosusi, A. A., & Agyekum, E. B. (2022). Toward a sustainable environment and economic growth in BRICS economies: Do innovation and globalization matter? *Environmental Science and Pollution Research International*, *29*(38), 57740–57757. doi:10.1007/s11356-022-19742-6 PMID:35352228

Paulet, E., & Relano, F. (2023). Fintech seen through a sustainability lens: Transformative potential and actual achievements. *Management International / International Management / Gestiòn Internacional, 27*(1), 131–140. https://doi-org.ezproxy.myucwest.ca/10.7202/1098927ar

Pawłowska, M., Staniszewska, A., & Grzelak, M. (2022). Impact of FinTech on Sustainable Development. *Financial Sciences / Nauki o Finansach, 27*(2), 49–66. https://doi-org.ezproxy.myucwest.ca/10.15611/fins.2022.2.05

Petróczy, D. G., & Csató, L. (2021). Revenue allocation in Formula One: A pairwise comparison approach. *International Journal of General Systems*, *50*(3), 243–261. doi:10.1080/03081079.2020.1870224

Putra, R. D., Mulyani, S., Poulus, S., & Sukmadilaga, C. (2022). Data quality analytics, business ethics, and cyber risk management on operational performance and fintech sustainability. *International Journal of Data and Network Science*, *6*(4), 1659–1668. doi:10.5267/j.ijdns.2022.4.008

Redahan, E. (2022, July 5). *Will Formula 1's drop-in fuel actually reduce carbon emissions?* SciBlog.org. https://www.soci.org/blog/2022/6/will-formula-1s-dropin-fuel-actually-reduce-carbon-emissions

Schneider, S., & Clauß, T. (2020). Business Models for Sustainability: Choices and Consequences. *Organization & Environment*, *33*(3), 384–407. doi:10.1177/1086026619854217

Storm, R. K., Jakobsen, T. G., & Nielsen, C. G. (2020). The Impact of Formula 1 on Regional Economies in Europe. *Regional Studies*, *54*(6), 827–837. doi:10.1080/00343404.2019.1648787

Swart, K., Cazorla Milla, A., & Mataruna-Dos-Santos, L. J. (2021). From the desert to the city: How is Dubai branding itself through sustainable sport events? *Worldwide Hospitality and Tourism Themes*, *13*(1), 34–48. doi:10.1108/WHATT-08-2020-0101

Taherdoost, H. (2022). *Data Collection Methods; An Essential Guide to Plan, Design and Develop Data Collection Tools*. Kindle Edition.

Walk, G. A. (2023). Money and Financial Technology (FinTech) History. *International Lawyer*, *56*(2), 227–331.

Wang, D., Peng, K., Tang, K., & Wu, Y. (2022). Does Fintech Development Enhance Corporate ESG Performance? Evidence from an Emerging Market. *Sustainability (2071-1050), 14*(24), 16597. doi:10.3390/su142416597

Wang, D., Peng, K., Tang, K., & Wu, Y. (2022). Does Fintech Development Enhance Corporate ESG Performance? Evidence from an Emerging Market. *Sustainability (2071-1050), 14*(24), 16597. https://doi-org.ezproxy.myucwest.ca/10.3390/su142416597

Wang, S. (2022). Improved Blockchain Technology for Performance Optimization Model Design of Sports Clubs. *Journal of Electrical and Computer Engineering*, *2022*, 1–8. doi:10.1155/2022/4436471

KEY TERMS AND DEFINITIONS

Carbon-Neutral: Balance between emission and absorption of carbon in the atmosphere.

ESG: Environmental, Social, and Governance strategy for businesses seeking to have less harmful impact on the environment and society.

Fintech: The use of technology to facilitate common financial practices.

Green Bonds: A financial instrument issued to raise money for programs and projects that benefit the environment.

Impact Investments: The practice of making investments with the goal of producing both financial returns and beneficial social or environmental impact.

Sponsorship: Financial support received (in this case by F1 Teams) to cover expenses and salaries of those involved.

Sustainability: The goal of positive coexistence between humans and the environment.

Chapter 12
Fintech-Enabled Telemedicine:
Global Healthcare Advancement

Shadi Askari
Hamta Business Corporation, Canada

Alireza Ghofrani
Quark Minded Technology Inc., Canada

Hamed Taherdoost
https://orcid.org/0000-0002-6503-6739
University Canada West, Canada

ABSTRACT

This chapter examines the transformative collaboration between financial technology (Fintech) and telemedicine, highlighting their combined potential to enhance global healthcare accessibility, affordability, and efficiency. Addressing regulatory, privacy, and ethical considerations, the chapter explores how Fintech contributes to overcoming challenges and proposes secure frameworks for a Fintech-enabled telemedicine ecosystem. It also investigates the role of digital currencies and blockchain in facilitating cross-border healthcare transactions. The chapter concludes with recommendations for policymakers, healthcare professionals, and Fintech innovators to harness this collaboration's full potential, aiming to shape a more accessible and advanced future for global healthcare.

INTRODUCTION

The intersection of fintech and telemedicine has the potential to revolutionize healthcare delivery and payment systems. Fintech, or financial technology, encompasses a wide range of digital innovations in the financial sector, including mobile payment solutions, blockchain technology, and digital currencies. Telemedicine, on the other hand, involves the remote delivery of healthcare services using telecommunications technology (Alt, Beck, & Smits, 2018; Haleem, Javaid, Singh, & Suman, 2021). The convergence of these two fields holds promise for improving access to healthcare, streamlining payment processes,

DOI: 10.4018/979-8-3693-1561-3.ch012

and enhancing overall patient experience. The integration of fintech and telemedicine can facilitate the seamless delivery of healthcare services, particularly in remote or underserved areas. By leveraging digital payment solutions, patients can easily settle medical bills for telemedicine consultations, prescription refills, and remote monitoring services (Akinola & Telukdarie, 2023). This can help overcome financial barriers to accessing healthcare and improve patient compliance with treatment plans. Fintech solutions such as mobile wallets, peer-to-peer payment platforms, and digital currencies can simplify the payment process for telemedicine services (Cai, Marrone, & Linnenluecke, 2022). This can lead to faster and more secure transactions, reducing administrative burdens for healthcare providers and improving overall efficiency in the healthcare system. The intersection of fintech and telemedicine has the potential to enhance the overall patient experience by offering convenient and secure payment options for healthcare services. Patients can benefit from the flexibility of making payments through mobile apps, online portals, or digital wallets, eliminating the need for traditional payment methods such as cash or physical credit cards (Singh & Rana, 2017). However, the convergence of fintech and telemedicine also raises important regulatory and security considerations. As financial transactions become increasingly integrated with healthcare services, it is essential to ensure compliance with data protection regulations, patient privacy laws, and financial industry standards to safeguard sensitive information and prevent fraud. The intersection of fintech and telemedicine presents exciting opportunities to transform healthcare delivery and payment systems. By leveraging digital financial technologies, healthcare providers can streamline payment processes, improve access to care, and enhance the overall patient experience. However, it is crucial to address regulatory and security challenges to ensure the responsible and ethical implementation of these innovations (Leung, 2023).

In the 21st century, technological advancements have become the catalysts for a paradigm shift in the field of healthcare, transcending geographical boundaries and reshaping the landscape of medical practices worldwide (El-Swaify, 2022). The intersection of technology and healthcare has not only improved patient outcomes but has also enhanced the accessibility, efficiency, and overall quality of healthcare services on a global scale. One of the key contributions of technological advancements to global healthcare is the revolution in diagnostics and the emergence of precision medicine. Cutting-edge technologies such as genomics, artificial intelligence (AI), and machine learning have paved the way for a more personalized approach to patient care (Ahmed, Mohamed, Zeeshan, & Dong, 2020). Genetic sequencing allows clinicians to decipher an individual's unique genetic code, enabling tailored treatment plans that consider genetic predispositions and responses to specific therapies (Chan & Ginsburg, 2011). AI-driven diagnostics enhance accuracy and speed in identifying diseases, leading to early detection and intervention. In an era of globalization, technological advancements have bridged the gap between patients and healthcare providers, overcoming geographical barriers through telemedicine. Telehealth platforms enable remote consultations, making healthcare services accessible to individuals in remote or underserved areas (Goel, Alam, Eggert, & Acharya, 2017). Furthermore, wearable devices and sensors facilitate remote patient monitoring, allowing healthcare professionals to track vital signs and disease progression in real-time. This not only improves patient outcomes but also reduces the burden on healthcare infrastructure by minimizing the need for frequent in-person visits (Kakria, Tripathi, & Kitipawang, 2015). The advent of big data analytics has empowered healthcare professionals and policymakers with the tools to analyze vast datasets and derive meaningful insights. By harnessing the power of big data, healthcare systems can identify trends, track disease outbreaks, and formulate evidence-based strategies for public health interventions (Dolley, 2018). This proactive approach not only enhances the efficiency of healthcare delivery but also plays a crucial role in preventing and managing global health crises. In an age where the security of health data is paramount, blockchain technology has emerged as a revolutionary force. Blockchain ensures the integrity and security of health records, protecting sensitive information from unauthorized access or tampering. Additionally, blockchain facilitates interoperability, allowing seamless and secure sharing of medical data across different healthcare providers and systems. This interconnectedness promotes continuity of care and facilitates collaborative efforts on a global scale.

FINTECH IN HEALTHCARE

Fintech refers to the innovative use of technology with respect to financial services, and fintech in healthcare refers to the utilization of financial technologies within the healthcare industry (Giglio, 2021). Fintech in healthcare encompasses various technologies that are developed, used, or refined for the finance sector, including digital identification, mobile money, artificial intelligence, robotics, and Blockchain. Fintech plays a pivotal role in improving access to timely healthcare services through innovative solutions, and it enables easier access to procedures that involve complex payment schemes and operations, ultimately improving the overall healthcare experience (Stojakovic-Celustka, 2020). Fintech interventions are addressing the inefficiencies and knowledge gaps inherent in many healthcare payment systems, and they are introducing new and improved digital financial service models. Fintech in healthcare has the potential to solve healthcare's most pressing issues, from minimizing medical debt to drastically improving patient satisfaction. Fintech companies are also tied up with telemedicine and provide services and insurance on the same platform (Grassi & Fantaccini, 2022).

Table 1 outlines the multifaceted role of Fintech in enhancing patient outcomes within the healthcare landscape. Fintech innovations play a pivotal role in streamlining various aspects of the healthcare ecosystem, from facilitating seamless payments for medical services to optimizing insurance management through insurtech solutions. The table elucidates how these fintech interventions positively impact patient outcomes, ensuring improved financial accessibility, efficient telehealth services, and enhanced coordination of care through secure health record sharing. Additionally, it highlights the role of fintech in promoting proactive healthcare management, with features such as healthcare savings accounts (HSAs) and personalized financial planning. By addressing financial stress, improving access to treatments, and fostering investments in healthcare innovations, fintech emerges as a key enabler in the quest for a patient-centric and technologically advanced healthcare system.

Fintech has significantly streamlined payment processes, billing, and insurance claims in the healthcare industry. For instance, Mastercard's partnership with HealthLock aims to bring clarity to patients' medical bills, addressing the issues of billing errors, fraud, and confusion. HealthLock uses machine learning and industry expertise to help patients keep track of their healthcare payments, focusing on privacy, control, and savings ("Mastercard and HealthLock partner to help protect consumers from healthcare fraud and billing errors," 2023). The lack of healthcare-specific systems for accounting and financial planning has led to a real-time, action-oriented engine that ingests financial data from various sources to become the financial system of record for the practice, providing predictive analytics and serving as a trusted source of truth for lenders, vendor partners, and insurance companies. Fintech has introduced easy-to-use apps and digital solutions to simplify patient payments, reducing the workload of the billing department and enhancing the billing and payment processes in healthcare organizations worldwide. Fintech aims to cut overhead costs spent on payment processing, claims submission, and reconciliation, providing a significant benefit to healthcare organizations amidst economic uncertainties.

Table 1. Fintech contributions to improving patient outcomes in healthcare

Aspect	Fintech Contribution	Impact on Patient Outcomes	Ref
Healthcare Payments	**Mobile Wallets and Digital Payments:** Fintech facilitates seamless, secure transactions for medical services, reducing administrative burdens.	**Improved Financial Accessibility:** Patients can easily manage medical bills, reducing financial stress and ensuring timely payments, leading to better access to healthcare.	(Shaikh, Memon, Dhomeja, & Dahri, 2023)
Insurance Management	**Insurtech Solutions:** Fintech streamlines insurance processes, offering real-time claims processing and policy management.	**Enhanced Coverage and Claim Efficiency:** Patients experience quicker claims processing, reduced administrative hassles, and better understanding of their insurance coverage, ensuring optimal utilization of benefits.	(Nicoletti & Nicoletti, 2021)
Telehealth Billing	**Automated Billing Systems:** Fintech automates billing for telehealth services, ensuring accuracy and prompt reimbursement.	**Efficient Telehealth Services:** Healthcare providers can focus on delivering quality care, knowing that the billing process is streamlined, leading to increased adoption of telehealth and improved patient outcomes.	(Bhat, AlQahtani, & Nekovee, 2023)
Medical Loans and Financing	**Healthcare Financing Platforms:** Fintech enables easy access to medical loans, allowing patients to manage unexpected medical expenses.	**Timely Access to Treatment:** Patients can afford necessary treatments without delay, preventing the exacerbation of health conditions and improving overall health outcomes.	(Modgil, Dwivedi, Rana, Gupta, & Kamble, 2022)
Patient Health Records	**Blockchain for Secure Data Sharing:** Fintech employs blockchain for secure and interoperable health data sharing across providers.	**Enhanced Care Coordination:** Seamless and secure access to patient health records ensures healthcare providers have comprehensive information, leading to more informed decisions and coordinated care.	(Shaikh et al., 2023)
Health Savings Accounts (HSAs)	**Fintech Integration with HSAs:** Fintech platforms enhance the management of HSAs, allowing patients to save for healthcare expenses tax-efficiently.	**Encouraging Preventive Care:** Patients can proactively manage their health by using HSAs for preventive services, leading to early detection and intervention, thereby improving overall health outcomes.	(Mhlanga, 2023)
Personalized Financial Planning	**AI-driven Financial Advice:** Fintech leverages AI to provide personalized financial planning, considering healthcare expenses.	**Reduced Financial Stress:** Patients receive tailored financial guidance, ensuring they can afford necessary treatments and medications, ultimately contributing to better mental and physical health.	(Lau & Leimer, 2019)
Healthcare Investment Platforms	**Fintech Investment Opportunities:** Fintech introduces healthcare investment platforms, allowing individuals to invest in healthcare innovations.	**Advancing Medical Research and Innovation:** Increased investments drive medical research and innovation, leading to the development of cutting-edge treatments and technologies that can positively impact patient outcomes.	(Jarvis & Han, 2021)
Fraud Prevention	**Biometric Authentication and AI Algorithms:** Fintech employs advanced security measures to prevent healthcare fraud.	**Ensuring Data Integrity:** Patient data remains secure, reducing the risk of identity theft and ensuring the integrity of healthcare information, contributing to better patient trust and outcomes.	(Xu, 2022)

These examples demonstrate how fintech is revolutionizing the healthcare industry by addressing billing errors, simplifying patient payments, and modernizing financial service models to streamline payment processes, billing, and insurance claims.

TELEMEDICINE REVOLUTION

Telemedicine, also known as telehealth or e-health, refers to the use of telecommunication and information technology to provide clinical healthcare services from a distance. The concept of telemedicine was introduced in the 1970s, and it has since evolved significantly, with the delivery of healthcare services becoming more accessible and convenient for patients (Bashshur & Shannon, 2009). The evolution of telemedicine can be traced through stages in Figure 1.

Current applications of telemedicine include provider and patient education, behavioral treatment, physical therapy, and general health information. Telemedicine has been used in various settings, such as rural areas, urban communities, and military settings, to provide healthcare services to patients remotely (Chen, 2017). As technology continues to evolve, telemedicine will likely play an increasingly important

Figure 1. The evolution of telemedicine

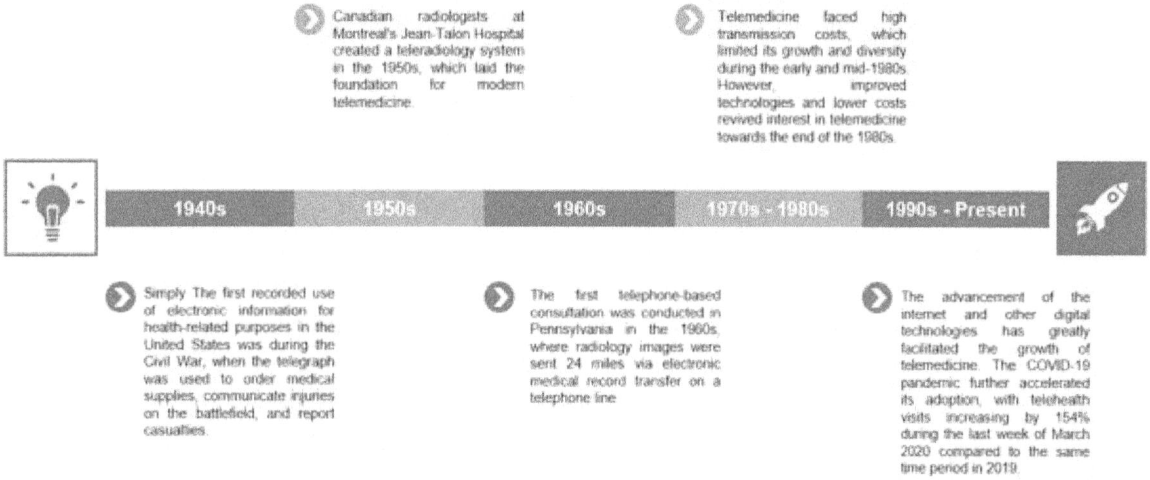

role in the delivery of healthcare services, offering patients more convenient and accessible care options. Telemedicine plays a crucial role in making healthcare accessible to remote and underserved areas. It enables people in remote or underserved areas to access medical specialists and healthcare services without the need for physical travel, reducing time and costs associated with hospital visits. Some of the key benefits of telemedicine in these areas include: Increased access to care, cost savings, improved monitoring and communications, reduced transportation burdens, and enhanced flexibility for providers (Workforce et al., 2015). However, there are also barriers to the adoption of telemedicine in healthcare, such as limited broadband access, equipment failures, and patient technological capability. To improve telehealth equity and access for underserved patients, healthcare providers can focus on improvements to telehealth workflow, staff training, and community resources. Overall, telemedicine has the potential to revolutionize healthcare access for remote and underserved areas, offering a more sustainable and cost-effective solution for providing quality healthcare services (Haleem et al., 2021).

The convergence of fintech and telemedicine enhances healthcare services by streamlining financial processes. Fintech facilitates seamless payment transactions for telemedicine consultations, offering patients convenience and efficiency. Integration with insurtech expedites insurance-related processes, ensuring quicker reimbursement for healthcare providers and a smoother experience for patients (Bhat et al., 2023).

Digital health wallets, developed by fintech companies, serve as centralized repositories for health and financial information. These wallets integrate with telemedicine platforms, allowing patients to access services, make payments, and share health information securely. Innovative payment models, such as subscription-based healthcare plans, are enabled by fintech, providing individuals with comprehensive and flexible telemedicine coverage (Maher, Khan, & Prikshat, 2023).

Fintech contributes to data security and privacy, crucial in maintaining the confidentiality of patient information in telemedicine. Moreover, it supports financial inclusion by offering accessible payment options, especially beneficial for individuals in remote areas. Mobile payment solutions and digital wallets enhance accessibility to telemedicine, promoting healthcare inclusivity (Govindarajan, Singh, & Gohel, 2023).

Fintech's advanced analytics capabilities benefit healthcare finance, helping providers optimize financial strategies, identify cost-saving opportunities, and enhance operational efficiency. Additionally, fintech tools enable secure cross-border transactions, facilitating international collaboration in the healthcare industry. In essence, the collaboration between fintech and telemedicine improves the financial aspects of healthcare, making services more efficient, accessible, and secure. This convergence has the potential to reshape the landscape of healthcare delivery (Jameaba, 2020).

The integration of digital payment solutions within telemedicine platforms is essential for providing seamless and convenient care to patients. Some telemedicine software providers have already addressed this issue by incorporating payment processing features into their platforms. For example, Doxy.me allows healthcare providers to collect payments directly from patients during their appointments or in the virtual waiting room, using a premium plan. Other telemedicine platforms, such as Mend, offer a comprehensive suite of patient engagement tools, including automated payments, digital forms, and appointment scheduling (McClure, 2020). However, there are still challenges to overcome in the integration of digital payment solutions in telemedicine platforms. Some of these challenges include state-specific licensure requirements, reimbursement options, adoption, technology, and patient access/awareness. To address these challenges, telemedicine platforms need to focus on full integration of Electronic Medical Records (EMR) with telehealth technology, ensure compliance with regulations, and continuously improve their platforms to meet the evolving needs of healthcare providers and patients (Lau & Leimer, 2019; Williams & Boren, 2008).

The integration of digital payment solutions within telemedicine platforms is crucial for providing efficient and convenient care. Some telemedicine software providers have already taken steps to address this issue, but there are still challenges to overcome. By focusing on integration, compliance, and continuous improvement, telemedicine platforms can better serve the needs of healthcare providers and patients in the digital age of healthcare.

IMPROVING ACCESS TO HEALTHCARE

Fintech-enabled telemedicine has the potential to improve access to healthcare services globally. Telemedicine can make it easier for people to get preventive treatment and help their long-term health, particularly for those who face financial or regional causes to receiving quality treatment (Bashshur & Shannon, 2009). Telemedicine can improve the quality of medical practice, allowing doctors to spend less time on rural assignments and providing more care to patients. It also enables private healthcare specialists to practice and enhances the patient experience. Patients will no longer have to stand in long queues, and physicians will be able to access patient information more conveniently and efficiently with electronic files and eliminating overall wait times. Telemedicine can significantly improve health care delivery for patients with limited access to medical services, providing services from radiology to dermatology to at least some of the millions of patients who lack adequate health care (Maddukuri, Patel, & Lipoff, 2021). Fintech solutions can be powerful in helping long-excluded low- and middle-income populations gain access to healthcare and buttress them. Fintech is revolutionizing the financial aspect of telemedicine by providing ad hoc payment solutions such as dedicated credit cards and apps that allow patients to create tailored payment plans remotely. Fintech and InsurTech allow consumers to make better-informed decisions about their coverage plan and make comprehensive resources available, such as a Health Information Platform and insurance comparison apps (Antony, Menon, RD, & Varghese, 2022). Several case studies highlight successful implementations in different regions, showcasing the effectiveness of various approaches and strategies in various contexts. Some notable examples include: Fogarty's Center for Global Health Studies, in collaboration with the Cincinnati Children's Hospital Medical Center and the National Cancer Institute, is commissioning a collection of implementation science case studies in LMICs. These case studies describe key components of conducting implementation research, including selecting, adapting, and applying implementation science models, theories, and frameworks to these settings, developing and testing implementation strategies, and evaluating implementation processes and outcomes (Beecroft, Sturke, Neta, & Ramaswamy, 2022)

FINANCIAL INCLUSION AND HEALTH EQUITY

Fintech and telemedicine contribute to financial inclusion in healthcare by providing digital financial services, improving access to healthcare financing, and reducing disparities in health care access. Fintech, which combines finance and digital technologies, offers innovations such as mobile money, blockchain, and artificial intelligence to improve convenience, financial inclusion, and data analytics. It enables people to pay for and access healthcare using digital financial services, addressing high out-of-pocket payments for high-quality care and working with partners to adopt systems technologies that can bring down the cost of care. Additionally, fintech can increase financial resources for health, improve planning and participation in financial protection programs, and create operational efficiency and transparency in health facilities and across the health system (Nathan, Setiawan, & Quynh, 2022). Furthermore, fintech revolutionizes the financial aspect of telemedicine by providing ad hoc payment solutions, such as dedicated credit cards and apps, that allow patients to create tailored payment plans remotely. Fintech and telemedicine play a crucial role in expanding financial access to meet the healthcare needs of underserved communities and reducing financial barriers to health care access (Khezr, Moniruzzaman, Yassine, & Benlamri, 2019).

The impact of fintech and telemedicine on health equity and bridging the healthcare gap is significant. Telehealth, enabled by digital technology, plays a crucial role in enabling health equity by disrupting and rebuilding health systems around the care needs of individuals and populations, thus empowering underserved communities. It addresses inequities fostered by the implementation of global telehealth services and emphasizes the importance of proactive measures to reduce system-wide barriers for access to telehealth, ensuring that underserved populations can take advantage of telehealth to improve access to healthcare services (Kuziemsky et al., 2022).

On the other hand, digital financial services, including fintech, impact health system performance by increasing financial resources for health, improving planning and participation in financial protection programs, and creating operational efficiency and transparency in health facilities and across the health system. Fintech's role in reducing disparities and financial barriers to healthcare access is particularly pertinent for low-income countries and regions where out-of-pocket spending for healthcare is high, and bank account ownership is not widespread. It has the potential to bridge accessibility gaps and increase the scale, reach, and sustainability of access to healthcare funds for those in need (Cambaza, 2023). Both telemedicine and fintech contribute to health equity by addressing disparities in access to healthcare services and financial resources. They play a crucial role in bridging the healthcare gap by empowering underserved communities, improving access to healthcare financing, and reducing financial barriers to healthcare access.

DATA SECURITY AND PRIVACY

Addressing concerns related to data security and privacy in fintech-enabled telemedicine is crucial to ensure the protection of patient information and build trust in telehealth systems. Several studies and articles highlight the challenges and factors associated with privacy and security in telehealth services.

Privacy and Security Concerns in Telehealth

The use of telemedicine has raised concerns about privacy and security risks related to patient health information. A systematic review identified challenges and factors for privacy and security related to telehealth visits, including concerns about privacy and confidentiality, lack of familiarity with technology, and issues protecting confidentiality and data security (Watzlaf, Zhou, Dealmeida, & Hartman, 2017). Additionally, the risks posed to the privacy and security of patients' health information in telehealth systems can affect the level of trust and willingness to adopt and use the system (Dhagarra, Goswami, & Kumar, 2020).

Data Security in Telemedicine

As the use of telemedicine increases, concerns over data security and confidentiality issues have also grown. Patient data must be kept confidential and secure at all times to protect both patients and doctors. Healthcare providers can ensure data security by using the latest technologies and following best practices (Thapa & Camtepe, 2021). Common types of data security threats in telemedicine include data breaches, which pose a risk to patient safety and confidentiality (Pramanik, Pareek, & Nayyar, 2019).

Policy Interventions and Digital Health

Policy interventions in the health care sector, particularly in the context of digital interventions, need to address concerns about security, privacy, and surveillance. The implementation of the "Internet of Health Care Things" framework requires careful consideration of patient data privacy requirements and the safe and well-regulated collection and use of health care data (Hossain et al., 2021).

Addressing Privacy Concerns in Telehealth Software Development

Healthcare organizations have an ethical responsibility to address privacy and security risks in telehealth software development. Understanding the privacy and security risks is the first step in protecting patients' information, and conducting a risk assessment can help identify weak points in telehealth services. Best practices for safeguarding privacy in telehealth software development include implementing a robust system of security measures to ensure user privacy and protect sensitive data (Watzlaf et al., 2017). Addressing concerns related to data security and privacy in fintech-enabled telemedicine requires a comprehensive approach that encompasses technological, operational, and regulatory aspects. By implementing best practices, staying informed of privacy and security policies, and conducting risk assessments, healthcare providers can mitigate the risks and build trust in telehealth systems.

Telemedicine and Fintech are two rapidly growing industries that have the potential to revolutionize healthcare delivery and financial services, respectively. The integration of these two industries can lead to innovative solutions that improve access to care, reduce costs, and enhance patient outcomes. However, the integration of Fintech and Telemedicine also presents unique challenges related to regulatory frameworks, privacy, security, and ethical considerations (Cambaza, 2023). Regulatory frameworks for Telemedicine vary widely across different countries and regions. In the European Union, for example, the recent European Commission proposal on the regulation of digital health aims to harmonize legal frameworks to enable cross-border telemedicine practices (Raposo, 2016). In the United States, the Centers for Medicare and Medicaid Services (CMS) has issued guidelines for the reimbursement of telemedicine services (Brotman & Kotloff, 2021). In China, the government has implemented policies to promote the development of telemedicine, including the establishment of telemedicine centers and the provision of financial incentives (Ma et al., 2022). Best practices for the integration of Fintech and Telemedicine include the establishment of standardized guidelines and best practices for telemedicine to ensure consistency and quality in care delivery. Policymakers can work with professional medical organizations to develop guidelines for telemedicine, covering areas such as patient evaluation, prescribing medications, documentation, and privacy and security standards (Krupinski & Bernard, 2014). Policymakers should also establish guidelines and regulations to protect patients' rights and ensure ethical telemedicine practice. This includes safeguarding against fraud, ensuring informed consent, addressing issues of medical malpractice, and establishing mechanisms for handling patient complaints or disputes related to telemedicine services. Regulatory frameworks for Fintech also vary widely across different countries and regions. In the European Union, for example, the European Commission has proposed a regulatory framework for digital currencies to ensure the protection of consumers and the prevention of money laundering (Vandezande, 2017). In the United States, the Consumer Financial Protection Bureau (CFPB) has issued guidelines for the regulation of digital currencies and other Fintech services (Levitin, 2012). In China, the government has implemented policies to promote the development of digital currencies and other Fintech services, including the establishment of regulatory sandboxes and experimental legal regimes (Elizaveta & Tjaša, 2020). Best practices for the integration of Fintech and Telemedicine include the establishment of clear and comprehensive information to patients on the types of services that can be provided through telemedicine and their timing, as well as costs and access methods. Policymakers should also ensure the ability to manage security and data protection as early as the design phase of the application (so-called privacy by design). A clear and complete identification of the figures responsible for data processing within the structure providing the telemedicine service is also important. The integration of Fintech and Telemedicine has the potential to revolutionize healthcare delivery and financial services. However, it also presents unique challenges related to regulatory frameworks, privacy, security, and ethical considerations. Policymakers can address these challenges by establishing standardized guidelines and best practices for telemedicine and Fintech, protecting patients' rights and ensuring ethical practice, and promoting the development of innovative solutions that improve access to care and financial services, reduce costs, and enhance patient outcomes.

CHALLENGES AND OPPORTUNITIES

Implementing fintech-enabled telemedicine involves the convergence of financial technology and healthcare services, offering promising solutions but also encountering several challenges. One key challenge is the need for robust cybersecurity measures to protect sensitive patient data and financial transactions. As telemedicine relies heavily on digital platforms, ensuring the confidentiality and integrity of personal health information becomes paramount (Frumento, 2019). Cyber threats such as data breaches and hacking incidents pose a significant risk to the seamless operation of fintech-enabled telemedicine, potentially compromising patient privacy and financial security (Govindarajan et al., 2023).

Interoperability issues between different fintech and telemedicine platforms present another hurdle. Integrating diverse technologies to create a seamless and efficient system for both financial transactions and medical consultations requires standardized protocols and interfaces. Without proper interoperability, the user experience may suffer, leading to frustration among both healthcare providers and patients. Additionally, achieving regulatory compliance in the rapidly evolving landscape of fintech and telemedicine is complex. Striking the right balance between innovation and adherence to regulations is crucial to prevent legal challenges that could hinder the widespread adoption of these technologies (Ramzan et al., 2022).

The digital divide is a significant challenge in the implementation of fintech-enabled telemedicine. Not all populations have equal access to the necessary technology or reliable internet connectivity, limiting the reach of telemedicine services. This issue exacerbates existing healthcare disparities, as those in underserved or rural areas may face difficulties accessing both financial services and telemedicine. Moreover, there are concerns related to the ethical use of patient data in fintech-enabled telemedicine. Balancing the potential benefits of data-driven insights with the ethical responsibility to protect patient privacy is an ongoing challenge that requires careful consideration and regulation (Agate, 2017).

Financial inclusion is a critical aspect that cannot be overlooked. While fintech-enabled telemedicine aims to provide convenient and affordable healthcare services, there is a risk of excluding individuals who do not have access to traditional banking services or who are unfamiliar with digital transactions. Overcoming these barriers requires addressing issues of financial literacy and creating user-friendly interfaces that accommodate a diverse range of users (Tsai, Lin, & Liu, 2020). Another challenge is the potential for increased healthcare costs associated with the implementation of fintech-enabled telemedicine. While these technologies can streamline processes and reduce administrative overhead, there is a need for careful consideration to ensure that cost savings are passed on to patients and do not contribute to the rising healthcare expenses (Cai et al., 2022).

Resistance to change within the healthcare industry and among healthcare professionals poses a substantial challenge. Many practitioners may be hesitant to embrace new technologies, requiring comprehensive training programs and strategies to demonstrate the benefits of fintech-enabled telemedicine. The delicate balance between human touch in healthcare and the efficiency offered by technology must be carefully navigated to gain acceptance among both healthcare providers and patients. Additionally, the risk of algorithmic bias in fintech-enabled telemedicine poses ethical concerns. If not properly addressed, biased algorithms could lead to disparities in healthcare outcomes, disproportionately affecting certain demographic groups (Alrahbi, Khan, Gupta, Modgil, & Chiappetta Jabbour, 2022).

While fintech-enabled telemedicine holds great promise for improving healthcare accessibility and efficiency, its implementation is not without challenges. From cybersecurity concerns to issues of interoperability, digital inclusion, and ethical considerations, a multifaceted approach is required to overcome these obstacles. Striking the right balance between innovation and regulatory compliance, addressing healthcare disparities, and ensuring the ethical use of patient data are essential steps toward the successful implementation of fintech-enabled telemedicine. In the realm of fintech-enabled telemedicine, challenges are apparent, but there are concurrent opportunities for growth and improvement. One avenue for advancement lies in the realm of cybersecurity. Instead of viewing security concerns as obstacles, the industry can innovate by investing in advanced technologies such as blockchain to fortify data storage and transmission, thus heightening overall platform security.

A crucial opportunity arises in the push for standardization and interoperability. Establishing industry-wide standards can create a common framework, promoting seamless integration between fintech and telemedicine platforms. This not only enhances the user experience but fosters the development of a more cohesive ecosystem (Kerber & Schweitzer, 2017).

Collaboration and partnerships represent another significant opportunity. By building strong relationships between fintech companies, healthcare providers, and regulatory bodies, the industry can develop comprehensive solutions that address both financial and healthcare needs. Partnerships can provide the support needed to navigate regulatory complexities and promote a more supportive growth environment (Anagnostopoulos, 2018). Government incentives can play a pivotal role in propelling the growth of fintech-enabled telemedicine. Advocating for regulatory support and exploring avenues such as tax incentives for companies investing in secure healthcare technology can provide the necessary impetus (Ennew, Waite, & Waite, 2013). Bridging the digital divide is an opportunity that aligns with the goal of making telemedicine accessible to all. Initiatives aimed at improving digital literacy and expanding internet access, especially in underserved areas through public-private partnerships, can extend the reach of telemedicine services (Chang et al., 2004). Ethical considerations surrounding patient data use offer an opportunity to build trust. Developing and adhering to comprehensive ethical frameworks, along with trustworthy option for patients (Shadbolt et al., 2019). Addressing concerns about financial inclusion is paramount. Fintech-enabled telemedicine platforms can incorporate strategies to cater to individuals without traditional banking services, exploring partnerships with mobile payment providers or the development of alternative payment models. Emphasizing the cost-effectiveness of telemedicine presents another avenue for growth. Demonstrating how these technologies lead to overall cost savings in healthcare delivery can be a compelling argument for adoption by both providers and patients. Overcoming resistance to change requires robust education and training programs for healthcare professionals. Investment in initiatives that familiarize practitioners with the benefits and proper use of fintech-enabled telemedicine can contribute to a smoother implementation process. Figure 2 illustrates the landscape of challenges, opportunities, and best solutions within the realm of fintech-enabled telemedicine. The Challenges section highlights regulatory compliance, data security, interoperability, user adoption, and payment integration. The Opportunities section presents areas such as remote patient monitoring, blockchain for security, AI-driven diagnostics, telehealth expansion, and global reach. Solutions include compliance automation, advanced encryption, standardized protocols, user-friendly interfaces, and blockchain integration.

FUTURE TRENDS

The fintech and telemedicine industries are experiencing significant trends that are shaping their future. In fintech, emerging trends include AI and machine learning, embedded finance, open banking, and IoT, which are revolutionizing banking, payments, investments, and risk management (Feyen, Natarajan, & Saal, 2023). Additionally, the use of fintech apps is increasing, and fintech is acting as a bedrock for financial guidance and stability during uncertain times (Chiu, 2016). In telemedicine, trends such as the "digital first" approach, the adoption of mHealth, and the use of artificial intelligence as a standard of care are advancing the "new normal" in healthcare (Marx & Padmanabhan, 2020). These trends are driven by the growing prevalence of telemedicine and the increasing interest in remote patient care (Wahezi et al., 2021). The future of both industries is promising, with a focus on sustainability, customer activation, and the integration of new technologies to meet evolving consumer needs. The future

Figure 2. Navigating the Fintech-telemedicine horizon: Unveiling challenges, opportunities, and innovative solutions

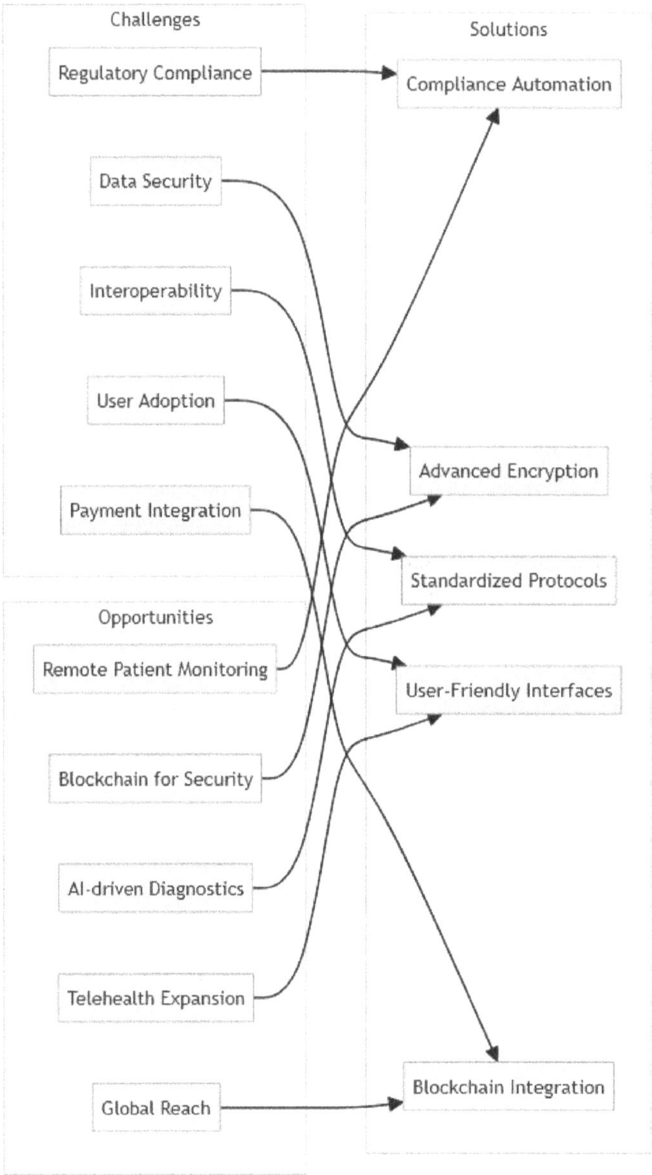

of fintech and telemedicine is shaped by several emerging trends and potential breakthroughs. In the fintech industry, predictions for the future include the rise of embedded finance, open banking, and the increasing use of AI and machine. Additionally, the adoption of sustainable payment solutions and the wider range of AI applications are anticipated to influence the fintech landscape. In telemedicine, the "digital first" approach, the adoption of mHealth, and the use of artificial intelligence as a standard of care are expected to advance the "new normal" in healthcare. Furthermore, the growth of telehealth is predicted to continue, with a focus on fair payment for services and the evolution of the telehealth system to meet patient needs. These predictions are driven by technological progress, customer activation, and the integration of new technologies to meet evolving consumer needs in both industries.

CONCLUSION

The key points discussed in the chapter emphasize the transformative potential of fintech-enabled telemedicine for global healthcare advancement. Fintech innovations are converging with telehealth to change the financial side of healthcare, making payments more efficient, innovative, and predictable, providing greater transparency and control. Fintech solutions are revolutionizing the financial aspect of telemedicine by providing ad hoc payment solutions such as dedicated credit cards and apps that allow patients to create tailored payment plans remotely. Telemedicine can significantly improve healthcare delivery for patients with limited access to medical services, and it can cost-effectively provide services to millions of patients who lack adequate healthcare. Despite its promise, telemedicine still faces barriers to wide-scale acceptance, such as lack of transnational regulatory standards, biases against technology-based medicine, and little to no interoperability between initiatives. The global public health response to manage and contain the pandemic has placed a paramount emphasis on telemedicine toward remote delivery of care, and the adoption of telemedicine has been seen in various regions around the world. Overall, the integration of fintech and telemedicine has the potential to improve healthcare affordability and accessibility across the globe.

REFERENCES

Agate, S. (2017). Unlocking the power of telehealth: Increasing access and services in underserved, urban areas. *Harvard Journal of Hispanic Policy*, *29*, 85.

Ahmed, Z., Mohamed, K., Zeeshan, S., & Dong, X. (2020). Artificial intelligence with multi-functional machine learning platform development for better healthcare and precision medicine. *Database (Oxford)*, *2020*, baaa010. doi:10.1093/database/baaa010 PMID:32185396

Akinola, S., & Telukdarie, A. (2023). Sustainable Digital Transformation in Healthcare: Advancing a Digital Vascular Health Innovation Solution. *Sustainability (Basel)*, *15*(13), 10417. doi:10.3390/su151310417

Alrahbi, D. A., Khan, M., Gupta, S., Modgil, S., & Chiappetta Jabbour, C. J. (2022). Challenges for developing health-care knowledge in the digital age. *Journal of Knowledge Management*, *26*(4), 824–853. doi:10.1108/JKM-03-2020-0224

Alt, R., Beck, R., & Smits, M. T. (2018). *FinTech and the transformation of the financial industry* (Vol. 28). Springer.

Anagnostopoulos, I. (2018). Fintech and regtech: Impact on regulators and banks. *Journal of Economics and Business*, *100*, 7–25. doi:10.1016/j.jeconbus.2018.07.003

Antony, A., Menon, G., RD, K., & Varghese, S. (2022). A study on the digital transformation of insurance industry. Academic Press.

Bashshur, R. L., & Shannon, G. W. (2009). *History of telemedicine: evolution, context, and transformation*. Mary Ann Liebert, Inc., Publishers.

Beecroft, B., Sturke, R., Neta, G., & Ramaswamy, R. (2022). The "case" for case studies: Why we need high-quality examples of global implementation research. *Implementation Science Communications*, *3*(1), 15. doi:10.1186/s43058-021-00227-5 PMID:35168672

Bhat, J. R., AlQahtani, S. A., & Nekovee, M. (2023). FinTech enablers, use cases, and role of future internet of things. *Journal of King Saud University. Computer and Information Sciences*, *35*(1), 87–101. doi:10.1016/j.jksuci.2022.08.033

Brotman, J. J., & Kotloff, R. M. (2021). Providing Outpatient Telehealth Services in the United States: Before and During Coronavirus Disease 2019. *Chest*, *159*(4), 1548–1558. doi:10.1016/j.chest.2020.11.020 PMID:33245875

Cai, C., Marrone, M., & Linnenluecke, M. (2022). Trends in fintech research and practice: Examining the intersection with the information systems field. *Communications of the Association for Information Systems*, *50*(1), 40. doi:10.17705/1CAIS.05036

Cambaza, E. (2023). The Role of FinTech in Sustainable Healthcare Development in Sub-Saharan Africa: A Narrative Review. *FinTech*, *2*(3), 444–460. doi:10.3390/fintech2030025

Chan, I. S., & Ginsburg, G. S. (2011). Personalized medicine: Progress and promise. *Annual Review of Genomics and Human Genetics*, *12*(1), 217–244. doi:10.1146/annurev-genom-082410-101446 PMID:21721939

Chang, B. L., Bakken, S., Brown, S. S., Houston, T. K., Kreps, G. L., Kukafka, R., Safran, C., & Stavri, P. Z. (2004). Bridging the digital divide: Reaching vulnerable populations. *Journal of the American Medical Informatics Association : JAMIA*, *11*(6), 448–457. doi:10.1197/jamia.M1535 PMID:15299002

Chen, E. T. (2017). Considerations of Telemedicine in the Delivery of Modern Healthcare. *American Journal of Management, 17*(3).

Chiu, I. H. (2016). Fintech and disruptive business models in financial products, intermediation and markets-policy implications for financial regulators. *J. Tech. L. & Pol'y*, *21*, 55.

Dhagarra, D., Goswami, M., & Kumar, G. (2020). Impact of Trust and Privacy Concerns on Technology Acceptance in Healthcare: An Indian Perspective. *International Journal of Medical Informatics*, *141*, 104164. doi:10.1016/j.ijmedinf.2020.104164 PMID:32593847

Dolley, S. (2018). Big data's role in precision public health. *Frontiers in Public Health*, *6*, 68. doi:10.3389/fpubh.2018.00068 PMID:29594091

El-Swaify, M. A. (2022). The Global Nexus: Bridging Science, Technology, and Business in the International Landscape. *International Multidisciplinary Journal Of Science. Technology & Business*, *1*(01), 22–28.

Elizaveta, G., & Tjaša, I. (2020). Regulatory sandboxes (experimental legal regimes) for digital innovations in BRICS. *BRICS Law Journal*, *7*(2), 10–36. doi:10.21684/2412-2343-2020-7-2-10-36

Ennew, C., Waite, N., & Waite, R. (2013). *Financial services marketing: An international guide to principles and practice*. Routledge. doi:10.4324/9780203521649

Feyen, E., Natarajan, H., & Saal, M. (2023). *Fintech and the Future of Finance: Market and Policy Implications*. World Bank Publications. doi:10.1596/978-1-4648-1914-8

Frumento, E. (2019). Cybersecurity and the evolutions of healthcare: challenges and threats behind its evolution. *M_Health Current and Future Applications*, 35-69.

Giglio, F. (2021). Fintech: A literature review. *European Research Studies*, *24*(2B, 2B), 600–627. doi:10.35808/ersj/2254

Goel, N. A., Alam, A. A., Eggert, E. M., & Acharya, S. (2017). *Design and development of a customizable telemedicine platform for improving access to healthcare for underserved populations.* Paper presented at the 2017 39th Annual International Conference of the IEEE Engineering in Medicine and Biology Society (EMBC). 10.1109/EMBC.2017.8037404

Govindarajan, U. H., Singh, D. K., & Gohel, H. A. (2023). Forecasting cyber security threats landscape and associated technical trends in telehealth using Bidirectional Encoder Representations from Transformers (BERT). *Computers & Security*, *133*, 103404. doi:10.1016/j.cose.2023.103404

Grassi, L., & Fantaccini, S. (2022). An overview of Fintech applications to solve the puzzle of health care funding: State-of-the-art in medical crowdfunding. *Financial Innovation*, *8*(1), 1–27. doi:10.1186/s40854-022-00388-9 PMID:36158456

Haleem, A., Javaid, M., Singh, R. P., & Suman, R. (2021). Telemedicine for healthcare: Capabilities, features, barriers, and applications. *Sensors International*, *2*, 100117. doi:10.1016/j.sintl.2021.100117 PMID:34806053

Hossain, M. J., Wadud, M. A. H., Rahman, A., Ferdous, J., Alam, M. S., Bhuiyan, T. M. A.-U.-H., & Mridha, M. F. (2021). *A Secured Patient's Online Data Monitoring through Blockchain: An Intelligent way to Store Lifetime Medical Records.* Paper presented at the 2021 International Conference on Science & Contemporary Technologies (ICSCT). 10.1109/ICSCT53883.2021.9642537

Jameaba, M.-S. (2020). Digitization revolution, FinTech disruption, and financial stability: Using the case of Indonesian banking ecosystem to highlight wide-ranging digitization opportunities and major challenges. *FinTech Disruption, and Financial stability: Using the Case of Indonesian Banking Ecosystem to highlight wide-ranging digitization opportunities and major challenges*.

Jarvis, R., & Han, H. (2021). Fintech Innovation: Review and Future Research Directions. *International Journal of Banking. Finance and Insurance Technologies*, *1*(1), 79–102.

Kakria, P., Tripathi, N., & Kitipawang, P. (2015). A real-time health monitoring system for remote cardiac patients using smartphone and wearable sensors. *International Journal of Telemedicine and Applications*, *2015*, 8–8. doi:10.1155/2015/373474 PMID:26788055

Kerber, W., & Schweitzer, H. (2017). Interoperability in the digital economy. *J. Intell. Prop. Info. Tech. & Elec. Com. L.*, *8*, 39.

Khezr, S., Moniruzzaman, M., Yassine, A., & Benlamri, R. (2019). Blockchain Technology in Healthcare: A Comprehensive Review and Directions for Future Research. *Applied Sciences (Basel, Switzerland)*, *9*(9), 1736. Advance online publication. doi:10.3390/app9091736

Krupinski, E. A., & Bernard, J. (2014). Standards and Guidelines in Telemedicine and Telehealth. *Health Care*, *2*(1), 74–93. doi:10.3390/healthcare2010074 PMID:27429261

Kuziemsky, C., Hunter, I., Udayasankaran, J. G., Ranatunga, P., Kulatunga, G., John, S., . . . Basu, A. (2022). Telehealth as a Means of Enabling Health Equity. *Yearb Med Inform, 31*(1), 60-66. doi:10.1055/s-0042-1742500

Lau, T., & Leimer, B. (2019). The era of connectedness: How AI will help deliver the future of banking. *Journal of Digital Banking*, *3*(3), 215–231.

Leung, R. (2023). *Leveraging AI and Blockchain for Streamlining Healthcare Payments.* Paper presented at the 2023 5th Blockchain and Internet of Things Conference. 10.1145/3625078.3625086

Levitin, A. J. (2012). The consumer financial protection bureau: An introduction. *Rev. Banking & Fin. L.*, *32*, 321.

Ma, Q., Sun, D., Tan, Z., Li, C., He, X., Zhai, Y., Wang, L., Cui, F., Li, M., Gao, J., Wang, L., & Zhao, J. (2022). Usage and perceptions of telemedicine among health care professionals in China. *International Journal of Medical Informatics*, *166*, 104856. doi:10.1016/j.ijmedinf.2022.104856 PMID:36037593

Maddukuri, S., Patel, J., & Lipoff, J. B. (2021). Teledermatology addressing disparities in health care access: A review. *Current Dermatology Reports*, *10*(2), 40–47. doi:10.1007/s13671-021-00329-2 PMID:33747638

Maher, M., Khan, I., & Prikshat, V. (2023). Monetisation of digital health data through a GDPR-compliant and blockchain enabled digital health data marketplace: A proposal to enhance patient's engagement with health data repositories. *International Journal of Information Management Data Insights*, *3*(1), 100159. doi:10.1016/j.jjimei.2023.100159

Marx, E. W., & Padmanabhan, P. (2020). *Healthcare digital transformation: How consumerism, technology and pandemic are accelerating the future*. CRC Press. doi:10.4324/9781003035695

Mhlanga, D. (2023). Financial Technology, Artificial Intelligence, and the Health Sector, Lessons We Are Learning on Good Health and Well-Being. In *FinTech and Artificial Intelligence for Sustainable Development: The Role of Smart Technologies in Achieving Development Goals* (pp. 145–170). Springer. doi:10.1007/978-3-031-37776-1_7

Modgil, S., Dwivedi, Y. K., Rana, N. P., Gupta, S., & Kamble, S. (2022). Has Covid-19 accelerated opportunities for digital entrepreneurship? An Indian perspective. *Technological Forecasting and Social Change*, *175*, 121415. doi:10.1016/j.techfore.2021.121415 PMID:36536802

Nathan, R. J., Setiawan, B., & Quynh, M. N. (2022). Fintech and Financial Health in Vietnam during the COVID-19 Pandemic: In-Depth Descriptive Analysis. *Journal of Risk and Financial Management*, *15*(3), 125. Advance online publication. doi:10.3390/jrfm15030125

Nicoletti, B., & Nicoletti, B. (2021). Platforms for insurance 4.0. *Insurance 4.0: Benefits and Challenges of Digital Transformation*, 173-259.

Pramanik, P. K. D., Pareek, G., & Nayyar, A. (2019). Security and Privacy in Remote Healthcare: Issues, Solutions, and Standards. In H. D. Jude & V. E. Balas (Eds.), *Telemedicine Technologies* (pp. 201–225). Academic Press. doi:10.1016/B978-0-12-816948-3.00014-3

Ramzan, S., Aqdus, A., Ravi, V., Koundal, D., Amin, R., & Al Ghamdi, M. A. (2022). Healthcare applications using blockchain technology: Motivations and challenges. *IEEE Transactions on Engineering Management.*

Raposo, V. L. (2016). Telemedicine: The legal framework (or the lack of it) in Europe. *GMS Health Technology Assessment*, *12*, Doc03. doi:10.3205/hta000126 PMID:27579146

Shadbolt, N., O'Hara, K., De Roure, D., Hall, W., Shadbolt, N., O'Hara, K., . . . Hall, W. (2019). Privacy, trust and ethical issues. *The Theory and Practice of Social Machines*, 149-200.

Shaikh, Z. A., Memon, S. A., Dhomeja, L. D., & Dahri, K. (2023). Blockchain-Based Fintech Architecture for Enhanced Interoperability in Health Insurance. *The Asian Bulletin of Big Data Management*, *3*(1).

Singh, S., & Rana, R. (2017). Study of consumer perception of digital payment mode. *Journal of Internet Banking and Commerce*, *22*(3), 1–14.

Stojakovic-Celustka, S. (2020). *FinTech and its implementation.* Paper presented at the International Workshop on Measuring Ontologies in Value Environments.

Thapa, C., & Camtepe, S. (2021). Precision health data: Requirements, challenges and existing techniques for data security and privacy. *Computers in Biology and Medicine*, *129*, 104130. doi:10.1016/j.compbiomed.2020.104130 PMID:33271399

Tsai, C.-H., Lin, C.-F., & Liu, H.-W. (2020). The diffusion of the sandbox approach to disruptive innovation and its limitations. *Cornell Int'l LJ*, *53*, 261.

Vandezande, N. (2017). Virtual currencies under EU anti-money laundering law. *Computer Law & Security Report*, *33*(3), 341–353. doi:10.1016/j.clsr.2017.03.011

Wahezi, S. E., Kohan, L. R., Spektor, B., Brancolini, S., Emerick, T., Fronterhouse, J. M., ... Anitescu, M. (2021). Telemedicine and current clinical practice trends in the COVID-19 pandemic. *Best Practice & Research. Clinical Anaesthesiology*, *35*(3), 307–319. doi:10.1016/j.bpa.2020.11.005 PMID:34511221

Watzlaf, V. J. M., Zhou, L., Dealmeida, D. R., & Hartman, L. M. (2017). A Systematic Review of Research Studies Examining Telehealth Privacy and Security Practices used by Healthcare Providers. *International Journal of Telerehabilitation*, *9*(2), 39–59. doi:10.5195/ijt.2017.6231 PMID:29238448

Williams, F., & Boren, S. A. (2008). The role of the electronic medical record (EMR) in care delivery development in developing countries: A systematic review. *Informatics in Primary Care*, *16*(2). PMID:18713530

Workforce, C. P., Rimsza, M. E., Hotaling, A. J., Keown, M. E., Marcin, J. P., Moskowitz, W. B., ... Simon, H. K. (2015). The use of telemedicine to address access and physician workforce shortages. *Pediatrics*, *136*(1), 202–209. doi:10.1542/peds.2015-1253 PMID:26122802

Xu, J. (2022). Biometrics in FinTech: A Technological Review. *Future And FinTech, The: Abcdi and Beyond, 361*.

Compilation of References

. Al Suwaidi, M. E. Y. M., Sidek, S. B., & Al-Shami, S. A. (2022). *A Conceptual Framework of FinTech Laws and Regulations on the Risk Management of Financial Institutions in UAE.* Mathematical Statistician and Engineering Applications, 71(3), 01-07.

. Mehdi, B. A. (2022). Can Qatar become a fintech hub? SWOT analysis. *FIIB Business Review,* 1-9.

2p. (2022). *Popular Payment Methods in Thailand: What Consumers Want.* Retrieved from https://2c2p.com/blog/thailand-payment-methods

Ab Razak, M. I., Dali, N. A. M., Dhillon, G., & Manaf, A. W. (2020). Fintech in Malaysia: Anappraisal to the need of shariah-compliant regulation. *Pertanika Journal of Social Science & Humanities*, *28*(4), 3223–3233. doi:10.47836/pjssh.28.4.40

Abdeldayem, M., & Aldulaimi, S. (2023). Entrepreneurial finance and crowdfunding in the Middle East. *The International Journal of Organizational Analysis*, *31*(4), 927–944. doi:10.1108/IJOA-03-2021-2684

Abdillah, L. A. (2019). An overview of Indonesian Fintech application. *Social Science Research Network.* https://papers.ssrn.com/sol3/papers.cfm?abstract_id=3512737

Abdul-Rahim, R., Bohari, S. A., Aman, A., & Awang, Z. (2022). Benefit–Risk Perceptions of FinTech Adoption for Sustainability from Bank Consumers' Perspective: The Moderating Role of Fear of COVID-19. *Sustainability (2071-1050), 14*(14). doi:10.3390/su14148357

About Us. (n.d.). Golomt Bank. https://www.golomtbank.com/en/about-bank

About Us: MineSec white-label softpos. MineSec. (n.d.). https://www.theminesec.com/about-us

Abu Alruz, J., Khasawneh, O. Y., Al-Jamal, D., Talafha, F., & Almajali, D. (2021). Financial inclusion in Saudi Arabia: An analysis of influencing factors. *Heliyon*, *7*(9), e08056. PMID:34632138

Acclime. (2023, August 31). *Fintech in Cambodia: An overview*. Retrieved from https://cambodia.acclime.com/insight/Fintech-overview/

Acemoglu, D., & Restrepo, P. (2020). Robots and jobs: Evidence from US labor markets. *Journal of Political Economy*, *128*(6), 2188–2244. doi:10.1086/705716

Adeleye, B. N., Bengana, I., Boukhelkhal, A., Shafiq, M. M., & Abdulkareem, H. K. (2022). Does human capital tilt the population-economic growth dynamics? Evidence from Middle East and north African countries. *Social Indicators Research*, *162*(2), 863–883. doi:10.1007/s11205-021-02867-5

Adrian, T., & Mancini-Grifoli, T. (2019b, September 19). *Digital Currencies: The Rise of Stablecoins.* Retrieved from https://blogs.imf.org

Afif, M., & Samsuri, A. (2022). Integration of Fintech and Islamic Banking in Indonesia: Opportunities and Challenges. *Cakrawala: Jurnal Studi Islam*, *17*(1), 27–38. doi:10.31603/cakrawala.7051

AgarwalS.QianW.RenY.TsaiH. T.YeungB. Y. (2020). *The real impact of Fintech: Evidence from mobile payment technology*. doi:10.2139/ssrn.3556340

Agarwal, S., & Zhang, J. (2020). FinTech, lending and payment innovation: A review. *Asia-Pacific Journal of Financial Studies*, *49*(3), 353–367. doi:10.1111/ajfs.12294

Agate, S. (2017). Unlocking the power of telehealth: Increasing access and services in underserved, urban areas. *Harvard Journal of Hispanic Policy*, *29*, 85.

Agrawal, A., McHale, J., & Oettl, A. (2018). *The Impact of Artificial Intelligence on Innovation*. National Bureau of Economic Research, Working Paper 24284. February 2018.

Ahmad, S. M., & Al Mamun, A. (2020). Opportunities of Islamic fintech: The case of Bangladesh and Turkey. *CenRaPS Journal of Social Sciences*, *2*(3), 412–426. doi:10.46291/cenraps.v2i3.39

Ahmed, Z., Mohamed, K., Zeeshan, S., & Dong, X. (2020). Artificial intelligence with multi-functional machine learning platform development for better healthcare and precision medicine. *Database (Oxford)*, *2020*, baaa010. doi:10.1093/database/baaa010 PMID:3218539

Airfunding. (2019). *5 kinds of Taiwan Crowdfunding Platforms*. Airfunding Blog. https://blog.airfunding.net/crowdfunding/5-kinds-crowdfunding-platform/#:~:text=flyingV%20is%20a%20typical%20comprehensive,and%20divided%20into%2012%20categories

Airpay. (n.d.). *About us*. Retrieved from http://www.airpay.co.th/

Akinola, S., & Telukdarie, A. (2023). Sustainable Digital Transformation in Healthcare: Advancing a Digital Vascular Health Innovation Solution. *Sustainability (Basel)*, *15*(13), 10417. doi:10.3390/su151310417

Akmal, S., Talha, M., Faisal, S. M., Ahmad, M., & Khan, A. K. (2023). Perceptions about FinTech: New evidences from the Middle East. *Cogent Economics & Finance*, *11*(1), 2217583. doi:10.1080/23322039.2023.2217583

Akselaran. (n.d.). *Blog*. Retrieved from: https://www.akseleran.co.id/blog/

Al Jaber, K. (2022). Qatar Leads Fintech Adoption in Middle East and Africa. *Gulf Times*. https://www.gulf-times.com/story/717150/Qatar-leads-FinTech-adoption-in-Middle-East-and-A

Al Jazeera. (2023, April 11). *Cambodia deports 19 Japanese cybercrime scam suspects*. Retrieved from https://www.aljazeera.com/news/2023/4/11/cambodia-deports-19-japanese-cybercrime-scam-suspects

Al Karim, R., Rabiul, M. K., Taskia, A., & Jarumaneerat, T. (2023). Millennial customer engagement with Fintech services: The mediating role of trust. *Business Perspectives and Research*, 1–19. doi:10.1177/22785337231183275

Al-Afeef, M., Fraihat, B., Alhawamdeh, H., Hijazi, H., AL-Afeef, M. A., Nawasr, M., & Rabi, A. M. (2023). Factors affecting middle eastern countries' intention to use financial technology. *International Journal of Data and Network Science*, *7*(3), 1179–1192. doi:10.5267/j.ijdns.2023.5.006

Al-Amry, A., & Al-Harbi, O. (2019). The impact of fintech on financial inclusion in Saudi Arabia. *Journal of Financial Services Research*, *38*(4), 487–507.

Alarifi, A. E., Sedera, D., Al-Jabri, I. M., & Sohaib, O. (2021). Predicting fintech adoption in Saudi Arabia: The modified unified theory of acceptance and use of technology (UTAUT2) model. *Information Systems Frontiers*, 1–17.

Al-Awadhi, A., & Jantan, A. (2019). Cybersecurity Challenges and Recommendations for the Financial Sector in Qatar. *Journal of Cybersecurity and Information Management*, *12*(3), 25–38.

Al-Awadhi, M., & Al-Obeidallah, A. A. (2020). The role of fintech in enhancing the efficiency of business transactions in Saudi Arabia. *International Journal of Financial Research*, *11*(2), 273–290.

Albarrak, M. S., & Alokley, S. A. (2021). FinTech: Ecosystem, opportunities and challenges in Saudi Arabia. *Journal of Risk and Financial Management*, *14*(10), 460. doi:10.3390/jrfm14100460

Alblooshi, F. S. A. K. (2022). FinTech in the United Arab Emirates: a general introduction to the main aspects of financial technology. In Entrepreneurial Rise in the Middle East and North Africa: The Influence of Quadruple Helix on Technological Innovation (pp. 163-178). Emerald Publishing Limited. doi:10.1108/978-1-80071-517-220221010

Al-Chalabi, A., & Al-Qudah, S. (2022). FinTech: Ecosystem, Opportunities and Challenges in Saudi Arabia. *MDPI, 14*(10).

Alda, T. (2022b, October 24). FinTech in China. *Statista.* https://www.statista.com/topics/6893/FinTech-in-china/#editorsPicks

Al-Dosari, A., & Al-Sulaiti, A. (2023). Cybersecurity Awareness Training for Employees in the Financial Sector of Qatar. *International Journal of Information Management*, *76*, 102070.

Al-Ghaith, W. (2020). User adoption of fintech in the Kingdom of Saudi Arabia: Are women more influenced by ease of use, trialability, and effectiveness? *Journal of Open Innovation*, *6*(4), 128.

Al-Ghamdi, A. (2021). Cybersecurity in Saudi Arabia: Challenges and opportunities. *Journal of Cybersecurity*, *6*(1), 1–12.

Al-Ghamdi, A. A. (2021). Cybersecurity challenges and opportunities in Saudi Arabia. *International Journal of Information Technology and Management*, *20*(4), 573.

Al-Ghamdi, A. A. (2021). Cybersecurity challenges and opportunities in Saudi Arabia. International Journal of Information Technology and Management, 20(4), 573-589. Al-Khateeb, M., & Alzahrani, E. (2022). Cybersecurity awareness among Saudi employees in the banking sector. *Journal of Financial Crime*, *39*(4), 484–500.

Al-Ghamdi, R. (2020). The impact of technology on the Saudi economy. *Journal of King Abdulaziz University: Islamic Studies*, *32*(1), 1–20.

Alhababi, W.A.H. & Barnes, S.J. (2022). FinTech in Saudi Arabia: evolution, policy implications and future directions. *Digital Policy, Regulation and Governance*.

Al-Haddad, M. (2022, February 21). The rise of FinTech in Saudi Arabia. *Arab News*. Retrieved from https://www.arabnews.com/node/2221566/business-economy

Al-Hamad, A., & Mahmoud, A. (2021). Vulnerability Assessment and Penetration Testing for Fintech Applications in Qatar. *Journal of Cyber Security and Information Management*, *14*(1), 1–12.

Al-Harbi, M. A. (2021). Fintech and its impact on job creation in Saudi Arabia. *International Journal of Business and Economics Research*, *10*(2), 213–222.

Al-Hashimi, S. (2023). Fintech regulations in Saudi Arabia: A harmonized approach with US regulations? *Journal of Financial Regulation*, *26*(1), 235–252.

Al-Hashimi, S., & Mehmood, A. (2022). The impact of smartphone usage on social connections among Saudi Arabian youth. *Journal of Islamic Marketing*, *13*(3), 387–405.

Al-Haya, M., Malik, A., & Abu-Salih, N. (2018). Cybersecurity Challenges and Recommendations for Fintech Companies in Qatar. *Journal of Financial Innovation*, *15*(1), 1–14.

Al-HussainiR.AlamroM. (2023). Neobanks in Saudi Arabia: A case study of STC Pay. SSRN: 4349084.

Al-Hussain, M., & Al-Shami, M. F. (2022). The rise of fintech innovation in Saudi Arabia. *Journal of Innovation and Entrepreneurship*, *11*(1), 1–15. PMID:35036286

Ali, H., Abdullah, R., & Zaini, M. Z. (2019). Fintech regulation. *Fintech and Islamic Finance: Digitalization, Development and Disruption*, 137-158.

Ali, H., Abdullah, R., & Zaini, M. Z. (2019). Fintech and its potential impact on Islamic bankingand finance industry: A case study of Brunei Darussalam and Malaysia. *International Journal of Islamic Economics and Finance*, *2*(1), 73–108. doi:10.18196/ijief.2116

Al-Jaber, A., & Al-Marzouqi, A. (2022). Data Encryption and Security for Fintech Companies in Qatar. *International Journal of Computer Applications*, *186*(3), 1–6.

Al-Kaabi, N., & Abushaiba, I. (2022). An empirical investigation into the determinants of mobile commerce adoption in Qatar. *Information Technology & People*.

Al-Khateeb, M. F., & Alzahrani, A. M. (2022). Cybersecurity awareness and practices in Saudi Arabia: A comparative study between public and private sectors. *International Journal of Information Security and Privacy*, *16*(2), 175–192.

Al-Khateeb, M., & Alzahrani, E. (2022). Cybersecurity awareness among Saudi employees in the banking sector. *Journal of Financial Crime*, *39*(4), 484–500.

Alkhazaleh, A. M. K. (2021). Challenges and Opportunities for FinTech Startups: Situation in The Arab World. *Academy of Accounting and Financial Studies Journal*, *25*(3), 1–14.

Al-Kuwari, A., & Hassan, A. (2020). Access Control Mechanisms for Fintech Applications in Qatar. *Journal of Network and Computer Applications*, *162*, 102624.

Al-Kuwari, D. (2020). The impact of emerging technologies in Qatar's fintech industry. *Global Policy*, *12*(1), 46–53.

Al-Monitor. (2023, September 12). Saudi Arabia fastest growing crypto economy globally amid regional drive. *Al-Monitor: The Pulse of the Middle East*. https://www.al-monitor.com/originals/2023/09/saudi-arabia-fastest-growing-crypto-economy-globally-amid-regional-drive

Almurshidi, G. H., Alserhan, B. A., & Al-Nory, M. T. (2018). The emergence of Fintech in Saudi Arabia: Antecedents, implications and future directions. *The Journal of High Technology Management Research*, *29*(2), 258–267.

Al-Qahtani, A. (2021). The role of technology in the development of the Saudi Arabian economy. *International Journal of Economics and Business Research*, *18*(1), 1–10.

Alqahtani, M., & Mohammad, H. (2017). Mobile Applications' Impact on Student Performance and Satisfaction. *The Turkish Online Journal of Educational Technology*, *14*(4), 102–112.

Al-Qarni, A. S., & Alamri, Y. (2023). The role of smartphone usage in the spread of misinformation among Saudi Arabian youth. *Journal of Media Studies*, *14*(1), 54–72.

Alrahbi, D. A., Khan, M., Gupta, S., Modgil, S., & Chiappetta Jabbour, C. J. (2022). Challenges for developing health-care knowledge in the digital age. *Journal of Knowledge Management*, *26*(4), 824–853. doi:10.1108/JKM-03-2020-0224

Al-Saidi, A., Al Barghouthi, H., Arvas, M., Erol, O., & Al-Emran, M. (2021). Risk management practices for fintech startups in Qatar. *Risks*, *9*(11), 209.

Al-Sartawi, A., & Shamsudin, S. (2022). FinTech in the Saudi Context: Implications for the Industry and Skills Development. International Journal of Business Information Systems (IJBIS), 42(1), 72-84.

Al-Shami, S. (2022). Digital wallets in Saudi Arabia: A review of the current landscape. *Journal of Financial Services*, *12*(2), 103–115.

Al-Shammari, A. (2022). Cybersecurity in Saudi Arabia: A review of the current state and future directions. *Journal of Cybersecurity and Information Management*, *16*(4), 273–293.

Al-Shammari, N. (2022). The impact of cybersecurity on national security in Saudi Arabia. *Journal of Information Security*, *7*(1), 1–12.

Alsharif, M. H., Alhosain, A., Alghamdi, R., & Alharbi, N. S. (2021). Digital transformation in the Saudi banking industry: Evaluating performance, challenges and opportunities. *Banks and Bank Systems*, *16*(3), 27–35.

Al-Somali, A. (2022). The impact of technology on the Saudi Arabian labor market. *Journal of Labor Economics*, *40*(2), 351–378.

Alt, R., Beck, R., & Smits, M. T. (2018). *FinTech and the transformation of the financial industry* (Vol. 28). Springer.

Alzahrani, N. & Skinner, G. (2022). FinTech in Saudi Arabia: Challenges and recommendations for sustainable growth. *Digital Policy, Regulation and Governance*.

Alzahrani, A., Ahmad, S., & Alamri, A. (2023). The impact of smartphone addiction on the academic performance of university students in Saudi Arabia. *Journal of Applied Business and Social Sciences*, *13*(2), 1–12.

Al-Zahrani, R. (2022). Saudi Arabia's cashless society drive: A key to economic growth and financial inclusion. *Arab Journal of Economics*, *16*(2), 201–220.

Anagnostopoulos, I. (2018, November). Fintech and Regtech: Impact on regulators and banks. *Journal of Economics and Business*, *100*, 7–25. doi:10.1016/j.jeconbus.2018.07.003

Andrushia, A. D., Neebha, T. M., Patricia, A. T., Sagayam, K. M., & Pramanik, S. (2023). Capsule Network based Disease Classification for VitisVinifera Leaves. *Neural Computing & Applications*. Advance online publication. doi:10.1007/s00521-023-09058-y

Angrish, A., Craver, B., Hasan, M., & Starly, B. (2018). A case study for blockchain in manufacturing "FabRec": A prototype for peer-to-peer network of manufacturing nodes. *Procedia Manufacturing*, *26*, 1180–1192. doi:10.1016/j.promfg.2018.07.154

Anh, N. (2021, November 10). *Why do many Vietnamese people prefer to buy goods from Taobao and other Chinese e-commerce websites?* Vietnam Media Corporation Joint Stock Company - Vccorp. https://genk.vn/vi-sao-nhieu-nguoi-viet-thich-mua-do-tu-taobao-va-cac-trang-tmdt-trung-quoc-20210102101619171.chn

Antony, A., Menon, G., RD, K., & Varghese, S. (2022). A study on the digital transformation of insurance industry. Academic Press.

Antwi, S. K., & Hamza, K. (2015). Qualitative and Quantitative Research Paradigms in Business Research: A Philosophical Reflection. *European Journal of Business and Management*, *7*(3), 217–226.

Apollo.io. (2022). https://www.apollo.io/companies/Mongol-iD/556cf15c73696412081d5a00?chart=count

Aquarii. (2022, February 16). *Fintech And E-Commerce In Cambodia. Retrieved from*https://aquariibd.com/Fintech-and-e-commerce-in-cambodia/

Arab Gulf States Institute. (2021). *The Development of Fintech Regulations in the Gulf Arab States.* Arab Gulf States Institute in Washington. https://agsiw.org/development-fintech-regulations-gulf-arab-states#qatar

Arab Monetary Fund. (2022). *FinTech in Saudi Arabia: A Landscape Analysis*. Author.

Arab News. (2022). *Qatar allowing cryptocurrency trading in special zone*. https://www.arabnews.com/node/2089696/business-economy

Arab News. (2022, October 24). *Digital Payments in Saudi Arabia: The Rise of a Cashless Society - Cybersecurity ASEE.* Retrieved from https://www.arabnews.com/node/1456136/business-economy

Aschi, M., Bonura, S., Masi, N., Messina, D., & Profeta, D. (2022). Cybersecurity and fraud detection in financial transactions. In *Big Data and Artificial Intelligence in Digital Finance: Increasing Personalization and Trust in Digital Finance using Big Data and AI* (pp. 269–278). Springer. doi:10.1007/978-3-030-94590-9_15

Ashisha, G. R., Anitha Mary, X., George, T., & Martin Sagayam, K. (2023). Unai Fernandez-GamizHatıraGünerhan, M. N.Uddin and S. Pramanik, Analysis of Diabetes disease using Machine Learning Techniques: A Review. *Journal of Information Technology Management.*

Ashta, A. (2023). How Can Fintech Companies Get Involved in the Environment? *Sustainability (2071-1050), 15*(13), 10675. doi:10.3390/su151310675

Asian Banking & Finance. (2021). *Digital-savvy Thais push banks' Fintech adoption: S&P.*Retrieved from https://asian-bankingandfinance.net/banking-technology/news/digital-savvy-thais-push-banks-Fintech-adoption-sp

Asian Banking & Finance. (2023, May). *Cards & Payments financial technology*. Retrieved From https://asianbank-ingandfinance.net/cards-payments/in-focus/filipinos-spent-over-4-million-hours-using-e-wallets-in-2022-study

Asian Development Bank. (2022). Mongolia: Developing Financial Technology Legal and Regulatory Frameworks for Mongolia. Asian Development Bank.

Ata, S. N., Hassan, A. K., Selim, H. S., Hammad, B. E., Abdelhalim, H. M., & Abdelhalim, A. M. (2023). The Use of Blockchain Technology and Its Reflection in the Financial Performance of Investment Projects Developed by the Ministry of Sports. *Economies*, *11*(5), 140. doi:10.3390/economies11050140

Aulia, M., Yustiardhi, A. F., & Permatasari, R. O. (2020, January 1). An overview of Indonesian regulatory framework on Islamic financial technology (Fintech). *Jurnal Ekonomi & Keuangan Islam*, *6*(1), 64–75. doi:10.20885/jeki.vol6.iss1.art7

Australian Government. (n.d.). .https://www.austrade.gov.au/ArticleDocuments/4569/digital-banking-vietnam-report.pdf.aspx

Autoriti Monetari Brunei Darussalam. (2020). *The state of Fintech in Brunei Darussalam.* Retrieved from https://www.moneylaundering.com/wpcontent/uploads/2021/01/Brunei.NA_.Fintech.2020.pdf

Aya Pay. (n.d.). *Features*. Retrieved from https://www.ayapay.com/

Aye, T. (2020). *Adoption of Fintech and policy recommendations: The case for digital lending platform in Myanmar.* Retrieved from https://scholarbank.nus.edu.sg/handle/10635/192617

Baabdullah, A. M., Alalwan, A. A., Rana, N. P., Kizgin, H., & Patil, P. (2022). Perceived risk towards fintech products and services in an emerging market. *The Journal of High Technology Management Research*, *33*(1), 100397.

Baabdullah, A. M., Rana, N. P., Alalwan, A. A., Patil, P., & Dwivedi, Y. K. (2021). Adoption of FinTech applications during a developing country perspective. *International Journal of Bank Marketing*.

Baabdullah, A. M., Rana, N. P., Osmani, M., & Alalwan, A. A. (2022). Cognitive computing capabilities of artificial intelligence systems: A systematic literature review. *Journal of Cognitive Systems Research, 73*, 36–49.

Bachman, J. R. (2020). Motorsport Event Attendees: Who are They, What is Their Environmental Worldview, And How Does It Relate to Trip Spending? *Event Management, 24*(5), 629–644. doi:10.3727/152599519X15506259856264

Bacuilima, E., Morocho, J., Aguirre, J., Coronel-Pangol, K., & Mora, P. (2023). Financing Ecuadorian Social Enterprises: What Is the Role of Impact Investment? *Sustainability (2071-1050), 15*(14), 11210. doi:10.3390/su151411210

Bag, S., Gupta, S., Kumar, S., & Sivarajah, U. (2021). Role of technological dimensions of green supply chain management practices on firm performance. *Journal of Enterprise Information Management, 34*(1), 1–27. doi:10.1108/JEIM-10-2019-0324

Bain & Company, & Google, & Temasek Holdings. (2022). *E-commerce market size in the Philippines in 2019 and 2021, with a forecast for 2022 and 2025 (in billion U.S. dollars)* [Graph]. Statista. Retrieved August 26, 2023, from https://www.statista.com/statistics/1125455/e-commerce-market-size-philippines/

Bains, P., & Wu, C. (2023). *Institutional Arrangements for Fintech Regulation: Supervisory Monitoring*. Academic Press.

Baird, N., Blevins, J., Scheerschmidt, T., Vecchi, N., & Weiße, L. (2023). Dubai: A City of Contradictions. In *The Strategic Management of Place at Work: Why, What, How and Where* (pp. 377–393). Springer Nature Switzerland. doi:10.1007/978-3-031-29463-1_20

Bajwa, I. A., Rehman, S. U., Iqbal, A., Anwer, Z., Ashiq, M., & Khan, M. A. (2022). Past, Present and Future of FinTech Research: A Bibliometric Analysis. *SAGE Open, 12*(4), 1–22. doi:10.1177/21582440221131242

Bake. (n.d.). *Control your financial destiny*. Retrieved from https://bake.io/about-us/

Bakkar, A. (n.d.). *FinTech and the Future of Finance. The Global Advisory and Account in Network.* https://www.hlb.global/FinTech-and-the-future-of-finance

Bakker, B. B. (2023). *The rise and impact of fintech in Latin America*. Imfsg. doi:10.5089/9798400235474.063.A001

Banerjee, A. (2020). FinTech revolution in the gulf countries and mena region. *Entrepreneurial Finance in Emerging Markets: Exploring Tools, Techniques, and Innovative Technologies*, 335-344.

Banga, K., & te Velde, D. W. (2020). *Cambodia, COVID-19 and inclusive digitaltransformation: a seven-point plan.* Supporting Economic Transformation.

Bank of Thailand. (2021). *Fintech in Thailand.* Retrieved fromhttps://www.bot.or.th/en/financial-innovation/digital-finance/Fintech-in-thailand.html

Bank of Thailand. (2023). *Virtual Bank.* Retrieved from https://www.bot.or.th/en/financial-innovation/digital-finance/virtual-bank.html

Banking and Fintech. (n.d.). Invest in Mongolia | Ministry of Economy and Development. https://investmongolia.gov.mn/banking-and-FinTech/

Banking. (n.d.). https://www.boj.or.jp/en/about/press/koen_2016/data/ko161118a.pdf

Barker, T., & Üngör, M. (2019, January). Vietnam: The next Asian Tiger? *The North American Journal of Economics and Finance, 47*, 96–118. doi:10.1016/j.najef.2018.11.010

Barroso, M., & Laborda, J. (2022). Digital transformation and the emergence of the FinTech sector: Systematic literature review. *Digital Business*, *2*(2), 100028. doi:10.1016/j.digbus.2022.100028

Barsallo Rodríguez, R. (2018). *Propuesta De Regulación De Las Fintech En Panamá* (Doctoral dissertation). Universidad Santa María La Antigua.

Bashshur, R. L., & Shannon, G. W. (2009). *History of telemedicine: evolution, context, and transformation*. Mary Ann Liebert, Inc., Publishers.

Batunanggar, S. (2019). *Fintech Development and Regulatory Frameworks in Indonesia. ADBI Working Paper 1014*. Asian Development Bank Institute. Retrieved from https://www.adb.org/publications/Fintech-development-regulatory-frameworks-indonesia

Bayram, Talay, & Feridun. (2022). Can FinTech promote sustainable finance? Policy lessons from the case of Turkey. *Sustainability, 14*(19), 12414.

Bayram, O., Talay, I., & Feridun, M. (2022). Can FinTech promote sustainable finance? Policy lessons from the case of Turkey. *Sustainability (Basel)*, *14*(19), 12414. doi:10.3390/su141912414

BCG. (2023). *The future of Neobanks in GCC's Finance Industry*. Retrieved from: https://www.bcg.com/publications/2022/future-of-neobanks-in-gcc-finance-industry

Beecroft, B., Sturke, R., Neta, G., & Ramaswamy, R. (2022). The "case" for case studies: Why we need high-quality examples of global implementation research. *Implementation Science Communications*, *3*(1), 15. doi:10.1186/s43058-021-00227-5 PMID:35168672

Beijing's intentions. (n.d.). China Briefing News. https://www.china-briefing.com/news/a-close-reading-china-FinTech-development-plan-for-2022-2025/

Belanche, D., Casaló, L. V., & Flavián, C. (2019). Artificial Intelligence in FinTech: Understanding robo-advisors adoption among customers. *Industrial Management & Data Systems*, *119*(7), 1411–1430. doi:10.1108/IMDS-08-2018-0368

Belaws Cambodia. (2022). *The rise of Fintech in Cambodia*. Retrieved fromhttps://www.belaws.com/cambodia/Fintech-in-cambodia/

Ben Hassen, T. (2021). The state of the knowledge-based economy in the Arab world: Cases of Qatar and Lebanon. *EuroMed Journal of Business*, *16*(2), 129–153. doi:10.1108/EMJB-03-2020-0026

Bentler, P. M. (1990). Comparative fit indexes in structural models. *Psychological Bulletin*, *107*(2), 238–246. doi:10.1037/0033-2909.107.2.238 PMID:2320703

Bhat, J. R., AlQahtani, S. A., & Nekovee, M. (2023). FinTech enablers, use cases, and role of future internet of things. *Journal of King Saud University. Computer and Information Sciences*, *35*(1), 87–101. doi:10.1016/j.jksuci.2022.08.033

Bhattacharya, A., Ghosal, A., Obaid, A. J., Krit, S., Shukla, V. K., Mandal, K., & Pramanik, S. (2021). Unsupervised Summarization Approach with Computational Statistics of Microblog Data. In D. Samanta, R. R. Althar, S. Pramanik, & S. Dutta (Eds.), *Methodologies and Applications of Computational Statistics for Machine Learning* (pp. 23–37). IGI Global. doi:10.4018/978-1-7998-7701-1.ch002

Bhattacherjee, A. (2001). Understanding Information Systems Continuance: An Expectation- Confirmation Model. *Management Information Systems Quarterly*, *25*(3), 351–370. doi:10.2307/3250921

Biçak Hukuk ve Danışmanlık. (2023, June 28). *Fintech businesses legal framework in Turkey*. Retrieved from https://www.bicakhukuk.com/en/fintech-businesses-legal-framework-in-turkey/

Bitkub. (n.d.). *About us*. Retrieved from https://support.bitkub.com/en/support/solutions/articles/151000034649-who-is-bitkub-

Bito.Ex. (2023). *About Us*. Bito.Ex. https://www.bitoex.com/?locale=en

Bittini, J. S., Rambaud, S. C., Pascual, J. L., & Moro-Visconti, R. (2022). Business Models and Sustainability Plans in the FinTech, InsurTech, and PropTech Industry: Evidence from Spain. *Sustainability (2071-1050), 14*(19), 12088. https://doi-org.ezproxy.myucwest.ca/10.3390/su141912088

BKM. (2022*). Report on the Number of POS, ATM, ÖKC Software*. bkm.com.tr

Blockchain Turkey Platform. (2023). *Blockchain Turkey Platform*. https://bctr.org/en/

Bloomberg. (2023, July 25). *Turkey tightens the screws on credit boom with new lending rules*. Retrieved from https://www.bloomberg.com/news/articles/2023-07-25/turkey-tightens-the-screws-on-credit-boom-with-new-lending-rules

Bodie, Z. H., & Merton, F. (2015). Design of financial systems: Towards a synthesis of functionand structure. *Journal of Investment Management, 3*(1), 1–13.

Bongloy. (n.d.). *About us*. Retrieved from https://www.bongloy.asia/

Boost Capitals. (n.d.). *About us*. Retrieved from https://www.boostkh.com/

Borneo Bulletin. (2022, September 27). *Brunei sees acceleration of Fintech products, andservices*. Retrieved from https://borneobulletin.com.bn/brunei-sees-acceleration-of-Fintech-products-services/

Boston Consulting Group. (2023). *Saudi Arabia's wealth management market: Opportunities and challenges*. Author.

Bottiglia, R. (2016). Competitive frontiers in P2P lending crowdfunding. *Crowdfunding for SMEs: A European Perspective*, 61-92.

Boulevard, S. (2023). *An Overview of Cybersecurity Issues Faced by the FinTech Industry*. [https://securityboulevard.com/2023/01/an-overview-of-cybersecurity-issues-faced-by-the-fintech-industry

Boulieris, P., Pavlopoulos, J., Xenos, A., & Vassalos, V. (2023). Fraud detection with natural language processing. *Machine Learning*, 1–22.

Bouteraa, M., Chekima, B., Lajuni, N., & Anwar, A. (2023). Understanding Consumers' Barriers to Using FinTech Services in the United Arab Emirates: Mixed-Methods Research Approach. *Sustainability (Basel), 15*(4), 2931. doi:10.3390/su15042931

Briefing, C. (2018b, January 22). China's FinTech Industry. *China Briefing News*. https://www.china-briefing.com/news/chinas-FinTech-industry/

Briefing, C. (2022, July 21). *China's Fintech Development Plan for 2022-2025: Understanding Beijing's intentions*. China Briefing News. https://www.china-briefing.com/news/a-close-reading-china-FinTech-development-plan-for-2022-2025/

Brochado, A., Dionísio, P., Leal, C., Bouchet, A., & Conceição, H. (2021). Organizing sports events: the promoters' perspective. *Journal of Business & Industrial Marketing*. doi:10.1108/JBIM-10-2020-0451

brokerchooser. (2023). *Best Online Brokers in Saudi Arabia*. Author.

brokerchooser.com. (n.d.). *Best Brokers: Best International Online Brokers for Citizens in Turkey*. Retrieved from https://brokerchooser.com/best-brokers/best-international-online-brokers-for-citizens-in-turkey

Brokers, C. (n.d.). *Turkey Brokers*. Retrieved from https://comparebrokers.co/compare/turkey-brokers/: https://comparebrokers.co/compare/turkey-brokers/

Bromberg, L., Godwin, A., & Ramsay, I. (2017). Fintech sandboxes: Achieving a balancebetween regulation and innovation. *Journal of Banking and Finance Law and Practice*, *28*(4), 314–336.

Brotman, J. J., & Kotloff, R. M. (2021). Providing Outpatient Telehealth Services in the United States: Before and During Coronavirus Disease 2019. *Chest*, *159*(4), 1548–1558. doi:10.1016/j.chest.2020.11.020 PMID:33245875

Brown, M. (2023, March 30). Inside the numbers that show formula 1's popularity and financial growth. *Forbes*. https://www.forbes.com/sites/maurybrown/2023/03/29/inside-the-numbers-that-show-formula-1s-popularity-and-financial-growth/?sh=3288d45d4df6

Brunei Darussalam Central Bank. (n.d.). *Islamic Finance*. Retrieved fromhttps://www.bdcb.gov.bn/regulatory/islamic-finance

Brynjolfsson, E., Rock, D., & Syverson, C. (2018). Artificial Intelligence and the Modern Productivity Paradox: A Clash of Expectations and Statistics. *The American Economic Review*, *108*(6), 1259–1266.

Buchak, G., Matvos, G., Piskorski, T., & Seru, A. (2018). Fintech, regulatory arbitrage, and the rise of shadow banks. *Journal of Financial Economics*, *130*(3), 453–483. doi:10.1016/j.jfineco.2018.03.011

Buchholz, K. (January 19, 2022). *The End of Natural Population Growth?* [Digital image]. Retrieved November 12, 2023, from https://0-www-statista-com.biblioteca-ils.tec.mx/chart/26634/start-year-of-negative-net-births-by-country

Budzinski, O., & Muller-Kock, A. (2018). Is the Revenue Allocation Scheme of Formula One Motor Racing a Case for European Competition Policy? *Contemporary Economic Policy*, *36*(1), 215–233. doi:10.1111/coep.12247

Bui, M. T., & Luong, T. N. O. (2023). *Financial inclusion for the elderly in Thailand and the role of information communication technology*. Borsa Istanbul Review. doi:10.1016/j.bir.2023.02.003

Business World. (2023, June 12). *More than 400 small businesses in the Philippines accept Bitcoin payments — Fintech firm*. Retrieved from https://www.bworldonline.com/sparkup/2023/06/12/527873/more-than-400-small-businesses-in-the-philippines-accept-bitcoin-payments-Fintech-firm/

Business, A. (2022). *BitOasis becomes one of the first globally regulated Crypto Asset businesses in MENA*. Retrieved from https://www.arabianbusiness.com/banking-finance/466749-bitoasis-becomes-one-of-the-first-globally-regulated-crypto-asset-businesses-in-mena

Byrne, B. M. (2016). *Structural equation modeling with AMOS: Basic concepts, applications, and programming*. Routledge. doi:10.4324/9781315757421

Cafe, F. (2021). *Breakdown of Fintech startups in Vietnam in 2020, by category*[Graph]. In Statista. Retrieved July 23, 2023, from https://www.statista.com/statistics/1229955/vietnam-Fintech-startups-by-category/

CAG. (2021). DERIN, The FinTech revolution in China: opportunities and threats. *FinTech Magazine*. https://FinTechmagazine.com/financial-services-finserv/FinTech-revolution-china-opportunities-and-threats

Cai, C., Marrone, M., & Linnenluecke, M. (2022). Trends in fintech research and practice: Examining the intersection with the information systems field. *Communications of the Association for Information Systems*, *50*(1), 40. doi:10.17705/1CAIS.05036

Cambaza, E. (2023). The Role of FinTech in Sustainable Healthcare Development in Sub-Saharan Africa: A Narrative Review. *FinTech*, *2*(3), 444–460. doi:10.3390/fintech2030025

Campanella, F., Serino, L., Battisti, E., Giakoumelou, A., & Karasamani, I. (2023). FinTech in the financial system: Towards a capital-intensive and high competence human capital reality? *Journal of Business Research*, *155*, 113376. doi:10.1016/j.jbusres.2022.113376

Cao, L., Yuan, G., Leung, T., & Zhang, W. (2020). Special issue on AI and FinTech: The challenge ahead. *IEEE Intelligent Systems*, *35*(2), 3–6. doi:10.1109/MIS.2020.2983494 PMID:35935446

CapBay. (n.d.). *The #1 Supply Chain Finance Company*. Retrieved fromhttps://capbay.com/about-us/

Capgemini. (2023). *World Wealth Report 2023: Middle East*. Author.

Carare, A., Franco, L., Hadzi-Vaskov, M., Lesniak, J., Vasilyev, D., & Yakhshilikov, Y. (2022). *Digital Money and Remittances Costs in Central America, Panama, and the Dominican Republic*. Academic Press.

Caschili, S., & Medda, F. R. (2020). Customer perceptions of digital banking risks. *International Journal of Bank Marketing*.

Caspcr, S., & Matthias, Y. (2021). *Orientation in a New World of Technology and Finance Integration*. Exploring the Concept of Embedded Lending.

CCAF. (2021). *Fintech Regulation in Sub-Saharan Africa*. CCAF. www.jbs.cam.ac.uk/faculty-research/centres/alternative-finance/publications/fintech-regulation-in-sub-saharan-africa

Cengiz, S., Atmiş, E., & Görmüş, S. (2019). The impact of economic growth oriented development policies on landscape changes in Istanbul Province in Turkey. *Land Use Policy*, *87*, 104086. doi:10.1016/j.landusepol.2019.104086

Central Bank of Malaysia. (2013a, March 22). *Financial Services Act 2013*. Retrieved fromhttps://www.bnm.gov.my/-/financial-services-act-2013

Central Bank of Malaysia. (2013b, March 22). *Islamic Financial Services Act 2013*. Retrievedfrom https://www.bnm.gov.my/documents/20124/8102422b-e6dd-d149-8db0-e3637e89ed5c

Central Bank of Malaysia. (2023c, March 29). Let's Go Digital Confidently. Annual Report 2022.Retrieved from https://www.bnm.gov.my/documents/20124/10150308/ar2022_en_box6.pdf

Central Bank of Myanmar. (2016). *Regulation on Mobile Financial Services*. Retrieved fromhttp://www.myanmar-embassy-tokyo.net/eco2017/Finance/Mobile-Financial-Services-regulation-2016.pdf

CFMI - China Fintech market insights. (n.d.). https://www.mordorintelligence.com/industry-reports/china-FinTech-market#:~:textChina%20Fintech%20Market%20has%20generated,the%20FinTech%20space%20in20China

Chainalysis. (2023). *2023 Geography of Cryptocurrency*. Retrieved from https://go.chainalysis.com/2023-crypto-crime-report.html

Chainalysis. (2023, September 12). *2023 Global Crypto Adoption Index*. Chainalysis. https://www.chainalysis.com/blog/2023-global-crypto-adoption-index/

Chaitanya, C., & Gupta, D. (2017). Factors Influencing Customer Satisfaction with Usage of Shopping Apps in India. *International Conference on Recent Trends in Electronics, Information and Communication Technology,* 1483–1486. 10.1109/RTEICT.2017.8256844

Chambers and Partners. (2023, March 23). *Thailand - Fintech Trends and Developments*. Retrieved from https://practiceguides.chambers.com/practice-guides/Fintech-2023/thailand/trends-and-developments

Chang, B. L., Bakken, S., Brown, S. S., Houston, T. K., Kreps, G. L., Kukafka, R., Safran, C., & Stavri, P. Z. (2004). Bridging the digital divide: Reaching vulnerable populations. *Journal of the American Medical Informatics Association : JAMIA*, *11*(6), 448–457. doi:10.1197/jamia.M1535 PMID:15299002

Chan, I. S., & Ginsburg, G. S. (2011). Personalized medicine: Progress and promise. *Annual Review of Genomics and Human Genetics*, *12*(1), 217–244. doi:10.1146/annurev-genom-082410-101446 PMID:21721939

Chen, E. T. (2017). Considerations of Telemedicine in the Delivery of Modern Healthcare. *American Journal of Management, 17*(3).

Chen, L., Meservy, T. O., & Gillenson, M. (2012). Understanding Information Systems Continuance for Information-Oriented Mobile Applications. *Communications of the Association for Information Systems*, *30*(9), 127–146. doi:10.17705/1CAIS.03009

Chen, M. A., Wu, Q., & Yang, B. (2019). How valuable is FinTech innovation? *Review of Financial Studies*, *32*(5), 2062–2106. doi:10.1093/rfs/hhy130

Chen, X., Huang, Q., & Davison, R. M. (2017). Economic and social satisfaction of buyers on consumer-to-consumer platforms: The role of relational capital. *International Journal of Electronic Commerce*, *21*(2), 219–248. doi:10.1080/10864415.2016.1234285

Chen, Z., Li, Y., Wu, Y., & Luo, J. (2017). The transition from traditional banking to mobile internet finance: An organizational innovation perspective-a comparative study of Citibank and ICBC. *Financial Innovation*, *3*(1), 1–16. doi:10.1186/s40854-017-0062-0

Chepurnoy, A., Larangeira, M., & Ojiganov, A. (2016). A prunable blockchain consensus protocol based on non-interactive proofs of past states retrievability. *arXiv preprint arXiv:1603.07926.*

Cherif, R. (2022). *How Qatar is emerging as a global fintech hub*. World Economic Forum. Retrieved from https://www.weforum.org/agenda/2022/05/how-qatar-is-emerging-as-a-global-fintech-hub/

Chinnasamy, G., Madbouly, A., & Reyad, S. (2021). FinTech: A pathway for MENA region. *The fourth industrial revolution: implementation of artificial intelligence for growing business success*, 135-151.

Chiu, I. H. (2016). Fintech and disruptive business models in financial products, intermediation and markets-policy implications for financial regulators. *J. Tech. L. & Pol'y*, *21*, 55.

Choi, G., & Cho, S. H. (2022). Effect of market versus nonmarket environmental policy stringency on knowledge sourcing behavior for green technology: Evidence from OECD countries. *Review of International Business & Strategy*, *32*(1), 72–93. doi:10.1108/RIBS-09-2020-0113

Choi, Y., & Shin, Y. (2019, September 23). Feasibility of the Fintech Industry as an Innovation Platform for Sustainable Economic Growth in Korea. *MDPI*, *11*, 5351. doi:10.3390/su1119535

Chong, S. (2023, June 28). *Rising Cyber Crime, Financial Losses Will Test The Role Of Banks.Business Today*. Retrieved from https://www.businesstoday.com.my/2023/06/28/rising-cyber-crime-financial-losses-will-test-the-role-of-banks/

Chou, C., & Lee, J. (2013). *Understanding Mobile Apps Continuance Usage Behavior and Habit: An Expectance-Confirmation Theory*. Academic Press.

Choudhury, M. D. (2020). *NIC sets-up CoE for Blockchain in Karnataka to enhance citizen services*. Express Computer. Available at https://www.expresscomputer.in/egov-watch/nic-sets-up-coe-for-blockchain-in-karnataka-to-enhance-citizen-services/45650/

Chueca Vergara, C., & Ferruz Agudo, L. (2021). Fintech and Sustainability: Do They Affect Each Other? *Sustainability (2071-1050), 13*(13), 7012. doi:10.3390/su13137012

Clements, R. (2019). Fintech in Canada. In Research Handbook on the Law of Fintech. Digital Innovation and Technology Law Lab, Digital Law Network, University of Padova.

Cobbs, J. B., Jensen, J. A., & Tyler, B. D. (2022). The sponsorship performance cycle: Longitudinal evidence of sponsors' contribution to Formula One team achievement. *Journal of Business and Industrial Marketing*, *37*(1), 103–114. doi:10.1108/JBIM-06-2020-0299

Cobbs, J., Tyler, B. D., Jensen, J. A., & Chan, K. (2017). Prioritizing Sponsorship Resources in Formula One Racing: A Longitudinal Analysis. *Journal of Sport Management*, *31*(1), 96–110. doi:10.1123/jsm.2016-0115

CoFarm. (n.d.). *About us*. Retrieved from https://cofarm.la/#about

Coindesk. (2016). *State of Blockchain q1 2016: Blockchain Funding Overtakes Bitcoin.* https://www.coindesk.com/state-of-blockchain-q1-2016/

CoinGecko. (2023). *Turkey Crypto Exchanges*. https://www.coingecko.com/research/publications/turkey-crypto-exchanges

Coins.ph. (n.d.). *About us*. Retrieved from https://coins.ph/about

Cointelegraph. (n.d.). *Latest News on Saudi Arabia*. Retrieved from https://cointelegraph.com/tags/saudi-arabia

cointelegraph.com. (2023, October 4). *Turkey's central bank completes first CBDC test with more to come in 2023.* Retrieved from https://cointelegraph.com/news/turkey-s-central-bank-completes-first-cbdc-test-with-more-to-come-in-2023

Comin, D., & Mestieri, M. (2022). Artificial Intelligence and Economic Growth: A Review of the Literature and Directions for Future Research. *Annual Review of Economics*, *14*, 743–767.

Communications and Information Technology Commission (CITC). (2020). *Cloud Computing Regulations.* Retrieved from: https://www.cst.gov.sa/en/RulesandSystems/RegulatoryDocuments/Pages/CCRF.aspx

Communications Regulatory Authority. (2021). *ICT Sector Performance Report Q4 2021.* https://cra.gov.qa/en/documents/ICT_SPR_Q42021Eng.pdf

Connell, A. (2022). 33 Latest WeChat Statistics And Trends For 2022. *Blogging Wizard.* https://bloggingwizard.com/wechat-statistics/

Consortiumadmn. (2023). *Estado de la Regulación Fintech en la Región Centroamericana.* Consortium Legal. https://consortiumlegal.com/2022/09/30/estado-de-la-regulacion-fintech-en-la-region-centroamericana/

Cooper, A. (2023, June 14). *F1 reports progress towards 2030 net zero target. Motorsport.com: F1 News, MotoGP, NASCAR, Rallying and more.* https://www.motorsport.com/f1/news/f1-reports-progress-towards-2030-net-zero-target/10482379/#:~:text=Formula%201%20says%20that%20the,with%20much%20more%20to%20come.&text=F1%20reduced%20its%20carbon%20footprint,figures%20yet%20to%20be%20finalised

Cornwell, N., Bilson, C., Gepp, A., Stern, S., & Vanstone, B. J. (2023). The role of data analytics within operational risk management: A systematic review from the financial services and energy sectors. *The Journal of the Operational Research Society*, *74*(1), 374–402. doi:10.1080/01605682.2022.2041373

Cortis, D., Debattista, J., Debono, J., & Farrell, M. (2019). InsurTech. *Disrupting finance:Fintech and strategy in the 21st century*, 71-84.

Creación del marco regulatorio para Fintech en Costa Rica. (n.d.). https://revistas.uned.ac.cr/index.php/rna/article/view/4785/6664

Crowe, M. D., Rysman, M., & Stavins, J. (2010). *Mobile payments in the United States at retail point of sale: current market and future prospects*. FRB of Boston Public Policy Discussion Paper (10-2).

Crunchbase News. (2023). *Saudi Arabia Investment Is Increasing In US-Based Startups*. Retrieved from https://news.crunchbase.com/venture/saudi-arabia-startup-investment-nile-axiom/

Crunchbase. (2023) *Grab Funding*. Retrieved from https://www.crunchbase.com/organization/grabtaxi/company_financials

Crunchbase. (2023). *BitFlyer*. Crunchbase Website. https://www.crunchbase.com/organization/bitflyer

Crunchbase. (2023). *Paidy*. Crunchbase Website. https://www.crunchbase.com/organization/paidly

Cruz Rambaud, S., & López Pascual, J. (2023). Insurtech, Proptech, and Fintech Environment: Sustainability, Global Trends and Opportunities. *Sustainability (2071-1050), 15*(12), 9574. https://doi-org.ezproxy.myucwest.ca/10.3390/su15129574

Crypto.com. (n.d.). *Cryptocurrency in every wallet*. Retrieved from https://crypto.com/ca/about

CSA (Singapore). (2022, August 29). *Cybercrime as a share of total crimes in Singapore from2014 to 2021* [Graph]. Statista. Retrieved July 29, 2023, from https://www.statista.com/statistics/1267252/singapore-cybercrime-as-share-of-total-crime

Cudjoe, A. G., Anim, P. A., Gerald, J., & Tetteh, N. (2015). Determinants of Mobile Banking Adoption in the Ghanaian Banking Industry : A Case of Access Bank Ghana Limited. *Journal of Computer and Communications*, *3*(February), 1–19. doi:10.4236/jcc.2015.32001

Cung, N. H. (2019, November 30). Gross Domestic Product and Foreign Direct Investment: Empirical Evidence from Vietnam. *European Scientific Journal*, *15*(31). Advance online publication. doi:10.19044/esj.2019.v15n31p38

Cusolito, A. P., Gévaudan, C., Lederman, D., & Wood, C. (2022). *The upside of digital for the Middle East and North Africa: how digital technology adoption can accelerate growth and create jobs*. World Bank Publications.

Cyber Security Brunei. (2020, February 6). *Brunei reports 39% rise in cyber attacks in 2018*.Retrieved from https://www.csb.gov.bn/brunei-reports-39-rise-cyber-attacks-2018#:~:text=BANDAR%20SERI%20BEGAWAN%20%E2%80%93%20Brunei%20has,its%20'Smart%20Nation'%20plans

Cyr, D., Head, M., & Ivanov, A. (2006). Design aesthetics leading to m-loyalty in mobile commerce. *Information & Management*, *43*(8), 950–963. doi:10.1016/j.im.2006.08.009

Cywinska, M., & Zawadzki, K. (2018). Performance appraisal system for administrative staff: A pilot implementation study at the University of Warsaw. *Economic and Social Development: Book of Proceedings,* 332-340.

DANA. (n.d.). *About DANA*. Retrieved from https://www.dana.id/en/about

Das, A., & Das, S. (2020). Perception, adoption, and pattern of usage of FinTech services by bank customers: Evidence from Hojai district of Assam. *Emerging Economy Studies*, *6*(1), 7–22. doi:10.1177/2394901520907728

Data&StorageAsean, (2022, August 9). *2022 Press Releases*. Retrieved fromhttps://datastorageasean.com/news-press-releases/digitalisation-being-bolstered-laos-countrys-government-which-concerned-about

Datareportal. (2021). *Internet users in Ghana*. Retrieved July 10, 2021, from https://datareportal.com/reports/digital-2020-ghana

DataReportal. (2023). *Digital 2023: Qatar*. Retrieved from https://datareportal.com/reports/digital-2023-qatar

Daza Jaller, L. S., & Molinuevo, M. (2020). *Digital Trade in MENA: Regulatory Readiness Assessment.* World Bank Policy Research Working Paper, (9199).

de Araujo Silva, C., & Walter Wildauer, E. (2023). Modelo De Expansão Sustentável Para Um Ecossistema De Fintech. *Revista Gestão & Tecnologia*, *23*(1), 298–315.

Decision Lab. (2022). *The Connected Consumer.* https://www.decisionlab.co/connected-consumer#download

Degerli, K. (2019). Regulatory challenges and solutions for fintech in Turkey. *Procedia Computer Science*, *158*, 929–937. doi:10.1016/j.procs.2019.09.133

Deloitte. (2017). *Blockchain technology in India Opportunities and challenges.* Deloitte and he Associated Chambers of Commerce of India. Available at https://www2.deloitte.com/content/dam/Deloitte/in/Documents/strategy/in-strategy-innovation-blockchain-technology-india-opportunities-challenges-noexp.pdf

Deloitte. (2017, October 23). *How does FinTech in Japan compare to the rest of the world.* Deloitte. https://www2.deloitte.com/jp/en/pages/financial-services/articles/bk/jp-fi-FinTech-in-japan.html

Deloitte. (2023). *FinTech Ecosystem in Turkey.* Available at: https://www2.deloitte.com/tr/en/pages/finance/articles/fintech-ecosystem-in-turkey.html

Deloitte. (2023). *The Fintech Ecosystem in Saudi Arabia.* Retrieved from https://alj.com/en/perspective/digital-future-for-saudi-financial-services/

Demirgüç-Kunt, A., Klapper, L., Singer, D., & Ansar, S. (2022). *The Global Findex Database 2021: Financial inclusion, digital payments, and resilience in the age of COVID-19.* World Bank Publications. doi:10.1596/978-1-4648-1897-4

Dennis, Q., Divina, I., Neonette, P., & Kristina, N. (2022). *Law and Practice. Quisumbing Torres.* Retrieved from https://www.quisumbingtorres.com/-/media/minisites/quisumbing-torres/files/2022/quisumbing-torreschambers-and-partnersFintech-guid.pdf?sc_lang=en&hash=1ED0840A6D5998C2FC4F5C3330693962

Department of Banking Regulation Banking Policy Division. (n.d.). *Enabling Framework for Regulatory Sandbox.* the Reserve Bank of India. https://rbidocs.rbi.org.in/rdocs/PublicationReport/Pdfs/ENABLING79D8EBD31FED47A-0BE21158C337123BF.PDF

Dhagarra, D., Goswami, M., & Kumar, G. (2020). Impact of Trust and Privacy Concerns on Technology Acceptance in Healthcare: An Indian Perspective. *International Journal of Medical Informatics*, *141*, 104164. doi:10.1016/j.ijmedinf.2020.104164 PMID:32593847

Didenko, A. N. (2020). Cybersecurity Regulation in Singapore's Financial Sector: Protecting Fintech 'Ants' in a Jungle Full of 'Elephants'. *UNSW Law Research Paper*, 20-45.

Diep, C. (2023, August 31). *E-commerce in Japan - statistic & facts.* Statista. Retrieved September 3, 2023, from https://www.statista.com/topics/5262/e-commerce-in-japan/#topicOverview

DigFin. (2020, October 6). *Red app, blue app: KBZPay notches 6m Myanmar users.* Retrieved from https://www.digfingroup.com/kbz-pay/

Digital Financial Services. (n.d.). Bain & Company. Retrieved from https://www.bain.com/insights/fufilling-its-promise/

Digital Investment - Mongolia. (n.d.-a). *Statista market forecast.* Statista. https://www.statista.com/outlook/dmo/FinTech/digital-investment/mongolia

Digital remittances - Mongolia: Statista market forecast. (n.d.). Statista. https://www.statista.com/outlook/dmo/FinTech/digital-payments/digital-remittances/mongolia

Dobberstein, L. (2022, September 22). *Cambodian authorities crack down on cyber slavery amid international pressure.* Retrieved from https://www.theregister.com/2022/09/22/cambodian_authorities_crack_down_on/

Dogan, E., & Stupar, A. (2017). The limits of growth: A case study of three mega-projects in Istanbul. *Cities (London, England)*, *60*, 281–288. doi:10.1016/j.cities.2016.09.013

Doha Bank. (2022). *Doha Bank launches Doha Bank Oasis.* Retrieved from https://dohabank.qa/who-we-are/news/doha-bank-launches-doha-bank-oasis

Dolley, S. (2018). Big data's role in precision public health. *Frontiers in Public Health*, *6*, 68. doi:10.3389/fpubh.2018.00068 PMID:29594091

Dubai Islamic Economy Development Centre. (2018). *Islamic Fintech report 2018: current landscape & path forward.* Retrieved from https://www.dinarstandard.com/wp-content/uploads/2018/12/Islamic-Fintech-Report-2018.pdf

Dwivedi, P., Alabdooli, J. I., & Dwivedi, R. (2021). Role of FinTech adoption for competitiveness and performance of the bank: A study of banking industry in UAE. *International Journal of Global Business and Competitiveness*, *16*(2), 130–138. doi:10.1007/s42943-021-00033-9

Dzhondzhorov, D. (2023, March 18). *Crypto Flourishes in Vietnam With 16.6 Million Holders (Report).* CryptoPotato. https://cryptopotato.com/crypto-flourishes-in-vietnam-with-16-6-million-holders-report/

Dziawgo, T. (2021, September 1). Wealth Tech Impact on Wealth Management Sector. *European Research Studies*, *24*(3B), 141–151. doi:10.35808/ersj/2463

E.SUN. (2023). *Brand Story.* E.SUN FHC. https://www.esunfhc.com/en/about-esun/intro/commitment

E-commerce Driving Force for Growth. (n.d.). *Vietnam Business Forum of Vietnam Chamber of Commerce and Industry (VCCI)-Economy.* https://vccinews.com/news/48958/e-commerce-driving-force-for growth.html#:~:text=Shopee%20is%20the%20largest%20e,1%25%20of%20the%20market%20share.

Ecommerce Market Mongolia - Data & Trends | ecommercedb.com. (n.d.). https://ecommercedb.com/markets/mn/all

eCommerceDB. (2023). *eCommerce market in Myanmar.* Retrieved fromhttps://ecommercedb.com/markets/mm/all

EdgePoint. (2021). *How Qatar is transitioning into an eCommerce hub.* Retrieved from https://edgepointlearning.com/blog/ecommerce-in-qatar/

Eileen, Yu. (2019, March 6). *Hacker Group Behind SingHealth Data Breach Identified, Targeted Mainly Singapore Firms.* Retrieved from https://www.zdnet.com/article/hacker-group-behind-singhealth-data-breach-identified-targeted-mainly-singapore-firms/

El Madany, S. (2021). *Qatar-ained fintech seeks slice of region's billions in remittances.* Arab News. https://www.arabnews.com/node/1788016/business-economy

Eldon, Y. (2016). *Information Security Challenges in the New Era of Fintech.* AIS Electronic.

El-Haddad, A. (2023). Fintech up-coming in Saudi Arabia: Study, analysis, and recommendations. *International Journal of Business Information Systems*, *42*(1), 85–104.

Elizaveta, G., & Tjaša, I. (2020). Regulatory sandboxes (experimental legal regimes) for digital innovations in BRICS. *BRICS Law Journal*, *7*(2), 10–36. doi:10.21684/2412-2343-2020-7-2-10-36

Elmorshidy, A. (2018). Factors Affecting Mobile Applications of Remote Security Cameras at Home and Office : An Empirical Investigation in Southern California. *The International Technology Management Review*, *7*(1), 93–111. doi:10.2991/itmr.7.1.9

El-Swaify, M. A. (2022). The Global Nexus: Bridging Science, Technology, and Business in the International Landscape. *International Multidisciplinary Journal Of Science. Technology & Business*, *1*(01), 22–28.

Emara, N., & Mohieldin, M. (2021). Beyond the Digital Dividends: FinTech and Extreme Poverty in the Middle East and Africa. *Topics in Middle Eastern & North African Economies: Proceedings of the Middle East Economic Association*, 23.

Empaxis. (2023). *Saudi Arabia Wealth Management: Outlook & Solutions to Operations Challenges*. Author.

Ennew, C., Waite, N., & Waite, R. (2013). *Financial services marketing: An international guide to principles and practice*. Routledge. doi:10.4324/9780203521649

Eqtor. (2023). *We're here to make investing easy for everyone*. Retrieved from https://eqtor.com/qa

Erinç Yeldan, A., & Ünüvar, B. (2016). An Assessment of the Turkish Economy in the AKP Era. *Research and Policy on Turkey*, *1*(1), 11–28. doi:10.1080/23760818.2015.1099779

Ernest, W., Gutiérrez, P., & Schneider, C. (2019). *FINTECH en Costa Rica: hacia una evolución de los servicios financieros* (Vol. 732). Inter-American Development Bank. doi:10.18235/0001754

Ernst & Young Global Limited. (2019). *Global Fintech adoption index 2019*. Retrieved fromhttps://www.ey.com/en_gl/ey-global-Fintech-adoption-index

Ernst & Young. (2011). *The economic impact of the 2011 Formula 1TM Australian Grand Prix*. Retrieved from https://www.tourism.vic.gov.au/images/stories/Documents/FactsandFigures/2011_gp_eco_impact_final_21_07_11.pdf

Ernst & Young. (2019). *Thailand Fintech Landscape Report*. Retrieved fromhttps://www.researchgate.net/profile/Varun-Mittal-9/publication/337971279_Thailand_Fintech_Landscape_Report_Sanitized_by_Global_Markets_EY_Knowledge/links/5df8527aa6fdcc283726a7b3/Thailand-Fintech-Landscape-Report-Sanitized-by-Global-Markets-EY-Knowledge.pdf

Ernst, Y. (2014). *Landscaping UK Fintech*. Ernst and Young LLP.

ETDA. (October 13, 2021). *E-commerce market value in Thailand from 2017 to 2020, with a forecast for 2021 (in trillion Thai baht)* [Graph]. Statista. Retrieved August 19, 2023, from https://www.statista.com/statistics/1115125/thailand-e-commerce-market-value/

Etikan, I., Musa, S. A., & Alkassim, R. S. (2016). Comparison of Convenience Sampling and Purposive Sampling. *American Journal of Theoretical and Applied Statistics*, *5*(1), 1–4. doi:10.11648/j.ajtas.20160501.11

Evron, Y., Kowner, R., & Kumaraswamy, P. R. (2024). East and West Asia in the Twenty-First Century: From Bilateral to Interregional Relationships. In East-West Asia Relations in the 21st Century (pp. 3-14). Routledge.

Expat Guide Korea. (2020, July 23). How to Set Up Kakao Pay: the best mobile payment service in Korea. *Expat Guide Korea*. https://www.expatguidekorea.com/article/how-to-set-up-kakao-pay-the-best-mobile-payment-service-in-korea.html

Export.gov. (2018). *Turkey - Information and Communications Technology*. https://legacy.export.gov/article?id=Turkey-Information-and-Communications-Technology

EY. (2021). *How Qatar is paving the way for a bright fintech future*. https://www.ey.com/en_qa/digital-banking-fintech/how-qatar-is-paving-the-way-for-a-bright-fintech-future

Failory. (2023). *Top 16 Startups in Saudi Arabia in 2023*. Retrieved from https://www.failory.com/startups/saudi-arabia

Falgright. (2023). The Future of Reg Tech in Taiwan. *Fintech Global*. https://FinTech.global/2023/05/22/the-future-of-regtech-in-taiwan

Fallahpour, A., Yazdani, M., Mohammed, A., & Wong, K. Y. (2021). Green sourcing in the era of industry 4.0: Towards green and digitized competitive advantages. *Industrial Management & Data Systems*, *121*(9), 1997–2025. doi:10.1108/IMDS-06-2020-0343

Fayda, S. N. A., Sencan, A., Aksoy, O., & Yazici, S. (2020). A Qualitative Research on Selected Performance Indicators for Investment Decision Process: A Framework for FinTech Startups in Turkey. *Journal of Business Economics and Finance*, *9*(1), 28–41. doi:10.17261/Pressacademia.2020.1190

Feyen. (2023). Fintech and the Future of Finance. *World Bank Group*. https://documents1.worldbank.org/curated/en/099450005162250110/pdf/P17300600228b70070914b0b5edf26e2f9f.pdf

Feyen, E., Natarajan, H., & Saal, M. (2023). *Fintech and the Future of Finance: Market and Policy Implications*. World Bank Publications. doi:10.1596/978-1-4648-1914-8

Filofteia, T. M. (2018). Mobile Applications for Tourism. Study Regarding Their Use by Romanians. *Brâncuşi, Annals of the Constantin. Economic S*, (4), 78–84.

FIN/SUM. (2023). *Fintech, the era of "Neoteric Individual"*. FIN/SUM 2023. https://www.finsum.jp/en_index.html

Financial Service Agency. (2023). *Laws & Regulations: FSA*. FSA. https://www.fsa.go.jp/en/laws_regulations/index.html

Fintech - Mongolia: Statista market forecast. (n.d.). Statista. https://www.statista.com/outlook/dmo/FinTech/mongolia

Fintech Energy. (2022). *Myanmar's 8 Fastest Growing Fintech Startups*. Retrieved from https://Fintech.energy/myanmars-8-fastest-growing-Fintech-startups/

Fintech Malaysia. (2022, July 18). *Fintech Report 2022: Malaysia Charts a New Path for Fintech Growth*. Retrieved from https://Fintechnews.my/31945/malaysia/Fintech-report-malaysia-2022/

Fintech Malaysia. (2022, May 11). *Top 5 Funded Fintechs in Malaysia*. Retrieved fromhttps://Fintechnews.my/31200/malaysia/top-5-funded-Fintechs-in-malaysia/

Fintech News Hong Kong. (2020, February 10). *Fintech In South Korea: Regulators Step In To Boost Innovation*. Fintech Hong Kong. https://FinTechnews.hk/4823/FinTechkorea/FinTech-south-korea-regulators-step-boost-innovation/F6s.com

Fintech News. (2022). *Distribution of Fintech companies in Singapore in 2022, bysector* [Graph]. Statista. Retrieved July 29, 2023, from https://www.statista.com/statistics/1294130/singapore-Fintech-companies-share-by-sector/

Fintech News. (2022, December 8). All 5 Singapore Digital Banks Are Now Members of the Credit Bureau. Lending Virtual Banking. Retrieved from https://Fintechnews.sg/67599/virtual-banking/all-5-singapore-digital-banks-are-now-members-of-the-credit-bureau/

FinTech sector? (n.d.). *McKinsey & Company*. https://www.mckinsey.com/~/media/mckinsey/industries/financial%20services/our%20insights/whats%20next%20for%20chinas%20booming%20FinTech%20sector/whats-next-for-chinas-booming-FinTech-sector.ashx

Fintech Show, D. A. T. E. (2023). *Shaping Saudi Arabia's Financial Tech Future*. Retrieved from https://datewithtech.com/ksa/ai/

Fintechnews. (2023, January 10). *Laos' Fintech Revolution is Still Bank-Led, For Now*. Retrieved from https://Fintechnews.sg/68354/laos/laos-Fintech-revolution-is-still-bank-led-for-now/

Firn, M. (2021, July 15). *TrueMoney goal for 2 mn 2021 e-wallet transactions on target*. Retrieved from https://www.khmertimeskh.com/50894147/truemoney-goal-for-2-mn-2021-e-wallet-transactions-on-target/

Fonseca-Argüello, H. (2021, November 22). *Estado y tendencias del sector Fintech en Costa Rica*. http://201.196.25.14/index.php/actas/article/view/1328

Forbes Middle East. (2023). *Top 20 Fintech Startups in the Middle East*. Retrieved November 13, 2023, from https://www.forbesmiddleeast.com/list/top-20-FinTech-startups-in-the-middle-east

Forbes. (2020). *Share of investment banks worldwide using artificial intelligence (AI) as of 2020, by types of application* [Graph]. Statista. Retrieved November 18, 2023, from https://0-www-statista-com.biblioteca-ils.tec.mx/statistics/1246874/ai-used-in-investment-banking-worldwide-2020

Fortumo. (2021, July 27). *Market share of leading mobile wallet applications in the Philippinesin 2020* [Graph]. Statista. Retrieved August 26, 2023, from https://www.statista.com/statistics/1258098/philippines-mobile-wallet-apps-market-share/

Fortumo. (2021, September 28). *Number of mobile wallet users in Indonesia in 2020, with aforecast for 2025 (in millions)* [Graph]. Statista. Retrieved August 16, 2023, from https://www.statista.com/statistics/1327354/indonesia-mobile-wallet-users/

Fortune Pay. (n.d.). *About us*. Retrieved from https://fortunepay.com/about-us/

Fosso Wamba, S., Kala Kamdjoug, J. R., Epie Bawack, R., & Keogh, J. G. (2020). Bitcoin, Blockchain and Fintech: A systematic review and case studies in the supply chain. *Production Planning and Control*, *31*(2-3), 115–142. doi:10.1080/09537287.2019.1631460

Francis, D. (2014). Should the US & Canada merge? Journalist Diane Francis argues that it would create an unstoppable North American superpower! *New York Times Upfront, 147*(6), 8-13.

Frumento, E. (2019). Cybersecurity and the evolutions of healthcare: challenges and threats behind its evolution. *M_Health Current and Future Applications*, 35-69.

Fuster, A., Goldsmith-Pinkham, P., Ramadorai, T., & Walther, A. (2022). Predictably unequal? The effects of machine learning on credit markets. *The Journal of Finance*, *77*(1), 5–47. doi:10.1111/jofi.13090

Fuster, A., Plosser, M., Schnabl, P., & Vickery, J. (2019). The role of technology in mortgage lending. *Review of Financial Studies*, *32*(5), 1854–1899. doi:10.1093/rfs/hhz018

Futures, C. (2022, October 2). *The Future of Fintech in Japan: Top Fintech Trends to watch in 2023*. Computer Futures. https://www.computerfutures.com/en-jp/knowledge-hub/financial-technology/the-future-of-FinTech-in-japan-top-FinTech-trends-to-watch-in-2023/#jobs

Gai, K., Qiu, M., & Sun, X. (2018). A survey on FinTech. *Journal of Network and Computer Applications*, *103*, 262–273. doi:10.1016/j.jnca.2017.10.011

Galaxy, F. (2022). *Qatar FinTech Hub launches equity crowdfunding platform for startups and SMEs*. Retrieved from https://fintechgalaxy.com/qatar-fintech-hub/

Galaxy, F. (2023). *Qatar fintech startups and companies on Fintech Galaxy*. Retrieved from https://fintechgalaxy.com/location/qatar/

Gantès, G. D., Gerson, H., & Romano, K. (2023, May 3). *On the verge of a digital bankingrevolution in the Philippines.* McKinsey & Company. Retrieved from https://www.mckinsey.com/industries/financial-services/our-insights/on-the-verge-of-a-digital-banking-revolution-in-the-philippines

Gao, F. (2018). Leveraging a mega sport event: Lessons for the 2019 FIBA world cup. *Sport & Entertainment Review*, *4*, 59–63.

Garrouch, K. (2021). Does the reputation of the provider matter? A model explaining the continuance intention of mobile wallet applications. *Journal of Decision Systems*, *30*(2-3), 150–171. Advance online publication. doi:10.1080/12460125.2020.1870261

Gayabazar, U. (2021). Future tendencies in the financial markets in Mongolia and worldwide. *Int. J. Foresight and Innovation Policy, 15*(1-3), 187–203.

Geloso, V. (2022). The Historical Evolution of Canadian Living Standards. In Oxford Research Encyclopedia of Economics and Finance. doi:10.1093/acrefore/9780190625979.013.791

General Authority for Statistics. (2023). *Statistical yearbook 2023.* Retrieved from https://www.stats.gov.sa/en

General Secretariat for Development Planning. (2022). *Qatar National Vision 2030.* Retrieved from https://www.psa.gov.qa/en/qnv1/Pages/default.aspx

General Statistics Authority of Saudi Arabia. (2023). Retrieved from https://www.stats.gov.sa/en/43

George, D., & Mallery, M. (2003). *Using SPSS for Windows step by step: a simple guide and Reference.* Academic Press.

Giang, H. (2022, July 28). *Elevating the startup ecosystem through the innovative policies of the Government.* Government News. https://baochinhphu.vn/nang-tam-he-sinh-thai-khoi-nghiep-tu-nhung-chinh-sach-kien-tao-cua-chinh-phu-102220728140305108.htm

Giang, H. (2023, March 13). *E-commerce Driving Force for Growth.* Vietnam Business Forum.https://vccinews.com/news/48958/e-commerce-driving-force-for%20growth.html

Giglio, F. (2021). Fintech: A literature review. *European Research Studies*, *24*(2B, 2B), 600–627. doi:10.35808/ersj/2254

Glancy, F. H., & Yadav, S. B. (2011). A computational model for financial reporting fraud detection. *Decision Support Systems*, *50*(3), 595–601. doi:10.1016/j.dss.2010.08.010

Global, E. (2022). What is next for Asia in FinTech adoption. *EY - Global.* https://www.ey.com/en_gl/banking-capital-markets/what-is-next-for-asia-in-FinTech-adoption

Globe. (2023, August 9). *GCash: Everything You Need To Know To Make Life Easier.* Retrieved from www.globe.com.ph/go/technology/article/gcash-everything-you-need-to-know.html

GMA. (2023, April 12). *Philippines 4th in the world with most incidents of cyber attacks — DICT.* Retrieved from https://www.gmanetwork.com/news/scitech/technology/866755/philippines-4th-in-the-world-with-most-incidents-of-cyber-attacks-dict/story/

Gochhwal, R. (2017). Unified payment interface—An advancement in payment systems. *American Journal of Industrial and Business Management*, *7*(10), 1174–1191. doi:10.4236/ajibm.2017.710084

Godoy-Troya, J. R., & de Velazco, T. (2022). Modelos de negocios basados en fintech y su impacto en el ecosistema financiero panameño. *Revista Científica Orbis Cógnita*, *6*(1), 111–127.

Goel, N. A., Alam, A. A., Eggert, E. M., & Acharya, S. (2017). *Design and development of a customizable telemedicine platform for improving access to healthcare for underserved populations.* Paper presented at the 2017 39th Annual International Conference of the IEEE Engineering in Medicine and Biology Society (EMBC). 10.1109/EMBC.2017.8037404

Golomt bank - banking - overview, competitors, and employees. (n.d.). Apollo.io. https://www.apollo.io/companies/Golomt-Bank/5f3db67ee06ba3000173b9e1?chart=count

GoPay. (n.d.). *About us.* Retrieved from https://www.gopay.com/en/about-us/

Gotrade. (n.d.). *Making investing fun, fair and simple.* Retrieved from https://www.heygotrade.com/

Gottfried, J., & Shearer, E. (2022). *Tech adoption and the future of the internet.* Pew Research Center.

Govindarajan, U. H., Singh, D. K., & Gohel, H. A. (2023). Forecasting cyber security threats landscape and associated technical trends in telehealth using Bidirectional Encoder Representations from Transformers (BERT). *Computers & Security, 133*, 103404. doi:10.1016/j.cose.2023.103404

Grab. (2019, December 20). *Grab Primed to Drive Digital Economy in Malaysia through e-Tunai Rakyat Programme.* Press Center. Retrieved from: https://www.grab.com/my/press/business/grab-e-tunai-rakyat-programme/

Grab. (n.d.). *Charging forward together.* Retrieved from https://www.grab.com/sg/about/

Grassi, L., & Fantaccini, S. (2022). An overview of Fintech applications to solve the puzzle of health care funding: State-of-the-art in medical crowdfunding. *Financial Innovation, 8*(1), 1–27. doi:10.1186/s40854-022-00388-9 PMID:36158456

Greene, C. (2022, November 16). *Uproar in Mobile Financial Services.* Retrieved from

Griethuijsen, R. A. L. F., Eijck, M. W., Haste, H., Brok, P. J., Skinner, N. C., & Mansour, N. (2014). Global patterns in students' views of science and interest in science. *Research in Science Education, 45*(4), 581–603. doi:10.1007/s11165-014-9438-6

GSMA. (2022, July 4). *The Philippines is a Duopoly No More: Assessing DITO's Impact on 4G and 5G Performance.* Retrieved from https://www.gsma.com/membership/resources/the-philippines-is-a-duopoly-no-more-assessing-ditos-impact-on-4g-and-5g-performance/

Guevara, H. R. L., & Domínguez, J. N. C. (2023). *Fintech: Modelo de negocio para plataforma digital de financiamiento colaborativo en Honduras.* Academic Press.

Gulf Times. (2019). *Commercial banks asked not to deal in virtual currencies.* https://www.gulf-times.com/story/638730/Commercial-banks-asked-not-to-deal-in-virtual-curren

Gulf Times. (2022). *QIB launches open banking platform to boost financial inclusion.* https://www.gulf-times.com/story/716215/QIB-launches-open-banking-platform-to-boost-financ

Gupta, V., & Zhang, Y. (2020). Investigating Environmental Performance Management. *Revista Brasileira de Gestão de Negócios, 22*(1), 5–48. doi:10.7819/rbgn.v22i1.4034

Gur, N., Babacan, M., Aysan, A. F., & Suleyman, S. (2023). Firm Size and Financing Behavior during COVID-19. In *Pandemic: Evidence from SMEs in Istanbul.* Borsa Istanbul Review.

Hair, J. F., Black, W. C., Babin, B. J., Anderson, R. E., & Tatham, R. L. (2010). *Multivariate data analysis* (6th ed.). Pearson Prentice Hall.

Hair, J. F. Jr, Hult, G. T. M., Ringle, C. M., & Sarstedt, M. (2014). *A primer on Partial Least Squares Structural Equation Modeling (PLS-SEM).* SAGE Publications Ltd.

Hakala, K. (2019). *Robo-advisors as a form of artificial intelligence in private customers' investment advisory services*. Academic Press.

Halawi, L., Mccarthy, R. V., & Farah, J. (2018). Information Systems Continuance: Faculty Perceptions of Canvas. *Issues in Information Systems*, *19*(4), 171–175.

Haleem, A., Javaid, M., Singh, R. P., & Suman, R. (2021). Telemedicine for healthcare: Capabilities, features, barriers, and applications. *Sensors International*, *2*, 100117. doi:10.1016/j.sintl.2021.100117 PMID:34806053

Halme, M., Rintamäki, J., Knudsen, J. S., Lankoski, L., & Kuisma, M. (2020). When Is There a Sustainability Case for CSR? Pathways to Environmental and Social Performance Improvements. *Business & Society*, *59*(6), 1181–1227. doi:10.1177/0007650318755648

Hanjaya, M., Kenny, S. K., & Gunawan, F. (2019). Understanding Factors Influencing Consumer's Online Purchase Intention Via Mobile App: Perceived Ease Of Use, Perceived Usefulness, System Quality, Information Quality, And Service Quality. *MINIB*, *32*(2), 175–206. doi:10.2478/minib-2019-0035

Hao, V. (2020, January 1). Developing a Fintech Ecosystem in Vietnam: Opportunities and Challenges for Startups. *SHS Web of Conferences; EDP Sciences*. 10.1051/shsconf/20208904001

Haqqi, F. R., & Suzianti, A. (2020, June). Exploring risk and benefit factors affecting user adoption intention of Fintech in Indonesia. In *Proceedings of the 3rd Asia Pacific Conference on Research in Industrial and Systems Engineering* (pp. 13-18). 10.1145/3400934.3400939

Harris, A., Goodman, S., & Traynor, P. (2013). Privacy and Security Concerns Associated With Mobile Money Applications in Africa. *Washington Journal of Law, Technology and Arts*, *8*(3), 246–263.

Hasaka, K. (2019). *The Impact of Fintech innovations and financial standards on bank performance: Evidence from selected commercial banks in ASEAN*. Retrieved from https://ink.library.smu.edu.sg/cgi/viewcontent.cgi?article=1256&context=etd_coll

Hasanat, M. W., Hoque, A., Shamim, A., & Abuhammad, S. (2023). FinTech Disruption in the Financial Sector of Saudi Arabia: A Preliminary Inquiry. *Journal of Open Innovation*, *9*(1), 11.

Hasan, R., Islam, M. A., & Hossain, M. A. (2021). Evaluating drivers of fintech adoption in the Netherlands. *Global Business Review*, 1–14. doi:10.1177/09721509211027402

Hassan, J. (2022). *Recent regulatory moves suggest Qatar's leadership aims to adopt crypto assets in financial sector*. Retrieved from https://www.dailysabah.com/business/finance/recent-regulatory-moves-suggest-qatars-leadership-aims-to-adopt-crypto-assets-in-financial-sector

Hassan, M. K., Rahiman, H. U., Rabbani, M. R., & Alhomaidi, A. (2022). The future of finance and FinTech: Visualizing the opportunities for FinTech in the MENA region. In *FinTech in Islamic Financial Institutions: Scope, Challenges, and Implications in Islamic Finance* (pp. 89–111). Springer International Publishing. doi:10.1007/978-3-031-14941-2_5

HBR. (2022). *Cambodia - Overview*. Retrieved from https://www.halberdbastion.com/intelligence/countries-nations/cambodia

Heno. (n.d.). *Introduction*. Heno. https://heno.vn/about/about-heno

Heritage (2020). *2020 Index of Economic Freedom: Mongolia*. Author.

Hernàndez, P. (2019, Nov 19) Financial technology: the 150-year revolution. *Basel Committee on Banking Supervision and Governor of the Bank of Spain*. https://www.bis.org/speeches/sp191119.htm

Hidayat, S. E., & Alhabshi, S. M. (2022). Shariah-Compliant FinTech in Islamic Finance: A Review of the Literature. *Journal of Islamic Monetary Economics and Finance*, *8*(1), 131–150.

Hoang, L. (2021, December 21). *Vietnam e-wallet MoMo gains unicorn status with $200m investment.* Nikkei Asia. Retrieved from https://asia.nikkei.com/Business/Technology/Vietnam-e-wallet-MoMo-gains-unicorn-status-with-200m-investment

Holla, N., & Pasha, S. (2022). *The Qatar fintech ecosystem - Investment opportunities abound.* Retrieved from https://home.kpmg.com/qa/en/home/insights/2022/09/the-qatar-fintech-ecosystem-investment-opportunities-abound.html

Horton, J. (1979). *Financing North American economic cooperation.* Paper presented at the Forum for Social Economics.

Hossain, M. J., Wadud, M. A. H., Rahman, A., Ferdous, J., Alam, M. S., Bhuiyan, T. M. A.-U.-H., & Mridha, M. F. (2021). *A Secured Patient's Online Data Monitoring through Blockchain: An Intelligent way to Store Lifetime Medical Records.* Paper presented at the 2021 International Conference on Science & Contemporary Technologies (ICSCT). 10.1109/ICSCT53883.2021.9642537

Hoz, S. (2022). *Saudi Arabia Internet Penetration Rate 2022.* Available at: https://www.statista.com/statistics/484930/internet-user-reach-saudi-arabia/

https://www.myanmarinsider.com/uproar-in-mobile-financial-services/

Huang, Chiang FinTech in China: overview. (2021). *Practical Law.* https://uk.practicallaw.thomsonreuters.com/w-019-4896?transitionType=Default&contextData=(sc.Default)&firstPage=true#:~:text=The%20People's%20Bank%20of%20China%20(PBOC)&text=Control%20and%20supervision%20of%20the,finance%2Drelated%20laws%20and%20regulations

Hukuk. (2023). *Fintech Businesses Legal Framework in Turkey.* [https://www.bicakhukuk.com/en/fintech-businesses-legal-framework-in-turkey/].

Huong, A., Puah, C. H., & Chong, M. T. (2021). Embrace Fintech in ASEAN: A perception through Fintech adoption index. *Review of World Economics*, *12*(1), 1.

Hurriyet Daily News. (2022). *Artificial Intelligence Era Opportunity for Turkey.* [https://www.hurriyetdailynews.com/artificial-intelligence-era-opportunity-for-turkey-144960]

Huseien, G. F., & Shah, K. W. (2022, January). A review on 5G technology for smart energy management and smart buildings in Singapore. *Energy and AI*, *7*, 100116. doi:10.1016/j.egyai.2021.100116

Hussein, H. (2020). The impact of financial technology on financial inclusion: The case of Egypt. *IOSR Journal of Economics and Finance*, *11*(6), 35–51.

ICLG. (2023). *Fintech Laws and Regulations in Turkey.* https://iclg.com/practice-areas/fintech-laws-and-regulations/turkiye

iclg.com. (2023). *FinTech Laws and Regulations | Türkiye.* Retrieved from https://iclg.com/practice-areas/fintech-laws-and-regulations/turkiye

IFC. (2017). *Blockchain in Financial Services in Emerging Markets.* EMCompass Note 43, International Finance Corporation. Available at: https://www.ifc.org/wps/wcm/connect/a3559b7c-19b7-4f8d-94be-30d1cf7e172b/EMCompass+Note+43+FINAL+8-21.pdf?MOD=AJPERES&CVID=lU51Cxz

Igor Tomych. (2023). *Fintech Compliance In MENA: Navigating Regulations and Security Requirements.* Retrieved from https://dashdevs.com

IMF. (2022). Reaching New Heights: Qatar. *Economic Outlook, 2022*. https://www.imf.org/en/Countries/ResRep/QAT#countrydata

imtilak.net. (2023, October 5). *Banks in Turkey*. Retrieved from https://www.imtilak.net/en/turkey/articles/banks-in-turkey

Inside. (2022). *Major Blockchain Adoption Announced by LBank in Turkey*. [http://edgeservices.bing.com/edgesvc/redirect?url=https%3A%2F%2Fwww.bollyinside.com%2Fnews%2Fmajor-blockchain-adoption-announced-by-lbank-in-turkey%2F&hash=qvAcW63mfNHJqvxxkNL9UbBAqbo130lWqYqP3WQ6T3s%3D&key=psc-underside&usparams=cvid%3A51D%7CBingProd%7C1ED14F335B5CD360F9B03E42B6EB6E24521A7E16F69EF215EF7F49A570BA0BE1%5Ertone%3ABalanced].

Insider Intelligence. (2022). *Artificial intelligence (AI) adoption rate in financial businesses worldwide in 2022 and 2025* [Graph]. Statista. Retrieved November 13, 2023, from https://0-www-statista-com.biblioteca-ils.tec.mx/statistics/1346736/ai-function-adoption-rates-business-finance

Insider. (2020, October 30). Wave Money sets record breaking 1.1 Million Monthly ActiveUsers *of WavePay*. Market Insider. Retrieved from https://markets.businessinsider.com/news/stocks/wave-money-sets-record-breaking-1-1-million-monthly-active-users-of-wavepay-1029744558

Insights, L. (2022). *Turkey Blockchain Regulatory Sandbox*. Retrieved from https://www.computerworld.com/article/3261444/study-fintech-other-industries-should-open-blockchain-sandboxes-and-work-with-regulators.html

Insurance Regulatory and Development Authority of India (Regulatory Sandbox) Regulations, 2019.

Intelligence, G. S. M. A. (2023). *The Mobile Economy Middle East & North Africa*. Retrieved from https://www.gsma.com/mobileeconomy/mena/

Intelligence, M. (2022). *Qatar Fintech Market - Growth, Trends, COVID-19 Impact, and Forecasts (2022 - 2027)*. Retrieved from https://www.mordorintelligence.com/industry-reports/qatar-fintech-market

Intelligence, M. (2023). *FinTech Market in Saudi Arabia - Trends & Size*. Retrieved from https://www.mordorintelligence.com/industry-reports/saudi-arabia-fintech-market/market-size

International Finance. (2020, June 5). *5G is a logical solution to the Philippines*. Retrieved from https://international-finance.com/5g-is-a-logical-solution-to-the-philippines/

International Monetary Fund. (2020, September) *Republic of Korea: Financial Sector Assessment Program*. IMF Country Report No. 20/280.

International Telecommunication Union (ITU). (2023). *Qatar Profile*. Retrieved from https://www.itu.int/itu-d/apis/clients/res/pdfs/country_profile/report_QAT_web.pdf

International Trade Administration. (2022, April 20). *Singapore's e-commerce market*. Retrieved from https://www.trade.gov/market-intelligence/singapores-e-commerce-market

International Trade Administration. (2022, July 25). *eCommerce*. Retrieved from https://www.trade.gov/country-commercial-guides/philippines-ecommerce

International Trade Administration. (2022, July 26). *eCommerce*. Retrieved from https://www.trade.gov/country-commercial-guides/thailand-ecommerce

International Trade Administration. (2022, November 23). Malaysia - eCommerce. Retrieved from https://www.trade.gov/country-commercial-guides/malaysia-ecommerce

International Trade Administration. (2022, November 4). *Japan - Market Overview*. International Trade Administration. https://www.trade.gov/country-commercial-guides/japan-market-overview

International Trade Administration. (2023, February 7). Singapore cybersecurity market. Retrieved from https://www.trade.gov/market-intelligence/singapore-cybersecurity-marketInternational

International Trade Organization. (2020). *Taiwan Fintech Market*. Market Intelligence. https://www.trade.gov/market-intelligence/taiwan-FinTech-market

Internship golomt bank. (n.d.). https://app.emaze.com/1927358/internship-golomt-bank#/12

Intonti, M., Serlenga, L., Ferri, G., De Leonardis, M., & Starace, G. (2023). The "Greenium" in Green Bonds: How Did It Change with COVID-19? *Sustainability (2071-1050), 15*(7), 5631. https://doi-org.ezproxy.myucwest.ca/10.3390/su15075631

Intralink. (2020). *Fintech South Korea: Market Intelligence Report. Innovation is Great*. www.intralinkgroup.com/Syndication/media/Syndication/Reports/Korean-Fintech-report-Oct-2020.pdf

Inukollu, V. N., Keshamoni, D. D., & Kang, T. (2014). Factors Influencing Quality of Mobile Apps: Role of Mobile App Development Life Cycle. *International Journal of Software Engineering and Its Applications*, *5*(5), 15–34. doi:10.5121/ijsea.2014.5502

Invest.gov.tr. (2023). *The State of FinTech Ecosystem in Türkiye*. https://www.invest.gov.tr/en/news/news-from-turkey/pages/the-state-of-fintech-ecosystem-in-turkiye.aspx

iPrice Group. (2022, November 29). *Most visited e-commerce sites in Thailand as of 1st quarter 2022, by monthly traffic (in 1,000 clicks)* [Graph].In Statista. Retrieved August 24, 2023, from https://www.statista.com/statistics/1117797/thailand-popular-e-commerce-sites/

iPrice Group. (2022, November 7). *Leading e-commerce sites in Indonesia as of 2nd quarter 2022, by monthly traffic (in million web visits)* [Graph]. Statista. Retrieved August 05, 2023, from https://www.statista.com/statistics/869700/indonesia-top-10-e-commerce-sites/

iPrice Group. (2022, October 19). *Most visited e-commerce sites in Malaysia as of 2nd quarter 2022, by monthly traffic (in 1,000 clicks)* [Graph]. Statista. Retrieved August 12, 2023, from https://www.statista.com/statistics/869640/malaysia-top-10-e-commerce-sites/

Islam, R., Romdhane, L. B., Mouakhar, K., & Yousuf, S. (2021). Cyber risk Readiness in Qatar's Financial Sector. *Technology Innovation Management Review*, *11*(10).

ISP. (2023, June 27). *The growth of Fintech in mongolia: How telecommunications is shaping the financial sector*. https://isp.page/news/the-growth-of-FinTech-in-mongolia-how-telecommunications-is-shaping-the-financial-sector/

ITA. (2023). *Taiwan - Country Commercial Guide*. https://www.trade.gov/country-commercial-guides/taiwan-information-and-telecommunications-technology

Jaber, J., & Issa, H. (2022). Disruptive innovation in the middle eastern FinTech sector: Resource-based view. *International Journal of Technology and Human Interaction*, *18*(1), 1–21. doi:10.4018/IJTHI.299069

Jahmurataev, U. (2022). Fintech in Qatar: The highway to economic diversification beyond hydrocarbons. *International Review of Applied Economics*, *36*(2), 237–256.

Jain, R., Kumar, S., Sood, K., Grima, S., & Rupeika-Apoga, R. (2023). A Systematic Literature Review of the Risk Landscape in Fintech. *Risks*, *11*(2), 36. doi:10.3390/risks11020036

Jain, V., Rastogi, M., Ramesh, J. V. N., Chauhan, A., Agarwal, P., Pramanik, S., & Gupta, A. (2023). FinTech and Artificial Intelligence in Relationship Banking and Computer Technology. In K. Saini, A. Mummoorthy, R. Chandrika, N. S. Gowri Ganesh, & I. G. I. Global (Eds.), *AI, IoT, and Blockchain Breakthroughs in E-Governance*. doi:10.4018/978-1-6684-7697-0.ch011

Jameaba, M.-S. (2020). Digitization revolution, FinTech disruption, and financial stability: Using the case of Indonesian banking ecosystem to highlight wide-ranging digitization opportunities and major challenges. *FinTech Disruption, and Financial stability: Using the Case of Indonesian Banking Ecosystem to highlight wide-ranging digitization opportunities and major challenges.*

James. (2019, August 19). The future of FinTech in South Korea - QARA - Medium. *Medium*. https://medium.com/qara/the-future-of-FinTech-in-south-korea-37a0a1315742#:~:text=Compared%20to%20the%20U.S.%20or%20China%2C%20South%20Korea%E2%80%99s,2018%20and%2045%20million%20users%20expected%20by%202022

Jana Kapital. (n.d.). *About us*. Retrieved from https://www.janakapital.com/about

Japan External Trade Organization. (2017). Japan's Fintech Ecosystem Transformation Today and toward 2020. *JETRO*. https://www.jetro.go.jp/ext_images/canada/pdf/FinTechseminaroct1817maeda.pdf

Jarvis, R., & Han, H. (2021). Fintech Innovation: Review and Future Research Directions. *International Journal of Banking. Finance and Insurance Technologies*, *1*(1), 79–102.

Jayasingh, R. (2022). Speckle noise removal by SORAMA segmentation in Digital Image Processing to facilitate precise robotic surgery. *International Journal of Reliable and Quality E-Healthcare*, *11*(1), 1–19. Advance online publication. doi:10.4018/IJRQEH.295083

Jeník, I., Flaming, M., & Salman, A. (2020). *Inclusive digital banking: Emerging markets case studies*. Consultative Group to Assist the Poor Working Paper. Washington, DC.

Jensen, J. A., Cobbs, J. B., Albano, B., & Tyler, B. D. (2021). Analyzing Price Premiums In International Sponsorship Exchange: What Drives Marketing Costs In Formula One Racing? *Journal of Advertising Research*, *61*(1), 44–57. doi:10.2501/JAR-2020-018

JohnClements. (2023). *Fintech Frontier: Trends And Innovations*. Retrieved from https://www.johnclements.com/the-looking-glass/featured/Fintech-frontier-trends-and-innovations/

Jones, C. W., Byon, K. K., & Huang, H. (2019). Service Quality, Perceived Value, and Fan Engagement: Case of Shanghai Formula One Racing. *Sport Marketing Quarterly*, *28*(2), 63–76. doi:10.32731/SMQ.282.062019.01

Jorgenson, D. (2004). *Economic Growth in Canada and the United States in the Information Age*. Academic Press.

Joshi. (2021). *The Promise of Fintech Achieving Financial Inclusion*. International Monetary Fund. https://www.imf.org/external/pubs/ft/fandd/2021/06/what-is-fintech-basics.htm

Julian, H. L. C., Chung, T., & Wang, Y. (2023, January 6). Adoption of Metaverse in South East Asia. *Strategies and Opportunities for Technology in the Metaverse World*, 196–234. doi:10.4018/978-1-6684-5732-0.ch012

Kabulova, J., & Stankevičienė, J. (2020). Valuation of Fintech innovation based on patent applications. *Sustainability (Basel)*, *12*(23), 1–14. doi:10.3390/su122310158

Kagan, J. (2022, October 30). *Financial Services Agency (FSA)*. Investopedia. https://www.investopedia.com/terms/f/financial-services-agency-fsa.asp

Kajihara, A. (2023, February 20). FinTech in Japan. Trends for 2023. Wahl+Case. https://www.wahlandcase.com/blog/FinTech-predictions-2023

Kakria, P., Tripathi, N., & Kitipawang, P. (2015). A real-time health monitoring system for remote cardiac patients using smartphone and wearable sensors. *International Journal of Telemedicine and Applications, 2015*, 8–8. doi:10.1155/2015/373474 PMID:26788055

Kaleido Intelligence. (2023). FinTech Market Analysis.

Kalibrate. (2022). *Saudi Arabia's FinTech Landscape: A Comprehensive Overview*. Retrieved from https://medium.com/@ifinancemag/saudi-arabias-fintech-growth-and-cashless-transition-a04905f7bb28

Kapron, Z. (2023, April 12). *Incumbents Are Poised To Dominate Digital Banking In Thailand. Forbes*. Retrieved from https://www.forbes.com/sites/zennonkapron/2023/04/12/incumbents-are-poised-to-dominate-digital-banking-in-thailand/?sh=ef723811df9b

Karaman, H. D., Savaser, T., Tiniç, M., & Tumer-Alkan, G. (2021). Financial technology in developing economies: A note on digital lending in Turkey. *Economics Letters*, *207*, 110012. doi:10.1016/j.econlet.2021.110012

Karkkainen, T. (2023). *The FinTech Evolution: Technology Push, Market Pull Dynamics, and Inertia*. Tatja Karkkainen.

Kashyap, M. (2023, April 20). *Ecommerce in Malaysia: Growth, Trends & Opportunities. Capillary*. Retrieved from https://www.capillarytech.com/blog/ecommerce-in-malaysia-growth/

Katadata. (2022). *Most known digital banks among Indonesians in 2022*. Statista. Retrieved August 05, 2023, from https://www.statista.com/statistics/1326448/indonesia-leading-digital-banks/

Kem, B., Sou, J., Ng, Z., & Chan, P. (2019, January 1). *Cambodia's Vibrant Tech Startup Ecosystem*. Retrieved from https://static1.squarespace.com/static/56a87acd05f8e263f7b16c7f/t/5c9b0762085229887ba9af72/1553663849501/Cambodian_Tech_Startup_Report_Final_250319.pdf

Kerber, W., & Schweitzer, H. (2017). Interoperability in the digital economy. *J. Intell. Prop. Info. Tech. & Elec. Com. L.*, *8*, 39.

Khanh, P. T., Ngọc, T. H., & Pramanik, S. (2023). Future of Smart Agriculture Techniques and Applications. In A. Khang & I. G. I. Global (Eds.), *Advanced Technologies and AI-Equipped IoT Applications in High Tech Agriculture*. doi:10.4018/978-1-6684-9231-4.ch021

Khan, M. A., Alqahtani, F., Alqahtani, M., Alharthi, A., & Alghamdi, A. (2022). Utilizing the collective wisdom of FinTech in the GCC region: A systematic mapping approach. *Measurement and Control*, *56*(3-4), 717–725. doi:10.1177/00202940211042411

Kheira, T. (2021). Financial technology prospects in the Middle East and Africa. *Journal of Economic Growth*, *4*(3), 14–25.

Khezr, S., Moniruzzaman, M., Yassine, A., & Benlamri, R. (2019). Blockchain Technology in Healthcare: A Comprehensive Review and Directions for Future Research. *Applied Sciences (Basel, Switzerland)*, *9*(9), 1736. Advance online publication. doi:10.3390/app9091736

Khoroshilov, E. (2018). New Technologies in Canadian Financial Sector: Artificial Intelligence and Big Data. *Ekonomika, Politika, Kultura*, (10), 50-65.

Khue, D. T. T. (2021, July 1). Recommendations contributing to the development of financial technology (Fintech) in Vietnam. *International Journal of Research in Finance and Management*, *4*(2), 74–80. doi:10.33545/26175754.2021.v4.i2a.110

Khurana, K. (2023). A bibliometric study of publications on the adoption of FinTech using VOSviewer. *Journal of Educational Technology Systems*, *51*(4), 505–514. doi:10.1177/00472395231165715

Kijkasiwat, P. (2021). Opportunities and challenges for Fintech Startups: The case study of Thailand. *ABAC Journal*, *41*(2), 41–60.

King, B. (2018). *Bank 4.0: Banking everywhere, never at a bank*. John Wiley & Sons. doi:10.1002/9781119506515

Kishi, M. (2019). *Project Stella and the impacts of FinTech on financial infrastructures in Japan*. ADBI Working Paper Series.

Klenow, P. (2019). How valuable is e-commerce. *Stanford Institute for Economic Policy Research (SIEPR)*. Retrieved from https://siepr.stanford.edu/publications/policy-brief/how-valuable-e-commerce

Kompas. (2022, July 21). *Most used e-wallet apps by consumers in Indonesia as of July 2022* [Graph]. Statista. Retrieved August 05, 2023, from https://www.statista.com/statistics/1327316/indonesia-most-used-e-wallet-apps/

Kowsmann, P., & Ostroff, C. (2023, August 2). Crypto is illegal in China. Binance does $90 billion of business there anyway. *WSJ*. https://www.wsj.com/articles/crypto-is-illegal-in-china-binance-does-90-billion-of-business-there-anyway-2a0af975

KPMG. (2023). 100 Questions: FinTech Development In Taiwan. *KPMG International Cooperative*. https://assets.kpmg.com/content/dam/kpmg/tw/pdf/2020/07/tw-100-Questions-FinTech-Development-in-Taiwan.pdf

KPMG. (2023). *Qatar Fintech Ecosystem Study 2023*. Retrieved from https://home.kpmg/qa/en/home/insights/2023/02/qatar-fintech-ecosystem-study.html

KPMG. (2023). *Saudi Arabia FinTech Landscape 2023*. KPMG.

KPMG. (2023). *The fintech revolution in Saudi Arabia*. Retrieved from https://assets.kpmg.com/content/dam/kpmg/sa/pdf/2020/fintech-saudi-annual-report.pdf

Krupinski, E. A., & Bernard, J. (2014). Standards and Guidelines in Telemedicine and Telehealth. *Health Care*, *2*(1), 74–93. doi:10.3390/healthcare2010074 PMID:27429261

Kukreja, G., Gupta, R., & Gupta, A. (2021). FinTech in Oman: Present and future scenario. *Applications of Artificial Intelligence in Business, Education and Healthcare*, 173-183.

Ku-Mahamud, K. R., Abu Bakar, N. A. M., & Omar, M. (2018). Blockchain, cryptocurrency and Fintech market growth in Malaysia. *Journal of Advance Research in Dynamical & Control Systems, 10*(14 SI), 2074-2082.

Kumar, S., Li, A., Wong, H., Chauhan, H., Shubhankar, S., & Oetama, I. (2023, April 19). *Indonesia's Fintech Industry Is Ready to Rise. Canada - EN*. https://www.bcg.com/en-ca/publications/2023/Fintech-industry-indonesia-growth

Kumar, A., Adlakaha, A., & Mukherjee, K. (2018). The effect of perceived security and grievance redressal on continuance intention to use M-wallets in a developing country. *International Journal of Bank Marketing*, *4*(September), 1–22. doi:10.1108/IJBM-04-2017-0077

Kuratko, D. F., & Hornsby, J. S. (1999). Corporate entrepreneurial leadership for the 21st century. *The Journal of Leadership Studies*, *5*(2), 27–39. doi:10.1177/107179199900500204

Kurniasari, F., Tajul Urus, S., Utomo, P., Abd Hamid, N., Jimmy, S. Y., & Othman, I. W. (2022). Determinant factors of adoption of Fintech Payment Services in Indonesia using the UTAUT approach. *Asian-Pacific Management Accounting Journal*, *17*(1), 97–125. doi:10.24191/APMAJ.V17i1-04

Kuziemsky, C., Hunter, I., Udayasankaran, J. G., Ranatunga, P., Kulatunga, G., John, S., . . . Basu, A. (2022). Telehealth as a Means of Enabling Health Equity. *Yearb Med Inform, 31*(1), 60-66. doi:10.1055/s-0042-1742500

Kyaw, E. N. (2022, June 3). *The revolution of Myanmar Fintech: Mobile payment applications.* Retrieved from https://www.myanmore.com/2022/06/the-future-of-myanmars-Fintech/

La Estrella De Panamá, G. -. (2023, December 1). *El futuro de las "fintech" en Panamá. La Estrella De Panamá.* https://www.laestrella.com.pa/cafe-estrella/tecnologia/230112/futuro-fintech-panama

Lagna, A., & Ravishankar, M. N. (2022). Making the world a better place with fintech research. *Information Systems Journal, 32*(1), 61–102. doi:10.1111/isj.12333

Laik, D. M. N., & Wei, C. M. H. (2019). *Creating a unique mobile financial services framework for Myanmar: A Review.* Retrieved from https://arxiv.org/ftp/arxiv/papers/1910/1910.03793.pdf

Lainez, N. (2021, January 6). *Navigating Vietnam's Lending App Maze. Fulcrum - Analysis on Southeast Asia.* https://fulcrum.sg/navigating-vietnams-lending-app-maze

Lankton, N. K., & Mcknight, H. D. (2012). Examining Two Expectation Disconfirmation Theory Models : Assimilation and Asymmetry Effects Models : Assimilation and Asymmetry Effects. *Journal of the Association for Information Systems, 13*(2), 88–115. doi:10.17705/1jais.00285

LaoPay. (n.d.). *About us.* Retrieved from https://www.laopay.app/en/about-us

Latif, K. F., Afzal, O., Saqib, A., Sahibzada, U. F., & Alam, W. (2021). Direct and configurational paths of knowledge-oriented leadership, entrepreneurial orientation, and knowledge management processes to project success. *Journal of Intellectual Capital, 22*(1), 149–170. doi:10.1108/JIC-09-2019-0228

Lau, T., & Leimer, B. (2019). The era of connectedness: How AI will help deliver the future of banking. *Journal of Digital Banking, 3*(3), 215–231.

Lee & Li. (2023). First-step analysis: FinTech regulation in Taiwan. *Lexology.* https://www.trade.gov/market-intelligence/taiwan-FinTech-market

Leesa-nguansuk, S. (2023, August 1). *Thailand feels the force of cyber-attacks.* Bangkok Post. Retrieved from https://www.bangkokpost.com/business/general/2621385/thailand-feels-the-force-of-cyber-attacks

Legal500. (2023). *Turkey: Data Protection & Cybersecurity.* Retrieved from https://www.legal500.com/guides/chapter/turkey-data-protection-cybersecurity/

Legal500. (2023). *Turkey: Lending & Secured Finance.* Retrieved from https://www.legal500.com/guides/chapter/turkey-lending-secured-finance/

Le, T. T., Mai, H. N., & Phan, D. T. (2021, April 24). Fintech Innovations. *The Impact of.*

Leung, R. (2023). *Leveraging AI and Blockchain for Streamlining Healthcare Payments.* Paper presented at the 2023 5th Blockchain and Internet of Things Conference. 10.1145/3625078.3625086

Levitin, A. J. (2012). The consumer financial protection bureau: An introduction. *Rev. Banking & Fin. L., 32*, 321.

Li, A., Sun, Y., Yang, X., & Guo, J. (2019). Exploring the Relationship between Perceived Ease of Use and Continuance Usage of a Mobile Terminal: Mobility as a Moderator. *Sustainability (Basel), 11*(1128), 1–15. doi:10.3390/su11041128

Li, B., & Xu, Z. (2021). Insights into financial technology (FinTech): A bibliometric and visual study. *Financial Innovation, 7*(1), 1–28. doi:10.1186/s40854-021-00285-7 PMID:35024290

Library (AISeL). (n.d.). https://aisel.aisnet.org/cgi/viewcontent.cgi?article=1038&context=iceb2016

Li, C., Khaliq, N., Chinove, L., Khaliq, U., & Oláh, J. (2023). Consumers' Perception of Risk Facets Associated With Fintech Use: Evidence From Pakistan. *SAGE Open*, *13*(4), 1–17. doi:10.1177/21582440231200199

Lien, N. T. K., Doan, T. T. T., & Bui, T. N. (2020, September 30). Fintech and Banking: Evidence from Vietnam. *The Journal of Asian Finance. Economics and Business*, *7*(9), 419–426. doi:10.13106/jafeb.2020.vol7.no9.419

Lightcastle Partners. (2021). *Fintech Trends in Qatar*. https://www.lightcastlebd.com/insights/2021/11/24/fintech-trends-in-qatar

Lim, X., Cheah, J.-H., Ng, S. I., Kamal Basha, N., & Liu, Y. (2021). Are men from mars, women from venus? examining gender differences towards continuous use intention of branded apps. *Journal of Retailing and Consumer Services*, *60*, 102422. Advance online publication. doi:10.1016/j.jretconser.2020.102422

Lin, L., & Chen, C. (2020, March). The promise and perils of InsurTech. *Singapore Journal of Legal Studies*, 115-142.

Linh, D. H. (2022, April 18). P2P Lending's Credit Risk in Vietnam: Determinants and Discussions. *Journal of Economics. Finance and Management Studies*, *5*(4). Advance online publication. doi:10.47191/jefms/v5-i4-18

LinkAja. (n.d.). *About LinkAja*. Retrieved from https://www.linkaja.id/about-us

Linklaters. (2023, August 10). *Data protected - Turkey*. Retrieved from https://www.linklaters.com/en/insights/data-protected/data-protected---turkey

Liu, G., & Tai, P. T. (2016). A Study of Factors Affecting the Intention to Use Mobile Payment Services in Vietnam. *Economics World*, *4*(6), 249–273. doi:10.17265/2328-7144/2016.06.001

Liu, X., & Nie, W. (2022). Study on the coupling coordination mechanism of green technology innovation, environmental regulation, and green finance. *Environmental Science and Pollution Research International*, *29*(47), 71796–71809. doi:10.1007/s11356-022-20905-8 PMID:35599286

Li, Z., Zhong, R. Y., Tian, Z.-G., Dai, H.-N., Barenji, A. V., & Huang, G. Q. (2021). Industrial Blockchain: A state-of-the-art Survey. *Robotics and Computer-integrated Manufacturing*, *70*, 102124. doi:10.1016/j.rcim.2021.102124

Loca. (n.d.) *Loca Pay*. Retrieved from https://loca.la/locapay/

Long, T. Q. (2023, June 11). *Financial literacy, behavioral traits, and ePayment adoption and usage in Japan*. Financial Innovation. https://jfin-swufe.springeropen.com/articles/10.1186/s40854-023-00504-3

Loo, M. K. L. (2019). Enhancing financial inclusion in ASEAN: Identifying the best growth markets for Fintech. *Journal of Risk and Financial Management*, *12*(4), 181. doi:10.3390/jrfm12040181

Lowrey, T. (2020). *Sustainability*. Formula One World Championship Limited. https://corp.formula1.com/corporate-responsibility/sustainability/

Lowry, P. B., Gaskin, J. E., & Moody, G. D. (2015). Proposing the multimotive information systems continuance model (MISC) to better explain end-user system evaluations and continuance intentions. *Journal of the Association for Information Systems*, *16*(7), 515–579. doi:10.17705/1jais.00403

Lukonga, I. (2021). Fintech and the real economy: Lessons from the Middle East, North Africa, Afghanistan, and Pakistan (MENAP) region. The Palgrave handbook of fintech and blockchain, 187-214.

Lwin, N., Ameen, A., & Nusari, M. (2019). Mobile Banking Adoption among Customers within Private Commercial Banking Sector in Yangon, Myanmar. *International Journal of Management and Human Science*, *3*(2), 44–59.

Mad. (2022). *The Landscape of Digital Banking in Cambodia*. Retrieved from https://www.mad.co/insights/the-landscape-of-digital-banking-in-cambodia

Maddukuri, S., Patel, J., & Lipoff, J. B. (2021). Teledermatology addressing disparities in health care access: A review. *Current Dermatology Reports*, *10*(2), 40–47. doi:10.1007/s13671-021-00329-2 PMID:33747638

Magnitt. (2022). *UAE H1 2022 Venture Investment Report*. magnitt.com.

Mahalakshmi, V., Kulkarni, N., Kumar, K. P., Kumar, K. S., Sree, D. N., & Durga, S. (2022). The Role of implementing Artificial Intelligence and Machine Learning Technologies in the financial services Industry for creating Competitive Intelligence. *Materials Today: Proceedings*, *56*, 2252–2255. doi:10.1016/j.matpr.2021.11.577

Mahapatra, J. (n.d.). *South Korea - The Fintech Growth Story*. https://www.linkedin.com/pulse/south-korea-FinTech-growth-story-jagdish-mahapatra/

Maher, M., Khan, I., & Prikshat, V. (2023). Monetisation of digital health data through a GDPR-compliant and blockchain enabled digital health data marketplace: A proposal to enhance patient's engagement with health data repositories. *International Journal of Information Management Data Insights*, *3*(1), 100159. doi:10.1016/j.jjimei.2023.100159

Mahmud, K., Joarder, M. M. A., & Sakib, K. M. U. (2022). Adoption factors of FinTech: Evidence from an emerging economy country-wide representative sample. *International Journal of Financial Studies*, *11*(1), 9. doi:10.3390/ijfs11010009

Makhija, A. K. (2019). *Accelerating Financial Inclusion in Cambodia Using Artificial Intelligence & Machine Learning*. Retrieved from https://ebook.cam-ed.com/public/images/sarana_file/1627893780.pdf

Malaa. (2023). *Malaa: Your Gateway to Smart Investing*. Retrieved from https://play.google.com/store/apps/details?id=tech.malaa.personal&hl=en_US

Malaai. (2023). *Meet Malaai: Your Personal Islamic Robo-Advisor*. https://www.malaai.com/

Malaysian Communications and Multimedia Commission. (2022, August 25). *Population coverage of 4G LTE mobile network in Malaysia from 2016 to 2021* [Graph]. Statista. Retrieved August 12, 2023, from https://www.statista.com/statistics/1051191/malaysia-4g-lte-population-coverage/

Malyshev. (2021 Oct 25) Regulatory quality and competition policy in Korea. *OECD*. https://www.oecd.org/country/korea/thematic-focus/regulatory-quality-and-competition-policy-in-korea-e5b4137d/

Mandal, A., Dutta, S., & Pramanik, S. (2021). Machine Intelligence of Pi from Geometrical Figures with Variable Parameters using SCILab. In D. Samanta, R. R. Althar, S. Pramanik, & S. Dutta (Eds.), *Methodologies and Applications of Computational Statistics for Machine Learning* (pp. 38–63). IGI Global. doi:10.4018/978-1-7998-7701-1.ch003

MandaV.PolisettyA. (2018). Status Check on Blockchain Implementations in India. doi:10.2139/ssrn.3265654

Manila Bulletin. (2023, July 12). *Fueling the country's digital shift with the 'real 5G'*. Retrieved from https://mb.com.ph/2023/7/12/fueling-the-country-s-digital-shift-with-the-real-5-g

Ma, Q., Sun, D., Tan, Z., Li, C., He, X., Zhai, Y., Wang, L., Cui, F., Li, M., Gao, J., Wang, L., & Zhao, J. (2022). Usage and perceptions of telemedicine among health care professionals in China. *International Journal of Medical Informatics*, *166*, 104856. doi:10.1016/j.ijmedinf.2022.104856 PMID:36037593

MarCoPay. (n.d.). *About us*. Retrieved from https://www.marcopayinc.com/AboutUs

Marek, S. (2020, April). *Myanmar - Mobile Network Experience Report*. Retrieved from https://www.opensignal.com/reports/2020/04/myanmar/mobile-network-experience

Market Report. (2021, December 31). *Vietnam Fintech Report In 2021: Viet Nam*. Retrieved from https://marketreport.io/Fintech-vietnam-report

Marqués, J. M., Ávila, F., Rodríguez-Martínez, A., Morales-Reséndiz, R., Marcos, A., Godoy, T., Villalobos, P., Ocontrillo, A., Lankester, V. A., Blanco, C., Reyes, K., Lopez, S. I., Fernández, A., Santos, R., Maza, L. Á., Sánchez, M., Domínguez, C., Haynes, N., Panton, N., ... Francis-Pantor, M. (2021). Policy report on FinTech data gaps. *Latin American Journal of Central Banking*, *2*(3), 100037. doi:10.1016/j.latcb.2021.100037

Marry, K., Nguonly, T., Makararavy, T., & Leakhena, C. (2020). *Financial Technology Landscape in the Kingdom of Cambodia*. Technical Report. Retrieved from https://digitaleconomy.gov.kh/public/images/mediahub/Fintech_Landscape_Report_in_Cambodia_Final_Submission.pdf

Martina, M. (2022). *Fintech and Financial Inclusion for MSMEs in Lao PDR* (Doctoral dissertation, School of Public Policy, The University of Tokyo). Retrieved from https://www.pp.u-tokyo.ac.jp/wp-content/uploads/2016/02/R8_Marsili-Martina.pdf

Martin-Bariteau, F., & Scassa, T. (2021). *Artificial intelligence and the law in Canada. Artificial Intelligence and the Law in Canada*. LexisNexis Canada.

Marx, E. W., & Padmanabhan, P. (2020). *Healthcare digital transformation: How consumerism, technology and pandemic are accelerating the future*. CRC Press. doi:10.4324/9781003035695

Masocha, R. (2018). Adoption of Mobile Money Services and the Performance of Small and Medium. *Academy of Accounting and Financial Studies Journal*, *22*(3), 1–11.

Mason, R. (2022, July 14). *Philippines' digital transformation could make it a new crypto hub. Cointelegraph*. Retrieved from https://cointelegraph.com/news/philippines-digital-transformation-could-make-it-a-new-crypto-hub

Mason, A., Lee, R., & Network, N. T. A. (2022). Six ways population change will affect the global economy. *Population and Development Review*, *48*(1), 51–73. doi:10.1111/padr.12469

Mastercard. (2022). *In Qatar, Mastercard joins hands with Doha Bank to advance digital payment infrastructure*. Retrieved from https://newsroom.mastercard.com/middle-east-africa/press-releases/in-qatar-mastercard-joins-hands-with-doha-bank-to-advance-digital-payment-infrastructure/

Maya. (n.d.). *About us*. Retrieved from https://www.maya.ph/about

Mazrekaj, E., Dehghantanha, A., Dargahi, T., & Choo, K. K. R. (2023). How Regulatory Sandboxes Enabled Fintech Innovation in Qatar. *Computer Law & Security Review*.

Mazrekaj, E., Dehghantanha, A., Parizi, R. M., & Choo, K. K. R. (2021). Adoption of fintech by women entrepreneurs in Qatar. *Entrepreneurship and Sustainability*, *8*(2), 525–546.

Mazreku, I., Mori, N., Mahmood, T., Cristiana, J., & Ventura, S. (2022). FinTech Use and Financial Inclusion in Qatar. *Economies*, *10*(2), 68.

Mbawuni, J., & Joshi, M. P. (2023). Economic impact of fintech sector development in Qatar: An integrated input–output approach. *Technology in Society*, *67*, 101800.

Mbawuni, J., & Nilashi, M. (2023). Challenges for sustainable fintech growth in Qatar: Implications for policymakers and practitioners. *Technology in Society*, *67*, 101990.

McKinsey & Company. (2021). *The Future of FinTech in Saudi Arabia*. Author.

McKinsey & Company. (2023). *Fintech in the Middle East: The Next Frontier*. Author.

McKinsey & Company. (2023). *The Future of Work in Turkey*. https://www.mckinsey.com/featured-insights/future-of-work/the-future-of-work-in-turkey

Medina, A. (2023, July 25). *Indonesia Launches World's First State-Backed Cryptocurrency Bourse*. ASEAN Briefing. Retrieved from https://www.aseanbriefing.com/news/indonesia-launches-worlds-first-state-backed-cryptocurrency-bourse/

Medina, A. F. (2023, August 17). *Laos Launches Digital Currency Trial*. ASEAN Briefing. Retrieved from https://www.aseanbriefing.com/news/laos-launches-digital-currency-trial/

Mehdi, B. A. (2021). Cryptoassets in Qatar: Evolution and prospects. *International Journal of Ethics and Systems*.

Mehdi, B. A. (2021). *How Qatar punches above its weight in fintech startups*. The Conversation. https://theconversation.com/how-qatar-punches-above-its-weight-in-fintech-startups-168088

Mehdi, B.A. & Kamal, S.M. (2022). *Cryptocurrency Regulation in Qatar: Promises and Challenges*. Academic Press.

Melhim, S., & Ahmad, A. (2021). Cryptocurrency regulation in the GCC countries: Focus on Saudi Arabia. *The Journal of International Trade & Economic Development*, 1–25.

MENA Fintech Association. (2022). *BitOasis receives in-principle approvals as a fully regulated Virtual Asset Service Provider from two of the largest financial centres in the world*. https://menafintech.org/bitoasis-receives-in-principle-approvals-as-a-fully-regulated-virtual-asset-service-provider-from-two-of-the-largest-financial-centres-in-the-world/

Mention, A.-L. (2019). The future of fintech. *Research Technology Management*, *62*(4), 59–63. doi:10.1080/08956308.2019.1613123

Meta Platforms, Inc, and Bain & Company, Inc. (2022, September). *Southeast Asia's digital consumers: A new stage of evolution*. Retrieved September 17, 2022, from https://www.edb.gov.sg/en/business-insights/market-and-industry-reports/southeast-asias-digital-consumers-a-new-stage-evolution.html

Metain. (n.d.). *What is Metain*. Metain Co-investment platform. https://metain.io/

Mhlanga, D. (2023). Financial Technology, Artificial Intelligence, and the Health Sector, Lessons We Are Learning on Good Health and Well-Being. In *FinTech and Artificial Intelligence for Sustainable Development: The Role of Smart Technologies in Achieving Development Goals* (pp. 145–170). Springer. doi:10.1007/978-3-031-37776-1_7

Mikhaylov, A., Dinçer, H., & Yüksel, S. (2023). Analysis of financial development and open innovation oriented FinTech potential for emerging economies using an integrated decision-making approach of MF-X-DMA and golden cut bipolar q-ROFSs. *Financial Innovation*, *9*(1), 1–34. doi:10.1186/s40854-022-00399-6

Milken Institute. (2019). *The Rise of FinTech in the Middle East*. Retrieved from https://milkeninstitute.org

Miller, C. (2022). The Chips That Make Taiwan the Center of the World. *TIME*. https://time.com/6219318/tsmc-taiwan-the-center-of-the-world/

Miller, T. (2016). Greenwashed sports and environmental activism: Formula 1 and FIFA. *Environmental Communication*, *10*(6), 719–733. doi:10.1080/17524032.2015.1127850

Milne, A., & Parboteeah, P. (2016). *The business models and economics of peer-to-peer lending*. Academic Press.

Minh, P. (2023, June 17). *Lending money through the app is flourishing, but the risk of "falling into a trap" of black credit*. Vietnam Economic Association. Retrieved from:https://vneconomy.vn/cho-vay-tien-qua-app-no-ro-nguy-co-sap-bay-tin-dung-den.htm

Ministry of Development Planning and Statistics (MDPS). (2022). *Labor Force Sample Survey*. Retrieved from https://www.mdps.gov.qa/en/statistics/Statistical%20Releases/Social/LaborForce/2022/Statical_analysis_labor_force_2022_En.pdf

Ministry of Finance Saudi Arabia. (2023). *Government Initiatives*. Retrieved from https://www.mof.gov.sa/en/

Ministry of Industry and Trade (Vietnam). (2022, December 26). *E-commerce market value in Vietnam from 2014 to 2022 (in billion U.S. dollars)* [Graph]. Statista. Retrieved October 14, 2023, from https://www.statista.com/statistics/986043/vietnam-ecommerce-market-value-revenue/

Mobile Banking Apps on Bank Performance in Vietnam. (n.d.). *International Journal of Research and Review, 8*(4), 391–401. doi:10.52403/ijrr.20210446

Modgil, S., Dwivedi, Y. K., Rana, N. P., Gupta, S., & Kamble, S. (2022). Has Covid-19 accelerated opportunities for digital entrepreneurship? An Indian perspective. *Technological Forecasting and Social Change*, *175*, 121415. doi:10.1016/j.techfore.2021.121415 PMID:36536802

Moenjak, T., Kongprajya, A., & Monchaitrakul, C. (2020). *Fintech, financial literacy, and consumer saving and borrowing: The case of Thailand (No. 1100)*. ADBI Working Paper Series.

Mohamed, H. Y., Hamdan, A., Karolak, M., Razzaque, A., & Alareeni, B. (2021). FinTech in Bahrain: The role of FinTech in empowering women. In The Importance of New Technologies and Entrepreneurship in Business Development: In The Context of Economic Diversity in Developing Countries: The Impact of New Technologies and Entrepreneurship on Business Development (pp. 757-766). Springer International Publishing. doi:10.1007/978-3-030-69221-6_57

MoneyMatch. (n.d.). *About us*. Retrieved from https://moneymatch.com.bn/about-us

Mongolia GDP. (n.d.). Worldometer. https://www.worldometers.info/gdp/mongolia-gdp/#:~:text=GDP%20Growth%20Rate%20in%202022,3.3%25%20in%20GDP%20per%20capita

Mongolian FinTech Association. (2023, May 11). *Fintech statistics*. www.mongoliaFinTech.org. https://www.mongoliaFinTech.org/52/bitem

Monix. (n.d.). *About us*. Retrieved from https://www.monix.co.th/about-us

Monteiro, L. (2023, February 15). *3 FinTech companies in Japan to watch out for in 2023*. IBS Intelligence. https://ibsintelligence.com/ibsi-news/3-FinTech-companies-in-japan-to-watch-out-for-in-2023/

Moore, J. F. (1996). *The Death of Competition: Leadership and Strategy in the Age of Business Ecosystems*. HarperBusiness.

Mordor Intelligence. (n.d.). China Fintech Market Size. *Mordor Intelligence Industry Reports*. https://www.mordorintelligence.com/industry-reports/china-FinTech-market/market-sieç

MorganP. L.TrinhL. Q. (2019). Fintech and Financial Literacy in the LAO PDR. *Social Science Research Network*. doi:10.2139/ssrn.3398235

Mougayar, W. (2016). *The business blockchain: promise, practice, and application of the next Internet technology*. John Wiley & Sons.

Mourao, P. R. (2018). Smoking Gentlemen—How Formula One Has Controlled CO2 Emissions. *Sustainability (Basel)*, *10*(6), 1841. doi:10.3390/su10061841

Næss, H. E. (2019). Investment Ethics and the Global Economy of Sports: The Norwegian Oil Fund, Formula 1 and the 2014 Russian Grand Prix. *Journal of Business Ethics*, *158*(2), 535–546. doi:10.1007/s10551-017-3751-8

Nagaraji, S., & Gardeaszabal Monsalue, A. (2023). *Digital ecosystem in Guatemala*. Intl Food Policy Res Inst.

Nair, K. (2023, June 7). *Fahmi: Malaysia's 5G coverage now at 62.1%.* The Star. Retrieved from https://www.thestar.com.my/business/business-news/2023/06/07/fahmi-malaysias-5g-coverage-now-at-621

NamY.LeeS. T. (2022). Behind the growth of FinTech in South Korea: Digital divide in the use of digital financial services. *Social Science Research Network*. doi:10.2139/ssrn.4295694

Nathan, R. J., Setiawan, B., & Quynh, M. N. (2022, March 06). Vietnam during the COVID-19 Pandemic: In-Depth Descriptive Analysis. *Journal of Risk and Financial Management*, *15*(3), 125. doi:10.3390/jrfm15030125

National Cyber Security Agency. (2023, April 20). *Number of cyber threats detected and settled by ThaiCERT in Thailand in 2022, by type of threat* [Graph]. Statista. Retrieved August 26, 2023, from https://www.statista.com/statistics/1154735/thailand-number-of-cyber-threats-by-type-of-threat/

National Cybersecurity Authority (NCA). (2017). *Cybersecurity Law*. Retrieved from: https://www.pwc.com/m1/en/services/consulting/technology/cyber-security/cybersecurity-compliance-handbook-kingdom-of-saudi-arabia.html

National Cybersecurity Authority (NCA). (2023). *Cybersecurity Awareness*. Retrieved from: https://nca.gov.sa/en

National Cybersecurity Authority (NCA). (2023). *Cybersecurity Law*. Retrieved from: https://www.pwc.com/m1/en/services/consulting/technology/cyber-security/cybersecurity-compliance-handbook-kingdom-of-saudi-arabia.html

Naz, F., Karim, S., Houcine, A., & Naeem, M. A. (2022). FinTech growth during COVID-19 in MENA region: Current challenges and future prospects. *Electronic Commerce Research*, 1–22. doi:10.1007/s10660-022-09583-3

Neobanks.app. (2023). *Neobanks in Turkey*. https://neobanks.app/neobanks/turkey

Netsmart. (n.d.). *Netsmart: Information Security Solutions*. Retrieved from https://www.netsmart.com.tr/?utm_source=Tech-Behemoths&utm_medium=Profile&utm_campaign=viewprofile

Newswire, P. R. (2023, March 16). *MINESEC empowers Mongol ID as Mongolia's pioneering FinTech with softpos launch*. https://www.prnewswire.com/apac/news-releases/minesec-empowers-mongol-id-as-mongolias-pioneering-FinTech-with-softpos-launch-301771327.html

nfcw.com. (2022, October 28). *Turkey to Integrate Digital Currency with National Digital Identity System.* Retrieved from https://www.nfcw.com/2022/10/28/380006/turkey-to-integrate-digital-currency-with-national-digital-identity-system/

Ng Pilipinas, B. S. (2020). *BSP digital payments transformation roadmap 2020-2023*. Retrieved from https://www.bsp.gov.ph/Media_And_Research/Primers%20Faqs/Digital%20Payments%20Transformation%20Roadmap%20Report.pdf

Ngoc, M. (2023, April 7). *MoMo and ZaloPay are leading the market for digital wallets*. Financial & Monetary Market Review. https://thitruongtaichinhtiente.vn/momo-va-zalopay-dan-dau-thi-truong-vi-dien-tu-trong-nuoc-45105.html

Nicoletti, B., & Nicoletti, B. (2021). Platforms for insurance 4.0. *Insurance 4.0: Benefits and Challenges of Digital Transformation*, 173-259.

Nicoletti, B. (2017). *The Future of Fintech: Integrating Finance and Technology in Financial Services*. Palgrave Macmillan. doi:10.1007/978-3-319-51415-4

Norton Rose Fulbright. (2021). *Turkey's Digital Services Tax Developments: USTR Report and Pillar One*. https://www.nortonrosefulbright.com/en/inside-turkey/blog/2021/03/turkeys-digital-services-tax-developments-ustr-report-and-pillar-one

Norton Rose Fulbright. (2023). *Fintech in Turkey: An Overview*. https://www.nortonrosefulbright.com/en/knowledge/publications/86be2daf/fintech-in-turkey-overview

NUGPay. (n.d.). *About.* Retrieved from https://nugpay.app/

Nugraha, D. P., Setiawan, B., Nathan, R. J., & Fekete-Farkas, M. (2022). Fintech adoption drivers for innovation for SMEs in Indonesia. *Journal of Open Innovation*, *8*(4), 208. doi:10.3390/joitmc8040208

Nurlatifah, H., Saefuddin, A., Nanere, M., & Ratten, V. (2022). Muslimpreneur: Entrepreneur potential characteristics in Indonesia as the country with the largest Muslim population in the world. *Entrepreneurial Innovation: Strategy and Competition Aspects*, 129-139.

Nurunnabi, M. (2017). Transformation from an oil-based economy to a knowledge-based economy in Saudi Arabia: The direction of Saudi vision 2030. *Journal of the Knowledge Economy*, *8*(2), 536–564. doi:10.1007/s13132-017-0479-8

O'Hanlon, J. (2020, May 18). *FINOLAB: driving innovative startups in FinTech.* FinTech Magazine. https://FinTechmagazine.com/company-reports/finolab-driving-innovative-startups-FinTech

Oi, R. (2023, February 21). *Digital Banks Could Be the Key to Promoting Financial Inclusion for Malaysia's B40.* Fintech Malaysia. Retrieved from https://Fintechnews.my/34216/financial-inclusion/digital-banks-could-be-the-key-to-promoting-financial-inclusion-for-malaysias-b40/

Ojekemi, O. S., Rjoub, H., Awosusi, A. A., & Agyekum, E. B. (2022). Toward a sustainable environment and economic growth in BRICS economies: Do innovation and globalization matter? *Environmental Science and Pollution Research International*, *29*(38), 57740–57757. doi:10.1007/s11356-022-19742-6 PMID:35352228

Omarini, A. (2023). From Digital Technologies to New Economics in Banking: How to Drive the Future of Digital Money and Data Information Knowledge. In Digital Transformation and the Economics of Banking (pp. 31-49). Routledge.

Omolade, A. O. (2017). Predictors of Use of Mobile Applications by University Students in Oyo. *Journal of Information Science. Systems and Technology*, *1*(1), 34–47.

Ooredoo. (2021). *Ooredoo brings 5G to 95% of Qatar's population.* Retrieved from https://www.ooredoo.qa/portal/OoredooQatar/5g-population-coverage

OpenGov Asia. (n.d.). https://opengovasia.com/expediting-4g-coverage-for-socio-economic-growth-in-indonesia/

Orpheus Capital. (n.d.). *About us.* Retrieved from https://orpheuscapital.com.my/en/about-us/

Osetskyi, V., Vitrenko, A., Tatomyr, I., Bilan, S., & Hirnyk, Y. (2020). Artificial intelligence application in education: Financial implications and prospects. *Financial and Credit Activity Problems of Theory and Practice,* *2*(33), 574-584.

Oxford Business Group. (2020, September 23). *Covid-19 and Fintech: Myanmar's chance to expand financial inclusion?* Retrieved from https://oxfordbusinessgroup.com/articles-interviews/covid-19-and-Fintech-myanmars-chance-to-expand-financial-inclusion

Oxford Business Group. (2021). *Forecasted contribution of artificial intelligence to gross domestic product in the Middle East and North Africa region in 2030, by industry* [Graph]. Statista. Retrieved November 18, 2023, from https://0-www-statista-com.biblioteca-ils.tec.mx/statistics/1272197/mena-ai-contribution-to-gdp-by-industry

Oxford Business Group. (2022). *Fintech poised for faster growth in Qatar on regulation evolution.* Retrieved from https://oxfordbusinessgroup.com/news/fintech-poised-faster-growth-qatar-regulation-evolution

Oxford Business Group. (2023). *Increased mobile and internet penetration supports Qatar's digital ambitions.* Retrieved from https://oxfordbusinessgroup.com/analysis/increased-mobile-and-internet-penetration-supports-qatar's-digital-ambitions

Özdemir, H. (2023). Cybersecurity in Turkey: Challenges and opportunities. In The Routledge Handbook of Turkish Cyberspace (pp. 153-172). Routledge.

Paggo App | Crece tu negocio. (n.d.). https://www.paggoapp.com/

Pal, A., Herath, T., De', R., & Raghav Rao, H. (2021). Why do people use mobile payment technologies and why would they continue? An examination and implications from india. *Research Policy*, *50*(6), 104228. Advance online publication. doi:10.1016/j.respol.2021.104228

Pan, M., & Gao, W. (2021). Determinants of the behavioral intention to use a mobile nursing application by nurses in china. *BMC Health Services Research*, *21*(1), 228. Advance online publication. doi:10.1186/s12913-021-06244-3 PMID:33712012

Park, A. J. (2023, August 31). Korea Fintech Week 2023 brings financial giants and startups together. *Koreatimes*. https://www.koreatimes.co.kr/www/biz/2023/08/126_358142.html

Paulet, E., & Relano, F. (2023). Fintech seen through a sustainability lens: Transformative potential and actual achievements. *Management International / International Management / Gestiòn Internacional, 27*(1), 131–140. https://doi-org.ezproxy.myucwest.ca/10.7202/1098927ar

Pawłowska, M., Staniszewska, A., & Grzelak, M. (2022). Impact of FinTech on Sustainable Development. *Financial Sciences / Nauki o Finansach, 27*(2), 49–66. https://doi-org.ezproxy.myucwest.ca/10.15611/fins.2022.2.05

Paxful. (n.d.). *Buy Bitcoin in Saudi Arabia – Secure & Fast*. Retrieved from https://paxful.com/buy/bitcoin/saudi-arabia

Pay, S. T. C. (2023). *Corporate Profile*. Retrieved from https://stcpay.com.qa/about

Pay.com. (2023). *Top payment methods in Turkey*. Retrieved from https://pay.com/blog/top-payment-methods-in-turkey

Payd. (n.d.). *Empowering Everyday People*. Retrieved from https://www.justpayd.com/about

Payfort. (2023). *Online Payment Gateway and Fraud Prevention Solution*. Retrieved from https://www.payfort.com/

PayK. B. Z. (n.d.). *About us*. Retrieved from https://www.kbzpay.com/en/about/

Payments, S. (2021, May 12). *Saudi Instant Payment System (Sarie)*. Retrieved from https://www.saudipayments.com/

Payments, S. (2022, November 7). *e-Payment Channels in the Kingdom of Saudi Arabia*. Retrieved from https://www.saudipayments.com/

PaymentsS. (2023, March 16). *Home Page*. Retrieved from https://www.saudipayments.com/

PayPal. (2023). *Bringing Secure Digital Payments to Qatar*. Retrieved from https://www.pymnts.com/news/international/2022/paypal-launches-services-in-qatar/

Payverse. (2023). *A look at Brunei and Timor's major ewallets*. Retrieved from https://blogeromnet.com/brunei-and-timor-ewallets/?ckattempt=1

PayWatch. (n.d.). *About us*. Retrieved from https://www.paywatch.com.my/about-us

PayWay. (n.d.). *About us*. Retrieved from https://www.payway.com.kh/about-us

Pease, W., & Rowe, M. (2005). An overview of information technology in the tourism industry. *Conference Proceedings-ICT Networks-Building Blocks for Economic Development*, 1–13. Retrieved from https://eprints.usq.edu.au/245

Peddlr. (n.d.). *About the product*. Retrieved from https://www.peddlr.io/en/faqs

Pei, S. F. (2018). Singapore approach to develop and regulate Fintech. In T. T. Kuo (Ed.), *R. H.*

Perlman, L. (2017). *Technology inequality: Opportunities and challenges for mobile financial services.* Retrieved July 10, 2021, http://www.ruralfinanceandinvestment.org/sites/default/files/CFI_MFS_Tech_FINAL.pdf

PerlmanL.GurungN.TrujilloV. (2021). Regulatory Technology ("RegTech") Readiness in Honduras. Available at SSRN 3887874.

Perols, J. (2011). Financial statement fraud detection: An analysis of statistical and machine learning algorithms. *Auditing*, *30*(2), 19–50. doi:10.2308/ajpt-50009

Perols, J. L., Bowen, R. M., Zimmermann, C., & Samba, B. (2017). Finding needles in a haystack: Using data analytics to improve fraud prediction. *The Accounting Review*, *92*(2), 221–245. doi:10.2308/accr-51562

Personal Information Protection Commission Japan. (n.d.). *Roles and Responsibilities*. Roles and Responsibilities |PPC Personal Information Protection Commission, Japan. https://www.ppc.go.jp/en/aboutus/roles/

Petróczy, D. G., & Csató, L. (2021). Revenue allocation in Formula One: A pairwise comparison approach. *International Journal of General Systems*, *50*(3), 243–261. doi:10.1080/03081079.2020.1870224

Philippon, T. (2016). *The fintech opportunity. No. w22476*. National Bureau of Economic Research. doi:10.3386/w22476

Philstar Global. (2023, August 10). *Maya dominates digital banking*. Retrieved from https://www.philstar.com/business/2023/08/10/2287452/maya-dominates-digital-banking

Pi Pay. (n.d.). *Who we are*. Retrieved from https://www.pipay.com/#who-we-are

Pillay, T. (2018). *The influence of insurance on the existing insurance business model.* University of Pretoria.

Pitchbook. (2023). *Lend & Borrow (Taiwan) overview*. Pitchbook. https://pitchbook.com/profiles/company/266998-15#overview

Pluang. (n.d.). *About us*. Retrieved from https://pluang.com/id/tentang-pluang

Postigo, A. (2023). *Governing the Digital Economy in Thailand: Domestic Regulations and International Agreements (No. 58/2023)*. Perspective.

Pramanik, S., Sagayam, K. M., & Jena, O. P. (2021). Machine Learning Frameworks in Cancer Detection. ICCSRE 2021, Morocco. doi:10.1051/e3sconf/202129701073

Pramanik, H. S., Kirtania, M., & Pani, A. K. (2019). Essence of digital transformation—Manifestations at large financial institutions from North America. *Future Generation Computer Systems*, *95*, 323–343. doi:10.1016/j.future.2018.12.003

Pramanik, P. K. D., Pareek, G., & Nayyar, A. (2019). Security and Privacy in Remote Healthcare: Issues, Solutions, and Standards. In H. D. Jude & V. E. Balas (Eds.), *Telemedicine Technologies* (pp. 201–225). Academic Press. doi:10.1016/B978-0-12-816948-3.00014-3

Pramanik, S., & Bandyopadhyay, S. (2023). Identifying Disease and Diagnosis in Females using Machine Learning. In I. G. I. John Wang (Ed.), *Encyclopedia of Data Science and Machine Learning*. Global. doi:10.4018/978-1-7998-9220-5.ch187

Pramanik, S., Galety, M. G., Samanta, D., & Joseph, N. P. (2022). Data Mining Approaches for Decision Support Systems, *3rd International Conference on Emerging Technologies in Data Mining and Information Security*. 10.1007/s11042-023-16762-3,2023

Praveenkumar, S., Veeraiah, V., Pramanik, S., Basha, S. M., Lira Neto, A. V., De Albuquerque, V. H. C., & Gupta, A. (2023). *Prediction of Patients' Incurable Diseases Utilizing Deep Learning Approaches, ICICC*. Springer., doi:10.1007/978-981-99-3315-0_4

Presidency of the Republic of Türkiye Finance Office. (2023). *The State of FinTech Ecosystem in Türkiye*. Retrieved from https://www.invest.gov.tr/en/news/news-from-turkey/pages/the-state-of-fintech-ecosystem-in-turkiye.aspx

PricewaterhouseCoopers (PwC). (2023). *Doing Business in Saudi Arabia: Cybersecurity.* Retrieved from: https://taxsummaries.pwc.com/saudi-arabia

PricewaterhouseCoopers (PwC). (2023). *Doing Business in Saudi Arabia: Tax.* Retrieved from: https://taxsummaries.pwc.com/saudi-arabia

PricewaterhouseCoopers. (n.d.). *A comparison of cybersecurity regulations: China*. PwC. https://www.pwc.com/id/en/pwc-publications/services-publications/legal-publications/a-comparison-of-cybersecurity-regulations/china.html#:~:text=China%20is%20increasingly%20emphasising%20government,for%20cybersecurity%20and%20data%20protection.pymnts

PricewaterhouseCoopers. (n.d.). *Tech start-up funding trends and outlook: Singapore*. PwC. https://www.pwc.com/sg/en/financial-services/venture-hub/tech-startup-funding-trends-and-outlook.html

Privacy Shield Framework. (n.d.). *Cambodia - e-commerce*. Retrieved from https://www.privacyshield.gov/ps/article?id=Cambodia-eCommerce

Priyaranjan, N., Roy, M., & Dhal, S. (2020). Distributed Ledger Technology, Blockchain and Central Banks. *RBI Bulletin.* Available at https://rbidocs.rbi.org.in/rdocs/Bulletin/PDFs/03AR_11022020510886F328EB418FB8013FBB684BB5BC.PDF

PSA (Philippines). (2022, December 2). *Total number of overseas Filipino workers (OFWs) from 2017 to 2021 (in 1,000s)* [Graph]. Statista. Retrieved September 02, 2023, from https://www.statista.com/statistics/1287067/philippines-number-of-overseas-filipino-workers/PwC

Puig, S. (2019). *The United States-Mexico-Canada Agreement: a glimpse into the geoeconomic world order*. Academic Press.

Purani, K., Kumar, D. S., & Sahadev, S. (2019). E-loyalty among millennials: Personal characteristics and social influences. *Journal of Retailing and Consumer Services*, *48*, 215–223. doi:10.1016/j.jretconser.2019.02.006

Puriwat, W., & Tripopsakul, S. (2017). Mobile Banking Adoption in Thailand : An Integration of Technology Acceptance Model and Mobile Service Quality. *European Research Studies*, *20*(4), 200–210. doi:10.35808/ersj/885

Putra, R. D., Mulyani, S., Poulus, S., & Sukmadilaga, C. (2022). Data quality analytics, business ethics, and cyber risk management on operational performance and fintech sustainability. *International Journal of Data and Network Science*, *6*(4), 1659–1668. doi:10.5267/j.ijdns.2022.4.008

PwC Türkiye. (n.d.). *Asset and Wealth Management*. Retrieved from https://www.pwc.com.tr/asset-and-wealth-management

PwC. (2018). *Forecasted contribution share of Artificial Intelligence to GDP in the Middle East and North Africa in 2030, by region* [Graph]. Statista. Retrieved November 18, 2023, from https://0-www-statista-com.biblioteca-ils.tec.mx/statistics/1181489/mena-forecasted-gdp-contribution-of-ai

PwC. (2021). *US$320 billion by 2030? The potential impact of AI in the Middle East*. Retrieved from https://www.pwc.com/m1/en/publications/potential-impact-artificial-intelligence-middle-east.html

PwC. (2022). *Neobank Licensing Sets Stage for Saudi FinTech Acceleration.* Retrieved from: https://www.pymnts.com/digital-first-banking/2022/neobank-licensing-sets-stage-for-saudi-fintech-acceleration/

PwC. (2022). *Unlocking the potential of Open Finance in Qatar*. https://www.pwc.com/m1/en/publications/documents/unlocking-potential-open-finance-qatar.pdf

PwC. (2023). *FinTech in Saudi Arabia: A Rising Force*. PwC.

PYMNTS.com. (2022, June 28). *Brand consolidation key amid proliferation of payment options in Turkey*. Retrieved from https://www.pymnts.com/news/payments-innovation/2022/brand-consolidation-key-amid-proliferation-of-payment-options-in-turkey/

Qatar Central Bank. (2022). *Qatar fast payment system marks a milestone in advancing state-of-the-art fintech infrastructure in Qatar*. Retrieved from https://www.qcb.gov.qa/English/MediaandNews/News/Pages/News557.aspx

Qatar Development Bank. (2023). *Finance Solutions*. Retrieved from https://www.qdb.qa/en/products-solutions/finance

Qatar Digital Government. (2020). *Qatar National Cybersecurity Strategy*. http://motc.gov.qa/sites/default/files/documents/ncs_english_v21.pdf

Qatar FinTech Hub. (2023). *Qatar FinTech Hub launches "Embedded FinTech" program to catalyze innovation in the financial services sector*. Retrieved from https://qatarfintechhub.com/embedded-fintech-catalyze-innovation/

Qatar Fintech Landscape. (2023). *QNB*. https://thefintechtimes.com/fintech-landscape-of-qatar-in-2022/

Qatar Free Zones. (2022). *Qatar at cutting edge of global fintech revolution*. https://qfz.gov.qa/English/MediaCenter/Pages/NewsDetails.aspx?NID=1047

Qatar Investment Authority. (2021). *Qatar's Commitment to Tech Start-ups Continues*. Retrieved from https://www.qia.qa/News/Qatar-commitment-to-tech-startups-continues

Qatar, S. (2023). *Fintech in Qatar*. Retrieved from https://www.startupq8.com/ecosystem/fintech/

QCB Fintech Initiative. (2023). *Qatar Central Bank*. http://www.qcb.gov.qa/English/strategicplan/Pages/FintechStrategy.aspx

QDB. (2023). *Qatar Fintech Report 2023*. Retrieved from https://www.qdb.qa/en/Documents/Fintech%20Report%20 2023.pdf

QFC Regulatory Authority. (2020). *QFC Fintech Regulations and Guidance*. https://www.qfcra.com/en/documents/Regulations-Guidance/QFC-Fintech-Regs-Guide.pdf

QFZA. (2021). *Qatar Free Zones Authority Offers 100% Foreign Ownership*. Retrieved from https://qfz.gov.qa/English/MediaCenter/Pages/NewsDetails.aspx?NID=453

Qing, T., & Haiying, D. (2021). How to achieve consumer continuance intention toward branded apps—From the consumer–brand engagement perspective. *Journal of Retailing and Consumer Services*, *60*, 102486. Advance online publication. doi:10.1016/j.jretconser.2021.102486

QNB. (2023). *Digital Wallet*. Retrieved from https://www.qnb.com/cs/sites/qnb/en/mobile-banking/digital-wallet.html

Q-Post. (2022). *New Postal Code System in Qatar*. Retrieved from https://www.qpost.qa/NewPostCodeSystemLaunchingSoon

Quang, D. P., Huu, T. K., & Manh, H. P. (2022). Fintech Development and Cooperation Strategies of Vietnamese Commercial Banks. *International Journal of Advanced Engineering and Management Research*, *07*(01), 53–65. doi:10.51505/IJAEMR.2022.7104

Quimba, F. M. A., Barral, M. A. A., & Carlos, J. C. T. (2021). *Analysis of the Fintech Landscape in the Philippines (No. 2021-29)*. PIDS Discussion Paper Series.

Qureshi, A. A. (2023). The role of payment gateways in facilitating e-commerce growth in Saudi Arabia. *International Journal of Electronic Business Management*, *21*(1), 1–12.

Rabaa'i, A. A. (2021). FinTech in Kuwait: A survey study. *International Journal of Business Information Systems*, *1*(1), 10042271. doi:10.1504/IJBIS.2021.10042271

Rabbani, M. R., Hassan, M. K., & Rashid, M. (2022). Introduction to Islamic FinTech: a challenge or an opportunity? In *FinTech in Islamic Financial Institutions: Scope, Challenges, and Implications in Islamic Finance* (pp. 1–27). Springer International Publishing. doi:10.1007/978-3-031-14941-2_1

Rabbit Line Pay. (n.d.). *About us*. Retrieved from https://pay.line.me/portal/th/main

Rain. (n.d.). *Buy & Sell Bitcoin, Ethereum & more in the Middle East*. Retrieved from https://www.rain.com/en-ae

Rakuten. (2023). *About Us*. Rakuten. https://global.rakuten.com/corp/about/company/FinTech.html

Ramadan, M. Z., Levchenko, A. A., & Hachicha, N. (2022). The Impact of FinTech on Economic Growth: Insights from MENA Countries. *Journal of Risk and Financial Management*, *15*(2), 72.

Ramzan, S., Aqdus, A., Ravi, V., Koundal, D., Amin, R., & Al Ghamdi, M. A. (2022). Healthcare applications using blockchain technology: Motivations and challenges. *IEEE Transactions on Engineering Management*.

Raposo, V. L. (2016). Telemedicine: The legal framework (or the lack of it) in Europe. *GMS Health Technology Assessment*, *12*, Doc03. doi:10.3205/hta000126 PMID:27579146

Razavi, H., Sarabadani, H., Karimisefat, A., & Lebraty, J. F. (2019, February). Profitability prediction for ATM transactions using artificial neural networks: A data-driven analysis. In *2019 5th Conference on Knowledge Based Engineering and Innovation (KBEI)* (pp. 661-665). IEEE.

Razavi, H., & Ghasemi, A. (2017). Multi-Objective Optimization of a QoS-Aware Channel Allocation in Cognitive Radio Networks using NSGA-II Algorithm. *Journal of Control*, *11*(1), 1–9.

Razavi, H., Jamali, M. R., Emsaki, M., Ahmadi, A., & Hajiaghei-Keshteli, M. (2023, September). Quantifying the Financial Impact of Cyber Security Attacks on Banks: A Big Data Analytics Approach. In *2023 IEEE Canadian Conference on Electrical and Computer Engineering (CCECE)* (pp. 533-538). IEEE. 10.1109/CCECE58730.2023.10288963

Razavi, H., Jamali, M. R., Emsaki, M., Gholian-Jouybari, F., Bonakdari, H., & Hajiaghaei-Keshteli, M. (2023, September). Statistical and Data Analytics Approaches to Parameter Tuning for Enhancing QoS of E-Banking Transactions: A Case Study of Sample Bank. In *2023 IEEE Canadian Conference on Electrical and Computer Engineering (CCECE)*. 10.1109/CCECE58730.2023.10288713

Razzaque, A., Cummings, R. T., Karolak, M., & Hamdan, A. (2020). The propensity to use FinTech: Input from bankers in the Kingdom of Bahrain. *Journal of Information & Knowledge Management*, *19*(01), 2040025. doi:10.1142/S0219649220400250

Realbox. (n.d.). *The future of real estate investment*. Realbox. https://realbox.io/en

Redahan, E. (2022, July 5). *Will Formula 1's drop-in fuel actually reduce carbon emissions?* SciBlog.org. https://www.soci.org/blog/2022/6/will-formula-1s-dropin-fuel-actually-reduce-carbon-emissions

Reed, J. (2022, January 20). *Thailand's Bitkub plans crypto expansion in SE Asia*. Financial Times. Retrieved from https://www.ft.com/content/0aa3acff-e6c2-4482-8761-991f76cee7f7

ReportB. C. G. (2022). Available at https://web-assets.bcg.com/e7/ab/51644cf944d686cd121d9c3f4bb4/future-of-fintech-july2022.pdf

Republic of Turkey Ministry of Treasury and Finance. (2023). *Türkiye Foreign Direct Investment Strategy 2021-2023.* Retrieved from https://www.invest.gov.tr/en/library/publications/Lists/InvestPublications/Turkiye-Foreign-Direct-Investment-Strategy-2021-2023.pdf

Reuters. (2022). *Qatar allows financial firms at regulated QFC centre to trade crypto assets.* Retrieved from https://www.reuters.com/technology/qatar-allows-financial-firms-regulated-qfc-centre-trade-crypto-assets-2022-10-03/

Reuters. (2023, May 16). *Indonesia's biggest Islamic bank says customer data safe amid reports of breach.* Finance. Retrieved from: https://www.reuters.com/business/finance/indonesias-biggest-islamic-bank-says-customer-data-safe-amid-reports-breach-2023-05-16/

Reyes, E. D. (1999). Regionalism: The Case of North America. In Economic Integration in NAFTA and the EU: Deficient Institutionality (pp. 161-177). Springer.

RHB. (n.d.). *Who we are*. Retrieved from: https://www.rhbgroup.com/others/about-us/who-we-are.html

Rock, D., & Sorkin, I. (2021). *Artificial Intelligence and the Future of Work: The Role of Corporate Social Responsibility.* National Bureau of Economic Research, Working Paper 29992.

Roy, S. (2017). App Adoption and Switching Behavior: Applying the Extended Tam in Smartphone App Usage. *Journal of Information Systems and Technology Management, 14*(2), 239–261. doi:10.4301/S1807-17752017000200006

Ruan, J., Wang, Y., Chan, F. T. S., Hu, X., Zhao, M., Zhu, F., Shi, B., Shi, Y., & Lin, F. (2019). A life cycle framework of green IoT-based agriculture and its finance, operation, and management issues. *IEEE Communications Magazine, 57*(3), 90–96. doi:10.1109/MCOM.2019.1800332

Rugman, A. M. (2004). *North American Economic and Financial Integration.* Emerald Group Publishing Limited. doi:10.1016/S1064-4857(2004)10

Ruslan, R. A. H. M., Ibrahim, M. A., & Abd Hamid, N. H. (2022). Application of artificial intelligence in FinTech: the decision of youth investors to use robo-advisor platform as micro-investing alternative. *Journal of Entrepreneurship, Business and Economics, 10*(2S2), 38-54.

Saba, I., Kouser, R., & Chaudhry, I. S. (2019). FinTech and Islamic finance-challenges and opportunities. *Review of Economics and Development Studies, 5*(4), 581–890. doi:10.26710/reads.v5i4.887

Saffa, A. (2023, June 13). *Expediting 4G coverage for Socio-Economic growth in Indonesia.* Academic Press.

Sakarya, Ş., & Aksu, M. (2021). *Fintech ecosystem in Turkey: an evaluation in terms of financial markets and financial stability. The Impact of Artificial Intelligence on Governance* (Vol. I). Economics and Finance.

Sakarya, Ş., & Aksu, M. (2021). FinTech ecosystem in Turkey: An evaluation in terms of financial markets and financial stability. *The Impact of Artificial Intelligence on Governance, Economics and Finance, I*, 11–31.

Salah, K., MacDonald, M., Qaddoumi, I., Abusalem, M., & Ventura, S. (2023). The crucial role of AI, machine learning and big data in Qatar's FinTech rise. *Technological Forecasting and Social Change, 177*, 121629.

Salama, V. (2022). *Qatar based FinMkt raised $3M in Seed funding.* Wamda. Retrieved from https://www.wamda.com/2022/05/qatar-based-finmkt-raised-3m-seed-funding

SAMA. (2020, June 21). *SAMA Announces the Deployment of Blockchain Technology.* Saudi Arabian Monetary Authority. https://www.sama.gov.sa/en-US/News/pages/news-575.aspx

Sangwan, V., Prakash, P., & Singh, S. (2020). Financial technology: A review of extant literature. *Studies in Economics and Finance*, *37*(1), 71–88. doi:10.1108/SEF-07-2019-0270

Santosdiaz, R. (2023). *Fintech Hubs In The Middle East and Africa.* Retrieved April 24, 2023, from http://thefintech-times.com

Santosdiaz, R., & Santosdiaz, R. (2023). How China became a leader in digital payments and wider digitalisation. *The Fintech Times*. https://theFinTechtimes.com/how-china-became-a-leader-in-digital-payments-and-wider-digitalisation/#:~:text=However%2C%20with%20its%20population%20of,for%20innovation%2C%20technology%20and%20adoption

Sarwa. (2022). *Why Sarwa is launching in Qatar and what to expect.* Retrieved from https://www.sarwa.co/blog/why-sarwa-is-launching-in-qatar-and-what-to-expect/

Sarwa. (2023). *Sarwa: Investing Made Easy*. Retrieved from https://www.sarwa.co/

Saudi Arabian Data Protection Authority (SDPA). (2023). *Personal Data Protection Law*. Retrieved from: https://sdaia.gov.sa/en/SDAIA/about/Documents/Personal%20Data%20English%20V2-23April2023-%20Reviewed-.pdf

Saudi Arabian Fintech Association. (2022). *The Saudi Arabian Fintech Market: A Report by the Saudi Arabian Fintech Association*. Author.

Saudi Arabian General Investment Authority (SAGIA). (2023). *Tax Exemptions in Saudi Arabia*. Retrieved from: https://www.argaam.com/en/article/articledetail/id/513727

Saudi Arabian Monetary Authority. (2023). *Fintech initiatives*. Retrieved from https://www.sama.gov.sa/en-us/regulatory%20sandbox/pages/permitted-fintechs.aspx

Saudi Arabian Monetary Authority. (2023). *New regulations for fintech companies*. Retrieved from https://www.sama.gov.sa/en-us/laws/pages/bankingrulesandregulations.aspx

Saudi Arabian Monetary Authority. (2023). *SAMA Supports Fintech Development in Saudi Arabia*. Retrieved from https://www.sama.gov.sa/en-us/pages/default.aspx

SaudiF. (2023). Retrieved from https://fintechsaudi.com/

SBI Holdings. (n.d.). Japanese Site. https://www.sbigroup.co.jp/english/

SCB. (2020). *Myanmar E-Commerce Market - Growing Trade Opportunities*. Retrieved from https://www.scb.co.th/en/personal-banking/stories/business-maker/myanmar-e-commerce.html

SCB. (2020). *Penetrate Cambodian Market through E-Commerce to Fight Against COVID-19*. Retrieved from https://www.scb.co.th/en/personal-banking/stories/business-maker/cambodia-e-commerce.html

Schellhase, J., & Garcia, A. (2019). *Fintech in the Philippines: Assessing the state of play*. Milken Institute.

Schilirò, D. (2021). FinTech in Dubai: Development and Ecosystem. *International Business Research*, *14*(11), 61–70. doi:10.5539/ibr.v14n11p61

Schneider, S., & Clauß, T. (2020). Business Models for Sustainability: Choices and Consequences. *Organization & Environment*, *33*(3), 384–407. doi:10.1177/1086026619854217

Secretariat, C. (n.d.). *Regulatory Sandbox|Cabinet Secretariat Website*. 内閣官房. https://www.cas.go.jp/jp/seisaku/s-portal/regulatorysandbox_e.html

SESE. (2019, November 11). *Mongolia's emerging it sector leads economy in New Direction*. Nikkei Asia. https://asia.nikkei.com/Business/Technology/Mongolia-s-emerging-IT-sector-leads-economy-in-new-direction

Setav. (2021). *Turkey's National Artificial Intelligence Strategy: A Comprehensive Analysis*. https://www.setav.org/en/assets/uploads/2021/08/P66-AI.pdf

S-GE. (2021). *Guide to Turkey Smart Cities Clean2*. Retrieved from https://sls.gatech.edu/smart-and-sustainable-cities

Shadbolt, N., O'Hara, K., De Roure, D., Hall, W., Shadbolt, N., O'Hara, K., . . . Hall, W. (2019). Privacy, trust and ethical issues. *The Theory and Practice of Social Machines*, 149-200.

Shahriar, A., Alabdullah, M., Al-Emadi, N., Godsell, J., Hussain, O.K., Jurayev, M., & Saif, Z. (2023). Role of cloud computing in enabling FinTech innovations in Qatar: managerial perspective. *Digital Policy, Regulation and Governance*.

Shahzad, K., Takala, J., Helo, P., & Phuyal, S. (2022). Fintech startup success factors: The case of Qatar. *Digital Policy, Regulation and Governance*.

Shahzad, K., Takala, J., Hietajärvi, A. M., & Tuunainen, V. K. (2021). The Development of Fintech in Qatar: Phases and Role of Regulatory Sandbox. *Journal of Promotion Management*, *27*(6), 965–983.

Shaikh, Z. A., Memon, S. A., Dhomeja, L. D., & Dahri, K. (2023). Blockchain-Based Fintech Architecture for Enhanced Interoperability in Health Insurance. *The Asian Bulletin of Big Data Management*, *3*(1).

Sharafi, A. (2022). A survey of the innovation ecosystem in the United Arab Emirates. *Journal of Economic and Social Thought*, *9*(3), 163–177.

Sharma, T. K. (2018). *Blockchain technology in India – opportunities and challenges*. Available at <https://www.blockchain-council.org/blockchain/blockchain-technology-in-india-opportunities-and-challenges/

Shop. (n.d.). *About us*. Retrieved from https://pages.shop.com.mm/wow/i/mm/about-us/about-us

Simms, T. (2020). *India ban overturned, BTC owners warned they'll lose everything, holder's digest, Mar 2-8, Cointeregraph-the future of money*. Available at https://cointelegraph.com/news/india-ban-overturned-btc-owners-warned-theyll-lose-everything-hodlers-digest-mar-28

Singapore, H. G. B. S. D. (2022, November 29). *Mobile wallet users Singapore 2020-2025*. https://www.statista.com/statistics/1325918/singapore-number-of-mobile-wallet-users

Singh, S., & Rana, R. (2017). Study of consumer perception of digital payment mode. *Journal of Internet Banking and Commerce*, *22*(3), 1–14.

Singtel. (n.d.). *About 5G*. Retrieved from https://www.singtel.com/personal/products-services/mobile/5g

Sironi, P. (2016). *FinTech innovation: from robo-advisors to goal-based investing and gamification*. John Wiley & Sons. doi:10.1002/9781119227205

Smart, D. (2023). *Derayah Smart: Your Sharia-compliant Robo-advisor*. Retrieved from https://derayahsmart.com/

Smartphone os market share in Saudi Arabia 2009-2023. (n.d.). Retrieved from https://gs.statcounter.com/os-market-share/mobile/saudi-arabia/#monthly-200906-202310

Soft Space. (n.d.). *About us*. Retrieved from https://www.softspace.com.my/about-us/

Softinyo. (n.d.). *Softinyo: Digital Services and Cyber Security Solutions*. Retrieved from https://softinyo.com/?utm_source=Tech-Behemoths&utm_medium=Profile&utm_campaign=viewprofile

Solecki, I., Porto, J., Alves, N. D. C., Gressevon, C., Hauck, J., & Borgatto, A. F. (2020). *Automated assessment of the visual design of Android apps developed with the app inventor.* Paper presented at the Annual Conference on Innovation and Technology in Computer Science Education. 10.1145/3328778.3366868

Song, N., & Appiah-Otoo, I. (2022). The Impact of Fintech on Economic Growth: Evidence from China. *Sustainability (Basel), 14*(10), 6211. doi:10.3390/su14106211

Soriano, M., Ziegler, T., Umer, Z., Chen, H., Jenweeranon, P., Zhang, B. Z., & Liu, K. (2019). *The ASEAN Fintech ecosystem benchmarking study*. Academic Press.

South China Morning Post. (2023, July 20). *China far outpaces the US in 5G base-station construction*. https://www.scmp.com/video/technology/3228390/china-has-built-6-times-number-5g-towers-3-months-us-has-installed-2-years

Srivastava, S., & Vishnani, S. (2021). Determinants of mobile bank usage among the bank users in north India. *Journal of Financial Services Marketing, 26*(1), 34–51. doi:10.1057/s41264-020-00083-9

Standard Insights. (2022, September 13). *Share of Indonesians who owned a banking or insurance app on their phone in 2022* [Graph]. Statista. Retrieved August 16, 2023, from https://www.statista.com/statistics/1338322/indonesia-ownership-of-mobile-banking-or-insurance-app/

Stanford University. (2023). *Artificial intelligence (AI) private investment worldwide in 2022, by industry* [Graph]. Statista. Retrieved November 15, 2023, from https://0-www-statista-com.biblioteca-ils.tec.mx/statistics/1381487/ai-private-investment-focus-worldwide

Statcounter. (2023). *Mobile Operating System Market Share in Turkey*. Available at: https://gs.statcounter.com/os-market-share/mobile/turkey/#monthly-200901-202310

Statcounter. (2023). *Mobile operating system market share Qatar - Jan 2009 to Oct 2023*. Retrieved from https://gs.statcounter.com/os-market-share/mobile/qatar

Statista & Statista Digital Market Insights. (2022). *Digital & Trends: FinTech in Japan*. Statista. https://www-statista-com.ezproxy.myucwest.ca/study/111372/FinTech-in-japan/

Statista. (2020). *Share of total population with 3G mobile network coverage in Vietnam from 2017 to 2020*. Retrieved from https://www.statista.com/statistics/1291551/vietnam-population-with-3g-mobile-network-coverage

Statista. (2021a). *Online banking penetration forecast in Ghana 2010-2025*. Retrieved July 10, 2921, from https://www.statista.com/forecasts/1169529/online-banking-penetration-by-country

Statista. (2021b). *Penetration rate of Internet users in Ghana 2017-2021*. Retrieved July 10, 2021, from https://www.statista.com/statistics/1171435/internet-penetration-rate-ghana/

Statista. (2022). *Countries & Regions: Japan*. Statista. https://www-statista-com.ezproxy.myucwest.ca/study/10007/japan-statista-dossier/

Statista. (2022). *Fintech - Singapore*. Retrieved July 29, 2023, from https://www.statista.com/outlook/dmo/Fintech/singapore

Statista. (2022). *Fintech In Vietnam - Statista Digital Market Outlook – Market Report*. Author.

Statista. (2022). *Fintech industry market value Thailand 2018-2021*. Retrieved from https://www.statista.com/statistics/1284830/thailand-market-value-of-the-Fintech-sector/

Statista. (2022, June 27). *Cashless payments adoption rate SEA 2021, by country*. Retrieved from https://www.statista.com/statistics/1234061/sea-cashless-payments-adoption-rate-by-country/

Statista. (2022, November 29). *Mobile wallet users Singapore 2020-2025.* https://www.statista.com/statistics/1325918/singapore-number-of-mobile-wallet-users

Statista. (2022, November). *Funding value for cryptocurrency companies in Singapore.* Retrieved from https://www.statista.com/statistics/1294117/singapore-cryptocurrency-funding-by-deals-and-value/

Statista. (2023). *Average fixed broadband speed in Saudi Arabia from 2018 to 2023.* Available at: https://www.statista.com/statistics/518942/fixed-broadband-subscriptions-per-100-inhabitants-in-saudi-arabia/

Statista. (2023). *Average monthly cost of 50 GB of mobile data in Saudi Arabia from 2015 to 2023.* Available at: https://www.statista.com/statistics/489169/canada-united-states-average-data-usage-user-per-month/

Statista. (2023). *Digital payments in Turkey.* Retrieved from https://www.statista.com/topics/10877/digital-payments-in-turkey/

Statista. (2023). *eCommerce - Cambodia.* Retrieved from https://www.statista.com/outlook/dmo/ecommerce/cambodia

Statista. (2023). *eCommerce - Myanmar.* Retrieved from https://www.statista.com/outlook/dmo/ecommerce/myanmar

Statista. (2023). *eCommerce - Taiwan.* Statista. https://www.statista.com/outlook/dmo/ecommerce/taiwan

Statista. (2023). *E-commerce market in Saudi Arabia from 2019 to 2025.* Available at: https://www.statista.com/topics/7723/e-commerce-in-saudi-arabia/

Statista. (2023). *Fintech - Brunei.* Retrieved from https://www.statista.com/outlook/dmo/Fintech/brunei-darussalam

Statista. (2023). *Fintech - Cambodia.* Retrieved from https://www.statista.com/outlook/dmo/Fintech/cambodia

Statista. (2023). *FinTech - China | Statista market forecast.* https://www.statista.com/outlook/dmo/FinTech/china#analyst-opinio

Statista. (2023). *Fintech – Indonesia.* Statista Market forecast. https://www.statista.com/outlook/dmo/Fintech/indonesia#transaction-value

Statista. (2023). *Fintech - Laos.* Retrieved from https://www.statista.com/outlook/dmo/Fintech/laos#transaction-value

Statista. (2023). *Fintech - Myanmar - Transaction Value.* Retrieved from https://www.statista.com/outlook/dmo/Fintech/myanmar

Statista. (2023). FinTech – Taiwan. *Statista.* https://www.statista.com/outlook/dmo/FinTech/taiwan#key-market-indicators

Statista. (2023). *FinTech in Saudi Arabia.* Retrieved from https://www.statista.com/outlook/dmo/fintech/saudi-arabia

Statista. (2023). *FinTech in Turkey: Market Overview.* Retrieved from https://www.statista.com/outlook/dmo/fintech/turkey

Statista. (2023). *Internet penetration rate in the Philippines.* Retrieved from https://www.statista.com/statistics/975072/internet-penetration-rate-in-the-philippines

Statista. (2023). *Neobanking in Turkey.* https://www.statista.com/outlook/dmo/fintech/neobanking/turkey

Statista. (2023). *Number of internet users in Thailand from 2017 to 2020 with a forecast through 2026.* Retrieved from https://www.statista.com/statistics/553730/number-of-internet-users-thailand/

Statista. (2023). *Predicted internet user penetration rate in Turkey 2023-2028.* https://www.statista.com/statistics/567686/predicted-internet-user-penetration-rate-in-turkey/

Statista. (2023). *Predicted Smartphone User Penetration Rate in Turkey*. Available at: https://www.statista.com/statistics/568281/predicted-smartphone-user-penetration-rate-in-turkey/

Statista. (2023). *Robo-advisors in Turkey*. https://www.statista.com/outlook/tmo/robotics/turkey

Statista. (2023). *Robo-Advisors: Saudi Arabia | Statista Market Forecast*. Retrieved from https://www.statista.com/outlook/fmo/wealth-management/digital-investment/saudi-arabia: https://www.statista.com/outlook/fmo/wealth-management/digital-investment/saudi-arabia

Statista. (2023). *Total population of the ASEAN countries from 2018 to 2028*. Retrieved from https://www.statista.com/statistics/796222/total-population-of-the-asean-countries/

Statista. (2023). *Transaction Value. Fintech in the Philippines*. Retrieved from https://www.statista.com/outlook/dmo/Fintech/philippines

Statista. (2023). *Turkey: Outlook for the digital investment market size and number of users in robo-advisors from 2023 to 2027*. Retrieved from https://www.statista.com/outlook/fmo/wealth-management/digital-investment/robo-advisors/turkey

Statista. (2023, April). *Cryptocurrencies in Thailand*. Retrieved from https://www.statista.com/outlook/dmo/Fintech/digital-assets/cryptocurrencies/thailand724market. (n.d). About us. Retrieved from https://insure.724.co.th/about

Statista. (2023, April). *Transaction Value. Fintech – Malaysia*. Retrieved from https://www.statista.com/outlook/dmo/Fintech/malaysia#transaction-value

Statista. (2023, August 14). *Internet penetration rate in Thailand 2019-2028*. Retrieved from https://www.statista.com/statistics/975067/internet-penetration-rate-in-thailand

Statista. (2023, August 8). *Fintech adoption rate South Korea 2017-2019*. https://www.statista.com/statistics/1125349/south-korea-FinTech-adoption-rate/

Statista. (2023, February 13). *Internet penetration rate in Brunei from 2011 to 2020*. Retrieved from https://www.statista.com/statistics/767584/internet-penetration-rate-brunei/

Statista. (2023, June 26). *Number of users of digital payments in Malaysia 2018-2027 (in million users)* [Graph]. Statista. Retrieved August 12, 2023, from https://www.statista.com/forecasts/1367668/malaysia-digital-payment-users

Statista. (2023a, March 13). *Main information channel when looking for information South Korea 2022*. https://www.statista.com/statistics/1115944/south-korea-main-service-used-to-search-for-information/#:~:text=According%20to%20a%20survey%20in%202022%2C%20close%20to,Korean%20website%20to%20feature%20its%20own%20search%20engine

Stoeckli, E., Dremel, C., & Uebernickel, F. (2018). Exploring characteristics and transformational capabilities of InsurTech innovations to understand insurance value creation in a digital world. *Electronic Markets*, *28*(3), 287–305. doi:10.1007/s12525-018-0304-7

Stojakovic-Celustka, S. (2020). *FinTech and its implementation*. Paper presented at the International Workshop on Measuring Ontologies in Value Environments.

Storm, R. K., Jakobsen, T. G., & Nielsen, C. G. (2020). The Impact of Formula 1 on Regional Economies in Europe. *Regional Studies*, *54*(6), 827–837. doi:10.1080/00343404.2019.1648787

Suryono, R. R., Budi, I., & Purwandari, B. (2020). Challenges and trends of financial technology (Fintech): A systematic literature review. *Information (Basel)*, *11*(12), 590. doi:10.3390/info11120590

Susanto, H., Ibrahim, F., Rosiyadi, D., Setiana, D., Susanto, A. K. S., Kusuma, N., & Setiawan, I. (2022). Securing Financial Inclusiveness Adoption of Blockchain FinTech Compliance. In FinTech Development for Financial Inclusiveness (pp. 168-196). IGI Global. doi:10.4018/978-1-7998-8447-7.ch010

Susanto, A., Chang, Y., & Ha, Y. (2016). Determinants of Continuance Intention to Use the Smartphone Banking Services : An Extension to the Expectation-Confirmation Model information. *Industrial Management & Data Systems, 116*(3), 508–525. doi:10.1108/IMDS-05-2015-0195

Swart, K., Cazorla Milla, A., & Mataruna-Dos-Santos, L. J. (2021). From the desert to the city: How is Dubai branding itself through sustainable sport events? *Worldwide Hospitality and Tourism Themes, 13*(1), 34–48. doi:10.1108/WHATT-08-2020-0101

Syfe. (n.d.). *The leading all-in-one digital investment platform for Asia-Pacific*. Retrieved from https://www.syfe.com/about-us

Tabachnick, B. G., & Fidell, L. S. (2007). *Using Multivariate Statistics* (5th ed.). Allyn and Bacon.

Taherdoost, H. (2023a). Fintech: Emerging trends and the future of finance. *Financial Technologies and DeFi: A Revisit to the Digital Finance Revolution*, 29-39.

Taherdoost, H. (2022). *Data Collection Methods; An Essential Guide to Plan, Design and Develop Data Collection Tools*. Kindle Edition.

Taherdoost, H. (2023b). Drivers of Financial Technologies. In *Mainstreaming Cryptocurrency and the Future of Digital Finance* (pp. 1–30). IGI Global. doi:10.4018/978-1-6684-8368-8.ch001

Tao, J., & Azhgaliyeva, D. (2018). *The role of green Fintech for Singapore: Risks and benefits*. https://scholarbank.nus.edu.sg/bitstream/10635/151199/1/4_Jacqueline_TAO_and_Dina_

Tech Collective. (2023, April 14). *Fintech trends: The rise of digital loans in Malaysia*. Retrieved from https://techcollectivesea.com/2023/04/14/Fintech-trends-digital-loans-malaysia/

Techloy. (2023). *Saudi Arabia's backing startups with a $200 million fund.* Retrieved from https://www.wamda.com/2023/08/saudi-arabia-launches-200-million-fund-local-foreign-high-tech-startups

Thanthong-Knight, R. (2021, November 30). *Thai Crypto Unicorn Plots Expansion in Bid to Be Asia's Coinbase*. Bloomberg. Retrieved from https://www.bloomberg.com/news/articles/2021-11-30/thai-crypto-unicorn-plots-expansion-in-bid-to-be-asia-s-coinbase?in_source=embedded-checkout-banner

Thapa, C., & Camtepe, S. (2021). Precision health data: Requirements, challenges and existing techniques for data security and privacy. *Computers in Biology and Medicine, 129*, 104130. doi:10.1016/j.compbiomed.2020.104130 PMID:33271399

THBL. (2018). Karnataka to use blockchain technology for e-governance. *The Hindu Business Line*. Available at https://www.thehindubusinessline.com/news/karnataka-to-use-blockchain-technology-for-egovernance/article10035777.ece#

The Asian Banker. (2022, May 26). *BIBD maintains leading market position in retail loans and deposits*. Retrieved from https://www.theasianbanker.com/updates-and-articles/best-retail-bank-in-brunei-bank-islam-brunei-darussalam-bibd-2022#:~:text=The%20bank's%20NEXGEN%20Wallet%20rec

The Australian Trade and Investment Commission. (2020). *Digital Banking in Vietnam*. Author.

The Banker. (2022). *Saudi venture investment on the rise*. Retrieved from https://www.thebanker.com/World/Middle-East/Saudi-Arabia

The Fintech Times. (2022, October 4). *Fintech landscape of Turkey in 2022*. Retrieved from https://thefintechtimes.com/fintech-landscape-of-turkey-in-2022/

The International Trade Administration. (2022, July 30). *Laos - eCommerce*. Retrieved from https://www.trade.gov/country-commercial-guides/laos-ecommerce

The Peninsula. (2021). *QIB unveils electronic account opening solution as part of digital transformation*. https://www.thepeninsulaqatar.com/article/05/12/2021/QIB-unveils-electronic-account-opening-solution-as-part-of-digital-transformation

The Peninsula. (2022). *Commercial Bank implements security solutions to adhere to compliance*. https://thepeninsulaqatar.com/article/13/09/2022/Commercial-Bank-implements-security-solutions-to-adhere-to-compliance

The Peninsula. (2022). *QIB launches open banking platform to boost financial inclusion*. https://thepeninsulaqatar.com/article/05/04/2022/QIB-launches-open-banking-platform-to-boost-financial-inclusion

The World Bank in Mongolia. (2023, June 19). World Bank. https://www.worldbank.org/en/country/mongolia/overview

The World Bank. (2020). *Mobile cellular subscriptions (per 100 people) – Lao PDR, World*. Retrieved from https://data.worldbank.org/indicator/IT.CEL.SETS.P2?locations=LA-1W

thefintechtimes.com. (2022). *Fintech landscape of Turkey in 2022*. Retrieved from https://thefintechtimes.com/fintech-landscape-of-turkey-in-2022/

Themefisher. (n.d.). *About Orda*. ORDA. https://orda.mn/about/

Thunes. (2023). *Is the Kingdom of Saudi Arabia the next fintech hotspot*. Retrieved from https://www.thunes.com/news/thunes-partners-with-saudi-arabias-new-digital-bank-d360-to-power-instant-cross-border-payments-across-mena-and-key-global-markets/

Thunes. (2023, August 1). *Digital Payments In Saudi Arabia | Thunes*. Retrieved from https://www.thunes.com/

Thusi, P., & Maduku, D. K. (2020). South African millennials' acceptance and use of retail mobile banking apps: An integrated perspective. *Computers in Human Behavior*, *111*, 106405. Advance online publication. doi:10.1016/j.chb.2020.106405

Tomas, J. (2022, October 25). *Thailand to reach 5G coverage of 85% by end-2022*. Retrieved from https://www.rcrwireless.com/20221025/5g/thailand-reach-5g-coverage-85-end-2022-true

Tomás, J. P. (2022, October 26). *XL Axiata expects 5G momentum in Indonesia to start around 2025*. RCR Wireless News. https://www.rcrwireless.com/20221026/5g/xl-axiata-expects-5g-momentum-indonesia

Toplist Joint Stock Company. (n.d.). *Top 10 biggest FinTech companies in China - Toplist.info*. toplist.info. https://toplist.info/top-list/biggest-FinTech-companies-in-china-by-market-cap-10577.htm

Tracxn. (2023). *Fintech Start Ups in Taipei*. Tracxn. https://tracxn.com/explore/FinTech-Startups-in-Taipei

Tracxn. (2023, July 9). *FinTech Startups in Japan*. Tracxn. https://tracxn.com/explore/FinTech-Startups-in-Japan

Tracxn. (2023, September 2). South Korea. *Geographies | Tracxn*. https://tracxn.com/d/geographies/south-korea/__us6k-b0pJxXgamA9AipJbdHh7DP6AZ-jAWckbXbAmAhQ/companies

TradeArabia. (2021). *TerraPay ties up with Commercial Bank of Qatar for instant global payments*. https://www.tradearabia.com/news/BANK_396713.html

Tribune, Q. (2021). *Microsoft launches its first data centres in Qatar*. Retrieved from https://www.qatar-tribune.com/news-details/id/226004/microsoft-launches-its-first-data-centres-in-qatar

TrueMoney. (n.d.). *About us*. Retrieved from https://www.truemoney.com/about/

Truong, N. (2023, June 20). *Employees of 13 banks questioned about selling customer data*. Academic Press.

Tsai, C.-H., Lin, C.-F., & Liu, H.-W. (2020). The diffusion of the sandbox approach to disruptive innovation and its limitations. *Cornell Int'l LJ*, *53*, 261.

Tseng. (n.d.). Taiwan Fintech. *The Legal 500.* https://www.legal500.com/guides/chapter/taiwan-FinTech/

Turkish Competition Authority. (2021). *Number of fintech startups in Turkey in 2021, by activity* [Graph]. Statista. Retrieved November 17, 2023, from https://0-www-statista-com.biblioteca-ils.tec.mx/statistics/1295524/turkey-fintech-startup-number-by-activity

Turkish Ministry of Finance. (2023). *Istanbul Finance Center*. Retrieved from https://ifm.gov.tr/

Turkish Statistical Institute. (2023). *Results of Population Censuses, 1935-2000 and results of Address Based Population Registration System, 2007-2022*. Retrieved from https://www.tuik.gov.tr/en/

UN DESA. (2019). *Total population across the Middle East and North Africa from 1990 to 2050 (in million)* [Graph]. Statista. Retrieved November 12, 2023, from https://0-www-statista-com.biblioteca-ils.tec.mx/statistics/978535/mena-total-population

United Nations Escap. (2018, April) Potential of financial technology in East and North-East Asia. *MPFD policy briefs. No.73.* https://www.unescap.org/sites/default/d8files/knowledge-products/MPFD%20Policy%20Brief%2073_FinTech%20in%20ENEA.pdf

United Overseas Bank Limited. (2021, November). *Fintech in Thailand 3Q2021: Thailand 4.0 plots way forward*. Retrieved from https://www.uobgroup.com/techecosystem/news-insights-Fintech-in-thailand-3q-2021.html

United Overseas Bank Limited. (2022, April). *Shifting consumer habits drive Malaysia Fintech growth*. Fintech in ASEAN 2021 report. Retrieved from https://www.uobgroup.com/techecosystem/news-insights-consumer-research-malaysia.html

United Overseas Bank Limited. (2022, November). *Fintech in ASEAN 2022: Finance, Reimagined*. Retrieved from https://www.uobgroup.com/techecosystem/news-insights-Fintech-in-asean-2022.html

United Overseas Bank. (2021, November 22). *Distribution of financial technology (Fintech) firms in Thailand in 2021, by type of firm* [Graph]. Statista. Retrieved August 19, 2023, from https://www.statista.com/statistics/1293999/thailand-distribution-of-Fintech-firms-by-firm-type/

United Overseas Bank. (2022, November 1). *Number of operating Fintech companies in the Philippines from 2017 to 2022* [Graph]. Statista. Retrieved August 26, 2023, from https://www.statista.com/statistics/1247613/number-of-Fintech-firms-philippines/

UOB. PwC, SAF. (2021). *Fintech in ASEAN 2021: Digital takes flight*. https://singaporeFintech.org/Fintech-in-asean-2021/

Vandezande, N. (2017). Virtual currencies under EU anti-money laundering law. *Computer Law & Security Report*, *33*(3), 341–353. doi:10.1016/j.clsr.2017.03.011

Veeraiah, V., Thejaswini, K. O., Dilip, R., Jain, S. K., Sahu, A., Pramanik, S., & Gupta, A. (2023). *The Suggested Use of Big Data in Medical Analytics by Fortis Healthcare Hospital. In Adoption and Use of Technology Tools and Services by Economically Disadvantaged Communities: Implications for Growth and Sustainability*. IGI Global.

Velmie. (2023). *Middle East Digital banking Outlook.* www.velmie.com

Venkatesh, V., Thong, J. Y. L., Chan, F. K. Y., Hu, P. J., & Brown, S. A. (2011). *UTAUT predictors and the role of context.* doi:10.1111/j.1365-2575.2011.00373.x

Venkatesh, V., Thong, J. Y. L., & Xu, X. (2012). Consumer Acceptance and Use of Information Technology: Extending the Unified Theory of Acceptance and Use of Technology. *Management Information Systems Quarterly*, *36*(1), 157–178. doi:10.2307/41410412

Ventures, H. A. L. A. (2023). *Neobanks and Saudi Arabia Banking Industry.* Retrieved from: https://www.hala.vc/neobanks-and-saudi-arabia-banking-industry/

Vesty, G., Kokshagina, O., Jansson, M., Cheong, F., & Butler-Henderson, K. (2023). Accounting, valuing and investing in health care: Dealing with outdated accounting models. *Meditari Accountancy Research*, *31*(1), 52–77. doi:10.1108/MEDAR-06-2021-1334

VidyaChellam. (2023). *A Machine Vision-based Approach for Tuberculosis Identification in Chest X-Rays Images of Patients, ICICC.* Springer. doi:10.1007/978-981-99-3315-0_3

Vietnam as of October 2022 [Graph]. (n.d.). Statista. Retrieved July 23, 2023, from https://www.statista.com/statistics/1105406/vietnam-leading-e-payment-services/

Vietnam Social Security Portal. (2022, February 20). *Vietnam records nearly 1,400 cyber-attacks in January.* Retrieved from https://vss.gov.vn/english/news/Pages/external-information.aspx?ItemID=10306&CateID=184

Vietnam, I. (2021, October 28). *5 Reasons Peer-to-Peer Lending is Really Hot in Vietnam.* InCorp Vietnam. https://www.cekindo.vn/blog/reasons-peer-to-peer-lending-hot-vietnam/

Vietnam's service ecosystem. https://www.generalatlantic.com/media-article/vnlife-announces-series-b-funding-round-led-by-general-atlantic-and-dragoneer/

Vigilia, C. (2023, April 4). Thailand moves closer to the launch of digital-only banks. *The Asian Banker.* Retrieved from https://www.theasianbanker.com/updates-and-articles/thailand-moves-closer-to-creation-of-digital-banks

Visa Inc. (2022). *Cashless payments adoption rate in Southeast Asia in 2021, by country* [Graph]. Statista. Retrieved July 29, 2023, from https://www.statista.com/statistics/1234061/sea-cashless-payments-adoption-rate-by-country/

Vives, X. (2019). Digital disruption in banking. *Annual Review of Financial Economics*, *11*(1), 243–272. doi:10.1146/annurev-financial-100719-120854

VK, A. (2019). 5 Indian banks That Are Rewriting The Payments Field With Blockchain. *Analytics India Magazine.* Available at: https://analyticsindiamag.com/5-indian-banks-rewriting-payments-field-blockchain/

VNExpress. (n.d.). Retrieved from: https://e.vnexpress.net/news/news/employees-from-13-banks-investigated-for-allegedly-selling-customers-data-4619893.html

Volopay. (n.d.). *The financial control centre to manage.* Retrieved from https://www.volopay.com/sg/

Vyshnavi - StartupTalky. (2023, June 20). StartupTalky. https://startuptalky.com/author/pv/

Wahezi, S. E., Kohan, L. R., Spektor, B., Brancolini, S., Emerick, T., Fronterhouse, J. M., ... Anitescu, M. (2021). Telemedicine and current clinical practice trends in the COVID-19 pandemic. *Best Practice & Research. Clinical Anaesthesiology*, *35*(3), 307–319. doi:10.1016/j.bpa.2020.11.005 PMID:34511221

Walk, G. A. (2023). Money and Financial Technology (FinTech) History. *International Lawyer*, *56*(2), 227–331.

Waloan. (n.d.). *About us*. Retrieved from https://www.waloan.app/en.html

Wamda. (2022). *Fintech in Qatar*. https://www.wamda.com/research/whitepaper/the-state-of-fintech-in-qatar

Wamda. (2023). *Saudi Arabia launches $200 million fund to back local, foreign high-tech startups*. Retrieved from https://www.wamda.com/2023/08/saudi-arabia-launches-200-million-fund-local-foreign-high-tech-startups

Wang, D., Peng, K., Tang, K., & Wu, Y. (2022). Does Fintech Development Enhance Corporate ESG Performance? Evidence from an Emerging Market. *Sustainability (2071-1050), 14*(24), 16597. doi:10.3390/su142416597

Wang, D., Peng, K., Tang, K., & Wu, Y. (2022). Does Fintech Development Enhance Corporate ESG Performance? Evidence from an Emerging Market. *Sustainability (2071-1050), 14*(24), 16597. https://doi-org.ezproxy.myucwest.ca/10.3390/su142416597

Wang, S. (2022). Improved Blockchain Technology for Performance Optimization Model Design of Sports Clubs. *Journal of Electrical and Computer Engineering*, *2022*, 1–8. doi:10.1155/2022/4436471

Wang, Y., & Collins, W. B. (2021). Systematic evaluation of mobile fitness apps: Apps as the tutor, recorder, game companion, and cheerleader. *Telematics and Informatics*, *59*, 101552. Advance online publication. doi:10.1016/j.tele.2020.101552

Wang, Y., Xiuping, S., & Zhang, Q. (2021). Can fintech improve the efficiency of commercial banks?—An analysis based on big data. *Research in International Business and Finance*, *55*, 101338. doi:10.1016/j.ribaf.2020.101338

Watzlaf, V. J. M., Zhou, L., Dealmeida, D. R., & Hartman, L. M. (2017). A Systematic Review of Research Studies Examining Telehealth Privacy and Security Practices used by Healthcare Providers. *International Journal of Telerehabilitation*, *9*(2), 39–59. doi:10.5195/ijt.2017.6231 PMID:29238448

Wave Money. (n.d.). *About us*. Retrieved from https://wavemoney.com.mm/about-us

WE ARE SOCIAL. (2023). *Digital 2023: Saudi Arabia*. Retrieved from https://datareportal.com/reports

WE ARE SOCIAL. (2023). *Digital 2023: Turkey*. Retrieved from https://datareportal.com/reports/digital-2022-turkey

Webenertia_Admin. (2016, April 6). *White Paper: How China Telecom's transformation enables growth*. China Telecom Americas. https://www.ctamericas.com/blog/china-telecoms-transformation-enables-growth/#:~:text=Telecommunications%20growth%20has%20also%20been,fastest%20growing%20sectors%20in%20China

Weelago. (n.d.). *Sellers center*. Retrieved from https://weelago.com/seller-center/#:~:text=Weelago.com%20is%20Brunei's%20No,and%20largest%20online%20shopping%20mall

Wilkins, C. (2016). *Fintech and the Financial Ecosystem: Evolution or Revolution?* Remarks to Payments Canada.

Williams, M. D., Rana, N., & Dwivedi, Y. K. (2015). The unified theory of acceptance and use of technology (UTAUT): A literature review. *Journal of Enterprise Information Management*. doi:10.1108/JEIM-09-2014-0088

Williams, F., & Boren, S. A. (2008). The role of the electronic medical record (EMR) in care delivery development in developing countries: A systematic review. *Informatics in Primary Care*, *16*(2). PMID:18713530

Wiyono, G., & Kirana Kusuma, C. (2021). Digital transformation of SMEs financial behaviour in the new normal era. *Jurnal Keuangan Dan Perbankan*, 191-211.

Woffenden, C. (2022, October 20). *Digital Transformation in mongolia: Insight from the Ministry of Digital Development*. The Fintech Times. https://theFinTechtimes.com/digital-transformation-in-mongolia-insight-from-bolor-erdene-battsengel/

Wojcik, D. (2021). Financial Geography I: Exploring FinTech – Maps and Concepts. *Progress in Human Geography*, *45*(3), 566–576. doi:10.1177/0309132520952865

Workforce, C. P., Rimsza, M. E., Hotaling, A. J., Keown, M. E., Marcin, J. P., Moskowitz, W. B., ... Simon, H. K. (2015). The use of telemedicine to address access and physician workforce shortages. *Pediatrics*, *136*(1), 202–209. doi:10.1542/peds.2015-1253 PMID:26122802

World Bank. (2017). *The Global Findex Database.* Available online: https://globalfindex.worldbank.org/

World Bank. (2022). *GDP per capita (current US$) – Vietnam* [Data file]. Retrieved from https://data.worldbank.org/indicator/NY.GDP.PCAP.CD?locations=VN

World Bank. (2022). *Global Findex Database 2021.* https://globalfindex.worldbank.org/

World Bank. (2022). *World Development Indicators. GDP per capita (current US$) – Vietnam* [Data file]. Retrieved from https://data.worldbank.org/indicator/NY.GDP.PCAP.CD?locations=VN

World Bank. (2023). *Mena FinTech: Embracing financial inclusion and innovation for the digital era.* https://www.worldbank.org/en/news/press-release/2022/07/21/world-bank-support-to-the-middle-east-and-north-africa-exceeds-us-5-billion-helping-to-mitigate-impacts-of-covid-19-and-

World Bank. (2023). *Population - total Thailand.* Retrieved from https://data.worldbank.org/indicator/SP.POP.TOTL?locations=TH

World Bank. (2023). *Population, total - Brunei Darussalam.* Retrieved from https://data.worldbank.org/indicator/SP.POP.TOTL?locations=BN

World Bank. (2023). *Population, total - Cambodia.* Retrieved from https://data.worldbank.org/indicator/SP.POP.TOTL?locations=KH

World Bank. (2023). *Population, total - Lao PDR.* Retrieved from https://data.worldbank.org/indicator/SP.POP.TOTL?locations=LA

World Bank. (2023). *Population, total - Myanmar.* Retrieved from https://data.worldbank.org/indicator/SP.POP.TOTL?locations=MM

World Bank. (2023). *Population, total - Philippines.* Retrieved from https://data.worldbank.org/indicator/SP.POP.TOTL?locations=PH

World Bank. (2023). *Saudi Arabia Overview.* Author.

World Bank. (2023, June 29). *Value of remittances received in Myanmar from 2013 to 2022 (in billion U.S. dollars)* [Graph]. Statista. Retrieved September 09, 2023, from https://www.statista.com/statistics/880741/myanmar-value-of-remittances/

Writer, S. (2021, July 6). *SBI invests in AI-powered microlender serving Mongolia.* Nikkei Asia.https://asia.nikkei.com/Business/Finance/SBI-invests-in-AI-powered-microlender-serving-Mongolia

Wyman, O. (2020). *Singapore Fintech Landscape 2020 and Beyond.* Singapore Fintech Association (SFA). Retrieved from: https://www.oliverwyman.com/content/dam/oliverwyman/v2/publications/2020/dec/singpore-Fintech-landscape-2020-andbeyond.pdf

Xu, J. (2022). Biometrics in FinTech: A Technological Review. *Future And FinTech, The: Abcdi and Beyond, 361.*

Xu, Y., & Bao, H. (2023). FinTech regulation: Evolutionary game model, numerical simulation, and recommendations. *Expert Systems with Applications*, *211*, 118327. doi:10.1016/j.eswa.2022.118327

Yahaya, M. H., & Ahmad, K. (2018). Financial inclusion through efficient zakat distribution for poverty alleviation in Malaysia: Using fintech & mobile banking. In *Proceeding of the 5th International Conference on Management and Muamalah* (pp. 15-31). Academic Press.

Yaokumah, W., & Amponsah, R. A. (2017). Examining the Contributing Factors for Cloud Computing Adoption in a Developing Country. *International Journal of Enterprise Information Systems, 13*(1), 17–37. doi:10.4018/IJEIS.2017010102

Yasin, N., & Khansari, Z. (2022). Exploring the Enterprise Landscape for Business Incubators in the UAE. In *Entrepreneurship and Change: Understanding Entrepreneurialism as a Driver of Transformation* (pp. 191–208). Springer International Publishing. doi:10.1007/978-3-031-07139-3_8

Yavuz, A. (2012). Competing Paradigms : The Dilemmas and Insights of an ELT Teacher Educator. *International Education Studies, 5*(1), 57–66. doi:10.5539/ies.v5n1p57

Yazici, S. (2019). The analysis of Fintech ecosystem in Turkey. *Journal of Business Economics and Finance, 8*(4), 188–197. doi:10.17261/Pressacademia.2019.1162

Young El Salvador. (2019). *Retos de la industria: Banca tradicional vs. Fintech*. Realidad Empresarial, Recuperado el 25 de Octubre de 2020. doi:10.5377/reuca.v0i7.7831

YukselB. (2020). *Future of Fintech in Turkey in the Absence of Mandatory Open Banking Regulations and the Possible Role of Competition Law*. doi:10.2139/ssrn.3622317

Yunus, K. (2021). The analysis of FinTech sector in Turkey. *Journal of Politics Economy and Management, 4*(2), 128–139.

Zaghlol, A. K., Ramdhan, N. A., & Othman, N. (2021). The Nexus between Fintech Adoption and Financial Development in Malaysia: An Overview. *Global Business and Management Research, 13*(4).

Zheng, A. H. Y., Ab-Rahim, R., & Jing, A. H. Y. (2022). Examining the Fintech Ecosystem of ASEAN-6 Countries. *Asia-Pacific Social Science Review, 22*(2). Retrieved from https://www.dlsu.edu.ph/wp-content/uploads/pdf/research/journals/apssr/2022-June-vol22-2/2-zheng.pdf

Zheng, H. (2023). China's experience with mobile payments highlights the pros and cons of a cashless society. *The Conversation*. https://theconversation.com/chinas-experience-with-mobile-payments-highlights-the-pros-and-cons-of-a-cashless-society-201177#:~:text=Leading%20mobile%20payment%20platforms%20Alipay,credit%20card%20and%20buy%20i

Zhou, M., Zhou, Y., Zhang, J., Obschonka, M., & Silbereisen, R. K. (2019). Person–city personality fit and entrepreneurial success: An explorative study in China. *International Journal of Psychology, 54*(2), 155–163. doi:10.1002/ijop.12451 PMID:28804917

Zhou, T. (2013). An empirical examination of continuance intention of mobile payment services. *Decision Support Systems, 54*(2), 1085–1091. doi:10.1016/j.dss.2012.10.034

ZigWay. (n.d.). *Who we are*. Retrieved from https://www.zigway.co/

Ziwen, C. (2023, September 5). *Police in China and Myanmar detain 269 in cyber scam crackdown*. Retrieved from https://www.scmp.com/news/china/diplomacy/article/3233506/police-china-and-myanmar-detain-269-cyber-scam-crackdown

About the Contributors

Hamed Taherdoost is an award-winning leader and R&D professional. He is founder of the Hamta Group | Hamta Business Corporation, and Associate Professor at University Canada West. He has over 20 years of experience in both industry and academia sectors. He has worked at international companies from Cyprus, the UK, Malta, Iran, Malaysia, and Canada and has been highly involved in development of several projects in different industries; healthcare, transportation, residential, oil and gas and IT. Apart from industry, he has been a university lecturer in three different parts of the world, Southeast Asia, the Middle East, and North America. Currently, he is an Adjunct Professor at Westcliff University, mentor at Futurpreneur Canada, Advisory Board of Cambridge Scholars Publishing, UK, Senior Technical Consultant at CI Solutions Ltd, Innotek Consulting Ltd & Quark Minded Technology Inc and Chair of Research and Scholarly Activities Committee at University Canada West. He is a certified cybersecurity technologist and a senior member of IEEE, IAEEEE, IASED, & IEDRC, Fellow Member of ISAC, WGM of IFIP TC11, member of CSIAC, ACT-IAC and AASHE.

Nam Phuong Le is an Assistant Professor of Business Management at University Canada West (UCW). Dr. Le received his Doctor of Business Administration from Walden University (USA), Master of Business Administration from Vancouver Island University (Canada), and Master of Science in International Business from the University of Hertfordshire (UK). Dr. Le also holds the CITP®|FIBP® - a professional designation in international business. His research interest includes globalization, emerging economies, global migration, internationalization of SMEs, and doing business with East Asia. Besides UCW, Dr. Le also taught at Fairleigh Dickinson University - Vancouver campus, Kwantlen Polytechnic University (KPU), Yorkville University, University of Petroleum and Energy Studies, India (visiting professor), and other colleges in Vancouver, BC, Canada.

Mitra Madanchian possesses a Ph.D. in Business Management and a Master's degree in Human Resource Administration, she currently assumes multiple professional roles, serving as the CEO at Hamta Business Corporation, as well as holding a full-time position as an Assistant Professor Faculty Member at University Canada West and a Sessional Faculty member at Fairleigh Dickinson University. With an extensive tenure exceeding 15 years encompassing both industry and academia, she has established herself as an influential figure in the field of management. She has actively contributed to notable projects for internationally acclaimed companies such as KPMG, demonstrating her proficiency in business development roles. Complementing her industry experience, she has achieved noteworthy accomplishments in the academic arena, boasting a portfolio of over thirty scientific articles published in esteemed peer-reviewed international journals and conferences. As a dedicated researcher specializing in business management, leadership, Human Resource Management, and marketing, she has made substantial and impactful contributions to the academic domain.

* * *

Giovana Castanho, hailing from Brazil, has found her educational journey in the vibrant city of Vancouver as an international student. Currently, she is pursuing a Bachelor's in Commerce at University Canada West, where her passion for ESG practices continues to grow. Giovana actively engages in volunteer work and proudly serves on the board of One Vancouver, a local non-profit organization. In the early stages of her career, she is committed to delving into the ever-evolving landscape of sustainability and social responsibility, driven by her personal values and ambitious aspirations.

Ali Habibnia is an Assistant Professor in the Department of Economics and the Computational Modeling and Data Analytics, College of Science, Virginia Tech. His research focuses on the intersection of statistical machine learning and big data econometrics, with a particular interest in high-dimensional nonlinear time-series analysis and their applications in macroeconomic/financial forecasting and estimation of big financial networks. He received his Ph.D. (2017) from the London School of Economics and Political Science, Department of Statistics. Ali also works occasionally as a consultant for financial firms and governmental organizations for all businesses related to pattern recognition and knowledge discovery, especially computer modeling and forecasting. He has been in the industry for a few years, working as a trader and portfolio strategist and developing different algorithmic trading strategies.

Jay Israni from India is a dynamic author and finance enthusiast, armed with a Bachelor's degree in Commerce and a Diploma in Financial Management. With a fervent passion for the finance industry, Jay has honed his skills in financial analysis, budgeting, and project management. Currently serving as an accountant at PCL Construction, Jay seamlessly integrates his academic knowledge with practical expertise, contributing significantly to the organization. Known for his ability to follow through on his vision and achieve tangible results, Jay is a dedicated professional with a keen interest in the world of finance.

Eric Kuada is a Senior Lecturer and the former head of department at the Department of Computer Sciences at the Ghana Institute of Management and Public Administration. He is also a Senior Member of the Institute of Electrical and Electronic Engineers (IEEE) and a past chairman of the IEEE Ghana Section. He received his PhD degree in Information Technology in 2014 from Aalborg University, Denmark. He has prior to that received his MSc. degree in Network Services and Systems in 2009 from the Royal Institute of Technology, Sweden; and a BSc. degree in Electrical and Electronic Engineering (with first class honours) in 2003 from the Kwame Nkrumah University of Science and Technology, Ghana. He has worked as a lecturer in several universities in Ghana and Denmark and has also held engineering and technology specialist positions in these two countries.

Peace Kumah holds a doctorate degree in Business Administration and MBA (Human Resource Management) degree from Wisconsin International University College, Accra, Ghana. She has several years of teaching experience and occupies leadership positions in various educational institutions. Her research interest includes organizational leadership and motivation, change management, and employment relations.

Sunil Kumar is currently serving as Assistant Professor at Department of Commerce, University of Jammu. He has completed his Ph.D in the area of Marketing. He is having nine years of teaching and research experience. He teaches various subjects i.e., Marketing Management, Business-to-Business

Marketing, International Marketing, GST Law and Practice and Financial Planning. He has presented papers in National and International conferences and has also published papers in journals of national and international repute. He has also co-edited a book on Managing the impact of COVID-19 on Financial Services Industry.

Amir Najafi currently works at the Department of Industrial Engineering, Islamic Azad University - Zanjan Branch (Associate Professor), Also works as a Head of Technology, Productivity, and Entrepreneurship Development Research Center.

Behzad Najafi, was born in 1992. He received B.Sc. degree in industrial engineering from Payam Noor University of Zanjan, Zanjan, in 2014. He received M.A. degree in Industrial Management from Azad University of Zanjan, Zanjan, in 2022. His research interests are industry 4.0, operational excellence (OPEX), business analysis, artificial intelligence, operation management, and information systems.

Sabyasachi Pramanik is a professional IEEE member. He obtained a PhD in Computer Science and Engineering from Sri Satya Sai University of Technology and Medical Sciences, Bhopal, India. Presently, he is an Associate Professor, Department of Computer Science and Engineering, Haldia Institute of Technology, India. He has many publications in various reputed international conferences, journals, and book chapters (Indexed by SCIE, Scopus, ESCI, etc). He is doing research in the fields of Artificial Intelligence, Data Privacy, Cybersecurity, Network Security, and Machine Learning. He also serves on the editorial boards of several international journals. He is a reviewer of journal articles from IEEE, Springer, Elsevier, Inderscience, IET and IGI Global. He has reviewed many conference papers, has been a keynote speaker, session chair, and technical program committee member at many international conferences. He has authored a book on Wireless Sensor Network. He has edited 8 books from IGI Global, CRC Press, Springer and Wiley Publications.

Hooman Razavi is a researcher in the School of Engineering Science at Tecnologico de Monterrey, where his primary focus lies at the crossroads of applied machine learning, big data analytics, and FinTech. Currently pursuing his Ph.D. at Tecnologico de Monterrey, he has already obtained his DBA from Shahid Beheshti University in 2022. Hooman's academic journey includes a Master's degree in Artificial Intelligence earned in 2015 and a Bachelor's in Computer Engineering received in 2012, both from K. N. Toosi University of Technology. In addition to his academic pursuits, Hooman extends his expertise as a consultant for financial firms and banks on an occasional basis, contributing to the practical application of his research in the industry.

Rodrigo Romero is an aspiring student, writer, and photographer completing his Bachelor of Commerce at University Canada West. Originally from El Salvador he moved to the city of Vancouver, Canada with hopes of leading a new life and starting businesses from his passions: Research, Visual Arts, and Design. Rodrigo holds multiple awards for public speaking and investigative essays, as well as working as a consultant for the government of his country despite his short age, all led by a passion to question and educate himself in as many subjects as possible. His work also includes his graduating thesis "Challenges of the implementation of Fintechs in El Salvador", an extensive research paper which aided in the development of the country´s own crypto wallet: Chivo. He is currently amidst founding and starting his own magazine, dedicating himself to mastering his craft as a photographer and writer, as well as focusing greatly on his degree with hopes of later on pursuing an MBA or a Doctorate Degree.

Jigmet Stobdan is an Assistant Professor in the Department of Commerce, University of Ladakh (India). He is a Ph.D. Scholar and has presented papers at various national and international conferences. He has also published his articles in reputed journals.

Winfred Yaokumah is a researcher and senior faculty at the Department of Computer Science of the University of Ghana. He has published several articles in highly rated journals including Information and Computer Security, Information Resources Management Journal, IEEE Xplore, International Journal of Human Capital and Information Technology, International Journal of Human Capital and Information Technology Professionals, International Journal of Technology and Human Interaction, International Journal of e-Business Research, International Journal of Enterprise Information Systems, Journal of Information Technology Research, International Journal of Information Systems in the Service Sector, and Education and Information Technologies. His research interest includes cyber security, cyber ethics, network security, and information systems security and governance. He serves as a member of the International Review Board for the International Journal of Technology Diffusion.

Index

G

H

I

J

M

N

O

P

Q

R

S

T

U

www.ingramcontent.com/pod-product-compliance
Lightning Source LLC
LaVergne TN
LVHW080630011026
849160LV00014B/1171